Viking Burial in the North of England

Viking Burial in the North of England

A Study of Contact, Interaction and Reaction between Scandinavian Migrants with Resident Groups, and the effect of Immigration on Aspects of Cultural Continuity

Angela Z. Redmond

BAR British Series 429
2007

Published in 2016 by
BAR Publishing, Oxford

BAR British Series 429

Viking Burial in the North of England

ISBN 978 1 4073 0050 4

BAR Publishing is the trading name of British Archaeological Reports (Oxford) Ltd. British Archaeological Reports was first incorporated in 1974 to publish the BAR Series, International and British. In 1992 Hadrian Books Ltd became part of the BAR group. This volume was originally published by John and Erica Hedges Ltd. in conjunction with British Archaeological Reports (Oxford) Ltd / Hadrian Books Ltd, the Series principal publisher, in 2007. This present volume is published by BAR Publishing, 2016.

Printed in England

BAR
PUBLISHING

BAR titles are available from:

BAR Publishing
122 Banbury Rd, Oxford, OX2 7BP, UK
EMAIL info@barpublishing.com
PHONE +44 (0)1865 310431
FAX +44 (0)1865 316916
www.barpublishing.com

ABSTRACT

VIKING BURIAL IN THE NORTH OF ENGLAND.

A STUDY OF CONTACT, INTERACTION AND REACTION BETWEEN SCANDINAVIAN MIGRANTS WITH RESIDENT GROUPS, AND THE EFFECT OF IMMIGRATION ON ASPECTS OF CULTURAL CONTINUITY

BY ANGELA Z REDMOND

Keywords - Viking, Funerary Rites, Contemporary Accounts, Migration, Assimilation, Culture, Archaeological Record

The north of England is home to a plethora of Scandinavian influenced cultural remains. However, against this background is an apparent paucity of burials. To understand why, a multidisciplinary approach was adopted, utilising the archaeological record, contemporary documents, anthropological research and theoretical modelling of culture contact during periods of migration and assimilation. Archaeological and historical records show that the settlement and assimilation of Viking groups followed a distinct pattern of contact, interaction and reaction. The successful settlement of Viking groups was determined by the specific type of person able to migrate and manner of assimilation undertaken by them and their descendants throughout the period. The production of Scandinavian influenced remains, including the funerary record, is an image of the socio-cultural milieu in which they were created. To set the research in context the Viking graves of Ireland, Scotland and the Isle of Man were studied. An extensive evaluation of the resources pertaining to Scandinavian type burials in the north of England established a complete database. Analysis of these records combined with the model constructed using migratory principles allowed tripartite sub-division. Each type reflected the degree of assimilation surrounding those performing the funerary rites. Comparison of these and the other burials in the British Isles and Ireland identified differences due to the settlement and assimilation processes being undertaken. Recognition of cultural reactions during the process of assimilation proved the Scandinavian type funerary record of the north of England to be expected, and illustrated numbers to be superfluous in understanding culture contact.

CONTENTS

TABLES

FIGURES

APPENDICES

APPENDICES - FIGURES

ACKNOWLEDGEMENTS

It is often said that the process of research involved in the production of a PhD is a highly isolating and lonely undertaking, however, from my own experience the whole project would have been an insurmountable challenge without the personal and professional support of a great many people. The first person I would like to thank unreservedly is my supervisor, Julie Bond, whose unstinting support and kindness has guided me through the past three years. For setting me on the road to PhD, untiring friendship and faith, I am deeply indebted to John McIlwaine. For the wise counsel and the company provided across the miles walked searching for Norse sites in the Northern Isles I am truly grateful to Nigel Melton. Responsibility for providing the opportunity to take archaeology beyond night-school enthusiasm and the support provided since rests with John Buglass. The generous help of Steve Dockrill, Sonia O'Connor, Gerry McDonnell, Tim Taylor, Holger Schutkowski and Jane Hammond from the Department of Archaeological Sciences, at the University of Bradford is gratefully acknowledged. Thanks to Caroline Clarke, Julie Milns, Kirran Kline, Janet Montgomery, Yvonne Wolfram and Amanda Forster whose support via friendship has been so important. I am also grateful for the assistance provided by Kevin Leahy, Richard Hall, Peter Cardwell, Greg Speed and the staff of Northern Archaeological Associates, Tim Padley and the staff of the Tullie House Museum, Carlisle, and Ros Watson and the staff of Harrogate Art Galleries and Museums. Finally, I'd like to thank Mum and Dad for firing my interest in history and archaeology at an early age and to Andrew Coote, without whom none of this would have been possible.

This research was funded between October 2001 and October 2003 by the Arts and Humanities Research Board.

CHAPTER ONE – VIKING BURIAL IN THE NORTH OF ENGLAND. AN INTRODUCTION TO THE RESEARCH

1.0 Introduction

The north of England is home to a plethora of Scandinavian influenced cultural remains, ranging from language and place-names to sculpture and artefact designs. Contemporary historical documents attest to periods of war and settlement during the eighth to eleventh centuries, and modern day excavations in towns such as York continue to reveal facets of Anglo-Scandinavian life. Against this backdrop of settlement and cultural influence it is to be expected that the funerary remains of the period would similarly incorporate many of the non-Christian rites of Scandinavia, as the Anglo-Saxon migrations had done in the previous centuries. However, this is not the case. As Richards' (2000*a*: 142) comments,

"It is one of the most remarkable aspects of Viking Age England that…there are very few Viking graves."

It is the main aim of this research to understand why there are apparently so few Scandinavian influenced burials in the Viking period north.

1.1 Objectives of the research

In order to achieve this aim, a multi-disciplinary approach was applied. This utilised the archaeological record, historical documents, and theoretical modelling of culture contact during periods of migration and assimilation between immigrant and resident groups. By not treating funerary rites as an isolated occurrence within the archaeological record, but as an event subject to a whole array of factors (social, cultural, personal, legal, economic, *etc*) it proved possible not only to explain the burial evidence but add significantly to the understanding of settlement and assimilation in the north of England during the Viking period.

The area chosen to base the study incorporates the most intensely Scandinavian influenced districts of the north, and covers Northumbria, Cumbria, Westmorland, Lancashire, Yorkshire and Derbyshire. These modern counties also contain the majority of Scandinavian type burials in England.

Tantamount to the understanding of the burial record is the acceptance of the fact that all obsequies are directly influenced by a milieu of multi-faceted factors which are at work within the social environment. Some of these factors are recognisable from within the historical and archaeological records. In order to address this, a detailed examination of contemporary historical accounts was made, to identify occasions of contact, interaction and subsequent reaction between Viking groups (be they raiders, traders or settlers) and the resident population of England. This was then expanded to encompass evidence of contact and cultural interaction between the two groups identifiable in the archaeological record, employing detailed consideration of sculpture, place-names, language and the growth of towns in the north of England.

Recognising that these people were an immigrant population seeking to settle within a far from empty landscape, is also a vital component in the understanding of the period. For this reason a study of migration, immigration and assimilation, coupled with issues of real and perceived ethnic identities of cultural groups was undertaken. The results of this, combined with the archaeological and historical data provided the foundation from which meaningful conclusions could be drawn and applied to the burial evidence.

In order to place the research in context it was necessary to study the types of burial practices undertaken by immigrant Viking groups in Ireland, Scotland and the Isle of Man. With this in place work was undertaken to extensively research and re-evaluate all possible burials of Scandinavian-type within the study area. In the majority of cases the burials had been excavated during the eighteenth and nineteenth centuries, leading to problems of accurately disseminating information from non-modern excavation techniques, alongside the loss in many cases of skeletal and artefactual evidence. However, an in-depth study was made, and the results and conclusions discussed in chapter eight, with a table of all burials appended and illustrated gazetteer (appendices 5 & 6).

1.2 The Viking Period: towards a definition and a chronology

The first, and often quoted historical account of contact between Scandinavian and Anglo-Saxon occurred in 789 AD at Portland Harbour, Dorset, where the reeve was killed in a skirmish with men from Hordaland, now part of Western Norway (Anglo-Saxon Chronicles). This marks the beginning of almost three hundred years of documented accounts of contact between Viking groups and the residents of Anglo-Saxon England via warfare, trade and settlement.

Throughout the period there occurred the migration of predominantly Scandinavian people, especially into the north of England, following the success of the military campaigns of the Viking war-bands against local kings. Over the next three centuries they, and their descendants were to become indelibly involved with the formation of the English state, as well as influencing laws, social structure, cultural practice and the English language itself (Hadley 1997: 70, Stenton 1998: 502-25). In 1017 England became entirely subject to a Scandinavian ruler, following the campaigns of Cnut, king of Denmark. This study will be bound between these two important historical dates of first contact and overall conquest.

Since the first literal mention of marine launched coastal attacks in 789 the raiders have been subject to a number of names. The etymology of the word *Viking* has been, and continues to be the subject of research and discussion amongst linguistic scholars (Jesch 2001*b*: 47). The Old Norse words *víkingr* and *víking* refer to a person and an activity, respectively (Jesch 2001*b*: 47). In modern English, history and archaeology the word has become both erroneously associated with a homogeneous cultural group and synonymous with a particularly long chronological period of mid-to-late Anglo-Saxon England. Ironically, the term *Viking* is hardly used at all by contemporary Anglo-Saxon authors, the word occurring only five times in the entire corpus of the Anglo-Saxon

Chronicles (Fell 1986, 1987). From the highly informed identification of the first raiders of 789 their names within contemporary Anglo-Saxon documents are multiple, *Danes* perhaps being the most commonly used term alongside *Northmen*, *Norwegians*, *pirates*, *heathens* and *pagans*, depending on what activity was taking place at the time or the personal bias of the author.

The modern study of culture and acculturation within modern archaeology has shown that the use of such ethnic tags can be misleading (Griffiths, forthcoming, pers. comm., Richards 2000*a*: 295-309, Thomas 2000: 237-255). For the purpose of this study it has been decided that the term *Viking* will be used as a general description encompassing all ethnic groups and cultural identities of active participants, whose origins, encompassed not only Scandinavia, but the entire northern European continent, the North Atlantic, as well as the British Isles and Ireland. For these reasons the word will only be used in a euphemistic sense, and where more specific and helpful terms are demanded from the evidence it will be replaced accordingly.

Similarly, the north of England has become synonymous with the term *Danelaw*, an expression that is notoriously fluid and probably impossible to define either politically or geographically (Holman 2001). In this study the difficulty will be circumvented by defining the north of England as representative of the modern day counties of Northumbria, Cumbria, Westmorland, Yorkshire, Lancashire and Derbyshire, as described above.

1.3 Past Work on Viking Burial

Although there is a huge corpus of work devoted to aspects of Viking studies (particularly stone sculpture and place-name research) surprisingly little has been directed towards the funerary record in the north of England. As Graham-Campbell (1989: 72) pointed out, this may be due to the perceived limitation of data available for analysis; which, as this study shows, is indeed a perception.

The designation of almost all known Viking burials is wholly due to the surviving records of eighteenth and nineteenth century antiquarians. Many are limited to a few scanty lines in journals, and some are second-hand accounts, however, no matter how woefully inadequate they now seem, these records are sadly now the only basis of our knowledge of a good many sites, the artefacts and skeletal remains long since lost or destroyed. The first real scholarly attempt to assess Viking burial within England was carried out by Bjørn and Shetelig who, by examination of museum collections, identified some nine Viking burial sites in the north of England (Bjørn & Shetelig 1940: 11-22)[1]. Because of the artefactual base of the study some sites were neglected, and the burial of the female at Bedale wrongly attributed to a site at Northallerton. Beyond these points, and the fact that it is now over sixty years out of date, it still remains a seminal artefactual study, and a vital component to beginning research into Viking period England. However, this being said, the mistake with the Bedale site resulted in the perpetuation of the error in at least two papers (Wilson 1967: 43, 1968: 295).

In 1948 Cowen appended the work of Bjørn & Shetelig in a paper containing details of artefactual and descriptive accounts of a further five sites in the north west of England.[2]

Almost twenty years later Wilson sought specifically to identify all known Viking burials in the north of England, not just to provide a complete artefactual reference as other studies had done, but to use the data in an effort to further understanding of the relationship between Viking settler and resident Anglo-Saxon, or more exactly, to highlight the conversion of non-Christian groups (Wilson 1967). The lists of Bjørn and Shetelig and Cowen were further contributed to by the inclusion of Wensley (Yorks.) and Ingleby (Derbys.) (Wilson 1967: 43-4). Worryingly, these additions were accompanied by the omission of Repton and Rampside, both included in the earliest lists (Bjørn & Shetelig 1940).

In his assessment of the burials, Wilson concluded that the Viking raiders were, "...*poverty stricken*..." and that they were unreliable within a historical context (Wilson 1967: 44, 38). Such conclusions can only be reached via consideration of the funerary record as a discrete entity within the socio-cultural milieu. The study of funerary rites should go beyond ideas of religious affiliation (see chapter three, for full consideration), and it is wrong to solely attribute the evangelising nature of Christianity to what he saw as an "...*already run-down Viking religion*..." for the apparent paucity of Scandinavian type burials (Wilson 1967: 46). During this period the burial record within recognised Christian cemeteries is far from regular, and in some cases transcends ideas of Christian burial, and if treated as an isolated event, may even be described as pagan. Radiocarbon dates from recent excavations of unaccompanied (and therefore artefactually undatable) burials have revealed early medieval interments within prehistoric sites, for example, at Ash Hill Neolithic long barrow (Lincs.), and the cemetery within a Bronze Age enclosure at Thwing (Yorks.) (Phillips 1989: 169, Geake 1997: 159). Similarly, unaccompanied graves and the reuse of prehistoric barrows are both common in *pagan* Viking Age Scandinavia (Brøndsted 1936).

His rejection of the burial record as evidence for further understanding of the settlement of Viking groups continued in a subsequent paper the following year (Wilson 1968). Again the list of Viking burials was increased, this time to include Brigham (Cumbria), Heysham, (Lancs.), and Repton (Derbys.) (Wilson 1968:295). Wilson's comment that, "*The grave finds are hardly capable of historical interpretation*", is difficult to substantiate, given that Repton appears in contemporary sources as the site of the winter camp of the Great Army in 873-4, and illustrates again that the study is being undertaken within a very narrow scope (Wilson 1968: 293). However, his critique of the difficulties associated with typological chronologies and their correspondingly wide dates of historical association is very important, and not only for Viking period studies (Wilson 1968: 296, Morris 1998: 88). The dates associated with Viking period artefacts are for all intents and

[1] Cambois, Northumbria: Hesket-in-the Forest, Rampside, & West Seaton, in Cumbria: Ormside, Westmorland: Camp Hill & Northallerton, in Yorkshire: Claughton Hall, in Lancashire: Repton, in Derbyshire.

[2] Aspatria, Brigham, Eaglesfield, Whitbarrow Scar, in Cumbria: Hasty Knoll, Blackrod, near Wigan, Lancashire.

purposes floating chronologies, based on parallel Scandinavian finds, which are entirely dependent on estimated dates themselves (Morris 1998: 88). The problems of dating are far more evident with the limited, and largely historically accountable two hundred years of later Anglo-Saxon England, in comparison for example to the acceptable scope for a prehistoric burial. A case in point is the boat burial from Scar, Sanday (see chapter seven), where a series of radiocarbon and artefactual dates provided very different results, which prove vital in understanding the movement and settlement of people in the North Atlantic (Owen & Dalland 1999).

Overall, however, Wilson concludes that the grave finds are of extremely limited historical value, and that their distribution is meaningless (Wilson 1968: 293-4). Both conclusions would be true if the burial record was a discrete dataset, totally separate from any influence of society, which of course, could never be the case.

Wilson's final map to date (1976: 394) corrects his original error of identifying the female burial at Bedale with Northallerton, and adds to it the nineteenth century discovery of a series of burials from Kildale Church (Yorks.). This map, including omissions (for corrections and additions see chapter eight, and appendices 5, 6 & 7) has been faithfully reproduced by all subsequent accounts regarding Viking burials (for examples see Graham-Campbell 2001: 107, 1989: 71, 1980, Richards 2000*a*: 143 and Halsall 2000: 260). His hypothesis that the *uninformative* group of Viking burials were limited due to the evangelising process of Christianity was unanimously accepted, and in effect hamstrung any further research for over twenty years. This problem was highlighted as early as 1980 by Graham-Campbell, who saw the need for an, "*...attempt to collate critically the available evidence for all known and suggested Scandinavian burials in England, however putative, in order to establish a nucleus of proven sites...*", which as illustrated above, forms one of the primary objectives of the research (Graham-Campbell 1980: 379). His call for greater research was still being given in 1989, and up until now has still remained unaddressed (Graham-Campbell 1989: 72).

More recently assessments of Viking settlement in England have moved away from the strict limits of artefactual analysis and cautiously begun to consider questions of ethnicity, culture and assimilation (see Hadley 1997, Kershaw 2000, Innes 2000, Trafford 1997, 2000). Innes (2000) has shown quite clearly in his study of historical accounts that recognition of ethnicity between resident and incoming groups existed, and produced complex interaction across all social levels throughout the time period. To a more limited extent these theories have been applied to the archaeological record, although the studies have been handicapped from the beginning by incomplete data and the inability to satisfactorily define a Viking burial (see below).

Hadley dealt with the problems of cultural identification with the suggestion that burials throughout this period should be considered as elite or non-elite, rather than Scandinavian or Anglo-Saxon because of the large variation in funerary traditions (Hadley 2000*a* & *b*). This view was expounded to suggest that the earliest graveyard monuments of Scandinavian influenced design were erected by elite members of the immigrant community as a way of expressing social dominance over resident groups (Hadley 2000*b*: 121). She then saw the use of such grave-markers setting a trend, one which was subsequently adopted by the indigenous population (Hadley 2000*b*: 121). This may well be a valid and interesting observation, and one carried further by Stocker, who suggests that they are in fact the grave-markers of wealthy Scandinavian traders, although it does contradict Hadley's stance on the impossibility of knowing the cultural/ethnic identification of those lying beneath (Hadley 2000*b*: 121, Stocker 2000). However, as well as circumventing issues of culture and ethnicity, neither author elucidates the defining characteristics of a non-elite burial, examples of which abound in pre-Christian Anglo-Saxon cemeteries and Viking period burials in, for example, the Northern Isles of Scotland, or consider the vitally important effects of immigration and assimilation.

The inability of modern scholars to actually define a Viking burial is a recurrent and pernicious problem that effectively hamstrings the construction of any valid hypothesis drawn from the archaeological evidence. This has been perfectly illustrated in a paper by Halsall, who after consideration of the artefacts recovered from the traditionally associated Viking-type graves (above) and the wide variation in funerary traditions practiced by resident Anglo-Saxon groups, arrived at the conclusion that there were no positively identifiable Scandinavian-type burials, a result he was himself uncomfortable with (Halsall 2000: 268-269)

Despite this failure to organise the archaeological evidence, Halsall continued to use the data in order to understand the settlement of Viking groups (Halsall 2000). He rightly dismisses the accepted theory of a swift conversion to Christianity as the reason for the apparent paucity of Scandinavian-type burials as shallow, along with the temptation of using them as an indicator of the limited numbers of settlers (Halsall 2000: 270-2). However, his overall conclusion that the burials were representative of power and social dominance (see Hadley (2000*b*) above) over the local populace is unconvincing (Halsall 2000: 270-2).

The latest papers to address Viking burials by Richards and Hadley also conclude that they were representations of power and social display (Richards 2002, Hadley 2002). This suggests that the hypothesis is fast becoming the replacement to the rapid Christianisation theory as an explanation for the differences within the funerary rites. Once more, reliance for the foundation of the studies is firmly placed on Wilson's map, although Richards does refer to the incompleteness of the data (Wilson 1976, Hadley 2002, Richards 2002). Worryingly, Hadley manages even to transpose this data, by stating Cambois and Bedlington (Northumbria) to be two separate sites, when in fact they are the site and the geographical location, respectively.

The problems of identification are discussed by Richards, who takes the data beyond the limit of artefactual analysis and begins to look at the situations of the burials within the landscape (Richards 2002). Vitally, he also carries forward the perceived problem of recognition via artefact analysis, by suggesting that there may be identified new funerary rites within Viking period archaeology due to interaction between settlers and residents, such as the use of hogback tombstones

(Richards 2002: 162, 165). His suggestion that the study of Scandinavian type burials be less polarised and limited by artefactual limitations is extremely significant, and one taken further by this research (Richards 2002).

From this critique of the work directly concerned with Viking burial it can be seen that the hiatus in the field remains highly visible and confused, still lacking an in-depth study of all the available evidence (archaeological and historical, geographical and demographic), and persistently treating the disposal of the dead as an isolated incident within the archaeological record. By acknowledging that funerary rites are not a separate component of the socio-cultural milieu, and adopting a multi-disciplinary approach which embraces the archaeological record, it is possible to move closer towards understanding the manner of contact and interaction between immigrant and national groups, and propose a hypothesis as to why there are apparently so few Scandinavian type burials in the north of England.

CHAPTER TWO – TOWARDS A SOLUTION: METHODOLOGY.

In order to achieve the main aim of the research two key issues had to be addressed; firstly, and most fundamentally, that the Viking groups were immigrants into a far from empty landscape; and secondly, that funerary rites are subject to a whole array of factors, indelibly connected to the socio-cultural milieu in which the deceased had lived. The core theme of the research, therefore, was firmly grounded in aspects of contact and interaction between immigrant and resident groups.

In order to set the research in context it was necessary to study just how and why society and personal belief can affect funerary rituals. This was achieved by examining the belief systems of both ancient and modern societies, and how everyday life influences reactions to death and burial. This was then expanded to consider how migration and subsequent settlement of immigrant communities in a new homeland alters funerary practice, something which was to prove key in understanding the Viking burial record in the north of England.

With this in place, it was then necessary to consider the society of the Viking homelands and the type of funerary practice carried out there during this period. This was accomplished by a survey of the archaeological and historical records of Denmark, Norway and Sweden.

As already discussed, Viking groups (be they raiders, traders or settlers) were not entering into a landscape devoid of human populace, and unlike many areas of archaeological research the period is reasonably well served by a series of contemporary Anglo-Saxon documents. Although this section does not attempt to break new ground in historical research, it was vital to study the primary accounts in order to understand the manner of contact, interaction and subsequent reaction between Viking groups and the indigenous Anglo-Saxons. The historical overview was then combined with an examination of the archaeological resource created directly as a result of contact, and included sculptural traditions in the north of England, place-names, language, settlement and the growth of towns. A combination of both archaeological and historical evidence provided a much fuller picture of the period, which is not normally attempted, and allowed the opportunity to examine the magnitude and depth of social and cultural interaction at work during this highly dynamic period.

With this background in place, the research then moved on to the crux of the study, that of migration, immigration, ethnicity and culture, and their direct application to the Viking period. Utilising modern studies made by sociologists and demographers, alongside archaeological theory, it was possible to build a migration model, which was subsequently applied to the artefactual and historical research of the previous chapters. The results of this provided an in-depth understanding of the type of person likely to migrate, the problems and the benefits, and the critical need to assimilate into the resident populace. The archaeological and historical resources enabled periods of migration and assimilation to be identified throughout the Viking period, and in many cases demonstrated quite clearly the cultural response to the contact of immigrant and national groups. This section provided the opportunity to explore new hypotheses as to the manner and extent of settlement. It also gave a crucial insight into the socio-cultural milieu of the period, which would directly affect the funerary rituals of immigrant groups.

Although work had been undertaken on the archaeological funerary record of the Viking homelands, the results from the research so far illustrated even more clearly that the Viking migrants were far from a culturally homogeneous group. With this in mind, it was absolutely vital to make a detailed study of the funerary record of immigrant Viking groups in Ireland, Scotland and the Isle of Man, from which more meaningful comparisons and conclusions could be drawn. To this end every Scandinavian type burial from Ireland and the Isle of Man was examined, along with over one hundred sites from Scotland and its islands. Combined with historical overviews of the regions, this analogous dataset was to prove pivotal.

As illustrated in the previous chapter, the most fundamental shortcoming of previous work concerning Scandinavian type funerary practice in England is the inability of scholars to satisfactorily identify a Viking burial. In order to address this fully a new system of categorisation was derived:

i. Traditional Burials – the burial parallels those found in Scandinavia and/or other areas of the British Isles and Ireland. They contain identifiable Scandinavian goods of the period and conform to some aspects of the funerary rite practiced within the Scandinavian homelands

ii. Accompanied Burials in Christian Cemeteries – inhumations recovered from Christian graveyards accompanied by items associated with uses other than dress-fittings or small personal goods (Scandinavian or unattributable)

iii. Accompanied Burials of Viking Period Date in Christian Cemeteries – as ii., but accompanied by only dress-fittings and small personal goods (Scandinavian or unattributable)

vi. Possible sites of Viking burial identified via stray finds and antiquarian records (appendix 7)

Work could then proceed with the identification and analysis of the Scandinavian type graves identified in the north of England. Utilising the core research with the graves gave a fascinating insight into social interaction of the period and provided the means to answer fully one of the conundrums that has troubled Viking period archaeology for years.

CHAPTER THREE – DEATH AND SOCIETY. DEALING WITH THE DEAD IN THE VIKING HOMELANDS.

3.0 Introduction

Across all societies and all time periods people have created religion to explain unanswerable questions or insurmountable problems. Most of these difficulties pertain to the general lifestyle of the society in question, but all have a particular tenet devoted to death, which after all covers both unanswerable question and insurmountable problem.

It is acknowledged that religion, despite its many forms and ritual customs, is indelibly linked with the structure of society in which it is practiced (Radcliffe-Brown 1968: 163, Murray Parkes *et al* ed. 1997). It follows therefore, that reactions to death are similarly governed and influenced, and that in order to understand at least part of the archaeological funerary record, a study of society should be made.

This chapter begins by looking at the structure and manner of belief systems practiced by groups both today and in the past. A brief overview is then given of the historical landscape of the Viking period homelands, before moving on to consider the type and manner of social structure of the resident population. With this background in place, a detailed study was then made of both the historical and archaeological records pertaining to the funerary rites of the Viking homelands.

3.1 The Structure of Belief Systems

Religion, in all its many ritual guises, is indelibly linked with the structure of society in which it is practiced (Radcliffe-Brown 1968: 163, Murray Parkes *et al* ed. 1997). The simplest religions are found amongst hunter-gatherer communities, and are based on animism, progressing in complexity amongst settled farming communities, whose beliefs extend to mystical protectors of hearth and harvest, and finally to the rise of the city-states, where religion becomes professionally organised and structured, in essence mirroring the way the state itself was run (Murray Parkes *et al* 1997: 16). As it will be shown, the Viking homelands were beginning to undergo a fundamental change at this time within society and religion, as the smaller, clan owned areas of land were being swallowed up into larger, countrywide kingships, supported by a new state maintained cult of Christianity (Randsborg 1980: 13, Roesdahl 1991: 74-7, Foote & Wilson 1979: 14, 40).

The religious base of farming groups revolves around older members of the community, who are responsible for carrying out necessary rituals and communicating these beliefs to the younger generations (Murray Parkes *et al* 1997: 16). Alongside their ritual obligations these people have other everyday occupations within the community; the specialised profession of priesthood unknown (Murray Parkes *et al* 1997: 16). Priests, temples and written dogma only appear with the rise of city-states, which makes it possible for a very large area to adopt a single religion and allow church and state to combine (Murray Parkes *et al* 1997: 16). In farming communities religion is perpetrated by the people: in nations it is perpetuated by the state. Farming societies tend to be clan based, and amongst these groups there is a strong tendency towards ancestor worship, which provides social stability by cementing relationships within communities (Radcliffe-Brown 1968: 164, Haley 1999: 5). This form of ancestor veneration can be seen to be taking place in the Viking world, as recorded in later sagas and poetry. Where the understanding of religion becomes difficult is in the dissemination of the rituals themselves, the perfect appreciation of which must derive from fundamental belief. Unfortunately fundamental belief does not include the scope for unbiased comparative evaluation; so complete understanding of ritual and religions can never truly be achieved. What can be identified, however, is change, an indication that corresponding transformations within the social fabric are likely to be taking place. Strong cases can be made for the identification of and reasons for these changes within the socio-cultural milieu by archaeologists and anthropologists studying the physical remains of burial ritual.

One of the most important rituals of any religion are those which pertain to death and burial, and encompass not only the corpse, but other members of the community, to a greater or lesser extent (usually depending on status of or relationship to the deceased) who are left to deal with what is often seen to be a highly dangerous (physically or spiritually) receptacle of an unquiet soul (van Gennep 1977: 146-165). In the modern day West death has been highly sanitised (regardless of religious beliefs and associated cultural practices) and in effect become the polar opposite to what it once meant to a society in times past, and to other societies in different parts of the modern world (see van Gennep 1977, Murray Parkes *et al* eds. 1997). In the west it is increasingly rare for someone to die at home surrounded by family and friends, indeed this would be treated by society with suspicion. The end of life is determined by medical practitioners relating to the termination of perceptible physical functions, not by religious belief. In Hinduism a person is not regarded as truly dead until their soul has been released through the cranium, the breakage of which takes place within the cremation fire, days after being 'scientifically' pronounced dead (Laungani 1997: 61). In other cultures definitions of death are also at odds with the scientific community. The Tapirapé of Brazil regard anyone unfit for work as dead, and the Dogon of Africa believe any person who has gone missing to be dead, even if they subsequently return (Haley 1999: 2). All of which may seem to western eyes difficult to understand, until, as Metcalf and Huntington say, the burial rituals are,

"*Placed in context of a particular ideological, social and economic systems,...(they)...begin to make sense in a way that they cannot if we pursue elusive cultural universals*" (1993: 75).

In the modern West, this pursuit of 'cultural universals' has contributed to the destruction of many cultural norms when dealing with death, and is an influence that must be borne in mind by all western archaeologists and anthropologists when trying to recreate and understand the rituals involved in the past or the present.

Across all cultures and not too long ago in the West, the immediate family, the extended family group and community were all directly or indirectly involved with the ritual surrounding preparation of the corpse (see Murray Parkes *et al* ed. 1997, Hertz 1907 (1960), Metcalf & Huntington 1993, van Gennep 1977: 146-165). It is perhaps safe to say that the idea of washing and preparing a corpse at home for burial and leaving him or her in an open coffin in a modern English sitting room would be treated by most people today with horror and repugnance, despite the practice being normally adhered to within living memory. This treatment of the dead has not occurred because of changes in religious belief, but through other aspects of perceptions of normality, that is, changes in culture that reflect and adapt to changes in all aspects of life. It is perhaps surprising that the rituals involved with something so intrinsically linked with religion should be so easily and quickly abandoned by both cults and practitioners alike. However, these changes are not limited to nationals. This rapid casting off of ritual practice is especially visible amongst immigrant communities in Britain today.

Laungani's (1997) paper illustrates this cultural stripping of aspects of burial ritual in Hindu communities by comparing the obsequies carried out in India to those in England. The speed at which major elements of the funeral ritual (one of the strongest cultural acts) are lost is quite startling. Large parts of the ceremony are foregone and others severely truncated (Laungani 1997: 68-9). This is not due to changes in religious practice by those involved in carrying out the ritual duties associated with the treatment of the dead, but a case of the assimilation of the rites practiced in Britain, the physical shift away from the cultural homeland, and proportionately fewer members of the older generation who are generally more observant of rituals and cultural practice (Laungani 1997, Rosenblatt 1997: 38). This change and the cultural implications of it are vital in our understanding of Viking burial in England, when one considers that Viking groups in the British Isle were an immigrant population. These will be dealt with fully in the following chapter.

3.2 The Historical Landscape of Viking Scandinavia

3.2.1 Denmark

The geographical position of Denmark in the midst of northern Europe dominating as it does the route linking the Baltic and North Sea, made it a major influence in European politics and trade. By the eighth century it was a centralised power, and by the beginning of the ninth, it was strong enough to pose a threat to Carolingian Empire at its southern border (Jones 1973: 98). The latter half of the ninth and beginning of the tenth century bore witness to the fragmentation of political power as a series of dynasties contended for the throne of a united kingdom (Randsborg 1980: 13). In the early part of the tenth century parts of Denmark were under Swedish control, including the important commercial centre of Hedeby (Foote & Wilson 1979: 14). It was during this time that the first Danish attacks were made on other European countries, and settlements established (Randsborg 1980: 13). From the mid tenth century a continuous dynasty of kings was established by the ascension of Gorm the Old, and the Swedish hold on parts of the country overthrown (Roesdahl 1991: 74, Foote & Wilson 1979: 14). By 987 his son and successor, Harald Bluetooth, had become overlord of Norway and in 1013 his grandson, Sven Forkbeard had conquered England (Roesdahl 1991: 74, Foote & Wilson 1979: 14.). The acceptance of Christianity as the official religion in Denmark occurred in during the 970's, under Harald after his defeat at the hands of the Frankish emperor Otto II in 974 (*Adam of Bremen*: bk. 2, pt. 22). At the height of Danish influence, and towards the end of this remit, in 1027, a letter from Gorm's great-grandson, Cnut, referred to himself as king of England, Denmark, Norway and part of Sweden (Roesdahl 1991: 74, Foote & Wilson 1979: 14.).

3.2.2 Norway

Before the end of the ninth century, Norway was made up of a series of tribal polities, the richest of which occupied the arable areas of Vestfold, site of the busy commercial centre of Kaupang (Foote & Wilson 1979: 40). Up until the late ninth century much of Norway was controlled by Denmark (Jørgensen 2000: 75). It was first unified during the final decades of the ninth century by Harald Finehair, whose dynasty was to rule both in their own right, and as vassals to Danish kings in return for their support during almost constant internecine warfare (Roesdahl 1991: 74-76). Eric Bloodaxe, one of Harald's sons, and his immediate successor, was ousted soon after his father's death, and went on to play a major role in England until he was killed in 954 (Roesdahl 1991: 74). He was replaced in Norway by his brother Hakon Æthalsteinsfostri, who was, as his name suggests, the foster son of the English king Æthelstan (Roesdahl 1991: 75). It was his defeat around 960 by an alliance of his nephews and the Danes that paved the way for Danish over lordship (Roesdahl 1991: 75). Norway seemed to be beyond the missionaries' remit, and evidence from a runestone in Dynna, Hadaland puts the official recognition of Christianity as the state religion during the 1020's (*Adam of Bremen*, bk. 4, pt. 30 Gräslund 2000:61).

3.2.3 Sweden

During the early Viking period Denmark controlled much of southern Sweden (Price 2000: 33). Very little is known about its political history, Olaf Skötkonung (*c.* 995-1020) being the first known king of a united country, although its modern geographical boundaries were not established until the Reformation (Randsborg 1980: 77, Price 2000: 34). Several petty kings are mentioned as having met the Christian missionaries in Birka during the ninth century, although later on there are two recognised main tribal groups, the Svear and the Götar (Roesdahl 1991: 76-77). The existence of the runic king-lists of the Svear at the royal capital and religious centre of Uppsala attest to a number of rulers in the region, but little else is known about them (Foote & Wilson 1979: 28). The events surrounding the Danish king Cnut's rise to power in Sweden during the lifetime of king Anund Jacob, a grandson of Olaf Skötkonung, during the late 1020's are similarly obscure (Foote & Wilson 1979: 32). Some things are known however about the social organisation from the Västergötland laws, which record the right of the Svear to accept or veto a new king, differences in wergilds for the killing of a person from Svear or Götar, and marked contrasts in land measurement systems and customs, where the Svear used the hundred and the Götar the Danish *herreds* (Foote & Wilson 1979: 29). Missionary activity in Sweden seems to have been established around the time of Ansgar, with a church being built in Birka, after king Olaf consulted the casting of lots, although conversion was much slower, and only officially acknowledged as being Christian during the middle of the eleventh century (*Adam of Bremen*, bk. 1, pt. 17, Gräslund 2000: 61, Roesdahl 1991: 77).

3.3 Social Structure in the Viking Homelands

In common with other northern European communities within the early medieval period Scandinavian society was hierarchical and based around the three social groupings of nobles, freemen and slaves (Dommasnes 1991: 66). Rank was generally determined by birth, although social and economic standing within each group could be wide. For example, amongst the ranks of nobles could be kings, jarls or holds and amongst the freemen could be those who owned large farms, the people who worked on them and those in possession (owned or rented) of more modest property. These ranks are visible in Viking myths and legends, law codes, sagas and the archaeological record (Dommasnes 1991: 66).

The basic unit was that of the family, linked usually back to a common great-great grandfather, with both male and female sides given equal preference (Foote & Wilson 1979: 4-5). Men were essentially responsible for women, but both sexes were equal in the eyes of the law and the family, and a woman was entitled to own land, although she had no political rights (Foote & Wilson 1979: 108-11, Crossley-Holland 1980: xviii). Land, profit, honour and shame were all shared between family members (Foote & Wilson 1979: 5). Feuds between kin groups were common, and could either be settled between themselves, or in a specially convened court (Crossley-Holland 1980: xviii). Friendships were also cultivated between kin groups for mutual benefit, and were probably the base of many a ships crew (Crossley-Holland 1980: xviii).

The freemen made up the bulk of society and were responsible for upholding and maintaining the law, and for occasional selection and support of a king or chief, generally a landowner like themselves, who was himself responsible to the laws and his subjects (Foote & Wilson 1979: 82). The larger farms were not simply homes to a single family, but were an extended household unit, and could comprise of owners, parents, siblings, children, foster-children, servants and slaves (Jørgensen 2000: 82). Freemen also had the right to bear arms (Foote & Wilson 1979: 82). The title of jarl was both dynastic and conferred by a king, and covers major landowners or sub-kings (Foote & Wilson 1979: 135-136).

The thrall, or slave, played an important role in Viking society, both for their labour and trade value. In fact, the value of a slave as a trade commodity cannot be underestimated in the Viking world. Many Viking raids were undertaken specifically to take slaves (see for example, the slave raids described across Ireland and Scotland in the *Annals of Ulster*). No distinction was made between selling other Vikings captured during in-fighting, or those captured in raids on other countries (Foote & Wilson 1979: 66-69). Slaves had no rights, and people could be reduced to slavery by voluntary submission, as a punishment or as a temporary measure to pay off part of a debt or simply be born the child of slaves (Foote & Wilson 1979: 66-69). It was possible to become free, either by self-redemption, or at the will of the slave's owner, but in parts of Norway three and sometimes four generations had to pass before the thrall family no longer had any obligation to former masters (Foote & Wilson 1979: 71-74).

As illustrated above, society within the Viking homelands was a mixture of both tribal and proto-feudal, which was finally to tip towards the latter with the rise of kingship, by putting loyalty to one's lord in the growing struggle for land and prestige above that of the family, resulting finally in the breakdown of kin-groups (Foote & Wilson 1979: 6). It is likely that this shift in social focus was one of the reasons for the expansion of the Vikings across Europe as these overlords struggled to found and settle kingdoms of their own.

3.4 Dealing with Death in the Viking Homelands

As it has been shown, society within the Viking homelands was predominantly made up of farming communities comprised of kin groups. In such societies the people themselves perpetrate religion, rather than the state, and the beliefs and rituals passed on to younger generations by the older members of the community (Murray Parkes *et al* 1997: 16). An example of this is to be found in *Eirik the Red's Saga*, where it is recounted that a young woman had been taught to chant ritual incantations by the older women in her kin group when she had been a girl (pt. 4, pp658-660). There is no indication in the surviving accounts pertaining to Norse religion that cult practice was strictly controlled by the state (despite many of the elite families claiming descent from the gods) or ecclesiastical groups until the advent of Christianity. It was, however, hierarchical. While it is known from surviving sources that there were ritual specialists within Viking society (for example the gođi in Iceland, the Angel of Death from Ibn Fadlan's account, soothsayers), these people had other, everyday occupations within the community.

The most basic and fundamental form of worship was carried out at household level and incorporated ancestor worship and personal spirits of the home (Craigie 1914: 43, Simek 2000: 60, Turville-Petrie 1964: 269). A common theme running through the written sources is the existence of the 'living dead', where the deceased actually lives inside his/her burial mound (Turville-Petrie: 269). The dead were still able to eat, drink, speak, help, injure or pester the living, and so had to be placated (Turville-Petrie 1964: 269). The dísir, were the female spiritual protectors of the home (Craigie 1914: 43, Simek 2000: 60). Sacrifices to these spirits are mentioned in the *Ynglinga Saga*, the *Landnámabok*, *Egil's Saga* and the *Saga of Víga-Glum* (Simek 2000).

The gođi (male) or gođja (female) were members of the community of high social rank who were responsible for organising the rituals involved with the worship of the major gods of the Vanir (such as Freyr or Thor) (DuBois 1999: 65-7, Byock 2001: 94). They were also responsible for the upkeep of the temple to their god, where worship took place at a community level (Byock 2001: 94, DuBois 1999: 66). It has been suggested that the major landowners amongst the gođi/ gođja were highly influential in the manner of worship of their tenants, something that was to become more obvious with the arrival of Christianity, which concentrated on converting elite members of society, and the ownership of churches on their estates (Byock 2001: 94, 303).

It is possible that the temple on the Isle of Nerthus at Uppsala, Sweden, played host to a number of communities' spiritual needs, especially on significant holy days (*Adam of Bremen*, bk. 4 pt. 26, Turville-Petrie 1964: 172). The temple was principally dedicated to Thor, although Odin and Freyr were also worshipped there (*Adam of Bremen*, bk. 4, pt. 26). Every nine years a major ceremony took place at the temple, attended by all people from all levels of society from the king downwards (*Adam of Bremen*, bk. 4, pt. 26).

As it can be seen, Norse religion was very personal and at the same time hierarchical, taking place within the home, at the estate of a chief at community level, and at a large temple at regional level (Gräslund: 2000: 56). The whole process is one of a dendric pattern. While not strictly institutionalised, it did need adherents at every level of society in order to perpetuate it. If breaks and gaps appeared, especially at the upper end of society (where Christian conversions were initially targeted and achieved) or within the home, then the delicate branches of interaction would be broken and the religion become fragmented and lost.

When immigrants left the Viking homelands to settle in other parts of what was Christian Europe, the connections that tied the religious community at home and local level would be stretched and in most cases fragmented, hastened by intermarriage with the people of the Christian faith, and by the fact that only a very particular part of the population migrate, who would not be representative of their culture and may not contain those capable of or interested in perpetuating their religious beliefs (see chapter six).

From surviving historical accounts the immediate family of the deceased were ultimately responsible for the treatment and burial of a member of their family. The only ritual specialist connected with funerary practice in historical sources is the Angel of Death, in Ibn Fadlan's account of the burials of a Rus chief on the Volga during the tenth century (transl. Sass in Warmind 1995: 136-7). It does seem likely that Ibn Fadlan witnessed the obsequies of a follower of Odin (who, along with Freyja seems to be the only god in the Norse pantheon directly associated with death and eschatology) and that the formidable figure was a priestess of the cult, although no reference is made to the god by name. What is clear from the account is that the whole war band were involved with the funerary rites, the man's closest kin playing the key roles in the rituals carried out. An insight into perceptions of eschatology of at least this war band is given by one of its members, and it is clear that the idea of body and soul being separate entities is pervasive; the soul being freed to go to paradise upon cremation of the body. While the preparations were being made for the cremation, the body and the trapped soul must have been seen to hold an awful danger to the living.

Other surviving accounts of death and burial are brief and limited, often to a couple of lines in the Icelandic Sagas. Most refer to the building of mounds and the insertion of the deceased with goods to accompany them in the world of the dead (for example, *Egil's Saga*, *Saga of the People of Laxardal*). In the *Ynglinga Saga*, Odin decrees that all his followers should be marked by a spear at the point of death, and after death, cremated and the ashes scattered or buried (chpt. VIII: 12, chpt. XII). However, his son and successor, Freyr, was inhumed in a burial mound, perhaps evidence of culture legitimising one of the older fertility gods into a later Norse pantheon led by Odin (chpt. XII: 14).

Throughout all mentions of death and burial, from the Icelandic Sagas to Ibn Fadlan, one thing is fundamentally clear – that of the involvement of both immediate family, kin group and the community as a whole in carrying out funerary rites. The consideration of any burial within the Viking homelands in this period (rich or poor) was ultimately dependent on the particular situation (social, economic, political, cultural), and is a reflection of this. Quite simply, an archetypal, Scandinavian Viking burial does not exist, only a series of common types (as shown below), each moment of burial affected and altered by the humans involved in the rites.

3.5 The Burial Record in Viking Period Scandinavia

This section will provide a concise précis of the types and manner of burial customs practiced in Denmark, Norway and Sweden during the Viking period. A selection of sites has been chosen in order to provide comparative data from which analogies with sites in the British Isles might be made. It is acknowledged that there are a great many different funeral rites occurring during this period across Scandinavia both at a local and national scale, producing complex issues which have been analysed by modern day Scandinavian scholars (for example Pedersen 1997 *a* & *b*, Randsborg 1980, Gräslund 1980).

3.5.1 Burial Practice in Viking Period Denmark

The predominant type of burial rite practiced in Denmark in this period was inhumation, with the deceased being placed in a flat grave or more rarely, a mound (Randsborg 1980: 122, Brøndsted 1936: 214). Generally, where a Viking grave has been identified within a mound it has been a secondary inhumation, involving the use of a Bronze Age barrow (Brøndsted 1936: 215). In primary barrow burials of this period the body was interred below ground level before a mound was raised over it (Brøndsted 1936: 215). Variation of burial practice across the country is illustrated on the island of Bornholm where mound burial predominates over all other methods of grave markers (Randsborg 1980: 122, Jørgensen 1987: 18). Stone settings of various regular shapes were often used to mark flat graves, and are also especially visible on the island of Bornholm (Jørgensen 1987: 18).

Viking period graves tend to be very simple, and in most cases contain a wooden coffin, although many of the dead were laid directly in the ground (Brøndsted 1936: 215). Unlike Norway, the use of cists with grave-cuts is unknown in Denmark (Brøndsted 1936: 215).

As a rule graves had very few inclusions, weapons and tools occurring very rarely in stark contrast to Norway and Sweden during this period (Randsborg 1980: 126). Female graves were far more likely to contain burial goods than male, and were for the greater part items of personal jewellery (Brøndsted 1936).

In western Denmark are a series of richly accompanied female graves where the incumbent was placed on a wagon inside a chamber, but these are limited to only this geographical area (Randsborg 1980: 125-6). Exceptions to the rule of normally poor, weaponless male graves occur during the tenth century, but are again limited in geographical terms, this time to Jylland, Fyn and Langeland (Pedersen 1997*a*: 124). These inhumation graves are accompanied by weaponry, horses and riding gear (Pedersen 1997*a*: 126). Many of these 'cavalry' graves were secondary burials in either Neolithic or Bronze Age mounds (Pedersen 1997*a*: 126). Plain weapon graves also occur in cemeteries, the most common weapon being the axe in contrast to the sword in the 'cavalry' burials (Pedersen 1997*a*: 126-7). Wealth, social standing and regional differences have been suggested for these different types of burial (Pedersen 1997*a*: 127).

Beside the horses of these 'cavalry' graves, dogs occur rarely, beside other bones of domestic farm animals that had been placed in graves as food offerings (Brøndsted 1936: 220, 224).

Cremation is a comparatively rare phenomenon in Viking period Denmark, and is mostly limited to the Jylland area up until the tenth century (Ramskou 1950, Randsborg 1980: 121). Most survive as areas of bones and charcoal covered by a small regular shaped barrow (round, oblong or triangular), with a surrounding kerb of regular shape, although cremated remains have been found in urns in south-west Jylland (Ramskou 1950, Randsborg 1980: 121). The cremations may be primary or secondary deposits and there are very many variations in the way the cremated remains were dealt with after burning (Ramskou 1950). Some were covered in stones, others collected together into a small pile, while some cremated remains were edged with kerbs (Ramskou 1950). As with the inhumation burials, inclusions are few, if any, the burials appearing poor to modern eyes (Ramskou 1950, Randsborg 1980: 121).

Boat graves (which include coffins made of boat timbers) are relatively common, continuing a tradition in Scandinavia dating back to the Iron Age (Birkedahl & Johansen 1994: 163). Boat burials continue into the eleventh century, and are especially visible in the churchyard at Sebbersund, north Jylland (Birkdahl & Johansen 1994).

The most spectacular ship burial to be found in Denmark to date was recovered from a barrow in the small cemetery at Ladby (Thorvildsen 1975). The burial dated from the mid-tenth century, and contained eleven horses, dogs, a bundle of arrows, tack and spurs, an iron bound wooden bucket, a silver plated iron whip handle, a gaming board, a silver eighth century Frankish belt buckle, a gilt silver plate and a bronze dish (Thorvildsen 1975: 8-12). Despite the survival of several fabrics and furs and a painted wooden plaque, no human skeletal remains were recovered (Thorvildsen 1975: 13-15).

A further ship grave was recovered from Hedeby and contained the rich burial of a man and two armed male retainers (Jørgensen 2000: 76-7). The burial dates to around 850, and each man was accompanied by a horse and weaponry (Jørgensen 2000: 76-7).

Excavations of the two large mounds in the churchyard at Jelling, Jutland, during the early nineteenth century hoped to recover the remains of the last pagan king and queen of Denmark, Gorm and Thyra (Jørgensen 2000: 76-8). However, despite recovery of many rich grave goods no human remains were found, and evidence suggests that Gorm at least, was removed from the burial mound by his son Harald Bluetooth and re-interred in the recently constructed church (Krogh 1983).

3.5.2 Burial Practice in Viking Period Norway

The main type of burial rite in Norway during this period was cremation, although inhumation was also practised (Price 2000: 39). Mortuary rituals seem to be delineated within particular regions, and could possibly be dictated by local traditions, with different customs appearing on adjacent farms (Dommasnes 1982: 71-72).

During the Viking period more effort seems to have been put into the mortuary ritual (cremation or inhumation), with an increase of grave goods from the eighth century onwards, including the poorest graves (Shetelig 1910: 195). This can either be interpreted as strength of the pagan belief in afterlife or a reaction to the encroachment of Christianity in Northern Europe. Generally, cremation burials are found beneath mounds or cairns, and are not usually in containers, the bones found mixed with charcoal, left apparently where they fell with the pyre (Shetelig 1910). Cremations found at Liten and Naterstad had been in part collected and placed in a soapstone bowl, as were cremations in the west of Norway studied by Dommasnes (Shetelig 1910: 197, 200, Dommasnes 1982: 80). In some, though not all cremations, grave goods were either put on the pyre or deliberately damaged, for example, at Markestad or Vestre Berg (Shetelig, 1910: 197, Dommasnes 1982: 71). Cremation burials also seem to have a higher percentage of horse tack than inhumations (Shetelig 1910: 196-208).

There is no evidence for the deliberate damage of grave goods included with inhumations (Shetelig 1910:203-208). Inhumations could either be laid directly in the ground, in a stone coffin, or in a boat (Shetelig 1910: 203-308). In both inhumation and cremation burials there is a very high percentage of weaponry (which may reflect laws compelling males to bear arms in life), along with iron tools (such as the boat builders' tools at Hopperstad, Vik), weights and scales, weaving implements, whetstones, combs, iron cooking pans and soapstone vessels (Shetelig 1910: 203-208, Dommasnes 1982: 73, 77). There are also instances of double graves occurring in both cremation and inhumation contexts (Shetelig 1910, Dommasnes 1982: 79).

The greatest of all Viking period graves to be discovered in Scandinavia was excavated at Oseberg, during 1904 (Jørgensen 2000: 76). The mound was found to contain a ship which carried the bodies of a noblewoman and her slave, along with a highly decorative wagon, four sledges, at least twelve horses, five beds, a chair, chests, tents, buckets, kitchen utensils, lamps, items for spinning and weaving, food and sumptuous textiles (Jørgensen 2000: 76).

3.5.3 Burial Practice in Viking Period Sweden

As in Norway the more predominant funerary practice in Sweden was that of cremation (Price 2000:39). Discussions will centre of the cremation cemetery at Helgö, and the mixed cremation and inhumation cemeteries at Birka (Holmqvist 1970, Gräslund 1980).

The latest graves at Helgö date to the mid-ninth century, and incorporate twelve firmly dated cremations (Holmqvist 1970: 221-222). All consisted of small turf mounds over circular or oval stone-settings (Holmqvist 1970: 218). The cremations were apparently done *in-situ*, with some grave goods showing evidence of fire damage, although graves fifty-one and fifty-two A, the larger pieces of cremated bone had been collected and placed in urns (Holmqvist 1970: 168-197). Eleven of the twelve graves contained animal/bird bones, especially dog which was recovered from eight (Holmqvist 1970: 168-197). Male burials seem to be associated here with horse bones, and in three of the female graves were found stone funerary globes (Holmqvist 1970: 218, 168-197). Generally speaking, the grave goods are quite poor, and limited to pottery, pieces of iron and austere jewellery (Holmqvist 1970: 168-197).

The seven cemeteries on Birka offer wide scope for comparative analogies to be made, containing both inhumation (five-hundred and forty-four) and cremation (five-hundred and sixty-six) burials (Gräslund 1980:5-6, 50). The majority of interments are covered by a mound and stone-settings of various regular shapes (Gräslund 1980: 5-6). There are three main inhumation types, coffined, coffinless, and chamber graves into which the deceased are directly placed unlike examples in Denmark where they are interred within a coffin inside the chamber (Gräslund 1980: 5, 30). Other than at Birka chamber graves are very rare in Sweden (Gräslund 1980: 34). The only animal bones found with inhumations at Birka were those of horses (Gräslund 1980: 60).

The majority (86.5%) of cremations were carried out *in-situ*, with over two-thirds being placed in urns (Gräslund 1980: 51). Commonly associated with the cremations placed in vessels were rings with Thor's hammer pendants and uncremated poultry bones and eggs (Gräslund 1980: 54). Some of the cremations at Birka followed the central Swedish tradition of placing the remains of the funeral pyre in a pit (Gräslund 1980: 58). Out of all the cremations only four graves contained unburnt grave goods (Gräslund 1980:79).

3.6 Death and Society: conclusions

As with all societies, past and present, society in the Viking period homelands was indelibly linked to religion. The funerary rituals enacted were a product of personal and socio-cultural factors at work on the kin of the deceased as they performed their responses to death. It has been shown in this study that the perpetuation and the perpetration of the Norse religion and the rituals involved depended on the basic unit of society, that of the family. Within the Viking homelands burial practice was wide and varied, differing not only between geographically and historically differentiated areas but also between adjacent farms. Each burial was unique, simply because it was the product of a communal reaction to death at a particular moment in time. Each person involved in the funerary rite would have been subject to a whole array of factors, both personal and from the surrounding socio-cultural milieu, all of which would be partially reflected in the funerary rites.

Changes in burial practice are not however, dependent on changes in religious belief, but occur due to changes in culture, which reflects and adapts to the influences experienced in any aspect of life. Rituals associated with death and burial are the first parts of religious practice to be subject to change, and are especially likely to be cast off completely amongst immigrant groups in a new homeland. This is not due to changes in religious belief, but to processes of assimilation, the physical shift away from the cultural homeland and the fact that there are proportionately fewer older members of the community to pass on details of rituals and cultural practice (Laungani 1997, Rosenblatt 1997: 138).

All these points discussed above are vital to the consideration of the funerary record of immigrant Viking groups in the north of England, and will be further explored in the following chapters.

CHAPTER FOUR – VIKING PERIOD ENGLAND. TOWARDS A DEFINITION AND A CHRONOLOGY

4.0 Introduction

It has been shown in the previous chapter that funerary rituals are a product of the personal and socio-cultural factors at work on the people responsible for the disposal of the deceased. These factors vary at an exponential rate, and are not governed by changes in religious beliefs, but by reactions to the constant shifts within the socio-cultural milieu.

In order to understand why there are apparently so few Scandinavian-type burials in the north of England it is critical that an understanding of the socio-cultural background is attained. During this period England is well served by both a corpus of contemporary historical documents and material remains, which relate directly to the interaction between Viking and Anglo-Saxon groups. Both sets of data can be seen as a result, or more properly a *reaction* to *contact* and *interaction*. By consideration of both types of evidence it is possible to understand the socio-cultural influences at work at different time periods amongst resident and incoming groups.

The documentary sources of the period can be sub-divided into three sections, historical accounts, law codes and legal documents, and miscellaneous accounts of historical interaction. Each source was examined for evidence of contact and interaction between Viking and Anglo-Saxon groups, and the subsequent reaction analysed for the effect on the socio-cultural milieu at that time and its later effects. For clarity a reference system of initials has been used for the primary sources, a glossary of which follows:

Æ – *The Chronicle of Æthelweard*
ASC – *The Anglo-Saxon Chronicles*
Asser – *Asser's Life of King Alfred*
AU – *Annals of Ulster (to AD 1131)*
EHD – *English Historical Documents, c500-1042*
FW – *Florence of Worcester*
HCD – *History of the Church of Durham*
HK – *A History of the Kings of England*
HSC – *History of St Cuthbert*
RW – *Roger of Wendover's, Flowers of History*
Saxo – *The History of the Danes Books I-IX*
WM – *William of Malmesbury, The History of the Kings of England, and of his own times*

The stipulated archaeological remains of the period are those that bear influences of both Viking groups and the resident Anglo-Saxon population. These have been sub-divided into two sections, place-names and language, and material remains conveying hybrid-designs. The effects of Scandinavian influence on place-names are considered here for reasons of clarity and evidence of interaction.

On a more basic, but highly critical level, this chapter will also provide a fixed chronology of what was a highly dynamic era, covering a period of two-hundred and twenty-eight years from the first historically documented contact in 789 until the ascension of the Dane Cnut to the English throne in 1017. For ease of reference an abridged, tabulated chronology is appended (appendix 1). Where not specifically stipulated the main historical account used was the Anglo-Saxon Chronicles.

4.1 Primary Historical Accounts of Interaction between Viking and Anglo-Saxon Groups in England (appendix 1)

As already described, the first documented contact between Viking and Anglo-Saxon groups took place at Portland Harbour, Dorset in 789 (ASC, Æ). An altercation took place and Beaduheard, reeve of King Beorhtric of Wessex, was killed (ASC, Æ). It is extremely unlikely that this was the first contact between the people of England and Scandinavia. That trade and contact had been practiced between England and the Continent (north and south) for hundreds, if not thousands of years is beyond doubt (see especially Carver 1999: 365, Braudel 1972). The fact that the residents of Portland knew the group also supports this, the chronicler recording precisely that their origins lay in Hordaland, Western Norway.

Trade, exploration or adventuring could account for a multitude of unrecorded movements between England and Scandinavia, especially one would expect, in the North Sea area. Reports and first hand sightings of potential areas to raid undoubtedly initiated the beginning of Viking attacks aimed at ecclesiastical targets, a period that was to last some eleven years in the north of England and encompass three recorded raids. The sack of Lindisfarne in 793 was followed a year later by attacks at the Tyne harbour and Jarrow monastery, where the raiders were eventually killed by local levies (HK). In 795 the Annals of Ulster record the sacking of the monasteries on Iona and Skye, and in 800 the churches of Hartness and Tynemouth were plundered (AU, RW). Following this spate of attacks England seems to have then been free of recorded Viking aggression for some years, a very different situation to that of Scotland and Ireland, where attacks continued unabated throughout the eighth and ninth centuries (AU). The limited time period of eleven years is suggestive that these initial forays into piracy could be traced to a single group, whose activities waned with the deaths of their leaders.

According to the surviving English historical sources, 835 marked the resumption of piratical attacks after a break of some thirty-five years, when Sheppey was raided.[1] This attack marked the beginning if one-hundred and nineteen years of struggle between the Anglo-Saxon kings and Viking raiders.

The attacks along the south coast of England from 835 are mirrored in France and continued from then on almost yearly, progressing as far north as Lindsey in 841 (Logan 1991: 114ff, Wallace-Hadrill 1975). In 850-1 the Viking raiders spent their first recorded winter in Britain, on either Thanet or Sheppey, and so established the first permanent raiding base (ASC, Swanton 2000: 64 fn. 7). The raids across the south of England by various war bands continued, and in 860 Winchester itself was sacked by a Viking army actually based on the Somme, before being driven off by Anglo-Saxon forces (*Annals of St Bertin* in Swanton 2000: 68 fn.. 1).

[1] There does survive, however, two charters referring to the threat of Viking raids, one from 804, the other from 822, which will be discussed below.

4.1.1 The Great Army

In 865 the manner of assault against the kingdoms of Anglo-Saxon England changed with the gathering together of at least six[2] war bands to form a single force, known to history as the *Great Army*. The reasons for the formation (and the logistics involved) must be manifold and not limited to revenge, settlement or the creation of new Viking kingdoms. Each leader can be seen to have had his own personal agenda, but what was common throughout is the continuing pursuit of profit and glory. According to two contemporary sources the army was ultimately led by Ivar the Boneless, a notorious Viking leader, who had been operating from a Dublin base since 857 (Æ, AU).

Already active in England at the time was the Viking war band based at Thanet, and it seems likely that East Anglia provided a rendezvous point. It was certainly where the war bands over-wintered. At this point it seems no attempt was made to overthrow Edmund of East Anglia, the Viking leaders apparently content with protection money and perhaps wary of risking their limited forces in an effort to control an English kingdom. It seems their interest lay in the possibility of further expansion into Northumbria, where a civil war was currently being fought between rival claimants to the throne, Ælla and Osberht. York was captured by the Great Army in 866 and the two warring kings killed. Raids were then undertaken across the surrounding countryside, before the kingdom was divided (RW, HK). The Viking leaders established an Anglo-Saxon by the name of Egbert, as king north of the Tyne, a position he was to hold for six years (RW, HK).

The army then moved south into Mercia and wintered in Nottingham, where a combined army of Wessex and Mercia failed to expel them, resulting in the Mercians making peace with them. This allowed the army to leave Nottingham and return to York, before moving back across Mercia and into East Anglia to winter at Thetford in 869. From this base East Anglia was raided and conquered and its king, Edmund, killed. The names of two Viking leaders are mentioned here for the first time as an insertion in the Anglo-Saxon Chronicles manuscript F as Ivar and Ubba, the two who killed the king (ASC Swanton 2000: 70, fn. 2)[3]. In the same year Ubba's war band was responsible for the destruction of the monastery at Peterborough (*John of Peterborough*, in Swanton 2000: 71, fn. 16). In 870 the Great Army then moved on to Reading, in Wessex itself (ASC).

By 870 Ivar had left the Great Army and rejoined his Dublin ally Olaf at the siege of Dumbarton, the capital of the Strathclyde Britons (AU, Smyth 1977: 149). Presumably he took his war band with him, perhaps satisfied with the profit they had made, and thus depleting the Great Army of men further. By this time the leadership of the Great Army in England seems to lose its sense of direction and they seem undecided whether to attack Wessex properly or consolidate earlier gains. During 870 a series of skirmishes took place, resulting in the death of one of the two remaining Viking kings, Bagsecg; the second, Halfdan, survived. The following year the Great Army was bolstered by the arrival of the *Summer Fleet*, which landed at Reading. The combined force then marched on London, and the Mercian rulers allowed them to winter there.

In 872 the Northumbrians expelled the Viking puppet-king Egbert and replaced him with Ricsige (RW). Egbert sought refuge at the court of the Mercian king Burgred, where he died the following year. (RW).

In 872-3 the Great Army moved across country from their winter base in Torksey to Repton. During 873, Burgred was defeated, and Ceolwulf established as king of Mercia by the Viking leaders. At this point, Halfdan, one of the original leaders of the Great Army, took his force and left for Northumbria, where they established winter quarters on the mouth of the Tyne. Between 873 and 875 raids were undertaken against the Pists and the Strathclyde Britons, and also against the Norse colonies in Ireland (AU). In 876 it is recorded that the settlement was acknowledged some long term permanence, when Halfdan began the process of dividing Northumbria between his men (ASC). No mention is made about any land being given to Ricsige, the king of Northumbria, unlike had been to Ceolwulf, suggesting still more strongly he was not chosen or backed-up by the Viking army, but was rather an impotent Anglo-Saxon figurehead – something probably enforced in Roger of Wendover's account, which reads,

"...*Halfdeane, king of the Danes, occupied Northumbria, and divided it among himself and his thegns, and had it cultivated by his army; then the king of the same province, Ricsige, struck to the very heart with grief, ended his last day and Egbert*[4] *succeeded him.*"

It does seem that the Anglo-Saxon nobility still wielded strong influence in the appointment of their kings in York, while allowing Halfdan and his followers to settle.

However, his over-lordship of Northumbria was not to last, and in 877 Halfdan left for Ireland again. According to the *History of the Church of Durham*, he was expelled by his own followers from the Tyne, accompanied by only three ships and died shortly after. *Saxo Grammaticus* also has an account of Halfdan's failure to rule Northumbria successfully, and records his destruction of both people and farmland before he left in an act of vicious retribution (*Saxo*, Smyth 1977: 260-1). The entry for the *Annals of Ulster* in 877:5, records a small battle on Strangford Loch between the fair heathens (*finn gaill*) and the dark heathens (*dub gaill*), in which Albann or Halfdan, the king of the *dub ghaill* was killed.

With Halfdan gone, it does seem plausible that the army should then have chosen a new leader, something that the *History of St Cuthbert* picks upon and inter-weaves with legend in 883,

[2] Those of Ivar, Halfdan, Ubba, Guthrum, Oscytel and Anund.

[3] A list of the Viking kings and dukes is given by Simeon of Durham in his History of the Church of Durham, and reads, Halfdene, Inguar, Hubba, Beicgsecg, Guthrun, Oscytell, Amund, Sidroc, Sidroc, Osbern, Frana and Harold (p654).

[4] *ie* Egbert II

when the slave[5] Guthfrith Hardacnutson was chosen as king of the Northumbrian Danes, and was crowned in a ceremony combining both pagan and Christian elements (HCD).

Returning south to the actions of the remainder of the Great Army, its further division in 874 after the conquest of Mercia is recorded in the Anglo-Saxon Chronicles. As well as Halfdan the Chronicles also record the names of three further Viking kings, Guthrum, Oscytel and Anund, all of whom went on to Cambridge. It is common belief that these three men led the summer army of 871, although as mentioned above, their names appear in historical documents as early as 865 (HCD).

The intention to subdue Wessex was continued until 876, when after a series of defeats, the Great Army retreated back into Mercia where land was apportioned between Ceolwulf and themselves (ASC, Æ). However, the prospect of defeating Alfred and Wessex proved too great, and after an initial period of success, the Great Army was resoundingly defeated at Edington (Wiltshire). This defeat was to prove final, and peace terms were made between kings Guthrum and Alfred, the former being baptised into the Christian church as part of the settlement. No mention is made of the other kings, Oscytel and Anund; it is possible that they had been killed in intervening battles.

In 879 the army moved from Cirencester into East Anglia, where areas of land were distributed. Meanwhile, other raiding parties were still active, including one in Fulham that subsequently left to fight the Franks in Ghent.

4.1.2 The Resumption of Raids

After a respite of six years Wessex was again subjected to a series of Viking attacks from groups that had been raiding in France. It is more than likely that they were also joined by Vikings from East Anglia, since after the defeat of this new army Alfred launched an attack on the kingdom (ASC, E).

In 886 Alfred captured London, and put it under the charge of his Mercian brother-in-law Æthelred, and there was a brief respite until 892.

In 891 the Frankish annals were reaching the end of their account of the notorious Viking leader Hæsten, who after twenty years of raiding in France was attempting to settle in the Piccardy region, but was defeated at Louvain (Leuven) in 892 (Logan 1991:132). Setting sail from the Frankish Empire, the Anglo-Saxon Chronicles then pick up his story as he, along with another large fleet of Vikings, landed on the English coast. The largest force was made up of some two hundred and fifty ships landed at Appledore in Kent. It is not known who led this force (Stenton 1998: 266). Hæsten, who was leading a smaller force of some eighty ships, also landed in Kent and made a fort at Milton Royal. This landfall south of the recently established settlement areas seems almost to suggest that Hæsten and his compatriots were intent on carving out a new kingdom for themselves in Wessex rather than settling within Viking held East Anglia, Northumbria or Mercia.

Meanwhile the Anglo-Saxon Chronicles contains details of the continuing raids in Wessex from Viking held territory despite promises and exchanges of hostages. In 893 persistent harrying by the Anglo-Saxon army saw the defeat of the larger army at Farnham and the infliction of serious injury to its leader forced it to take up a defensive position on Thorney Island, Buckinghamshire (Æ, Stenton 1998: 266). In the meantime Hæsten had sailed from Milton Royal to Benfleet, which he established as another base for raiding into Wessex. Obviously aware of these movements Vikings from Northumbria and East Anglia formed a force of some one hundred and forty ships, a hundred going to lay siege to Exeter, and the remainder attacking the Devonshire coast and Bristol estuary. Alfred then turned his attention to Benfleet, where Hæsten was raiding from and had recently been joined by the remains of the larger raiding army from Appledore. While Hæsten was away raiding, Benfleet was captured, the fortress destroyed and plunder taken along with all the women and children sheltering there. From the account in the Anglo-Saxon Chronicles it seems that Hæsten and Alfred had met or even had been in some negotiation at a time previous to this, as the two sons of Hæsten were named as godsons of Alfred and Æthelred (Alfred's son-in-law). Alfred subsequently released Hæsten's family along with an amount of money, perhaps to divert further raids. The king then turned his attention to Exeter, and the siege seems to have been lifted without a fight, the force of Anglo-Vikings returning to their ships and sailing off to join the remnants of the raiding army on the Thames, with reinforcements from East Anglia and Northumbria. Some followed a Northumbrian jarl, Sigfrith, who had been part of the force, to Dublin, where he succeeded in dividing the Vikings there in 893 before being expelled back to Northumbria by Sihtric Ivarson (Æ, AU).

Sailing up the Thames, the raiding army crossed country to join the Severn and set up a fortress at Buttington, where they were eventually starved out. Those who managed to escape the battle with the Anglo-Saxon force regrouped at Benfleet. The Anglo-Saxon Chronicles then recounts how the Viking army, again bolstered by their fellows living in England, placed their families and valuables in East Anglia and marched for the deserted city of Chester, probably via Watling Street. Pursued by the army of Wessex, they were again starved out, and set off raiding across Wales in 894 before marching on to Essex via Northumbria and East Anglia, to arrive on the island of Mersea.

In 895 the Viking king Guthfrith of Northumbria died and was buried in a church now on the site of the Minster in York, his successors being the shadowy figures of Siefred and Cnut (Æ, Stenton 1998: 262-263).

The raiding army in the south meanwhile left Mersea in favour of a new fortification twenty miles north of London, thought possibly to be at Hertford (Swanton 2000:89 fn.. 7). Again Alfred cut off their food supplies and also blocked the rivers so they could not get their boats out. The raiders subsequently abandoned Hertford and unable to remove their ships they marched to Bridgenorth where another fortification was set up. Sometime during 896 Bridgenorth was abandoned, and the army disbanded, some going into East Anglia and Northumbria, and those without provisions to set themselves

[5] It is extremely unlikely that within the highly socially stratified society of the time that a slave would be taken as a king of a Viking war band.

up, sailing for France to join raiding parties on the Seine. Even after the army had dispersed raids on the seaboard of Wessex continued unabated throughout the year, the raiders engaged by an Anglo-Saxon fleet on several occasions.

4.1.3 The Reclamation of the North (table 4.1)

The death of Alfred in 899 and ascension of his son Edward to the kingdom of Wessex, led to a power struggle between him and his cousin Æthelwold, who along with his retainers had thrown in their lot with the Vikings of East Anglia and Northumbria and began raiding across Mercia and Wessex. Edward sent his own raiding army into East Anglia to ravage the countryside, and during its withdrawal part of the force became engaged with the Viking army. The small Anglo-Saxon group was defeated; however, amongst the dead of the Viking army were Eohric the king of East Anglia, Æthelwold, and one Beorhtsige, son of ætheling Beorhtnoth (a possible landless descendent of the Mercian royal house) (Stenton 1998: 322). Also killed were holds Ysopa and Oscytel. This use of the Viking armies in England by an English prince marks a historically accountable change in relationship between the two groups (Stenton 1998: 322). In 905 Edward negotiated a peace treaty with the leaders of Northumbria and East Anglia, which was signed at Tiddingford, a crossing point of the river Ouzel at Linslade (Swanton 2000: 94 fn. 8).

The reclamation of Viking held territory had started politically and economically before the military advances by Edward begun in 909. Before Alfred's death, his son-in-law was ruler over a large part of Mercia, covering the land south of the Mersey, encompassing the midlands and bounded by the Welsh Kingdoms to the west and Watling Street to the east (Stenton 1998: 321). Whether this southern part of Mercia had been the thegn Ceolwulf's portion in the division of land in 877 is open to speculation, however, what is clear is that a large part of the old kingdom of Mercia had returned to Anglo-Saxon hands with the Alfred Guthrum Treaty (see below), so it is quite possible that Æthelred had had some land returned then. Edward and Æthelred, had also ordered the buying of land from Viking owners along the border at Chalgrave and Tebworth in Bedfordshire, a fact attested to in later surviving charters of Æthelstan (see below, EHD: 103, Stenton 1998: 322-323). These purchases made by the thegn Ealdred cannot have been the only land transactions carried out by the English nobility (EHD: 103, Stenton 1998: 322-323). This is also the earliest reference to the buying and selling of land, an alien concept to Anglo-Saxon society before the advent of Viking influence (see below).

Military reclamation began in 909 when Edward marshalled both Mercian and Wessex forces to raid Northumbria, and over a period of five weeks great damage was done to the countryside. In retaliation the army of Northumbria raided deep into Mercian territory the following year, and were heavily defeated at Tettenhall, a defeat the Northumbrian army would not recover from. The Anglo-Saxon Chronicles (Manuscript D) lists the deaths of two Viking kings Halfdan and Eowils[6] and many leading jarls and holds, the names of many known to contemporary writers[7]. No mention is made of a corresponding raid or even an alliance with the East Anglian army as had occurred in earlier encounters. Following the battle Edward again took his forces into Northumbria and raided across the countryside, killing many Viking settlers.

Within six years three Viking kings had been killed, along with very many leading lords known to the authors of the Anglo-Saxon annals, which no doubt created a power vacuum and great instability across society. This apparent power vacuum was ripe to be subsequently exploited by the leaders of the Dublin Vikings (see below).

Between the years 912-917 Edward and his sister Æthelflæd, who had taken over the lordship of Mercia after the death of her husband Æthelred in 911, undertook to build a series of fortresses specifically to control communication routes (land or river) and face establish Viking held fortresses (Stenton 1998: 324). The chain of garrisoned fortresses inflicted the desired strangle hold on the Viking armies of Mercia and East Anglia stretching between the towns of Cambridge, Bedford, Huntingdon, Northampton, Stamford, Leicester, Nottingham, Derby, and to a certain extent, Lincoln. By engaging each army at each town and cutting off the routes of contact and reinforcements the fall of Viking held Mercia and East Anglia came very swiftly.

In 913 punitive raids were undertaken from Leicester and Northampton into the surrounding Anglo-Saxon held lands, only to be driven back by local levies. The following year fortresses at Eddisbury Hill, Cheshire, and Warwick were made secure and garrisoned. The Wye Valley, meanwhile fell prey to a Viking attack from Jarls Ohtor and Hroald, fresh from Brittany, and captured Bishop Cameleac of Archenfield. He was subsequently ransomed to Edward for the sum of forty pounds, and raids further inland were halted by the garrisons of Hereford and Gloucester alongside local Mercian levies (ASC). In the fighting Jarl Hroald was killed along with Jarl Ohtor's brother, before they were driven away to Ireland where the *Annals of Ulster* recorded their arrival on Loch dá Caech, Waterford, Munster. The establishment by Edward of a fort at Buckingham no doubt prompted the surrender of Thurcytel and his Bedford army that winter, along with some men of rank from Northampton.

The following year's account tells of how Edward gave money to Thurcytel and whoever wanted to follow him, to fund his move to France. During 916 Edward proceeded to fortify Maldon, perhaps to secure the coast from Viking raids from France and prevent them from reinforcing the Viking armies still resident in English towns. In 917 these remaining Viking towns were to collapse with surprising ease to the advancing English army. The two armies of Northampton and Leicester combined to attack the newly founded Anglo-Saxon fort at Towcester. The siege lasted only a day, before the armies gave up and resorted to pillaging the surrounding countryside. Similarly, the armies from East Anglia and Huntingdon

[6] Who *FW* calls brothers of king Hinguar (Ivar), as does Æ, which is unlikely, given the time depth.

[7] The others killed mentioned in the ASC were Jarls Ohtor and Scurfa, Holds Athulf, Agmund, Benesing, Thurferth, Guthferth, Olaf the Black, Osferth Hlytte (*Soothsayer*), and Guthferth – the *Annals of St Neots* also adds Eagellus (Swanton 2000: 97 fn. 14).

combined to build a fortress at Tempsford, abandoning Huntington altogether. Attacks on the English held Bedford by this force also failed. Viking armies from East Anglia and Mercia (general terms given in the *Anglo-Saxon Chronicles*) united to attack the newly founded Anglo-Saxon fort at Wigingamere (possibly Wigmore – Swanton 2000: 101 fn. 12), but yet again they were driven off.

The Anglo-Saxon army later that year went on to lay siege to Tempsford, and take it, killing the king (presumably of Viking East Anglia), one Jarl Toglos, his son Jarl Manna, and an unnamed brother. Colchester was briefly taken by a Viking army, but was recaptured before very long. Maldon was also attacked, but again the Viking army was repulsed. In the north Æthelflæd captured Derby. In the autumn Jarl Thurferth and the holds of Northampton and surrounding land surrendered to Edward. He then moved to fortify the town of Huntingdon, and the local people surrendered to him. Soon after the people of East Anglia, Essex, and the Viking armies of East Anglia and Cambridge submitted.

Throughout the whole military campaign of reclamation the picture painted of the Viking settlers is one of fragmentary groups loyal to their own leader of a particular area, rather like the war bands of 865. This time, however, there was no single ruler or group of co-operating leaders to draw together the disparate groups and form the formidable fighting machine that had come so close to capturing the whole of Anglo-Saxon England during the late ninth century. There is no doubt that this fundamental difference is due to the cultural and ethnic changes within the social fabric of the people within these areas of Viking control, a vital consideration and one that will be fully discussed in chapter six.

By 918 the English crown had reclaimed the kingdoms of Mercia and East Anglia. Only Northumbria remained. Nowhere in this struggle for survival did the army of Northumbria appear as it had done without fail in previous attacks on Wessex held England. Apparently leaderless after the battle of Tettenhall and subjected to a heavy defeat, the military might of Viking Northumbria had been extinguished, a fact not lost on the Dublin based Viking leader Ragnald. It is known that Ragnald was active in the far north of England and Scotland during the period 912-14 (HCD, HSC), but no mention was made of him when the leading men of York submitted peace terms to Æthelflæd in 918. It seems unlikely that the chroniclers would ignore a person of his standing had he been in York at the time.

4.1.4 The Viking North. The Arrival of the Dublin kings

The interest of the Hiberno-Norse Viking leaders in the north of England was no doubt exacerbated by their temporary expulsion from their Dublin headquarters in 902 by Mael Finnia, king of Ireland (AU). The Irish *Three Fragments* recounts the arrival of the Viking Hingamund and his followers on the Wirral where he was granted land to settle by Æthelflæd, who was ultimately repaid by an attack on Chester by his mixed army of Norse, Irish and Danes (transl. in Wainwright 1942 (2000)). There can be little doubt that there were many Norse raids and settlements on the western seaboard of northern England, from bases in Ireland, the Isle of Man and the Scottish Isles, although they remain unrecorded in English chronicles until the arrival of Ragnald, the grandson of Ivar the Boneless *c*913-14 (HSC). After their expulsion the *Annals of Ulster* continued to keep track of the leaders who were trying their hand in Scotland, and records the death of Ivar, one such man (another of Ivar's grandsons), in a battle there in 904.

In 912 the northern English annals record the sacking of Dunblane by King Ragnald, Jarl Ottar and Oswulf Crakabain (HK). Ragnald then proceeded to defeat King Constantine of Scotland and Eadred of Bamburgh in the first battle of Corbridge (*HSC*). Sometime following this, probably between 912 and 914 Ragnald reappears in the *Annals of Ulster*, defeating Bárdr Óttarsson in a sea battle off the coast of the Isle of Man (Smyth 1978: 9, *AU*). Unusually, this, the first battle at Corbridge mentioned in *The History of St Cuthbert* is not even alluded to in the *Annals of Ulster*, which covers the second battle in 918 in great detail, as well as mentioning many raids inflicted on the different kingdoms of Scotland by various Viking leaders in previous years. According to the *History of St Cuthbert* the battle is caused by Ragnald driving out the Anglo-Saxon Ealdorman Ealdred from his lands at Bamburgh, causing him to flee, not to the court of King Edward, but King Constantine of Scotland. In the subsequent battle Ragnald is victorious, and succeeds in killing a number of English aristocracy including one Alfred who had fled Norse attacks from the west of the Pennines during 910 (HSC).

Ragnald then proceeded to divide up the land he had conquered between his followers as Halfdan had done some forty years earlier. It is tempting to equate these as being identical landscapes; only this time the land seems to have been the redistribution of existing estates, ruled by a single man instead of small parcels of land given to troops to farm (Morris 1981). No doubt their new tenants included the descendents of Halfdan's war band. The *History of St Cuthbert* is of course concerned with the losses of church holdings, and describes how an estate stretching from the River Wear to the River Tees was divided between Scula and Olaf Ball (HSC). Scula's portion reached from the Eden in the north, to the Tees in the south: Olaf's was bounded by the Wear to the north and the Eden to the south (HSC). Quite what happened to the land following Olaf's sudden death after casting disparaging remarks about Christianity in a church in Chester-le-Street (identified as the wrath of God, by the author) is unknown (HSC).

In 917 The *Annals of Ulster* recorded the return of Ragnald and his cousin Ivar to Ireland, and their successful reclamation of Norse territory, including Dublin. The following year Ragnald returned to Northumbria, possibly of a mind to take York (AU). Battle was again convened at Corbridge, and again a combined force of Scots and English were defeated (AU, HSC). Once more the ecclesiastical community found itself deprived of land, losing an estate it had given to Eadred, a sanctuary-seeking criminal, who had been killed in the battle (HSC). Rather ironically Ragnald gave the land to the English brothers Esbrid, and Ealdorman Ælstan sons of Eadred, who had fought bravely for him in the battle (HSC). The following year Ragnald took York by force (HK).

With the capture of York Ragnald was to fall within the remit of Edward of Wessex, whose gradual reclamation of England was beginning to close its grip around the southern edges of Northumbria. In 920 Ragnald along with Constantine, king of Scotland, Eadwulf's sons (King Alfred's appointed reeve of Bamburgh), their fellow Northumbrians[8], and the king of the Strathclyde Britons[9] accepted Edward as high king. Meanwhile the *Annals of Ulster* record Ragnald's brother Sihtric leaving Dublin in 920, and the northern English annals picks up his progress when he lands in England and sacks Davenport (HK). This may have been a result of Ragnald's death, and it appears Sihtric took the crown or assumed the vacant throne of Northumbrian without opposition (AU). According to William of Malmesbury's account he paid little heed to Edward, but when Æthelstan acceded to the West Saxon throne in 924, a peace treaty was made between the two kings at Tamworth in 925, and Sihtric married Æthelstan's sister, Ædgyth (WM). Perhaps unsurprisingly the marriage was not to last, and seems to have been undertaken as a placatory measure alongside that of becoming a token Christian, as his continued adherence to paganism showed (RW). How long Æthelstan was willing to tolerate this is not known, since Sihtric died within two years of the marriage, and left as heir a son, Olaf (presumably by an earlier wife or concubine). After Sihtric's death in 927 Æthelstan assumed the Northumbrian crown after putting down an uprising, probably sourced from Bamburgh, and driving off Guthfrith[10], Sihtric's Dublin based brother, who went to Scotland (WM). Sihtric's son, Olaf, fled to Ireland (WM). After narrowly avoiding being handed over to Æthelstan by the king of Scotland at Dacre, Guthfrith (after apparently collecting a war band) attempted an unsuccessful siege of York, but eventually submitted to the English king before returning to Ireland (WM). From then on Guthfrith remained in Ireland, and continued to raid across the countryside until his death in 934 (AU).

According to the surviving historical sources the kingdom of Northumbria remained free from any attempt at the recovery of Viking leadership until 937, when Olaf Guthfrithsson attempted to reclaim York, held for a limited period by his father in 927. Accompanied by a large army Olaf Guthfrithsson began to raid and pillage across the north of England, before combining with the forces of Scotland and Strathclyde (WM, HK). Æthelstan marched north to meet them, and defeated the combined forces at Brunanburh. The poetical account given in the *Anglo-Saxon Chronicles* (A) describes a very heavy defeat, with the death of five kings, seven of Olaf's jarls, and the son of the king of Scotland. Olaf escaped back to Dublin. The *Annals of Ulster* record the large losses inflicted on both sides in the battle and Æthelstan's victory, along with Olaf's return in 938.

Æthelstan died in 939, and the northern chronicles record Olaf's return to York the following year (HK). He then moved south with his army and failing in an attempt to take Northampton, turned to pillaging the countryside around Tamworth (HK). Æthelstan's brother and successor Edmund, met them at Leicester, and peace was brokered between them by Wulfstan, Archbishop of York, and Oda, Archbishop of Canterbury (HK). In effect the peace treaty re-divided England along the old Alfred-Guthrum boundary, Watling Street (HK). In this single treaty Edmund gave up everything Edward and Æthelstan had struggled to re-conquer and hold. In the account given by *Roger of Wendover* for 940 Olaf married Aldgyth (an English name, possibly a daughter of an Anglo-Viking and an English wife), the daughter of Jarl Orm, who had masterminded the success of his campaign (RW). However, his reign in York was not to last long. He died in 941 after raiding the church of St Bealdhere and burning Tyninghame near Dunbar (HK, Stenton 1998: 357). Within the year his cousin Olaf Sihtricson/Cuarán, king in Dublin (son of Sihtric, Ivar's grandson who had held York 921-927) had succeeded to the crown (HK).

In 942 Edmund began to re-conquer the north of England, beginning with the Five Boroughs (Leicester, Lincoln, Nottingham, Stamford and Derby). In 943 Olaf sacked Tamworth, accompanied by Wulfstan, Archbishop of York, only to be chased and besieged by Edmund at Leicester. They escaped the siege, but Olaf later approached Edmund in friendship, and received baptism. The succession in York after the death of Olaf Guthfrithson must have been open to challenge since Olaf Sihtricson had been followed from Ireland more or less immediately by Ragnald Guthfrithson, Olaf's younger brother. Quite who held the reigns of power in Northumbria is unclear. It seems highly likely that they were figureheads, and the real power held by resident Viking and Anglo-Saxon nobles. Shortly after Olaf Sihtricson's baptism in Edmund's court Ragnald followed suit. In 944 Edmund retook Northumbria and drove both Ragnald and Olaf back to Ireland where Blacair Guthfrithsson ceded Dublin to Olaf (ASC, AU).

On the death of Edmund in 946, the people of Northumbria took as their new ruler Eric, deposed king and son of Harald Finehair of Norway (HK, Stenton 1998: 360). Two years later Eadred, successor of Edmund, invaded Northumbria and forced Eric to flee and the local nobles to accept him as king. The throne of York, now more than ever obviously a figurehead role controlled by Northumbrian nobles, was ceded in 949 to Olaf Sihtricsson until 952, when the council replaced him with the returning Eric Bloodaxe (ASC, E). Eric's reign was again destined to be short, and he was driven out in 954 and murdered at Stainmore by Earl Maccus as he attempted to flee Northumbria (RW, ASC, E). He was to be the last Viking king of York. No further attempts were made by Olaf Sihtricsson, or any other Dublin Viking to take the kingdom of Northumbria, and Eadred of Wessex became king of England.

The kingdom of England was then ruled by a series of strong kings until the death of Edgar in 975. The Viking attacks beginning in the ill-fated reign of Æthelred during 981 were of a different type, led by the kings and sons of kings of Denmark and Norway, bent on annexing their kingdoms, rather than independent war bands and their leaders seeking plunder. This was eventually to succeed, and in 1017 the Dane Cnut was accepted as king of England.

[8] Who the ASC list as English, Danish Norwegian and others

[9] Probably Yawain, (Swanton 2000: 104 fn. 5)

[10] According to the *Chronicle of John of Wallingford* he was invited by the Northumbrian nobles because they wanted their own king (Whitelock 1959: 71)

4.1.5 Historical Accounts: discussion

The predominant sources for this section have been the historical texts recording the martial contact between Viking raider and Anglo-Saxon national, or more precisely, the Viking war-band leaders and the kings of Wessex. As argued above, it would be naive to think that the first contact the people of England had with Scandinavia occurred during the initial piratical forays of a few ships' crews in the late ninth century. Rather, it would be safe to propose a steady and long lasting link via trade and migration, which was to both pre and post-date Viking raids.

The initial aims of the Viking war bands were no doubt centred on plunder and glory. Although contact would have been predominantly aggressive, any army must be fed, equipped and entertained, factors not perpetually sustainable from within the group. These factors must have taken on a greater urgency when the army first over-wintered in Kent in 850-1. Supplies must have been acquired from the surrounding countryside, and no doubt fresh influences of entrepreneurial traders and hawkers who swelled the ranks of the camp followers, eager to chance risk against profit; a practice still evident around armies today. It is without doubt that the army had permanent camp followers, hawkers, traders, slavers, families (like Haesten's), prostitutes *et cetera*, some of whom may have been predominantly Scandinavian or Anglo-Saxon, or have roots in the myriad of the cultures in Europe the Vikings had come into contact with. All these people would have interacted with the army and the surrounding native population to a greater or lesser extent and had corresponding influence. Rather than a place to be avoided the army camps must have acted like an economic magnet, profit and need transcending incidental cultural differences. With this in mind it can be seen that contact did not begin pristinely during the settlements of the north during the late ninth century. Rather, it had been going on for a great number of years, simply changing in manner and intensity, as the needs and situations propelling it dictated the manner of interaction between Viking and native Anglo-Saxon at a particular time.

This manner of interaction is of course determined at a personal level, defined by the wants and needs of both parties. In 865 the formation of the Great Army by the grouping of several independently led war bands, has given rise to the speculation that it was intended to conquer England. It is in fact difficult to ascertain the ultimate intention of this war machine, as on the outset, its subjugated Anglo-Saxon kingdoms were ultimately used as banks and safe houses for further raids. Ultimately mantles of kingship were carved out by some of the leaders later on, no doubt mirroring the ruling elite of Wessex and utilising the remaining upper echelons of Anglo-Saxon nobility in the area by merging social strata of both groups. However, these are the predilections of only a few men. The greatest amount of contact, interaction and reaction would have occurred between the rank and file of the army and native groups, for food, equipment, entertainment and so on. The provision of social maintenance for the Viking troops must have been vital for success, morale and keeping the war bands together, beyond the highly tractable oath giving and kin-loyalty, and would have been recognised by the leaders. These had to be provided, or at least the opportunity for acquiring them.

As argued above, the pre-requisite of every army the camp followers, could have provided a certain amount, but what better place to camp than in or within the immediate vicinity of a town? The use of towns by the Viking war bands is specifically referred to throughout Anglo-Saxon accounts. On the surface, and quite true, is the fact that they were also chosen for their defensive potential, access to riverine and land routes as well as for the social maintenance of a large group. What tends to be overlooked however, are the people living in the towns at the time. It could be argued that a vast majority upped and fled. But where would they go, especially during the winter months? Would they abandon everything and risk starvation, or chance staying at home and interacting with the Viking host? It seems likely that at the higher end of the social scale some may have fled, as the *History of St Cuthbert* records, the likelihood being that they had somewhere else to go, or could at least be granted haven within another large household (secular or monastic). For the rest it seems the choice was rather bleaker. However, forced or not, contact had been initiated between the Viking armies and the people of the towns and satellite settlements. Interaction would logically follow, with reaction from Viking and native. Although for all intents and purposes the towns would have been controlled by the martial law of the invading host, neither the Anglo-Saxon Chronicles nor other contemporary sources allude to the flight of refugees into Anglo-Saxon Wessex from Viking held areas (ironically, the only record surviving alludes to movement the other way, and is discussed below), or the destruction of foodstuffs to make winter for the army harder to survive, or the raising of local levies to employ stings against an army at its most vulnerable. Neither does it mention the destruction of towns as had been done in France throughout the period. It does seem likely that the interaction was highly successful, and mutually profitable. The reaction was to maintain the *status quo*; retain a kind of symbiotic relationship. Whereas the Viking army possessed the power to wreak huge destruction and murder, should it be used against the local populace unrest was likely to follow within the ranks during the winter months as money, somewhere to spend it, food and entertainment were irrevocably removed.

Beyond the winter camps, (which no doubt retained parts of the army, its followers, sick and wounded when the bulk of the force moved on) the movement of war bands around England would initiate social contact at every turn, as they were by no means marching through an empty landscape. There is no doubt that this involved killings, rape, slaving and pillage, but equally likely that other modes of less insalubrious interaction took place.

An initial examination of table 4.1 illustrates that the direct influence of Viking rule seems decidedly short. According to the *Anglo-Saxon Chronicles*, Mercia was settled from 877, and reclaimed by Æthelflaed in 918, forty-one years later, or socially speaking, after one generation (taking one generation as the standard thirty-three years). Mercia had been lost to Viking control during the lifetime of her father Alfred, but was

Anglo-Saxon Kingdom	Conquered by Viking Army in	Settled by Viking Army in	Reconquered by Anglo-Saxon kings in	Number of Years Under Viking Control	Number of Generations (taking one generation = 33 years)	Years of Contact
Northumbria	866/873 (Great Army)	876	927	43 (from settlement) 8 (919-927 Norse)	1⅓	61
East Anglia	869 (Great Army)	879 (Summer Army of 871)	917	38 (from settlement)	1	48
Mercia	874 (Great Army)	877	918	41 (from settlement)	1	44

Table 4.1 *The Conquest and Reclamation of Viking England*

successfully reclaimed by her. The scene is repeated in East Anglia. In Northumbria, things are slightly different, mostly due to the resurgence of piratical activities instigated by the leaders of the Dublin Vikings. Had Æthelflaed not died in 918 there is little doubt that Northumbria would have been under the Wessex umbrella nine years earlier. This aside, the kingdom of York was only beyond the remit of Anglo-Saxon kingship for a single generation, the same as Mercia and East Anglia. It is acknowledged that the Viking 'rule' of York ended with the expulsion and death of Eric Bloodaxe in 954, however, what is evident from the historical sources is that these men, supported by a limited personal retinue, were accepted as kings by the Anglo-Scandinavian nobility of Northumbria, rather as the Anglo-Saxon figureheads appointed by their Viking predecessors during the 860's and 870's. It does seem likely that they were chosen to maintain some sort of independence, albeit limited, from Wessex who, as history showed, was militarily capable of subduing the north when politically expedient. The importance of the arrival of the Dublin leaders, however, lies again in contact and interaction, as their political knowledge and desire for wealth and status no doubt provided extra impetus to trade between York, Dublin and the rest of the North Sea World.

Remaining with the idea of contact and interaction, and setting aside the historically recorded benchmarks for the origins of settlement, the opportunity for contact really begins when the Great Army embarks on its campaign across England. This dramatically increases the timescale, moving Mercia to forty-four years, East Anglia to forty-eight and Northumbria sixty-one years, where two generations of people could have lived within the sphere of Viking influence.

The historical accounts of the reclamation also reiterates the use of towns by those who would be the descendents of the first Viking settlers in northern England, maintaining contact with places such as the Five Boroughs[11], York, Torksey, Northampton, Bedford, Huntington, Cambridge and Thetford. All these towns were a focal point for the satellite communities in the surrounding countryside where great interaction must have gone on between native Anglo-Saxon, Vikings, settlers and their descendents. Each town seemed to have its own leader, mirroring the days of the jarl and his war band but in more peaceful circumstances. The final collapse of Viking held districts was surprisingly swift and points to the scattered nature of their rule. Although the army of Northumbria was resoundingly defeated at Tettenhall in 910, and a large proportion of its nobility apparently killed, there is no effort made by the war bands of Mercia and East Anglia to combine as they had in 865 to form a single army. No doubt this is due to the different cultural and, to a certain extent, the ethnic make-up of the 'Viking' settlers. It is without doubt that those members of the Great Army and primary settlers were dead, and their successors to the settlement sites were derived from a very different cultural and social background. Some may have been secondary settlers from Scandinavia joining kin; others may be tertiary settlers. Intermarriage was extremely likely, producing descendents with a mixture of Viking and Anglo-Saxon ancestors. The incentives for survival and glory in a foreign land had long since gone, as these people were no longer invaders from a foreign shore, but were intensively integrated within communities, and were for all intents and purposes Anglo-Saxons in an Anglo-Saxon sub-kingdom. Defeat to the Great Army meant expulsion from England and a deflated ego for the Viking warriors. Protracted resistance and inevitable defeat for their successors meant death, and death for their families. They no longer had boats to run to, or an overseas homeland to return to. Mercia, East Anglia and Northumbria were now home and reactions to the threat of hostility had to be tempered accordingly. That is not to say cultural identity was lost by the Scandinavian settlers along with the ability to recognise cultural and ethnic differences between the two groups, something that is addressed in chapter six. This ethnic recognition may be alluded to in the description of Edward's raids into Northumbria and purposeful destruction of Scandinavian settlement sites (ASC). How such sites were identified can only be guessed at. It does, however, seem more likely that the raid was not ethnically selective, but rather a term of propaganda.

[11] Lincoln, Derby, Nottingham, Leicester and Stamford.

4.2 Viking and Anglo-Saxon Interaction: law codes and legal documents

As it has been shown above, the history of the Vikings in England survives for the most part within the Anglo-Saxon Chronicles and other less complete accounts, as a yearly list of interactions between established kingdoms and apparently recalcitrant Vikings. This section will continue the theme of investigation of contact, interaction and reaction and their implications through the surviving contemporary law codes and legal documents between Anglo-Saxon and Viking groups, be they raiders or settlers. As with all contemporary Anglo-Saxon sources these documents have long been subject to large amounts of scholarly attention in their own right, and correspondingly produced a huge corpus of written work on various themes. It is not the intention here to critique or discuss any of the documents, but solely to continue the theme of investigating the contact and interaction behind the reactions contained within these resources.

4.2.1 Primary Contact

Reference to the Vikings first appear in charters as early as 804, when King Cenwulf of Mercia and King Cuthred of Kent granted the Abbess of Lyminge an area of land in Canterbury to be used as a refuge should their institution be attacked by raiders (EHD 82: 514). Such raiders are again mentioned in a grant dated to 822 made by King Ceolwulf of Mercia to Archbishop Wulfred, retaining a charge against the land to cover military service against pagan enemies (EHD 83: 514-5). Some surviving charters record details of Viking presence hitherto unknown in other contemporary annals, such as that of King Burgred of Mercia granting lands in 855 to the Bishop of Worcester which refers to the presence of pagans in the Wrekin area of Shropshire (EHD 90: 526-7).

4.2.2 The Great Army and the Law

Charters and coins surviving from the reign of Ceolwulf, the Viking appointed king of Mercia, attest to the acceptance of his role by the highest-ranking members of both secular and ecclesiastical society (EHD 95: 533). Laws and treaties issued by Ceolwulf II, as he was styled, were also upheld by later Anglo-Saxon overlords of Mercia (Whitelock 1979: 533).[12]

Perhaps the most well known of all Anglo-Viking documents is the Alfred-Guthrum treaty, drawn up sometime between 866, when the Anglo-Saxons reclaimed London, and 890, the death of the East Anglian king, Guthfrith (Whitelock 1979: 416, Thorpe 1840: 152-7). It is without doubt an Anglo-Saxon construct, written and delivered by Alfredian lawmen, the secular equivalent perhaps of the king's taking of Guthrum as his spiritual kinsman by standing sponsor and godfather to him at his baptism (Kershaw 2000: 46, Fletcher 1997: 224, 278). Interestingly enough, unlike later law codes or treaties, it makes no attempt to further the evangelical process, perhaps covertly referring to followers of a non-Christian faith in the prologue, which ends; "*... who care to have God's grace and ours*", perhaps threatening non-Christians with martial retaliation rather than the not applicable heaven sent wrath (EHD 34: 416-7).

For the most part the treaty is mainly interested in establishing a boundary between Viking held East Anglia and Wessex, the regulation of trade across this boundary and the movement of men, especially those who might be pre-deposed to change sides (EHD 34: 416-7, Thorpe 1840: 152-7). The acknowledgment and need to control the trade is extremely important when considering interaction. The switching of sides may not be as far-fetched as it seems, an occurrence suggested in a charter of Edward the Elder (dated 901) which dealt with the disposal of an area of land forfeited to King Alfred by Ealdorman Wulfhere when he broke oath and deserted both Alfred and his *fatherland* (EHD 100: 541-3).

The boundary, while logically geographical, is also recognition of Guthrum's right to rule a particular area and perhaps an acknowledgment of equal rank between the two kings. Physically, the East Anglian boundary rectified in the treaty seems only to secure the immediate north of Alfred's kingdom. This was to become more fluid and temporary during the Anglo-Saxon period than its modern incarnation as the marker of *Danelaw*, the term Danelaw being an eleventh century construct (Whitelock 1941: 8). It reads:

'First, concerning their land-boundaries: along the Thames, then up on the Lea, along the Lea unto its source, thence right to Bedford, thence upwards on the Ouse unto Watling-street' (Thorpe 1840: 152-7).

How the Treaty affected people living around or even on this boundary, or even if they were aware of it, will probably never be known. Neither is it clear what happens when Watling Street was reached. All in all it seems to be more of a secular face-saving exercise, written only to incorporate Guthrum's Vikings into Anglo-Saxon law, to give credence to a series of bartered oaths needed to protect on paper at least, the northern border of Wessex while Alfred continued to do battle with other Viking groups. Quite how seriously the Vikings of East Anglia took the treaty is illustrated over the following years when they joined other raiding groups from the continent and their Northumbrian compatriots in attacks against Wessex at every given opportunity.

The final part of the treaty covers the establishment of wergild prices and the equality of Englishman and Danes. The fact that the wergild value of free, landowning men is valued in marks (eight half marks of gold) a Scandinavian measurement of weight is interesting and could mean one of three things. Firstly, that the Anglo-Saxon court recognised the mark as a unit of measurement; secondly, that it was used as a concession to enable recognition of the law by the Vikings (whether they adhered to it or not) and thirdly, that the surviving copy of the treaty was written much later than claimed when Scandinavian nomenclature and style were becoming more widespread. It could also be taken to mean that all Viking settlers were recognised to be of this rank. The acceptance of the higher wergild value for a freeman by the Anglo-Saxons may also lend weight to the idea that the Viking settlers still held the balance of power over Wessex. What is clear, however, is that the treaty recognised two different groups of ethnic origin,

[12] Coins were also issued in his name (Whitelock 1979: 533).

Dane and Anglo-Saxon, and attempts to deal with them within the confines of its remit. Whether in fact the Vikings (be they Danes, Frisian, Norse, English, British or Irish) in East Anglia actually adhered to any of it is another question entirely.

4.2.3 Reclamation

Alfred's immediate successors, Edward and Æthelstan provided England with two strong military kings who, as illustrated above, reclaimed between them all Viking held territory. Edward's laws given at Exeter (*II Edward*), which probably date to the latter years of his reign, in the section regarding the protection of a convicted offender, refer to different forms of punishment carried out in the eastern and northern kingdoms for the offences set out in the *frith-gewritu* (written peace settlement), a reference to a treaty between Anglo-Saxon Wessex and the Viking settlers in East Anglia and Northumbria which is now lost (Lieberman 1903-16 in Attenborough 1922: 205, Thorpe 1840: 158-165 @ 165, Kershaw 2000: 44). The 901 charter of Edward that refers to the Alfred-Guthrum Treaty in the case of Ealdorman Wulfhere defecting to Viking held East Anglia, and has been discussed above. Both show continuing interaction between Anglo-Saxon Wessex and the Viking held territories of England.

This section cannot be complete without reference to the *Laws of Edward and Guthrum* an eleventh century document purporting to date from the time of Guthrum's rule in East Anglia (Whitelock 1941). It has been convincingly argued that the laws were written by Wulfstan II, Archbishop of York, and bear uncanny similarities to the laws of Æthelred, most of which he was involved with and have been discussed below (Whitelock 1941).

The surviving six series of the laws of Æthelstan have no particular reference to any Viking groups or kingdoms, suggestive that as the king of England Æthelstan saw himself as ruler of one resident geographically identified nationality (Attenborough 1922: 122-169). At the meeting at Eamont Bridge, near Dacre in 927 where the remaining independent kings of Britain[13] met with Æthelstan to accede to his over-lordship, the reference to pagans in the north no doubt applied to Viking groups, but is used instead of an ethnic tag applied in previous historical documents (Stenton 1998: 340).

What is particularly relevant to the overall study of Viking burial is contained in II Æthelstan issued at Grately Hampshire (926-30), where section 13.1 decrees that all burials are to take place within towns (EHD 35: 417-422 @ 419). This is a very important point, and can only have been a reaction to a common practice of burial close to rural settlement sites. The law seems to have been put in place to enforce control of church and state over funerary rituals and practice, no doubt aimed at incoming groups, whose obsequies may have been more pagan influenced than was acceptable to an evangelising king. By essentially removing cult practice from families and local groups it no doubt had the effect of standardising and enforcing the Christian ideals of dealing with death.

[13] Hywel, king of the West Welsh, Constantine, king of Scotland, Owain, king of Gwent, Ealdred of Bamburgh, Owain, king of the Cumbrians (ASC, WM)

The surviving charters of Æthelstan's reign attest to the purchase of land from Viking owners, a transaction introduced into England by the immigrants themselves. The first, dated to 926, refers to land at Chalgrave and Tebworth, Bedfordshire and recounts how it had been purchased on the orders of King Edward from the *pagans* for ten pounds of gold and silver (EHD 103: 546-7). The second charter involves the presentation of Amounderness to the church at York in 934, after Æthelstan had purchased it from the *pagans*, and was witnessed by six high-ranking men bearing Scandinavian names ending the list of the Anglo-Saxon named ealdorman and coming above the thegnly ranks (EHD 104: 548-51). It seems likely that they were jarls of Scandinavian descent and shows a differentiation between Viking groups (at the very least by the scribe) and levels of integration within England at the time within the upper echelons of society.

Further charters from Æthelstan's reign bear witness to the large number of people of Scandinavian descent at his court. For example, in March of 931 at his council at Colchester six of the thirteen earls present bore Scandinavian names, as did seven in November of 931 at Lifton, Devon (Stenton 1998: 351-2)[14]. All must have been substantial landowners possibly within East Anglia or the north of England, and as such would have had direct influence over people living there, be they Anglo-Saxon or those of Viking descent. It is worth emphasising that these men were up to three generations removed from the initial recorded settlers of the Great Army, and very probably the sons of the men defeated by Edward the Elder during his reclamation of the north (see table 4.2 below). Again, as pointed out above, this is likely to be a demonstration of his political power, by maintaining and accepting members of his kingdom at his court despite their recognisable ancestry. This presence and manipulation of ethnicity by immigrant groups will be discussed in chapter six.

Calendar Year (taking 1 generation=33 years)	Generation	Date range of birth
870	1st	830-855[15]
903	2nd	870-902
936	3rd	903-935

Table 4.2 *Generational Time-Span of Viking Settlers in England*

The first occurrence of a Scandinavian loan word in an English law text occurs in *II Edmund* (939-46), which deals with the suppression of the blood feud (Whitelock 1979: 428, EHD 38: 427-9). The word is *hamsocn* and translates as an attack on a farmstead (Whitelock 1979: 428, EHD 38: 427-9). This is surely evidence for integration across all levels of society of Scandinavian settlers and the native population.

[14] At Lifton – Urm, Guthrum, Haward, Gunner, Thurferð, Hadd and Scule. Other Scandinavian earls witness to Æthelstan's charters were Styrcær, Grim, Fræna, Regnwald, Inwær & Healfdean (Stenton 1998: 351).

[15] Taking 15 to be the youngest age from the Norwegian laws when a youth is given the right to bear arms, & a hypothetical 40 year old maximum (Frostathing Law, transl. Larson 1935: 240)

The code known as the '*Hundred Ordnance*' written between 939 and 961, and quite possibly has its origins during Edmund's reign lays instructions for the four weekly meetings of the hundred courts across England, and there is no doubt that this is an effort to bring into line at least the management of all the laws across a recently united England if not the laws themselves, whether they be Scandinavian influenced or older Northumbrian (Whitelock 1979: 429, EHD 39: 429-30).

A grant of land made by King Eadred in 946 illustrates again as with Æthelstan's Amounderness charter, the presence of Viking (quite possibly Hiberno-Norse) settlers in England and their continuing adherence to other religions other than Christianity, alongside the other named ethnic groups of Anglo-Saxons, Northumbrians and Britons (EHD 105: 551-2, Whitelock 1979: 429). As with Æthelstan's earlier charter it also illustrates a pattern of discrimination between different Viking groups in society, the grant being witnessed by Oda, Archbishop of Canterbury, who was a descendent of Danish settlers in East Anglia, and the earls (jarls) Orm (probably the father-in-law of Olaf Guthfrithson) and Morcar (EHD 105: 551-2, Whitelock 1959: 73). It is very likely that the Jarl Orm of this charter is one and the same as the Jarl Orm, who aided his son-in-law Olaf Guthfrithson's wars with Edmund around 940. This can be seen as illustrative of the fluidity of politics and how easily he was able to interact, presumably for his own best interests, with the new king.

The recognition of different Viking groups is also apparent in the will of King Eadred (dated 946-955), whish stipulates that sixteen hundred pounds be used to protect his people from famine or the heathen; the heathen presumably referring to the Vikings operating in the Irish Sea region (EHD 107: 554-5). A charter if his successor Eadwig in 856, granting Southwell to Oscytel Archbishop of York, illustrates that the estate had many places attached to it with sake and soke, an important fact to scholars of *Danelaw* tenure and landholding practices (EHD 108: 556-7)[16]. The identification of the 'rank' or position of a sokeman in Anglo-Saxon and later Anglo-Norman society is a contentious issue amongst historians; some of whom see the sokemen as descendents of Viking settlers, while others put forward arguments for its origins to lie prior to the advent of Viking settlement. Current consensus tends towards the latter point of view. If sokemen were indeed the descendents of Viking immigrant groups, existence of such charters again illustrate the interaction across all levels of society and acceptance of culturally different procedures of rank and estate management in the north by the Anglo-Saxon monarchy. If the converse is true, and the origins of sake and soke lay far earlier, then it seems more than likely that the settlers had assimilated into the major resident systems of land management.

4.2.4 Laws and Charters of a United Kingdom

The laws of Edgar, who was acknowledged King of England from the late 950's until his death in 975, legislates that the Danes under his rule should choose the best laws as they see fit, (Laws of Edgar, in Thorpe 1840: 273-77). This suggests that while Edgar is in some sense a high-king in England, there still exists a separation within society, acknowledged both by Anglo-Saxon elites and resident Anglo-Scandinavians, who had their own ruling and justice system, and enough power and political influence to maintain it despite a Wessex overlord. However, rather than equating Danes as a specific ethnic cultural group, perhaps the term should be regarded as those areas captured by the Great Army (*ie* Northumbria and East Anglia), which as discussed, had different laws to Wessex, either prior to or as a result of Viking settlement. It hardly seems likely that a group of Danish merchants living in London or Winchester should be allowed to practice their own laws in what was the Wessex heartland. In part 15 of *IV Edgar* dated 962-63, the Anglo-Scandinavian settlers in Northumbria are referred to by the Anglo-Saxon term *here* a word once used to describe a Viking army, but now used to described Anglo-Scandinavian settlers within the aldormanry of Earl Oslac of Northumbria who gave their support to the laws of the king (Thorpe 1840: 279, EHD 41: 437). While not an entirely derogatory term, the word is used to define the origins of and illustrate the differences still recognised within England at the time.

These differences while alluded to in Edgar's laws are expanded in the laws during the less stable rule of Æthelred, and although were constructed over one hundred years following the arrival of the first documented Viking settlers, are included here for sake of completeness (978-1016).

In his code at Wantage, or *III Æthelred*, written between 978 and 1008, the terminology is essentially Scandinavian, and while intends to represent the will of a king of all England, pays enormous adherence to local customs, and could quite possibly have been written by someone who understood Scandinavian law practices very well, a rouse perhaps to ingratiate the crown with the influential lords of Viking descent against the continual threats against England made by Norway and more especially Denmark (*EHD* 43:439-442, Stenton 1998: 508, 511). The fines stipulated for breaking the peace at meetings within the area of the Five Boroughs are so large, it is thought that they were levied on a group of people rather than the single offender (Stenton 1998: 510). The document is also important because it is the first time that a sworn jury of twelve men appears in English law, a tradition brought from Scandinavia, alongside the first appearance in English law that if the views of the jury differ than the views of the majority must prevail (Stenton 1998: 511, Thorpe 1840: 292-99). Part three deals with the purchase of land, a concept introduced to Anglo-Saxon England by the Vikings, and perhaps understandably therefore illustrated in Anglo-Saxon law by Scandinavian phraseology (Thorpe 1840: 293-295). This concept of using Scandinavian terms was not limited to secular practice; a private memo relating to a transfer of land written in Peterborough Abbey during the tenth century adheres completely in both word and deed to Scandinavian tradition (Stenton 1998: 512).

The fines in *III Æthelred* also imply Scandinavian influence, using the unit of the ora [17] alongside that of the mark (Stenton 1998: 510).

[16] See also Hadley 2000*a* for a modern study of Danelaw landholding.

[17] 1 ora = 16 pence. 8 orae = 1 mark. 120 orae = 8 English pounds = a *hundred* of silver. (Stenton 1998: 510).

In Æthelred's treaty with the Viking army (*II Æthelred*, 991 or 994) peace was drawn up between the English king and three Viking leaders, Anlaf (Olaf Tryggvason, later king of Norway), Justin (Olaf's maternal uncle) and Guthmund Stegita's son (EHD 42: 437-9, Thorpe 1840: 284-91). Following the payment of tribute[18], Æthelred sought to make it legally binding, by acknowledging *Danes* of this new army as having equal wergilds as Anglo-Saxons, as the Alfred-Guthrum Treaty had a hundred years earlier, and by allying this army with his own against subsequent raiding groups (EHD 42: 437-39, Thorpe 1840: 284-91).

An insight into the laws current in Anglo-Scandinavian northern England are alluded to in *V Æthelred*, dated to 1008, part 32.4, where he abolishes the practice carried out in 'the North' of not allowing a person charged with murder chance to prove his innocence if the victim died on the day the oath sworn accusation had been made (EHD 44: 442-6, Stenton 1998: 508). That there were more differences is tantalisingly alluded to in part 32.5, which reads, '*But our lord has suppressed that abuse. May he do more*' (*EHD* 44: 442-6, Stenton 1998: 508). However, again it is unknown whether these practices had their roots in Viking laws or those of Northumbria.

It is worthy of note that the first time the term *Danelaw* is used occurs in the eleventh century *VI Æthelred* part 37: it does not occur in any other earlier texts and is not used again until Cnut's laws (Whitelock 1941: 8).

Charters during this later period include the use of land to raise money to pay off Viking raiders (dated to 994), including some from a Dane (whether Danish born or of Anglo-Danish descent is unknown) by the name of Toti who had given a pound of gold towards tribute money. Ethnic identity, duplicity and confusion is illustrated in the confirmation of the will of Æthelric of Bocking (dated to 995-9), who had previously been suspected aiding the cause of Sven Forkbeard (Williams 1986: 1, EHD 117: 569-70, EHD 121: 579-580). The concluding paragraph reads:

'*...and all the thegns who were gathered there from far and wide, both West Saxons and Mercians, Danes and English*' (Whitelock 1930: 44-7).

Whether the Danes referred to be those descendents and scion of the original Viking raiders, or his more recent allies, can only be guessed at.

Witness lists are a record of those present at the king's court at the time, and the mention of *Danes*, however vague is very important in this instance owing to the scarcity of Danish names found on surviving charters of this period (Stenton 1998: 551). There are only two diplomas of Æthelred (S911[19] and S922[20]), which include Scandinavian names amongst the witnesses, and these only occur at very large meetings (Keynes 1980: 162). This may be illustrative of the distrust Æthelred and his council had for the nobles of Viking descent, or perhaps families were adopting more Anglo-Saxon names for their children. In favour of the latter it would perhaps have been more prudent to keep potentially recalcitrant Anglo-Viking nobles at court, rather than ostracize them and give rein for internal revolt. If it was the former, it shows that they were still recognised as socially, culturally and ethnically different by at least the upper-echelons of Anglo-Saxon society during this period. This apparent segregation could also be a reflection within society of the recognition of ethnically different groups living in England at the time and the inability to interact with them by the rulers when threatened by what was a totally different group from their perceived 'homeland', or rather the homeland of their grandparents or great-grandparents.

The will of a high-ranking Anglo-Saxon noble, Wulfric Spott (*c*1002-1004), whose Mercian mother, Wulfrun, had been captured by the Vikings in Tamworth in 943, records his landholdings as being in Lincolnshire, Leicestershire, Nottinghamshire, South Yorkshire, South Lancashire and Cheshire, all areas traditionally associated with the *Danelaw* (EHD 125: 586-589). The only mention of purchased land is that of Appleby (Leicestershire), so could it be possible that his family held on to the majority of their land throughout Viking attacks and the rule of the Hiberno-Norse or perhaps bought it back earlier or even took it by force (EHD 125: 586-589). Either way, the family of Wulfric Spot maintained control of their large estate within the boundaries of what is recognised by traditional history as Viking territory.

Perhaps the most famous charter issued in Æthelred's reign is the renewal of lands and privileges of the monastery of St Fridewide, Oxford, (1004) which recalled the king and his council's decree in 1002 that all the Danes in England were to be killed on St Brice' Day (EHD 127: 590-593). During the apparent slaughter in Oxford, a group of Danes had taken sanctuary in the church, and unable to get them out, the townspeople had burned the building down with them in it (EHD 127: 590-593). This is recounted in the charter, not as reparation for the act, but rather the irritating factor that caused the king to rebuild and refurbish the destroyed church (EHD 127: 590-593). No mentioned is made of the murdered people (EHD 127: 590-593). It is unknown whether these people were settlers of Danish descent, first or second generation, or even Danish merchants based in the town, whose links to earlier Viking raiding groups or those of the day were highly unlikely. They may have been very recent settlers in the city. It is known that the sister and brother-in-law of King Sven of Denmark were killed in the St Brice's Day massacre, which does suggest these people were recent immigrants and not the descendents of earlier settlers (see below) (ASC, WM, EHD 127: 590-3).

In the sixteenth century translation of *The North People's Law* a lost Anglo-Saxon text dating to the very early eleventh century, a list of wergilds are given which illustrates that there existed a class between that of the thegn and the ealdorman known as a *hold* (Lambarde 1568 in Thorpe 1840: 186-189, Stenton 1998: 509, Whitelock 1979: 468). The term *holdr* is of Scandinavian origin and used to describe a landowner of status below that of a jarl (ASC: 94). In *The North People's Law* the

[18] Twenty-two thousand pounds of gold and silver.

[19] Æthelred to Eynsham Abbey: confirmation of foundation & endowment in various counties d1005 (Keynes 1980: 96).

[20] Diploma in favour of Morcar, d1009 (Keynes 1980: 123).

wergild of the hold is four thousand thrymsas[21], half that of an ealdorman, and twice that of a thegn (Lambarde 1568, in Thorpe 1840: 186-189). The term is used in the *Anglo-Saxon Chronicles* for example in 904 when Edward defeated the combined force of Ætholwold and the Viking king Eohric of East Anglia, in its abridged list of the slain, and again in 910 for the battle of Tettenhall. The incorporation shows that Scandinavian social strata had been adopted by and legalised through the insertion into a list of ancient Northumbrian laws. This shows influence within the upper echelons of society and acceptance by the Northumbrians of an Anglo-Viking cultural practice and a willingness to accept and legitimise it at the highest level. This difference in social strata between the Viking influenced north and the Anglo-Saxon south is one of the very few that can be linked undisputedly to Viking settlement, rather than earlier Northumbrian laws.

4.2.5 Later Laws of the Danish Kings of England

In the later laws of the Anglo-Danish and Norman kings of England other differences are referred to and can be remarked upon. For example, in society the wergild of a man from the *Danelaw* payable to his lord depended on his rank, not that of his lord as it did in the laws of Wessex and Mercia (Stenton 1998: 507). The fines for such crimes as the king considered to be within his own remit, such as breach of the peace, attacks on the highways or houses were very heavy, far heavier than the rest of England, and possibly, as has been suggested, were to be levied on communities rather than individuals as mentioned above (Stenton 1998: 507). Less serious crimes were punishable in *Danelaw* by the payment of *lahslit,*[22] a Scandinavian loanword for a socially variable fine, first used in *III Æthelred* (EHD 44: 442-446, 49: 454-467 @ 456, Thorpe 1840: 358-425). The amount is once again far greater than the equivalent fines in the rest of England[23], and may have been payable by the family group or the larger community (EHD 44: 442-446, 49: 454-467 @ 456, Thorpe 1840: 358-425). However, the heriots payable to King Cnut (pt. 17) for a king's thegn within *Danelaw* are less than those without, which perhaps illustrates recognition and preferential treatment of people of Scandinavian descent, or at least those who had come to England with Cnut (Thorpe 1840: 454-467 @415, EHD 49: 454-467 @ 465). However, once again, it must be pointed out, that these laws may indeed have originated with the ninth century Viking settlers, or could have had their roots in deeper antiquity. Either way, it gives a sense of self-policing along with a feeling of how closely-knit communities were during the later Anglo-Saxon period in the north.

4.2.6 Law Codes and Legal Documents: discussion

What is immediately clear from the study is just how quickly Viking settlers became involved in English law and practice. It is especially visible during the consolidation of their new kingdoms by the Viking kings to secure recognised legal as well as military control. Initially their involvement or contact was seen to be unlawful (piratical), and laws were set in place as reactions to this (EHD 82, 83, 90: 514-5, 526-7). The establishment of Ceolwulf in Mercia was a reaction by both Viking and Anglo-Saxon nobles to replace the defeated King Burgred and an attempt at stability. There can be little doubt he was put in place by the support of both the leaders of the Great Army and the Mercian nobility, an example of swift interaction between the highest ranks of society to enable the Vikings to hold politically what they had taken militarily and the Mercian nobles to retain as much land and influence as they could under the new regime. It seems that the arrangement worked very well indeed, with Ceolwulf retaining at least some of his power and land after the 877 division of land, and the continuing adherence to the legal documents ratified by him by successive rulers of Mercia (EHD 95: 533, Whitelock 1979: 533). However, it seems more than likely that he was supported initially, not only by the threat of attack by the highly active Great Army (the threat of which conversely would surely have ensured his compliance to the whim of the Viking leaders), but no doubt there remained behind a military contingent from the Viking army to support and remind both him and the other Mercian nobles of the likely calamity of non-compliance. The presence of a force in Mercia would also retain contact links with the main group.

The Alfred-Guthrum Treaty continues the illustration of the links between the ruling ranks of society within Wessex and the remainder of the Great Army under Guthrum's leadership (EHD 34: 416-7). Although written by Anglo-Saxon scribes the use of Scandinavian terminology apparently so early in the historical settlement process is very important (that is, within the first generation). It could mean immediate acquiescence to the Viking army, or and more likely, the reaction to a long knowledge of terminology in use in England due to periods of long contact dating to the Great Army and earlier to incorporate normal, everyday trade and movement. Either way, it was constructed so that both parties knew what it meant and could not be misconstrued. The Alfred-Guthrum Treaty, or more properly, the people writing it, recognised two groups of different ethnic origin (something occurring in later contemporary documents) and attempted to deal with them within the confines of its remit. Ideas of ethnicity and cultural identity are indelibly woven into the fabric of archaeological inference (and none more so than in this period), and consideration of what it meant in the Anglo-Saxon period and what it means to today's scholars will be fully explored in chapter six, as it has a fundamental effect on the interpretation of the archaeological record during this period of intense interaction between two groups.

In a way, by laying down the law, the Alfred-Guthrum Treaty authorises contact and interaction between Anglo-Saxons of Wessex and the 'Danes' of East Anglia, and can be seen either as a reaction to the events of the past twenty years or a ratification of continual interaction. The East-Anglians themselves are not mentioned, their ethnic identity as a whole (in the eyes of the authors at least) changed to Danish, a reflection of the ethnicity of the new king. As argued above, it is likely that by the time that the Alfred-Guthrum Treaty was written (*c*886-90) contact and interaction between the Great

[21] Thrymsas = 3 silver pennies (Stenton 1998: 509).

[22] Lahslit-breach of the law, varies with rank of offender; 10 half-marks for a kings thegn, 6 half-marks for other landowners, 12 ores for the ceorl (EHD 44: 446)

[23] For example see Cnut 15, d. 1020-1023, EHD 49: 456, or Thorpe 1840 at 385 for unabridged version, where a thegn under English jurisdiction is to pay 120 shillings, a thegn under Danelaw 10 half-marks, which is rather more.

Army and its followers and settlers had been well under way for close on thirty years.

The boundary fixed between Wessex and the North of England in the Alfred-Guthrum Treaty can in no way be described as a Berlin Wall, although one would expect a least some sort of military presence (for defence or taxation) at major river crossings and road junctures. The boundary did not stop the movement of people, and resettlement took place within Viking held territory even by high-ranking Anglo-Saxon nobles. Diplomatic contact of sorts continued after the Alfred-Guthrum Treaty throughout Edward's reign, a fact alluded to in his law codes (EHD 34, 100: 416-7, 541-3). What this demonstrates is the continuing interaction between the two kingdoms and knowledge of the differences within the laws of the two areas, some which may or may not pre-date Viking influence.

Treatment or even acknowledgement of Danes as a separate ethnic identity does not occur in Æthelstan's laws, indicating perhaps a change in relationship of Viking settlers and native groups. By the time Æthelstan accedes the throne in 924 almost sixty years has gone by since the arrival of the Great Army, and the descendents of the earliest settlers must have been three or four generations removed. Instead of laws and charters drawn up governing the differences between the two groups as were done in the reigns of his predecessors, Anglo-Viking nobles were appearing consistently as signatories on his legal documents, indicating a major change in relationship, and close contact within certain areas of the highest levels of society (EHD 104, 105: 48-51). Æthelstan's charters also attest to the adoption of the Scandinavian practice of land purchase and ownership, the king himself being a buyer (EHD 103, 104: 546-7, 548-51). Such an acquisition is surely an indicator for a large amount of interaction between many people negotiating between vendor and purchaser. Doubtless many other tracts of land changed hands in similar circumstances.

Recognition and differentiation between ethnic and cultural groups do still occur in Æthelstan's documents, but are seemingly directed at Norse settlers in the northwest of England, who are persecuted not because of their ethnicity, but because of their religion (Stenton 1998: 340). This continues into the reign of Eadred and occurs in a charter of 946. A reversal as such occurs in Edgar's reign (late 950's-975) where Danes are once more dealt with as a distinct ethnic group (Laws of Edgar, in Thorpe 1840: 273-7). This is surely a reaction to some historically lost occasion of interaction, and rather than an acknowledgement to the descendents of Viking settlers (now four to five generations removed from the Great Army) it shows that there is going on within England a huge amount of contact with Scandinavia, no doubt fuelled by the constant interaction between the descendents of Vikings settlers, new migrants and their original homelands. This idea is confirmed in the reign of Æthelred, where there seems to be an underlying confusion within Anglo-Saxon society (the rulers at least) on how to deal with English born people of Scandinavia descent, now settlers, farmers, tradesmen and merchants, in the wake of the attacks by Sven and Cnut.

Overall, while the legal documents of the period show an immediate and lasting influence by Viking groups at all levels of society and in all manner of transactions, as contact and interaction was played out. Crucially, they are also a barometer for the success of the integration of settled groups.

4.3 Miscellaneous Historical Interaction

As already illustrated Viking leaders became directly embroiled in Anglo-Saxon politics almost as soon as they had a foothold on English soil. Profit, and ultimately survival, were no doubt underlying causes, but as time went on these were replaced by the search for prestige and influence, which runs hand in hand with political control. As discussed above, contemporary sources bear witness to such interaction, both secular and ecclesiastical.

4.3.1 Church and Viking

The interaction between church and Viking is perhaps most visible in the Anglo-Saxon kingdom of Northumbria. When the Great Army took York in 866 the then Archbishop, Wulfhere, supported the Anglo-Saxon puppet-king Egbert, and was driven into Mercia by his own people in 872, only to return in 874 after agreeing to support Ricsige, the king chosen by the Northumbrians (HK).

In the *History of St Cuthbert*, (pt. 13) relays the account of the saint appearing in a dream to the Abbot of Carlisle, ordering him to cross the Tyne to the army of the Danes where he was to select the slave of a certain widow, named Guthfrith Hardacnut's son, whom the army would (and apparently did) accept as king (HSC). The story almost takes the form of a creation myth to validate the ties of the church to what must have been predominantly pagan invaders. The alliance and accompanying myth was no doubt created to secure the rights/power base of the church with the new secular power. The piece records that Cuthbert ordered him to be ordained king by the thoroughly pagan tradition of placing him on a mound, generally an ancestor mound, Oswiu's Hill, and the placing of a gold ring on his right arm (HSC). Rather than the burial mound of his ancestors, Oswiu's Hill was named after a seventh century saint and king of Northumbria (Innes 2000: 79). Whether the manner of Guthfrith's rise to power is to be believed or not, it seems he was if not a Christian at the time, he was at least favourable towards the wandering monks of St Cuthbert, by allowing them to re-establish their monastery at Chester-le-Street, and being buried in a church below the later site of York Minster (HSC, Stenton 1998: 262).

Perhaps the most infamous prelate of York was Archbishop Wulfstan I, nominated to his see by King Æthelstan, and after his death a strong ally of the Norse kings of York, representing Olaf Guthfrithson as ambassador in the treaty made with Oda, Archbishop of Canterbury (himself a son of Danish settlers in East Anglia), representing King Edmund in 940 (Stenton 1998: 436). Wulfstan swore fealty to Eadred in 947 alongside other Northumbrian magnates, after Eric Bloodaxe had been taken as king in Northumbria in 946, but as the *Anglo-Saxon Chronicles* recounts, soon broke his oath and accepted Olaf Sihtricson in 949. In 952 Eadred ordered Wulfstan's arrest, and he was only partially re-instated to his see in 954 when Northumbria was restored to the English crown, but was never physically allowed to return, dying near Dorchester in 956 (Whitelock 1959: 73). It seems that Wulfstan was interested in keeping Northumbria an independent kingdom, no matter who was on the throne, whether they be Christian or not, an interest no doubt backed by the Northumbrian nobles of Anglo-Saxon and Viking descent.

That the Viking rulers of Northumbria allowed strong prelates to partake in mutually advantageous power politics is understandable, and is illustrated in contemporary documents and briefly discussed above. However, they may have left the monks of Lindisfarne to wonder across the north of England for seven years, but happily asset –stripped the ecclesiastical community not only of portable wealth, but more importantly land, a fact attested to in a memo of St Oswald, Archbishop of York, (*c*975-992) which bemoans the loss of land from Ripon, Otley and Sherburn-in-Elmet and in the earlier *History of St Cuthbert* which describes the dividing up of church land by the Dublin based Ragnald (EHD 114: 565, HSC, Stenton 1998: 436).

It is interesting to note that Wulfstan's successor was one Oscytel, a man with roots in the Eastern Danelaw (Whitelock 1959: 75). Oscytel is not only a Scandinavian name, but research has shown he was a kinsman of Oda, Archbishop of Canterbury, a man of Anglo-Danish parentage fostered into an Anglo-Saxon household (Whitelock 1959:73, Whitelock 1941: 169-170). Oscytel's successor at York was Oswald, a nephew of Oda (Whitelock 1959: 75). It is ironic that the English kings chose churchmen of Scandinavian extraction to become ecclesiastical leaders in an area of later Viking settlement because they were having more trouble with the local Anglo-Saxon prelates. It also had the added advantage of being better able to relate to the lifestyles of the large immigrant Scandinavian populace and encourage them to comply with the kings of Wessex (Whitelock 1959: 76). Neither had they any ties within Northumbria to benefit them by raising rebellion amongst the independent spirited Northumbrians (Whitelock 1959: 76).

4.3.2 Scandinavian Visitors and Anglo-Vikings

During the period of heaviest conflict in Alfred's reign contemporary writers attest to the presence of people of Scandinavian descent present at his court. Alfred's biographer, Asser, also recounts the presence of *pagans*, perhaps the most celebrated of which being the merchant-explorer Othere, proof enough of contact beyond the military type with Scandinavia at the height of the Viking assaults on England (Asser pt. 76: 91, Lund & Fell 1984). Asser also mentions the presence of a young monk of Viking (pagan) descent at Alfred's foundation at Athelney, and remarks that there were more who followed in his footsteps (Asser pt. 94: 103). Alfred was also godfather to the children of the Hæsten, before the ultimate defeat of the Viking leader at his hands.

As in the time of Alfred there were Scandinavian dignitaries who visited Æthelstan's court, such as Osfrid and Helgrim sent by Harald Fairhair of Norway who were received in York (WM).

In 918, the History of St Cuthbert records the presence of two Englishmen, Esbrid, son of Edred, and the Ealdorman Ælstan, his brother, as fighting with Ragnald against the Scots and the Bernicians at Corbridge (HSC, ASC). The battle won, Ragnald rewarded the two Englishmen with tracts of land taken from the monastery of St Cuthbert (HSC). While surprising at it may seem, Esbrid and Ælstan must not have been the only English men to throw in their lot with a Viking army. As discussed above in the case of Æthelwold, it was not beyond those members of the highest echelons of society to try to improve their lot with a Viking army who were happy to oblige in the pursuit of mutual profit.

Further interaction, albeit at a lower social scale, is referred to in a story connected to the battle of Brunanburh (937), where William of Malmesbury reports how Æthelstan's life is saved by a man in his retinue who at one time served his adversary Olaf Guthfrithson.

Perhaps a less reliable historical source is the contemporary *Egil's Saga* which despite some questionable mixing of dates, gives useful insights into life in the north of England during the period (Scudder 1997: 91, Jesch 2001*a*: 316). Part of the saga tells of how he and his brother Thorolf took three hundred of their men as mercenaries to join Æthelstan's army and fought for him at the battle of Brunanburh (*Egil's Saga* pt. 54-5: 87-92). This is analogous to the use of Anglo-Saxon men in Viking armies, as mentioned above, as Egil and his men were employed in fighting against the Viking king Olaf Guthfrithson. It is interesting to note that in order to join Æthelstan's army the king made a common request, and:

"...*asked Thorolf and Egil to take the sign of the cross, because that was a common custom amongst both merchants and mercenaries who dealt with Christians. Anyone who had taken the sign of the cross could mix freely with both Christian's and heathens, while keeping the faith that they pleased.*" (Egil's Saga pt. 50: 80-1).

Earlier in the saga are accounts of such trading trips from Norway to England, where they purchased wheat, honey, wine and cloth in exchange for fish and animal skins (*Egil's Saga* pt. 17: 28). In the saga is what only can be described as an ethnic depiction of the people living in Northumbria during the tenth century, and claimed that:

"...*the only people there of any standing were of Danish descent on their father's or mother's side, and there were many of each.*" (*Egil's Saga* pt. 50: 81).

In the account of *William of Malmesbury* this observation is repeated by his statement that by the tenth century the people of Northumbria (that is Anglo-Saxons and Scandinavians) were of one race (WM: 108). A later description of the populace of York from the *Life of St Oswald* (*c*1000) illustrates the continuing contact between Denmark and the north of England with its very large population of Danish merchants (Logan 1991: 165).

During the reclamation of the Five Boroughs by Edmund, Æthelstan's successor, in 942, the poetical account in the Anglo-Saxon Chronicles is quite clear in its description that prior to the capture by the Hiberno-Norse the Viking settlers there had considered themselves to be subjects of the English crown and were glad to be repatriated (ASC, A). That the English crown considered them to be subjects there can be no doubt. Exactly how the people of the Five Boroughs felt can only be assumed.

Other Vikings in Anglo-Saxon armies can be found in the troubled reign of Æthelred, and were most famously Thorkell the Tall, a member of the Jómsberg Vikings, and Pallig, the brother-in-law of Sven, king of Denmark (Stenton 1998: 382). Thorkell subsequently rejoined the Danish army and Pallig was killed along with his wife during the St Brice's Day massacre in 1002 (ASC, WM, EHD 127: 590-3). Æthelred was also plagued by the cultural mixing and with it the confused allegiance of the leaders of his armies. In 993 the three men[24] ordered to attack a Viking raiding army in Northumbria fled because they were Danes on their father's side (FW). Just how far back their Danish ancestry ran is unknown, although it does seem likely that it lay with their fathers, illustrative of a continuing pattern of migration. It is hard to imagine that folk memory would have stretched back a hundred years to a progenitor from within the Great Army.

A fragment of a letter written during the Anglo-Saxon period describes in no uncertain terms the feeling of the anonymous author towards the incoming settlers, and is an excellent example of linking culture with ethnicity (EHD 232: 895-6). In the letter the author complains bitterly of the English people taking up the practices of the heathen settlers, such as dress and hairstyles, stating that those who do will be, "*cursed and dishonours his own race*" (EHD 232: 895-6). This use of fashion and personal habits of male Viking settlers was also condemned in the writings of *John of Wallingford*, who saw their practice of bathing every week and combing their hair as nothing but a ruse to attract Anglo-Saxon wives, drawn by their attention to personal hygiene (*John of Wallingford* in Williams 1986: 14). This is surely an example of cultural mixing between immigrant and national.

Finally, evidence of cultural interaction between immigrant and settlers can be seen in historical records as late as the thirteenth century which show that peasants in what was northern Mercia were still giving their children Scandinavian names and nicknames to each other (Stenton 1998: 254). However, the use of Danish personal names did become fashionable during and after the reign of Cnut, so it is likely that the use of such names was perhaps given new impetus during this period (Williams 1986: 11-12).

4.3.3 Miscellaneous Historical Interaction: discussion

As with the historical sources and other contemporary records of the period this collection of historically documented interaction displays a length and depth far greater than the usual study of the Great Army settlement period. As argued above, it is apparent that interaction between the Anglo-Saxon and Scandinavian populace was carried out via trade prior to, during and after the Viking wars.

Again, as to be expected, more is recorded about the interaction between the upper echelons of society. This is especially so within the church, but shows an intense and swift political association for mutual benefit. Allied with this is perhaps the most interesting piece of miscellany relating to Oda, Archbishop of Canterbury, who was born in England of Danish parents, and fostered into the home of a neighbouring Anglo-Saxon nobleman (Whitelock 1959). It is unlikely that Oda would have been the only child of Danish descent fostered in this traditionally northern European manner. Through this action it shows a level of integration between settlers and native, and the swiftness of which it had taken place. The manner Oda was to subsequently rise and use his position within the church no doubt had its roots in his Anglo-Saxon upbringing, but he did not forget his blood-kin, placing family members in comparable positions of power within the ecclesiastical community while maintaining strong ties with the Wessex crown (Whitelock 1959).

The maintenance of homeland ties with Scandinavia and other areas of Viking settlement within the British Isles and Ireland, was no doubt bolstered by the thriving populations of Danish merchants known to have been operating out of York and Oxford during the tenth century, and no doubt elsewhere, especially within the Five Boroughs (Logan 1991:165). As merchants, these settlers would have been powerful, having wealth and control over supplies (food and goods) locally and especially luxury goods from further afield. They would also be a part of a wide information network. The fact that the merchants and, one would expect, their families were based in towns and the very nature of their work, gives a greater propensity for contact, interaction and reaction with all manner of people at all levels of society. It also has serious implications for the integration of communities, which will be fully explored in chapter six.

The surviving fragments of the Anglo-Saxon letter and the writings of John of Wallingford recount much about the adoption by ordinary Anglo-Saxon people of Danish cultural practice and the custom of intermarriage between settlers and native. Both can only be seen as successful integration between the groups.

4.4 Viking Period England: overall conclusions and discussions

From the above discussion points it can be seen that the settlement and integration of Viking groups in England followed a distinctive pattern of contact, interaction and reaction. The law codes and charters reflect the feelings of secular authority at the time towards the Vikings and begin with a sense of accommodation with the Alfred-Guthrum Treaty, and the acceptance of the puppet king Ceolwulf II by the Mercian elite. As Edward began his reclamation of East Anglia, Mercia and Northumbria using military and economic means, a series of peace treaties were drawn up with the leaders within the north of England, which while acknowledging him as king of England, allowed day-to-day governance to continue at local level as it had since the first settlements had taken place. No doubt these laws were a combination of Scandinavian (as shown in later English laws) and the earlier laws of the northern Anglo-Saxon kingdoms.

[24] Fræna, Godwine & Frithugist; Fræna (Frani) & Frithugist are Scandinavian names (Swanton 2000: 127 fn. 12).

During Æthelstan's reign there first appears a recognition of cultural and ethnic differences between Viking groups, by the Anglo-Saxons, into Danes and Norse, spurred no doubt by the expansive interests of the Hiberno-Norse and their Dublin-based kings. While his predecessor Edward fortified his recaptured towns with a mixture of Anglo-Saxon and Viking soldiers (ASC, A: 918), Æthelstan had Anglo-Scandinavian jarls present at his courts. He did not, however, suffer competition for the Northumbrian crown, and had no truck with the Hiberno-Norse kings and their attempts to wrest the north of England from his control. Following his reign there occurs the first written cultural indicators in the laws of Edmund (939-46), which is surely evidence for integration and cultural mixing across all levels of society within both the Anglo-Saxon communities and groups of Scandinavian descent. There are also efforts during his reign, if not to enforce a common law across England, to regulate and manage the dispensing of justice and to maintain his responsibility as head of state to enforce law and order (EHD 39: 429-30). By this time the established Viking settlers within what was Mercia and East Anglia saw themselves as English subjects, a fact plainly stated in the normally hostile *Anglo-Saxon Chronicles* when Edmund reclaimed the Fives Boroughs from the Hiberno-Norse in 942 (ASC).

Patterns of selective discrimination and delicate political manipulation based on the relationships of Viking groups and settlers with the kings of England continued throughout the reign of Eadred (946-55). In his will (946-55), it is stipulated that sixteen hundred pounds be set aside to be used to protect his subjects from the famine and the heathen, the heathen referring presumably to the Vikings operating in the Irish Sea region (EHD: 107: 554-5). Despite this, laws and charters issued by him continue to be witnessed by settlers of Scandinvian descent (EHD 105: 551-2). These include Jarl Orm, who had been instrumental in Olaf Guthfrithsons's seizure of Northumbria in 940 (ASC).

The reign of Edgar (*c*959-975) saw repeated the actions of Edward twenty years previously with the acknowledgment that districts of Viking settlement had their own laws (Laws of Edgar, in Thorpe 1840: 273-7). This is evidence for a continuing separation within English society, acknowledged by the Anglo-Saxon elite and resident Anglo-Scandinavians who co-existed with their own justice system (most likely a mixture of the old laws of the northern Anglo-Saxon kingdoms and Scandinavian legislation) within English law with the blessing of the king (Laws of Edgar, in Thorpe 1840:273-7).

While England was ruled by a strong king, the northern sub-kingdoms, governed by their own laws and customs, posed a lesser threat to political stability. This symbiotic relationship began to fall apart during the reign of Æthelred, when more and more Scandinavian cultural traits (laws, measurements, language, *et cetera*) became incorporated into the laws of England, perhaps exacerbated by new Danish settlers known to have been migrating there at the time (Williams 1986). Although English law became increasingly Scandinavian in form there were very few members of the Anglo-Scandinavian elite ever present at Æthelred's court, unlike those of his predecessors Æthelstan and Edgar (Stenton 1998: 551). This is perhaps illustrative of Æthelred trying to physically distance himself from those of Scandinavian descent, owing perhaps to the Danish attacks, while trying to placate these subjects by officially recognising their practices. This reaction is surely evidence for the continuing recognition within the ruling elite of those descended from Viking immigrants, some one hundred and fifty years after the first settlements. This could be due to folk memory, but is more than likely representative of continuing migration between Scandinavia and England of new settlers, two, three, maybe four generations after the arrival of the Great Army (see chapter six).

What is clear from this study is that the Viking settlers, from all levels of society made efforts to actively integrate themselves within the receptive area of the north of England. Later English kings encouraged this, so that cultural traits became shared and over time ethnic boundaries became blurred. The picture emerging from the historical record is one that displays evidence for contact, interaction and the positive reaction of both native and immigrant populace to each other. The following chapter will examine the archaeological record in order to ascertain whether such reactions between immigrant and national are visible in the surviving cultural remains of the Viking-period.

CHAPTER FIVE – HYBRID DESIGNS AND SETTLEMENT

5.0 Introduction

As with the historical documents there are very many scholarly studies devoted to Viking-period sculpture and settlement in the north of England. In addition to the historical resource examined in the previous chapter these remains can be seen as the physical evidence of a reaction to contact and interaction between resident and incoming groups, and must be utilised as remnants illustrative of change and negotiation within the socio-cultural milieu. This chapter is not intended to break new ground, but give an insight into the perspectives these resources provide of Viking period settlement in the north of England.

The first part of this chapter will explore the large corpus of Viking-period stone sculpture before moving on to consider the influence of the Scandinavian-language on place-names and epigraphic form. The final part of the chapter will examine the archaeological sites which may represent the domestic dwellings of incoming groups. Where appropriate with the area of discussion the associated Viking-period artefacts bearing evidence of Scandinavian-influence will be included where appropriate throughout, augmented by a map of major finds in appendix four (fig. A4.1).

5.1 Viking–period Stone Sculpture (figs. A3.1-5)

5.1.1 Introduction

One of the largest, and most enduring, collections of pre-Conquest objects are an indelible reminder of the impact incoming Scandinavian groups had on the social, economic and religious lives of the resident Anglo-Saxon groups. They are, of course, the collections of stone monuments, found in consistent numbers in the churches and churchyards of many towns and villages of northern England. A series of maps illustrating the sites of these sculptures is to be found in appendix 3.

Their recognition and study originated, after almost a thousand years of neglect, in the hands of the Victorian antiquarian, such as the Cumbrian luminary, WS Calverley. A rising awareness and interest in the past, combined with a period when very many old country churches were 'renovated' revealing early sculptural fragments provided the foundations on which modern studies are built.

Early studies were largely art-historical based, rather than archaeological (see for example Calverley 1899, Collingwood 1907, 1911, 1927). Mainly as a result of the work of WG Collingwood and JR Allen, the potential of the sculpture both as a discrete archaeo-historical tool and as a valuable piece of accompanying evidence to other historical and artefactual remains has allowed their inherent potential to be utilised to further understanding of the period.

As already pointed out, the subject has been well-studied by specialist researchers[1], but is included here as it represents a vivid example of cultural and social reaction between incoming Scandinavian groups and resident Anglo-Saxons in the north of England. It will be shown how the sculptural traditions of the period can not only be used to illustrate social and economic systems at a micro and macro geographical level, but also provide insights into the functions of the early medieval church and the transfer of cultural knowledge via iconographic representation.

5.1.2 Pre-Viking Traditions

Stone sculpture has a long tradition in the north of England prior to the arrival of Viking groups (Cramp 1978, Bailey 1980). Generally, Anglian stone sculpture seems to have been linked to monastic foundations, (such as Hexham, Ripon and Carlisle) where the traditional forms consisted of crosses and decorated slabs (Cramp 1984: 174-93, Lang 2001: 7, Bailey 1980: 79). These sculptures only carry firmly religious iconography, confirming that they were created for a strictly ecclesiastical complex (Bailey 1980: 79, Cramp 1984). During this period slabs were used to demarcate graves, whereas crosses were employed as an object of commemoration, either to the dead or to saints (Bailey 1980: 82). Beyond the boundaries of monastic settlements crosses were even more unlikely to have been used to mark the graves of the dead, church canons and histories of the period instructing that a cross be erected on the site of the altar should a church be moved and referring to the practice of landowners raising preaching crosses on those estates which lacked a church (Bailey 1980: 82).

Monastic control unsurprisingly kept designs remarkably constant and of a high standard, with further consistencies of type being found between mother and daughter houses, which in some cases could be geographically very far apart (for example, Lindisfarne and Crayke, in North Yorkshire) (Bailey 1980: 83, Cramp 1984: 194-208, Lang 2001: 7). However, the Anglian system of monasticism in the north began to fail during the ninth century and was all but obsolete by the tenth, a situation no doubt exacerbated by Viking raids and the accompanying social and economic upheaval, as landownership and power sources changed (Bailey 1980: 84). Rather than catastrophic for the perpetuation of the stone sculptural traditions of the north, however, the arrival of Scandinavian groups provided the basis of a renaissance, if not always in quality, then certainly quantity.

Conversely, there is no tradition of stone sculpture in Scandinavia prior to the Viking period, the only occasion it occurs being on the Swedish island of Gotland (Bailey 1980: 76). However, it would be unwise to suggest that the first experience of stone sculpture for groups of Scandinavian origin was during the settlement periods, piratical raids against monastic settlements in the north of England and Irish Sea region providing an obvious introduction. Similarly, the

[1] The primary resource for this section is the *Corpus of Anglo-Saxon Stone Sculpture*, published on behalf the British Academy, and any number associated with a piece of sculpture within the text relates directly to the catalogues within this work.

raiders and settlers of the Northern and Western Isles of Scotland would have been exposed to Pictish symbol stones and early Christian monumental sculptures, which were decorated with mythical scenes and/or interlaced patterns (Bond pers. comm.).

5.1.3 Identification of Sculpture in the Viking-period

The recognition and dating of sculpture allocated to the Viking period is for the most part subjective, based on inter-comparison, using amalgamation and developments of local Anglian traditions, the widespread use of figures, the utilisation of new motifs from Scandinavia (such as Borre, Jellinge, Mammen and Ringerike styles) and the Irish Sea region (ring-headed crosses) (Bailey 1980: 53-74, Cramp 1978: 14, Wilson & Klindt-Jensen 1966). While this self-regulation is inherently open to doubt, scholars have produced logical chronologies, aided by the few stone sculptures recovered from archaeologically dated levels, such as those recovered from the excavations in the Minster graveyard at York where almost fifty pieces of pre-Conquest sculpture were recovered *in-situ* (Lang 1995: 434, Lang 1991: 39-40). Inter-disciplinary association may also assist in allocating dates to sculptural motifs, such as the alliance of the introduction of the ring-headed cross to north-west England in the early tenth century following the historically attested piratical activity in the Irish Sea region with the expulsion of the Viking elite from Dublin (see chapter four) (Bailey 1980: 213). Such alliances can be extremely useful in furthering our understanding of the period, and will be further considered below. However, such insights may just as easily provide chronological blips from what is normally expected. For example, following recent research, there are reasons to suggest that a group of sculptured crosses in the Peak District of Derbyshire bearing apparently non-Scandinavian influenced designs were likely to have been created during the later Viking period, rather than Anglo-Saxon, albeit under a specific set of socio-political circumstances (Sidebottom 2000).

Similarly, the dating and chronology of stone sculpture via typology and art history must be considered circumspectly (Bailey 1980, Lang 1988, Sidebottom 2000: 213-17). An example of this problem is illustrated in the literature by the dating of the Middleton Cross (Yorks) (no. 2) (fig. 5.1), which has variously been placed in either the ninth or tenth century (Lang 1991: 182-4, Sawyer 1971: 163-4, Wilson & Klindt-Jensen 1966:104, Bailey 1980: 211-3, Lang 1973). Current consensus tends towards the latter date, based on the presence of a ring-headed cross, the introduction of which is believed to stem from the Irish Sea region during the period 920-50 (Bailey 1980: 212-3). The earlier date was attributed on the basis of the apparently simplistic representation of a warrior surrounded by his weapons carved on the shaft, and a Jellinge-style beast, all of which were interpreted as an Anglian sculpture struggling to cater for the whims of a patron of unfamiliar cultural tastes in the form of a new Viking overlord, freshly installed as a result of Halfdan's conquests in the region (Sawyer 1971: 163-4, Wilson & Klindt-Jensen 1966: 104). An early date was also suggested by the acceptance that the depiction of the warrior actually showed him in his grave, surrounded by grave goods, implying that the production of the cross represented a physical manifestation of the assimilation

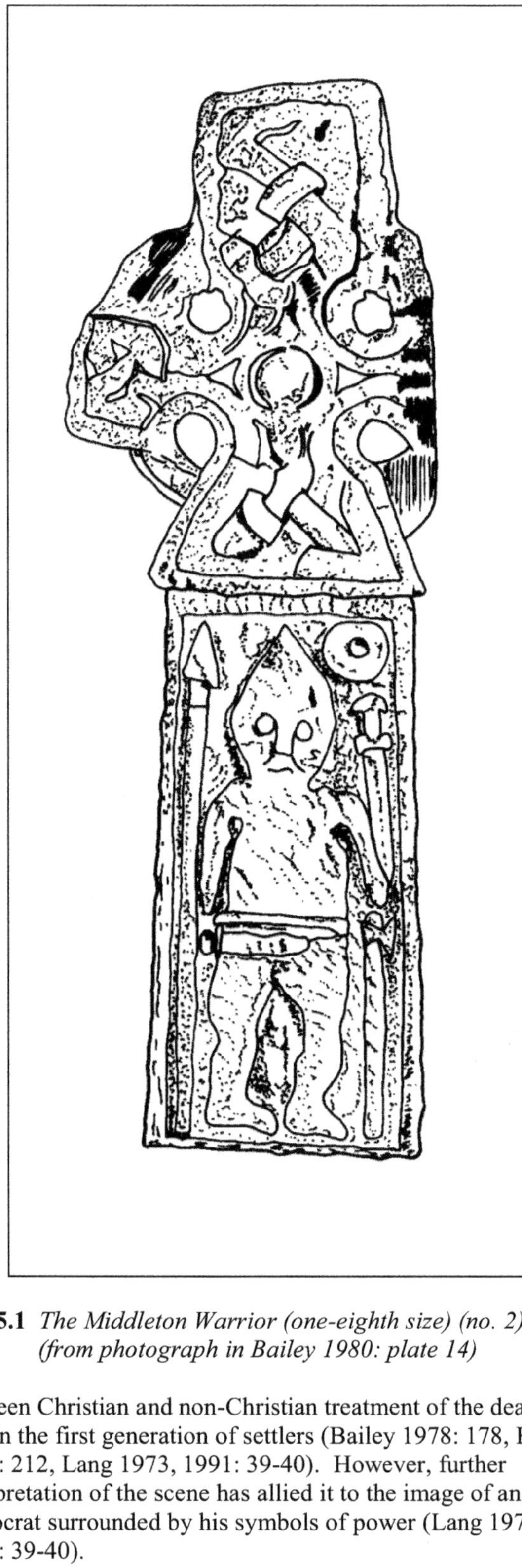

Fig. 5.1 *The Middleton Warrior (one-eighth size) (no. 2) (from photograph in Bailey 1980: plate 14)*

between Christian and non-Christian treatment of the dead, within the first generation of settlers (Bailey 1978: 178, Bailey 1980: 212, Lang 1973, 1991: 39-40). However, further interpretation of the scene has allied it to the image of an aristocrat surrounded by his symbols of power (Lang 1973, 1991: 39-40).

This being said, stone sculpture is only another facet of archaeological artefacts of the period, datable typologically, and prone to correction when found in association with items of fixed chronological value such as coins or historical documents. It is perhaps the acknowledgement of such chronological problems by scholars involved within the field of pre-Conquest sculpture-research which allows for uninhibited experiment and the inevitable discourse that follows, producing, as it will be shown, possibilities for deeper understanding of the period.

5.1.4 Changes in Sculptural Traditions during the Viking-period

As mentioned above, Anglian sculptural traditions in the north of England were by and large limited to monastic institutions, and as such were regulated in numbers, design and production (Bailey 1980: 79-84, Cramp 1978, 1984). With the arrival of settlers of Scandinavian origin all this was to change.

The most basic and obvious difference was the increase in the sheer quantity of stone monuments. For example, within the modern county of Cumbria there are between fifteen and seventeen sites containing twenty-five monuments of Anglian date (Bailey 1985: 54). In comparison, there are some thirty-six Viking period sites with at least one hundred and fifteen monuments (Bailey 1985: 54). Broadly speaking, during the Viking-period there is a doubling of the number of sites where carvings are found and an increase of the number of sculptured stone monuments by a factor of five (Bailey 1980: 80). What must be made very clear though, is that despite the boom of stone sculpture production during this period of Scandinavian influence, less than ten percent of the monuments display *Scandinavian* styles (Bailey 1985: 55). A somewhat similar situation occurs across the Pennines in the Yorkshire and Cleveland districts, with ninety Anglian monuments from forty-one sites, compared to three-hundred and twenty-five from sixty-five in the Viking-period (Bailey 1980: 80). This increase in numbers is thought to represent a shift in patronage from monastic to a more secular driven market, stone-sculpture being found in local church precincts rather than closed monastic settings (Bailey 1980: 55). There is little doubt that the creation of these objects were funded by wealthy members of the lay community keen to mark socio-cultural affiliations in a very visible and lasting manner in the landscape. The increase in quantity (and also retention of Anglian designs, see below) suggests very strongly that the resident Anglo-Saxon population had as much influence on the enthusiastic adoption of secular patronage as their incoming Scandinavian peers.

The production of friezes, panels, grave-slabs grave-markers and crosses continued traditions of the Anglian period, although the creation of the hogback tombstone was a very particular variant on an older theme, and will be discussed below and in the following chapters. Whether stone crosses actually marked graves is a moot point, although it would be safe to say that they continued in their Anglian form as commemorations of the dead. Other pieces of sculpture, the stone slabs, ornamental grave-markers and coped grave-covers, most definitely did, indisputable archaeological proof being provided by those burials found *in-situ* in the Minster cemetery at York (Lang 1995: 433-67, Lang 1991: 39-40). Quite clearly the presence of Viking-period monumental stone sculpture is indelibly linked with the dead, albeit those belonging to certain wealthy social groups. It is to the patrons we must now turn in order to understand how and why these changes in sculptural traditions came about.

In crude economic terms the shear time and effort necessary for the quarrying and transport or purchase of stone suitable for sculpture would have been large. Similarly, the cost of employing a craftsman to transform the natural stone into an art form must have been prohibitive to most people. This is without consideration of the social position of the individual(s) commissioning or purchasing a piece, and with it the influence to enable its deposition within an area of sacred space. Monumental commemoration in stone was strictly a preserve of the socio-economic elite of the period, not the common man. This assessment is clearly illustrated by the limited numbers per cemetery, although there are a few exceptions due to particular sets of economic circumstance, linked directly to enclaves of wealthy merchants within large northern towns (Stocker 2000).

By and large most monuments were cut, carved and painted from quarries and workshops within the vicinity of the church or graveyard where it was going to be set up, although there are a few instances of finished monuments being transported from their place of manufacture (for example, York to Crowle, Lincs) (Lang 1978: 11, Bailey 1980: 21-4, Stocker & Everson 2001: 229). The blurring of Anglian traditions and Scandinavian influences make it well-nigh impossible to ascertain whose taste is more on show, sculptor or patron, the Halton Cross in Cumbria being a fine example of Anglian patterns while at the same time bearing scenes from the *Volsunga Saga* (Cramp 1978: 11). Studies of the collection of stone sculpture at Gosforth, (Cumbria), suggest that the scenes depicted are in direct response to the instructions of a single patron, the large cross (no. 1), the Fishing Stone (no. 6) and a cross head (no. 3), all displaying the influence of Scandinavian legends and all carved by a single highly skilled sculptor; the contemporary Saint's Tomb (no. 5) was obviously carved by another craftsman, but still maintains Scandinavian mythological scenes (Bailey 1980: 255, Bailey & Lang 1975, Cramp & Bailey 1988:100-5, 106-9).

In Chester, York and Lincoln there appear to be sculptural workshops, which provided monuments of standard quality and design to their mainly municipal customers (Bailey 1980: 254-5, Lang 1978: 146, Stocker & Everson 2001). The very nature and position of the workshops within a town such as York must have introduced the sculptors to a myriad of new motifs via trade and fashion, and sparked trends which were to be copied in the provinces (Lang 1978: 146). It is the presence of these trends or styles of sculpture, both forms and decoration, which provide the key investigative opportunity within Viking period stone monuments.

Overall, while we can never be entirely sure, it seems highly suggestive that the settlement of wealthy immigrants of Scandinavian origin was responsible for the burgeoning interest in monumental sculpture in the Viking-period. The continuation of Anglian traditions and the amalgamation of some of the artistic styles from both groups illustrate lively interaction, and ultimately assimilation, clearly demonstrated by the subsequent development of a distinct cultural facet, which will be further explored below.

5.1.5 Regional Links

Across the corpus of Viking-period stone monuments in the north of England, certain regional groupings can be ascertained from styles of decoration and forms of sculpture. In some cases associations are clear, such as the appearance of ring-headed crosses on the north-west coastal plain, or the presence of round shafts in the Peak District of Derbyshire, or type of scroll work found in the Wharfe valley of West Yorkshire (Bailey 1980: 185-9). Sometimes related elements are more subtle, and require more careful detection, such as the stags depicted on the crosses at Brompton (Yorks) (no. 4a) and Sockburn (Durham) (no. 7) (Bailey 1980: 246-9, Lang 2001: 68, Cramp 1984: 138-9). While the reasons for these associations and others are different and will be considered below, the vital point is one of interaction and the movement of people and ideas.

Such movement and interaction can be identified within the regionally distinctive group of ring-headed crosses in the north-west. Within this particular group lies further stylistic variations at a local level, which has been carefully recorded and rigorously analysed elsewhere (see Cramp & Bailey 1988), and lies beyond the remit of this study. At a regional level these distinctive designs have been shown to originate in Ireland, and arrived in the north-west via the monastic communities of the Western Isles (Bailey 1980: 177-182). Their distribution hints very strongly at a tight-knit cultural unity to the west of the Pennines, very much influenced by sea-borne contacts to the Hiberno-Norse influenced areas of the Irish Sea region (Bailey 1980: 182). This is corroborated by both historical accounts (see chapter four) and by archaeological discoveries, such as the Fluskew/Flusco thistle brooches (and further penannular brooches) found near Penrith (Cumbria), the Irish manufactured bossed penannular brooch of the period from Orton Scar (Westmorland) and of course the famous Cuerdale Hoard (Lancs) discovered on the banks of the Ribble, part of the Viking period thoroughfare between the Irish Sea and York (see below and appendix 5) (Edwards 1998).

Further cultural links are illustrated through the appearance of 'hammer-head' cross designs (Bailey 1980: 183). These are found in the Eden Valley, Cumbrian coast and the upper river valleys of North Yorkshire as well as in Solway, weakly linked perhaps when planned in map form, but more strongly united when associated with corroborating place-name evidence, which shows the sculptures to be associated with pockets of Hiberno-Norse influenced nomenclature (Bailey 1980: 183, Cramp & Bailey 1988, Lang 2001, 1991).

The widespread use of figures during the Viking-period, in marked contrast to earlier Anglian traditions, can also be used to pinpoint regional styles (Cramp 1978: 14, Bailey 1980: 191). A preference for the use of figures, perhaps as a result of the Scandinavian legends, resulted in a tapping of these limited older sources by Viking-period craftsmen. The distinct smocked and belted figures found on sculptures of the Tees district draws from one of these limited situations of tradition, apparently influenced by the characters still visible today on the Anglian cross from St Andrew's, Aukland (Durham) (no. 1) (Bailey 1980: 191, Cramp 1984: 41-3). Similarly conspicuous characters, thought to represent saints, whose dished haloes flow stylistically into trailing hair, are found within churches along the Wharfe Valley (Yorks) and Leeds; the earliest an eighth century representation occurring at Collingham, the other Viking period copies being at Ilkley and Otley (Lang 1978: 146).

There are many other instances of shared traits and copying of motifs across the north of England, which include the use of aids in the form of templates (Bailey 1980: 246-9). The same single template of a stag was used to cave the animals on the crosses at Brompton (no. 4a), Kirklevington (Yorks) (no. 11) and Sockburn (no. 7) (Bailey 1980: 246-252, Lang 2001: 68, 146-7, Cramp 1984: 138-9). Similarly, a template of a warrior figure was used twice on surviving sculptures at Middleton (nos. 1 & 2) (fig. 5.1) (Bailey 1980: 246-252). The production, distribution and use of such objects again indicate lively interaction between regional groups of craftsmen and patrons; the manufacture and availability of templates allowing motifs to be widely copied, perhaps by less skilled sculptors.

These groupings of designs within regions can only be as a result of internal reaction to external stimuli, brought about by exposure or introduction to original forms, or more simply, contact between people and the subsequent spreading of ideas through culturally receptive groups.

5.1.6 Myths, Legends and Figurative Depictions

Within the field of iconographic representation it is the appearance of figures apparently allied with Scandinavian mythology that invite most interpretation, carved as they are on objects of such Christian affiliation. Such juxtaposition of faiths could perhaps be used as evidence for their co-existence, however, on closer inspection things are not quite as they might at first appear. Take for example the representation of a very well known Scandinavian myth. Illustrations relating to the story of Sigurd the Volsung and the dragon abound across the north of England. Depictions of the legend are to be found on the Halton cross (Lancs), a grave-slab from York Minster (YM 34, site report) (no. 34, corpus), fragments from Ripon Cathedral and Kirby Hill (Yorks), the crosses from Kirby Hill and Nunburnholme (Yorks) (no. 1), and the hogback from Heysham (Lancs) (Bailey 1980: 120-22, Lang 2001: 130, Lang 1995: 457-8, Lang 1991: 189-93, Lang 1991: 71-2, Lang 1976*a*: 88, Lang 1976*b*). While there is no doubt that the Sigurd legend was given new life in this form by the presence of Scandinavian groups in the north of England, it would be harder to prove that the resident Anglo-Saxon population had no knowledge of the story: elite families claimed descent from the Volsungs, and there is also the reference to Sigmund's father, Sigemund, as the dragon slayer, in Beowulf (Bailey 1980: 116). Before further consideration of what the scenes could represent in their physical context it is worth keeping in mind that those depictions of Sigurd are by no means clear indicators of a Scandinavian cultural origin or religious beliefs of either sculptor or patron. Fundamentally, the appearance of Sigurd as a recognisable icon to both resident and immigrant groups is an important indicator of assimilation. It is the amalgamation of his depiction within monumental sculpture that has the potential to reveal the negotiations going on within society that allowed successful assimilation to take place.

Further complications related to such shared cultural sources will also become apparent.

Similarly depicted, and just as well known to both Anglo-Saxon and Scandinavian groups, is the story of Wayland. In contrast to Sigurd, there already existed within Anglo-Saxon iconography a tradition of depicting the heroic smith (for example, the Northumbrian, early eighth century Franks Casket, which carries an eclectic mix of the Wayland legend, the Magi and the Virgin Mary), alongside the legends and associated place-names in the landscape (Lang 1976*a*: 90, Bailey 1990: 103). Viking period sculpture bearing depictions of Wayland have been found in Leeds, Sherburn (Yorks) and on the Bedale hogback (Yorks) (no. 6) (Lang 1976*a*, Bailey 1980:104, Lang 2001: 61-2). The Yorkshire demography of Wayland is interesting, and may represent evidence of stronger Anglo-Saxon cultural traditions at work through a preference of hero by the patron. However, this being said, representations of Wayland are to be found in the unique area of sculpture on Gotland, dating to the early ninth century (Bailey 1980: 105-6). Setting aside for the moment the religious implications behind the depiction of two mythological heroes within a Christian milieu, it is important to realise that the influence of incoming Scandinavian groups not only released perhaps latent knowledge of Sigurd within Anglo-Saxon society, but allowed the representation of Wayland to continue from earlier periods, assimilation introducing the new artistic medium of monumental sculpture. Without this interaction between groups none of this could have taken place and developed into a distinct cultural form.

However, the question still remains: what are legendary heroes of pre-Christian origin doing so blatantly displayed on objects of strictly Christian association? The answer lies not down the tempting route of pagan iconography debasing Christian doctrine, but once more as a continuance of tradition and juxtaposition of ideas, which was ultimately strengthening ecclesiastical ties within the secular community. From surviving records of the *Second Council of Nicaea* in 787, the power of iconographic representation in the spreading and perpetuation of Christian teachings was acknowledged as extremely important, and vigorously encouraged (Bailey 1980: 144). However, by representing literal teachings in this form, it was necessary to ally specific pictorial representations of limited scale to illustrate critical tenets. The most obvious of all Christian iconography in Viking-period stone sculpture would be a cross, with or without further elaboration upon it. Other symbolic representations include the cross as a tree (death and resurrection), Christ and his church as a vine, raised embosses to signify the five wounds of Christ and of course the crucifixion scene itself, which may or not include the witnesses to the act as described in the Bible (Bailey 1984: 143-54). There also occurs whole set-piece panels which depict stories from Biblical texts or Church history, for example the inverted crucifixion of St Peter at St Andrew's, Aycliffe (Durham) (no. 1), or the figure of Christ on a cross at Burton (Westmorland) (no. 1) bearing his rods of power on the Day of Judgement, standing on the Devil who is in the form of a snake (Cramp 1984: 41-3, Bailey 1980: 157, Cramp & Bailey 1988: 82). Incidentally, this form of Christ draws inspiration from those found on Irish cross-heads, for example at Clonmacnoise (Co. Offaly), and may once again illustrate the contacts between the north west of England and Ireland via the Hiberno-Norse (Bailey 1980:157, Cramp & Bailey 1988: 82).

All these truncated representations of Church tenets were produced to promote and propagate Christianity in a recognisable context on a striking medium. Pope Gregory in his letter to Mellitus in the late sixth century ordered the appropriation of non-Christian religious practice and buildings into church doctrine (EHD 151: 654-5). The idea was perpetuated and used by the eighth century missionary Boniface, who recognised the importance of the amalgamation of non-Christian belief into Christian dogma for the acceptance of Christianity (Bailey 1984: 130). The image of Wayland on the Franks Casket is one contemporary example of this. Ultimately incorporation meant manipulation and control of pre-Christian beliefs by the Church. The adoption of Sigurd was a small step, a continuation of established evangelical activity. The associations with the *Volsunga Saga* with dragons/serpents, mystic feasts and trees draws immediate parallels with the Biblical manifestations of evil, the Eucharist and sources of knowledge (Bailey 1980: 124-5). Depiction of these key juxtaposing scenes could result in explanations being sourced from theological tenets of vastly different origin.

However, Wayland and Sigurd are not the only characters of apparently pagan extraction to appear on Viking-period sculpture within a Christian context. Some, but by no means all, can again be allied directly with Christian dogma, (for example those further dragon slayers depicted at Gosforth (no. 1) and Penrith (no. 4), Great Clifton (no. 1) (all Cumbria)), while others such as the scene on a hogback from Sockburn (no. 21) depicting Tyr losing his hand to the wolf Fenrir, and Thor's hooking of the world serpent on the Fishing Stone at Gosforth (no. 6), may not (Cramp 1984: 143-4, Bailey 1980: 135, Cramp & Bailey 1988:101-4, 136-7, 110, 106-8). However, arguably the presence of Tyr enacting his part in the build-up to Ragnarok is analogous once more to the Biblical Doomsday (see below) (Cramp 1984: 143-4). Closer examination of the Fishing Stone (no. 6) reveals the scene immediately above Thor and Hymir depicts the hart and the snake, a familiar tableau from Christian narrative (Bailey 1980: 132, Cramp & Bailey 1988: 106-8). Taken in context it is apparent that both the major Scandinavian god and his giant counterpart have been re-assigned a new status within the Christian church, as heroes battling evil in the form of the devil/serpent, possibly at Doomsday itself. An eleventh century grave-marker from Bolton-le-Sands made up of a Viking-period grave-slab and part of a hogback still carrying the representation of a figure battling a serpent brings still closer the suggestion that the transmogrification of older non-Christian images was taking place, when one considers the rising popularity of St Michael and the dragon at the time (Lang 1984: 110).

Other representations of Scandinavian gods are perhaps unsurprisingly hard to find, and even more difficult to substantiate as specifically pagan iconography. There are depictions of Ragnarok, but as shown above, the arrival of the apoplectic doomsday is paralleled in Christian doctrine. It has been suggested that the apparently hanging figure on a fragment from Kirkbymoorside (Yorks) (no. 3) shows Odin as described in the *Hávamál*, where the god sacrifices himself to himself in order to receive mystic knowledge (Lang 1991: 156). However, this is not convincing. Too much of the original sculpture is missing, and one would expect at the very least if the rope was being depicted then the spear or certainly the wound left by the spear would also have been shown. Again it does seem likely that this image is to be viewed in a Christian context, perhaps as Bailey suggests, drawing inspiration from the Old English homily, *The Vision of Hell*, which describes the souls in hell as being hung from trees (Bailey 1980: 134). Never-the-less, the panel on the Oseberg tapestry which depicts a group of men hanged on the boughs of trees is seen purely as a reference to Odinic worship (Price 2002: 159). Although the particular scene is devoid of spears, the weapon is depicted throughout the rest of the tapestry alongside ravens, a further Odinic symbol (Price 2002: 159). Examination of the corpus of Viking period stone sculpture provides no real evidence for the depiction of any of the other major members of the Scandinavian pantheon, Odin, Freyr or Freyja (Cramp 1984, Cramp & Bailey 1988, Lang 1991, 2001). Other than the Gosforth Fishing Stone (no. 6) there is no evidence for Thor occurring on any other piece of sculpture elsewhere in the north of England (Cramp & Bailey 1988: 106-8, Cramp 1984, Cramp & Bailey 1988, Lang 1991, 2001).

Depictions of Ragnarok as alluded to above, of course display representations of the lesser Scandinavian gods. However, this Scandinavian interpretation of a possibly analogous Christian event is most clearly represented on the large Gosforth cross (no. 1), allied with a most graphic representation of the crucifixion. The apoplectic scenes depicted draw immediate parallels with the *Edda*, showing Viðarr slaying Fenrir, Heimdallr with his Gjallar horn, and most strikingly Loki is pictured bound beneath the dripping jaws of the serpent, his wife Sigyn beside him catching the venom in a bowl (Cramp & Bailey 1988: 101-4). Critically for the amalgamation of pagan myth by Christianity, Viðarr, one of the very few to survive Ragnarok, is placed above the crucifixion scene, a telling link perhaps of the hope of resurrection shared between two faiths.

However helpful the application of interdisciplinary research derived from Norse myths and Christian theology to the understanding of the depictions of scenes on Viking-period stone sculpture, the perils of subjective analogy remain. It is crucial to remember that our readings of the tableaux are essentially etic, and that our experiences are very far removed from those involved in the creation of the scene at that particular moment in time. It could very well be that the Biblical connections suggested by Ragnarok, serpents and mystic feasts are in fact a product of our own metaphysical world view, the depictions of Scandinavian-influenced mythology simply being just that, albeit in a new medium. There are certainly other figural representations on Viking-period stone sculpture that defy analogous compartmentalisation.

Such representations can be found on a cross fragment at Sockburn (no. 3) (Cramp 1984: 136-7). The panel depicting a serpent and a rider holding a bird, above a scene of a female pouring drink from a horn into the mouth of a further figure invites an Odinic interpretation (Cramp 1984: 136-7). However, there is nothing to prevent the scene being a representation of a nobleman hunting in the field, before retiring for sustenance from either his wife or female servant. Similarly the figure on the shaft at Kirklevington (no. 2a) pictured with a bird on each shoulder could easily be recognised as being Odin with his ravens Huginn and Muninn (Lang 2001: 142). Or is the man Elijah being fed by the ravens, and the picture a representation of God's Providence? Or a portrait of an unknown man? Similar scenes occur on Pictish slabs, and are interpreted analogously with Anglo-Saxon poems which described the victims of battle being preyed upon by ravens or wolves (Bond pers. comm.). The precise definition of intention behind the production of many sculptured scenes can never be recouped. What can be recaptured is the sense of human agency involved in their production. Whether or not they represent physical examples of theological manipulation needed for the control of incoming groups, or simply the delighted representation of myths, legends and everyday scenes via a new and striking medium, the fact remains that they were created from a fusion of traditions, given life as a results of the successful assimilation of Scandinavian settlers and resident population.

5.1.7 Hogbacks

Perhaps the most symbolic representation of Viking-period sculpture is the hogback tombstone. Unlike contemporary crosses, there is no doubt that these monuments were grave-markers, evidence existing for their function within the archaeological record at Heysham, Brigham (Cumbria) and Penrith (see chapter eight). The source of inspiration behind these images of Viking-period settlement has long been, and continues to be a cause of debate. Whether their creation came as a result of copying contemporary dwellings of the living to represent the houses of the dead, imitating the shrines on Irish crosses or other portable metalwork shrines of the period, or a variation of the extant Anglo-Saxon tradition of placing shrines over the body of a saint (for example, Hedda's Tomb, Peterborough) can never be entirely convincingly answered (Lang 1984: 90-1, Bailey 1980: 93-5). It seems likely that their origins lie within a multifarious set of cultural objects, but what is pertinent to this study is what the creation of these monuments conveys about the society in which they were produced. However, before this can be considered it is necessary to examine the historiography of the monument itself.

Essentially, the hogback is a large stone monument, very much like an up-turned boat in shape. Often over a metre in length and displaying regional variation in basic form, their particularly Scandinavian influenced designs fixes them all exclusively to the Viking period (Bailey 1980: 91). Geographical planning of the hogbacks in the British Isles and Ireland clearly shows them to be a phenomenon centred in the north of England, being found in greatest numbers in Cumbria and Westmorland and North Yorkshire (see fig. 8.4, Lang 1984: 86-7). The major centres of hogback production or at least visible consumption seem to be along the Tees and Eden river valleys; the most being found at Lythe (Yorks) (nos. 17-33), Brompton (nos. 16-26) and Sockburn (nos. 14-21, 28), with seventeen, eleven and nine monuments, respectively (Lang 1984: 87-8, Lang 2001: 159-66, 173-79, Cramp 1984: 140-4, 156).

Over fifty of the hogbacks have bear-like beasts gripping the gable-ends, some of which are very naturalistic in their depiction (as at Brompton, nos. 17a, 17c), while others survive in stylised form (Sockburn, no. 20) (Lang 1984: 106, Lang 2001: 74-5, Cramp 1984: 142-3). While hogback shapes, styles and motifs vary, from the tall cross-sections of the Gosforth Saint's Tomb type (no. 5), to the squat example from Ingleby Arncliffe (Yorks) (no. 3), the various Jellinge beasts (at Brompton, (no. 26) and Pickhill (no. 4a) (Yorks), for example) and the simple birds in the tree of the Sigurd myth at Heysham, the main commonality is the abhorrence by the sculptors of empty space (Cramp & Bailey 1988: 108-9, Lang 1984: 109, Lang 2001: 125-7, 178-9, 193-4).

Unlike the crosses or grave-slabs found alongside them in churchyards, the appearance of obvious Christian iconography on hogbacks is extremely rare (Lang 1984: 110). From his corpus of one-hundred and eleven distinct hogback forms in England, only Dewsbury (Yorks) (cross on one gable-end), and the Saint's Tomb at Gosforth (crucifixion scenes on each gable) (no. 5) bear surviving identifiable Christian motifs (Lang 1984: 112-172, Cramp & Bailey 1988: 108-9). The cross etched on the gable of hogback number 3 from Ingleby Arncliffe reported by Collingwood early in the last century is no longer discernable (Lang 1984: 142, Lang 2001; 125-7). Similarly recorded and now lost is the possible crucifixion scene on a hogback forming part of the Giant's Grave at Penrith (no. 9) (Cramp & Bailey 1988; 139, Lang 1984: 158). The gable of a hogback (YM 46) destroyed during the reconstruction work in York Minster during the nineteen-seventies showed a likely crucifixion scene, the figure having outstretched arms, coiled by snakes, with further serpents depicted below the armpits (Lang 1995: 463, Lang 1976*a*: 93-4).

It has been suggested that one of the figures on the Lowther (Westmorland) hogback (no. 5) is depicted in the attitude of prayer (Cramp & Bailey 1988: 130-1, Lang 1984: 146), although a compatriot in the tableau is seen to be holding a ring, prompting the suggestion that rather than a Christian religious enactment, the sculptor is illustrating a ring-giving ceremony. A similar explanation may also perhaps be allied to the scene depicted on the hogback at Bedale (no. 6) (Lang 2001: 61-2, Lang 1984: 116), where a seated figure with a bowl on his lap is depicted surrounded by further men, one of whom seems to be holding a ring. Hogback number 9 from Penrith, part of the Giant's Grave group, was recorded by Collingwood as also having a figure depicted with arms outstretched, possibly praying, or even part of a crucifixion scene (Cramp & Bailey 1988: 139, Lang 1984: 158). However, the figure is now indiscernible (Lang 1984: 158).

There are other hogbacks where active figures are displayed. Those thought to represent parts of the Sigurd and Wayland legends at Heysham and Bedale (no. 6) have been discussed above; but also depicted on the Lancashire monument is a hunting scene, complete with stags, a pack of hounds and four huntsmen (Lang 1984: 116, 138, Lang 1976*a*: 86). This tableau has been associated with Ragnarok and the triumph of Víðarr, the equivalent of Christ and the deer, the divine hart (Lang 1976*a*: 86), although as pointed out above, this could simply be an illustration of a hunt. Similarly the possible combination of iconographic representation of Ragnarok on Sockburn twenty-one (Durham) has been discussed above, although the fragment hogback fifteen seems entirely Scandinavian in its depiction of eschatology, if Lang is correct in his identification of the broken remains of female figure bearing a horn and bird at her feet with a valkyrie and raven serving dead warriors in Valhalla (fig. 5.2) (Lang 1984: 109, 166, Cramp 1984: 141).

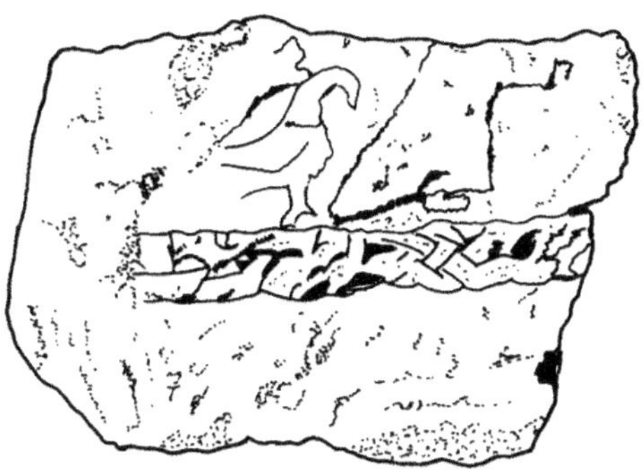

Fig. 5.2 *Sockburn 15, Valkyrie and Raven? (quarter size) (from photograph in Cramp 1984: vol. II plate 138)*

West of the Pennines depictions of men battling serpents are a common motif (for example, Penrith no. 7, and the Saint's Tomb at Gosforth, no. 5) (Cramp & Bailey 1988: 108-9, Lang 1984: 110). As demonstrated above explanations as to the narratives behind these scenes could incorporate both Christian and non-Christian themes. The Saint's Tomb (no. 5), for example, with its crucifixion scene at each end, depicts two warriors battling a serpent, the duo making it an unlikely representation of Thor fighting the Midgard serpent (Cramp & Bailey 1988: 108-9, Lang 1984: 110, 136).

Pictorial representations of contemporary culture may also be found. The martial scenes on hogbacks continue with the two vying war bands of the Warrior's Tomb at Gosforth (no. 4), and the ship-load of warriors bound for land and a waiting warlord at Lowther (no. 4), a scene paralleled on the Gotlandish stones Stenkyrka Smiss I and Larbro St Hammars 1 (Cramp & Bailey 1988: 105-6, 130, Lang 1984: 110, 134-6, 146-8). The two mounted figures carrying spears on Sockburn number 14 could be either huntsmen or warriors (Cramp 1984: 140-1). Other figures occur on hogbacks in almost portrait form, for example the cloaked man from Cross Canonby (Cumbria) (no. 5), and possibly also from the Warrior's Tomb at Gosforth (no. 4), the very faint impression of a man bearing an axe just visible (Cramp & Bailey 1988: 89-90, 105-6, Lang 1984: 110, 134).

The association of pictorial representations with either non-Christian or Christian myth can easily become a pre-occupation, and hide the fact that hogback research can be juxtaposed with other archaeo-historical research. For example, an association of hogbacks has been made with Hiberno-Norse place-names in the north-west (see also association of hammer-head crosses, above), and although there does seem to be a link between both sets of evidence there is nothing to suggest that the hogback was a product of Irish influence (to date only one hogback has been found in Ireland, at Castledermot, Co. Kildare), and care must be taken with the establishment of place-names before any conclusions may be drawn (see below) (Lang 1971, 1984: 89, Fellows-Jensen 1978).

The unique nature of the hogback and its firm dating to the Viking period makes it an invaluable tool in the understanding of the socio-cultural interaction being played out in the north of England. The use of hogback tombstones (fig. 8.4) is alien to both immigrant and national groups, and appears to be an extremely visible, iconographic representation of the assimilation of two communities through cult practice at a particular period in time (Richards 2002: 165). These monuments are perhaps more important than the accompanied burials themselves (see chapter eight), some of which may or may not have been marked above ground as different to the other non-accompanied interments of the graveyard. The concealment of items during the burial process could mean that only those directly involved with the deposition of the goods, or witness to the burial would know that they were there. Hogbacks were above ground, and permanently on display. Recognition and an understanding of these hybrid Anglo-Scandinavian monuments within the community would have been vital, and their constructions involve many members from within the community. Firstly, there must have been a patron wealthy enough to pay for the carving of such a monument, who also had the corresponding social influence to enable the hogback to be erected within a churchyard. Secondly, the patron or the sculptor must have had access to or knowledge of the Scandinavian myths and legends, and in some cases artistic style of representation (for example, Sockburn no. 15 and the Warrior's Tomb, Gosforth, no. 4) in order for them to be recorded in this form (Cramp & Bailey 1988: 105-6, Cramp 1984: 141, Lang 1984: 166, 134). Finally, and most importantly, the priest and the majority Christian community would also have had to be willing to allow the erection of the hogbacks within their sacred space.

5.1.8 Stone Sculpture: conclusions

Although this study of Viking-period monumental sculpture has had to be concise, the theme of contact and interaction between incoming settlers of Scandinavian origin and resident Anglo-Saxon groups is shown in every aspect of their production and use. Whereas it would be difficult to identify a Scandinavian origin for each patron of a stone-sculpture, there is no doubt that elite Scandinavian settlers were the catalyst behind the boom in production and shift in the market from majority ecclesiastical to secular consumption. The adoption of stone sculpture as a commemorative technique and the introduction of new motifs by incoming groups, along with the continuation of Anglian traditions combined to form a new cultural facet; an artistic schema entirely induced by the assimilation of immigrant and resident population.

Examples of this mixing are in evidence on the Gosforth cross and a tenth century cross-shaft fragment from York Minster (YM 4, site report) (no. 4, corpus) (Bailey 1980: plate 32, Lang 1995: 447, Lang: 1991*b*: 56-7). Below a depiction of the crucifixion on the Gosforth cross stands a female form which is directly analogous with pre-Christian figures depicted in Scandinavian art (such as on the Oseberg tapestry) (Bailey 1980: plate 32). The cross fragment from York Minster (YM 4, site report) (no. 4, corpus) carries both designs of Jellinge style and the dished-haloed nimbus head drawn from the earlier Anglian traditions of West Yorkshire monastic settlements (Lang 1991: 56-7, Lang 1995: 447).

Whatever their ultimate inspiration, the design and use of the hogback must be recognised as the physical manifestation of the interaction between two groups during the assimilation process. The negotiation involved in the establishment of these monuments, the majority of which bear no identifiable Christian indications, in Christian graveyards, cannot be underestimated or ignored.

As discussed above, the translation of figurative motifs is fraught with difficulty, due to its subjective nature. Our modern-day interpretations are essentially etic and despite all protestations to the contrary, tainted by our own experiences of life, which are very far removed from those of the sculptor or his patron. Viking-period sculpture tells us far more about the machinations of a highly dynamic period, showing through their own limited artefactual scope how cultural and ethnic indicators were successfully negotiated and realigned between resident and incoming groups to produce a highly iconographic representation of successful assimilation.

5.2 Place-names and Language

5.2.1 Introduction

The place-names of northern England provide the largest corpus of evidence for the influence of Scandinavian settlers, existing in most cases where archaeological evidence from the Viking-period is nil. Throughout the history of modern Viking-period research their uses in understanding Scandinavian settlement has been, and remains, contentious. Broadly speaking, scholars can be split into two camps: those who expound the merits of place-name research, and those who believe place-name research can offer very little in the way of sound constructive reasoning. The differing points of view stem ultimately from a single fundamental source; that of accepting the presence of Scandinavian place-names is equated directly with the presence of Scandinavian settlers, or that they are not. A simple division, but one which stirs heated debate.

In many cases when and how a topographical feature or settlement name (be they English, Scandinavian or an amalgamation of the two languages) appeared in spoken form will never be known. What is absolutely certain though is that Scandinavian influenced place-names could not exist without speakers of a Scandinavian language (Townend 2000). This simple fact must replace the place-names-equals-settlers and its derived arguments in order to better understand settlement processes by trying to discern how and why a place-name became preserved in written evidence. As with other facets of the cultural resource, place-names are a product of interaction between groups, not governed by time, but specific and peculiar social pressures at a particular time. As it will be shown, these influences are not just restricted to the people living in a particular area during the Viking-period, but come into play on the person actually responsible for physically recording the settlement name or reference to topology.

This chapter does not intend to break new ground in Viking-period place-name research, but intends to examine the resource not from traditional positivist/negativist viewpoints, but from one which recognises the creation and recording was a result of interaction between two communities where English and Scandinavian survived as two distinct languages (Townend 2000).

5.2.2 Identification of Scandinavian Influenced Place-names

Before surviving forms of Scandinavian influenced place-names can be discussed it is important to establish what kind of linguistic environment must have existed in which they were formed. Anglo-Saxon chroniclers show quite clearly that Scandinavian settlers in England spoke Scandinavian, which on the surface may seem to be a facile point, but proves that two distinct languages were being spoken: Scandinavian and English (Townend 2000: 93-4). The acknowledgement of the fact may be taken further by examining Æthelweard's account of the burial of Ealdorman Æthelwulf in 871: not only had his source given the place of burial as *Norðorþig* (Old English (OE), northern enclosure), but included the name by which it was known in the Danish language, Derby (from Old Scandinavian (OScand) *diurby* or *diuraby*, *-bý* where deer are seen or *-bý* with a deerpark, where *bý* is a Scandinavian habitative generic) (Townend 2000: 93, Æ 871: 37, DEPN[2]). From this account it is clear that amongst Scandinavian speakers the settlement was referred to as Derby, and to the English speaking Anglo-Saxon populace, Northworthy. This acknowledgement of linguistic difference and application of the Scandinavian version of the place-name is surely historical evidence for the presence of a bi-lingual society in late tenth century northern England (Townend 2000).

Philological research indicates that Scandinavian and English were of equal prestige, unlike later Norman-French, which was predominantly spoken by the ruling elite post 1066 (Townend 2000: 96). Over time Scandinavian ceased to be spoken, however, many loan words and grammatical forms passed into the English language and continue to be used in modern English,[3] that is, adopted by English speakers in the south and west of England, beyond areas of traditional Scandinavian settlement, unlike place-name traditions (Parsons 2001: 299, Townend 2000: 98). Briefly then, the general linguistic environment of the Viking-period North seems to have been one where two distinct, albeit mutually comprehensible, languages were spoken before Scandinavian eventually died out, but not before influencing English in its uptake of many loanwords and grammatical forms (Townend 2000).

As place-names are first and foremost sources for linguistic research, their association or rather identification as a Scandinavian influenced toponymic depends on the recognition of certain very distinct phonological, morphological and lexical diagnostic features (Styles 2001: 298, Townend 2000: 94). Inferences only begin during the subsequent analysis and equation with settlement patterns of immigrant Scandinavian groups. Bearing this in mind, and that the survival of a place-name is ultimately dependent on its use within the language community that created it, it is now time to examine the evidence.

5.2.3 Common Habitative Place-name Forms (fig. 5.3)

The most commons Scandinavian habitative element in the north of England is *–bý*, a general term to indicate settlement (Fellows-Jensen 2001: 282, 1985, 1972) (fig. 5.3). The specifics can be of Scandinavian or English form, and include anthroponymics, adjectives or appellatives (Fellows-Jensen 1972: 10-22). For example:

> Eppleby (N Yorks) – first recorded in Domesday (DB), is made up of the OE appellative *æppel* (apple) and the Scandinavian generic *–bý* (settlement);
>
> Willerby (E Yorks) – first recorded in Charter Rolls of 1262, is made up of the OE personal name *Wilheard* and the Scandinavian generic *–bý* (settlement);
> Wetherby (W Yorks) – first recorded in DB, is made up of the Scandinavian appellative *veðr* (wether-sheep) and the Scandinavian generic *–bý* (settlement);
>
> Thormanby (N Yorks) – first recorded in DB, is made up of the Scandinavian personal name *Þormóðr* and the Scandinavian generic *–bý* (settlement);

(DEPN, Fellows-Jensen 1972: 14, 40-1).

Although it will never be known when the names were originally used (that is, spoken), it is safe to assume that their roots lie amongst Scandinavian speaking communities in each area during the Viking-period. It is hard to subscribe to the idea of coining, which implies fixed cognitive behaviour and in some way enforcing the settlement name on resident communities (see for example Fellows-Jensen 1972, 1985 *etc*). Instead, it is perhaps safer to propose that each form grew from the interaction and amalgamation of a bi-lingual community during the process of assimilation. The preservation of purely Scandinavian forms (Wetherby, Thormanby) indicates that they were adopted into common use.

The second most common Scandinavian habitative generic in the north of England is *–þorp*, an appellative used to describe a secondary settlement (Fellows-Jensen 1972, 1985). The use of *–þorp* in advocating Scandinavian influence is muddied by the fact that the word/term is common throughout all Germanic languages, and so its appearance in an English place-name could be a result of either English or Scandinavian speaking communities, or both (Fellows-Jensen 1995: 180). Some scholars have even gone so far as to argue that *–þorp* (Scandinavian)/*-þrop* (OE) was an entirely English construct (Lund 1976: 182-3). However, its existence in Middle English is more likely due to its source being within a Scandinavian language speaking community, that is, the North of England as the occurrence of *–þorp* names are rare in southern and western England (Fellows-Jensen 1995: 180, 1972: 42-4). As with –*býs* above, the specifics can be of Scandinavian or English

[2] DEPN – Dictionary of English Place-Names, by E Ekwall 4th edition 1981
[3] such as, they, their, them, skull, sky, skin, low, happy, dream, *etc* (Townened 2000: 98, Jespersen 1967)

Fig. 5.3 *Map to show the distribution of –býs and –þorps in England (after Richards 2000a: 44)*

form, and may be anthroponymic, adjectives or appellatives (Fellows-Jensen 1972: 42-51). For example:

> Milnthorpe (We) – first recorded in 1348, is made up of the OE appellative *myln* (mill) and the Scandinavian appellative *–þorp* (secondary settlement);
>
> Crackenthorpe (We) – first recorded in 1202, is made up of the OE verb *cracian* (to crack) and the Scandinavian appellative *–þorp* (secondary settlement);
>
> Copmanthorpe (W Yorks) – first recorded in DB, is made up of the Scandinavian appellative *kaupmann*

(merchant) and the Scandinavian appellative *–þorp* (secondary settlement);

Helperthorpe (E Yorks) – first recorded in DB, is made up of the Scandinavian female anthroponymic *Hjalp* and the Scandinavian appellative *–þorp* (secondary settlement);

(DEPN, Fellows-Jensen 1985a: 204, 202, Fellows-Jensen 1972: 56, 60).

By and large the position of *–þorp* names are to be found on poorer, less profitable land, and their actual physical survival into modern day in many cases fails, as settlements became deserted and lost (for example, Danthorpe, E Yorks), or simple shrink (for example Easthorpe, (E Yorks) (Fellows-Jensen 1972:42-71, 57). Although this seems to be the general rule, there are however, some exceptions, such as Fridaythorpe, also in East Yorkshire, which was assessed in DB at sixteen carucates and three bovates (the average *–þorp* being assessed at four carucates) (Fellows-Jensen 1995: 180, Fellows-Jensen 1972: 223). It has been suggested that its prosperity was due to successful sheep farming (Fellows-Jensen 1995: 180, Fellows-Jensen 1972: 223).

As is has been shown above, there are many different examples of OE specifics combined with the Scandinavian habitative terms, the generic *–bý* and appellative *–þorp*. There is a third large group of names formed from a Scandinavian or Scandinavianised first element of the OE habitative generic *tūn*, meaning homestead or village (Ekwall 1981: xiv). When *tūns* are combined with a Scandinavian personal name they are known as *Grimston* or *Toton*-type hybrids (Fellows-Jensen 2001: 285-6). By and large these settlements seem to be situated on prime land, leading place-name scholars to suggest that these were extant Anglo-Saxon villages *taken over* by Scandinavian settlers, and hence mark the earliest chronological *coining* of Scandinavian place-names (Fellows-Jensen 1972: 109, 1995). However, there is a growing acceptance that many of these settlements could have taken the modern forms of their names far later than the Viking-period and perhaps beyond. This is mainly due to the work of Nicolaison (1969) and Gelling (1973). Nicolaison's (1969) work in Scotland showed that such Grimston-type names were allocated there by English colonists, centuries after initial Scandinavian settlements in the north of England. In England, Gelling (1973) has pointed out that several such names have manorial significance, some of which relate to the transfer of land in the eleventh century from Cnut or his sons to men with Scandinavian names (Fellows-Jensen 2001: 286). However, the difficulty with ascertaining the exact chronology of place-names still permits an earlier date for those settlements bearing archaic Scandinavian personal names (Fellows-Jensen 2001: 286). This being so, there is no longer any fixed rules as to the foundation of Grimston-type settlements. This problem of association was a direct result of equating the survival of a Scandinavian influenced name with a Viking-period Scandinavian settler(s), who on arrival changed the name of the Anglo-Saxon village. As well as being hard to accept, the idea initiates the formation of speculative generalisations, which may well be true in a small number of cases in a particular area and moment in time, but largely leave place-name research vulnerable to attack when other disciplines illustrate inconsistencies within the hypotheses. As with the *–býs* and *–þorps* the only thing that can be said with any certainty is that the Grimston-type hybrid developed within a bi-lingual community (Townend 2000: 99). The perpetuation of use within the settlement and the surrounding area may be seen as evidence of assimilation between the two groups of language speakers, no matter when the name was introduced into the onomastic sphere.

As with *–býs* and *–þorps* above, the specifics can be of Scandinavian or English form, and may be anthroponymic, adjectives or appellatives (Fellows-Jensen 1972: 109-168,). For example:

Grimston (E Yorks) – first mentioned in DB, is made up of Scandinavian anthroponymic *Grímr* and the OE habitative generic *tūn*;

Orton (Cu) – first mentioned in Pipe Rolls of 1227, is made up of the Scandinavian anthoponymic *Orri* and the OE habitative generic *tūn*;

Watton (E Yorks) – first mentioned by Bede *c*730, the original OE place-name was **wēta-dūn* (wet hill). The first element was replaced by the Scandinavian *vátr* (wet), remaining combined with the OE habitative generic *tūn*;

Aikton (Cu) – first mentioned in 1200, is made up of the Scandinavian *eik* (oak) and the OE habitative generic *tūn*;

(DEPN, Fellows-Jensen 1972: 128, 167, 1985a: 185, 190).

In addition to these majorities of types, there also exist very many other place-names bearing Scandinavian influence. They could survive in their Middle English (ME) written sources in their purely Scandinavian form, such as The Biggins (ME noun *bigginge* – homestead) in Westmorland, which is derived from the Scandinavian loanword *byggja*, to build, (Fellows-Jensen 1985a: 201). Or display evidence for changes in phonology, as in Skipton (N Yorks), where the OE place-name *Scīptun*, sheep-farm, has been transformed by replacing the OE [ʃ] for the Scandinavian [*sk*] (DEPN, Fellows-Jensen 1972: 138).

Other hybrids than the Grimston-type occur widely, where Scandinavian words can form either first or second elements to English, British or other Celtic influenced place-names. For example:

Cummersdale (Cu) – first mentioned in 1227, is made up of a specific the Primitive Welsh folk-name *Cömmri* (the Welsh, British), and the generic is the Scandinavian appellative *dalr*, valley;

(DEPN, Fellows-Jensen 1985a: 225).

Other, more familiar, influences on onomastic traditions introduced by Scandinavian settlers such as *staðð* (landing point), *buð* (booth), *sǽtr* (shieling), *skáli* (shieling hut), *-þveits* (-thwaites) and the Gaelic words *kirk* (church), *kross*, (cross) and *áirge* (shieling) seem to appear in distinct regional groupings, and will be discussed below.

5.2.4 Regional Variations and Distribution Patterns

Whilst the briefest of glances at any place-name map of England will show the north widely peppered with Scandinavian influenced names, closer examination of the evidence provides some interesting regional differences. As already discussed above, the most common Scandinavian habitative elements in the north of England are the *-býs* and *-þorps*, however, when plotted in map form (fig. 5.3) it can be seen that these forms predominate to the east and south-east of the Pennines, with very few in Northumbria, Lancashire, Cumbria and Westmorland (fig. 5.3, Fellows-Jensen 1985a, 1972). Quite clearly the perpetuation of this tradition of naming was far stronger, and perhaps the manner of naming itself far more popular in this region of Yorkshire. Further analysis of the *-býs* and *-þorps* in Yorkshire has shown that well over fifty percent contain an anthroponymic specific (Fellows-Jensen 1972). Such forms are unknown in Lancashire and Westmorland, while only thirteen sites in Cumbria contain Scandinavian anthroponymic specifics (Fellows-Jensen 1992: 26-43). The cluster of *-býs* around Carlisle can be seen as an anomaly, their presence due to continental colonists settled in the district by William Rufus in 1092 (Fellows-Jensen 1992: 38). The importance of this group of continental anthroponymic specifics combined with the *-bý* generic is seen to lie within the amalgamation of place-naming tradition, although it's not known whether these names replaced earlier Scandinavian or English anthroponymics or indeed forms of any other sort (Insley 1986: 172, Roberts 1989: 90, 34-5, Fellows-Jensen 1985: 22-4).

It has been hypothesised that the larger presence of *-býs* and *-þorps* to the east of the Pennines reflects the Danish ethnic origin of the majority of settlers, *-býs* and *-þorps* being more commonly used in Denmark for naming settlements than Norway or Sweden (Fellows-Jensen 1972, 1985a). However, this idea is derived from the view that a Scandinavian influenced place-name equates directly to the presence of Scandinavian settlers. The offering of a blanket hypothesis of the Danes being resident in all the *-bý* and *-þorp* settlements during the Viking-period is perhaps a step too far, as place-names are primarily evidence for language (Styles 2001: 98), and the identification of ethnicity or ethnic groups a perilous one (see following chapter). It seems safe to say that east of the Pennines, there existed communities of Scandinavian speaking people, familiar with the use of the naming tradition using *-býs* and *-þorps*, a possible majority of whom had cultural links with Denmark.

It has also been suggested that the large numbers of anthroponymic specifics combined with *-býs* and *-þorps* were representative of Scandinavian settlers apportioning pieces of old Anglo-Saxon estates (Fellows-Jensen 1972: 19, 1992: 38, 1995: 180). Again this is a blanket hypothesis, which explains the lack of the generic in other areas of the north being due to large estates being taken over *en-bloc* by Scandinavian lords, or being held intact by Anglo-Saxon lords, the ecclesiastical communities, or in the case of Cumbria, being ruled by the Strathclyde Britons (Fellows-Jensen 1972: 19, 1992: 38, 1995: 180). A limited analogy to the first case is provided in the historical resource, when during the second decade of the tenth century Ragnald redistributed four component parts of a multi-estate belonging to the Lindisfarne Community to four of his followers, two English and two Scandinavian (see chapter four) (HSC, Morris 1977: 7). The estates lie in what is now eastern County Durham, an area where Scandinavian influenced place-names of any kind are very rare indeed (Watts 1995: 212-3). Three of the four estate-centres (Gainford, Staindrop and Auckland) bear evidence of Scandinavian linguistic influence; but within ten years the Aycliffe estate had been returned to the Lindisfarne Community, one of the Scandinavian lords had died, and combined with the political upheavals centred in the north during the 920's, all provides a very unique set of circumstances within a very tight time period, which would no doubt have influenced settlement patterns of any kind (Morris 1977: 7).

The acceptance that the presence or lack of *-býs* and *-þorps* as representative of fission or continuance of estate structures may be correct in some cases but by no means all. Their presence is certainly evidence of a Scandinavian speaking community, and therefore Scandinavian settlers in the area, but it would be difficult to say more than that. Scandinavian anthroponymics are a tempting foil to this, however, without any firm chronological indication for an actual name-change, the fact remains that a personal-name is not a firm indicator of ethnicity[4].

To the west of the Pennines Scandinavian influenced place-names are just as common as in the east, albeit showing a preference for descriptive rather than personalised forms of names (Fellows-Jensen 1985a). This difference has been linked not only to the survival of earlier estates, but to different naming traditions of a mainly Hiberno-Norse immigrant community, who widely colonised the Scottish Islands and founded trading ports on the east coast of Ireland, such as Dublin and Waterford (Fellows-Jensen 1985a). Correspondingly, there occurs a series of place-names of typical Norwegian origin, mirrored within Viking-period settlements of the Northern and Western Isles of Scotland, such as the appellatives *staðir*, landing place, and *búð*, booth (Fellows-Jensen 1992: 34, 1985a). Examples include:

> Toxteth (Lancs) – first recorded DB, is made up of the Scandinavian anthroponymic *Tóki* and Old Norse appellative *staðir* (landing place);
>
> Bewcastle (Cu) – first recorded 1178, is made up of the Old Norse *búð* (booth) and the OE appellative *cæster* (fort, reference to Roman fort there);

(DEPN, Fellows-Jensen 1972: 59-60, 201).

The Scandinavian words for shieling and shieling-hut, *sǽtr* and *skáli* respectively, are also often seen as indicators of Norwegian influence, and have many applications within place-names in the north-west (Fellows-Jensen 1985b: 68). This association with Norway is because of their rarity in Denmark, a likely product of the lack of need for a description for upland grazing areas in a country composed of flat, fertile

[4] A Scandinavian personal name does not necessarily guarantee Scandinavian ethnicity. Ulfcytel, the most Scandinavian of names, was carried by Æthelred's great warrior, whom the Danes respected and feared for his prowess in battles against them (ASC C & D, d1004).

plains (Fellows-Jensen 1985b: 68). The elements *sǽtr* and *skáli* are extremely rare in Yorkshire, occurring only as single examples, listed below (Fellows-Jensen 1972: 74, 88). Examples include:

> Salescale (lost village near Kirby Misperton E Yorks) – recorded in DB, made up of either the Scandinavian anthroponymic Sali, or appellative *selja* (willow) and the Scandinavian appellative *skáli* (shieling hut);
>
> Selside (N Yorks) – first recorded 1196, made up of the Scandinavian appellative *selja* (willow) and the appellative *sǽtr* (shieling);
>
> Hawkshead (Cu) – first recorded 1200 (*Hovkesete*), made up of the Scandinavian anthroponymic Haukr and the Scandinavian appellative *sǽtr* (shieling); the modern form shows the substitution of OE *hēafod*, for the originally recorded generic;
>
> Loudscales (Lancs) – first recorded 1219, made up of the OE river name Loud (*Hlūde* – the loud one) and Scandinavian appellative *skáli* (shieling hut);

(DEPN, Fellows-Jensen 1972: 74, 88, 1985a: 64, 209).

A further term for shieling which has been used as evidence for Hiberno-Norse linguistic influence in the north-west is *ǽrgi*, a loanword from the Gaelic *áirge*, (Fellows-Jensen 1985a: 48). There are thirty-eight examples across the north-west, eleven containing Scandinavian personal names, and three Gaelic; by comparison there are only seven examples in Yorkshire (Fellows-Jensen 1972: 74, 1985a: 48). However, whereas its linguistic origins appear to be Gaelic, its use in topographical identification seems to be a new application by the Hiberno-Norse settlers amongst the resident population, there being no convincing instance of its use in Ireland (Fellows-Jensen 1992: 38). The word use for shieling in Ireland is *búa(i)le* (Anglicised as *booley*), therefore suggesting that the origins of *ǽrgi* lay in the Hebrides or west coast of Scotland (Fellows-Jensen 1992: 38). A proposed west Scotland linguistic derivation is perhaps supported by the many shared sculptural traditions in the Viking-period between Cumbria and Galloway (Bailey 1980). Cumbria and Westmorland were also ruled by the Strathclyde-Britons during the mid-tenth century (see chapter four). It may even be that the use of *áirge* was a continuation of indigenous British traditions. Examples of *ǽrgi* place-names include:

> Goosnargh (Lancs) – first recorded in DB, made up of Irish anthroponymic *Gussān* and the Gaelic loanword into Scandinavian *ǽrgi* (shieling);
>
> Mansergh (We) – first recorded in DB, made up of Scandinavian anthroponymic Mans and the Gaelic loanword into Scandinavian *ǽrgi* (shieling);
>
> Golcar (W Yorks) – first recorded in DB, made up of Scandinavian anthroponymic *Guðlaugr* and the Gaelic loanword into Scandinavian *ǽrgi* (shieling);
>
> Airy Hill, Whitby (E Yorks) – first recorded *c*1090-6, made up of the dative plural of the Gaelic loanword into Scandinavian *ǽrgi* (shieling);

(DEPN, Fellows-Jensen 1985a: 64, 65, 1972: 86).

Research into the comparative positions in the landscape of places containing the shieling references show that *skáli,* and *sǽtr* seem to be used to describe shielings in the uplands, while *ǽrgi* is used in the comparative lowlands (Fellows-Jensen 2001: 285, 1985b: 73-5). As with other Scandinavian words their introduction into the north of England toponomy must have been a direct result of the words being spoken within a community, be they Hiberno-Norse, British, Irish, or a mixture of all three. What seems to be very clear, however, is that this language group was predominantly situated to the west of the Pennines, something confirmed in the occurrence of further Gaelic loanwords and word order, which will be discussed below.

Old English *cros* was introduced into the English language via the Hiberno-Norse, whose *kross*, was ultimately derived from the Irish *cross*, itself a derivative of the Latin *crux* (DEPN). As with other Irish-influenced names, there are more to be found west of the Pennines than the east, a reflection of the language speaking communities of the Hiberno-Norse. Some examples are:

> Crosby Ravensworth (We) – first mentioned *c*1160, made up of Hiberno-Norse appellative *kross* and the Scandinavian generic *bý*. Ravensworth is made up of Scandinavian anthroponymic *Hrafn* and Scandinavian appellative *vað* (ford);
>
> Crosby (Cu) – first mentioned 1123-50, made up of Hiberno-Norse appellative *kross* and the Scandinavian generic *bý*;
>
> Crosscanonby (Cu) – first mentioned 1285, made up of Hiberno-Norse appellative *kross* and the Scandinavian generic *-bý*, *canon* added in Middle English to mark the gift of land to the canons in Carlisle
>
> Crosland (W Yorks) – first mentioned in the DB, made up of Hiberno-Norse appellative *kross* and the Scandinavian or OE *land* (tract of land);

(DEPN, Fellows-Jensen 1985a 28, 1972: 93).

Hiberno-Norse influence is evident in the introduction of a further ecclesiastical place-name term, this time that of *kirkja*, church (DEPN). In the north-west particularly the word order in the naming of these settlements tends to be Gaelic, again showing quite clearly the influence and occurrence of Gaelic words being spoken within communities. However, this tradition was not limited to the north-west, with such naming techniques introduced east of the Pennines. Examples include:

> Kirkdale (Lancs) – first mentioned in DB, Gaelic word order, made up of the Scandinavian appellatives *kirkja* (church) and *dalr* (valley)

Bridekirk (Cu) – first mentioned in 1291, made up of Irish St Bride and Scandinavian generic *kirkja* (church);

Oswaldkirk (N Yorks) – first mentioned in DB, it was originally an OE place-name, **Ōswaldes-cirice*, (St Oswald's Church), with Scandinavian influence via substitution of [k] in later sources;

Kirkby Malham (N Yorks) – first mentioned DB, made up of Scandinavian appellative *kirkja* (church) and Scandinavian generic *–bý*. The second word is probably derived from the Old Norse *mol/melr* (gravely soil), combined with OE habitative generic –*ham*;

(DEPN, Fellows-Jensen 1985a: 140, 53, 1972: 32, 149).

–kirk names in the north-west further demonstrate their Celtic origins, with thirteen of them containing the names of Irish saints[5] (Fellows-Jensen 1985a: 45, 53-55). It has been suggested that these words could even be the scandinavianisation of pre-existing Celtic names by settlers familiar with the naming-traditions of Scotland and/or Ireland (Fellows-Jensen 1985a: 46). What does seem reasonably certain is that those *–kirk* names in Yorkshire (for example, Oswaldkirk and Romaldkirk) were introduced by the Hiberno-Norse, since place-names made up of a saint's name and then the word for church are extremely rare beyond areas of England which were non-Celtic speaking in the Anglo-Saxon period (Fellows-Jensen 1985a: 46, 1972: 149, Gelling 1981).

The survival of Anglian sculpture at some church sites within settlements bearing the *kirk-bý* name shows that the place-name has been adopted in some form, influenced by the Scandinavian language which had once been spoken by communities in those parts (Fellows-Jensen 1985b: 77). Such examples occur at Kirkby Stephen, or Kirkby Thore, Cumbria and the church itself at Kirby Hill, North Yorkshire (Fellows-Jensen 1985b: 77, 1995: 177, Bailey 1980: 83).

The final Scandinavian place-name generic to be considered here as a possible indicator of influence by Hiberno-Norse groups are *–þveits* (-thwaites), which denote a settlement established in a clearing of trees or scrub (Fellows-Jensen 2001: 284). The term is considered to have Norwegian origins, although it does occur occasionally in Denmark (Fellows-Jensen 2001: 284). There are considerably more occasions of use in the west of the Pennines than the east, with only five being recorded in Yorkshire in Domesday[6] (Fellows-Jensen 1972: 791995: 183). The cluster of *–þveits* on the North York Moors are all historically datable totheir formation as new settlements in the twelfth and thirteenth centuries a situation paralleled in thirteenth century Cumbria (Fellows-Jensen 1995: 183, Winchester 1987: 41-2). Examples include:

Hunderthwaite (N Yorks) – first recorded in DB, made up of Scandinavian anthroponymic *Húnrøðr* and Scandinavian appellative *–þveit* (clearing);

Micklethwaite (W Yorks) - first recorded DB, made up of Scandinavian adjective *mikill* (great), or OE form *mycel* and Scandinavian appellative *–þveit* (clearing);

Laithwaite (Lancs) – first recorded 1320, made up of Scandinavian appellative *hlaða* (barn) and Scandinavian appellative *–þveit* (clearing);

Waberthwaite (Cu) – first recorded c1200, made up of Scandinavian **veiði-búð* (hunting or fishing booth) and Scandinavian appellative *–þveit* (clearing);

(DEPN, Fellows-Jensen 1972: 99, 101, 1985a: 141, 173).

5.2.5 Place-names as Indicators of Ethnic Influence

Evidence for settlement of immigrants can also perhaps be recognised in the use of folk-names, such as Danes, in Danby or Denby Dale in Yorkshire (Fellows-Jensen 1972: 25). In the first case, the form is of recognisably Norse character (*Dana*), suggesting that the settlement was referred to at some point by a community with a background of Norwegian linguistic influence (Fellows-Jensen 1972: 25). In Denby Dale, the form is OE (*Denigea* or *Dena*), suggesting that the settlement was referred to at some point by a community with a background of Anglo-Saxon linguistic influence (Fellows-Jensen 1972: 25). Similarly Normanby (Yorks), is formed of the Scandinavian folk-name *Norðmenn* (Northmen, Norwegians), indicating a referral by a community of either Anglo-Saxon or Danish linguistic influence (Fellows-Jensen 1972: 34). The combination of *Norðmenn* with the Scandinavian habitative generic *-bý* is very interesting and shows assimilation of naming traditions through linguistic amalgamation.

Possible settlements of Irish or Hiberno-Norse are indicated by the presence of *Írar* the Scandinavian folk-name for Irishman/men (Fellows-Jensen 1972: 31). These occur most commonly as Irby/Ireton/Ireby in the north, with more sites to the east of the Pennines (Fellows-Jensen 1985a, Higham MC 1995). Again these names seem to have been sourced within a Scandinavian linguistic community.

The Scandinavian or OE folk-name *Skotar*, occurs in Scotby (Cumbria), its application made in similar circumstances as the other folk-names, sourced from within either Anglo-Saxon or Scandinavian linguistic community (Fellows-Jensen 1985a: 39). The limited occasions where the English are incorporated derive from the OE *Engle*[7] or Scandinavian *Engla,* although due to their similarity there seems to be differences of opinion between place-name scholars as to its linguistic origin (Fellows-Jensen 1972: 30-1, DEPN). Its scarcity and linguistic source is perhaps an indicator of the size of a Scandinavian speaking community needed to identify an area of resident population by immigrant groups.

[5] Five Bride's, three Conall's, two Patrick's, a Brynach, a Sanctán and a Mochoe (Fellows-Jensen 1985a: 53-55)

[6] Hunderthwaite, Inglethwaite, Kelsit, Langthwaite, Micklethwaite (Fellows-Jensen 1972: 79)

[7] For example, Ingleby Arncliffe (N Yorks) and Ingleby (Derbys) (Fellows-Jensen 1972: 30-1, DEPN)

Attempts have been made to fine-tune further possible sites of Scandinavian settlers, and stipulate their ethnicity, Dane, Norwegian, or Irish by examining anthroponymic specifics in place-names (Fellows-Jensen 1972: 189-194). As outlined above, the use of this method is riddled with problems, historical sources attesting to the most English of people having Scandinavian names from the Viking-period until the thirteenth century (Parsons 2001: pers. comm.). What is clear, however, is that place-name evidence reflects the historical resource discussed in the pervious chapter, by demonstrating recognition of cultural/ethnic identity within society.

5.2.6 Evidence of Name Replacement

In a few occasions the surviving written resource has provided evidence to show that the Anglo-Saxon names of villages and topography survive now in a form developed within a Scandinavian speaking community. This occurs most famously with Derby, where the original Anglo-Saxon name *Norðworþig* (northern enclosure) was replaced in common use by the Old Scandinavian, deer-park *–bý* (DEPN). As already mentioned above, the *Chronicle of Æthelweard* (c990), includes the dual Anglo-Saxon and Scandinavian names in spoken-currency in 871; the Scandinavian form appears in the *Anglo-Saxon Chronicles* C in 917 and the southern manuscript A in 942 (DEPN). *Norðworþig* last occurs in written form around 1000, suggesting perhaps the longevity of the dual reference by communities to the town (DEPN).

Another place which may have been preserved in the name used by Scandinavian speaking groups is Whitby (E Yorks); the first element either the Scandinavian or OE anthroponymic *Hvíti/Hwīta* or the Scandinavian/OE adjective *hvītr/hwīt* (white), and *–bý* (DEPN, Fellows-Jensen 1972: 41). It has been suggested that Whitby might have been the *Streoneshalh*, site of the synod in 664, mentioned by both Bede (673-735) in the *Historia Ecclesiastica* and also the *Anglo-Saxon Chronicles* (680) (Stenton 1998: 129). The presence of the abbey and Anglo-Saxon sculpture certainly provides more evidence through the archeological resource.

A case of an onomastic switch from Scandinavian to English is in evidence on the North York Moors; the hill *Othenesberg* (Odin's Hill) recorded in 1119, becoming Roseberry Topping (DEPN). It is also worth pointing out that Odin's Hill is one of the very scare instances of a direct transfer of a name from a contemporary site in Denmark, in this case from Onsbjerg on Samsø (Fellows-Jensen 1981: 135). However, without knowledge of the previous name, one could easily speculate that it was the Scandinavianisation of a pre-Christian Anglo-Saxon or British god, Woden perhaps. This being said, the Scandinavian form must have been established within a Scandinavian speaking local community, and preserved in local dialect/use until the twelfth century.

5.2.7 River Names

Where onomastics are concerned River names are the most resistant to change, with many, such as the Nidd, Derwent and Rye, preserving their prehistoric form through into modern day (Ekwall 1968: 302-3, 121-3, 349-50). The reasons for this must be multi-various, but it seems safest to suggest that generally the longevity of the name reflects the prominence of the feature, the name perpetuated by communities in its vicinity. However, despite this, there are some rivers in the north of England which carry Scandinavian names or show evidence of the influence of the Scandinavian language.

Cumbria and Westmorland have very many Scandinavian or Scandinavian influenced river and stream names, interspersed with OE and British names (Ekwall 1968). They are particularly numerous in the high ground of the modern day Lake District and range from the pure Scandinavian from of the River Liza[8] (ON *lióss* – light and *á* – river) which is identical with *Ljósá* in Norway and Iceland (DEPN), to the Eamont[9] (OE junction of streams) which shows the influence of the Scandinavian language in its written form (Ekwall 1968). On the modern boundaries of Westmorland and Yorkshire the Ure rises at Ure Head (SD806968) and joins the River Swale (OE) at Myton (SE431661) to form the Ouse (Ekwall 1968: 427, 314-17). As with the Eamont, the River Ure shows influence of the Scandinavian language in its recorded form, this time on a name which originally derives from a British term (Ekwall 1968: 427-8). Further east, the River Riccal rises in the Cleveland Hills (SE602968) and joins the Rye south-west of Salton (SE713788), Riccal being an amalgamation of the British word *Rye* and Scandinavian *kalfr*, forming the calf of the Rye (Ekwall 1968: 341-3, 349-50).

Of particular interest are the cluster of Scandinavian influenced rivers and stream names in the Cumbria-Westmorland - Yorkshire Dales border, which is strongly suggestive of a widespread community of Scandinavian speakers in the area. These include Bowderdale Beck[10] (Cu) (ON *búðar-dalr*, valley with a booth), the River Rawthey[11] (Scandinavian *rauði-ā* – red-one (Scandinavian term for trout) river), and the River Skirface[12] (Old Scandinavian *skīrr* – bright, clear, and brook, derived from *fara* - to go) (Ekwall 1968: 56, 382, 425). The area also has very many references to *gill*, which is derived from ON *gil* (ravine, narrow valley) (for example, West Gill[13], East Gill[14], Whity Gill[15]) (Ekwall 1968: 195). The topography too is dominated by Scandinavian influenced names, especially the Dales themselves, *dale* being the Scandinavian appellative *dalr* (valley) (for example, Garsdale, Coverdale, Langstrthdale Chase, Swaledale, Arkengartdale, Wensleydale, Birk Dale, *etc*) (Fellows Jensen 1972). This grouping of onomastic influence is highly significant, and suggests a very strong continuity of the Scandinavian language in the area. This area also encompasses the Viking-period settlement site of Ribblehead (SD766784) which will be considered below (King 1978).

Further to the north and east, the influence of the Scandinavian language on river names, as with settlement names, lessens. The appearance of *beck*, from the Old Scandinavian appellative *bekkr*, and Scandinavian influence of *sk* in the OE River

---

[8] Rises at Kirk Fell, empties into Ennerdale Water (NY204110-125143)
[9] Rises at Ulswater, joins Eden (NY467241-589310)
[10] Rises SD684979, joins River Lune at NY677049
[11] Rises SD733921, joins River Lune at SD628893
[12] Rises SD847740, joins River Wharfe at SD79690
[13] Rises SD815982, joins River Lune at SD835935
[14] Rises SD861963, joins River Lune at SD835935
[15] Rises SD885946, joins River Ure at SD945901

Skerne[16] (bright, clear) still indicates the presence of Scandinavian speaking communities; as does the River Gaunless[17] (ON unprofitable), the only purely Scandinvian named river in County Durham, replacing the older name Clyde (Ekwall 1968: 425, Watts 1995: 211).

It seems that the socio-cultural change involved in the altering of river names is considerable and the areas where it occurred must have contained many communities in which was spoken the Scandinavian language. The adoption and perpetuation of the Scandinavian name is vitally important in understanding contact and assimilation of Scandinavian and Anglo-Saxon resident communities. The group of topographical, river and place-names across the modern-day boundaries of Westmorland, Cumbria and the Yorkshire Dales are ripe for research in a multi-disciplinary environment; the study of the written word forms no doubt providing the linguistic scholar with the raw data to understand how dialect/local traditions developed within a bi-lingual community into modern forms.

5.2.8 Administrative Districts

During the Viking-period, England was divided into a series of administrative districts known as *hundreds* in the South and *wapentakes* in then North (Hart 1992: 281). The word wapentake is derived from the Scandinavian *vāpnatak*, which describes the symbolic flourishing of weapons following the confirmation of decisions at a public assembly (Stenton 1998: 504). Each wapentake or hundred had a well established boundary, and every four weeks the leading men of the district would gather at a designated open air meeting place to implement law and order, and provide witness to the sale of goods, animals or land (Hart 1992: 281-3). Although the business transacted at either wapentakes of hundreds were essentially similar, and the names occasionally used interchangeably, as in East Yorkshire, the fundamental difference was the type of laws adhered to; in the North, as discussed in chapter four, the wapentakes dispensed the *Danelage* (Hart 1992: 281). Unlike the hundreds in the South, of which each unit was made up of a hundred hides, wapentakes were made up of carucates, arranged duodecimally in groups of either six or twelve, with no regular consistent sizes across the region (Hart 1992; 282, Stenton 1998: 647-8). Hundreds were also in possessions of a reeve, a full-time administrator of the king, whereas the wapentakes were not (Hart 1992: 282).

Although the administrative differences and peculiarities of land division is beyond the scope of this study, they have been included here to highlight possible differences in the north of England that may have been a result of Scandinavian influence. Equally though, as discussed in the previous chapter, such practices may have in fact been a continuation of earlier Northumbrian traditions. What is pertinent here though is the use of a Scandinavian word to describe the regional court, sourced directly from the Scandinavian speaking community. The local courts within wapentakes also bore a Scandinavian name, thing, from *þing* (meeting, court of justice), and occurs in the landscape at for example Thingwall (*þingvollr* – assembly field) in Lancashire (DEPN).

Correspondingly the influence of the Scandinavian language is very evident in the names of the wapentakes. Taking Yorkshire as an example, of the seven wapentakes in the north of the county, one is Scandinavian and another scandinavianised:

> Maneshou – first mentioned DB, made up of Scandinavian or OE anthroponymic *Man* and Scandinavian appellative *haugr* (mound);
>
> Halikeld – first mentioned DB, made up of OE adjective *hālig* (holy) and the Scandinavian appellative *kelda* (spring, well), replacing or influencing OE *celde*;

(Fellows-Jensen 1972: 100, 156, 228-9).

Of the ten wapentakes in West Yorkshire, two are Scandinavian, and three bear influence of the Scandinavian language:

> Staincross – first mentioned DB, made up of the Scandinavian appellative *stein* (stone), which was to be replaced by OE *stān*, and the Hiberno-Norse appellative *kross*, (cross);
>
> Osgoldcross – first mentioned DB, made up of the Anglicised form of the Scandinavian anthroponymic *Ásgautr*, and the Hiberno-Norse appellative *kross* (cross);
>
> Agbrigg – first mentioned DB, made up of the Scandinavian anthroponymic *Aggi/Agi* and OE *brycg* (bridge), later versions have the Scandinavian form *bryggja*;
>
> Ainsty – first mentioned DB, made up of a scandinavianised version of OE *ānstiga* (path wide enough for one man);
>
> Barkston – first mentioned *c*1030, made up of Scandinavian anthroponymic *Borkr/Barkr*, an OE *tūn* (settlement);

(Fellows-Jensen 1972: 104, 101-2, 151, 125, 228-9).

Of the fifteen hundred names in East Yorkshire, five are Scandinavian and two are scandinavianised:

> Holderness – first mentioned DB, made up of Scandinavian appellative *holdr* (hold, as in social title), and the Scandinavian appellative *nes* (headland);
>
> Torbar – first mentioned DB, made up of Scandinavian anthroponymic *Þórr/Þórir*, and the Scandinavian/OE appellative *berg/beorg* (hill);
>
> Scard – first mentioned DB, made up of Scandinavian appellative *skarð* (cleft in the hills);

[16] Rises NZ357346, joins River Tees at NZ287101
[17] Rises NZ019245, joins River Wear at NZ214304

Toreshou – first mentioned DB, made up of Scandinavian anthroponymic *Þórr*/*Þórir*, and the Scandinavian appellative *haugr* (mound);

Snecvlfcros – first mentioned DB, made up of Scandinavian anthroponymic *Snækolfr*, and the Hiberno-Norse appellative *kross* (cross);

Howden – first mentioned in 959, the first element was originally OE appellative *hēafod* (head), but was replaced pre-DB by Scandinavian cognate **haubuð*, the second element is OE appellative *denu* (valley);

Huntou – first mentioned in DB, made up of OE appellative *hunta* (huntsman) or OE anthroponymic *Hunta*, and the Scandinavian appellative *haugr* (mound) or possibly OE *hōh*;
(DEPN, Fellows-Jensen 1972: 96, 106-7, 103-4, 158-9, 228-9)

Whether Scandinavian settlers were responsible for the re-organisation of laws and administration in the North is a moot point, but once again the influence of the Scandinavian language is clearly in evidence in the sites associated with the courts where justice was carried out. Such incorporation is a clear indicator of assimilation of communities via tradition, law and language.

5.2.9 Epigraphy

Physical indications for the use of the Scandinavian language beyond place-names occur in the small collection of runic inscriptions in the north of England, believed by Page to be the product of a bi-lingual community (Page 1971, Page 1989: 54). The most famous example occurs in Carlisle Cathedral (dated to the late eleventh century), and announces, '*Dolfin wrote these runes on this stone*' (Page 1989: 54). Other instances of graffiti have been found at Dearham (Cu) and Settle (Yorks) (Page 1989, Swanton 1969). Runic inscriptions also occur more legitimately in ecclesiastical contexts on the late eleventh-early twelfth century Bridekirk font, the Skelton-in-Cleveland sundial, an earlier (now lost) inscription from the Bridekirk Cross (see chapter six) and the hogback from Pippin Castle (Yorks) (Page 1989: 54).

Runic inscriptions have also been found on more portable goods, such as a comb case from Lincoln and two brooches from Cumbria and Westmorland, although their origins could of course lie external to the north of England (Page 1989: 54, Stephens 1884: 160). The majority of the monumental runic inscriptions are post-Conquest, and despite their Anglo-Scandinavian form, point to a tradition drawn from a Scandinavian cultural source, perhaps given new impetus by the arrival of Cnut and the establishment of his nobles over large tracts of land.

5.2.10 Place-names and Language: conclusions

Although this study has had to be concise, the theme of contact and interaction between incoming settlers of Scandinavian origin and resident Anglo-Saxon groups is shown through the use and perpetuation of Scandinavian influenced place-names and language. Whereas it would be impossible to say that every settlement name of Scandinavian influence was independently coined by a resident Scandinavian immigrant, there is no doubt that the words originated within a district where the Scandinavian language was spoken, and that their application and perpetuation arose from the interaction and amalgamation of a bi-lingual community during the process of assimilation.

The majority hybrid forms of place-names are reflections of the assimilation process, no doubt aided by the similarity of Anglo-Saxon and Scandinavian languages. Through variations in dialect and language use place-name analysis has enabled scholars to identify the presence of Hiberno-Norse speaking groups predominantly in the north-west of England. In a few cases primordial tendencies are in evidence at some point within local communities, as folk-names were applied to some settlements, such as Denby Dale (Dane) or Normanby (Northman-by), but their scarcity surely reflects little support for cultural segregation (Fellows-Jensen 1972: 25, 34). Whether the names were applied by Anglo-Saxon communities or not, both forms derive ultimately from the Scandinavian language, and by their existence confirm linguistic amalgamation.

The influence of the Scandinavian language on river names, whose forms are notoriously resistant to change, is a testament to the extent of Scandinavian linguistic use in their vicinity, their adoption and perpetuation in Middle English a clear affirmation of successful and active assimilation. The use of Scandinavian and Scandinavian-influenced place-names within wapentakes is not surprising, but they are not exclusive, and exist alongside districts bearing Anglo-Saxon names.

Over all, the place-name evidence of the north of England, once stripped of its pernicious links to numbers of settlers and name coining, provides a huge corpus of evidence illustrative of the assimilation processes at work during the Viking-period.

5.3 Viking-period Settlement: the Archaeological Evidence (fig. 5.4)

5.3.1 Introduction

In stark contrast to the place-name evidence of Scandinavian settlers in the north of England, the corresponding archaeological substantiation is slight. Very few rural sites have been excavated, and those that have cannot reasonably be assigned as residences of Scandinavian immigrants; the dates and physical remains only confirming with any certainty occupancy during the Viking-period. It has been pointed out that this lacuna is largely due to the Viking-period houses and villages being beneath modern day settlements, and that rural settlements rarely provide a corpus of artefactual remains capable of determining cultural affinities (Richards 2000*a*: 49). There is also the added problem of identifying immigrant groups via cultural remains, which is discussed fully in the following chapter, their segregation from an overseas homeland a major factor. Evidence for settlement within towns is similarly hamstrung, past landscapes buried or destroyed through a thousand years of subsequent heavy land-use. Even in York, only 0.025% of its pre-Domesday surface has been examined (Hall 2000: 315). Despite this, the Viking-period saw dramatic growth within English towns in both the north and the south, Scandinavian threat or settlement spurring nucleation through the fortification of sites by the kings of Wessex or by simple economics (Clarke & Ambrosiani 1995: 102).

This section will examine the four rural sites that show evidence of Viking-period occupation, Ribblehead (N Yorks), Bryant's Gill (Cumbria), Cottam (E Yorks), and Simy Folds (Co Durham), and provide an overview of the socio-economic impact of the Scandinavian settlers in the towns of northern England (fig. 5.4).

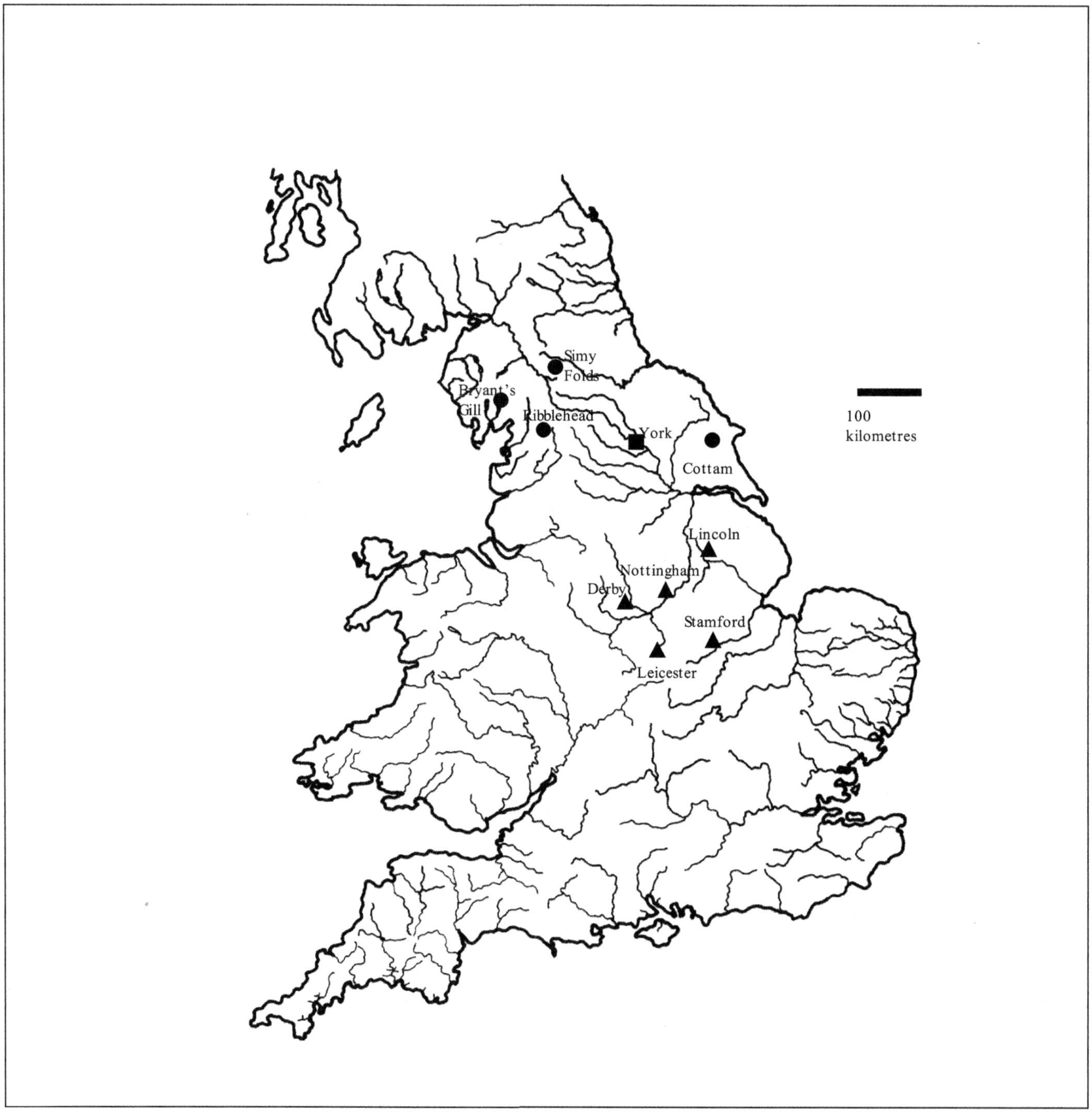

Fig. 5.4 *Map to show major towns and excavated Viking-period sites in the north of England*

5.3.2 Gauber High Pasture, Ribblehead (N Yorks) (SD766784) (figs. 5.4-5)

The remains of an isolated farmstead, high on the Ingleborough massif, underwent excavation during the mid-nineteen seventies prior to the extraction of limestone by a local quarry (King 1978: 21). The site consisted of three buildings, each with paved entrances leading from a central yard and an associated field system of 1.21 hectares (fig. 5.5) (King 1978: 21, Morris 1981: 71).The largest of the three buildings (A fig. 5.5) (19.52-18.91 x 3.96m, internal measurements) appears to be the farm house, from whose vicinity were found were found two angle-back knife blades, a fragment of an iron bridle-bit, a spear-head, and a small iron bell, of the type peculiar to areas of Viking period settlements in Eastern England and Scotland (King 1978: 22, Batey 1988). Also found within this building were three Northumbrian stycas, two of which date to the second half of the ninth century (King 1978: 22, 25). The third is illegible, as was a fourth, also recovered from just outside the northerly entrance farm site (King 1978: 22). The building was also thought to show evidence of a stone bench along the western wall (King 1978: 21).

The second building (B fig. 5.5) (6 x 3.3-7m, internal measurements), apparently linked to the southerly doorway of A by a paved walkway, was identified as a kitchen, being found to contain an oven, a quantity of butchered animal bone (horse, wild and domestic pig, hare fox, fowl, sheep and cattle) and a sandstone rotary quern (King 1978: 22, 25, King pers. comm.).

The third building (C fig. 5.5) (9 x 5m, internal measurements), more poorly built than A or B, was identified as a workshop, being found to have a central hearth which contained iron fragments and charcoal (King 1978: 25). Also recovered from the workshop were three whetstones and a green stone spindle-whorl (King 1978, King pers. comm.). Although it would be difficult to assign the farmstead as a home to Scandinavian (or Anglo-Saxon, for that matter) settlers, the coins place occupation during the late ninth century, and bell draws analogy with other Viking –period sites in the British Isles and beyond (King 1978, King pers. comm., Batey 1988).

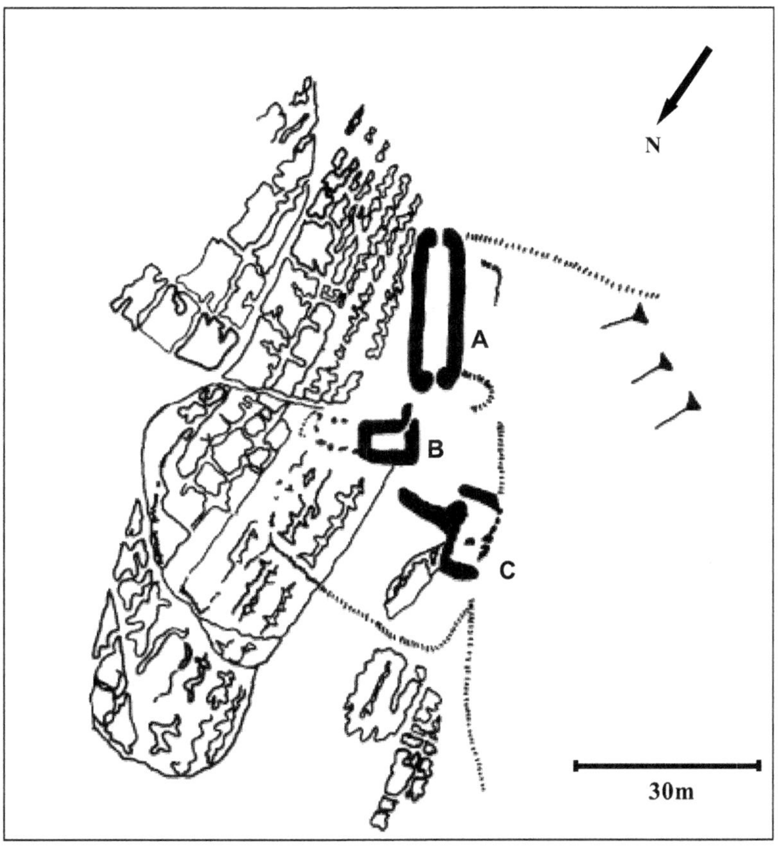

Fig. 5.5 *Gauber High Pasture, Ribblehead (N Yorks) (SD766784) (redrawn from King 1978: 23 fig. 5)*

5.3.3 Bryant's Gill, Kentmere (Cumbria) (NY456040) (fig. 5.4)

During the early nineteen-eighties and excavation was undertaken on a farmstead above the Kentmere Valley (Dickinson 1985: 85-6). As with Ribblehead, the buildings were associated with a field system, although a somewhat larger area of twenty hectares (Dickinson 1985: 85). The site was found to consist of a group of structural remains, including a rectangular building of approximately ten metres long by five wide (Dickinson 1985: 86). The building has a single entrance way, which leads inside to a strip of paving which runs the full length of the structure (Dickinson 1985: 85). Also within the structure are a series of post holes and a post trench, along with the remains of a hearth, from which charcoal was recovered for radiocarbon dating, producing a date of 700±80 (HAR 5944, uncalibrated) (Dickinson 1985: 85). Preliminary reports of the site also record some artefacts, which include eight lathe-turned shale spindle-whorls, over twenty whetstones, horse-shoe fragments, a knife, and auger, iron slag and a number of worked flints (Dickinson 1985: 85). There was also a very large amount of charcoal fragments found on the site, possibly illustrative of a manufacturing site (Dickinson 1985:86, 88). The similarity of structural form and geographical location to both Ribblehead (above) and Simy Folds (below), has allowed the excavators to form an analogy (Dickinson 1985). However, the final report of this complex site is still awaited, and until then its association with the Viking-period must remain speculative.

5.3.4 Cottam (E Yorks) (SE982668) (fig. 5.4)

Non-invasive examination of a deserted early medieval settlement site was initiated during the late nineteen-eighties following the recovery of a large number of Anglo-Saxon and Anglo-Scandinavian artefacts by metal-detectorists (Richards 2001: 271). The finds were considerable, and the evaluation produced some sixty-plus artefacts of eighth and ninth century date (Richards 1999). These and include twenty-two ninth century stycas, dress pins, strap-ends, seven finger-rings, four brooches and over thirty-five knife blades (Richards 1999). A series of Anglo-Scandinavian finds included two small iron bells (of the type recovered from Ribblehead), eight lead weights, a Jellinge-style brooch, and a buckle decorated in the Borre style (Richards 2001: 271). A further two Anglo-Scandinavian artefacts have been recovered close to the site, a chalk weight with ship graffito and another Jellinge-style brooch (Richards 2001: 271).

Magnetometer and invasion techniques were employed, and compared with plans of the artefact discoveries (Richards 2001: 271-4). The results of this analysis showed the site to have been occupied in two distinct phases; the southern end of the site abandoned sometime during the late ninth century (Richards 2001: 271-4). On the basis of the plentiful finds Richards recognised the site as a possible centre for a Northumbrian royal vill at Driffield (Richards 2000*a*: 53). After abandonment the settlement shifted a hundred metres to the north, where the Anglo-Scandinavian artefacts were predominantly recovered, and a substantial farmstead erected (Richards 2001: 271-4). The farmstead was found to consist of a number of sub-rectangular enclosures, dominated by a large decorative entranceway, made up of a truncated bank and ditch topped by a timber gate and palisade (Richards 2000*a*: 53). Archaeological evaluation of the site proved its occupation of the site to be short lived; after only fifty years the farmstead was abandoned again (Richards 2000*a*: 53, 2001: 271-4).

Although the site at Cottam differs substantially to the poorer dwellings of the Ribblehead and Bryant's Gill sites, the artefacts, magnetometer surveys and limited excavation all point to it as being a high status site, occupied during the Viking-period (Richards 2001: 271-4). The bowed walls of the rectangular structures draw immediate comparison to such Norse buildings at Jarlshof (Shetland), although it is impossible to assign ethnic origin to the owner of people living at the site.

5.3.5 Simy Folds (Co Durham) (NY888277) (figs. 5.4, 5.6-8)

The site at Simy Folds lies on the upland slopes of the Tees Valley amongst a series of early settlement sites dating from the prehistoric and through into the medieval period (Coggins *et al* 1983: 1). Excavation of three sites was undertaken over the period of 1976-81 (Coggins *et al* 1983: 1).

The three sites lay in a line along a narrow limestone band, and appeared to be dwellings associated with small stockyards (Coggins et al 1983: 1-4). The first site to be excavated in 1976 was *Site 2* (fig. 5.6) which was found to comprise of three buildings (1-3). The first building was rectangular in shape and entered via a long, narrow passage-way to the south-east (Coggins *et al* 1983: 6). It measured internally 13.5x3.5m, narrowing towards the entranceway, whose dimensions were 7m in length and 0.5m wide (Coggins *et al* 1983: 6). As at Ribblehead (above) the walls were made up of boulders, and varied in thickness between 1-2m, but stood now higher than 1m (Coggins *et al* 1983: 6). Along the central aisle of the dwelling had been laid a strip of limestone paving, which was extended at to cover the western end of the building (Coggins *et al* 1983: 6). The paving was truncated at each of the corners by the insertion of a hearth (Coggins *et al* 1983: 6). No evidence was found in the building for any post-holes (Coggins *et al* 1983: 6). There was some evidence to suggest that there may have bean a third hearth abutting the northern edge of the entranceway (Coggins *et al* 1983: 6). The only artefacts to be recovered were a stone spindle-whorl and an iron ring, from the floor of the building, and a whetstone in the southerly wall (Coggins *et al* 1983: 6).

Building 2 was found to be rectangular in shape, and measured internally 8x2.5m, and its boulder built walls were for the most part around 1.3m in width (Coggins *et al* 1983: 6). It was made up of two rooms, the most northerly of which had a paved floor and two entranceways, one to the yard, the other opposite the second smaller building (Coggins *et al* 1983: 6). A quantity of charcoal was recovered from the floor, and analysis gave a radiocarbon date of 1170±70 bp (HAR 1898) (Coggins *et al* 1983: 6). The second room possessed a cobbled floor, which lay 0.5m higher than that of the adjacent room, and a group of four flints were found in its north-west corner (Coggins *et al* 1983: 6).

Building 3 was excavated later in 1981, and was found to be comprised of two rectangular rooms, the smaller more northerly room being an addition to the larger southerly one (fig. 5.6) (Coggins *et al* 1983: 12). A lintelled doorway in the western wall was linked by a paved path to Building 2 (Coggins *et al* 1983: 12). A possible hearth in the north-east corner and post-hole close to the dividing wall covered by a series of flags were noted in the larger room (Coggins *et al* 1983: 12-4). Two quern fragments were discovered in the wall nearby, leading to the conclusion that the platform may have been used for grinding corn (Coggins *et al* 1983: 14). Artefacts found in the northern room were an iron buckle and socketed ferrule (Coggins *et al* 1983: 14).

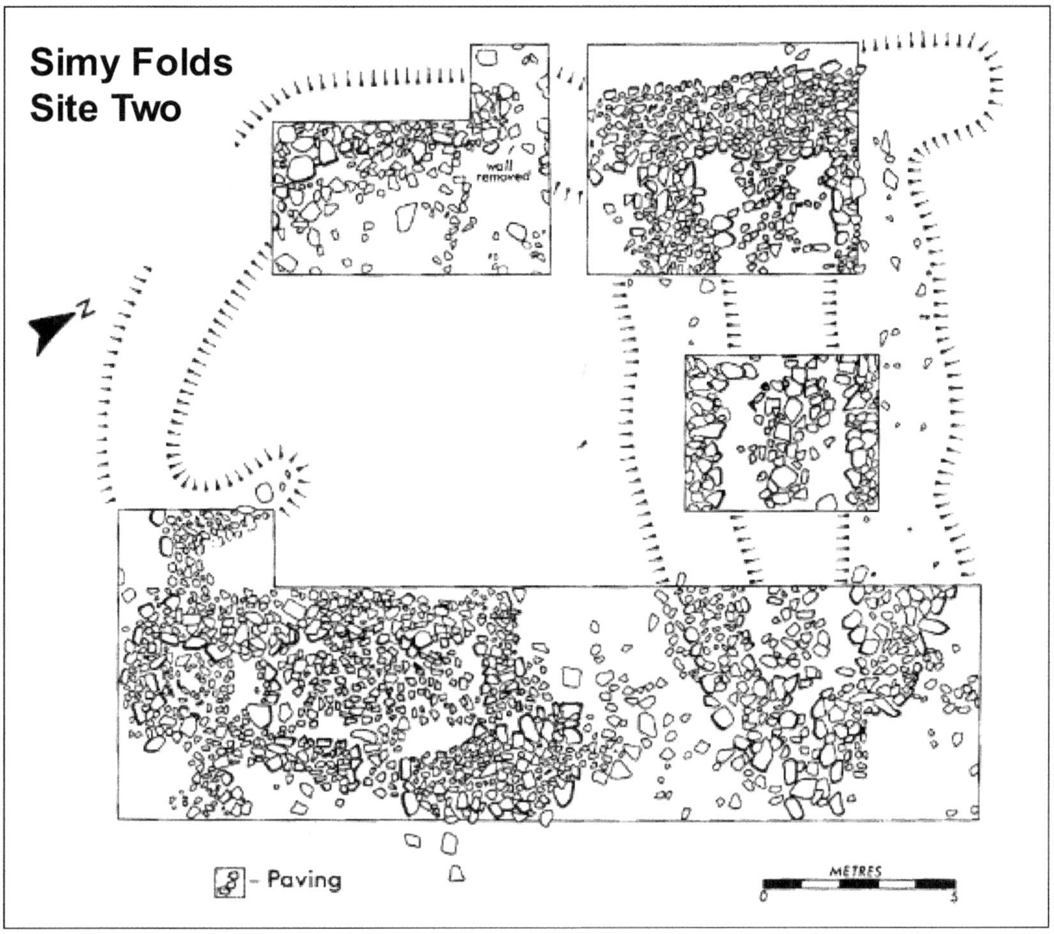

Fig. 5.6 *Simy Folds Site 2 (from Coggins et al 1983: 7 fig. 4)*

The second set of excavation examined the two buildings and yard which comprised *Site 1* (fig. 5.7) (Coggins *et al* 1983: 8). Building 1 was again rectangular in shape, and measured 9x4m internally, with walls on average 1.5m thick (Coggins *et al* 1983: 8). The floor was paved inside and two small benches had been inserted into the western corners (Coggins *et al* 1983: 6). A hearth containing charcoal, ash, burnt clay and slag lay between the south wall and the south-west bench (Coggins *et al* 1983: 8). Radiocarbon dates from the charcoal gave a date of 1210±80bp (HAR 4034) (Coggins *et al* 1983: 8). Re-examination of the site in 1981 resulted in the recovery of iron slag fragments amongst the fill of what covered the original western wall, and an adjacent pit (*c*50x40cm) which was found to contain pieces of prehistoric pottery(Coggins *et al* 1983: 12).

Building 2 of *Site 1* was found to be more sub-rectangular than all the others previously examined, and measured 8x4m internally (Coggins *et al* 1983: 8). The entranceway to the south was linked to the main building via a set of paving (Coggins *et al* 1983: 8). The walls of this structure were much more roughly constructed, and comprised mainly of earth and small stones (Coggins *et al* 1983: 8). A hearth had been cut into the bedrock 1m in from the western wall, and a sample of the charcoal recovered from it gave a date of 2330±100bp (HAR 4035) (Coggins *et al* 1983: 6-10).

The final series of excavations undertaken in 1981 also examined the rectangular building of *Site 3*, which proved to be of similar shape and construction of the main structures of the other two sites (fig. 5.8) (Coggins *et al* 1983: 10). It measured internally 5x3m, and its boulder constructed walls averaged in width around 2m (Coggins *et al* 1983: 10). The floor was partially paved and cobbled, and two post-marks in the centre suggested that it had at one time been split into two rooms (Coggins *et al* 1983: 11). A paved entranceway lay in the eastern wall, but there was found no evidence for a hearth (Coggins *et al* 1983: 11).

Also in the final excavation a sample was taken from the slag-heap which lay against the northern boundary wall; radiocarbon-dating of the charcoal producing a date of 820±80bp (HAR 4506) and the thermoluminescence-dating of some iron slag fragments a date of last usage of 640 AD (Coggins *et al* 1983: 14, Wright 1983: 18).

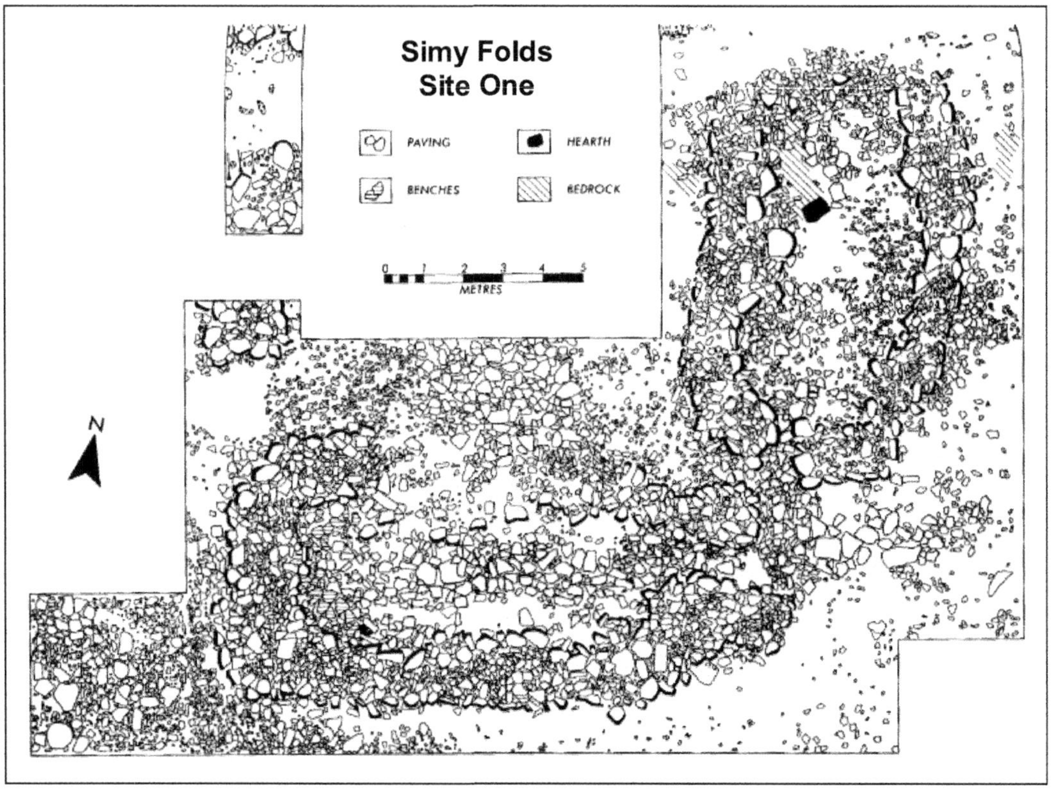

Fig. 5.7 *Simy Folds Site 1 (from Coggins et al 1983: 9 fig. 5)*

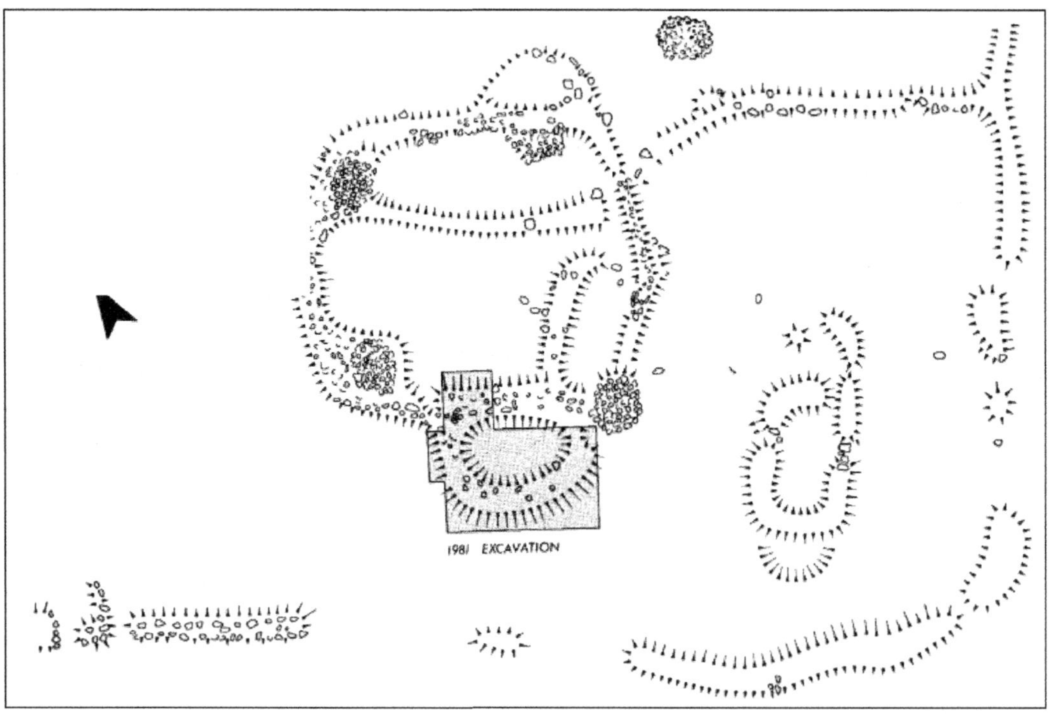

Fig. 5.8 *Simy Folds Site 3 (from Coggins et al 1983: 5 fig. 3)*

Although the similarity of *Site 2* with the buildings at Ribblehead is striking, neither complex can be described any more convincingly as an occupation area used during the late Anglo-Saxon period. Amongst the small number of artefacts there is nothing particularly culturally identifiable, nor are the buildings recognisable as Scandinavian-influenced in their construction. As discussed in chapter six, however, the apparent lack of Scandinavian-influenced goods should not preclude the presence of Scandinavian settlers; although the reproduction of traditional homesteads would require a larger cross-section of the society from the homelands to build than would be available in an immigrant population (see chapter six). The absolute-dates from the hearths show that the site at Simy Folds was occupied from prehistoric to the early medieval period, but offers no evidence at all to prove that the eighth century farmers were Scandinavian settlers.

5.3.6 Towns in the Viking-period (fig. 5.4)

This section cannot be complete without consideration of the effects Viking attacks and later Scandinavian settlement possibly had on the development of late Anglo-Saxon towns. The development of urban archaeology during the past thirty years has enabled a deeper understanding of the Viking-period in towns such as York and Lincoln, which continue to produce archaeological evidence of both structural and artefactual nature. There is no doubt that settlements in England developed real urban forms for the first time since the Roman era, beginning in the final decades of the ninth century and accelerating throughout the tenth, a period which also witnessed the movement of Scandinavian pirates, traders and settlers across northern Europe and beyond (Clarke & Ambrosiani 1995). It is tempting to equate the formation of the Anglo-Saxon town with Scandinavian settlement and trade impetus, however, as it will be shown this is not entirely the case.

The establishment of towns within the middle Anglo-Saxon period began largely as a result of the consolidation of secular and ecclesiastical control over settlements, a situation mirrored within the Carolingian Empire (Clarke & Ambrosiani 1995: 11). Most secular organisations were established within estate centers, whereas ecclesiastical communities commonly appropriated sites of Roman settlements, many diocese centres, then and now, owing their origins to the Roman period (Clarke & Ambrosiani 1995: 11). The establishment of these administrative centres allowed the establishment of specialised manufacturing and trade centres, supported by the surrounding agrarian economy (Clarke & Ambrosiani 1995: 11. Most trade was carried out within either temporary or permanent settlement sites called, *wics*, such as *Eoforwic* (York), *Hamwic* (Southampton) and *Lundenwic* (London) (Clarke & Ambrosiani 1995: 15). Modern excavations in York have identified the site of the *wic* to be in the area of modern day Fishergate, between the Rivers Ouse and Foss (Kemp 1996).

Excavations have shown that within these early *wic* sites trade was disrupted during the mid-ninth century, and in most cases ceased altogether, with a shift of operations to within defended sites nearby (Richards 2000*a*: 61). This was no doubt as a result of Viking assaults, the *Anglo-Saxon Chronicles* recording attacks on the commercial and administrative centres of London, Southampton, Canterbury and Sandwich during this period (Clarke & Ambrosiani 1995: 24, Richards 2000*a*: 61). The vulnerable site at Fishergate was duly abandoned entirely during this period; re-use of the land only beginning again during the eleventh and twelfth centuries (Kemp 1996). What is important here to note is that the Vikings were undertaking attacks against established settlements, the foundation of which (commercial, industrial or administrative centres) was a highly visible phenomenon across the north-western European continent at this time (Clarke & Ambrosiani 1995: 24).

A second likely response to the threat of attack was the creation in Mercia of a series of fortified towns, or *burhs*, in the late eighth century, established around major river crossings to act as civil and ecclesiastical centres of administration (for example, Tamworth and Chester) (Haslam 1987). As centres of population, they also became sites of markets (Haslam 1987, Richards 2000*a*: 67). The creation of such sites was mirrored and expounded in Wessex by Alfred and his son Edward, who were responsible for the establishment of a network of defensive settlements (Richards 2000*a*: 70). The establishment of these permanent *burhs* or towns acted as catalysts within regional economies, providing a safe haven for markets and industry, and also for taxation and control.

Some reference has been made to the Five Boroughs[18] in the previous chapter and their importance as centres of population during the Viking-period. Whether their establishment as fortified towns was undertaken by Scandinavian settlers in the late ninth century or by Edward the Elder during his reclamation of the north in the early tenth is a moot point, however, the growth and prosperity of these towns during and after this period is very clear (Hall 1989). All of the towns are situated on major transport routes, and have a history of use as administrative or ecclesiastical centres in the earlier Anglo-Saxon period; in Derby, Lincoln and Leicester the surviving Roman fortifications were utilised in their defensive structures (Hall 2000: 144-5). As with many of the *burhs* of Mercia and Wessex, the consolidation of the settlements within fortified boundaries enabled true urbanisation to take place (Richards 2000*a*: 76).

Of the Five Boroughs, the most available archaeological evidence comes from Lincoln, and has revealed the re-organisation of street systems around Flaxengate and Michaelgate[19], the former showing a large amount of industrial activity, including non-ferrous metalworking and glass manufacture, beginning in the late tenth century (Hall 1989: 184-5, Richards 2000*a*: 76).The mint at Lincoln (possibly begun in the late ninth century) produced as many coins as York (Hall 2001: 150). In Nottingham, Thetford and Stamford a number of Viking-period occupation sites have been discovered, along with areas of pottery production at both sites and iron-working at Stamford (Hall 2001: 149, Richards 2000*a*: 76-7). In Derby, and Leicester archaeological evidence of comparable nature is rather more scarce: and consists of a cess-pit and rubble-platform within the Roman fort at Derby, and a late tenth century pottery kiln in Leicester (Hall 1974*a*, Richards 2000*a*: 76).

By far the most archaeological features of the Viking-period have been recovered from York. As already described, excavations in the modern city have alluded to the original Anglian *wic* as being on the confluence of the Rivers Ouse and Foss, modern day Fishergate, before the trading site was shifted closer to the walls of the Roman fortress, which played their part in many ninth century sieges (Kemp 1996). Excavations at Lloyds Bank, Pavement uncovered timber buildings and the remains of workshops producing leather

[18] Derby, Leicester, Lincoln, Nottingham and Stamford.

[19] Both Flaxengate and Michaelgate bearing the Scandinavian appellative *gata*, road, similarly in York, with Coppergate, Micklegate, *etc*.

goods (Richards 2000*a*: 65). Tanning pits have been found on High Ousegate, and timber buildings and rubbish pits have been found along Micklegate and Skeldergate (Richards 2000*a*: 65). However, it was to be the Coppergate excavations which provided the most Viking-period archaeological remains. The four tenement buildings were found to have housed workshops producing craft activities on a commercial scale, and included ferrous and non-ferrous metal-working, glass manufacture, wood-working along with antler and bone carving (Ottaway 1992: 149-153). Associated with the buildings were wells, cess-pits and latrines, and piles of waste, whose peculiar state of environmental stasis allowed the recovery of very many organic remains, not normally preserved within archaeological contexts (Ottaway, 1992: 146-155, Richards 2000*a*: 65).

During the last quarter of the tenth century these buildings were demolished and the land re-used to accommodate the space more fully, with buildings being provided with small cellars (Ottaway 1992: 152). None of the buildings from either period could be particularly associated with Scandinavian influences, and all of their structural methods can be paralleled elsewhere in English towns of the period (Hall 2000: 315).

That there was a link with Scandinavia is undeniable, as the volume of artefacts and raw-materials sourced from within Norway, Denmark and Sweden attest. As referred to in the previous chapter, the presence of Scandinavian merchants in York are commonly alluded to contemporary historical documents, and it was they who no doubt played a central part in the import of particularly Scandinavian associated goods, such as soapstone, clubmoss and walrus ivory (Hall 2000: 316). The discoveries of silk and Kufic coins in York are also very likely a result of Scandinavian trading enterprises in the east (Hall 2000:316-7). However, these goods, along with other artefacts of Scandinavian type, such as weaponry, jewellery and combs cannot be attributed to Scandinavian owners. Such attribution of artefacts and alliance with ethnicity is discussed in the following chapter.

There is no-doubt that Vikings and Scandinavian settlers played a part in the establishment of the urbanisation of larger Anglo-Saxon settlements, with the creation of defensive settlements, increasing of populations through immigration and extension of trading contacts (Clarke & Ambrosiani 1995: 102). They were not however, wholly responsible for urbanization, merely a part of an ongoing process mirrored across Western Europe (Clarke & Ambrosiani 1995). The success of northern towns, however, is a testament to the assimilation of Anglo-Saxon and Scandinavian communities, an achievement reflected both in the historical and archaeological resource.

5.3.7 Viking-period Settlement: the Archaeological Evidence: conclusions

In contrast to stone-sculpture and place-names the evidence for Scandinavian-influence of settlements in actual physical form seems sparse. The most available archaeological data comes from modern excavations undertaken within towns, for example Lincoln or York, which provide not only artefactual evidence demonstrating designs drawn from both Anglo-Saxon and Scandinavian cultural milieus, but also domestic and manufacturing sites, which display the socio-economic vitality of the period. There is no doubt that Scandinavian raiders and settlers played a critical part in the establishment of the urbanization of larger Anglo-Saxon settlements, however, they were not wholly responsible, both historical (see chapter four) and archaeological resource demonstrating that the success of northern towns relied upon the successful assimilation of Anglo-Saxon and Scandinavian communities.

The picture in the countryside is somewhat different. Ignored for the most part by contemporary authors in the late Anglo-Saxon period, and relatively untouched by large-scale development and the precursive archaeological examination, the sum knowledge of Anglo-Saxon settlement sites in the north of England is very small indeed. It seems highly likely that many modern villages and farms overlie far older sites, thus depriving the archaeological resource; however, there are traces of very many deserted village sites (DMV), which could potentially provide a dataset of settlements for the late Anglo-Saxon period. They may or may not provide evidence of Scandinavian-influence via artefactual remains, building techniques or land use, but their archaeological value and use as test cases would be inestimable. Excavations at the DMV site at Wharram Percy (N Yorks) shows the huge potential on offer for this type of targeted excavation (where incidentally Borre style belt-fittings were recovered); and at Cottam itself, exploration of the DMV site by metal-detectorists paved the way for excavation (Stamper & Croft 2000, Richards 2001: 271). It does seem unlikely that there will ever be found a *Scandinavian farmstead* in the north of England, simply due to the nature of immigration and settlement (see chapter six). However, the settlement lacuna still remains and it should not preclude further investigation; as it has been illustrated throughout this work, any evidence of Scandinavian-influence, or even the lack of it can only further our understanding of settlement during the period.

The difficulties of not having any comparative reference are highlighted in the analyses of Ribblehead, Simy Folds, Bryant's Gill and Cottam. Despite the absolute dates provided by the excavations at Bryant's Gill and Simy Folds, placing use of the site during the Viking-period, neither site provided any clear evidence (structural or artefactual) for Scandinavian-influence. The bells recovered from Ribblehead and Cottam are, however, paralleled by similar finds across areas of Scandinavian settlement in the British Isles (King 1978, Richards 2001, Batey 1988). Other finds from Cottam also show evidence of Anglo-Scandinavian influence, although the number of discoveries in the area compared to the apparent paucity of objects from the remaining three sites may be due to the high status of the homestead (Richards 2001). Bryant's Gill, Simy Folds and Ribblehead are all poor small-holdings, situated on marginal land, whose occupants in the Viking-period would have been far removed both socially and economically from the landowner at Cottam (Dickinson 1985, Coggins *et al* 1983, King 1978, Richards 2001).

The similarities of construction of Bryant's Gill, Simy Folds and Ribblehead has been allied with a series of eleventh to thirteenth century Norse settlement sites in Scotland (Batey 1995), which although for the most part are later than the

English sites, is once again hampered because it is unknown whether this manner of settlement construction in upland situations during this period was the norm, or was in fact introduced by Scandinavian settlers. Consideration must also be given to the different types of settlement being undertaken in the two areas; colonisation in Scotland and assimilation in northern England (see chapter six). However, this being said, progress is restricted until researchers have more access to primary archaeological data from settlement sites in the north of England during the late Anglo-Saxon from which comparative results may be drawn.

Comparisons with the bowed structure at Cottam to that at Jarlshof (Shetland) is more favourable (Richards 2001). Allied with the large quantity of Anglo-Scandinavian artefacts recovered from the site, it may indeed be the case that the then occupier was a member of the Northumbrian social elite, descended from Scandinavian settlers. However, as will be discussed in chapter six, the equation of cultural objects with ethnic groups is far from clear cut. All that can be said with any certainty is that here was the home of a member of the Northumbrian social elite; whose household was linked to the Scandinavian-influenced world with the use of Anglo-Scandinavian artefacts and construction techniques.

Until further sites have been explored the level of knowledge surrounding Viking-period settlement sites in the north of England will remain static. There is little doubt, when one considers the impact of incoming Scandinavian groups upon language, place-names, sculpture, the growth of towns, law codes and practice, that there still awaits to be discovered a whole new facet of the Viking-period north of England.

5.4 Hybrid-designs and Settlement: conclusions

As with the previous chapter the analysis of Scandinavian-influenced stone-sculpture, language and settlement pattern has had to be concise, however, the theme of contact and interaction between immigrant and resident populations is very clearly in evidence throughout. In aspects of stone-sculpture, there is nothing to identify the patron of each example as being of Scandinavian descent, but there is no doubt that elite members of the immigrant community were the catalyst behind the boom in production and shift in market from majority ecclesiastical to secular consumption. Their continued display within churchyards also hints strongly of the manipulation of cultural fashion by the Anglo-Saxon clergy to facilitate the acceptance of Christianity, a method employed by missionaries since the earliest of times. The adoption of stone-sculpture as a commemorative technique, the introduction of new motifs by Scandinavian groups, combined with the continuation of Anglian traditions, fused to create an artistic schema entirely induced by the successful assimilation of immigrant and resident populations. The design and use of the hogback must also be recognized as a physical manifestation of the interaction between two groups during the assimilation process. The negotiations involved in the establishment of these monuments within churchyards, the majority of which bear no discernible Christian representations, cannot be underestimated or ignored.

This creation of a new cultural facet from two cultural origins is repeated in the study of place-names, and the recognition that a Scandinavian-influenced place-name arose within a district where both Old Scandinavian and Old English were spoken. The existence of a bi-lingual community is best illustrated by the fact that the majority of place-name forms are hybrid mixtures of the similar Old English and Old Scandinavian languages. This in itself reflects the level of assimilation taking place via the amalgamation of languages. The influence of Old Scandinavian on river names, whose forms are notoriously resistant to change, is a testament to the extent of its linguistic use in their vicinity; their adoption and perpetuation in Middle English a clear affirmation of successful and active assimilation. The use of Scandinavian and Scandinavian-influenced place-names within wapentakes is not surprising, but they are not exclusive and exist alongside districts bearing Anglo-Saxon names.

The most available archaeological evidence for Scandinavian-influence within settlement sites comes from the pre-construction archaeological evaluation work undertaken in towns such as York or Lincoln. Artefactual and structural remains demonstrate the use of Anglo-Scandinavian designs and economic vitality of the period; the growth and development of urban sites being depended on the successful interaction between resident and incoming groups. In the countryside the high status site at Cottam provides evidence for the consumption of Anglo-Scandinavian goods amongst elite members of society, and encourages the exploration of further DMV sites to widen the field of knowledge of late Anglo-Saxon settlements. Such expansion of the dataset would also aid in placing Ribblehead, Simy Folds and Bryant's Gill in context, and perhaps establish after all whether they are examples of traditional upland construction techniques (which is likely) or an introduction into northern England by Scandinavian settlers.

Overall the picture provided by the archaeological resource bearing influence of Anglo-Saxon and Scandinavian contact parallels that of the historical data, showing clear evidence of interaction and successful assimilation between resident and immigrant communities. The question that must now be addressed is how, and for that the answers lie in the process of migration and settlement of immigrant groups.

CHAPTER SIX – MIGRATION, IMMIGRATION, ETHNICITY & CULTURE

6.0 Introduction

"*...in highlighting the destructiveness of the Vikings, and the differences between Scandinavian and English society, we have not sufficiently addressed the very real issue of how and why the Scandinavians did eventually integrate themselves into native society and culture.*" (Hadley 1997: 95-6).

Before any attempt can be made to analyse what is perceived to be 'Viking' remains in the archaeological record or construct any sort of theoretical model to explain culture and contact it is absolutely vital to bear the following points in mind. Firstly that the 'Vikings' were not a single homogeneous cultural or ethnic group, and secondly that they were immigrant settlers in a far from empty landscape. Both points are fundamental and consideration of them has far-reaching effects for the understanding of the Viking period. This chapter does not attempt to '*highlight(ing)....the differences between Scandinavian and English* society..' or try to understand Viking settlement by projecting the perceived results backwards, it aims to understand who was coming and why, and how these people might have reacted to their new environment and settled in peace, by looking at theories of migration and integration between different ethnic and cultural groups. Using this as a basis it should then be possible to understand settlement and interaction between immigrant and local, and enable better evaluation of what is left of this contact in the archaeological record.

6.1 Current Paradigms

The large corpus of work devoted to the settlement of Viking groups in England is by and large devoid of foundation as scholars fail to address the study of migration, without which settlement could not take place (Trafford 2000: 17). This is exacerbated by the underlying assumption that all the Viking settlers were drawn from a single, culturally homogeneous group. This may largely be due to its predominant base in place-name research, which recognises the arrival of a migrant population in a landscape by the survival of some descriptive facets of a language other than that spoken by the resident population. However, the chronology of such events is generally floating somewhere between the historically perceived first arrival of Viking groups and the first written mention of the name. Hence in the vast majority of cases it is unknown when and how a particular part of the landscape received its Norse influenced name. Was it given by a first, second or third generation settler, an Anglo-Scandinavian, an Anglo-Saxon with knowledge of local usage of Norse words, or by a Viking who lived there briefly and is remembered in the landscape by the remaining locals? The list of predictions and efforts to understand the vagaries of the human psyche could go on and remain unproven, but does nothing to further understanding of settlement. As discussed in chapter five, surviving Norse place-names are a reaction by groups via the perpetuation of a word, and cannot be taken solely as an indicator of Viking settlers in the district.

Place-name studies tell us that the North of England in particular has very many topological features bearing names of Norse origin, which as Trafford (2000) has pointed out, has left Scandinavian settlement studies hamstrung by the pervading interest of scholars determined to pin-point the exact numbers of settlers to arrive. As well as being unanswerable, logically or via consideration of some of the most basic migratory principles, the debate has over-shadowed deeper exploration of settlement, and stunted the growth of studies which may have had the potential to provide answers to more conclusive and fruitful questions (see Hadley, above).

This preoccupation has its foundations firmly fixed within the whole paradigm of Viking studies, which is concerned with the assumed *results* of settlement, a case of splitting causality and effect, and ignoring the former (Trafford 2000: 20). Adherence to this has resulted in the stranding of Viking studies within archaeology, leaving scholars to struggle for new answers (and questions) amongst the same old datasets of Viking artefacts and historical sources. Within these datasets are of course Viking burials, which illustrate the problem perfectly. Their apparent paucity is seen as either an indicator for the rapid conversion to Christianity of the settlers or as evidence for their minimal numbers. Both are explanations of perceived results. This is not so much as a glass ceiling, but a glass floor. Viking settlers appear within the paradigm as a static, uniform mass, with no prior or subsequent socio-cultural, ethnic or economic links to anywhere or anybody.

This stranding of Viking archaeology is a direct result of the inability to come to terms with the visibility of historically recorded cultural interaction, and the insistence of treating immigrant Viking groups as discrete cultural and ethnic identities. This problem is highlighted when the logically expected corresponding pockets of Viking material remains (such as settlement sites) consistently fail to appear.

This period represents an ideal opportunity to apply insights into culture, ethnicity and migration developed by social scientists of various disciplines and combine them with the archaeo-historical evidence of the period. Such coalescence may bring understanding closer to the actual truth of how and why assimilation took place, and how this has affected or is possibly reflected in the archaeological record.

6.1.1 Towards an Answer

As argued above, appreciating why and how Viking and Anglo-Saxon social integration took place is not only important to Viking studies in general, but extremely pertinent in trying to understand the burial record.
The first part of this section examines the research of migration and migration theory undertaken by social scientists drawn from multiple disciplines, concerning the types of migration, the reasons for migration, the sort of person liable or able to migrate, and migration patterns. In light of this, the second part considers assimilation between immigrant and local populations and their expected outcome under certain conditions, and is expanded to analyse the identification of migration in the archaeological record. The third part of this section develops the theory of migration further by discussing the fundamental issues arising from the recognition of ethnicity

and culture within the archaeological record, and considers the danger and results of treating supposed cultural indicators as representative of discrete ethnic groups.

6.2 Migration

For the purpose of this study migration will be defined as the free, non-seasonal, movement of a person or people into a territory, other than their original homeland, and subsequent, permanent settlement there for a period of time.

The study of migration is far from being a modern academic construct, as Caesar's recording in 58 BC of the transhumance of the Helvetii from their homelands in Switzerland into France shows (Anthony 1990: 898-899). For over a hundred years social scientists from various disciplines have been studying migration, migration patterns and assimilation between national and immigrant, and this, for better or for worse, included archaeology until Kossinna's particular ill-based theories were used to validate sinister ends in Europe during the 1930's and 1940's (Lee 1966: 47-49, Anthony 1990: 896). Since then the migration of peoples has been the proverbial hot-potato, coming into and out of fashion with current political thought, rather than being used and developed as a discrete tool for understanding past populations (Chapman & Hamerow 1997, Anthony 1997). However, a recent resurgence in interest within theoretical archaeology will hopefully reverse this trend.

The various fields of social science interested in population movement recognise that there are broadly five categories of human migration.

> i. primitive – *ie* escape, from war, famine *etc.*
> ii. forced – *ie* the forced movement of one group by another
> iii. chain – *ie* the following of kin into areas already settled by family members
> iv. mass - usually beginning as free migrations (see below) *eg* the transhumance from Europe to America
> v. free - started by people who are neither pushed from their home or are strongly attracted to their destination.

(Encyclopaedia Britannica).

From the above categories it can be seen that migration is a social decision either undertaken as a free choice, or forced by factors beyond the individual or groups' control. There is some over-lap however, if one considers the movement of children and other familial dependents and slaves, who may not wish to move and have no say in the matter (Lee 1966: 51).

In any migration the decisions to migrate must be made from consideration of all the incentives and obstacles created by such a move. In the vast majority of migrations, this will depend on some knowledge (real or perceived) of the destination (Anthony 1990: 901). In order for migration to take place the positive benefits as seen to be offered by the destination must outweigh the personally envisaged difficulties or pressures of the home environment and the hardships to be encountered in trying to the reach the new destination (Lee 1966, Isaac 2000: 41). The incentives and obstacles involved in such a move will differ from person to person, group to group, and will be weighted accordingly during the decision to go or stay (Lee 1966: 50).

The specifics of a multitude of highly personal, sometimes irrational, socio-economic factors that influenced a person to migrate in the past can only remain speculative. However, researchers of population movement have gathered these positive and negative feelings towards homeland and destination into two non-specific, general clusters known as *push* and *pull* factors (Lee 1966). *Push* factors are what the potential émigré sees to be the downside of living in his homeland, and *pull* factors are the potential available benefits a new life as a result of migration to a new homeland may bring (Lee 1966). Each push or pull factor will be slightly different between different people, depending on socio-economic position or point of view (Lee 1966: 50). If the potential émigré recognises more positive pull factors outweigh those of home, he is more likely to take the decision to migrate. If, however, the negative push factors of his homeland are deemed not bad enough to take the risk of migration, the potential émigré will stay at home. Finally, indelibly connected with the push and pull factors, are the distance, the travelling involved between the two places, the cost and finally the viability of the person or people being able to undertake the journey successfully (Lee 1966: 50-51). Already the numbers of people economically, sociologically, psychologically and physiologically viable for the traumas of free migration are lessening. In a nutshell the type of person able to migrate must have capital, some knowledge of his destination, a strong inclination that what he is doing is right, be in good health (therefore probably young), and be of a social position within a community to do it (*ie* a freeman)[1]. In all cases the primary reason behind overcoming all the obstacles and natural propensity to stay put must be for gain, an envisaged improvement in lifestyle, either social or economic (Isaac 2000: 23-29, 41). Migration, rather than a chaotic leap into the unknown, is goal oriented and well planned and organised by its executors.

6.2.1 Migration Patterns

Studies made by social scientists of different peoples around the world in various historical time periods, show that there are a number of recurring elements shared between migrating groups making it possible to list a number of general regular patterns or rules (Anthony 1997: 22). These can be summarised as follows:

i. Primary migrations are more likely to be undertaken by young, adult males (Jansen 1969: 71-73, Morrison & Wheeler 1978: 79, Anthony 1990: 908).
ii. Settlement is done via 'information' stages; the transfer of knowledge from pioneers (scouts/traders/military personnel) to potential émigrés, and primary settlers to potential

[1] Although it could be argued that it is equally as likely for someone beyond the law to flee the country of their birth, they would still need the means to flee (money, transport) and to establish themselves within a settled group of émigrés or nationals.

secondary settlers still living in the homeland (Isaac 2000: 153, Anthony 1990: 902-903).

iii. The reasons to migrate can be for sociological or economic reasons, but usually are done to improve the socio-economic position of the migrant (Taylor 1969: 117, Jansen 1969: 65, Beijer 1969: 57, Isaac 2000: 23-29).

iv. Settlement areas often mirror a migrants' homeland (geographically, kin/friends, climate, employment type, *etc*) (Isaac 2000: 42, 53-4).

v. The choice or route of migration is very dependent on previously settled kin-groups or friends (Morrison & Wheeler 1978: 80, Taylor 1969: 127, Isaac 2000: 34, Anthony 1990: 899-903, Lee 1966: 54).

vi. Return migration occurs in very large numbers (Isaac 2000: 46, 63, Anthony 1997: 25, 1990: 897-898).

vii. Migration encourages further subsequent moves by the migrant (Morrison & Wheeler 1978: 79-80, Anthony 1997: 25, Taylor 1969: 110-112)

viii. Migration continues even after the cessation of the initial favourable conditions (Anthony 1997: 25).

ix. Culture does not migrate; a very particular and specific group of the population does (Anthony 1990: 908).

Although the list of trends above cover different facets of observable behaviour by immigrants there is a common theme of information. The importance of information flow in the decision to migrate cannot be over emphasised. Migrants to new homelands do not travel blindly into the unknown. As discussed above, there are a multitude of socio-economic factors bound up with the decision to migrate, and each factor has an element of risk. Such decisions cannot be made against the promise of an unknown land. Adventurers, traders or mercenaries, generally young adult males, some of whom may or may not have chosen to set up permanent bases there, relay reports and stories of new territories back to kin and friends at home (fig. 6.1). Such reports play a vital part in developing pull factors for the potential immigrant. The connection is made and the first link in *chain migration* is laid as émigrés take the decision to move to the areas these people have talked about, or set up home themselves (fig. 6.2). In turn some of these primary migrants will settle, usually close to others in the same migratory band, and the bridge of information between homeland and new land begins to take on more solid form (Anthony 1997: 26). The increased flow of information and the security of knowing that others who have gone before are safe, and perhaps more importantly, prospering, will induce others to follow. Over time new migrants heading for the primary centres settled by kin and/or friends will begin to establish homes in the landscape around it, and in effect create satellite communities (fig. 6.3) (Lee 1966: 55).

However, this is only the first of two fundamental traits found in the studies of migration. The first, as outlined above, is that migratory settlement is typically carried out by kin groups and the second that migration is really a two way event, with *stream* and *counterstream* of population moving between homeland and destination (Lee 1966: 54-56, Anthony 1990: 897). Studies show that sometimes as much as a third of a migratory population at any one-time return home (Isaac 2000: 63, Anthony 1997: 25). This phenomenon is illustrated by demographers using spatial interaction models, which also show that if a person has migrated in the last twelve months that person is highly likely to do it again (Anthony 1997: 25). This internal movement would be a very powerful and effective way of spreading language (which would have a profound effect on place-names) along with other facets of culture. Markov models, used to predict migration flows, show that once migratory flow has been established between two places movement continues even after the original incentives that encouraged initial migration have ceased (Anthony1997: 25).

This counter-stream of population to the homeland would also increase the knowledge base of potential émigrés of the new settlements being established in the new land. Whether the failed migrants and their information would encourage or dissuade further émigrés depends entirely on the prospective migrant.

From these series of factors and decision-making it can be seen that point nine, 'Cultures do not migrate', is true. Only a small section of people, generally younger adults, backed by suitable socio-economic conditions, will migrate. These people once settled within the new territory will have the propensity to move again within the new land, while maintaining contact with both other immigrants and kin-groups in the homeland. Migratory patterns are very fluid, and yet predictable, with their reliance on information.

6.2.2 Assimilation

For reasons of clarity the theories of migration discussed above has to a certain extent regarded the new homelands of the immigrant to be without nationals, which with very few exceptions in the history of mankind is untrue. The process of migration not only affects the immigrant but the national as well (Beijer 1969: 14). In all migrations there is a difference in culture between immigrant and national, and assimilation must be undertaken to guarantee successful settlement (Beijer 1969: 13). Assimilation will be harder for the older members of a migrant community, who due to their age will be more deeply influenced by the traditions of their homeland and cultural factors (Isaac 2000: 42). Studies show that second generations are often in conflict with their parents because of differences in social or cultural habits (Ross 1941: 583 in Beijer 1969: 52). The migrant is surrounded by a whole milieu of change, from language to religion, culture to politics, artistic to scientific, all of which will affect him on a personal level (Beijer 1969: 54). The greater the contact with nationals, the swifter integration takes place, studies showing that integration is quicker in an urban environment (Beijer 1969: 54, Jansen 1969: 68). Problems arise when migrant communities refuse or are prevented from extensive contact with nationals, something that can arise if groups settle closely together, maintain strong introspective cultural and ethnic ties and in effect form colonies within a new land (Price 1969: 187).

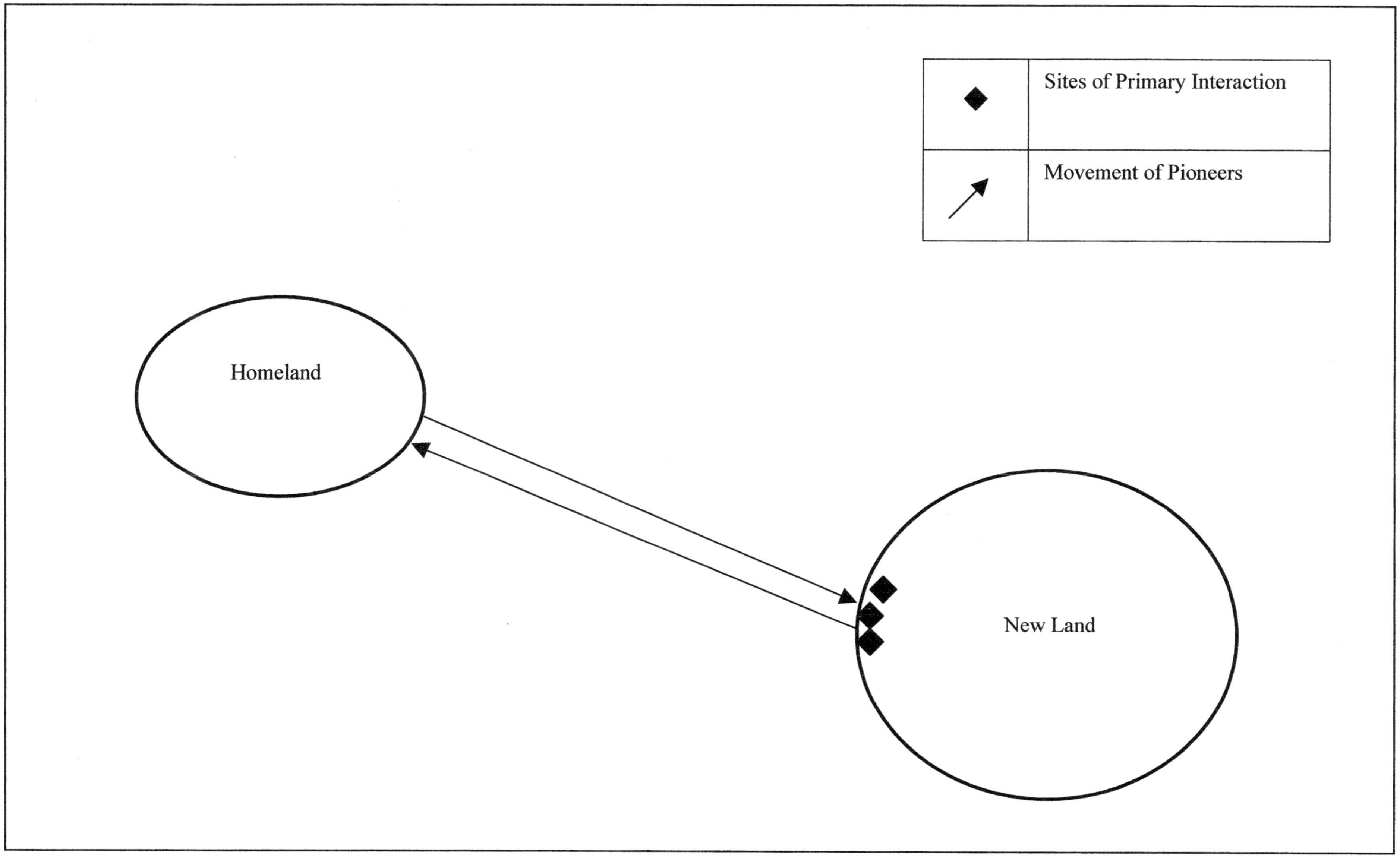

Fig. 6.1 *Primary Migration*

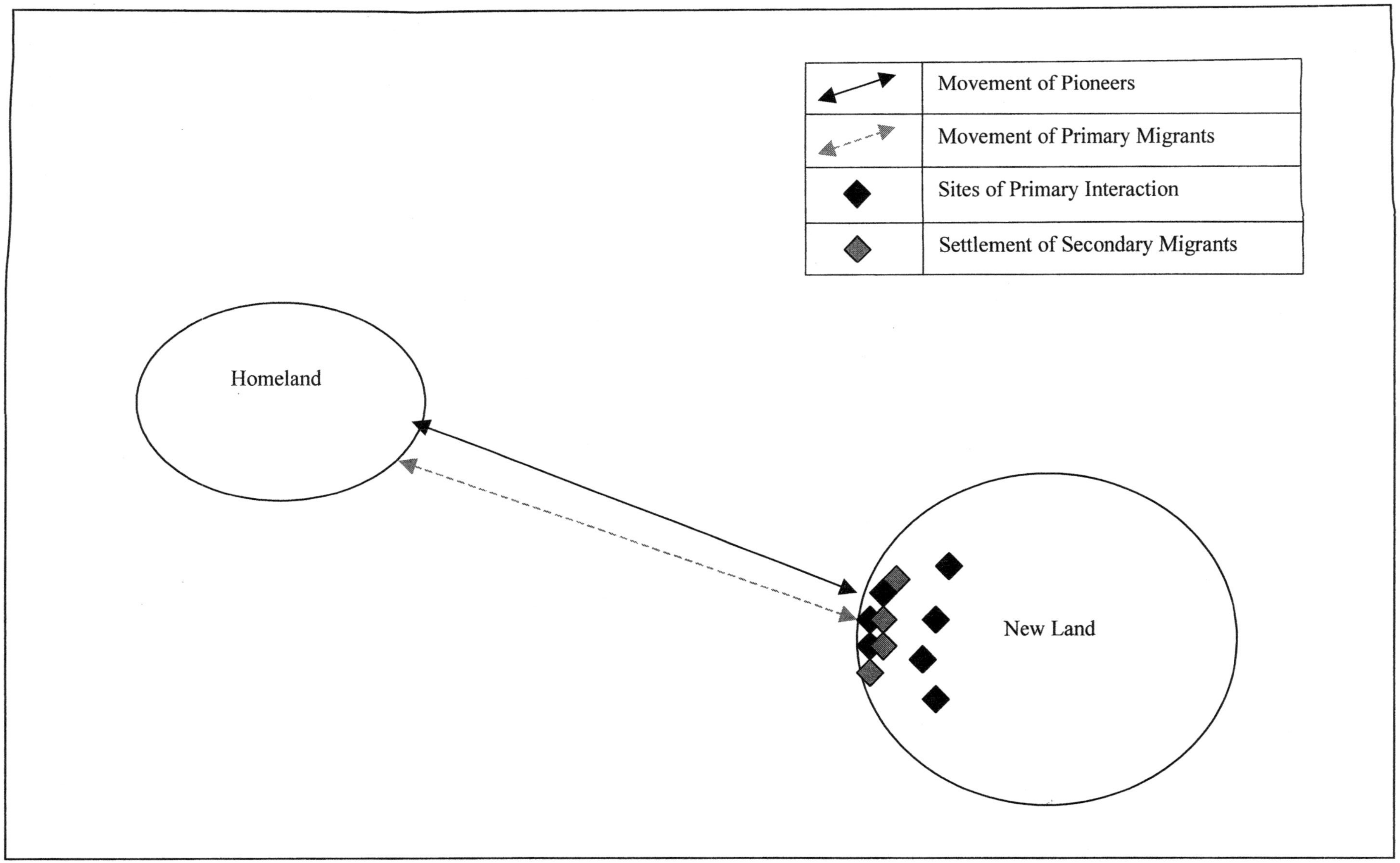

Fig. 6.2 *Secondary Migration*

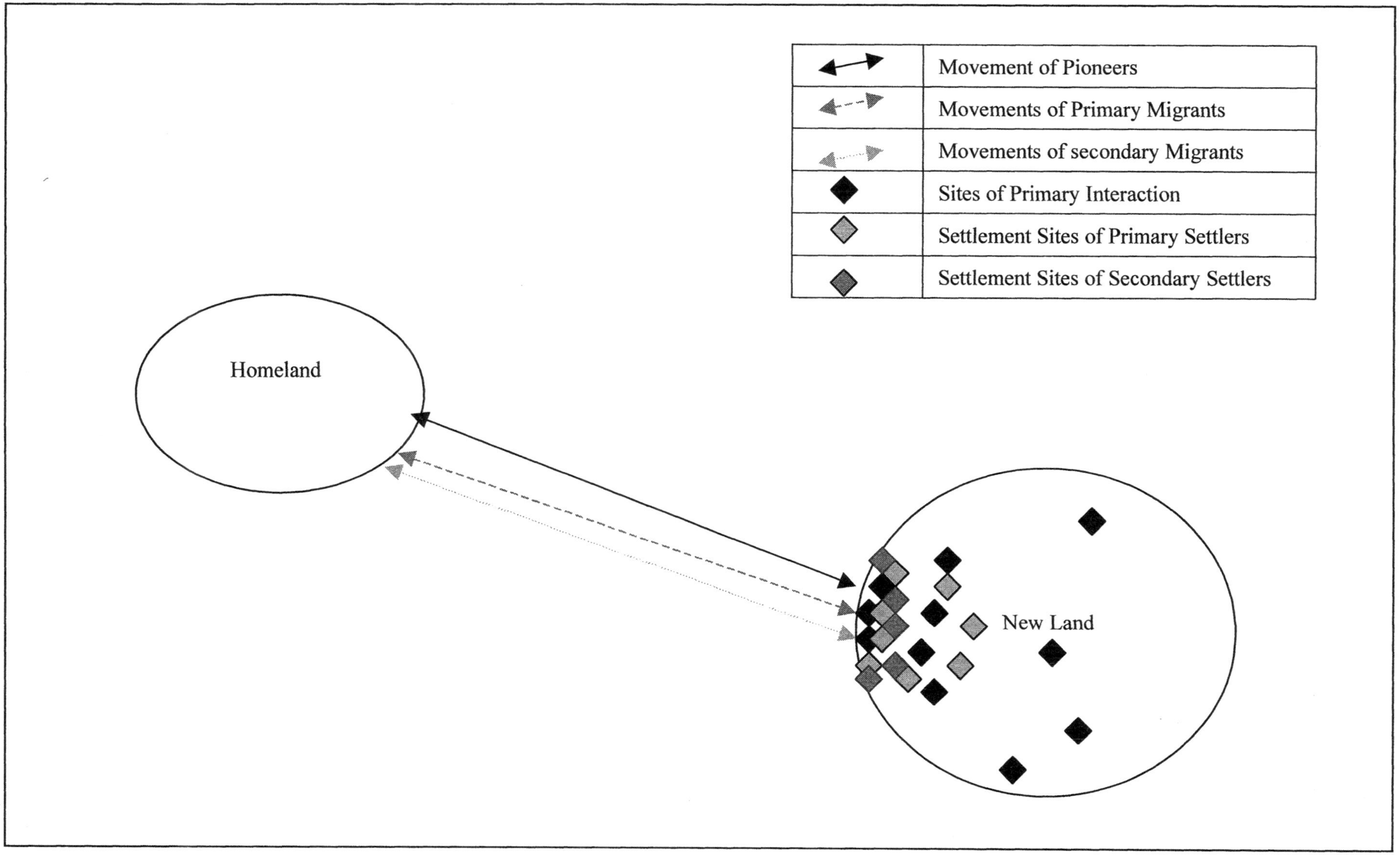

Fig. 6.3 *Tertiary Migration*

Similar to the very personal decisions and factors involved with the initial decision to migrate, the success or failure of assimilation of an immigrant is largely governed by personal factors, beliefs *etc.* Many processes and stages of assimilation have been suggested by social scientists, but most doubt, as with migration theory, that there could be a single hypothesis encompassing all aspects of assimilation (Price 1969; 235). However, three basic assumptions with regard to successful or unsuccessful assimilation can be made:

i. The attitude of nationals towards immigrants
ii. The attitude of immigrants towards nationals
iii. The size of the migrant population

(Price 1969: 185-187).

As well as the personal characteristics of the national and migrant which dominate the extent and hence success of integration, Beijer (1969: 55) identified seven further factors which influence acceptance:

i. The occupation of the migrant
ii. The availability to migrants of decent living accommodation
iii. The attitude of national neighbours and or work colleagues towards the migrant
iv. The ability to find and make friends
v. The migrant's cultural affinities
vi. How the migrant spends social and leisure time
vii. The acknowledgement by nationals of the strength of the cultural ties which may bind the migrant.

Each factor is different, and arguably as important as the rest, however each factor is dependent on the interaction between migrants and nationals. The success of the interaction is critical to the extent and speed of assimilation. Similarities in cultural acts and beliefs will ease and quicken assimilation, leading to more intermarriage and socio-cultural blending. This has been seen to happen within Northern European migrant groups settling in the United States (Price 1969: 206).

6.2.3 The Identification of Migration in the Archaeological Record

The logical, if rather crude method for the identification of migration in the archaeological record is done by recognising change within material remains, and being able to discriminate between internal changes within a population and changes introduced by migration in its various forms (Anthony 1990: 897). However, this method of identification is dependent on the assumption that the spatial patterning of associated remains is representative of an archaeological culture or ethnic group, an idea that underpins modern archaeological explanation despite recent anthropological and sociological work which shows it to be not strictly true (Shennan 1994: 5, Jones 1998). This section will consider ideas of culture and ethnicity, the problems of identification and their application to the archaeological record in an attempt to recognise population movement in the past.

6.3 Culture and Ethnicity

Although the earliest classical historians such as Caesar, Tacitus and Herodotus referred to many different tribal groupings and what we would consider to be their various ethnographic traits, the term *culture* only came into use during the seventeenth century (Dīaz-Andreu 1996: 51-52). The term was coined as a description of the intellectual characterisation and its subsequent developments within physical and academic fields of resident populations within particular geographically-political situations (Dīaz-Andreu 1996: 51-52).

The acceptance of *culture,* that is, the perceived defining traits of the present, led to the logical idea of projecting it onto the past, first by Gustav Kossinna and then Gordon Childe. Both Kossinna and Childe in their culture-historical approach believed that each group of past people had their own intrinsic beliefs and ways of doing things influenced by these beliefs, which consequently left their mark in a particularly recognisable way on the archaeological record (Kossinna 1911, 1914, Childe 1929). This paradigm of artefact style = culture = ethnic groups still dominates modern archaeological interpretations, despite criticism from many theoretical schools (Jones 1998: 5, 106-107). The main areas of criticism lies with equating archaeologically defined cultural areas, based on the spatial variation of certain assemblages, with ethnic groups (see Clarke 1978: 365, Jones 1998: 106, Shennan 1994). Aside from the natural inconsistencies of artefactual survival and recovery within the archaeological record, much less has been made of what is actually meant by *ethnic* group, and whether in fact it is archaeologically invisible. Two cases in point are DeCorse's modern study of tribal groupings and ethnicity in north-eastern Sierra Leone, and Osborn's similar study in the Andes which showed that although archaeologically their material remains would indicate a uniform cultural group, in reality there are very real ethnic differences to the members of the tribes resident within the area between themselves and other groups based on social behaviour and ritual (DeCorse 1994, Osborn 1994). Neither behaviour nor ritual practice can be read from archaeological remains with the degree of accuracy required to identify ethnicity in this case.

The acknowledgement of ethnicity as possibly being objectively unidentifiable from material remains further split the culture-ethnicity debate, into those assured of at least some relation between artefact groups and particular populations and those who see assemblages as simply surviving chronological remains (Bursche 1996: 228, Dolukhanov 1994: 266-267). The former view simply widens the field, and although indispensable when considering interaction, ignores ideas of ethnicity, the basic scale by which one group defines itself by recognising differences with others. The latter view is sterile and only succeeds in removing human life from archaeology.

This concept of defining oneself against the real or perceived differences of others is the crux of ethnicity, as illustrated by many recent anthropological and sociological studies (Graves-Brown 1996: 92, Jones 1998: 108). These differences may be racial or cultural (that is, different sociological practices) and may or may not leave recognisable traces in the archaeological record. It is therefore without doubt that although ideas of ethnic identity are essentially emic, it is a reaction to life that is taught, a lesson given against a cultural background (Graves-Brown 1996: 88). This is essentially the link between ethnicity and culture – as culture changes, so does ethnicity. The fluid and adaptive nature of ethnicity is used for survival and success in a social and environmental milieu (Shennan 1994, Hodder 1982), something key to swift and profitable assimilation following migration.

So where does this leave material culture? In effect material culture must be seen in the same light, changing, multi-faceted and affected by many different factors (sociological, environmental, *etc*) whose meaning and form may change through time as a result of being created during specific practices existing at the moment of its construction (Jones 1998: 118-125).

From the above discussion it can be seen that the actual identification of both cultural and, even more so, ethnic groups in the past from archaeological remains is very difficult. Many factors have to be taken into account and built into a chronological system, usually typological, which are then used to describe either the flow of people or ideas. The identification of migration usually involves seeing drastic changes from the norm across cultural assemblages, such as the introduction of agricultural practices in Europe during the Neolithic (Ammerman & Cavalli-Sforza 1984) and the accompanying change in land use, animal management and artefactual remains. Although even with this fundamental change in human behaviour it is hard to tell whether it was an example of migration on a huge scale or simply transference of ideas.

6.4 Viking Settlement

During the Viking Period some assistance in identifying migration is provided by the existence of historical sources. Contemporary writers attest to and in some cases describe in great detail the movements of people across the North Atlantic and Northern Europe, with some either settling new lands such as Iceland and Greenland, and others establishing colonies such as those at Dublin and Kiev. To these sources can be allied the archaeological record, which without the historical documents in England could just be seen as the results of trade and transference of ideas. This combination of historical and archaeological data can be used to show that a migration of people and settlement actually took place. The artefacts, allied with comparative finds of datable and typological similarity in Scandinavia lends support to a possible origin of some of the migrants, or more precisely evidence of contact and interaction of some means by people between the two areas. Norse place-names and loanwords also provide evidence for contact, their extent indicating possible migration or prolonged and intense contact with a new language group, or more properly the people who actually spoke it.

With this outline of migration and culture theory in place it should now be possible to ally it with the archaeological and historical record of Viking period England (as discussed in chapters four and five) in order to ascertain who was coming and why; and how these immigrants reacted to their new home and succeeded in the establishment of successful settlements.

6.4.1 The Pioneers (865-879)

Throughout the discussion on migration it can be seen that every aspect involved in the final decision by the potential émigré to leave his/her homeland relies entirely in the availability of information. Without knowledge of possible new homelands migration would not take place.

As argued above it is inconceivable to imagine that the first contact the people of eighth century England had with Scandinavia was via piratical raids. It is likely that trade and contact had been proceeding to a greater or lesser extent over hundreds if not thousands of years, movements suggested by both Braudel and more specifically Carver in his analysis of the cemetery at Sutton Hoo (Braudel: 1972: 760*ff*, Carver 1992: 363). It is not beyond the realms of possibility to suggest that allied to this had been an amount of migratory movement and settlement between England and northern Europe and *vice versa*. The knowledge of other lands and other cultures and peoples must have been reasonably well spread, but better known amongst those people with direct contact such as the traders, explorers and their kin groups.

It would have been this knowledge of the landscape (geographical, political, and economic) that would have precipitated the first Viking raids on English targets. The first recorded piratical attack at Portland Harbour perfectly illustrates this prior knowledge. At least one contemporary author knew the men for him to record their place of origin as Hordaland, part of Western Norway (Æ, ASC, E & F). They were not strangers to the coastline or the people of Wessex, and knew exactly where to lay anchor and make a profitable raid. A similar situation must be suggested for the raids carried out in Northumbria in 793 and 794. As already pointed out these initial forays into land piracy in England are, according to the historical sources, short lived, and it does seem likely that they were carried out by a particular kin-group. However, to dismiss the continuation of at least some raids would be presumptuous, particularly in the light of the historical records of Ireland, which continue to report seasonal attacks throughout the early ninth century. Despite this lacuna in the English historical accounts it is important to consider that contact and the associated knowledge would be maintained and built upon either through raids or via the continuance of more peaceful trade links. This sharing of knowledge with friends and kin within the Scandinavian countries after successful raids on Northumbria during the eighth century is thoroughly attested to in contemporary English accounts (WM, pt. 73).

According to the English historical accounts the resumption of raiding began again in 835 and continued almost yearly until 850. The manner of these attacks changed during the winter of 850-1 when the raiding parties did not return home for the winter as was usual, but set up camp on Thanet or Sheppey. The establishment of a semi-permanent settlement must have initiated a great deal of contact-interaction-reaction between resident and Viking groups, and not just martial, as discussed in the previous chapters. However, what is pertinent here is the accruing of further knowledge about the landscape and people by these Vikings that this contact would bring. This knowledge would have found its way back to the homelands as people returned, information passing from person to person, group to group. The situation was repeated in 855-6 when a raiding party again over-wintered in England, this time on Sheppey. It is not inconceivable to suggest that some of the men may have remained behind, or returned to the area of these semi-permanent camps after the main groups had moved on. From 865 the manner of attack changed again, with the arrival of the Great Army.

For the purpose of this study the people of the Great Army will be identified as the pioneers of the migration model, simply because they represent in the historical accounts the first arrival of extended permanence of a significant group of people with origins beyond the shores of Anglo-Saxon England. In order to understand them further, and integrate them into the archaeological and historical records, it is necessary to examine who these people were and how they reacted to their new environment.

As illustrated in chapter three the political boundaries of Scandinavia and Denmark during the Viking period were very different to those of today, and were increasingly subject to change as small polities and later larger kingdoms within them struggled for power and dominance. Each polity or subkingdom had its own identifiable cultural and ethnic communities who, while generally falling under the Scandinavian cultural umbrella, had their own particular traits (Price 2000: 39-41). It is highly likely that during the late eighth and early ninth centuries they still, economically speaking, functioned at a tribal level. The people in these areas probably identified themselves via familial or regional affiliations, rather than being Norse, Swedish or Danish, which was to come during the rise of the medieval kingdoms (Jones 1973: 2). It is these regional and familial associations that no doubt formed the core of many a ship's crew (Crossley-Holland 1980: xviii). In order to make any trip successful (that is, profitable) the owner and or captain of the ship or ships must have knowledge of his crew, and what better way than using friends and kin whose skills and trustworthiness was known?

As discussed above it takes a particular type of person backed by a specific set of socio-economic traits to be even a potential migrant. As the pioneers, in order to be successful, these traits must be polarised to an extent far greater than those found in a primary migrant. These personal socio-economic and physiological traits dictate the type of person likely to belong to a pioneer group and will dictate their reactions to the new homeland. In summary, the pioneers would:

i. Be primarily young adult males
ii. Be of a position to acquire knowledge and information about intended destinations
iii. Be in a social position to use the acquired information
iv. Be in an economic position to use the acquired information
v. Be freemen of social and economic position to enable them to leave their home for extended periods
vi. Be driven by a need for further social and/or economic gain
vii. Be highly adaptable (if only to be able to survive)
viii. Be highly motivated
ix. Be highly mobile
x. Be in possession of a strong recognition of 'self', and a great confidence in what he is doing is right.
xi. Recognise that what he is doing gives greater benefits than staying at home
xii. Have been probably encouraged by kin and or friends to go raiding as it was part of their culture and or lifestyle, and was seen as the right or acceptable thing to do
xiii. Not have much by the way of portable goods, since had to carry it. Accrued valuables would no doubt be periodically taken home
xiv. Not be as culturally imbued as the elders in their social group, simply because of their age
xv. Be psychologically able to cope and survive with a huge milieu of danger and cultural difference
xvi. Be physically able to cope with danger and hardship
xvii. Have some support amongst his peer group of pioneers
xviii. Be willing to interact with resident groups, in order to survive and eventually prosper
xix. Quite likely to have had some experience of other lands/cultures and peoples other than England, accrued by raiding or trading, and so has been open to a large amount of cultural influences and knows how to react within them.

As it can be seen, the pioneer has a very particular set of characteristics, and so is a very particular person and not by any means a cultural stereotype. As discussed above the actual identification of cultural and ethnic groups and migration in the archaeological record is fraught with difficulty. In Viking period England it can be seen that this is exacerbated by the fact that the earliest pioneer group (The Great Army) were:

i. Not a culturally homogeneous group,
ii. Not representative of their particular cultural group,
iii. Not a cross-section of their particular cultural group
iv. Not representative of a cross-section of society.

This suggests archaeological invisibility, and is in fact confirmed by the paucity of physical evidence dating from this period.

The continuing build-up of knowledge as people moved between England and the Scandinavian homelands from the raiding and over-wintering during the period 835-865, must have been directly responsible for the formation of the Great Army. There is no doubt that the Great Army increased the numbers of Vikings into England, but they were still pioneer types, with the above attributes, recruited by word of mouth on the promise of gain. The men of the army were no doubt drawn from all over Scandinavia, from continental war-bands, Europe, Ireland, Scotland and possibly even Anglo-Saxon England itself. While the leaders and arguably the majority of the men appear to be of Scandinavian origin it would be wrong to consider them as a culturally homogeneous group or culturally representative of their homelands.

When the Great Army arrived in East Anglia in 865, a large amount of contact and interaction, beyond land piracy, must have taken place between Viking and local resident groups at all levels of society, from the leaders agreeing a peace treaty with King Edmund through to acquiring provisions and accommodation for the soldiers and camp followers. The *Anglo-Saxon Chronicles* do not stipulate where in East Anglia the Great Army over-wintered during 865-6, though it seems a town would be likely, simply for logistical purposes. With its prominence as a site of later Viking camps it may well have been Thetford, a riverine town (on the River Little Ouse) where their boats could have been brought up and stored and repaired over the winter, ready for use in the spring. Modern archaeological excavations have also shown how Thetford expanded to a very large size during the Viking period, no doubt as a direct result of contact (Clarke & Ambrosiani 1995; 100). This initial site of over-wintering at a town is very important, as an urban environment speeds up assimilation, the two groups being in close contact and interacting on a daily basis for provisions and entertainment.

A similar situation must have been played out the following year when the Great Army left East Anglia to seize the kingdom of Northumbria. With the capture of York, a great amount of interaction would have been necessary between the Viking leaders and the remaining members of the Anglo-Saxon elite to establish and support their proposed candidate for king north of the Tyne (SD). Again, the placing of the Army in an urban environment would initiate intense and close contact and interaction between Viking and resident, and act as a catalyst for assimilation. As the Anglo-Saxon King Egbert was established as ruler in the north of Northumbria it seems at this early stage there was a Viking 'king' or at least Viking led council ruling in York who controlled the southern part. For this to be successful it would seem prudent to maintain a level of military force within the town after the Great Army felt able to move on in the spring of 867, and to establish mutually beneficial treaties between the Anglo-Saxon king to the north and the remaining Anglo-Saxon elites of York and the surrounding countryside. The balance must have been maintained by the threat of the Great Army returning, and regular contact thus necessitated between the leaders of the army and those who held Northumbria in York.

This establishment of a group from the Great Army in York in 866 must surely be seen as the first settlement of the Vikings in England, some ten years before the *Anglo-Saxon Chronicles'* description of Halfdan's division of Northumbria. As well as information passing between York and the Great Army, knowledge of the town becoming a Viking enclave would have been carried back to the Scandinavian homelands by stream and counter-stream of pioneers and traders, precipitating no doubt the beginnings of primary migration.

The use of urban settlements, the densest areas of populations, as winter camps continued in the following year when the Great Army arrived in Nottingham (later to become one of the Five Boroughs). The extent of contact and interaction was increased by the eighteen months spent there, further aiding and increasing acculturation processes between Viking and resident groups. Again, there is little doubt, that when the bulk of the Army moved on in 869, it left some of its followers behind.

The towns and the time spent in them would also act as a focal point for people and information, particularly the movement of men[1] (soldiers or traders) to and from the homelands and the army. The length of time the Great Army spent in Nottingham and their continued occupation in York must have created a hive of interaction between Viking and resident, and seen the movement of many men, all carrying information and knowledge tied in with their experiences in England. The brief visit to York by the Great Army in the following year may have been to bolster the military presence there before moving on to conquer East Anglia and winter once more in Thetford. Again, when the main force moved off the following year, it is more than likely that Thetford was garrisoned by an expedient military presence to maintain control over the newly captured kingdom.

The arrival of the Summer Army during 870 and its combination with the Great Army in Reading can only be the result of the transfer of knowledge between people moving regularly between England and the homelands, and the maintenance of contact between groups hundreds of miles apart.

The combined force wintered in London (871-2) after negotiating a peace treaty with the Mercians. Once more the picture of York, Thetford, Reading and Nottingham is repeated, with the stage set for intense interaction between residents and the Viking army across all social strata, the urban situations providing the greatest extent of contact with resident populations and cultural influences. As described in chapter four, the following two years saw the capture of Mercia and establishment of a Viking backed king, followed by the consolidation of Northumbria by Halfdan before its historically recorded division in 876 amongst his followers.

6.4.2 The Pioneers: discussion

It can be seen that the Viking mercenary of the earliest war bands and the later Great Army is perfectly representative of the pioneer in migration models. His knowledge of England no doubt began at home with tales from kin and family of earlier trading or raiding expeditions. This knowledge would have been developed and intensified through his own experiences, reports of which in turn would no doubt have been relayed home. The very manner by which the Great Army moved around England, from town to town, paved the way for the most intensive contact between resident and Viking, a very important factor in acculturation and later assimilation should the man decide to settle in England. The use of towns also provided the leaders with a means of controlling the population and economy of the surrounding landscape, which again would be vital for the success of later settlement.

[1] And to a lesser extent women. As discussed above Haesten's family travelled with his war band, & Frankish chroniclers attest to the presence of women in Viking camps.

Information would have continued to flow between England and the homelands as men moved backwards and forwards, increasing and spreading knowledge amongst friends and kin. Some men would of course have died in England, and some returned home after short periods with the army, but others could well have been based in England since 865 through to the settlement periods in the towns and to the historically recorded land divisions during the late 870's. Had they been the typical young adult males of the migration model, of around twenty years of age, then they would have spent over ten years in Anglo-Saxon England. That is, half of their lifetime or the majority of their adulthood. The influence extended contact with Anglo-Saxon culture would have cannot be underestimated. In short, their formative adult years would have been developed and created within the influence of an Anglo-Saxon cultural milieu, not that of their Scandinavian homelands.

What is also vitally important is that interaction and acculturation would have affected the resident Anglo-Saxon populations, who would have become familiar with at least some of the culturally influenced practices at work within the Viking group.

6.4.3 Settlement and Later Migrants (880-918)

As shown above, the first Viking settlements in England were to take place in the towns where the Great Army over-wintered or established military backed political control over newly conquered kingdoms, and not during the historically recorded land divisions of northern and eastern England during the late 870's. Recognition of this push settlement dates back ten years in Northumbria, nine years in East Anglia and seven years in Mercia. This should be allied to the possibility of the prior presence (permanent and semi-permanent) of Scandinavian traders in England, and the departure of at least some members of the Great Army into the landscape. The historically accounted dates of settlement simply mark the end of the campaign of the Great Army around England.

The division of land and estate structure in the north of England is beyond the remit of this study, and has been well researched elsewhere, with the production of sometimes contrasting hypotheses from the same sets of limited data. However, the land within the newly conquered Anglo-Saxon kingdoms must have been divided in such a way as to maintain control over the populace, economically, politically and militarily. With the removal of the Anglo-Saxon kings, the Vikings created a power vacuum, which their leaders neatly filled, backed by the military strength of the war bands. There can be no doubt that reward for the support of these men came in the form of land and rank within the new kingdoms. As already pointed out; however, the north was far from being an empty landscape, and there is no doubt that a great deal of interaction went on between Anglo-Saxon landowners and their new social superiors and peers. During this potentially volatile consolidation stage of conquest, control over towns would have proved vital. With their positions as receptacles of economy the town dominates the population of the surrounding landscape as well as providing a secure base for political and military control. As illustrated above, and in chapter four, knowledge of the Anglo-Saxon landscape and the use of towns was accrued and used to best advantage during the thirteen-year campaign of the Great Army. However, military domination of such a wide landscape could not have been a long-term option for the leaders; skilful, political manipulation was (see chapters four and five) and went hand-in-glove with assimilation into the Anglo-Saxon cultural milieu.

While this process of consolidation was being carried out, the movement of people around and between England and the Scandinavian homelands would have continued, carrying and spreading information about the fledgling Viking kingdoms. As the migration model shows, this transfer of knowledge would also include details of the pioneers' routes and places of residence, which subsequently determine the routes and settlement sites of primary and later migrants. The hypothesis of towns being the main areas of settlement, at least on the outset, is backed up by archaeological evidence which shows the great expansion of towns such as York, Lincoln, Thetford and Norwich (Clarke & Ambrosiani 1995: 92-102) during the late ninth and early tenth century, which is surely representative of a vibrant population increase. The arrival of immigrants to join kin or friends in the towns no doubt boosted economic interest, increasing trade as a result of population growth and by the widening of the contact base between the Scandinavian homelands that more people would bring. Contact and information would also be carried and maintained by returned migrants, who always figure in any migration pattern, and who may or may not influence decisions by others to go or stay. As discussed, migration continues within the new homeland, especially amongst pioneer groups, and this must have aided contact between the fledgling Viking communities in towns and later villages across the north of England. Trade links again, this time internal, would be a vital information and support network, and assist assimilation and integration between Viking settlers and resident groups. The discovery of a silk headscarf at Coppergate in York, and its subsequent matching with a piece form the same bale found in Lincoln illustrates such contact (Clarke & Ambrosiani 1995: 96).

As with the pioneers, it takes a particular type of person, backed by suitable socio-economic and physiological conditions to be a migrant. These personal traits dictate the type of person likely to belong to a migrant group and will influence their reactions to the new homeland. In summary, the primary settlers would:

- i. Have access to information about the potential new homeland
- ii. Have a belief that the destination would have more perceived benefits than the homeland, to enable social or economic improvement
- iii. Have confidence in what he is doing is right
- iv. Be predominantly young adult males
- v. Be capable of organising such a great move
- vi. Be in a social position to enable the move to take place
- vii. Have capital to fund the move
- viii. Be in good physical health
- ix. Be in good psychological health
- x. Follow previous routes used by pioneers to get to his destination

xi. Initially join pioneer settlements
xii. Settle near kin and or friends in new homeland
xiii. Be very likely to move again within the new homeland
xiv. Be very likely to return home
xv. Tend to settle in areas that mirror homeland, geographically and economically.
xvi. Settle somewhere where they can practice their trade (farmer, potter, fisherman, *etc*).

Every aspect of the migrant's move is still based on information and the access to that information about the potential new homeland. This does not matter whether they are primary, secondary or tertiary settlers spread across tens of years. Primary settlers will relay knowledge back to the homelands and so potentially induce secondary settlers to migrate, and so forth. It would be a highly active forum, involving a huge amount of movement, contact and information spread across not only the north of England, but the northern European continent as well.

The primary and later migrants differ from the pioneers in a number of ways. In the first place they have access to more readily available information about their potential destination courtesy of the pioneers. Secondly, they will be in contact with someone who could provide shelter when they arrived (temporary or permanent). Thirdly, they must be in a position, that is have the right contacts and money, to enable them to secure land, a house, or perhaps business premises in towns. This contact is illustrated in the description of the settlement of Hæsten's army and camp followers in Northumbria and East Anglia, which states that in order to establish residence the person had to have prior claim to property or the means to buy it (ASC: 896). Finally and perhaps most critically when considering issues of contact and assimilation with the resident Anglo-Saxon population, it is vitally important to remember that unlike the pioneers, later Scandinavian migrants did not have the extended contact with the nationals prior to settlement brought about by the campaigns of the Great Army. Contact, interaction and the subsequent reaction would all be quite new and different, albeit influenced to a certain extent by the knowledge of the experiences shared between pioneer and new settler. Increased numbers of migrants from a wider pool of potentials than the pioneer groups would also extend further knowledge of some Scandinavian cultural practices amongst nationals, although as with the pioneers, the following movement of settlers cannot be seen as representative of a cross-section of their culture or society. The migrant is a particular type of person with specific attributes. They were not a group made up of representatives of all trades, professions and walks of life. It does seem safe to suggest, however, that social status was a commonality shared between them, the Scandinavian settlers coming into England not likely to be the large landholders, who after all would have little to gain by abandoning estates in their homelands. This is perhaps visible in the establishment of the wergilds of freemen in the Alfred-Guthrum treaty, as discussed above.

The dates chosen to contain this section have been selected because of their historical significance; 880, following the recorded land division within what was to become known as the Danelaw, and 918, the year when Edward and Æthelflaed's military campaigns against the north were concluded. The dates, in migratory terms, are arbitrary; migration and settlement by Scandinavian groups no doubt taking place throughout this time period and afterwards. By 918 fifty-three years had passed since the arrival of the Great Army, and it is doubtful that any of the pioneers were still alive. A similar situation must be argued for the primary settlers. In their place were their sons and daughters, many no doubt of mixed Scandinavian and Anglo-Saxon parentage, and their grandchildren. There would also be the secondary, tertiary and later migrants and their families. However, despite this widening socio-cultural base the surviving records of the reclamation show that the towns within the Danelaw were still the focal point of the northern armies for a specific surrounding area, a fact that will be discussed below.

6.4.4 Settlement and Later Migrants: discussion

Throughout the following stages of migration it can be seen that the reliance on information increased exponentially with the knowledge of the pioneers. The information would be carried back to the Scandinavian homelands by the pioneers and would play a very large part in influencing the potential émigré. As shown in the migration model this information would be the reason why the primary and later migrants would follow the routes of travel of the pioneers. Settlement, initially at least, would be in close proximity to the pioneer groups, which as hypothesised, would be the towns used as camps by the Great Army. Where available this hypothesis has been supported by the archaeological record, which has shown a great expansion of towns such as York and Thetford during the late ninth and early tenth centuries (Clarke & Ambrosiani 1995). The arrival of later settlers following the pioneers into the towns and the associated increase in population would be directly responsible for a rush of economic opportunity and expansion. Later settlers would encourage the establishment of satellite communities around the towns. This settlement within the vicinity of these towns is also borne out by place-names. For example, study of the Norse place-names plotted around York shows a distinct cluster around the immediate environs, lessening with increasing distance (Higham 1992: 23). Whereas the use of place-names must be seen as the result of contact between settlers and resident groups, this clustering of Viking influenced communities is also representative of the spread of immigrants within the migration model after the initial settlements have taken place.

The arrival of immigrant groups would not be limited to a restricted time period or window of opportunity, but it does seem likely that the largest numbers would arrive after the consolidation of power in the north by the Viking kings. This securing of position by the Viking leaders was attained not by force (unsustainable over the long term) but by swift and adroit manipulation and assimilation of Anglo-Saxon laws and practice (see chapter four).

As illustrated above in the discussion of pioneers, it has been shown that the person likely to migrate has very specific attributes, and cannot be seen as representative of his or her culture or society. The same applies to a group of migrants, who even then cannot be expected to contain a representative cross-section of the culture and society of their homeland. This shows that the statement '*culture does not migrate; a very particular and specific group of the population does*', is true (Anthony 1990: 908). It does seem however, that one commonality these people shared was social status, an observation supported by the type of wergilds established for freemen in the Alfred-Guthrum Treaty (see chapter four).

During the period of reclamation it is important to realise that the Anglo-Saxon army of Wessex were no longer fighting against *Vikings*. Fifty-three years had passed since the Vikings of the Great Army had set foot on English soil. These people were the mixed population of an Anglo-Saxon kingdom, not members of a foreign mercenary band. They were involved in a fight for their homeland, which eventually resulted in a negotiation for their survival beneath the political umbrella of the kingdom of Wessex.

6.4.5 Assimilation of Viking and Scandinavian Settlers

From the above discussion it can be seen that the Viking settler in Anglo-Saxon England was a very particular type of person, and not one representative of his or her culture or the society of their homeland. While it has been shown that migratory patterns are very fluid and yet predictable with their reliance on information, it is impossible to tell how many people actually permanently settled, how many returned home or how many moved and re-settled within England. It has been illustrated through material remains and the historical record that Viking settlement was extremely successful. The questions are how and why. The answer lies in the final stage of successful migration, that of assimilation.

The type of person (as described above) likely to migrate is potentially suited for assimilation; and assimilation must be a priority if he is to firstly survive, and secondly, prosper within the new community, which is after all the whole point of free migration. However, what is equally important is the residents' attitude towards the migrant. In late Anglo-Saxon England Viking groups were initially at least vicious threats to home, life, family and the stability of whole kingdoms. Assimilation was no doubt helped by Viking leaders taking the mantle of Anglo-Saxon kingship, and the insertion of jarls and holds amongst local landowners and nobles to legitimise and establish control by law and force (the pioneer settlers were still mercenaries after all, and part of the Great Army). However, kingdoms cannot be held by threat of external force indefinitely, especially when the force involved had been a co-operation of individually led war bands now scattered across northern England. Assimilation must have been undertaken to guarantee successful settlement across all levels of society.

As shown above interaction had been going on for years at varying levels of intensity from trading, the first over-wintering of the earliest raiding parties, to the urban camps of the Great Army, and the occupation of the northern Anglo-Saxon kingdoms. Throughout this period the migrant was in constant contact with a different people, new language, different religion, different culture, art and politics, all of which would affect him at a personal level to a greater or lesser extent (Beijer 1969: 54). As argued above, the economic support and use of Anglo-Saxon towns as winter bases can only have aided and acted as a catalyst for assimilation, studies showing that integration and interaction is swifter in an urban environment (Beijer 1969: 54, Jansen 1969: 68). This was no doubt intensified by relationships of a personal nature between men of the army and Anglo-Saxon women of the towns and countryside.

The situation would be slightly different amongst the primary settlers, following in the footsteps of these pioneers, who would not have been exposed to the same amount of contact. This would no doubt increase the length of time for assimilation and make assimilation more difficult. They would, however, have the benefit of the pioneers' knowledge and experience.

Interaction between immigrant and national is absolutely vital to the speed and extent of assimilation (Beijer 1969: 54, Jansen 1969: 68). Interaction is also critical to the success of settlement. The Scandinavian settler had a vested interest in quick, peaceful assimilation with resident groups, and no doubt would have pursued it vigorously to survive and prosper. As discussed above, the mutual attitude of migrant towards national and *vice versa* determines the extent and success of assimilation. This is based by and large on cultural affinities, and the acknowledgement and maintenance of them (Beijer 1969: 55). Co-operation, flexibility and the fact that most migrants are young and therefore less culturally imbued than their elders will all play a great part in interaction and acceptance between migrant and national. The fact that the Scandinavian settlers were no longer a part of the cultural milieu of their own society, or represent a cross-section capable of sustaining all cultural practices would also speed up assimilation. The close association with nationals brought about by settlement in the population dense towns would also speed up assimilation via constant interaction (Beijer 1969: 54, Jansen 1969: 68).

Although the historical documents of the period deal predominantly with the upper echelons of society, chapter four has shown that integration into the political scene of the Anglo-Saxon world was extremely swift. Use of Scandinavian terminology in the Alfred-Guthrum Treaty shows evidence for a long knowledge and familiarity with the Norse language in use in England, which could only be the result of extended contact. The Alfred-Guthrum Treaty is also pertinent here since it deals with two ethnic groups, the Anglo-Saxons of Wessex and the Danes, the Anglo-Saxons resident in East Anglia apparently changing ethnicity to match that of their new overlords. There does not appear to have been any mass exodus of East Anglians, Mercians or Northumbrians into Wessex, or any uprisings against the Viking kings. In fact, the only mentioned movement was by an Anglo-Saxon noble who left Wessex for Viking East Anglia (EHD 100: 541-3). Within a generation of settlement Anglo-Saxon nobles from Wessex were claiming asylum and recruiting mercenary armies from Northumbria East Anglia to fight in their civil war (ASC).

That the Vikings were a victim of their own success is perhaps best illustrated during the reclamation of the north by Edward and Æthelflaed. Towns still appear to be the focal point of satellite communities in the countryside, held by its own leader and his followers, echoing the days of the Viking chief and his war-band. There seems to be no effort made to support the Northumbrian army at Tettenhall, suggestive that their commonality of cause and ultimate origins had gone. These people were the descendents of the pioneers and the later settlers, not mercenaries linked by membership of the Great Army. It is also more than likely that the majority were descendents of both Anglo-Saxon and Scandinavian parents. In essence they had become members of an Anglo-Saxon kingdom. The Vikings were gone. The people here were settled groups now and assimilated with the populace. Without doubt the members of the Great Army (pioneers) and the primary settlers were dead, and their successors to the settlement sites derived from a very different cultural and social background. Some may have been secondary or tertiary settlers from Scandinavia joining kin and or friends. As already mentioned intermarriage was extremely likely, producing descendents of Scandinavian and Anglo-Saxon ancestry. Incentives for survival and glory in a foreign land had long since gone as these people were no longer invaders from a foreign shore, but were intensely integrated communities, and were for all intents and purposes Anglo-Saxons in an Anglo-Saxon kingdom. Defeat to the Great Army meant expulsion from England. Protracted resistance and inevitable defeat for the descendents meant death and death for their families. They no longer had any boats to run to or an overseas homeland to return to. Mercia, Northumbria and East Anglia were now home and reactions to the threat of hostility had to be tempered accordingly.

That is not to say all cultural traits were abandoned by Scandinavian settlers and their descendents. The maintenance of many, particularly artistic, surviving within the archaeological record and as fashion trends in personal correspondence attest to retention and adoption by resident Anglo-Saxon populations. A combination was evident in a runic inscription (now lost) on the Bewcastle Cross (Camden 1685: 1030-1). A Latin translation of the inscription survives in Camden's *Britannia*, and reads:

> *"Latrones Ubbo Vicit"* - Ubba conquered the pirates.

Compelling evidence to suggest that a man of Scandinavian descent, now settled in the northwest was commemorated for defeating a group of Irish Sea Vikings (Camden 1685: 1030-1).

Swift assimilation is particularly evident between church and Viking leaders. The immediate concerns of the ecclesiastical community appear to be the retention of church lands and the maintenance of power and influence, all of which were beyond the religious predilections of the new rulers. After the period of consolidation by the war-band leaders the church was linked immediately to Guthrum, the first Viking king of East Anglia, and Guthfrith of Northumbria, both of whom were subsequently interred within an ecclesiastical complex (Æ, Swanton 2000: 82, fn. 7). As discussed in chapter three the cult practice associated with burial is one of the first things to be abandoned by immigrant groups, even though there is no actual change in religious beliefs (Laungani 1997, Rosenblatt 1997: 138). What is also important is the influence the church (a part of the cultural milieu) was able to have on them, the ready access it had to them, the nobles and their men, who would be doubly influenced in turn by both their social superiors and the ecclesiastical organisation. Most importantly perhaps for this study of burials is the point that some of these pioneers, the earliest Scandinavian settlers in England, were being buried in Christian cemeteries. This manner of burial rite is a physical manifestation of acculturation occurring within earliest settlers, albeit at a high level. Historical sources recount that both Guthfrith and Guthrum had been members of the Christian community, but it is impossible to tell how *Christian* they actually were (Æ, ASC, HSC). What is clear, however, is that the church had enough influence over the people responsible for their funerals to ensure burial in a Christian cemetery. This is surely proof enough of an extremely swift assimilation of a part of Anglo-Saxon culture by the Vikings, and an assimilation of the Anglo-Saxon ecclesiastical communities with the new secular rulers.

Other evidence of swift integration of immigrant and national again occurs in church writings of the period, and concerns Oda, Archbishop of Canterbury. As discussed above, it seems Oda was born around 900 in East Anglia of Danish immigrant parents. His date of birth makes it highly unlikely that his parents were amongst the pioneers of the Great Army as the historical accounts recount, or even amongst the primary settlers. It seems sensible to suggest that they were later settlers, following the routes of kin and or friends amongst the primary or secondary waves, arriving in East Anglia during the 890's. According to the church histories, Oda was fostered in what was the traditional Germanic (that is Scandinavian and Anglo-Saxon) cultural manner into a household beyond that of his immediate family (Whitelock 1959: 73, 1941: 169-70). In this case he was brought up in the household of not a fellow migrant, but an Anglo-Saxon nobleman of the district. He cannot have been the only one (Whitelock 1959: 73, 1941: 169-70). This is surely evidence of active integration and assimilation at a simple but highly critical social level, between immigrant and resident involving the lives of their children.

Oda's history is also pertinent as it follows the migration model. He had many family members in East Anglian, illustrating the fact that groups follow the same routes and lived close together, or in the vicinity of each other (Whitelock 1959: 73, 1941: 169-70). Again cultural influences were at work around Oda, undoubtedly more intensely with him growing up in an Anglo-Saxon household, resulting in him taking holy orders and rising to be the most powerful prelate in England. His rise to power seems to have been in no way inhibited by his ethnicity, or the cultural past of his parents, even though it was widely known and acknowledged (Whitelock 1959: 73, 1941: 169-70). Neither did it inhibit his appointment of other members of his family to positions of power within the Church (Whitelock 1959: 73, 1941: 169-70).

During the late ninth century Alfred's biographer Asser (pt. 94: 103) records that there were many monks in England of Danish descent, again pointing to a swift adoption of Anglo-Saxon religious cultural practice within the first generation of settlement.

6.4.6 Assimilation of Viking and Scandinavian Settlers: discussion

As discussed in chapters four and five the study of material remains and historical documents has proved that Viking and later Scandinavian settlement in the north of England was extremely successful. In order to achieve that settlement success, assimilation between resident groups and immigrant must have occurred. The propensity and drive necessary to be accepted into the society of the new homeland must originate within the migrant himself, in whose best interest it is, in order to survive and prosper. While the establishment of the Viking war band leaders as kings and members of the Anglo-Saxon aristocracy no doubt greatly influenced favourable settlement conditions via political manipulation, successful interaction and a good attitude between Anglo-Saxon and settler was still vital. This interaction would have been greatly aided by the settlement within towns where contact between immigrant and national would have been constant and unavoidable (Beijer 1969: 54, Jansen 1969: 68).

The extent of cultural maintenance within immigrant groups also affects chances of swift assimilation, but as the majority of émigrés are young people they are less likely to be as culturally imbued as their elders (Isaac 2000: 42). By leaving their homelands the émigré is also moving beyond the direct influence of his culture. The establishment of Viking and Scandinavian groups in the new homeland would place them within the influences of the Anglo-Saxon cultural milieu. Because of the nature of migration the Viking and Scandinavian settlers in England were not capable of maintaining the cultural practices of their homelands, as they cannot have been a representative cross-section of their society, encompassing all ages and walks of life. This would have ultimately aided integration by not appearing too different to resident groups, and easing tensions in social interaction (Price 1969: 187). In short, successful integration was totally dependent on the attitude of Anglo-Saxon residents towards Viking and Scandinavian settlers, and *vice versa* (Price 1969: 185-7, Beijer 1969: 55). From consideration of migration theories it has been possible to understand why.

6.5 Migration, Immigration, Ethnicity and Culture: conclusions

From this study of migration and assimilation it has been possible to move towards a deeper understanding of how and why Viking and Anglo-Saxon social integration took place during the late ninth and early tenth century. It can be seen that the Viking mercenary of the earliest war bands and later Great Army is perfectly representative of the pioneer in migration models. Their knowledge of England would have been provided by friends and kin, and intensified through their own experiences. The very manner by which the Great Army moved around England from town to town paved the way for the most intensive contact between resident groups and Viking, a very important factor in acculturation and later assimilation during settlement. The use of towns also provided the leaders with a means of controlling the population and economy of the surrounding landscape, which again would have been vitally important during the consolidation phase after conquest and for the success of later settlement. The overwhelming majority of these people would have been young adult males, who by the time of settlement would have spent the formative years of their adult lives within the influence of the Anglo-Saxon cultural milieu, rather than that of their homeland. The effect this influence would have cannot be underestimated.

The continuing movement of pioneers between England and the Scandinavian homelands would provide potential émigrés with further knowledge and information from which to make a decision on whether or not to emigrate. Travel routes, and settlement, initially at least, would be in close proximity to the pioneer groups, which as pointed out, would be the towns used by the Great Army. This hypothesis has been supported by the archaeological record, which shows great expansion of many Danelaw towns during the late ninth and early tenth centuries, which is likely be a result of the economic impetus an increasing population would provide. Again, patterns of migration show the development of satellite communities around sites of primary settlements, which are again borne out by the cluster of Norse influenced place-names around Danelaw towns.

In the case of both pioneer and later immigrants it has been shown that these people in no way represent the society or culture of their homeland. They are a very specific type of people and not a cross-section of their society, a major factor in the continuance or survival of some cultural traits. Cultural practices and the survival of them are determined by the society in which the practitioners live. With the current trend within archaeology to treat artefacts as cultural and ethnic indicators these Viking settlers are consequently archaeologically invisible.

The whole point behind free migration is to increase the socio-economic standing of the migrant, and in order to achieve this aim the migrant must successfully assimilate with the resident populace. The establishment of Viking kings and the integration of the war-band leaders amongst the rulers of Anglo-Saxon society no doubt greatly influenced favourable settlement conditions. However, the attitude of Anglo-Saxon nationals towards Viking settlers would have been critical. There is no doubt that residence within the towns speeded up and aided assimilation via constant contact and interaction. The maintenance of cultural practices can inhibit assimilation, although because of the nature of the migration of the Viking settlers in England this never took place.

Recognition of the type of migration and settlement undertaken by Scandinavian groups, and the corresponding cultural influences developed as a result of contact and interaction with the resident population, provides a platform for a deeper understanding of the archaeological record of the period. The next chapters will study the burial records of the British Isles and Ireland in this context in an effort to understand why there are so few diagnostically Scandinavian burials in the north of England.

CHAPTER SEVEN – VIKING BURIAL IN IRELAND, SCOTLAND AND THE ISLE OF MAN

7.0 Introduction

The archaeological remains of funerary rites represent a truncated element of a facet of material culture, which seemingly offers huge scope for understanding the past, despite being more difficult to interpret because of the ephemeral and variant nature of the personal and cultural factors involved in the act (chapter three). Despite this complicated milieu of influences, the majority of which are not preserved in the archaeological record, archaeologists still attempt to reconstruct what are perceived to be social norms and identities from these partial remains. This paradigm hinders understanding of Viking burial in the north of England since these migrants were beyond such limits as a 'social norm'. However, unlike the study of non-historic periods, where social norms are inferred from the archaeological record, details of society survive in contemporary documents and have been discussed in chapter four. By using these and the hypothesis proffered in the previous chapter it should be possible to better understand the Scandinavian type burial record in the north of England. To place the research in context detailed consideration has also be given to the burial practice of Viking immigrant groups in Scotland, Ireland and the Isle of Man. The chapter is also augmented by a quick reference database of sites and finds in appendix five.

7.1 Viking Burial in Ireland (fig. 7.1)

For Ireland, a complete list of all known (that is, published) data on Viking burials has been compiled. There are twenty-seven sites across the whole of Ireland, which contain upwards of eighty burials, the flexibility in terminology allowing for and accepting a low minimum figure of those recovered from the cemetery sites in Dublin (O'Brien 1998). Of the twenty-seven sites, thirteen fall within the city limits of Dublin.

Larne, Co. Antrim

During the early nineteenth century an inhumation was found close to the seashore at Larne, Co. Antrim (Smith 1841-44: 40-2, Fanning 1970: 71). There were no reports of any cist or mound covering the burial, only some two feet of sand (Smith 1841-44: 40-2, Fanning 1970: 71). Along with the remains were found a sword (Petersen Type X), dated to the tenth century, a spearhead, a copper-alloy ring-headed pin and a bone comb (Smith 1840-44: 40-2, Fanning 1970: 71, Bøe 1940: 76). From these grave goods it would be fairly safe to assume the incumbent was male. This burial seems to be a lone find, as no other accounts record any further discoveries amongst the sand dunes although Larne was known by the Norse place-name of Ulfrecksfjord (Ó Floinn 1998*a*: 145). See below for comparable dune burials in Scotland, for example at Pierowall, Carn a Bharraich, Ballinaby, and Reay.

Church Bay, Rathlin Island, Co. Antrim

At least two Viking burials were discovered in the late eighteenth and nineteenth centuries at Church Bay on Rathlin Island (Warner 1973-4: 61-62). The area seems to have been used as a cemetery since the Bronze Age and through into early Christian times, attested by the discovery of tumuli covered urned cremations and unaccompanied cist graves (Warner 1973-4: 61-62). The first inhumation to be found lay in a cist in one of the many Bronze Age tumuli, accompanied by a large silver penannular brooch and an unspecified number of beads (Hamilton 1822 & Gage 1851 in Warner 1973-4: 61). The grave was said to have been marked by a standing stone, which is still extant today (Warner 1973-4: 61 & Gage 1851 in Warner 1973-4: 61). The removal of a second tumulus during the nineteenth century revealed a further cist bound inhumation, accompanied by a sword that subsequently broke apart on handling (Gage 1851 in Warner 1973-4: 62). Also found in the vicinity of the cemetery was a copper-alloy pan of insular design, some copper-alloy rings and fragments of an iron cauldron, all items commonly found in Scandinavian graves (Gage 1851 in Warner 1973-4: 62, Ó Floinn 1998*a*: 145).

During the nineteen-twenties a Viking long-ship was also reputedly found to the west of the standing stone where the first burial was recovered (Northern Island Sites and Monuments Records).

These burials may well represent the remains of those who had lived at a temporary base, contemporary historical documents identifying Rathlin Island as a landing point of Viking groups (Smyth 1979: 113). The use of Bronze Age and Christian burial sites across the British Isles is a well-proven phenomenon; see especially Aspatria (Cumbria) and Claughton Hall (Lancs.), below.

Ballyholme, Co. Down

An inhumation was found just above the high-water mark on the beach at Ballyholme during the late nineteenth century (Smith 1906: 72-9, Bøe 1940: 73). The burial contained a pair of tortoise brooches, a small copper-alloy bowl and chain with pieces of wool inside it and a large piece of 'linen-like' cloth (Smith 1906: 72-9, Bøe 1940: 73-75). From the turn of the century account it seems that the burial lay in a v-shaped section of blackened earth and may have been covered by a mound, from which Ó Floinn suggests the possibility of it being a boat burial (Ó Floinn 1998*a*: 146-7, Smith 1906: 72-3). The burial is dated by the tortoise brooches, which place it in the late ninth century (Ó Floinn 1998*a*: 147). From the grave goods it may be safe to suggest that the inhumation was that of an important female, perhaps a settler in the area. It is also worth noting that the place-name Ballyholme is very likely to have its origins in the Norse language, one of very few in Ireland (Ó Floinn 1998*a*: 145).

Eyreport, Co. Galway

The burial at Eyreport is the first of only two known Viking burials on the west coast of Ireland (see below for Cloghermore Cave) (Sheehan 1987-8, Raftery 1960-1). It was found, as at Ballyholme, above the high-water mark of the beach amongst the sand dunes (Sheehan 1987-8, Raftery 1960-1). Accompanying the burial was a short sword datable to the mid-ninth century (Petersen Type K), a dagger, shield and spear

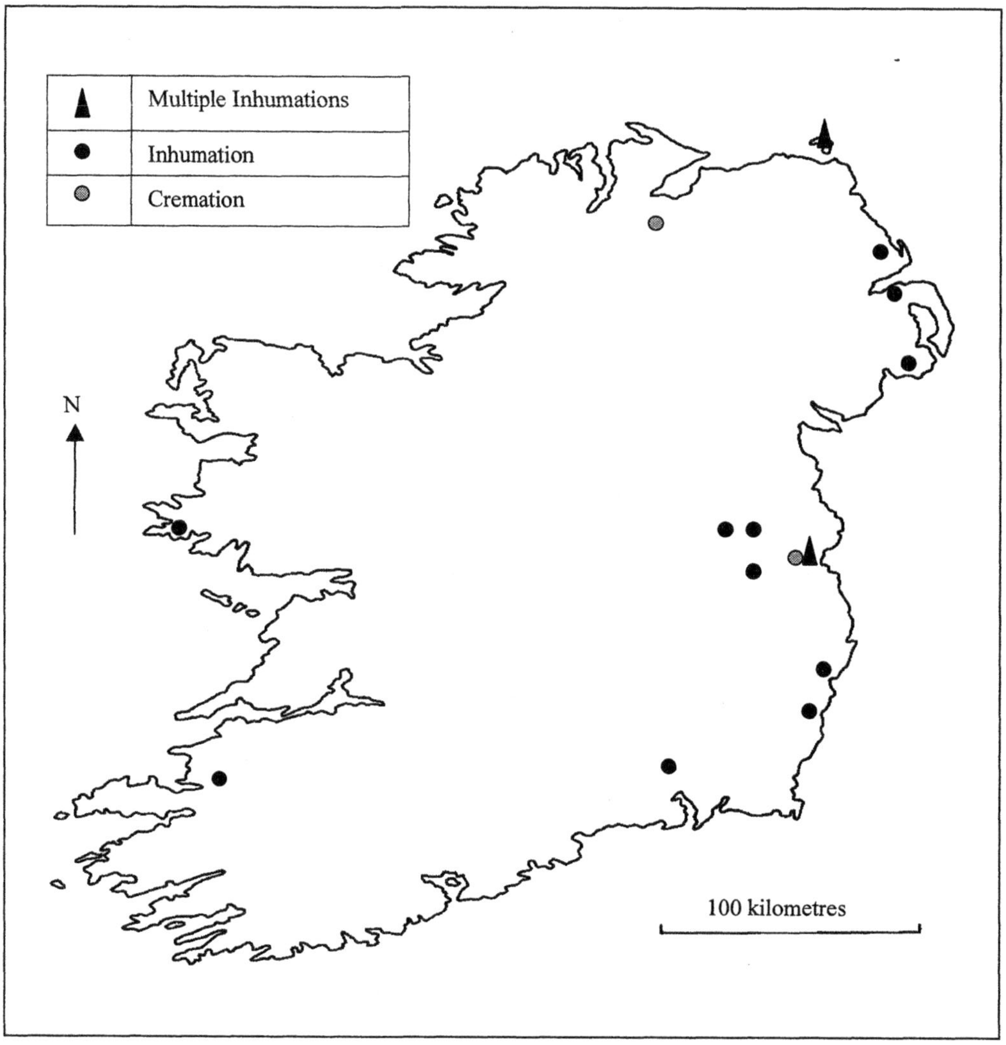

Fig. 7.1 *Viking Burials in Ireland*

(Sheehan 1987-8: 62-68). Examination of the skeletal remains in 1960 confirmed, as the artefacts suggested, that the incumbent was male (Sheehan 1987-8: 68). Due to its isolated nature, Sheehan suggested that the burial could represent a temporary base (Sheehan 1987-8: 68-70), although it is to be expected that even with a temporary raiding camp there would have been more burials.

Barnhill, Co. Kildare

Less is known of this Viking type burial found during the eighteenth century at Barnhill (Ó Floinn 1998*a*: 144-5, Walker 1788: 173 in Ó Floinn 1998*a*: 144-5). Accounts report the recovery of an inhumation along with an axe head and other 'weaponry' (Ó Floinn 1998*a*: 144-5, Walker 1788: 173 in Ó Floinn 1998*a*: 144-5). From the grave goods it is perhaps safe to assume that the incumbent was male. It is quite possible that this lone burial is representative of one of the many Vikings who must have fallen during the raids and skirmishes across Kildare, as recorded in Irish contemporary sources. It is also interesting to note that Barnhill is close to Leixlip, whose name originates from the Norse, one of the very few in Ireland (Ó Floinn 1998*a*: 145).

Near Milltown, Co. Kildare

Very little is known about a burial said to have been found between Milltown and Newbridge, other than a passing report that remains had been found interred with a horse in a brief note in the *Proceedings of the Royal Irish Academy* (Harrison 2001: 66, Anon 1859: 121). It may have been an interment of Scandinavian type, or possibly a pre-Christian Irish burial.

Three-Mile Water, Co. Wicklow

The details of the discovery of a pair of tortoise brooches (dated between 900-950) can only be described as sketchy, and their provenance is presumed to be originally a grave somewhere in the vicinity (Coffey 1902: 71, Ó Floinn 1998*b*). All that can be said with any amount of certainty is that they were found somewhere between Three-Mile Water and Arklow. No mention is made of them coming from a grave, although it is highly probable. The two brooches are very finely made, studded with silver and linked by a silver double chain made up of figure-eight links and decorated silver beads, similar to those found at Repton and Peel (see chapter eight) (Coffey 1902: 73). Suspended from the end of the chains is a silver decorated needle case (Coffey 1902: 73).

The Morragh, near Wicklow, Co. Wicklow

During the late nineteenth century stormy weather caused the erosion of a Viking period sword from the peat above a shingle beach on the Morragh (Ó Floinn 1998*b*). The reports of its recovery are scanty, but it does seem likely that it was once part of an interment (Ó Floinn 1998*b*). Parts of the blade and the highly decorated hilt survive and are on display in the National Museum of Ireland, Dublin.

Navan, Co. Meath

The discovery of several human and equine skeletons while building a railway in the nineteenth century gave rise to the suggestion of a Viking grave (Armstrong 1922). However, there is nothing in the recovered artefacts to suggest it is anything other than pre-Christian Irish (Armstrong 1922, Bøe 1940: 76).

Templemoyle, Limavady, Co. Londonderry

A description of a likely Viking cremation burial survives with old Ordnance Survey notes, which record a large cairn covering a cist that was found to contain bones and ashes (Northern Ireland Sites and Monuments Record). With the burial were found a pot, a sword, a whetstone, a small hammerhead and a 'speckled pebble' (Northern Ireland Sites and Monuments Record). From the brief description of the artefacts recovered it is reasonable to suggest that the incumbent was male.

Cloghermore Cave, Tralee, Co. Kerry

The remains of a male, aged around thirty to forty years, was recently discovered in a cave also thought to contain an area used for burial during pre-Christian times (Connolly & Coyne 2000). The head was laid to the south-east and there appeared to be vestiges of a stone-setting within the shallow depression containing the remains (Connolly & Coyne 2000: 17). Associated with the inhumation were a tinned copper-alloy ring-headed pin, a boat-shaped whetstone of Norwegian schist, a small knife, a tinned copper-alloy button and some iron fragments (Connolly & Coyne 2000: 18). Not far from the male were found the skeletal remains of a female and child (Connolly & Coyne 2000: 18-19). Radiocarbon and typological dating of the artefacts place the burial in the late ninth-early tenth centuries (Connolly & Coyne 2000: 19).

Croghan Erin, Co. Meath

A Viking period spear was recovered from within a Bronze Age burial mound during the nineteenth century, and may have come from a Viking burial (Larcom 1849: 388-9, in Harrison 2001:70).

Tybrough, Co. Kilkenny

Recorded here for sake of completeness. Harrison (2001: 68-9) reports an unpublished account of swords and human remains being recovered from a site here, which may represent a series of Viking burials or possibly pre-Christian Irish interments.

St. John's Point, Co. Down

Recorded here for sake of completeness. Harrison (2001: 68-9) reports an unpublished account of swords and human remains being recovered from a site here, which may represent a series of Viking burials or possibly pre-Christian Irish interments.

The Dublin Sites

As mentioned above, by far the highest concentration of burials and burial sites in Ireland fall within the modern city limits of Dublin. To date there are thirteen known sites, including the two well-known Viking cemeteries at Islandbridge and Kilmainham. All the burials were discovered as a result of building work, and none, save perhaps those found at College Green during the seventeenth century (which will be discussed below) seem to have been marked in any permanent way, although small cairns and stones settings along with the shadows of the rotted remains of wooden grave markers would very likely have been ignored by those disturbing the grave (Bøe 1940: 65, Ó Floinn 1998*a*: 135-7).

Kilmainham and Islandbridge

The Dublin localities of Kilmainham and Islandbridge are situated out towards Dublin Bay, on a gravel promontory between the River Liffey and River Camac (O'Brien 1998: 204). Prior to the Viking presence, the area had been the site of the early monastery of Cell Maignenn (O' Brien 1998: 206). Due to the manner of discovery and methods employed by early antiquarians the true extent and nature of each cemetery site will probably never be known. However, from the large corpus of surviving artefacts and nineteenth century records of the construction work, it has been possible to make some headway in understanding the sites. Through studies of nineteenth century contemporary accounts of discoveries and the surviving artefactual remains, O'Brien (1998) has identified a minimum of seventeen accompanied burials at Kilmainham, possibly fifteen male and two female. By far the most common objects to be recovered were weaponry, with thirteen shield bosses, ten swords and four spearheads reported (O'Brien 1998: 209-13). Also found at Kilmainham were a pair of tongs, weights and scales, two pairs of shears and some beads (O'Brien 1998: 213). There were also reports of skeletal remains interred without grave goods, who may well have been Christian members of the earlier monastery built at the site (O'Brien 1998: 213).

At Islandbridge O'Brien has identified a minimum of nineteen accompanied burials, possibly seventeen male and two female (O'Brien 1998: 213-14). Again, the dominant grave goods are items of weaponry, with eight swords, thirteen spearheads, four shield-bosses and two axe heads (O'Brien 1998: 211-4, Bøe 1940: 32-33). Also recovered were an insular zoomorphic mount, a belt buckle, several single-backed knives, hammers, tongs, sickles, whetstones, two pairs of weighing scales, ten decorated lead weights, two pairs of tortoise brooches, glass beads, spindle-whorls, and needle-cases (O'Brien 1998: 211). During the early nineteen-thirties further building work resulted in the discovery of three further Viking Graves (O'Brien 1998: 211-2). The fist two were found to contain between them two swords, a spearhead, an axe head, some iron nails and two bent metal rods, possibly parts of shield rims (O'Brien 1998: 211). The third grave was found to contain a sword, spearhead and a knife (O'Brien 1998:212). The accompanied graves were said to have been lying in a north-south direction (O'Brien 1998: 212).

There are a further sixteen swords, either in museum collections or written sources and four and a half pairs of tortoise brooches are listed as having either a Kilmainham or Islandbridge provenance, suggestive perhaps of least another twenty graves (O'Brien 1998: 214-6).

The artefacts, although dominated by weaponry, ally themselves to the idea of settlement, with the recovery of smithing tools, four sets of scales, bone gaming pieces, weights, knives, hammers, sickles, rings, pins and buckles, brooches, spindle whorls and a linen smoother, artefacts associated with both male and female graves (Bøe 1940: 38-57).

The discovery of a small copper-alloy axe (length 14.4cm), originally recorded as been covered by some 'white metal', may be compared to the larger axes recovered from some Viking period burials in Norway (Bøe 1940: 52-3, Trotzig 1985). They seem to have been an object of ritual, a symbol of male rank (Trotzig 1985). A similar, albeit larger, axe was recovered from a male grave in Southern Gotland, and although not cast solid like that from Islandbridge, had its shaft made of the soft wood maple, which although impractical if the axe was to be used as a weapon, would be very white in colour (Trotzig 1985). Unfortunately, nothing is known/recorded of the exact provenance of the Dublin example, or any accompanying grave goods. The two bone axes of similar size recovered from the high status settlement site at Jarlshof, Shetland may well have been amulets of analogous type.

From the examination of early descriptions of artefacts and surviving objects from Kilmainham and Islandbridge in the National Museum in Dublin, it seems very likely that there were at least four cremations. At least four swords appear to have been bent, along with two similarly damaged spears and four dinted shield bosses, one bearing the apparent effects of fire-damage (Bøe 1940:13-57). Unfortunately the only surviving accounts relating directly to burial refer to inhumations.

Bully's Acre, Kilmainham

A lost grave site from Kilmainham cemetery was recorded in a nineteenth century antiquarian account, which reports the discovery of an inhumation accompanied by a sword, spear, axe, copper-alloy pin and fragments of iron which may have been the remains of a shield (Bøe 1940: 58).

St Magnen's Churchyard, Kilmainham

Adjacent to the burial grounds of Kilmainham is situated the church of St Magnen, which had in the graveyard a carved stone of Viking type, beneath which Worsaae records were found several Hiberno-Norse coins and two swords, presumably from one or maybe two burials (Worsaae 1846-7 (1995) transl. Henry: 64).

Dollymount

The find of a single sword to the north of Dublin Bay during the late nineteenth century may represent a further lost Viking grave (Bøe 1940: 85, Ó Floinn 1998*a*: 134).

Cork Street

Find of a single sword (Ó Floinn 1998*a*: 132).

Kildare Street

Find of a single sword (Ó Floinn 1998*a*: 132).

Phoenix Park

More or less opposite Islandbridge across the River Liffey lays Phoenix Park, the site of another possible Viking cemetery (Ó Floinn 1998*a*: 132-3). A pair of tortoise brooches and a gilt mounting survive in museum collections alongside notes of provenance, which attest to at least one grave, although Worsaae's nineteenth century accounts of Viking antiquities in Ireland, record the discovery of a least one other, accompanied by tortoise brooches, along with the insinuation that more skeletons had been recovered similarly accompanied (Ó Floinn1998*a*: 132, Hall 1974*b*, Worsaae 1846-7 (1995) transl. Henry 64).

Aylesbury Road, Donnybrook

During the late nineteenth century workmen employed to prepare land for housing in the Donnybrook area of Dublin began to remove a low mound, which as work progressed was found to contain hundreds of human remains (Frazer 1879-88). At the southern end of the mound was found the only accompanied burial, that of a man, with a fine *Ulfberht* sword (Petersen Type D) dated to the first half of the ninth century, in its scabbard, a spear and three iron arrowheads (Frazer 1879-88, Hall 1978). The antiquarian account given by Frazer also mentions the discovery of two further skeletons apparently at the man's feet, but it does seem unlikely that these were the victims of a ritual killing, Frazer himself stating that they were, '*each a separate interment*' (Frazer 1879-88: 32-33). Although the skeletal remains of these two people were lost before he managed to arrive, there is no mention of any grave goods being recovered with them (Frazer 1879-88: 32-33).

A recent reassessment of the graves at Donnybrook has convincingly established that the site was originally an early Christian cemetery; perhaps abandoned by the time the Viking burial had taken place (O'Brien 1992). But what is also pertinent here is the re-use of an established place of burial, something that is repeated both at Kilmainham and

Islandbridge, and sites in the Isle of Man, England and Scotland.

Bride Street

Another possible cremation recorded as being found in Dublin was recovered from Bride Street, south west of College Green (Bøe 1940: 66). The burial was presumably male, and produced a sword, bent along its length, a shield boss, now very damaged, but showing it had been subjected by heat, and a broken spearhead (Bøe 1940: 66). It was apparently a lone find, no other records indicating otherwise (Bøe 1940: 66).

Royal Arcade, College Green

The site at College Green may well have once been the political focal point of Viking Dublin and the site of a further cemetery (Ó Floinn 1998*a*: 135-6). Antiquarian records and old paintings depict a large mound, known as *Thingmote*, since the twelve hundreds, and hence was regarded as being the *þing* site of the Dublin settlement (Ó Floinn 1998*a*: 135-6). The artefacts recorded as being found during the construction of the Royal Arcade on College Green during 1817-18 were two swords, four spearheads, a shield boss and a tinned-copper-alloy buckle (Bøe 1940: 65, Ó Floinn 1998*a*: 135-6). The two swords a spearhead and buckle are now the only surviving artefacts (Bøe 1940: 65, Ó Floinn 1998*a*: 135-6). It is very possible that College Green was the site of a further Viking cemetery. Records suggest a further inhumation accompanied by at least a shield was found in nearby Suffolk Street, along with silver fibulae and a gold ornamented sword (Ó Floinn 1998*a*: 136). Place-name evidence also suggests the site of a cemetery, in medieval times it was known as *Hoggen Green*, Hoggen drawn presumably from the Old Norse *haugr*, mound/burial mound (Ó Floinn 1998*a*: 136). It is also interesting to note that during the seventeenth and nineteenth centuries two prehistoric cremations were also recovered in the immediate vicinity (Ó Floinn 1998*a*: 136). This again is highly suggestive of the continuity of use of a burial site.

Palace Row (now Parnell Square North).

Another cluster of burials are known from the area around what is now known as Parnell Square (Walker 1788: 116, Bøe 1940: 67, Ó Floinn 1998*a*: 134). Antiquarian sources record the discovery of an inhumation while digging the foundations of a house in Palace Row, accompanied by a sword and shield boss (Walker 1788: 116, Bøe 1940: 67). Further remains were found at nearby Granby Row, accompanied by a sword, spear-head and iron rivets; in the same source human remains are recorded as being found stretched as far as Mountjoy Square, again accompanied by weaponry (Ó Floinn 1998*a*: 134).

7.1.1 Irish Burials: results

By far the most striking result from this study is that almost half (thirteen out of twenty-seven) of the Viking burial sites in Ireland were to be found within the limits of the Dublin settlement. If the doubtful burials at St John's Point, Tybrough, Navan, Milltown, The Morragh and Croghan Erin are excluded from the list, then the number of sites beyond Dublin falls to only eight (Armstrong 1922, Harrison 2001: 66-70, Ó Floinn 1998*a*).

The extensive use of the pre-Viking period cemeteries at Kilmainham and Islandbridge are unparalleled elsewhere in the British Isles. Continued use of Christian cemetery sites is common in areas of Britain, but not to the extent of the Dublin sites. Beyond Dublin the only other evidence for a cemetery, albeit small, are the remains of four people discovered at Church Bay, Rathlin Island, which may be linked to the historically attested presence of a Viking camp (Warner 1973-4: 61-3, Ó Floinn 1998*a*: 145). The remainder of the burials in Ireland are individual and limited to the vicinity of the coast, predominantly the eastern seaboard, with only two burials known so far on the Atlantic side (Sheehan 1987-8, Raftery 1960-1, Connolly & Coyne 2000).

Both within Dublin and beyond, Viking immigrants show their penchant towards the re-use of established burial grounds, both Christian (for example, Kilmainham and Islandbridge) and prehistoric (College Green and Church Bay), a trend repeated throughout the British Isles (see below and chapter eight) (O'Brien 1998, Bøe 1940: 65, Warner 1973-4: 61-2, Ó Floinn 1998*a*: 136).

The evidence for cremation is minimal, despite historical sources revealing that the majority of the settlers had their roots in Norway, where the predominant funerary rite was cremation, although the small number may be due to recovery technique. Recovery technique in years gone by also severely hampers analysis of individual funerary rites and comparisons, although it seems safe to suggest that there has yet to be found a Viking burial in Ireland comparable to those richly furnished burials of Ballateare (Isle of Man), Hesket-in-the-Forest (Cumbria) or Kiloran Bay (Colonsay) (Bersu & Wilson 1966: 46-62, Hodgson 1832, Anderson 1907: 443-8). By and large the grave-goods seem to echo what is known from the Irish documentary sources, that although the society was predominantly governed by endemic warfare, the presence of weights and scales, tools required for the manufacture of everyday objects, and gaming pieces indicate both trade and settlement (AU).

Although the burials in Ireland are predominantly male (at least sixty-three in total) there are at least fifteen archetypal female pagan burials of Scandinavian type, both singularly as at Ballyholme, and within the cemetery sites of Dublin (Smith 1905-6, O'Brien 1998).

7.1.2 Irish Burials: conclusions

In common with England at the same period, Irish history is well served by contemporary authors, who recorded much of the activity of the Vikings in Ireland, especially in and around Dublin (AU). As already discussed in chapter three, unlike England, Viking expansion in Ireland beyond the coast was consistently and successfully prevented by the Irish tribes (AU). This enforced limitation resulted in the foundation of colonies, the largest and most well known (historically and archaeologically) being Dublin. This containment severely curtailed assimilation between resident and settler. This segregation allowed parts of Viking culture to be maintained, for example, accompanied burials with various non-dress associated goods. However, as illustrated in the previous chapter, the Viking settlers in Ireland (as elsewhere) were not a representative cross-section of the society of their homeland and could not therefore be expected to maintain all aspects of their culture, which is shown in the burial record. The burials in Dublin are limited to the boundary of the colony, do not appear to have been demarcated by mounds, seem to have proportionately fewer cremations than expected, and use extensively sites of Christian burial, all in contrast with practices in the Scandinavian homelands (O'Brien 1998, Ó Floinn 1998*a*). Beyond Dublin the burials are scattered and isolated, and seem to be the results of skirmishes or temporary landfalls.

The presence of diagnostically Scandinavian type female burials can be taken as evidence of the migration of women from the Viking homelands, especially into the Dublin colony. As it will be shown below, this is very similar to the burial record found within Viking period Scotland, but in stark contrast to the north of England and the Isle of Man.

In effect it is apparent that the burial record in Ireland is mirroring the foundation of limited settlement, and more especially a colony by the immigrants, showing retention and perpetuation of some of their cultural traits because of the segregation of the settlers by the Irish tribes.

7.2 Viking Burial in Scotland (fig. 7.2)

For Scotland a general list of all easily accessible details of Viking burials has been compiled, as there is currently work in progress to document them all (Graham-Campbell & Paterson forthcoming). In it are sixty-three sites, which contain upwards of one hundred and three burials. For ease of dealing with such a large number of sites Scotland has been divided up into three areas; mainland Scotland, Western Isles and Northern Isles. Throughout this chapter there is repeated use of Graham-Campbell and Batey's 1998 publication *Vikings in Scotland*, which contains most sites and good up-to-date artefactual analyses.

7.2a Mainland Scotland

Reay, Caithness

At least two burials are known to have been found eroding from the sand-dunes to the north of Reay (Curle 1914b, Greig 1940: 19-24). It is highly likely that there were at one time many more, antiquarian reports dating to the eighteenth century and later recounting the exposure of stonework during the storms, which could be representative of cists or stone-settings (Graham-Campbell & Batey 1998: 125, Greig 1940: 19-24). It has also been suggested that they may mark the position of a one time Viking settlement (Graham-Campbell & Batey 1998: 125, Greig 1940: 19-24).

In 1913 the crouched remains of a female were exposed by erosion about four feet from the then ground level (Curle 1914: 295). Inspection of the site revealed that the woman had been buried with two tortoise brooches, though of a like type, not a pair, a copper-alloy ring-headed pin, a copper-alloy buckle with the plate decorated with a 'white metal', a small steatite spindle-whorl, and an iron snaffle bit (Curle 1914: 295-298, Greig 1940: 19). Also recovered close to the grave were an iron buckle and the top most part of a pair of iron tweezers (Curle 1914: 295-298, Greig 1940: 19). Also found in the vicinity were a large number of horse bones (Edwards 1928: 138).

In 1926 two young boys found a further inhumation exposed by the wind in the sand dunes (Edwards 1927: 202-3). The paved, cist lined grave lay around six feet below the then ground level, and was found to contain an iron axe head, a shield boss complete with rivets, a knife, a small sickle, an iron buckle, an iron mounting, a ring-headed pin, a slate whetstone and two small pieces of flint (Edwards 1927: 203, Greig 1940: 19). At the bottom of the grave was noted an area of dark sand mixed with pieces of 'burnt' iron (Edwards 1927: 203). From the grave goods it is assumed that the incumbent was male.

The following year further examination of the site was undertaken (Edwards 1928: 138). Several mounds were opened near Drill Hill at Reay village, but no further burials were found (Edwards 1928: 138). More cists were noted amongst the dunes and a bronze eighth-ninth century Anglo-Saxon strap-end was found on the surface of the sand (Edwards 1928: 138-40, Graham-Campbell & Batey 1998: 126).

From the surviving artefacts and reports of stone structures in the sand dunes at Reay at the very least bear witness to a Viking cemetery, probably situated amongst or adjacent to an earlier Christian cist cemetery, and possibly a settlement site nearby.

Torbeckhill, near Ecclefechan

The recovery of a Viking period sword of Petersen Type L (Anglo-Saxon type), dated to around nine-hundred, on the banks of the River Mein, may be supposed to have been a stray find as no other artefacts or skeletal remains were recorded as being found with it (Curle 1914a: 335, Greig 1940: 13-14). However, its discovery a couple of feet below the surface of a mound leaves the theory of a so far unrecovered interment entirely open to speculation (Curle 1914a: 335, Greig 1940: 13-14).

Boiden Mound, near Lower Bridge of Froon

In 1851 a series of weaponry was uncovered within a chamber two feet from the top of a mound near Loch Lomond (Anderson 1874: 569). Recovered from the chamber was a sword bent along its length, a shield boss and a spear (Anderson 1874: 569). There was no mention of any remains and with the condition of the sword it seems likely that the mound once held the cremated remains of a man (Anderson 1874: 569).

Gordon Bay, Argyll

The reported provenance (*c*1940) of the rivets surviving in the Highland Museum, Fort William is the only remaining indication for them coming from a boat burial in Gordon Bay (Greig 1940: 15).

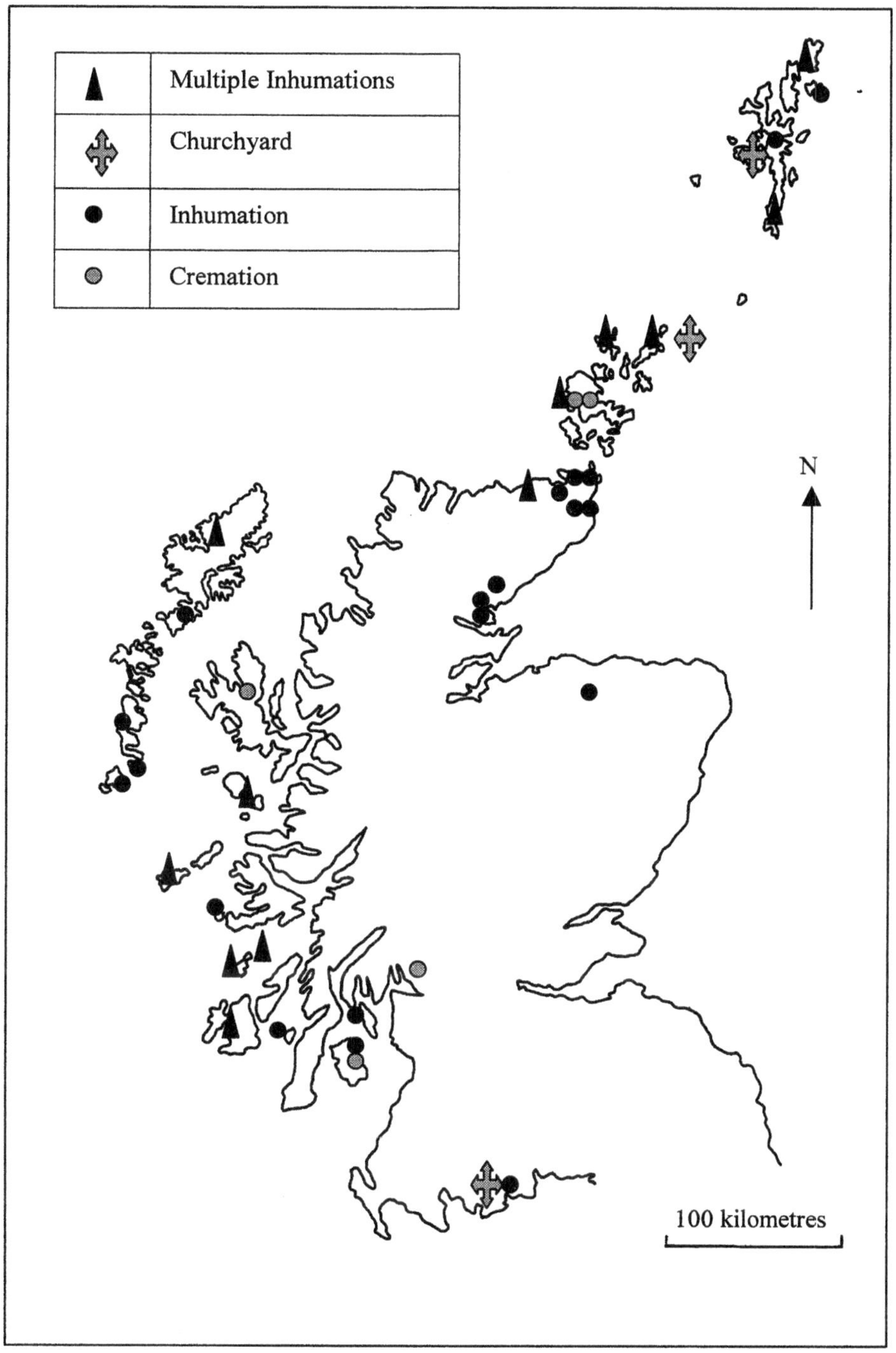

Fig. 7.2 *Viking Burials in Scotland*

Dunrobin Island, Golspie, Sutherland

From antiquarian reports and associated remains it seems highly likely that there were once a series of Viking graves near the site of Dunrobin Castle. A pair of tortoise brooches were said to have been recovered from a grave and a spear – head from another (Anderson 1874: 554, Greig 1940: 15-17). An iron axe-head and an iron ring were also recovered from the seashore, possibly also from a grave (Greig 1940: 17).

Opisdale House, Dornoch, Sutherland

The antiquarian accounts of the discovery of a single tortoise brooch and an urn (now lost) record them as being found near a standing stone (Anderson 1874: 554, Greig 1940: 17-18). No mention of any human remains was made (Greig 1940: 17-18).

Balnakeill, Durness, Sutherland

As with Reay above, the discovery of human remains in the sand-dunes at Balnakeill came about as a result of erosion (Graham-Campbell & Batey 1998: 140). The body of a boy aged between eight and thirteen years was recovered from a sand-dune, accompanied by a scabbarded sword, a spear, shield boss, a strap-end, three amber and glass beads, a copper-alloy brooch, a bag of antler gaming pieces, an antler comb, a needle-case and threaded needles, and a fish-hook (Graham-Campbell & Batey 1998: 141-2).

Examination of the surrounding area failed to identify any further burials (Graham-Campbell & Batey 1998: 141).

St Cuthbert's, Kirkcudbright

The discovery of a scabbarded sword, a copper-alloy ring-headed pin, and a small jet bead from the churchyard at St Cuthbert's near Kirkcudbright must surely be one of the few known Viking gráves from a Christian churchyard in Scotland (Greig 1940: 13). From the grave goods it is presumed the incumbent was male. To date, no further burials have been found.

Castletown, Caithness

In 1786 an inhumation grave was found beneath a large flagstone, inserted in the ruins of a broch (Anderson 1874: 549-550). Accompanying the skeletal remains was a pair of tortoise brooches, linked by a double row of silver chain (now lost), a lignite arm-ring (of Pictish type), and a bone bodkin (Greig 1940: 24, Batey 1987: 34, Graham-Campbell & Batey 1998: 68).

Longhills, in Westerseat, near Wick, Caithness

Two tortoise brooches (though not a pair) were recovered from a cist in the top of a gravel mound known as Longhills, near the Broch of Kettleburn in 1840 (Anderson 1874: 551-552). It is presumed they were found with human remains, although none were mentioned (Anderson 1874: 551-552). It was further reported that more cists were uncovered there, though no more artefacts were ever found (Greig 1940: 25). This may suggest the site of a pre-Norse Christian cemetery.

Haimer, near Thurso, Caithness

Antiquarian reports of the discovery of Scandinavian weaponry at Haimer may mark the one time existence of a further Norse period cemetery in Caithness (Anderson 1874: 563).

Huna, Caithness

A possible boat grave was exposed by sand erosion close to the high water mark in 1935 (Batey 1987: 38). Antiquarian notes of the discovery describe rivets, timber fragments, a piece of a human cranium, chain fragments and what seem to be rope restrainers (Batey 1987: 38). This is the only known boat burial in Caithness (Batey 1987: 38).

St Peter's Churchyard, Thurso

During 1896 the remains of a crouched adult inhumation was found beneath a runic cross slab in the graveyard (Batey 1987: 39-40). Beside the adult grave was found that of a child (Batey 1987: 39-40).

Ballindalloch, Morayshire

In 1829 a grave containing the skeletal remains of a man and horse were found along with '*a quantity*' of rings, iron fragments, a bridle-bit and a shield (Anderson 1874: 569-70).

7.2b Orkney

The importance of the Orkney Islands to Viking period studies cannot be overstated. Not only do they contain the highest number of Viking burials, but also chance finds and archaeological excavation have recovered a wealth of Viking artefacts and settlement sites. Historically it was on the centre of the Norse Earldom of Orkney and features in many sagas and contemporary accounts (Graham-Campbell & Batey 1998: 54). Perhaps unsurprisingly the islands also bear a wealth of Norse place-names (Graham-Campbell & Batey 1998: 54).

Lyking, Mainland

During the late nineteenth century a mound was opened at Lyking on Mainland (Donations to the Museum 1872-3, Greig 1940: 80). Inside the mound were found a layer of burnt bones, an unburnt comb fragment (as at Hesket-in-the-Forest, Cumbria, below), a small badly decomposed spearhead and an iron buckle (Greig 1940: 80). From consideration of the grave goods it appears that this was the cremation of a man.

Broch of Gurness, Mainland

A modern assessment of the excavations at Gurness had identified the possibility of at least six graves from early excavations (Hedges 1987: 73). Two shield bosses found in the fill of the broch tower may be representative of two male graves (Hedges 1987: 73). A dark green glass linen smoother, a folding copper-alloy balance and a large jet bead (now lost), a whetstone (now lost) and some iron fragments (now lost) were recovered from the north-western end of the Great Ditch (Hedges 1987: 73, 87). A copper-alloy ring-headed pin, an amber bead and parts of a human cranium were found close to the top of the southwest ramparts (Hedges 1987: 73). A lone amber bead found on top of a Broch Period level may indicate a further, disturbed burial, however, the recovery from a cist of two skeletal hands complete with five copper-alloy finger-rings *in-situ* close to the west of the broch tower surely does (Hedges 1987: 73).

It is very likely that there were far more burials within the broch mound, surviving records detailing the discovery of many human remains scattered across the site; however, the nature of their discovery and recording has effectively negated their worth (Hedges 1987: 73).

During the nineteen-thirties a skeleton was found in the northern part of the broch wall, surrounded by a stone setting and covered by flags and possibly a small mound (Robertson 1968-9: 289). Accompanying the deceased were a pair of tortoise brooches and around the neck was a necklace hung with pendants and amulets, one surviving sufficiently well enough to be identified as a Thor's hammer amulet (Robertson 1968-9: 290, Hedges 1987: 73, Graham-Campbell & Batey 1998: 128). Such Thor's hammers amulets on iron necklaces have been found in cremation graves dating from the ninth and early tenth century in the eastern Mälar region of Sweden, on the island of Åland in the Baltic and Russia (Gräslund 2000: 58-59). Also found in the grave was a small iron sickle, a knife and a bone pin (Robertson 1968-9: 290, Graham-Campbell & Batey 1998: 128). The artefacts have been dated to the late ninth, early tenth centuries, and would suggest that this was the burial of a woman (Graham-Campbell & Batey 1998: 129).

The discovery of scattered bones and artefacts within the broch mound would indicate the presence of further graves, disturbed now beyond recognition and evaluation (Graham-Campbell & Batey 1998: 128). It seems very likely though that the site had been a Norse cemetery, indicating the perhaps the continuity of settlement in the immediate vicinity of the broch.

Stenness, Mainland

In 1902 a mound at Stenness was opened to reveal an inhumation inserted into the remains of a ruined building (Charleson 1904: 565). Accompanying the body was found a large, copper-alloy ring-headed pin, with a flat, facet cut head (Charleson 1904: 566) The skull was identified to be that of a female by a leading physician of the time (Charleson 1904: 566). It is to be supposed that the pin held together a shroud, and the lack of further grave-goods has been seen as representative of a transition period between pagan and Christian cult practice (Graham-Campbell & Batey 1998: 61). It could just as well have been the grave of a poor person, the representation of a transitional period of assimilation more likely represented by an accompanied burial in a Christian graveyard.

Howe, Cairnton, Stromness, Mainland

The description of a possible grave opened during the nineteenth century is perhaps suggested by the *haugr* place name it carries. Little is known of the grave, and only a glass linen smoother survives from the artefacts said to have come from the mound (Marwick 1928: 121-122, Greig 1940:80). However, excavation during the nineteen-seventies and eighties showed it to have been a broch mound, and recovered no trace of any further artefacts associated with Viking burial (Graham-Campbell & Batey 1998: 60).

Gyron Hill, Sandwich-under-Skaill, Mainland (Skaill Bay)

There are several poorly recorded grave finds in the vicinity of Skaill Bay. One stone cist was found on Gyron Hill, which along with the human remains (presumably) was recovered a small, oblong steatite vessel (Greig 1940: 81).

A further cist grave, covered by a cairn was found to be holding an inhumation accompanied by an early Viking period spear head, and iron rivet, a knife, a small slate whetstone with suspension hole, a bone comb in its case, an iron rivet, iron fragments, a stone disc, an arrowhead and a leg bone of a horse (Watt 1888: 283-4, Greig 1940: 81-4). At the top of the northwest side of the grave were found bones from birds and a frogfish, as was a knucklebone of an unidentified mammal (Watt 1888: 284). It is likely that they were intrusive. Interestingly, *Skaill* is a Norse place-name, although there has been no settlement discovered to date, it is however, very close the prehistoric settlement of Skara Brae (Graham-Campbell & Batey 1998: 59), again suggesting the continuity of land-use.

Buckquoy, Mainland

Excavations of the Pictish and Viking period farmsteads at Buckquoy revealed a tenth century inhumation grave inserted into the ruins of a late Norse building (Ritchie 1976-7: 190). The grave was marked by a small mound and contained the remains of a crouched, middle-aged male, accompanied by half of a silver penny of Edmund (940-6), a knife, a spear, a whetstone, a ring-headed pin, a bone mount, and an iron buckle (Ritchie 1976-7: 190). The excavator also reported finds of neonatal bones scattered about the site at Viking period levels, perhaps illustrative of the lack of importance associated with infant burial (Ritchie 1976-7: 188). These included the skeletal remains of a newborn baby found beneath a flagstone in the northeast corner of the Norse farmstead, thought to represent a founding ritual (Ritchie 1976-7: 188).

Mainland (unprovenanced)

A poorly recorded burial recovered from a large mound by nineteenth century treasure hunters, '*from an island near Mainland*', is extremely important, as it is appears to have been a female cremation (Charleson 1904: 560). Laying in the centre of the mound was found a layer of burnt bones along with two copper-alloy tortoise brooches (Type R654), apparently unburnt with textile still attached (see Claughton Hall, Lancs., below) an amber spindle-whorl, an armlet of either jet or bone, and a fragment of a copper-alloy pin (Charleson 1904: 560-1, Greig 1940: 86). In the original account the brooches were said to have lain on top of the cremation deposit, some nine inches apart, with the other grave goods close by (Charleson 1904: 560).

Sweindrow and Westness, Rousay

The site at Westness, excavated between 1968 and 1984, embraced not only a Norse settlement but its cemetery as well (Kaland 1993, Graham-Campbell & Batey 1998: 135). At the adjacent area of Sweindrow nineteenth century antiquarian accounts describe a cemetery, and a sword (Petersen Type I, dated to 850-950) and scabbard and shield boss survived extraction to reach the collection of the National Museum in Edinburgh (Anderson 1874: 563-6, Greig 1940: 89-90). Although final site reports for Westness are awaited, the graves in the cemetery can briefly be summarised. It seems that the cemetery was originally in use during the Pictish period, and these earlier graves seem to have been respected by the Norse settlers (Kaland 1993, Graham-Campbell & Batey 1998: 136). All the burials appear to have been inhumations (Kaland 1993, Graham-Campbell & Batey 1998: 136). The first grave found which sparked modern investigation was that of a two females, one with a full-term infant, interred with amongst other things (full site report as yet unpublished), a pair of ninth century tortoise brooches, forty beads, a bejewelled silver annular brooch of eighth century Irish design, a gilt copper-alloy mount with animal ornamentation, two Anglo-Saxon strap-ends, a comb, a sickle, a copper-alloy basin, a weaving sword, shears and a pair of heckles (Kaland 1993, Graham-Campbell & Batey 1998: 136, Paterson in Sellevold 1999: 56). The other female was interred close by, but seemed to have had no accompanying grave goods (Paterson in Sellevold 1999: 56). Boat-shaped stone settings marked the graves of both the men and women (Kaland 1993, Graham-Campbell & Batey 1998: 136). One of the men was interred with a shield, arrows, sickle, ring-headed pin, a comb and a set of gaming pieces (Kaland 1993, Graham-Campbell & Batey 1998: 136-7). Another female grave was found to contain a sickle, a comb, a penannular brooch and two spindle-whorls (Kaland 1993, Graham-Campbell & Batey 1998: 137).

There were also discovered two boat burials at Westness (Graham-Campbell & Batey 1998: 137). Both incumbents were male, both having a sword, shield and arrows, one had a spear and an axe as well as a sickle and a ploughshare, both had a whetstone and a strike-a-light, one had a fishing weight (Kaland 1993, Graham-Campbell & Batey 1998: 137).

From the anthropological reports it seems that the cemetery was originally Pictish, before being use by Viking settlers (Sellevold 1999). It is also interesting to note that there is an occurrence of several specific congenital diseases that has enabled anthropologists to identify likely relationship between some of the people buried there (Sellevold 1999).

Lamba Ness, Sanday

The following two graves were said to have been found in the vicinity of the Broch of Lamba Ness (Greig 1940: 86-88). The first was a cremation, probably of a woman, found with a pair of tortoise brooches, a lignite arm-ring, a large amber bead and a copper-alloy ring-headed pin (Greig 1940: 86-7, Graham-Campbell & Batey 1998: 144). None of the objects were fire-damaged (Graham-Campbell & Batey 1998: 144).

The second possible grave was found by workmen digging in the ruins of a building (Greig 1940: 888). Although no remains were mentioned it seems likely that the sword, shield and spearhead that were recovered came from a male grave (Greig 1940: 88, Graham-Campbell & Batey 1998: 57).

Only the artefacts survive from a third grave, again, presumably that of a female, found at Braeswick, near Lamba Ness (Greig 1940: 88, Graham-Campbell & Batey 1998: 57). These were a pair of badly damaged tortoise brooches and three beads, including one of amber and one glass (Greig 1940: 88). From the grave goods it would seem reasonable to suggest that they originated from the grave of a female.

Other artefacts survive recorded as found while digging at *Lamaness* (Donations 1878: 599). Although no settlement site has been directly associated with these burials, it is interesting to note that the Norse settlement at Poole lies only across the bay.

Scar, Sanday

Erosion by the sea allowed one of the few Viking graves in the United Kingdom to be excavated by modern archaeological techniques. The boat burial had been dug down below ground level, and a cist laid out within it by lining the east end of the boat with stones (Owen & Dalland 1999). Into the boat had been placed three people, possibly a family group, with the prime position and most grave-goods belonging to an elderly female (Owen & Dalland 1999). Beside the woman had been placed a child of around ten, and at their feet, folded into the western tip of the boat was a male, around thirty (Owen & Dalland 1999). The woman had been buried with a whalebone plaque, a gilt copper-alloy equal-armed brooch, a sickle, bone comb, two spindle-whorls (one of steatite, the other sandstone), a weaving sword, a pair of shears, a needle case and a maple-wood box (Owen & Dalland 1999: 30-1). No grave-goods were assigned to the child by the excavators (Owen & Dalland 1999: 31). The man had been interred with a scabbarded sword (Petersen Type H, dated to 800-950), some arrows which had probably been in a quiver, a set of whalebone gaming pieces, leaf weights for scales and possibly shield, although only a mount remained (Owen & Dalland 1999: 29-30, 108). Radiocarbon dating of the human remains provided the interesting possibility of the three being buried at differing times, although the excavators rejected this and a date was set at 875-950 using both these results and typological analysis of the artefacts (Owen & Dalland 1999: 164-5).

Styes, Sanday

Excavation during the 1990's provided evidence for the existence of an extensive burial site on the headland (Bond 2003: pers. comm.). Antiquarian sources from the nineteenth century report the discovery of a sword of Scandinavian form from within a tumulus (Anderson 1874: 566).

Pierowall, Westray

Since the seventeenth century antiquarians have written about the discovery of graves amongst the sand dunes above the Bay of Pierowall (Graham-Campbell & Batey 1998: 129-30). A recent re-evaluation of the surviving artefacts and antiquarian accounts sets the figure at a minimum of sixteen graves[1] with many unprovenanced finds (Thorsteinsson 1968). All the burials appear to have been inhumations, and have the classic indicators of Norse burials. From examination of the grave-goods there appears to be both male and female burials, with associated weaponry and jewellery (Thorsteinsson 1968). From Thorsteinsson's reconstruction of the antiquarian accounts there appears to have been at least two groups of burials, one closer to the seashore, the other clustered around the remains of a ruined building (Thorsteinsson 1968: 166).

At least three of the burials were fund to contain the skeletal remains of a horse, and one of these also a dog (Thorsteinsson 1968: 167, 171). It also seems very likely from the survival of a series of rivets that there was also a boat burial (Thorsteinsson 1968: 171). The following accounts are a summary of Thorsteinsson's (1968) work.

The first burial was probably a secondary inhumation in an earlier grave. Accompanying what is presumed to be the crouched remains of a male was a sword, spear, a comb and a shield boss.

The second burial to be excavated was only a few yards to the north of the first, and contained the prone remains of a female, interred with a pair of tortoise brooches, a copper-alloy ring-headed pin, and what appeared to be a weaving sword that fell to pieces when handled.

The third grave was found beside number two, and contained a further female inhumation, accompanied by a pair of tortoise brooches and connecting chain, a sickle, bone comb, a large ring-headed pin, a bone needle case and needle inside and a stone spindle-whorl.

The fourth grave lay around thirty yards to the east of those mentioned above, and again seemed to contain the inhumed remains of a female. The crouched burial lay within a stone cist and was found to be accompanied by a pair of tortoise brooches, two bone combs, seven beads, and two ring-headed pins.

The following three graves were described as being found near to the shore, placed on a north-south alignment.

The first grave of this group was found to have been previously disturbed, although the skeletal remains survived along with a small axe head, half of a shield boss and several scattered fragments of iron.

The second grave of this seashore group was an inhumation accompanied by the skeletal remains of a dog and small horse. Also recovered were a bridle-bit (*in-situ*), a buckle, an object of iron thought to be either a spearhead or a short sword and fragments of bone with pieces of metal adhering and fragments of iron.

The third grave was also found to contain an inhumation accompanied by a harnessed horse (bridle-bit *in-situ*) and a small dagger.

The final grave of the group was said to have been found a considerable way to the north of the others. No artefacts were recovered with the crouched inhumation.

The following five graves were found clustered around a mound, further inland from the ones above, and running on a north-westerly line from them.

The first grave to be excavated was at the south of the mound and contained a square stone-setting into which had been place the crouched inhumation of a man. Found with the remains were a shield, a sword, a large whetstone, a bone comb and several glass beads.

The second grave opened, to the north of the mound, was presumably that of a female, and contained a small skeleton, with a pair of tortoise brooches apparently *in-situ*, a trefoil brooch and a pin.

The third grave, also on the north side of the mound, contained the remains of what was presumably a female, surrounded at each side by a row a small stones. Recovered from the grave were a pair of tortoise brooches, a ring-headed pin and a pair of decorated long bone combs and their cases.

The fourth grave, also on the north side of the mound, had been previously disturbed, although it was still found to contain skeletal remains laying with the head to the south.

The remains of a small skeleton, again presumably female, were then uncovered at the northeast side of the mound, accompanied by a pair of tortoise brooches, a ring-headed pin and two bone combs.

The final grave laying beside the mound was presumably that of a male, the skeleton reported to be large, and accompanied by a shield, an adze, a spear, and some iron fragments.

The provenance of the final two graves excavated at Pierowall during the nineteenth century is unknown, however, descriptions of the inhumations and their grave goods survive.

The first grave was found to contain two knives, an iron key, a sickle, the terminal mount of a drinking-horn, nails and nail-heads, a bead of burnt clay and several fragments of wood with iron adhering.

The second grave was described as being found in the lower part of the links, and was covered by a small mound. Inside was a ship burial, containing an inhumation, accompanied by a horse, two iron buckles, half a bone button, twenty-one boat rivets and several iron fragments. There are also several unprovenanced finds from the vicinity, including three tortoise

[1] Thorsteinsson's (1968) list is numbered incorrectly, missing what would have been his 'grave 5', therefore the final grave should be numbered 16 and not 17.

brooches, a bone comb, a ring-headed pin and a copper-alloy penannular brooch of Irish design.

7.2c Shetland

Unst

Little survives of the details of the recovery of a single tortoise brooch and a small circular copper-alloy box made possibly to hold a set of scales, other than they were recovered from a grave on Unst during the nineteenth century (Greig 1940: 103, Graham-Campbell & Batey 1998: 64). Also in the same list of donations to the National Museum in Edinburgh said to have been recovered from a Viking grave in Unst in 1861 was a small copper-alloy bowl and a serpentine button; it is quite possible that they all came from the same grave (Donations to the Museum 1893: 6).

Clibberswick, Unst

Work in a farmyard in Clibberswick during the mid eighteenth century led to the recovery of a pair of ninth century tortoise brooches, a Borre-style copper-alloy trefoil brooch, a silver armlet (now lost) and two white and blue coloured glass beads (now lost) (Anderson 1874: 556, Purchases for the Museum: 1882: 17-19, Greig 1940: 103-5, Graham-Campbell & Batey 1998: 64). From the description in the antiquarian accounts it seems that the artefacts (except the beads) were *in-situ*, placed in anatomically correct corresponding places even though the body seems to have decayed away (Greig 1940: 105). From the nature of the grave-goods it seems safe to suggest that the incumbent was female.

Clivocast, Unst

The opening of a large mound in 1875 at Clivocast was said to have revealed an inhumation accompanied by weaponry (Graham-Campbell & Batey 1998: 64). From this description it would seem safe to assume that the incumbent was male.

Sumburgh, Mainland

The possibility of a further cemetery is tantalisingly alluded to in records pertaining to the region around Sumburgh airport. While building the airport control tower during the Second World War an iron sword still in its scabbard, a small cooking pot (possibly a shield boss?) and part of a skull were found (NMRS). The artefacts and human remains are now lost (NMRS). Also during the War years a tortoise brooch was found while trenches were being dug on nearby Ward Hill, suggesting the possibility of a further, female, grave (Waugh 1996: 125).

St Olaf's, White Ness, Mainland

The discovery of an axe in a slab-lined tomb in the churchyard of St Olaf's during the nineteenth century surely marks one of the few known Viking type graves within a Christian churchyard in Scotland (Graham-Campbell & Batey 1998: 64, 144).

Housegord, Weisdale, Mainland

The discovery of a small whetstone pendant and a blue glass bead in the prehistoric burial mound at Housegord may represent a secondary interment during the Viking age (Graham-Campbell & Batey 1998: 64). Interestingly, the same artefact combination was recovered from a child's grave at Cnip on Lewis (see below) (Graham-Campbell & Batey 1998: 64).

Wick of Aith, Fetlar

The recovery of a quantity of boat rivets from beneath a mound above the beach at Wick is suggestive of a boat burial, although treasure hunters, fuelled by local legend had badly damaged the mound prior to the collection of the rivets (Graham-Campbell & Batey 1998: 64). During 2003 an excavation undertaken on behalf of *Time Team* recovered a late ninth century tortoise brooch, suggesting that this had once been the burial of a female.

7.2d The Western Isles

Ensay

During the early eighteenth century a grave was found at the westerly side of the island, from which was recovered a pair of copper-alloy scales and a small hammer, which could well have been a Thor's Hammer amulet (see Broch of Gurness, above) (Anderson 1874: 556).

Ardvonrig, Barra

During the mid-nineteenth century a mound marked with a standing stone was opened to reveal the late ninth-early tenth century grave of what seems very likely to have been a female (Anderson 1874: 555, Graham-Campbell & Batey 1998: 83, Greig 1940: 72-3). The many artefacts accompanying her were, a pair of tortoise brooches, a weaving sword in its scabbard, a pair of heckles, a bone comb, a copper-alloy penannular brooch, the copper-alloy terminal and mount of a drinking horn, a knife, an iron buckle, a copper–alloy needle-case and a slate whetstone (Anderson 1874: 555, Graham-Campbell & Batey 1998: 83, Greig 1940: 72-3). An Anglo-Saxon type sword said to have been found in the vicinity of the mound may point to the one time existence of a further burial (Graham-Campbell & Batey 1998: 83).

Barra (unprovenanced)

Also recorded as being found on Barra is a bone comb recovered from a stone cist somewhere on the island (Graham-Campbell & Batey 1998: 83).

Eriskay (unprovenanced)

The remains of a grave assemblage discovered somewhere on Eriskay during the eighteenth century were a sword (probably Petersen Type O, dated to 900-950) in its scabbard, an iron spearhead and a whetstone of grey slate (Greig 1940: 73). From the grave-goods it seems reasonable to suggest that this was the burial of a male.

South Uist

A fragmentary piece of carved antler comb is all that remains of a stone-lined burial beneath a sand mound somewhere on the coast of South Uist (Greig 1940: 73-4, Graham-Campbell & Batey 1998: 81-2).

Bhaltos, Lewis

In the coastal parish of Uig there is a particularly dense pocket of Norse place-names, which along with the recovery of several Norse period burials is surely a strong indicator for settlement (Graham-Campbell & Batey 1998: 74). At Bhaltos the remains of a female inhumation was found by school children after the erosion of a small mound of sand by the wind laid it bare (Macleod 1916: 181). The artefacts recovered were a pair of tortoise brooches, a copper-alloy brooch of Irish design, a silver-plated, niello decorated copper-alloy buckle also of Irish design, a copper-alloy penannular brooch again decorated in the Irish style, a piece of copper-alloy chain and an amber bead (Macleod 1916: 181-2). Also recovered later from the vicinity of the grave was a large broken iron knife along with other unidentifiable pieces of pierced iron sheets lined with copper-alloy (Macleod 1916: 182, Greig 1940: 78). It is also interesting to note that the adjacent area bears a Scandinavian influenced place-name, pertaining to a 'Norse fort' (Macleod 1916: 182).

Cnip, Lewis

Also in the parish of Uig lies the headland of Cnip, on which a large Norse cemetery has been partially excavated (Graham-Campbell & Batey 1998: 74). From radiocarbon dates of some of the organic remains recovered from the graves and artefactual analyses, it seems that the cemetery covers a period from the eighth to the tenth century (Graham-Campbell & Batey 1998: 74). The recent archaeological excavation recovered some seven inhumations from the site, including two females, two males and three children (Welander *et al* 1987). The richest grave of the group was that which belonged to one of the females, and contained a pair of tortoise brooches, a whetstone, a bone needle-case, a sheathed knife, a sickle, a necklace of multicoloured glass beads, an antler comb, a strap-end with copper-alloy studs and buckle, an iron rivet and a copper-alloy ring-headed pin (figs. 7.8 & 7.9) (Welander *et al* 1987). Isotopic research undertaken suggests a strong possibility that she grew up on the coast of Norway or quite possibly mainland Scotland (Montgomery 2002: 316, Montgomery 2003: pers. comm.).

The second female was discovered lying in an east-west aligned rectangular stone setting, accompanied by a bone pin and a perforated iron plate (Dunwell *et al* 1995). The male in the stone setting alongside her had no grave-goods (Dunwell *et al* 1995). Isotopic analysis of the female shows a very strong possibility that she came from the South Downs of England, and the male was of local origin (Montgomery 2003: pers. comm.). The second male inhumation lay in a north south direction at the feet of the fore-mentioned (Dunwell 1995). The only item recovered form his grave was a cow molar (Dunwell 1995). Isotopic analysis of his remains suggests a strong possibility that his origins lay in Co. Antrim, in the north of Ireland (Montgomery 2002: 315, Montgomery pers. comm.).

The first of the children lay in a shallow pit and was accompanied by an amber bead, three iron nails, and a light grey and pink sandstone pendant of the kind found at Birka (see also burial at Housegord, Mainland, Shetland above) (Dunwell *et al* 1995). The second child lay in a pit only fifty centimetres away from one of the males (Dunwell *et al* 1995). Associated with this interment was an amber bead, possibly along with two glass beads and a decorated bone pin which were found in the fill (Dunwell *et al* 1995). The third child was found in a coffinless pit along with a single iron rivet (Dunwell *et al* 1995). From isotopic analysis it was shown that all the children were of local origin (Montgomery 2003: pers. comm.).

Although the discovery of a cemetery is convincing evidence for Norse settlement nearby, to date no Norse period farmsteads have been found (Graham-Campbell & Batey 1998: 75).

Tarbert, Gigha

The circumstances surrounding the discovery of a set of copper-alloy weighing scales and bronze weights are cloudy, and the square stone box in which they were found has been described as a cist, whereas it could just have been as described – a stone box (Graham-Campbell & Batey 1998: 92, Greig 1940: 29-30). The only known grave to date in Scotland containing a set of scales and weights is the boat burial at Kiloran Bay, Colonsay (see below) (Graham-Campbell & Batey 1998: 92).

Ballinaby, Islay

From the survival of various antiquarian accounts from the eighteenth and nineteenth centuries relating the area of sand-dunes above the bay it seems that it was once a the site of a large Norse cemetery, with several of its graves marked with mounds and standing stones (Graham-Campbell & Batey 1998: 121).

In 1878 two cist-lined burials, complete with inhumations and accompanying grave-goods were exposed from beneath blowing sand (Anderson 1879: 51). The graves were said to have been lying side-by-side (Anderson 1879: 51). The first grave was found to contain a scabbarded sword (Petersen Type H, dated to 800-950), a shield of the Irish Sea conical boss type, the terminal and mounting of a drinking horn, a spearhead and ferrule, two axes, a pair of pincers, an adze, a smith's hammer, a fishing spear and a large iron cauldron (Anderson 1879: 51-2, 53-63, Greig 1940: 32-6, Graham-Campbell & Batey 1998: 122-4). From the grave-goods it seems safe to assume that the incumbent was male.

Accompanying the second inhumation was an iron heckle, a black glass linen smoother, a tinned copper-alloy needle-case and needle, a pair of silver decorated tortoise brooches, a silver ring-headed pin with a decorated spherical top and chain, a copper-alloy ladle of Irish type (of which similar examples have been found in Norway), three copper-alloy discs decorated with repoussé work, again possibly of Irish origin, four decorated glass beads and a copper-alloy edge mount (figs. 7.11 & 7.12) (Anderson 1879: 51-52, 63-72, Greig 1940: 36-40, Graham-Campbell & Batey 1998: 124). From the grave-goods it seems suggestive that the incumbent was female.

The links with Ireland and Norway this couple (perhaps) had is surely significant, perhaps charting their own progress, or simply having access to traded objects.

In 1932 a third grave was discovered, some four hundred yards west of those mentioned above (Edwards 1934: 74). The grave had been constructed into the side of a rising promontory, and seems to have been marked by two standing stones (Edwards 1934: 74 & Plate 1: 75). An area had been cut into the hillside and a cist inserted into the natural rock (Edwards 1934: 74). The grave had been previously disturbed, although the decayed inhumation inside was found to be lying in a supine position with the skull at the southwest end (Edwards 1934: 75). The incumbent was presumably male and was accompanied by a sword, shield, knife, axe, a gilt copper-alloy buckle set with red enamel and a copper-alloy ring-headed pin (Graham-Campbell & Batey 1998: 124-5).

Records survive of the disturbance of what appears to be a female grave at Ballinaby in 1778, when two tortoise brooches were recovered from beneath a standing stone close to where the preceding burials were found (Anderson 1874: 554, 1879: 71, Greig 1940: 41-2).

Newton Distillery, Islay

A cist grave was discovered close to the Newton Distillery sites in 1845 in a gravel bank beside the strath (Anderson 1879: 71, Greig 1940: 42). Accompanying the skeletal remains were a pair of tortoise brooches and an amber bead, suggesting that it was the burial of a female (Anderson 1879: 71, Greig 1940: 42).

Cruach Mhor, Islay

A series of artefacts recovered from a specific area at Laggan Bay may have once belonged to the grave of a wealthy female (Gordon 1990: 151). They comprise of a pair of tortoise brooches, beads, a spindle whorl, knives, sickle and the socket of what may have been a weaving sword (Gordon 1990: 151). They were found close to a building that is thought to be of Viking period date (Gordon 1990: 151).

Kiloran Bay, Colonsay

The ship-burial at Kiloran Bay was discovered beneath a mound in 1882, and was subject to two antiquarian explorations (Anderson 1907: 443-4). From the accounts it appears that the grave itself was below ground level and lined with stones before presumably the boat was place over the top, however, without the benefit of modern excavation the boat may have indeed lined the whole as was usual in Scandinavia (Greig 1940: 60). The interment also seems to be beside a rising mound, rather than beneath it, although this may be due to erosion (Anderson 1907: 444, Plate 8). Slabs at the east and west ends of the cist had been etched with a cross (figs. 7.13 & 7.14) (Anderson 1907: 447). The male interred within the grave was accompanied by a rich series of grave-goods, including three Northumbrian stycas, one dating to 808-40, another to 831-54 (see below for comparable coin found at King's Cross Point, Lamlash Bay, Arran), the third illegible, a sickle, iron buckles and a copper-alloy strap-mountings from harnesses (weapon or horse) similar to those found at Balladoole, a sword with a silver inlaid pommel (very deteriorated, possibly Petersen Type E, dated to 800-900) an axe, spear, a shield of the conical boss Irish Sea type, an iron cauldron, two arrowheads, a copper alloy pin, a copper-alloy ring-headed pin, a bridle bit, three knives, nine copper-alloy decorated mounts, boat rivets and nails, a whetstone, a set of copper-alloy scales and lead weights and the remains of a horse (Anderson 1907: 444-448, Greig 1940: 48-61, Graham-Campbell & Batey 1998: 118-22).

Ardskinish, Colonsay

A group of artefacts apparently discovered together at Ardskinish may be representative of a further possible boat burial. The artefacts are a ring-headed pin, a copper-alloy buckle and a small copper-alloy rivet hood (Greig 1940: 61).

Croc-Nan-Gill, Colonsay

A stronger contender for a boat-burial was found eroding from a sand mound at Croc-Nan-Gill (Greig 1940: 61-2). Recovered from the mound were twenty-five iron boat rivets of various sizes, some still with pieces of wood attached to them, a human tooth and a bovine tooth (Greig 1940: 61).

Machrins machair, Colonsay

During the late nineteenth century an exploratory north-south trench was put through an oval shaped mound at Machrins (M'Neill 1892: 61). The trench revealed the remains of a boat, the skeletal remains of a horse, an iron pot, an axe head and fragments of a sword (M'Neill 1892: 61). The horse was found to be lying within the boat and seems to have been fully tacked-up, although only a snaffle bit was recognised and recovered (M'Neill 1892: 61). Also found while sifting through the sand were a shield boss, a spearhead complete with a piece of shaft, an amber bead, a copper-alloy penannular brooch and a copper-alloy pin (M'Neill 1892: 61). The excavator made much of the 'damage' to the weaponry recovered, associating it with to ritual killing, although it does appear that it was due to degradation (M'Neill 1892: 61). No mention was made of any human remains (M'Neill 1892).

In 1978 an archaeological excavation of a settlement nearby discovered the remains of a female inhumation in a stone cist, accompanied by a copper-alloy plaque of Celtic design, a ring-headed pin, a knife, an iron nail, and a small dog (Ritchie 1981: 276, Graham-Campbell & Batey 1998: 90-91). Calibrated radiocarbon dates place the burial between 780+/-70, (Ritchie 1981: 276).

Colonsay (unprovenanced)

A collection of artefacts sent to the National Museum in Edinburgh at the end of the nineteenth century were said to have come from a series of Viking graves on Colonsay (Greig 1940: 48). However, no records survive, if there ever had been any, of which artefacts were found together and where (Greig 1940: 48). From the inclusion of many iron boat rivets it could be supposed that there was at least one boat burial (Greig 1940: 47-8). The other artefacts include a badly corroded sword, pieces of a further sword, the blade of a small knife, some pieces of fire-damaged copper-alloy (from a cremation?), an iron pot, a circular piece of iron plate, along with several fragments of iron (Greig 1940: 47-8). Also included in the collection was the wooden handle of a knife, carved to represent a female figure – it is doubtful whether it is of contemporary date (Greig 1940: 48).

Carn Nan Bharraich, Oronsay

The large mound of Carn Nan Bharraich was subject to a number of antiquarian excavations during the late nineteenth and early twentieth centuries, which although resulted in the preservation of a number of the artefacts, severely hamstrung further research by the non-stratigraphic excavation techniques used (Graham-Campbell & Batey 1998: 113-18). From careful dissemination of the surviving accounts it appears that there were at least three inhumations, quite probably inserted into the remains of a boat cremation, indicated by a large bed of charcoal and quantity of boat rivets (M'Neill 1891: 433). Initial exploration of the mound uncovered two stones, which seem to have been originally placed as markers on top of the mound (M'Neill 1891: 432). The mound also seems to have been lined, at least in some places by cist stones (M'Neill 1891: 432).

The first inhumations in the mound were positioned close together in the centre suggesting contemporaneous burial (M'Neill 1891: 432-33). The first skeleton appeared to be that if an elderly female, buried with a pair of gilt copper-alloy rectangular brooches, made from the clasps of a Celtic reliquary, a serpentine bead, a red amber bead, a bone object (now lost), and a Celtic style copper-alloy penannular brooch (M'Neill 1891: 432-33, Graham-Campbell & Batey 1998: 114).

Beside the woman lay the remains of an elderly man, accompanied by an iron knife and a limpet shell ring (M'Neill 1891: 433). A further trench put through the centre of the mound cut through a very large bed of charcoal containing boat rivets, six burnt pieces of bronze, a stone sinker, a bone finial, two flint pieces and a copper-alloy ring, possibly part of a pin (M'Neill 1891: 433, Grieve 1914: 273).

Subsequent erosion of the southern most edge of the mound led to the discovery in 1913 of a further female inhumation, accompanied by a pair of tortoise brooches, a knobbed ring-headed pin of Irish design, a bone needle and case, a pair of shears, a small iron socket, a bar of iron (remains of a weaving sword?) and iron fragments, along with four iron rivets and a clenched iron nail, which one would suspect were from the remains of the boat-burial (Grieve 1914: 275-77, Graham-Campbell & Batey 1998: 114-5, Greig 1940: 42-4).

Lochan Kill Mhor, Oronsay

A further possible boat cremation burial from Oronsay survives in the artefacts sent to the Edinburgh museum at the end of the nineteenth century (Greig 1940: 46). Nothing is known of their recovery (Greig 1940: 46). The surviving artefacts were eighteen small iron rivets, some fragments of iron plate, a hollow rod of iron, some teeth and fragments of charcoal (Greig 1940: 46).

Millhill, Lamlash Bay, Arran

During the late nineteenth century a small gravel mound some one hundred and seventy feet from the high water mark was levelled during construction of a house (Balfour 1910: 221). Three or four feet below the surface of the mound was recovered an iron shield boss of Merovingian or Anglo-Saxon design dated to the eighth-ninth century and a large scramasax (Balfour 1910: 221). No mention was made of any human remains, suggestive of the grave being either a cremation or a cenotaph, similar to that found at Claghbane near Ramsey on the Isle of Man (Balfour 1910: 221, Graham-Campbell & Batey 1998: 96, Cubbon 1983: 18).

King's Cross Point, Lamlash Bay, Arran

Across the bay at Lamlash to the south a further burial was discovered beneath a large mound at the crown of the headland (Balfour 1909: 371). The mound was constructed from pieces of red sandstone not naturally found in the area, and therefore suggestive that it had been brought specifically for its construction (Balfour 1909: 373). Inside the mound there was a ship-shaped stone setting (Balfour 1909: 372). Two feet above the centre of the mound towards the northern most end at the western side were found a pile of cremated human remains, part of a broken whalebone plaque, an iron hasp, a lock mount from a casket, four iron rivets, a large iron nail, some melted pieces of ornamented copper-alloy, a Northumbrian styca of Wigmund, Archbishop of York, dating to 837-54 (a coin of Wigmund was also found at Kiloran Bay), and two pieces of black vitrified rock (Balfour 1909: 372, Greig 1940: 26, Graham-Campbell & Batey 1998: 96). All the artefacts bore signs of fire damage except a single piece of copper-alloy (Balfour 1909: 373-4). The artefacts recovered from the burial suggest that the incumbent was a cremated female.

Tiree

The provenance of a female grave from which the surviving group of artefacts were recovered on Tiree is now unknown (Anderson 1874: 554-5, Greig 1940: 63). There was a pair of tortoise brooches decorated with silver wire (one now lost) and a copper-alloy pin with a perforated diamond-shaped head, suggesting that they were recovered from a female grave (Anderson 1874: 554-5, Greig 1940: 63).

It is possible, perhaps, that the grave was found amongst those regularly disturbed at Cornaigberg, where an eighteenth century account records the discovery of skeletal remains, both human and equine, swords, shields and spears (Anderson 1874: 555, Greig 1940: 63, Graham-Campbell & Batey 1998: 87). Also recorded in the account is the discovery of a skeleton holding the remains of an infant (Graham-Campbell & Batey 1998: 87).

Mull

Sadly the provenance and circumstances of a female grave from which a pair of tortoise brooches were taken during the nineteenth century is now unknown (Anderson 1879: 72, Greig 1940: 62).

Kildonnan, Eigg

There are three known Viking period burials from Eigg, all situated near to Kildonnan Chapel (Graham-Campbell & Batey: 84). The first mound, opened sometime during the eighteen thirties was found to contain a sword (Petersen Type D, dated to no later than 850) with a highly decorated copper-alloy hilt, complete with scabbard fittings, a whetstone, some decorated copper-alloy mounts from a bucket, and a small copper-alloy pot–leg, now believed to be medieval and therefore intrusive (MacPherson 1878: 586-8, Walsh 1998: 226, Graham-Campbell & Batey 1998: 84).

A second mound was opened in 1875, although it seems from the description of a depression in the top of the mound that the burial had been previously disturbed (MacPherson 1878: 589). The antiquarian record of the discovery of only a few pieces of bone in the remains of a cist may indicate that the skeletal remains had been removed and reburied in the nearby chapel, or simply poor excavation combined with acidic soil conditions (MacPherson 1878: 590). Recovered from the grave were a sword and scabbard, a whetstone, a copper-alloy penannular brooch, a piece of black cloth and fur with two charred pieces of bone (perhaps a charm bag?), a copper-alloy Carolingian style buckle, an axe, spear, sickle, a spindle whorl and some beads, including one of red amber bead (MacPherson 1878: 589-591, Graham-Campbell & Batey 1998: 84). The mix of artefacts may be illustrative of a male and female interment.

Adjacent to the above was a smaller mound a few yards to the south (MacPherson 1878:592). From this third mound was recovered a sword, a small whetstone with suspension hole, a jet bead, a copper-alloy buckle, a piece of flint, an amber bead and a copper-alloy penannular brooch (MacPherson 1878: 592). It is perhaps safe to assume that this was the burial of a male.

Tote, Sheabost, Skye

The only known (so far) Viking burial from Skye was found near the shore at Tote, Sheabost, in an area of Norse place-names (Graham-Campbell & Batey 1998: 78). A grass-covered cairn was opened in 1922 to reveal a primary cist lined, cremation burial of prehistoric date, with a Norse period burial higher up the mound over the top (Lethbridge 1920: 135). The fragmentary nature of the bones and the hole in the top of the mound is again suggestive of the skeletal remains either having been disturbed or removed at some point (Lethbrideg 1920: 136). The grave-goods do not show any indication of specific ritual or fire damage, thus ruling out cremation. The artefacts recovered were an axe, a copper-alloy pin, a bone bead, a sandstone hone, a piece of wood with a piece of iron attached to it, along with several iron fragments adhering to pieces of wood, which may have been a shield (Lethbridge 1920: 136). From the nature of the grave-goods it is likely that the burial was that of a male.

Sangay

The site of a female grave disturbed during the nineteenth century on Sangay is now unknown (Anderson 1874: 555). Accompanying the inhumation were two tortoise brooches, a copper-alloy pin and a copper-alloy needle, all of which are now lost (Anderson 1874: 555, Greig 1940: 79).

7.2.1 Scottish Burials: results

The first and most striking result of this research into Viking burials in Scotland is their sheer number in comparison to the rest of Britain and Ireland. By far the largest numbers are to be found on the islands, with at least fifteen in Orkney, seven in Shetland, twenty-six in the Western Isles, and fourteen sites on the mainland. All these are undoubtedly minimal totals. The larger number found on the Western Isles may be due to their geographical situation between Ireland and western Scotland, right on the sea route to Dublin, their position offering ease of accessibility to all points of the British Isles for raiding or trading. Although the presence of Norse settlers in the Northern Isles are both well attested to in both historical and archaeological sources, there has yet to be found any pagan burials associated with known settlement sites, for example at the Brough of Birsay[2], Skaill, Jarlshof and the Udal (Morris 1989, 1996, Gelling 1984, 1990, Hamilton 1956, Crawford & Switsur 1977, Crawford 1986, 1988). The trend may be reversed at Westness, but until full publication of the site report it cannot be assessed (Kaland 1993). However, there is evidence to suggest that continuity of settlement sites occurred at least in the close vicinity of earlier occupation, with the discovery of burials in broch mounds, for example at Howe, near Stromness, Orkney and Freswick Sands (Batey 2002). Similarly the burial inserted into the remains of an abandoned Norse farmstead at Buckquoy may also prove to be linked to a nearby later settlement (Ritchie 1976-7).

As with Ireland, the burials on mainland Scotland are clustered on the coast, again possibly as a result of the strength of the local rulers curtailing any attempt of settlement further inland, the Viking period coinciding with the rise of a particularly strong Scottish monarchy (Crawford 1987). However, central Scotland does remain largely unexplored archaeologically (Bond 2003: pers. comm.). The burials on the islands seem to have been situated on the least economically viable land (headlands, close to the sea shore amongst the dunes), arable/grazing land being at a premium. This being said, the burials do seem to be within areas of modern buildings,

[2] An inhumation in a cist grave was found accompanied by an antler comb and iron knife, and was radiocarbon dated to later Pictish to Viking period (Morris, with Pearson & Emery in Morris 1989: 114-127).

suggestive perhaps of further settlement sites being situated below today's farms.

By far the most common burial rite was inhumation, with only six cremations, three female (Lamba Ness Broch, King's Cross Point, Mainland Orkney), and three male (Lyking, Boiden Mound and Tote) (Greig 1940: 26-7, 70-1, 80, 86-8, Charleson 1903-4, Graham-Campbell & Batey 1998: 78, 144, 146-7, Balfour 1908-9, Anderson 1874-5: 569, Stewart 1853: 143, Lethbridge 1920). The cremation at Lamba Ness is associated with at least two other burials (Greig 1940: 86-8, Graham-Campbell & Batey 1998: 57, 144). The others are apparently singular, Tote being the only known Viking burial on Skye to date (Lethbridge 1920, Greig 1940: 70-1, Graham-Campbell & Batey 1998:78). All the cremations were marked by a mound, the Lamba Ness burial having been inserted into the remains of a wheelhouse (Greig 1940: 86-8, Graham-Campbell & Batey 1998: 57, 144).

The manner of demarcation is wide and covers all known methods of the Scandinavian homelands, including mounds, cists, stone-settings, cairns, standing stones, flat graves and boat burials. There is also evidence for the use of both prehistoric and Christian cemetery sites, such as at Pierowall (possibly late Iron Age), St Cuthbert's Kirkcudbright, Westness and Housegord (Thorsteinsson 1968, Batey 1993: 144, Greig 1940: 13, Kaland 1993, Graham-Campbell & Batey 1998: 64). This is mirrored in both Ireland and the north of England (see chapter eight).

Scotland differs from the north of England in the presence of cemeteries, similar to those found in Dublin, although these groups of burials seem to incorporate small family groups such as at Carn nan Bharraich or Scar, and a larger community at Pierowall and Westness, rather than the large mixed populations represented at Kilmainham and Islandbridge (McNeill 1890-1, Anderson 1907, Grieve 1913-4, Owen & Dalland 1999, Thorsteinsson 1968, Kaland 1993, O'Brien 1998). There is also evidence for cemeteries in the far north of mainland Scotland near Reay, Longhills in Caithness, and Dunrobin Island, Golspie (Curle 1913-4b, Edwards 1926-7, 1928-9, Anderson 1874-5: 551, 554). This must be representative of the manner of settlement, and will be discussed below in context with the results and implications from Ireland and the north of England.

These multiple burials, cemeteries and single graves provide a demography very different from the north of England. The first very obvious characteristic is the large number of diagnostically female burials, at least thirty-three compared to fifteen in Ireland and six in the north of England (see chapter eight). This is vitally important when considering settlement patterns, integration and cultural continuity. From this data it seems that in the Scottish Islands as in Ireland, there were many more female migrants from the Scandinavian homelands than there were in the north of England. The implications of this will be discussed below in the final conclusions to this chapter. It is also important to note that the remains of infants and children have also been recovered from Scar, Cnip and Westness, something unknown in England and Ireland, although it seems likely that if Kilmainham and Islandbridge cemeteries had been excavated under modern conditions young people would have been found there (Owen & Dalland 1999, Paterson 1999, Jørgensen *et al* 1987, Dunwell *et al* 1995).

7.2.2 Scottish Burials: conclusions

Unlike the situation on the Scottish mainland Viking settlers do not seem to have had much opposition to their take over from resident groups inhabiting the Scottish Islands (Graham-Campbell & Batey 1998: 54). There is evidence to suggest that some facets of the culture of resident groups were retained, such as pottery and agricultural systems (Bond 2003: pers. comm.). The settlement of the islands resulted in the foundation of colonies, not restricted in the way Viking Dublin was from the rest of Ireland, but because of their geography. This natural containment allowed the perpetuation of some parts of culture to be maintained. The almost complete replacement of native cultural indicators by those of the incoming Viking settlers suggests complete domination across all levels of society. This geographical segregation and establishment of parochial communities allowed the continuation of cultural traits, for example, the accompanied burials encompass all Scandinavian demarcation techniques, boat burials and small family cemeteries. There are however, still differences, and despite the majority of the settlers having links with Norway there are very few cremations, alongside the use of Christian graveyards. The lack of cremations may be due to the recognition and recovery techniques used in the past, although as discussed in chapters three and six, the abandonment of funerary rituals associated with the homelands is an extremely common trend within immigrant communities (Laungani 1997, Rosenblatt 1997).

The demography of the burials in the Scottish Isles differs from Ireland and the North of England by having large numbers of female burials, suggestive that there were more females migrating and settling in the area. This alongside the discovery of the graves of children and small cemeteries, could be evidence for the settlement of families, or at least the perpetuation of Norse cultural traits within a family unit. The different economic base, agrarian farming settlements rather than the trade based, martially-dominated, Dublin colony no doubt had a major role in determining the settlement sites of migrating women and children.

The larger presence of Scandinavian females is vitally important when considering the perpetuation of cultural traits, since it lessens the chance of marriage into resident groups. As discussed in chapter three, funerary rites in farming groups involves members of the family and community as a whole, male and female. It is also worth reiterating here that the ritual specialist in Ibn Fadlan's account was female, which may also have a bearing on the perpetuation of typically Scandinavian type burial practice by immigrant groups into the isles of Scotland, until the gradual acceptance of Christianity[3]. This perpetuation of knowledge within a family or community is perhaps best illustrated in the burial at Scar, where the old lady had been interred using traditional burial techniques, despite

[3] Until very recently in the United Kingdom it was traditionally older, generally widowed women who prepared bodies for burial and were called in by the family of the deceased (see chapter three).

the Northern Isles being officially Christianised at the time of her death (Owen & Dalland 1999).

As with Ireland, only to a greater extent because of the complete domination of the national resident populace, the Viking burials in the Scottish Islands reflect the foundation of long-lived colonies, showing retention and perpetuation of many cultural traits because of their parochial nature and continued links with the Scandinavian homelands.

7.3 Viking Burial in the Isle of Man (fig. 7.3)

Listed in the burial database from the Isle of Man are twenty-five burials from nineteen sites. Although upwards of forty Viking burials are claimed to exist on the Island, very few have been excavated, and only three reasonably recorded.

Ballateare, Jurby

The opening of a large burial mound at Ballateare was to provide the Isle of Man with one of its most famous and important Viking burials. It was coastally situated in the parish of Jurby, and was marked at the top by a wooden memorial post (Bersu & Wilson 1966: 46). On removal of the topsoil there was found to be a layer of cremated animal bone (cow, horse, sheep, dog), along with the skeletal remains of a female, with a hole in her skull, thought to represent a victim of ritual sacrifice (Bersu & Wilson 1966: 47). On removal of the mound, a rectangular pit was found dug into what was Viking period ground level, into which had been placed a wooden coffin, containing the inhumation of a man (Bersu & Wilson 1966: 48). With the man had been placed a sword (Petersen Type V, late ninth or more commonly dated to the tenth century), which was broken, its hilt lying on the blade along with the tip (Bersu & Wilson 1966: 50).The rest of the blade had apparently been left in its scabbard, which still bore its decoration of Anglo-Saxon mounts (Bersu & Wilson 1966: 51-2). There were three iron spearheads, one of which was half the size of the others and had its socket decorated with silver wire (see Hesket, Cumbria, chapter eight, appendix 6 for similarly decorated spearhead) (Bersu & Wilson 1966:57-59). The shield boss recovered from the grave was of the Irish Sea type, and bore signs of damage (Bersu & Wilson 1966: 59). An iron knife and sheath, a copper-alloy loop and plate, a copper-alloy strap-end and a copper-alloy ring-headed pin completed the grave-goods (Bersu & Wilson 1966: 54-7, 61-2).

As well as being important for providing evidence for the practice of graveside sacrifice (if indeed the injury was perimortem), Ballateare is a peculiar mix of funerary ritual, and may be evidence of the complexities of religious belief at the time. The killing of weapons is a hallmark of cremation ritual rather than inhumation, as is the presence of cremated animal bone in the grave. The manner of the breakages in the sword is peculiar, usually when swords are ritually damaged they are bent, rather than broken (see Hesket, below). In order to be bent or broken the sword must be reheated, the corresponding changes in the structure of the iron rendering it almost impossible to return the blade to the scabbard. It seems more likely that the sword and scabbard deteriorated together and were disturbed either by burrowing animals or the excavation itself. The sword, as the shield boss may equally have been damaged during their useful life.

Also, the sacrifice itself must be questioned. In the original account the skeleton was reportedly found towards the top of the mound, more than a metre higher the grave cut, and two metres above the inhumation (Bersu & Wilson 1966: 46, Plate 31). The woman was lying prone, with her arms at ninety degrees to her body (Bersu & Wilson 1966: 47). This suggests very strongly that she had been buried some time after death, allowing *rigor mortis* to set in. Whether she had been left in the position of death on a sacrificial platform suggested by the excavators, is open to speculation (Bersu & Wilson 1966: 47). However, in examples of the possible suttee ritual in Norway both male and females are buried together in the same grave cut (cremation or inhumation) and grave goods representative of both the incumbents are found (Shetelig: 1910). No grave-goods were found with this inhumation. Is it possible that the female recovered was a later insertion in the mound? Radiocarbon dates may prove instructive.

The mound at Ballateare was built on a Neolithic burial site of the Ronaldsway Culture, a further example of the re-use of established burial sites by the Vikings in the British Isles (Bersu & Wilson 1966: 46).

Cronk Mooar, Jurby

A second mound in Jurby one and a half kilometres north of Ballateare was found to be covering a sunken grave formed of either a wood-lined pit or containing a wooden coffin (Bersu & Wilson 1966: 63, 69). Mixed in with the fill of the mound were found pieces of burnt clay, charcoal, iron slag, bone, teeth and shells (Bersu & Wilson 1966: 63). Over the top of the coffin lay traces of a wooden beam, perhaps used to carry it to its final resting place (Bersu & Wilson 1966: 69). On top of the 'coffin' were found an iron spearhead and a shield (Bersu & Wilson 1966: 67-8). Inside the wooden structure was found a man wrapped in an animal skin cloak (Bersu & Wilson 1966: 83). Examination of insect paparia found around the body points to it having been buried some time after death, and that death took place during the spring or summer months of the year (Bersu & Wilson 1966: 70). It is tempting here to draw an analogy to Ibn Fadlan's account of the burial of the Rus chief, whose body lay in a separate grave during the preparatory rituals leading up to his actual 'burial event', that is in this case his cremation. Interred with the man was a sword (Petersen Type S, dated to the tenth century) and scabbard, complete with a copper-alloy strap distributor for attachment to a belt or baldric, a copper-alloy strap-end, an iron spearhead, a shield boss and nails, a knife and sheath and a bronze ring-headed pin (Bersu & Wilson 1966: 70-83). As with Ballateare, the incumbent's head lay to the west (Bersu & Wilson 1966: 89).

It is also interesting to note that the burial mound was built over a prehistoric settlement site, although it does seem that the area was under the plough during the Viking period (Bersu & Wilson 1966: 69-70).

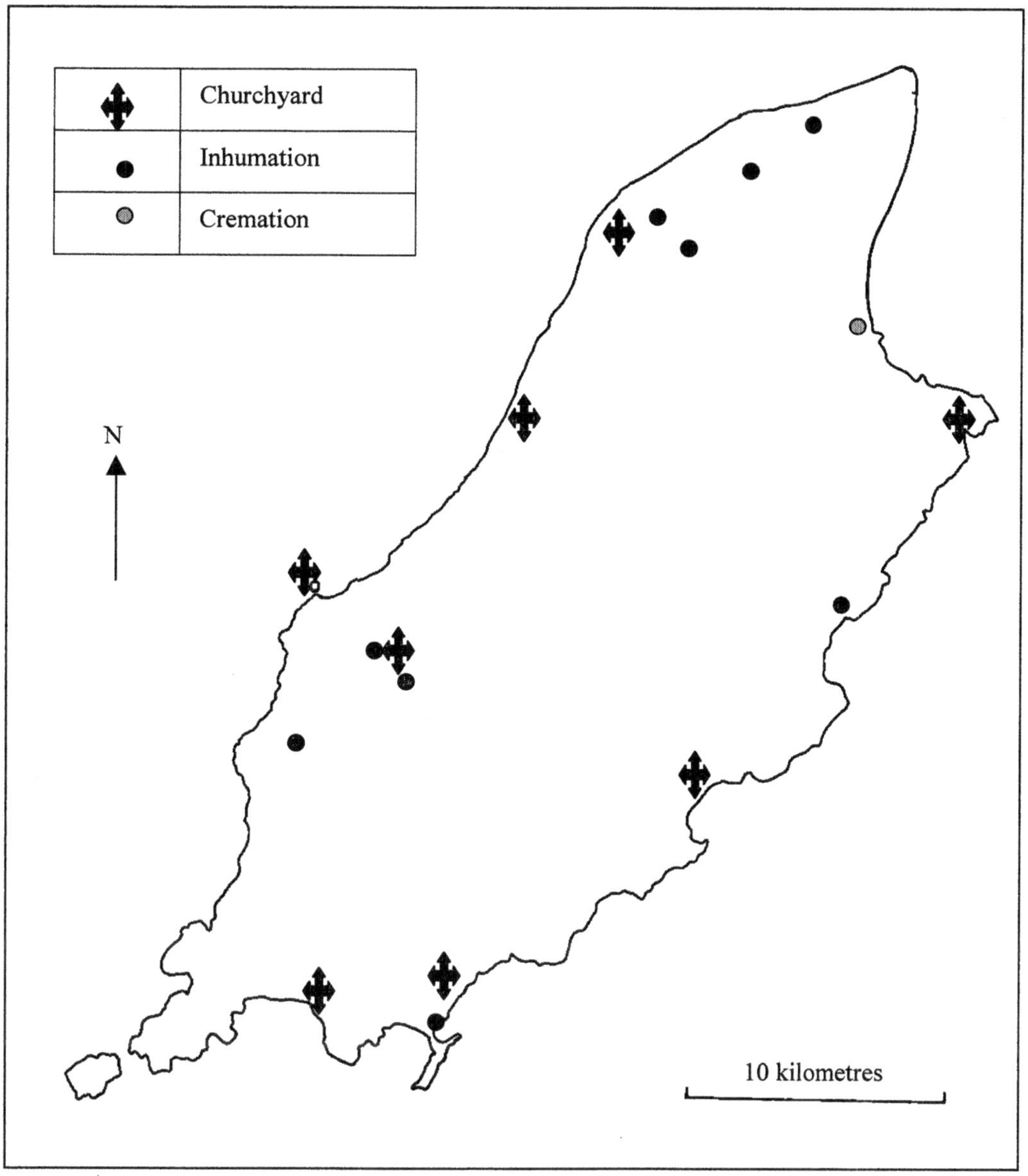

Fig. 7.3 *Viking Burials in the Isle of Man*

Balladoole, Arbory

Perhaps the most famous of the Viking burials to have been found on the Isle of Man is the boat burial at Balladoole. The burial had been deliberately placed right on top of the stone-lined graves of a Christian cemetery, deliberately disturbing and scattering inhumations that had not been interred for very long (Bersu & Wilson 1966: 4). The mound was surrounded by a kerb of large stones and the discovery of a large post-hole beside it is suggestive of a wooden marker (Bersu & Wilson 1966: 3). As with Ballateare, the funerary rites seem to be a peculiar mix of cremation and inhumation, the top most layersof the mound filled with the cremated remains of cattle, sheep, horse, cat and dog (Bersu & Wilson 1966: 10). Inside the centre of the mound was a flat-bottomed boat, packed with stones and found to contain the body of a male and two females, again supposed to be victims of sacrifice, although given the nature of the mound they could just as easily be the disturbed remains of prior inhumations (Bersu & Wilson 1966: 5-7). Also found amongst the fill were pieces of infant bone which were believed by the excavator to be intrusive (Bersu & Wilson 1966: 5-7). Accompanying the inhumations were a copper-alloy ring-headed pin, a knife and sheath, a whetstone, a flint strike-a-light, a silver belt buckle and strap-end, a pair of Carolingian style spurs complete with buckles and strap-ends, a bridle-bit and bridle mountings of Celtic design, a cylindrical iron object, a girth, a pair of iron stirrups, an iron cauldron, a further iron receptacle, pieces of linen and a shield of the conical Irish Sea type (see Ballateare, Islandbridge, Kilmainham and Kiloran Bay graves of comparable types) (Bersu & Wilson 1966: 13-44). Peculiarly there were no offensive weapons.

Again there is some mixing of burial rites with the inclusion of burnt animal remains, but there is no hint of Christianity, the incumbent laying with his head to the south-east (Bersu & Wilson 1966: 5). The dominance and disregard of the Christian cemetery is surely indicative of the power and influence this group of people had over the local populace.

The very obvious lack of offensive weapons is very interesting and may point to a person of particular social position within the group, or perhaps a specific wish. Also interesting is that horse bones appear to be missing from the burial, despite the presence of tack, other than those pieces found in the cremated layer towards the top of the mound. It could be that this later layer represents later ritual offerings of food to the dead.

Knock y Doonee, Andrea

Another boat burial was discovered beneath a mound, close to the church at Knock y Doonee (Kermode 1930). Inside the mound was found a cist-lined vault that covered the remains of a boat and the fragmentary remains of a human skeleton (Kermode 1930: 127-8). From the surviving grave goods it is perhaps safe to assume that the incumbent was male, although the human remains seem to have decayed away, leaving only pieces of crania and discolouration of the soil in the centre of the boat (Kermode 1930: 128). The boat appears to have been 'anchored' by a pile of stones (Kermode 1930: 128). The grave goods were a tenth century sword (Petersen Type X) and scabbard, a spearhead, an axe, a shield boss, an iron bowl, a hammer, tongs, two bone handled knives, the remains of a harness and copper-alloy mounts, a ring headed-pin, a set of copper-alloy belt mountings similar to those recovered from the burial at Kiloran Bay, Colonsay (see above) though finer, a lead fishing weight and many boat rivets (Kermode 1930: 128, Bjørn & Shetelig 1940: 23-4). In the northwest of the boat there was also recorded what seems to be the remains of a meal for the dead (Kermode 1930: 128-9). At the southwest end of the boat was found the skeletal remains of a horse, apparently buried wearing its tack (Bjørn & Shetelig 1940: 25).

Interestingly Bruce and Cubbon (1930) suggest that there is a further possible burial at Knock y Doonee, onto which the eleventh century church was built.

Claghbane, Ramsay

The discovery of a late ninth-early tenth collection of weaponry found beneath a wall without any mention of any accompanying human remains has given rise to the find being labelled a cenotaph (Cubbon 1983, Andersson 1998: 4). The group comprised of a sword, spearhead, shield boss, and bead (Cubbon 1983, Andersson 1998: 4).

Ballachrink, Jurby

During the late nineteenth century one of a pair of mounds set on the ridge of Ballachrink were taken down (Megaw 1937: 234-5, Bjørn & Shetelig 1940: 25). Inside the mound was found a cist that contained a sword, a spearhead and a perforated stone disc (Megaw 1937: 234-5 & Plate 2-3, Bjørn & Shetelig 1940: 25). The sword is of Anglo-Saxon type (Petersen Type L) and dates to around 900.

Ballaugh

In 1824 a fragmentary sword in its scabbard and a spearhead (lost during the nineteenth century) was discovered in a small gravel mound, six to seven feet below ground level, behind a cottage on the main street of the village (Megaw 1937: 235-6 & Plate 7, Anderson 1874: 567). The antiquarian source of the time attests to them as being laying parallel to each other, and the gravel around them discoloured, probably due to the decomposition of a body (Anderson 1874: 568). The sword is an Anglo-Saxon type (PetersenType L, dated to around 900). It would seem safe to assume that this was the burial of a male.

St Maughold

There are surviving accounts of many pieces of weaponry being recovered from the churchyard, which is famous for containing the largest collection of cross-slabs in the Isle of Man (Megaw 1937: 235). In 1824 part of the hilt of a sword was recovered and retrieved for posterity by a local antiquarian from a pile of refuse (Anderson 1874: 569, Megaw 1937: 235 & Plate 1). It is of Anglo-Saxon type (Petersen Type L) and dates to around 900. It is very likely that this was once part of an accompanied male grave placed in an established Christian cemetery, rather like the burials recovered from the parish church in Kildale, North Yorkshire (see chapter eight).

Kirk Michael

A thin iron spearhead was recovered from the churchyard during the late nineteenth century (Megaw 1937: 235 & fig 5, Bjørn & Shetelig 1940: 22). Again, it is highly likely that it formed, or was part of, the grave goods of a man buried in an established Christian graveyard.

Ballabrooie, Patrick

During 1964 a pattern-welded sword of Petersen Type L (*c*900) still in its scabbard was uncovered while ploughing rising land above the river Neb at Ballabrooie (Cubbon 1965:249-50). Although no human remains or other artefacts were found, it seems highly likely that this was once the site of a Viking grave (Cubbon 1965).

St John's, Kirk German

A small mound beside the megalithic tomb at the site of the Tynwald was opened during the nineteenth century (Megaw 1937: 235, Bjørn & Shetelig 1940: 25-6). Inside were found a stone cist, an axe, a stirrup and some beads of various colours and sizes (Megaw 1937: 235, Bjørn & Shetelig 1940: 25-6). These finds are now lost, although a sword (possibly Petersen Type P, dating to the first half of the tenth century) survives in the Manx museum which was said to have been found in the same field, and may perhaps have originated in this badly excavated tomb (Megaw 1937: 235 & fig. 4, Bjørn & Shetelig 1940: 26).

Ballelby, Kirk Patrick

This grave survives only as a verbal record as the farmer who disturbed the burial mound around eighteen-fifty reburied the human remains and accompanying axe (Megaw 1935: 232, Bjørn & Shetelig 1940: 25). A further vague account, which may or may not refer to the same burial whose exact site is now unknown, refers to the discovery of a stone cist containing an inhumation accompanied by a sword and axe (Megaw 1937: 235).

Old Kirk Braddan

Like those discussed above at Kirk Michael and St Maughold, a piece of a sword was discovered in a grave in 1865 while digging in the north of the churchyard at Braddan (Megaw 1937: 235 & Plate 6, Bjørn & Shetelig 1940: 23). Again, it could represent pagan elements of burial practice in a Christian graveyard, or perhaps the establishment of a Christian site on an earlier burial ground.

Malew Parish Church

During the mid-nineteenth century a brief account records the discovery of two '*Scandinavian*' swords in a grave in the churchyard (Megaw 1938: 13, Bjørn & Shetelig 1940: 25).

Ronaldsway, Kirk Malew

The site where the airport at Ronaldsway now stands was extremely disturbed before excavations got under way during the late nineteen-thirties (Neely 1940: 72). From the fragmentary remains of buildings and burials recovered it seems more than likely that this site was in continuous use from the Bronze Age until the early medieval period (Higgins 1999: 141-2, Neely 1940: 74). Across the site were found a great deal of artefacts of Norse type, including lignite arm-rings, ring-headed pins, strap-ends, brooches and mounts (Neely 1940: 81-86). Due to the disturbance of the site the original provenance of most of the artefacts are unknown. They may have originated in a burial context, or from a settlement site. There does survive a brief account of an accompanied inhumation, although all that remained was 'humus' and a spear-head (Neely 1940: 83). Amongst the site were very many early Christian lintel graves, in one of which was found a set of weights and scales, although not of recognisably Viking type, is a set of artefacts commonly recovered from Viking graves (see for example the burials at Tarbert, Kiloran Bay and Scar in Scotland, and Kildale in England) (Neely 1940: 77).

Orry's Grave, Gretch Veg, Kirk Lonan

Unfortunately the details of the mound opened at Kirk Lonan during the nineteenth century are very patchy, and report the discovery of a sword along with the skeleton of a horse, an iron horse-shoe some teeth and crumbling bones and a piece of Neolithic pottery (Megaw 1937: 236).

Jurby Parish Church, Jurby

A further sword was discovered, and re-interred, while grave digging in Jurby parish churchyard (Megaw 1937: 235 & Plate 8, Bjørn & Shetelig 1940: 22). Fortunately a sketch of the sword hilt survives, although it is difficult to match it to any type (Megaw 1937: Plate 8). It has a tri-lobed pommel, similar to a Viking period sword recovered from a well near the wharf at Jutwerd, Holland, which Bjørn & Shetelig place in Petersen Type K and dates to the mid-ninth century (Bjørn & Shetelig 1940: 117 & Plate 77).

Balladoyne Churchyard, St John's

A sword (Petersen Type M, dated to 850-950) and scabbard, spear and shield were recovered by workmen from an early Christian cemetery of cist graves in 1937 (Megaw 1938). They seemed to have been lying in a pit with only a piece of human pelvis by the spear, which could mean that either the weapons had been redeposited after an earlier disturbance or the body had been placed into a simple grave or coffin which had rotted away (Megaw 1938: 12-13, Bjørn & Shetelig 1940: 26). Accounts of the excavation recognised that the burial was at the same stratigraphic level as the cist graves, perhaps suggesting contemporaneity (Megaw 1938: 12-13). Either way, it seems that the churchyard once held the remains of a Viking male.

Peel Castle, St Patrick's Isle

Recent excavation of the large Christian cist cemetery at Peel recovered some seven accompanied burials from the Viking period (Freke 2002: 66-71). Of these seven, two were children, the first accompanied by a copper-alloy bell and a necklace of six glass and two amber beads, the second with a silver half-penny of Eadred (dated 946-55) in his/her mouth (Freke 2002: 71). There was also recovered a multicoloured glass bead from the up-cast of the latter burial, which may or may not have been a purposeful deposition (Freke 2002: 71).

Of the four adults recovered it was the burial of a female that commands the most attention. She had been placed in her stone-pillowed, lintel grave with a goose wing, an iron cooking spit wrapped in cloth with herbs on top, a knife with a decorated silver handle still in its scabbard, a plain knife, shears, pieces of fabric which were thought to be parts of a shroud and pillow, a work bag with two needles, a necklace of seventy-one glass and amber beads, an comb of insular design, a pestle and mortar amulet, a pendant of two amber beads, and a pierced ammonite charm (Freke 2002: 66-9). It has been suggested that she was a local Celt buried by a Viking husband (Freke 1995: 17) – although there is no reason to suggest why she was not of Viking stock and married to a Celtic Christian who was carrying out her wishes albeit in a Christian cemetery.

The second adult was buried with a ring-headed pin, eighteen silver wire balls, a copper-alloy buckle and a strap-end (Freke 2002: 70). A coin of Edmund (dated 939-46) was recovered from the grave-fill (Freke 2002: 69-70). The silver wire spheres may have been the edging of a cloak, a style known to be extant in Scandinavia at that time (Freke 1995, Biddle & Kjølbye-Biddle 2001: 85-86). Such items of clothing and decoration have also been recovered from the churchyard at Repton (Biddle & Kjølbye-Biddle 2001: 85-86).

A further adult was found with four similar spheres, possibly decorating the sleeves of a garment (Freke 2002: 71). The fourth adult was found to have a ring-headed pin, a strap-end and a buckle, a comb and an iron awl (Freke 2002: 70). The fifth adult had been buried with a knife in a scabbard decorated by a glass ball, a copper-alloy buckle, a strap-end with a gilded copper-alloy plaque decoration, the remains of what could have been a box, four small rivets and some copper-alloy fragments (Freke 2002:70). An amber bead and a blue glass bead were also recovered from the grave-fill (Freke 2002: 70).

7.3.1 Isle of Man Burials: results

By far the largest number of 'Viking' burial mounds are situated in the northernmost district of Jurby where the best agricultural land is to be found and include the spectacular confirmed burials at Ballateare and Cronk Mooar (Andersson 1998: 3, Bersu & Wilson 1966). As expected on an island the size of the Isle of Man the burials are coastal, but do seem to be specifically spaced (Cubbon 1983), as if they were founder burials marking claims to land. Pagan Viking burials have also been recovered from extant Christian cemeteries; some like those excavated at Peel respecting the previously interred and others such as Balladoole which cuts straight through the Christian graves (Freke 1986: 102-105, Cubbon 1983: 16-18). Somewhat surprisingly there has yet to be found a Viking cremation on the Isle of Man, although it is worth speculating had the cenotaph at Claghbane been recovered more recently modern techniques may have proved it to be a cremation (Cubbon 1983). As the results stand, however, the lack of cremations is an important consideration on an island so apparently Scandinavian-influenced in other historical and cultural respects.

The Isle of Man is similar to the North of England in that there have been many pieces of weaponry recovered from churchyards, strongly suggestive of a one time accompanied burial. What is particularly striking is the number of Anglo-Saxon type swords recovered from Viking graves on the island. From the fourteen swords recovered, ten can be identified typologically. Six are from different groups (Petersen Types V, S, M, K, P and X), the remaining four belonging to the Anglo-Saxon Type L. Could this be down to a weapon-smith of Anglo-Saxon training working in the Isle of Man, or mementoes of raiding/trading in England during the late ninth-early tenth century?

The penchant continues for reuse of burial sites is shown at Ballateare, the site of Neolithic interments, and the Christian graveyard at Balladoole (Bersu & Wilson 1966:46, 4).

From the available data it seems that the demarcation of burial sites was dominated by the use of mounds. The burials at Balladoole and Ballateare were covered by a mound and excavation found remains of large post-holes which were thought to have been grave markers, similar to those found at Repton, Derbyshire (see chapter eight) (Bersu & Wilson 1966: 3, 46, Biddle & Kjølbye-Biddle 2001).

Unlike the rest of the British Isles and Ireland, there has yet to be found a single diagnostically identifiable female burial of Scandinavian type. This suggests intermarriage with resident groups, something perhaps augmented by the 'Pagan Lady of Peel' who was buried within the Christian cemetery with goods of Anglo-Scandinavian/Irish Sea origins, and therefore thought by the excavator to represent a Christian Celtic woman buried by a Norse husband (Freke 1986: 102-105, Graham-Campbell 1998: 119). The females recovered from the burials at Ballateare and Balladoole, as discussed above, were more than likely separate interments. The theory of intermarriage of Hiberno-Norse settlers with the resident female population is also supported by the Celtic names mentioned in runic inscriptions found on tenth century Christian monuments (Graham-Campbell 1998: 119, Page 1983). Unlike the islands of Scotland where children have been found buried in diagnostically pagan Viking fashion, young people have only been recovered from the Christian cemetery at Peel.

To date no large cemetery sites such as those as Kilmainham and Islandbridge in Dublin have been found on the Isle of Man, nor have smaller extended family type burial grounds like those in the Scottish Isles, although there are indications that Ronaldsway may have possibly provided such a site (Neely 1940, Higgins 1999).

7.3.2 Isle of Man Burials: conclusions

Perhaps surprisingly the burial evidence from the Isle of Man differs quite substantially from both Ireland and Scotland. With its geographical position in the Irish Sea it would seem to be safe to suggest that the Isle of Man is perfectly situated for the foundation of a colony; however there is nothing to suggest this from the burial record. It is perhaps its vulnerability to raids from Dublin and the Scottish Isles that prevented this. To date there has yet to be found a female burial of diagnostically identifiable Scandinavian type, or any cemeteries. There are however, many surviving memorial stones in graveyards which indicate intermarriage amongst the higher echelons of society, those family members commemorated bearing both Norse and Gaelic names (Fellows-Jensen 1983: 43). This situation is perhaps identifiable with the 'Pagan Lady' of Peel.

The presence of the four richly accompanied burials at Ballateare, Cronk Mooar, Balladoole and Knock y Doonee, suggests men of high social standing, interred by their followers in the manner representative of the upper end of Scandinavian society (Bersu & Wilson 1966, Kermode 1930).

From the available data, the burials seem to reflect and enforce the hypothesis that the ruling elite of the Isle of Man was replaced by incoming Viking raiders, who found a land well-populated, but small enough to control, and succeeded in introducing and maintaining a very strong Norse cultural milieu through intermarriage and social dominance.

7.4 Viking Burial in Ireland, Scotland and the Isle of Man: conclusions

From the above discussions it can be seen that there is a direct correlation between the manner of settlement undertaken by immigrant groups and the burial record. In Ireland and mainland Scotland, settlement was limited to the coastal areas by military means employed by the resident populations, resulting in the creation of colonies and thus enabling the perpetuation of some, but by no means all, aspects of funerary practice employed in the Scandinavian homelands. The parochial nature of settlement on the Northern and Western Isles of Scotland also resulted in the foundation of colonies, the natural geographical containment also allowing the maintenance of some parts of cultural practice. The larger presence of female graves bearing evidence of Scandinavian-influence in the Scottish Islands is vitally important when considering the perpetuation of cultural traits, since the chance of inter-marriage with resident groups diminishes, and therefore lessens the direct influence of non-Scandinavian traditions within a family unit. The vulnerability of the Isle of Man to attacks from Ireland and the Scottish Islands deterred colonial-type settlement, the distinct lack of female Scandinavian-influenced burials and presence of richly accompanied male inhumations in what were in all likelihood the centres of appropriated estates, combined with epigraphic evidence of intermarriage, reflects the hypothesis that the ruling elite of the Island was replaced by incoming Viking raiders, who had the power to maintain a very strong Scandinavian cultural milieu through social dominance.

This evidence has shown that the manner of settlement and resulting contact and interaction between immigrant and national communities during the Viking-period is demonstrated in the burial record of incoming groups. Using this knowledge and the evidence of assimilation drawn from archaeological and historical sources it should now be possible to analyse and better understand the Scandinavian-influenced burial record of the Viking–period in the North of England.

CHAPTER EIGHT – VIKING BURIALS IN THE NORTH OF ENGLAND

8.0 Introduction

This section will cover the central theme of the work and consider Viking burials in the counties of Northumbria, Cumbria, Westmorland, Lancashire, Yorkshire and Derbyshire.

As discussed in chapter one, even the most cursory glance through papers discussing Viking burial in England reveals a shared problem between academic authors; that of definition. This conundrum is directly derived from the habitual practice of treating Viking groups as being static representatives of a perceived social norm. This is of course untrue, and has been proved to be so in the previous chapters.

All current arguments (for example, Halsall 2000) are primarily concerned with the *scandinavianess* of the artefacts included in the funerary rite. Self-perpetuating problems then arise, such as ascertaining the socio-cultural or ethnic origin of the deceased via the adjudged *scandinavianess* of the grave goods (the difficulties with such associations are discussed in chapter six), without considering the fact that the people involved in the funerary ritual were not from a homogeneous socio-cultural group. Should the funerary deposition be judged lacking in *scandinavianess*, then in England the burial becomes an extremely late burial of national origin in a society Christianised for hundreds of years, an unthinkable scenario for like burials in Ireland or the rest of the British Isles in the same period. As it can be seen, problems of identification and definition swiftly become a morass of Gordian proportions. In order to allay this problem and incorporate the results of the previous chapters certain parameter must be set, from which meaningful hypotheses may be drawn. Rather than defining a possible Viking burial strictly via artefactual evidence alone, the funerary rites will be divided, into four identifiable types:

i. Traditional Burials (Type I) – the burials parallel those found in Scandinavia and/or other areas of the British Isles and Ireland. They contain identifiable Scandinavian goods of the period and conform to some aspects of the funerary rite practiced within the Scandinavian homelands (fig. 8.1).

ii. Accompanied Burials in Christian Cemeteries (Type II) – inhumations recovered from Christian graveyards accompanied by items associated with uses other than dress-fittings or small personal goods (fig. 8.3).

iii. Accompanied Burials of Viking Period Date in Christian Cemeteries (Type III) – as Type II., but accompanied only by dress-fittings and small personal goods (fig. 8.5).

A final section in appendix seven covers those burials and artefact finds recorded by antiquarians during previous centuries that may or may not represent the one time presence of a Viking burial. This chapter is also augmented by the quick reference database in appendix five and an illustrated gazetteer in appendix six. References to illustrations will be given in the text as *fig. A6.**, describing their positions within the appendix.

8.1 Traditional Burials (Type I) (fig. 8.1)

Hesket-in-the-Forest, Cumbria

During road widening in 1822 workmen were forced to dismantle a mound beside the turnpike road running from Penrith to Carlisle at Hesket-in-the-Forest (Hodgson 1832: 106). From sketches done at the time it seems that the mound lay to the east of the road (if one were travelling north), close to and within sight of a house called Cross Gaps (fig. A6.10) (Hodgson 1832: 106 & plate 1). According to local accounts of the mound's destruction, the tumulus was for the most part constructed of large stones, which had been variously robbed by farmers and road builders almost down to natural level (Hodgson 1832: 106). When the workmen began removing the remains of the cairn it was noted that the stones had been laid in a circle of a diameter of around twenty-two feet below the then level of the field (Hodgson 1832: 107). These larger stones were found to be surrounding a layer of cremation deposit of bones, charcoal and ashes, resting on a layer of natural sand (Hodgson 1832: 107) (see below for comparable use of sand at Heath Wood). It is recorded that the sand bore testament to contact with fire, indicating that the cremation was carried out *in-situ* (Hodgson 1832: 107). The whole area of cremation deposit was said to have covered some fourteen feet, with the artefacts piled on top, and slightly off centre (Hodgson 1832: 107). The entire hearth had been covered by large stones and packed with smaller ones, three of which were identified as being part of millstones, and a fourth, having two holes through its centre surrounded by an inscribed irregular pentagon (Hodgson 1832: 107 & Plate 1). The grave goods recovered were three decorated bone combs and their cases (unburnt) (fig. A6.13), a whetstone, a pair of iron spurs, a sickle, shield boss, axe head (fig. A6.11), a sword dated to the first half of the tenth century (Petersen Type O, Plate A6.12), a small spear with a decorated socket, a larger plain spearhead, a snaffle bridle-bit with copper-alloy fittings and still retaining the iron rein and cheek-piece attachments, a buckle and strap along with two further broken buckles from the bridle (Hodgson 1832: 108 & Plate II, Bjørn & Shetelig 1940: 19). All the metallic items in the grave bore marks of fire damage (Hodgson 1832: 107). All the artefacts barring the original spurs are held by Tullie House Museum, Carlisle.

The sword has a silver plated lower guard, engraved with an interlaced chain, of a type found on stone monuments in the Isle of Man, and had been ritually damaged, almost folded in two, and its tip further bent round against the blade (fig. A6.12) (Cowen 1934: 175-6, Hodgson 1832: 107). Both spearheads had also been bent, and the shield boss severely dented; the sickle also appears to have been bent (Hodgson 1832: 107). Analysis of the grave goods suggests that the burial took place sometime during the first half of the tenth century (Cowen 1934: 174-180).

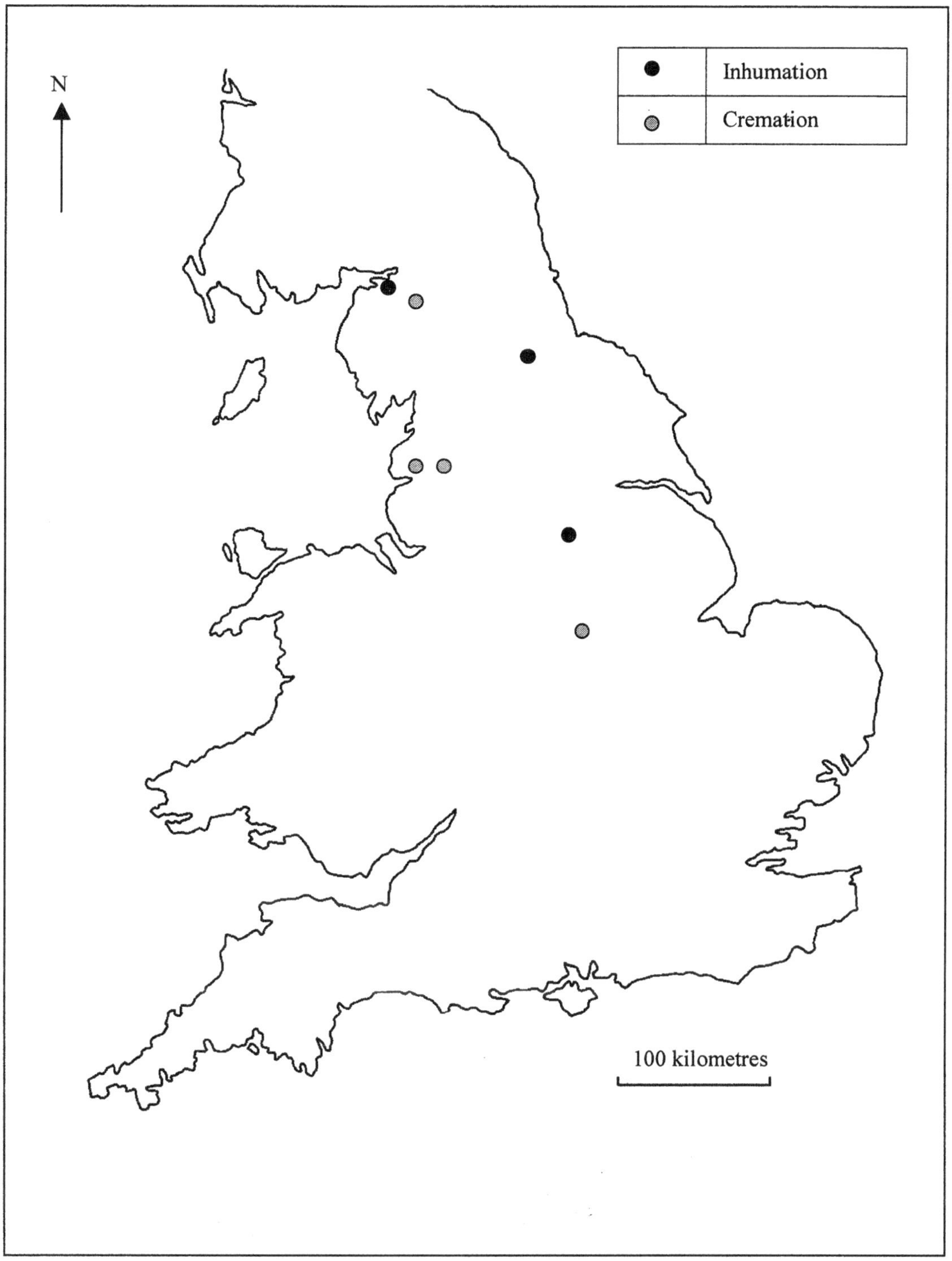

Fig. 8.1 *Traditional Viking Burials in the North of England*

The presence of the three bone combs and their cases in the burial is interesting, and may suggest that this had been the site of a dual cremation, that of a female and a male (fig. A6.13). Pairs of combs are generally found with female burials (for example, at Pierowall), whereas in male graves where combs are found they are always singular (for example, Skaill Bay). From the remaining grave-goods it is perhaps safe to assume that this was the cremation of a socially powerful man and most likely his horse. It is an archetypal Viking cremation grave. Its lone position beside what was in Viking times the Roman Road Watling Street (see also Bedale and Red House for comparative burials sites) is suggestive of a burial of a leader of a raiding band; buried in a fitting state by his followers and then left as they moved on across country to York or perhaps the Irish Sea, rather in the manner of Ibn Fadlan's description of the lone burial of the Rus Chief. It could also conceivably be a founder burial place near a boundary/liminal point of a claimed territory. On this point the place-name evidence is rather compelling, Hesket a word derived from the Norse, *hestr*, meaning horse and *skeið*, boundary (Fellows-Jensen 1985: 133).

Aspatria, Cumbria

In 1788 a large mound on top of Beacon Hill, Aspatria was levelled by the local landowner (fig. A6.1) (Rooke 1792: 112). The circumference of the tumulus was said to have been some ninety feet, giving a diameter of around twenty-eight feet, somewhat close to the size of the Hesket cairn (above) (Rooke 1792: 112). A cist was discovered some three feet below what was described as ground level (Rooke 1792: 112). Although not mentioned the cist seems to have been capped, as the account then clearly describes articulated remains of a large skeleton, accompanied by a sword (type unknown as the artefact is now lost and the surviving drawing shows it lacking the hilt) with a lower-guard ornamented by silver flowers similar to the hilt of the tenth century *Ulfberht* sword recovered from the Viking grave at Donnybrook (Petersen Type D, dated to the ninth-tenth century, see above) (fig. A6.2: 1) (Rooke 1792: 112, & Plate IV). Also recovered was an artefact of iron over eighteen inches long which was described as a dagger although from the contemporary drawings it appears to be either a single edged knife or more likely a spear, the grip/socket being found to have been studded with silver (fig. A6.2: 2) (see Ballateare above for similarly decorated spearhead) (Rooke 1792: 112, & plate IV). Close to the knife/spearhead was found a gold buckle and a gold ornamented strap-end of Carolingian style (fig. A6.2: 3 & 4) (Rooke 1792: 112). Also recovered were fragments of a shield, a damaged axe-head, an iron bridle-bit and part of an iron spur (fig. A6.2: 7 & 5) (Rooke 1792: 113). Unfortunately all these accompaniments of what appears to have been a male inhumation have been subsequently lost.

Two of the stones which formed part of the cist were found to be carved with prehistoric cup and ring marks, and various other linear and circular inscriptions, some of which were filled with crosses cut in relief to stand proud within four of the five circles, also carved in relief (fig. A6.2: 8) (Rooke 1792: 113 & Plate IV). The remaining marks on the stones are unintelligible, and probably still would be should the original stones ever be recovered, and may represent ritual carving or graffiti of a prehistoric or later date.

In 1997 two trenches were put into the top of Beacon Hill to precipitate the erection of a telecom mast (Abramson 2000). By chance the excavation fell within the exact area of the initial exploration and recovered many objects distributed through what appeared to be part of the infill of the original pit (Abramson 2000: 80). In the pit were found fragments of the left and right tibia of an adult (probably female) a copper-alloy ring-headed pin, an iron buckle and buckle-plate, a tin-plated strap guide, a folding knife, part of a spur, the top part of an axe head which appears to be that missing from the original, several unidentified pieces of iron, nails, and what are possibly the remains of an iron cauldron (fig. A6.3) (Langston 2000: 80-1, Ottaway 2000: 81-87).

From the surviving accounts and artefacts it seems that a late ninth, early tenth century Viking burial was placed into an earlier Bronze Age mound (see Claughton Hall, below). A less likely hypothesis is that there had been two people (male and female) interred in the Viking period, although the grave goods and antiquarian account do not seem to suggest this.

Again Aspatria seems to be a lone pagan burial, like Hesket, albeit a likely secondary inhumation. In the churchyard at Aspatria though there is a hogback tombstone, along with a Scandinavian style sculptured cross, suggesting perhaps a continuity of settlement (Lang 1984: 114, Bailey 1980). At least two items of Viking period jewellery have also been found in the Aspatria area, the terminal of a silver penannular brooch at Brayton, and a gold armlet found in a ditch, said to have been inscribed with the name '*Gerot*' in runes (Stephens 1884: 160). Aspatria as a place-name is recognised as Norse influenced by a Celtic word order and many surrounding places also bear Norse influenced names (Fellows-Jensen 1985).

Claughton Hall, near Garstang, Lancashire

In 1822 workmen employed in laying a new road close to Claughton Hall removed a small tumulus, and two to three feet below ground level found a pair of tenth century tortoise brooches (fig. A6.6), placed back to back in order to hold two beads (one blue glass, one red paste), a Carolingian style mount that had been converted into a brooch and a molar tooth (Jones 1849 in Edwards 1969: 109, Bjørn & Shetelig 1940: 15). Also found was an iron axe head, a hammer, sword, spear, a pot containing cremated bone and a small stone axe-hammer of Bronze Age date (Jones 1849 in Edwards 1969: 110). In the 1849 account read at the *Society of Antiquaries* it was said that the whole of the finds were enclosed in a 'wooden case' which may mean a coffin or perhaps a wooden chamber inside the mound (Jones 1849 in Edwards 1969: 110). The pot and stone axe head are undoubtedly Bronze Age and probably represent the primary burial. No mention was made of any further bones, cremated or otherwise, and it does seem likely that the bones were quickly destroyed by the sand which was said to have formed the mound (Edwards 1998: 15). The three brooches and beads are the only surviving artefacts, and are held in private hands (Edwards 1998: 16).

There can be little doubt that the Bronze Age tumulus at Claughton Hall contained a secondary burial of tenth century Viking type, possibly a double male and female burial, or a man buried with a keepsake of a female companion (Edwards 1998: 15).

Crossmoor, near Inskip, Lancashire

Workmen quarrying gravel at Crossmoor, near Inskip in 1889 discovered some ten feet below ground level an urn, parts of a sword and a dagger (fig. A6.7) (Fishwick 1891: 2-3). In the account of the discovery the pot was considered a funerary vessel even though no human remains were mentioned, although it apparently bore scorch marks presumably from a pyre (Fishwick 1891: 2-3). Of the artefacts only part of the sword remains (Petersen Type L, dated to around *c*900) (Edwards 1998; 21 fig. A6.7). The 'dagger' as Edwards suggests may have been a spearhead (Edwards 1998: 20-21). What is interesting is its proximity (around five miles) to the grave found at Claughton Hall (see above), which also contained a Viking-period sword, an urn and other artefacts of Viking period date (Edwards 1998: 20-21).

Leeming Lane, Bedale, Yorkshire

Early in the nineteenth century workmen on the road between Catterick and Piercebridge, near Bedale came across an inhumation buried in its centre at a very shallow depth of one to two feet (Anon 1848: 220). Accompanying the remains were a pair of mid-tenth century tortoise brooches and a spearhead (Anon 1848: 220). Contrary to the vivid description it seems unlikely that the incumbent had been murdered by use of the spear, despite its position in the centre of the chest (Anon 1848: 220). The mid-tenth century tortoise brooches were still *in-situ*, resting on the shoulders of the body (fig. A6.16) (Anon 1832: 220). The presence of the *in-situ* tortoise brooches suggests most strongly that this was the burial of a Viking female, made unusual with the addition of the spear to the grave-goods. As discussed above this mixing of male and female goods is not unusual, the cremation at Claughton containing both weaponry and tortoise brooches. There is also the possibility that the grave was at one time a double interment of male and female, the male remains disturbed and lost before the discovery of the latter, although there is nothing in the account that suggests disturbance.

The position of the burial in the centre of what was the line of the Roman road draws immediate parallels to the female interment at Red House Park, who lay beside a Romano-British track-way, very close to Dere Street (Speed 2003: pers. comm., see below).

Red House Park, Adwick-le-Steet, near Doncaster, South Yorkshire

During early 2001 archaeological excavation undertaken by Northern Archaeological Associates on behalf of Yorkshire Water discovered the poorly preserved remains of a diagnostically Scandinavian female grave (Speed 2003: pers. comm., NAA Archaeological Post-Excavation Assessment 2001). The remains were found lying in a south-westerly direction across a ditch running north beside what appeared to be a Romano-British track way (Speed 2003: pers. comm., NAA Archaeological Post-Excavation Assessment 2001: 01/64). The skeletal material was incomplete and damaged by ploughing; however, it was possibly to ascertain that they were that of a female around thirty-three to forty-five years at the time of death (Langston 2001: 51). Results of isotopic analysis from the teeth are still awaited (Cardwell 2003, pers. comm.). Accompanying the woman were two late ninth century tortoise brooches (fig. A6.20) (an unmatched pair, but of the same type), a severely plough-damaged decorated copper-alloy bowl (fig. A6.21), a small flat-backed knife and an iron latch-lifter (Speed 2003: pers. comm., NAA Archaeological Post-Excavation Assessment 2001: 01/64). The survival of textile fragments within the backs of the brooches strongly suggests they are the remains of the straps of a traditional Scandinavian type dress (Walton Rogers 2001: 46).

The burial is closely comparable to that of the female grave at Ballyholme, Co. Down, both containing tortoise brooches of the same type (Petersen Type 37/Rygh 647) and a copper-alloy bowl. A copper-alloy bowl and pair of tortoise brooches of the same type were also recovered from the rich female grave at Westness. Brooches of the same type have been recovered from Dublin, Three Mile Water Co. Wicklow, Valtos Uig, Pierowall Westray, Unst and a stray find of a pair from Orkney or the Hebrides (all sites discussed above).

The woman also lay in close proximity to a series of Romano-British burials, discovered prior to the excavation undertaken by NAA (Speed 2003: pers. comm., NAA Archaeological Post-Excavation Assessment 2001: 01/64).

Heath Wood, near Ingleby, Derbyshire (fig. A6.8)

The archaeological importance of the Viking cremation cemetery at Heath Wood cannot be underestimated. It is the only Viking cremation cemetery in the British Isles and Ireland, and the only dedicated Viking cemetery in England. It is also historically accountable being directly associated with the winter camp of the Great Army at Repton in 873-4.

Lying to the south of the River Trent on rising ground, the cemetery is made up of sixty-seven round barrows roughly arranged into four groups (fig. A6.8) (Richards 2003*a*: 170-1, Richards *et al* 1995: 58). Over the years approximately one third of the mounds have been subjected to some sort of archaeological investigation.

Bateman in his 1861 work, '*Ten Years Diggings…*' describes his opening of five of at least fifty mounds situated on the rising hillside, in 1855 (Bateman 1861 (1978): 72). He described the mounds as being consistent in shape and size, from seven to ten yards in diameter, at a height of two to three feet (Bateman 1861 (1978): 72). In the five mounds he opened were five cremation burials laying at ground level, with the human remains and ash gathered together to form a layer of an inch thick, evidence of being burned *in-situ* (Bateman 1861 (1978): 72). The cairns had apparently been built over the pyre before the fire was truly out, some of the stones still carrying scorch marks from where they had been placed on top (Bateman 1861 (1978): 72). The only artefacts Bateman recovered were an iron pin and a fragment of iron (Bateman 1861 (1978): 72).

The cemetery was again subjected to excavation during and just after the Second World War, when Clarke and Fraser (1946) opened seven of the mounds. In the first mound was the remains of a funeral pyre and skeletal remains which had apparently been subjected to crushing after cremation – something confirmed by modern analysis of the cremated animal bone recovered from the excavation during the nineteen nineties (Clarke & Fraser 1946: 4-6, Bond 2002, pers. comm.). The site of the cremation was surrounded by a ring of scorched stones, which had formed a hearth (Clarke & Fraser 1946: 4-6). Found with the bones were a sword of unusual type having the curved upper guard of a Petersen Type L (*c*900), but having a straight upper guard not found in Type L type classified swords (fig. A6.9), which bore the marks of ritual damage, a copper-alloy suspensory loop, an iron buckle and strap-slider, fragments of copper-alloy, four pieces of unidentifiable animal bone (thought to be possibly sheep and dog), seven ox teeth (unburnt) and a fragment of an ox's skull (also unburnt) (Clarke & Fraser 1946: 4-6, Leeds 1946: 14-16 & Plate

5: 15, Cave 1946: 10-21, Jackson 1946: 22). Unburnt fragments of an ox skull was also recovered from mound fifty during recent excavations (see below).

The second mound to be excavated was thought to be a natural feature, as no hearth, burial, grave-goods or any identifiable cairn structure was recognised (Clarke & Fraser 1946: 7).

The third mound, however, was found to contain a cremation, along with an iron buckle, two iron nails, pieces of copper-alloy sheets which may have been parts of a bucket, and a small piece of copper-alloy rod (Clarke & Fraser 1946: 3, Leeds1946: 16-17, Cave 1946: 20-1).

The fourth mound they excavated was by far the largest, and was constructed differently from the others being made of huge sandstone blocks and slabs (Clarke & Fraser 1946: 7-8). It was, however, apparently empty, devoid of hearth, bones or grave goods (Clarke & Fraser 1946: 7-8).

In the fifth mound the cremation had again been *in-situ*, and included the cremated remains of an ox or horse (Clarke & Fraser 1946: 8-9, Leeds 1946: 18, Cave 1946: 20-21, Jackson 1946: 22). The only artefacts recovered were two iron nails, possibly the remains of the funeral pyre (Clarke & Fraser 1946: 8-9, Leeds 1946: 18). Analysis of the human remains at the time suggested that they belonged to an adult female (Cave 1946: 21).

The sixth mound to be excavated was again found to contain an *in-situ* cremation, though this mound differed from the others as it had less pieces of sandstone incorporated within its structure (Clarke & Fraser 1946: 8-9, Leeds 1946:18, Cave 1946: 21-22). Whether this was consciously done by the people building the mound can only be guessed at. Animal bone was again present, probably the remains of a funeral feast or food for the deceased on their journey, in the form of unburnt ox and pig bones and a sheep's tooth (Cave 1946: 21-2, Jackson 1946: 22). Also surviving were three copper-alloy fragments, a small brooch that had been exposed to the fire, a copper-alloy strap-end, six iron nails and two iron buckles (Leeds 1946: 18).

The final mound to be excavated by Clarke *et al* (1949) contained a cremation hearth made of sandstone, a sword, again showing signs of damage, around twenty-four clenched iron nails that may have been part of a shield, or possibly part of the pyre construction, along with some fragments of iron (Clarke *et al* 1949: 78-79). The remains of the sword were sufficient to be ascribed to Petersen's Type H, the most common type of sword in Viking period Scandinavia, giving a wide date range of 800-950 (Leeds 1949: 80).

A further seven mounds were opened during the nineteen-fifties by Merrick Posnansky (Posnansky 1956). The first mound (mound nine) excavated was surrounded by a kerb, but on opening was found to have no hearth and no grave (Posnansky 1956: 43-44). Mound ten was again found to be built of substantial sandstone blocks, and was surrounded by a kerb, although like mound four was found to have no burial inside (Posnansky 1956: 44). In mound eleven a cremation hearth containing fragments of bone was found amongst the ashes of Holm oak, a tree species of Mediterranean origin (Posnansky 1956: 44-7, Levy 1956: 56). Rather than the pyre being built of this exotic species to the British Isles it is possible that something in the grave goods was made of it. Cremated animal bone was again found (from a dog, sheep or goat and a horse) along with an unburnt iron spade (perhaps used to build the mound) and a silver wire embroidered piece of head wear similar to those found at Birka, generally found on female headbands or male caps (Posnansky 1956: 44-47, Jackson 1956: 55, Crowfoot 1956: 52-53, Bond & Worley forthcoming). Analysis of the small amount of bone recovered from the pyre site suggests that the majority was removed after cremation (Bond & Worley forthcoming).

Mound twelve, although surrounded by a ditch and kerbstones was found to be empty (Posnansky 47-48).

Mound thirteen was constructed like mound ten, with large sandstone blocks and a surrounding ditch and kerb stones, although like ten it proved to be empty (Posnansky 1956: 48).

Mound fourteen was thought to have been a natural feature (Posnansky 1956: 43).

The final mound, fifteen, was found to be empty, although it had been surrounded by a ditch with a narrow berm between it and the tumulus (Posnansky 1956: 48).

During his excavations Posnansky noted that there was a V-shaped ditch running across the site, passing below mounds nine and twelve, and running in a north-easterly direction (Posnansky 1956: 48-49). A similarly shaped ditch was found during the excavations at Repton only two and a half miles away (see below). Several shards of rough handmade pottery were recovered from the fill of the ditch, which may be Viking or of an earlier date (Posnansky 1956: 48-50). It is not known whether the ditch forms part of a Viking entrenchment, as it was found to be at Repton, during their winter camp in 873-4.

It worth noting here that of the fifteen numbered mounds said to have been excavated between Clarke *et al* and Posnansky, neither record mound eight, which undoubtedly disturbed was not opened by them. It may have been one of those opened by Bateman (Richards *et al* 1995: 54).

During 1998-2000 the adjacent shallow mounds fifty and fifty-six were excavated (Richards 2003 *a* & *b*). Mound fifty was surrounded by a shallow ring ditch, and between a half and one metre of soil was removed before the original surface was revealed (Richards 2003*b*: pers. comm.). Directly above the cremation heath had been placed an unburnt jaw of a cow (Richards 2003*b*: pers. comm.). The unburnt pieces of an ox skull were also found in mound one by Clarke and Fraser (1946), discussed above. The cremation layer was found to contain the remains of a female and juvenile, accompanied by a silver sword mount decorated in the Trewhiddle style, parts of a shield, a knife, two copper-alloy tacks a hinge pivot from a chest, the complete remains of a horse, a dog, a side of pork, pieces of sheep or goat and cattle bone, along with many nails of three different sizes (Richards 2003*b*: pers. comm., Bond & Worley forthcoming). There were also recovered from the pyre tiny pieces of bone which may have come from a bird, or possibly a dog (Bond & Worley forthcoming). The whole deposit had been carefully raked together after cremation *in-situ* before the mound was built (Richards 2003*b*: pers. comm.). Beneath the cremation a layer of sand had been deposited (Richards 2003*a*: 184). A layer of sand beneath the cremation hearth was also reported at Hesket-in-the-Forest, discussed above. The use of sand in the cremation rite may be linked to the ancient ideas of resurrection associated with it, or more mundanely to prevent the spread of fire from the funeral pyre.

The smaller mound fifty-six was again surrounded by a ring ditch and excavated down to bedrock (Richards 2003*b*: pers. comm.). Unlike mound fifty there was no evidence for a funeral pyre, only a small deposit of burnt bone and charcoal and a ring-headed pin towards the edge of the mound (Richards 2003*b*: pers. comm., Richards 2003*a*). A small fragment of pig bone was identified from amongst the remains (Bond & Worley forthcoming). Richards suggests that the individual had been cremated elsewhere, and some of his or her remains from the funeral pyre was taken and deposited in the mound (Richards 2003*b*: pers. comm.). He also suggests therefore, that the partially excavated 'cenotaph' mounds from Heath Wood were in fact of this type, the single excavation trenches failing to include the small cremation deposits (Richards 2003*b*: pers. comm.). This view, however, is contra to the reports produced which deal with the cremated bone, the authors concluding that the human and animal bone both being removed from the pyre site (Bond 2003: pers. comm., Bond & Worley forthcoming).

In his conclusions Posnansky (1956: 50-51) saw the size of the cemetery at Heath Wood as the result of a settlement site of immigrants after the Alfred-Guthrum treaty, obviously finding it hard to come to terms with a winter camp accounting for some sixty deaths/mounds. However, there is no reason why not; injury, disease and starvation could all be responsible for the deaths of both soldiers and camp followers. The numbers of burials at Heath Wood may have been increased beyond 873-4 if Richards is correct in his hypothesis that the area became a kind of war cemetery where some of the ashes of people perhaps associated with the army who died and were cremated elsewhere were returned and buried by their friends or family (Richards 2003*b*: pers. comm.).

The paucity of artefactual remains along with the historically attested presence of the Great Army in the area provide no doubt that the cemetery at Heath Wood contains the remains of an itinerant people. It is likely that these people formed a separate group or perhaps a gathering of a particular sect across the army, whose primary funerary rite was cremation rather than inhumation, and preferred their dead to be treated differently than those interred within the Christian graveyard at Repton. Rather than perhaps displaying a threatening show of paganism to the resident Anglo-Saxon populace in the area they may have been enforcing their own identity within the Great Army itself.

8.1.1 Artefactual Analysis of North of England Traditional Burials

This section will consider the correlation and significance of the burials discussed above both as a discrete whole, and within the wider context of the rest of Britain and Ireland, and Scandinavia where appropriate. Owing to the nature of the analysis and in order to facilitate fluidity of structure where multiple sites will be compared within a sentence all general references to the sites are those listed in appendix five and will be provided at the end of the sentence in numerical form (for example, Hesket would be (1)). Where specific points are drawn from particular sources full references will be made in the standard fashion. Analysis of the sites will be undertaken in traditional comparative manner via burial rites and artefactual analysis. This has been done not only to glean information from the archaeological remains, but show that the divisions used above are extremely valuable and more helpful in understanding interaction between immigrant and settled groups.

From the discussion above it can be seen that Type I comprises of four cremations and three inhumation sites (fig. 8.1). Three of the four cremation sites are located in the north-west of England and the fourth, the cremation cemetery at Heath Wood, four kilometres south-east of the site of the winter camp of the Great Army over 873-4 at Repton (Richards *et al* 1995). There are no known Viking-period cremations east of the Pennines. Despite the numbers, the site at Heath Wood is a visible outlier, suggesting perhaps that those interments made in the north-west were carried out by people with links with the Hiberno-Norse, cremation being the predominant funerary rite in Norway during the Viking-period (see chapter three). As discussed in the previous chapter, cremations are similarly limited in number in Ireland and the Scottish Islands and to a single possible site on the Isle of Man (Claghbane), however, the rite was still being performed albeit in a much truncated form due entirely to the pervading socio-cultural influence of the time (chapter six). These influencing factors are discussed below.

Mounds marked the burials at Hesket, Aspatria, Claughton and the cemetery at Heath Wood (1, 2, 3, 7-23). No mound was remarked upon at Crossmoor, although the likelihood of the accompanying funerary urn being Bronze Age suggests that the burial was a secondary addition to an extant mound (4). Similarly at Claughton (less than eight kilometres away), the discovery of a Bronze Age stone axe-hammer, cinerary urn and bones also strongly suggest that this interment too was placed in a much older burial mound (3). The presence of the prehistoric cup and ring marked stones forming part of the cist within the mound at Aspatria, along with the recovery of a pair of female tibiae could also be seen as evidence of re-use of the site of an earlier burial (2).

From the available records it is apparent that the mound at Hesket was constructed in a way similar to those at the cemetery at Heath Wood, its hearth surrounded by a ring of large stones whose diameter of 6.7 metres falls within the range of 6.7-13.7 metres at the Derbyshire site (Clarke and Frazer 1948: 4, Hodgson 1832: 107). Unfortunately the robbing of stone from the mound at Hesket left it impossible to know the region of its original height; those at Heath Wood varying in modern times between 0.46 and 1.52 metres (Clarke and Frazer 1948: 4, Hodgson 1832: 106-7). No records survive pertaining to the dimensions of the mounds at Crossmoor and Claughton; although the 'depth' of 0.6-0.9 and 3 metres referred to in the earliest accounts of Claughton and

Crossmoor respectively may in fact refer to the height (Jones 1849 in Edwards 1969: 109, Fishwick 1891: 2-3).

The circumference of the mound at Aspatria was said to have been some 27.4 metres, giving a diameter of 8.5 metres, somewhat close to that of the Hesket cairn (Rooke 1792: 112). Within the mound the inhumation and grave goods were sealed in a capped cist, unlike any of the other accompanied Viking-period internments discussed in this chapter (2). A likely Viking cremation at Templemoyle, Limavady (Co. Londonderry) was found in a cist covered by a large cairn (NISMR, chapter seven), and the use of cists are frequently found in the Scottish Islands, for example the inhumations at Pierowall, Westray; Westness, Rousay and Machrins Machair, Colonsay (250, 133, 146, 215). Cists were also recorded on the Isle of Man at Knock-y-Doonee, Ballachrink and Ballelby (92, 101, 107). Interestingly there are no cist burials on Iceland, despite their use in Scandinavia, especially Norwegian graves (Eldjárn 1984: 8).

The use of mounds as a burial marker is extremely common in Scotland, Ireland and the Isle of Man, whether the mound was constructed at the time of the Viking-period internment, or the re-use of an earlier structure. Grave 1 at Pierowall, Westray, was a secondary burial in a prehistoric mound, as was that at Housegord, Weisdale, Shetland (130, 173). The remains of a broch was used to demarcate a female inhumation at Castletown, Caithness, and the ruinous mound of an abandoned Norse farmstead used at Buckquoy, Orkney (124, 161). At Westness, Rousay a Pictish cemetery was re-used by Norse settlers for the internment of their dead (146-7).

Re-use of earlier burial sites by Norse groups is also in evidence on the Isle of Man: at Ballateare, the Viking-period mound was built on a burial site of the Neolithic Ronaldsway-Culture; the burial at Balladoole badly disturbed an early Christian cemetery then in use; and the site of Ronaldsway itself, where an eclectic mix of Pre-historic and Viking-period remains have been found (89, 91, 110). In Ireland the burials at Church Bay, Rathlin Island (Co. Antrim), re-used an area devoted to burial from the Bronze Age to early Christian times; the cremation at Templemoyle, Limavady (Co. Londonderry), was a secondary interment in a prehistoric burial mound (218, 250). Prehistoric burials are also known form the area around Cloghermore Cave, Tralee (Co. Kerry); a further Bronze Age mound was used at Croghan Erin (Co. Meath); and the Dublin sites of Kilmainham, Islandbridge and Donnybrook were all used as Christian burial grounds before the establishment of the Longport (241, 249, 226-31, 225). Prehistoric burials were also recovered from the College Green, Dublin (233).

Clearly, across the British Isles and Ireland those Scandinavian people responsible for the disposal of dead members of their community were very aware of the ritual landscape, and were keen to re-use areas already containing burial sites; either to make a socio-political point with regard to power and control of people and land (past and present), or more simply a respect and adherence to the special places set aside to house the dead (this theme is continued with the use of extant Christian cemeteries, below Type II and III).

At Heath Wood, especially with its connection with the wintering of the Great Army at Repton nearby, there is a tendency to believe that the creation of the cemetery was pristinely undertaken during and immediately following 873-4. However, closer examination of the archaeological data may suggest otherwise. As argued above the evidence suggests that the Viking-period cremations at Claughton and Crossmoor have been placed within earlier Bronze Age mounds; meaning that the actual funeral pyre was built away from the place of deposition, the cremated bone and artefacts gathered and interred within the extant mound. At Hesket the hearth/pyre was *in-situ*, and the cairn and the mound constructed above. At Heath Wood there seems to be a combination of rites being carried out; some mounds containing funerary hearths like Hesket (for example, mound 1); and others apparently devoid of hearth, human or animal remains, or artefacts (for example, mound 9); and some containing partial remains of a cremation pyre (for example, mound 56) (1, 3, 4, 7-23). In the final case Richards suggests that these small collections of remains are being brought in and buried from elsewhere, contra to the researchers responsible for analysing the cremated animal and human bone, who see the remains being those left by people gathering pyre debris to take away (Richards pers. comm., Bond pers. comm.). Either way, the position of the cremation fragments at the edge of the mounds suggests that in some cases the mounds pre-date the cremated remains of the Viking-period, that is the secondary deposit of human remains. It is the author's view that many of the sixty-seven mounds (fig. A6.8) are in fact Bronze Age in date, some of which were re-used and the area interspersed with mounds constructed during the Viking-period. Full excavation of the Heath Wood site may validate or refute this claim. That the site was being used in the prehistoric period there was no doubt, Posnansky's excavations discovering the line of a V-shaped ditch, passing below mounds 9 and 12 in a north-easterly direction (fig. A6.8), the fill of which was found to contain fragments of prehistoric pottery (Posnansky 1956: 48-50).

A final point which also supports this hypothesis, and links with the re-use of burial sites by Scandinavian-influenced groups, lies with the site at Hesket. The mound appeared to be a pristine construction during the Viking-period, although examination of early eighteenth century topographical accounts describe it to be in the vicinity of four prehistoric tumuli, evidence to suggest the recognition and use of the ritual landscape by Scandinavian-influenced groups involved in the disposal of the dead man (and possibly female) (Hutchinson 1794-97 (1974) vol. I: 505).

The remaining two inhumations belonging to the Type I group, Leeming Lane and Red House, were not marked in any way (5, 6). They were both, however, directly associated with roads. The female inhumation found at Leeming Lane was discovered while road repair was being undertaken during the nineteenth century (5). The remains lay at a shallow depth in what was originally the line of the Roman road leading to Catterick and Piercebridge (Margary 1967, 5). Similarly, the female inhumation at Red House lay in a grave-cut across a ditch beside a Romano-British track-way, linking a settlement site to the road between the forts at Burghwallis and Castleford (Margary 1967, 6). Despite their lack of physical markers, the position in the archaeological landscape of Leeming Lane and Red House is directly linked with the other five sites of the Type I group via their association with transport routes. The mound at Aspatria overlooks the route from the Roman occupied sites of Maryport and Old Carlisle (fig. A6.1); Hesket, the route from Carlisle to Penrith (A6.10), and Claughton is adjacent to Galgate, the Roman road from Ribchester to Lancaster (Margary 1967). Crossmoor cannot be allied directly to any route, but lies eight kilometres west of Claughton, between the Roman roads running between Ribchester and Poulton-le-Fylde and the Preston to Lancaster route (Margary 1967: 374-7, 392). The cemetery at Heath Wood lies on the Trent Valley, the *Anglo-Saxon Chronicles* and excavations at Repton clearly illustrating the use of this riverine route by Scandinavian raiders (39-43, 81, 7-23).

Within the Type I group Heath Wood is the only cemetery (indeed, the only known Viking-period cremation cemetery in the British Isle and Ireland), although it is highly likely that both Claughton and Hesket contained multiple burials, as seen in mound 50 at Heath Wood (1, 3, 22). The recovery of female tibiae at Aspatria could suggest that there had been initially a male and female inhumation, although the description if the cist opening only refers to a single set of skeletal remains, and the artefactual evidence points to a male inhumation; a combination of goods being present in Scandinavian Viking-period graves where males and females have been interred together (contra Ballateare, see chapter seven) all of which points to a single Viking-period deposition (Shetelig 1910, chapter three) (2). Other than mound 50 at Heath Wood, where modern assessment of the cremation remains has identified the presence of a female and juvenile, sexing has been dependent of the type of artefacts interred with the deceased (the author knows of only one case in the whole of Scandinavia where a female was interred with a sword[1]). Where ascertainable the demographic spread at Heath Wood is three male, three female and a juvenile (7-23). At Crossmoor the sword and spearhead suggest the presence of a male (4). Similarly the weaponry at Hesket makes it extremely likely that the mound contained the cremation pyre of a socially powerful male, although the presence of three combs and their cases suggests that there might have also been a female present; single combs being found in male graves (see chapter seven and appendix five on the Scottish burials), pairs in females. The presence of weaponry and tortoise brooches at Claughton also suggests double interment, the selection of brooches (undamaged by fire) place into the mound after the cremation had been carried out (3). There are no comparable surviving finds of tortoise brooches from Heath Wood; suggesting either that the corroded fragments of earlier, pre-modern excavations were not recognised (damaged by fire or not); brooches were not placed in the interment or that tortoise brooches were not owned/worn by the females who were interred at Heath Wood. A final scenario is that the jewellery from Claughton (tortoise brooches, Carolingian mount and beads) were a keepsake, added to the burial of a cremated male; or perhaps *vice versa*, the weaponry interred with a female (3).

At Red House there is no doubt that the female inhumation was a single deposit in a single cut (6). The account of the recovery of the inhumation from Leeming Lane quite clearly relates the presence of a single skeleton, with the tortoise brooches *in-situ* just below the shoulders (5). The spear-head was laying amongst the bones of the rib-cage, leading to speculation that the female had been murdered, a hypothesis easily refuted (see above) (5). The fact still remains, however, that here is an inhumation with both male and female grave-goods, an occurrence repeated here and nowhere else in the British Isles or Ireland. It may well be that the spear-head was of some special significance to the woman, and was interred with her for reasons known only to herself and the people laying her to rest.

A final point relating to the physical positioning of the burials in the landscape is that all Type I burials lie beyond the boundaries of Viking-period settlements. Only the burial at Aspatria, lying just outside the village on the hill (fig. A6.1), can be associated with a settlement site. Interestingly, the place-name Apsatria (*Patrick's ash*) , first recorded *c*1160 is made up of elements reflecting Celtic word order; the specific being the Irish saint's name, Patrick, the generic being in some cases written as being derived either from the OE appellative *æsc* (ash tree) or the OScand. cognate *askŕ* (ash tree) (Fellows-Jensen 1985: 214). This is surely evidence of a place-name being used in a bi-lingual community, the speakers in this case influenced also by the Gaelic of the Irish Sea region (including Stratchclyde) (see chapter five). In the churchyard at Aspatria are also five Viking-period crosses and a hogback (see chapter five, Bailey 1980). Also a number of Viking-period artefacts are known to have been found in the area (see chapter five and appendix four), including a gold armlet bearing a runic inscription and a silver penannular brooch (see chapter five and appendix four).

All the sites except the inhumation at Red House produced items of weaponry. Swords were recovered from Hesket, Aspatria, Claughton, Crossmoor, and Heath Wood (1-5, 7, 13). Spears were recovered from Hesket (two), Aspatria, Claughton, Crossmoor and Leeming Lane (1-5). Somewhat surprisingly, given the numbers recovered from graves across the rest of the British Isles (including the Type II group) and Ireland, no evidence for any spear-heads has been forthcoming from the cremation cemetery at Heath Wood (7-23). It is possible that the many recorded iron fragments in early excavation reports contained spears, although the standards of excavation were high, and two spear-heads survived the funerary pyre at Hesket (7-23, 1). The spear-heads from Hesket are still extant (in the Tullie House Museum, Carlisle) and demonstrate evidence of both ritual damage (killing) and heat. The larger of the two spear-heads (L=44.8cm) (appendix six) (Petersen Type I) is missing its tip, although some of the seven rivet holes in its socket still contain fragments of copper-alloy rivets (1). The second spear-head is much smaller (L=27.9cm) and has been identified as belonging to the Petersen Type F group (1). It has been bent in the middle of the blade, and its socket is decorated by six closely spaced rings, each pierced by a pair of rivet holes, in one of which a single copper-alloy rivet remains (1). The author cannot at present identify similar type spears in the British Isles or Ireland, although the corroded nature of many surviving specimens and variation in manufacture of such a common weapon defies in many cases allocation of standard typologics. Sadly the spear-heads from Aspatria, Claughton, Crossmoor and Leeming Lane are all lost. The surviving drawings of the spear-heads from Aspatria and Claughton do not aid further identification (fig. A6.2: 2, Richards 2000: plate 19).

[1] Häme, Finland; female interred with two swords (Edgren 2000: 115). Carpenter's tools and arrowheads occur in female graves in western Norway (Dommasnes 1982).

Unlike spears, swords are more easily associated with standard typological groups, probably owing to their production being undertaken within a limited number of specialist workshops. As with the spears, the sword at Hesket (fig. A6.12) bears testament to ritual damage, the blade being folded almost flat, and also the heat of the pyre (1). Although the pommel knob is now missing it is identifiable as a Petersen Type O (900-50) (fig. A6.12) (1). The lower guard still bears traces of silver-plating decorated with a ring-chain pattern, the likes of which are found on Viking-period stone sculptured monuments in the Isle of Man (Cowen 1934: 175-6) (1). It is likely that the upper guard was also decorated in the same manner, but the heat from the pyre makes it hard to ascertain. The only other Petersen Type O sword recovered from a funerary context in the British Isles forms part of an unprovenanced grave assemblage found on Eriskay during the eighteenth century (see chapter seven) (202). There are no known Petersen Type O swords in Ireland (Walsh 1998). In England Type O swords have been dredged from the River Kennet at Reading and the River Thames at Kew (Peirce 2002: 90). Only eleven of this type was listed by Petersen in his 1919 Scandinavian corpus (Peirce 2002: 90).

The sword from the burial at Aspatria is now lost, the surviving sketch (fig. A6.2: 1) shows only the lower guard extant, which is described as being decorated with silver flowers (2). The information is not sufficient to allocate a specific type amongst the swords of the Viking-period. Similarly the surviving water-colour of the sword recovered from Claughton, which is now also lost, depicts a weapon which is of medieval rather than Viking-period date, suggesting a degree of artistic licence (Edwards 1969, Richards 2000: plate 19) (3).

The sword from Crossmoor still survives (fig. A6.7), and is of Petersen Type L (*c*900), the detached lower half of the blade perhaps owing to ritual damage (see fig. A6.12, Hesket sword, being similarly broken). Metallurgical analysis could be employed to ascertain whether or not the sword has been exposed to heat. A Petersen Type L sword bearing evidence of fire-damage was also recovered from mound 1 at Heath Wood (fig. A6.9) (7). The Type L sword is also known as the *Anglo-Saxon* type, and was introduced into Scandinavia via contact with the British Isles. Of the fourteen listed by Petersen (1919) in Norway, they are principally found in Vestfold (Walsh 1998: 233). They are a very common discovery within graves, occurring in Type II group sites at Repton and Camp Hill; and at Torbeckhill, Kirkcudbright (fig. 7.3), Ballachrink, Ballaugh, St Maughold and Ballabrooie on the Isle of Man (see below & chapter seven) (38-43, 118, 101-103, 105). There has yet to be found a Type L sword in a Viking-period burial in Ireand, although ten exist from other provenances (Walsh 1998: 233-4).

The most common type of Viking-period sword in Scandinavia are Petersen Types H (800-950) and its very similar derivative type I (850-900) (Petersen 1919). A fire-damaged sword of Type H was recovered from mound 7 at Heath Wood (13). A sword of Type H (or possibly the very similar I) accompanied the inhumation at Tendley Hill, (Type II, see below); and Type H swords were recovered from Scar, Sanday and Ballinaby, Islay (chapter seven) (26, 148-50, 183). Sixteen swords of Type H (two of Type I) were found at the cemetery sites of Kilmainham and Islandbridge, Dublin (Walsh 1998:230).
Shields were recorded as being found at Hesket, Aspatria and Heath Wood (1, 2, 7-23). The loss of the shield from Aspatria denies further evaluation. The surviving shield-boss from Hesket is of the Irish Sea conical type (850-900) and bears evidence of fire damage and ritual killing in the form of a large dint. A shield-boss of this type also survives from the inhumation at Ormside (Type II, below); Kiloran Bay, Colonsay; Ballinaby, Islay (fig. A7.10); and Lamlash, Arran (27, 179, 183, 187). At least twenty survive from the cemetery sites of Kilmainham and Islandbridge (Bøe 1940: 35-8). The fragmentary remains of the shield from mound 50 at Heath Wood may not be the only example from the site; the presence of clenched nails, charred-wood and iron fragments found during earlier excavations possibly all that remain of a fire damaged artefact (7-23).

Axes were recovered from Hesket, Aspatria and Claughton; unfortunately the weapons from the latter pair are now lost, although a fragment of the socket from Aspatria was recovered during the 1997 excavation (fig. A6.5: 5) (1-3). The axe-head from Hesket (fig. A6.11) belongs to the Petersen Type E group (Rygh 561) (late ninth, through to the eleventh century), a type commonly discovered as stray finds in England, but more specifically occurs in a likely grave at Repton and possibly at Pippin Castle (figs. A8.7, A8.8) (both Type II, see below) (43, 31). The surviving illustration of the axe from Kildale (fig. A6.15: 6) also appears to show a weapon of similar type (33-7). Two axes of this type were recovered from the cemetery sites of Kilmainham and Islandbridge (Bøe 1940:32-3). Axe-heads are a very common find from graves both in Scotland and the Isle of Man (see chapter seven).

The remaining artefact types found at more than one site are riding accoutrements (Hesket and Aspatria) and tortoise brooches (Leeming Lane, Red House and Claughton) (1-2) (5, 6, 3). The riding gear at Hesket is comprised of an iron bridle-bit, which like the other iron artefacts shows evidence of being on the funerary pyre, pieces of melted copper-alloy still adhering to the rings in places; iron buckle fragments from the bridle, and a pair of spurs which are now lost (1). The bit is of plain snaffle type with barred rings, and iron rein and cheek piece attachments surviving on the left ring. At Aspatria the bit survives only in pictorial form (fig. A6.2: 7). It is again of snaffle type, with this time a twisted mouth-piece from which are drawn the holes attaching the cheek-pieces and rein. Again there are bars, which appear to have been slotted through the mouth-piece at each end, just before the rings. Unlike the plain Hesket bars, they have been hammered into a design not unlike the two upward curling petals of a *fleur des lis* (fig. 6.2: 7). The iron spurs described, and pictured from Aspatria (fig. A6.2: 6) is of the plain prick type; there is no evidence of a rowel. A spur fragment was recovered from the 1997 excavation (fig. A6.3: 4) (2). Spurs were also reported as being found at Kildale (Type II, below), although they were subsequently stolen with the rest of the artefacts during the nineteenth century (37).

At neither Hesket nor Aspatria were any equine remains reported (1, 2). This may sound unlikely and horse-bones were recovered from alongside tack at Kiloran Bay, Colonsay; Pierowall, Westray and Ballindalloch, Morayshire (179, 135, 129). However, at

Balladoole, Isle of Man, no equine remains were reported alongside the discovery of riding equipment, including spurs of Carolingian type (91). Animal bones and a horse-shoe were found at Kirk Lonan, Isle of Man, and two horse-shoes (now lost) were recovered from the Pippin Castle site in Yorkshire (Type II, see below) (111, 31). There is of course the chance that the animal bone was disregarded at both Hesket and Aspatria, more especially at the former where it would have been cremated (1, 2). The remains of cremated horse bone has been identified at Heath Wood in mounds 5, 11 and 50, although no riding accoutrement have been discerned (11, 17, 22). Heath Wood is the only site of the Type I groups to have had animal bone finds recorded, probably owing to its more recent and modern excavations; a fact repeated at Repton (Type II, below), the only other site to have recorded animal bone from a Viking-period grave (39). The recovery of cremated animal bone (including horse) from the mound fill at Ballateare, Isle of Man, should be seen as the remains as an unrelated occurrence, perhaps an earlier disturbed burial (see chapter seven for discussion) (89). A piece of unworked rib from a whale (fig. A8.6) was recovered from the site at Pippin Castle, along with a bovine humerus from the right leg (see below & appendix 8).

The site at Heath Wood also produced the cremated bone of sheep and dog, and the uncremated bone of ox, pig and again sheep, which are probably representative of the remains of a funerary feast placed on the burnt-out pyre (11, 12, 17, 22, 23). The jaw-bone of a cow was recorded with an accompanied inhumation from Islandbridge, Dublin, in 1934, along with a further burial found to contain two teeth, one of a horse, the other an ox (Bøe 1940: 59).

The tortoise brooches in the female inhumations at Leeming Lane (fig. A6.16), Claughton (A6.6) and Red House (fig. A6.20) find parallel in England with those in the grave find at Santon Downham, Norfolk; where the double interment of a male and female was accompanied by a sword (Petersen Type L) and the tortoise brooches (Rygh 652-4) (Bjørn & Shetelig 1940: 12-13). The surviving brooch from Leeming Lane (fig. A6.16) and pair from Claughton (fig. A6.6) are also of type R652 (900-50), a very common design, also found in the graves at Reay, Caithness: Dunrobin Castle, Golspie, Sutherland; Opisdale House, Durnoch, Sutherland; one of the unmatched pair from Longhills in Westerseat, Caithness; Tiree; Cnip, Lewis (figs. A7.8-9); Ballinaby, Islay (fig. A7.11) and Three Mile Water, near Arklow, Co. Wicklow (114, 121, 123, 128, 198, 180, 207, 245). The tortoise brooches from Red House, although a pair of the same type (R647), are slightly different, one belonging to the sub-group Petersen 37.2 and the other P37.3 (6). Late ninth-century brooches of this type were also recovered from Unst (singly); Bhaltos, Uig and Pierowall, Westray (171, 204, 131). Three pairs and two further single examples were recovered from Kilmainham and Islandbridge (Bøe 1940: 38-40). Most strikingly, the Type R647 tortoise brooches were also found along with a copper-alloy bowl, like Red House, at Ballyholme, Co. Down and Westness, Rousay, suggestive perhaps of a common origin of all three women and the people responsible for the interments (222, 146).

The fragmentary remains of an iron cauldron, including the rim, were recovered from the site of the Aspatria burial during the excavations in 1997, and copper-alloy fragments though to be part of a vessel rim were found in mound 3 at Heath Wood (2, 9). Cauldrons were also recovered from the male inhumations at Kiloran Bay and Machrins Machair Colonsay; Ballinaby, Islay(fig. A7.10) and Knock-y-Doonee, Isle of Man (179, 216, 182, 92). It is worth speculating that the bowl recovered from the churchyard at Ormside, also site of a Type II burial (see below) once accompanied an inhumation (27).

Unlike the Scandinavian influenced burials of the Viking-period in Scotland, only Hesket within the Type I group was recorded as having combs amongst the funerary goods (1). The three bone combs and cases (fig. A6.13) were unburnt, apparently placed on the site o the hearth when the cremation pyre had ceased to burn (1). Bone combs were recovered from Cambois (fig. A6.4: 2), Ripon and Heysham (fig. A6.14) (Type III, see below). A fragment of a comb tooth was also recovered from the fill of a grave in York Minster (see below, YM 58). Bone combs are a common find in Viking-period burials and from the domestic contexts, for example, in York. Of the many recorded from the Scottish burials (see chapter seven & appendix five) a pattern can be ascertained; pairs of combs are generally found with female interments (for example, three at Pierowall, Westray) and single examples with male (for example, Skaill Bay, Orkney) (133, 165, 130, 165). It seems reasonable to suggest therefore, that Hesket may have contained the cremation of both a male and female. The single comb finds at Heysham, Cambois and Ripon are all within burial contexts far different from the Type I group and the Scottish burials, and variations in burial rite therefore expected (see above for definition of group type and below for association) (44, 52, 53).

Hesket was also the only one of the Type I sites from which a whetstone and sickle were recovered (1). Whetstones are a common find amongst the Scandinavian-influenced graves in Scotland (see chapter seven & appendix five); and in Ireland whetstones were found at Islandbridge, Dublin; Templemoyle, Limavady, Co. Londonderry; Cloghermore Cave, Tralee, Co. Kerry and on the Isle of Man at Balladoole (231, 250, 241,91). In England whetstones were recovered from Kildale (now lost), and Pippin Castle (fig. A8.3) (37, 31). A stone with a silver suspension mount at Carlisle Cathedral grave 251, and a smaller pendant form from the adolescent male inhumation at St Mary's Bishophill Junior, York (47, 72). The latter is paralleled by the inhumation of a child at Cnip, Lewis, where beads also accompanied the burial (208). It is also possible that the whetstone pendant and beads found at Housegord, Shetland, also formed the burial of a child (173). Such miniature whetstones may be particular to Scandinavian-influenced graves of children of the Viking-period in the British Isles.

The cremation at Hesket was also the only Type I site to produce a sickle, which, as with the other iron artefacts, shows evidence of fire damage (1). The only other recorded occasion in England where a sickle has been recovered from a Scandinavian-influenced Viking-period burial was from the inhumation in Wensley churchyard (Type II, see below) (32). They are, however, a common find in Scotland, occurring in the better appointed male and female graves (see chapter seven & appendix five). They have been recovered from at least nine sites; Reay, Caithness;

Broch of Gurness, Orkney; Wetness, Rousay (fig. A7.4); Scar, Sanday; Pierowall, Westray; Cnip, Lewis (fig. 7.8); Kiloran Bay, Colonsay; Cruach Mhor, Islay; and Kildonan, Eigg (115, 155, 146, 149, 144, 207, 179, 185, 188). Sickles were also recovered from the cemetery site at Islandbridge, Dublin; but as yet, no examples are known from the Isle of Man (231).

Although well-equipped with martial accoutrements, Hesket was apparently devoid of any personal ornaments, despite the suggestion that the cremation may have been of both a male and female (1). This may be due to recovery or the heat of the funeral pyre, although the perishable combs had been placed in the burial once the fires had been extinguished, as the brooches as Claughton had (1, 3). Similarly the cremation cemetery at Heath Wood has produced little in the way of jewellery, the remains of a small copper-alloy fibula recovered from mound 6, a ring-headed pin from mound 56, and a fragment of a silver-wire head-band from mound 11, which has no parallel in the British Isles or Ireland, but occurs within the Scandinavian homelands, for example in graves at Birka (Crowfoot 1956: 52-3) (12, 23, 17). No similar items were reported as being found at Crossmoor (4). A ring-headed pin was also recovered from Aspatria during the 1997 excavation (fig. A6.3:1) (2). Other than Heath Wood and Aspatria, ring-headed pins are found in only two other grave-contexts in England; Brigham (Type II) and Carlisle Cathedral grave 242 or 244 (Type III) (25, 48) (see below). They are extremely common in the graves of Scotland, occurring at fourteen sites (see chapter seven & appendix 5). Ring-headed pins are also found at five of the nineteen burial sites on the Isle of Man, and at Larne, Co. Antrim; Cloghermore Cave, Tralee, Co. Kerry; and at the Dublin cemetery sites Kilmainham and Islandbridge (see chapter seven & appendix five) (217, 241, 231). Ring-headed pins are found in pre-Viking Irish contexts, and it seems safe to suggest that the style was introduced into northern England by the Hiberno-Norse; correspondingly, Heath Wood is the only English site where a ring-headed pin was found that is not on the Irish Seaboard.

The tortoise brooches at Claughton (discussed above) were accompanied by a Carolingian silver-gilt and nielloed scabbard mount which had been converted into a brooch by the addition of a hinged pin (3). It is an original object within the British Isles and Ireland, although items with their origins within the Carolingian Empire are known from grave contexts, such as the gold buckle and strap-end from Aspatria (lost) (fig. A6.2: 3); the copper-alloy buckle from Kildonan, Eigg; and spear-heads from the Dublin sites of Kilmainham and Islandbridge (2, 188, 231). The disc-brooch from Cambois (Type II, see below) is also paralleled in Carolingian contexts (fig. A6.4: 1) (44). A pair of Carolingian style spurs were recovered from the boat burial at Balladoole, Isle of Man (91).

Small knives were recovered from Aspatria, Red House and Heath Wood (2, 6, 22). The knife from Aspatria recovered in 1997 is a folding type (A6.3: 3), similar to ones found at Repton (grave 511, Type II, see below) and Carlisle Cathedral (grave 251, Type III, see below) (2, 39, 47). The knives of domestic type from Red House and Heath Wood are similar to knives from the Type II group (see below) at Kildale (lost, fig. A6.15: 5), Wensley, Ormside (lost), and Type III group (see below) at Repton (grave 203) (whose wire bound handle draws immediate comparison to the description of the Kildale knife), Ripon (Ailcy Hill grave group 1064) and the grave of the adolescent male at St Mary Bishophill Junior, York (37, 32, 27, 81, 51, 72). Knives are extremely common in the graves across the rest of the British Isles and Ireland (see chapter seven & appendix five).

The recovery of an iron hammer-head from the Claughton cremation finds no parallel in the accompanied Viking-period graves of England. It is now lost, although the surviving watercolour of it (see Richards 2000: plate 19) shows it to be comparable to that recovered from Ballinaby, Islay (fig. 7.10) (182). Three hammer-heads were also recovered from the cemetery sites of Kilmainham and Islandbridge, Dublin; Templemoyle, Limavady, Co. Londonderry; and Knock-y-Doonee, Isle of Man (231, 250, 92).

Similarly, the only latch-lifter to be found in any burials in the British Isles and Ireland was recovered from the burial at Red House (6). Latch-lifters are a common find in early Anglo-Saxon accompanied burials of females (Lucy 2000:45). Keys have been recovered from Type II contexts at Repton (grave 511) (fig. A6.22: 8) and Type III at York Minster (grave 68) (39, 64). The only other key recovered from a Scandinavian-influenced burial of the Viking-period in the British Isles and Ireland occurred at Pierowall, Westray (144).

8.1.2 North of England Traditional Burials: results

In comparison to the other areas of the British Isles and Ireland there are very few traditional Viking burials. In all there are seven sites, encompassing recognisably traditional funerary rites. These contain sixteen burials, accepting a double interment at Claughton and nine from the seventeen excavated mounds at Heath Wood (Edwards 1969, Clarke & Fraser 1946, Clarke *et al* 1949, Posnansky 1956, Richards 2003 *a* & *b*).From consideration of the artefacts, the presence of three combs in the Hesket cremation may be indicative of a male and female interment, patterns of comb deposition in the Scandinavian-influenced burials in Scotland showing that generally males were accompanied by single combs and females, pairs. The funerary rites comprise of three inhumations and thirteen cremations. Where it can be ascertained, these are made up of two female and one male inhumation, and five male and four female cremations (Richards 2003 *a* & *b*). One of the female cremations identified at Heath Wood also included the remains of a juvenile (Richards 2003 *a* & *b*).

There are more cremations in the North of England than in the rest of the British Isles and Ireland combined. Scotland has the same number of cremation sites (four), but a lesser number of burials because of the presence of the cemetery at Heath Wood. Heath Wood represents the only known Viking cremation cemetery in the British Isles and Ireland, and is the only known Viking cemetery in England. The cremation cemetery at Heath Wood is also a geographical outlier (fig. 8.1), the other three cremation sites situated in the north-west of England. There are no known Scandinavian-influenced Viking-period burials east of the Pennines. This suggests that these interments were carried out by people with links to the Hiberno-Norse, cremation being the predominant funerary rite in Norway during the Viking-period (see chapter three). This also corresponds with the influence of

Hiberno-Norse groups on stone-sculpture and place-names in the north-west (see chapter five).

At four of the seven sites, mounds were used to demarcate the burials; the creations at Hesket, Claughton and Heath Wood, and the inhumation at Aspatria. While the mound at Hesket appears to have been an original Viking-period construction above the cremation hearth, it was situated close to the site of earlier barrows (Hutchinson 1794-97 (1974) vol. I: 505). At Heath Wood some of the mounds were found to be of similar construction to that of Hesket, that is, raised above an *in-situ* funerary hearth (for example, mound 1) (7). Others were devoid of hearth, human remains or artefacts (for example, mounds 9 & 50), and in some cases mounds were found to contain the partial remains of a cremation pyre at the very edge (for example, mound 56) (15, 22, 23). It has been suggested that, rather than cenotaphs, the mounds excavated and found to be empty in the nineteen-forties and fifties were not completely excavated to the edges where more modern excavation techniques allowed the discovery of partial remains (Richards pers. comm.). From this evidence it seems plausible that in some cases the mounds pre-date the Viking-period cremated remains, that is, the cremation was carried out away from the extant mound. It could well be that many of the sixty-seven mounds (fig. A6.8) are prehistoric in date, some of which were re-used, and the already extant ritual landscape interspersed with mounds constructed in the late-ninth century over cremation hearth, a theory given further credence by the discovery of a prehistoric ditch running below mounds 9 and 12 (fig. A8.8) (Posnansky 1956: 48-50). This hypothesis also has support from the burial at Claughton, where the remains of a Viking-period cremation rite were inserted into an extant Bronze Age mound. The cremation of what seems to be a male and a female took place away from the mound (that is, it was not constructed over the heart as at Hesket or Heath Wood 1) and the bones and artefacts collected and deposited alongside the Bronze Age remains inside.

There is also compelling evidence to suggest that the burial at Aspatria was a secondary interment in a prehistoric mound, the cup and ring-marked stones forming part of the cist, and the scattered remains of a female unassociated with the Viking-period found in the 1997 excavation (2). No mound was reported at the cremation site at Crossmoor, although the recovery of a cinerary urn along with the Viking-period sword and spear-head again points to secondary use of an extant monument. The recognition and continued use of the funerary ritual landscape by people of Scandinavian origin in the north of England is one mirrored in the rest of the British Isles and Ireland, were there are many examples if the re-use of prehistoric, pre-Christian and early Christian cemeteries (see above, chapter seven, appendix five).

The remaining two female inhumations at Leeming Lane and Red House were apparently unmarked (5, 6). They were, however, directly associated with roads; the Leeming Lane inhumation buried in the centre of what was the line of the Roman road leading to Catterick and Piecebridge; and the Red House burial lying across a ditch beside a Romano-British track-way linking a settlement site to the road between the forts at Burghwallis and Castleford (Margary 1967) (5, 6). This association with transport routes is directly linked with the other five sites of the Type I group. The mound at Aspatria overlooks the route from the Roman occupied sites of Mary Port and Old Carlisle (fig. A6.1); Hesket lies on the route from Carlisle to Penrith (fig. A6.10); and Claughton is adjacent to Galgate, the Roman road running between Ribchester to Lancaster (Margary 1967). Although the site at Crossmoor cannot be allied directly to a particular transport route, it is situated between the Roman roads running between Ribchester and Poulton-le-Fylde, and Preseton to Lancaster (Margary 1967: 374-7, 392). The cemetery at Heath Wood lies on the Trent Valley, the *Anglo-Saxon Chronicles* and excavations at Repton clearly illustrating the use of this riverine route by Scandinavian raiders (7-23, 39-43, 81).

This positioning in the landscape beside transport routes also links with the fact that all the burials of the Type I group are found beyond the limits of late Anglo-Saxon period settlement sites. A case may be made for the cemetery at Heath Wood being directly associated with the temporary settlement site of the Great Army over the winter of 873-4, although it hardly warrants correlation. A tenuous link may be made with the burial at Aspatria, which lay on the hill just beyond the village. The place-name, first recorded around 1160 reflects Gaelic word order, Patrick's ash, the specific being the Irish saint's name, and the generic derived from either the OE appellative *æsc* or OS *askŕ* (ash tree) (Fellows-Jensen 1985: 214). This is surely evidence of a bi-lingual community, the speakers influenced by the Irish Sea region. The presence of the Anglo-Scandinavian sculpture in the churchyard and discovery of a series of Viking-period artefacts in the area (see chapter five & appendix four) is also compelling evidence for the settlement and integration of Hiberno-Norse groups.

Amongst the artefacts recovered from the Type I sites weaponry predominates; of the seven sites only Red House was lacking in arms. The most common item was the sword, examples occurring at all the cremation sites and the inhumation at Aspatria. The ritually fire-damaged sword from Hesket belongs to the rare and highly decorative Petersen Type O group (900-50), and is only paralleled by a single other grave assemblage from Eriskay (unprovenanced) during the eighteenth century (202). (see chapter seven). A single example of the most common Scandinavian Viking-period sword, Petersen Type H (850-900), was retrieved from the hearth of mound 7 at Heath Wood (13). A sword of this type was also found with the Type II burial at Tendley Hill (below), and a further two are known from graves in Scotland and sixteen in Ireland (see chapter seven) (26,148-50, 183). The remaining swords which were possible to associate to a typological group belong to Petersen Type L or the Anglo-Saxon Type (*c*900), come from the cremations at Crossmoor (fig. A6.7) and mound 1 at Heath Wood (fig. A6.9) (4, 5).

Spear-heads were retrieved from five of the seven sites; the female inhumation from Red House perhaps expectedly devoid, but the martially associated cremation cemetery at Heath Wood was quite unexpected. Equally unusual was the recovery of a spear-head from the female inhumation at Bedale; the inclusion of a male gendered object with a female unparalleled in the British Isles and Ireland, although had the human bone survived from the cremation at Claughton the scenario may have been repeated.

Shields were recovered from three sites, Hesket, Aspatria and Heath Wood (1, 2, 7-23). Further evaluation of the shields from

Aspatria and Heath Wood is difficult, as the former is now lost, and because of the burnt nature of the others. The Hesket example belongs to the conical Irish Sea type (850-900), examples of which occur in the Type II burial at Ormside (fig. A6.17) (see below); three grave sites in the Scottish Islands; and at least twenty survive from the cremation sites of Kilmainham and Islandbridge in Dublin (27, 179, 183, 187, 231).

The final item of weaponry to be found was the axe, being recovered from Hesket, Aspatria and Claughton (1, 2, 3). The axe-head from Hesket is now the only surviving example, and is identifiable as the common Petersen Type E, which was also found at the Type II sites of Repton and Pippin Castle (figs. A8.7-8) (43, 43).

The remaining artefact types to be found at more than one site were tortoise brooches and riding gear. Tortoise brooches were recovered from the female inhumations at Red House (fig. A6.20), Leeming Lane (fig. A6.16) and the cremation at Claughton (fig. A5.6) (6, 5, 3). The brooches from Leeming Lane and Claughton are of very common type (R652, 900-50), and are paralleled in an English grave context at Santon Downham, Norfolk (Björn & Shetelig 1940: 12-13). Brooches of this type occurred in seven of the burials in the Scottish corpus (114, 121, 123, 128, 198, 180 figs. 7.8-9, 207 fig. 7.11). A single pair is known from Ireland, recovered from the grave at Three Mile Water, near Arklow (245). The brooches from Red House, although the same type (R647) are not a pair, one belonging to the sub-group P37.2, the other P37.3 (fig. A6.20) (6). Three and a half pairs have been recovered from Scottish grave sites, and four pairs and two single examples were recovered from sites in Ireland (Bøe 1940: 38-40) (131, 146,171, 204, 222, 231). Most strikingly the artefact pairing of the Type R647 tortoise brooches and copper-alloy bowl found at Red House is paralleled by those found at Ballyholme, Co. Down and Westness, Rousay, suggestive perhaps of a common origin of all three women and the people responsible for the interments (6, 222, 146).

The cremation at Hesket and inhumation at Aspatria were found to contain a bridle-bit and a pair of spurs (1, 2). There is no record of any animal bone being found in association with either burial (1, 2). Although it is usual to find horse bone alongside depositions of tack (see 179, 135, 129), they are not alone in the corpus, no equine remains being found at Balladoole on the Isle of Man, despite the presence of riding equipment (91). Of all the seven Type I sites, Heath Wood was the only place where animal bone was recovered, probably due to its excavation being undertaken in more modern times (7-23).

The remaining items from the Type I groups were individual to each site, albeit finding parallels with artefacts fro within the corpus. The only truly original pieces were the latch-lifter from Red House and the Carolingian scabbard mount from Claughton that had been converted to a brooch by the addition of a pin.

All the burials contain artefacts which allow a date range of deposition to be ascertained (fig. 8.2). Hypothetically, they could all fall around the 900 mark, although the probability is slight. The historical association of Heath Wood with the Great Army camp of 873-4, and the wide typological dating thresholds from the Hesket sword (900-50) (fig. A6.12) and Leeming Lane tortoise brooches (also 900-50) (fig. A5.16) could theoretically place a difference of between twenty-seven and seventy-seven years for dates of possible deposition, although the earlier date is probable for the Hesket burial with the inclusion of the shield-boss of Irish Sea type (850-900). From the artefactual evidence it seems likely that the interments at Heath Wood, Red House and Crossmoor could be grouped together chronologically earlier in the sequence, with Hesket and Claughton later (fig. 8.2). However, as already pointed out, real-time chronological comparison provides only a small part of the understanding of the settlement of Scandinavian groups.

8.1.3 North of England Traditional Burials: conclusions

Although on the surface the sites of Type I seem an eclectic mixture of Scandinavian influenced funerary practice, it has been shown that rather than displaying very few artefactual similarities and depositional traditions as seen in Ireland, Scotland and the Isle of Man, they are in fact linked primarily by the use of the physical landscape. There is strong evidence to suggest that the Viking-period depositions at Crossmoor, Claughton, Aspatria and some of the mounds at Heath Wood were secondary interments in extant prehistoric burial mounds. The Viking-period mound at Hesket continued the tradition of recognition and association with the ritual landscape by being placed close to a series of prehistoric barrows. This recognition by Scandinavian groups of the ritual-funerary landscape and predilection of use is repeated in the majority of sites across the British Isles and Ireland.

The association of the burial sites with transport routes is compelling, giving the circumstances surrounding the interments a very transient feel, as if the deceased and those performing the funerary rites were passing through the landscape. This is certainly a historically attested phenomenon at Heath Wood.

Other than the cremation cemetery at Heath Wood, which is unparalleled in the British Isles and Ireland, and was utilised by a specific group at a specific moment in time, the Type I burials are isolated occurrences, laying beyond areas of settlement. Unlike the Scandinavian-influenced burials of the Viking-period in Scotland and Ireland which depict all the signs of a colony, their residents retaining and perpetuating some cultural knowledge of the homeland within the limits of the parochial settlement, there is no evidence in England for the continuation of traditional funerary practice beyond a single event.

The predominant artefact type amongst the sites was weaponry, which is unsurprising when placed within the wider context of the Scandinavian-influenced burials of Ireland, Scotland and the Isle of Man. The rarity of the highly decorated sword (Petersen Type O) from Hesket enforces the theory that this was primarily the burials of an important man, and makes for a good comparison of social equality against the poor graves of the Great Army at Heath Wood. The copper-alloy bowl and tortoise brooch (R647) set found at Red House (figs. A6.21-1), Ballyholme, Co. Down, and Westness, Rousay, is very significant, suggestive perhaps of a common origin of all three women and the people responsible for the interments (6, 222, 146).

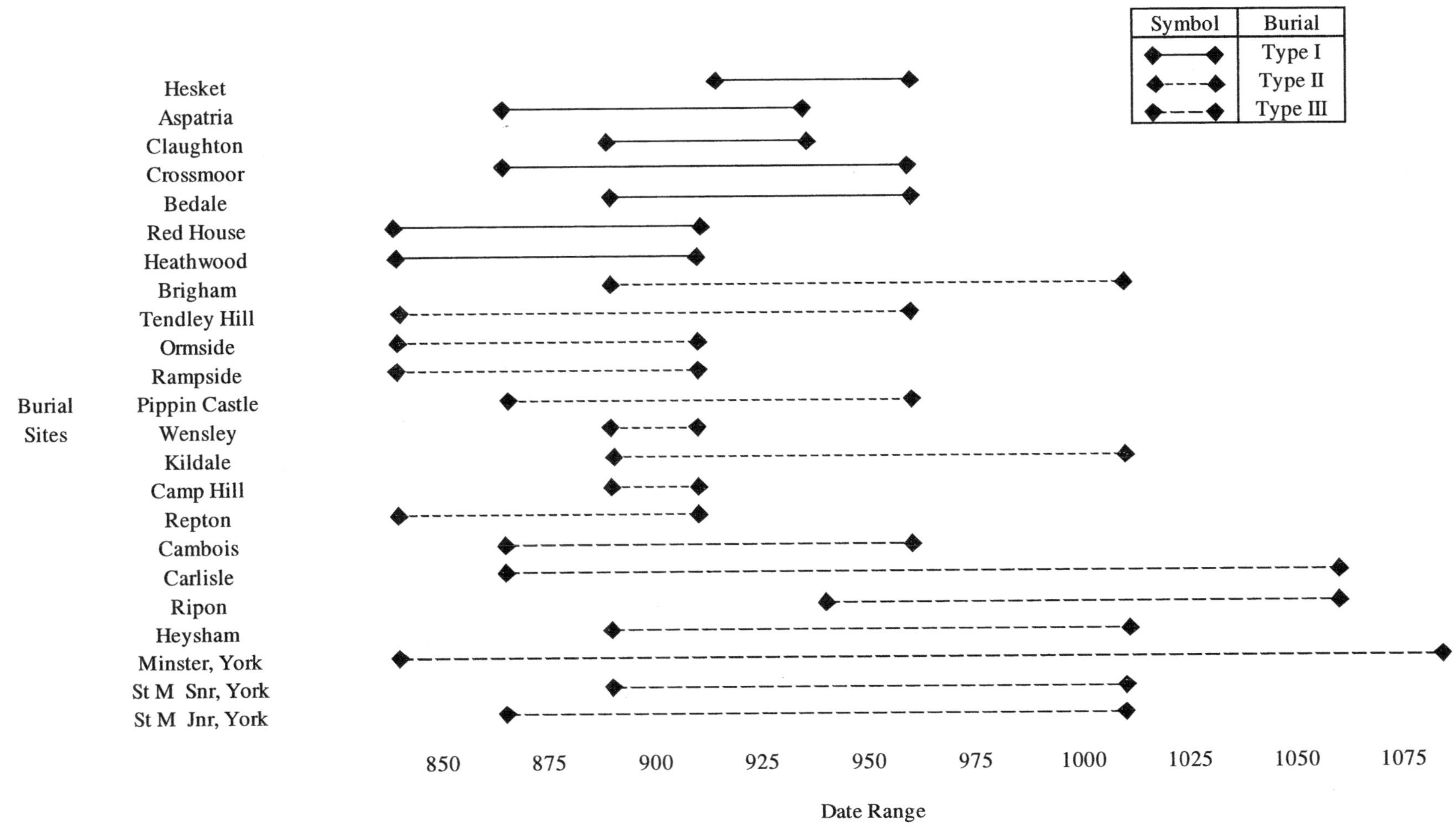

Fig. 8.2 *Chart to Show Comparative Date Ranges of Burials*

The use of identifiable Scandinavian artefacts and funerary rites of the period amongst the Type I sites shows reasonably strong link with the homelands or perhaps colonies in the Irish Sea region where more concepts of cultural knowledge of funerary rites still survived within the more socially insular settlements. The situation of the singular burials beyond the boundaries of settlement sites and the association of transport routes suggest a peripheral existence on the edge of society. These people could perhaps be reasonably linked with the pioneers of the migration model; living beyond the arrival of the primary migrants and preceding the settlement of their own group. As argued above, chronologically speaking, it is unlikely that these people where all contemporary, and they need not necessarily be so; the exploitation of wider territories undertaken by pioneer groups from the homelands being carried out at the sae time as settlement of secondary or tertiary migrants in other areas.

8.2 Accompanied Burials in Christian Cemeteries (Type II) (fig. 8.3)

Penrith, Cumbria

The parish churchyard at Penrith is perhaps best known in Viking studies as being the home of the 'Giant's Grave', the rectangular arrangement of four pieces of hogback stones and two Viking period crosses. It is obvious to modern eyes, and confirmed by old sources that all the pieces of sculpture have been moved several times before and after the sixteen hundreds when the first accounts appear, and excavation during the early part of the last century showed the ground beneath them to have been much disturbed (Lang 1984: 156). A folk story recounts the opening of the grave, possibly during the seventeenth century, and tells of the discovery of an inhumation accompanied by a sword (Edwards 1998: 96).

Brigham, Cumbria

The discovery of a ring-headed pin beneath Brigham Church tower suggests the presence of a possible Viking period burial (*Proceedings of the Cumberland & Westmorland Antiquarian Society,* 1904: 340). There was, however, no mention of it being associated with any human remains or other Viking type grave-goods, prompting the suggestion that the artefact may have simply been lost by its owner in the churchyard. More compelling support as to it being part of a funerary deposition was provided by the discovery of part of a hogback tombstone close to where the pin was found (Lang 1984: 116).

Tendley Hill, Eaglesfield, Cumbria

During the early nineteenth century a grave was found in a gravel quarry at Tendley Hill, Eaglesfield, just to the south of Brigham (fig. A6.23) (Dalton 1841 in Cowen 1967: 198, Wilson 1978: 47). The inhumation was recorded as being found at the highest point of the hill closest to the village (Dalton 1841 in Cowen 1967: 198, Wilson 1978: 47). Accompanying the burial was a sword with a silver inscribed hilt (fig. A6.23), a spearhead, and a copper-alloy penannular brooch described as being in the form of two gaping serpents (Dalton 1841 in Cowen 1967: 198). Thanks to the detective work of JD Cowen a hundred years later, the sword was traced and to the Black Gate Museum, Newcastle (Cowen 1967:199). The sword could either be Petersen Type H (800-950) or I (850-900), which are very similar, H being the most common Viking type sword (Cowen 1967: 201, Petersen 1919).

It seems however, that the burial was not alone on the hill, as attested to in the surviving notes of a local antiquarian writing in 1814 (Dalton 1814 in Cowen 1967: 202). Dalton described the disturbance of a series of inhumations, apparently both adults and children, in shallow coffinless graves, all interred without grave goods (Dalton 1841 in Cowen 1967: 202). There is nothing to suggest that these burials were Viking, but nothing to prevent them being Christian graves of the Anglo-Saxon period.

The site at Tendley Hill shares some similarities to that of Camp Hill, near Carthorpe (Yorks.), both being on a promontory and a Viking burial close, if not in, a Christian cemetery (see below). Sadly the whole site at Eaglesfield has since been destroyed by quarrying (Wilson 1978: 52).

Ormside, Westmorland

In 1898 while grave digging in the churchyard the sexton disturbed an inhumation, accompanied by a sword (fig. A6.18), a shield-boss (fig. A6.17) and part of the rim, and a small knife of domestic type (Ferguson 1899: 379-380). The human remains were left *in-situ* (Brunskill in Ferguson 1899: 379). The shield-boss (fig. A6.17) is of the Irish Sea conical type, similar to those recovered from Hesket, the cemetery at Kilmainham, the boat grave at Kiloran Bay, Colonsay and the grave at Ballinaby on Islay (fig. 7.10) (see above) and dates from the second half of the ninth century, a date also confirmed by the Petersen Type M sword (fig. A6.18) (Bjørn & Shetelig 1940: 18-19). The finds are still extant and on display in the Tullie House Museum, Carlisle.

Also recovered from the churchyard around the turn of the nineteenth century was the famous Ormside bowl (Collingwood 1899: 386), which allied with the discovery of the Viking burial has become indelibly linked with being part of Viking plunder hidden in the churchyard. Whether the highly ornate little bowl was part of piratical plunder or perhaps grave goods, it is certainly not Scandinavian in design, the fantastic birds and animals in repoussé seem almost Romano-Greek in their influence rather than northern European (Collingwood 1899). However, this does not preclude it from Viking ownership, their trade and transport links across mainland Europe being vast. One final point worth noting is that the church at Ormside is built on a manmade earthwork, set into a natural promontory, which is perhaps suggestive of it being built on an earlier, if not prehistoric site (Ferguson 1899: 377). This draws close parallel to the church at Rampside, which is thought to have been built on a Neolithic long barrow (Gaythorpe 1910: 300-301).

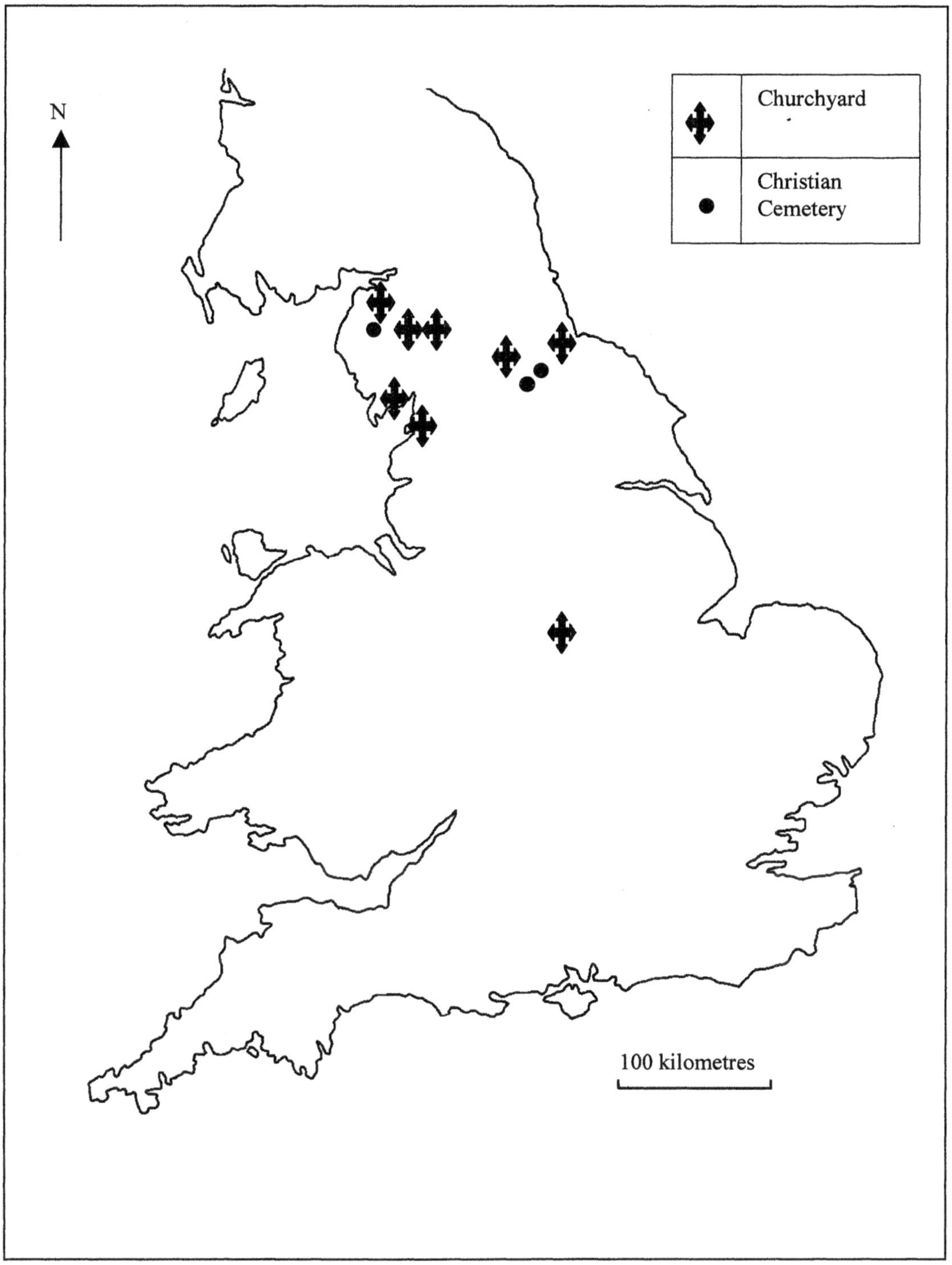

Fig. 8.3 *Accompanied Burials in Christian Cemeteries*

Rampside, Lancashire

The churchyard at Rampside has provided the site of a further two accompanied Viking burials. A gravedigger discovered the first burial in 1854-5 covered by a large slab, with what appeared to be the remains of a broken sword, the hilt and some of the blade surviving then to an overall length of twelve inches (Gaythorpe 1910: 300). Unfortunately this is now lost (Gaythorpe 1910: 300).

The second inhumation found at a slightly earlier date, was also accompanied by a sword in its scabbard (fig. A6.19), laying in the western part of the grave (Gaythorpe 1910: 300). This sword still survives, and is of Petersen Type M, and so dates to the second half of the ninth century (Bjørn & Shetelig 1940: 18).

Again the burials may represent inhumations of a pagan type in a Christian graveyard, or they may predate the establishment of the church and a Christian burial ground. In 1860 a Neolithic axe head was found amongst a '*heap of bones*', along with large slabs of stone, which is strongly suggestive of the site being in use as a burial site for a very considerable length of time (Gaythorpe 1910: 300-301).

Heysham, Lancashire

Some time before 1823 a hogback stone in St Peter's churchyard was disturbed while grave digging, and beneath it was found the remains of an iron spearhead (Whitaker 1823: vol. II 319). The spearhead is now lost, and presumably the bones were re-interred, but the hogback remains and is preserved inside the church (Lang 1984: 138). Although the account is scanty, it is one of the very few instances recorded in England (see Penrith, above) where an accompanied, apparently Viking grave, has been discovered beneath a hogback. This is surely a clear example of a pagan funerary rite taking place within a Christian graveyard.

Pippin Castle, Scargill, near Harrogate, Yorkshire

Prior to this research the artefacts associated with the site had never been analysed or published. A full report was compiled on behalf of Harrogate Museums and Arts (HARGM) who curate the artefacts, a copy of which is in appendix eight.

In 1901 a series of tumuli were destroyed at a site known locally as Pippin Castle in Haverah Park, an area of open moorland to the southwest of Harrogate in preparation for the construction of Scargill and Beaver Dyke reservoirs (Kaye 1902, 1928). Early topographical descriptions record the presence of three tumuli on rising ground, the largest of which incorporated the promontory into its construction (Grainge 1871: 347). On the Ordnance Survey map of 1851 'Pippin Castle' is represented by a large mound, with a further two tumuli on top, one centrally placed, and another, smaller mound , immediately to the south, overlapping its furthest edge (OS 1851, grid ref. SE221544). Twenty years later a local historian described the earthworks as three separate mounds, and records the folk memory that the area had once been a chapel and burial ground to 'John O'Gaunt's Castle', a medieval fortified tower some three-quarters of a mile to the north-west (Grainge 1871: 347).

The first mound to be described by Grainge was the largest of the three, and was oval in shape and around eighty yards long by forty across its widest point (Grainge 1871: 347). His description is consistent with the OS illustration, it being made up of partially at least by the natural promontory (Grainge 1871: 347). Grainge also observed that it was not overly high and was surrounded by a narrow ditch (Grainge 1871: 347).

The second mound was also oval in shape, but somewhat smaller, being around thirty yards long and eighteen across in its widest part (Grainge 1871: 347). The top of this mound he noted as being unnaturally flat, and struck him as always having been so (Grainge 1871: 347). The eastern edge of this mound was on the edge of the valley, the other sides being surrounded by a substantial ditch of some fifteen feet in depth, and ten feet in width (Grainge 1871: 347).

The third and smallest mound, Grainge described as being close to the second, a fact again confirmed by the 1851 map (Grainge 1871: 347). It was described as being conical in shape with a base of fifteen yards in diameter, and a cavity in the top, possibly the result of treasure hunters (Grainge 1871: 347). The mound was also described as being surrounded by a ditch of around ten feet in depth (Grainge 1871: 347).

In Kaye's later accounts of the site (1901 and 1928) he describes only two mounds. The larger of the two (given to be ninety feet by fifty) can be equated with the second mound described by Grainge (Kaye 1901: 55, 1928: 382, Grainge 1871: 347). The smaller mound appears to be the one of conical shape close by, although Kaye's measurements (fifteen feet in height, and fifteen in diameter) are a third of the earlier accounts (Kaye 1901: 55, 1928: 382, Grainge 1871: 347). This may simply be due to confusion in the reproduction of yards and feet.

Positioned at the northwest side of the conical mound Kaye discovered a stone inscribed with Norse runes (fig. A8.2) (Kaye 1928: 382, 1901: 55). The runes were dated to the eleventh or twelfth century and read '*SUNA*', which has variously been translated as either part of a name, or the word 'son' (Kermode in Kaye 1901: 55, Baldwin-Brown 1928: 384). The stone, while bearing many faded scratch marks other than the runic inscription, does not appear to have been smoothed, or any effort made to make it decorative or ornamental (Baldwin-Brown 1928: 383). It is impossible to tell whether the inscription related to a theological inscription (*i.e.* the son of God) or a commemoration by a parent.

The runestone survives in the collections of Harrogate Museums and Arts (HARGM), and on inspection there is the suggestion that it may have been a very crude attempt at the basic outline shape of half a hogback tombstone. The runes are very large and crude, and all but cover one surface. Its current length is 560mm, height 330mm, and is approximately 176mm wide at the base.

From mounds were recovered an axe-head, of the late-ninth century type Rygh 561/Petersen Type E[1] (figs. A8.7-8) (Bjorn & Shetelig 1940: 14-15, 20), two small horse-shoes, a four-feet long iron saw blade (figs. A8.9-11), fragments of glazed pottery (figs. A8.12-15), pieces of 'black oak' likened in his account to something used in building (fig. A8.5), some flints and the humerus of an ox (Kaye 1928: 382). No human bones were reported (Kaye 1928). Unfortunately Kaye did not stipulate from which of the mounds the artefacts were recovered.

[1] The same type as those recovered from the burials at Repton (Derbys.) and Hesket-in-the-Forest (Cumbria).

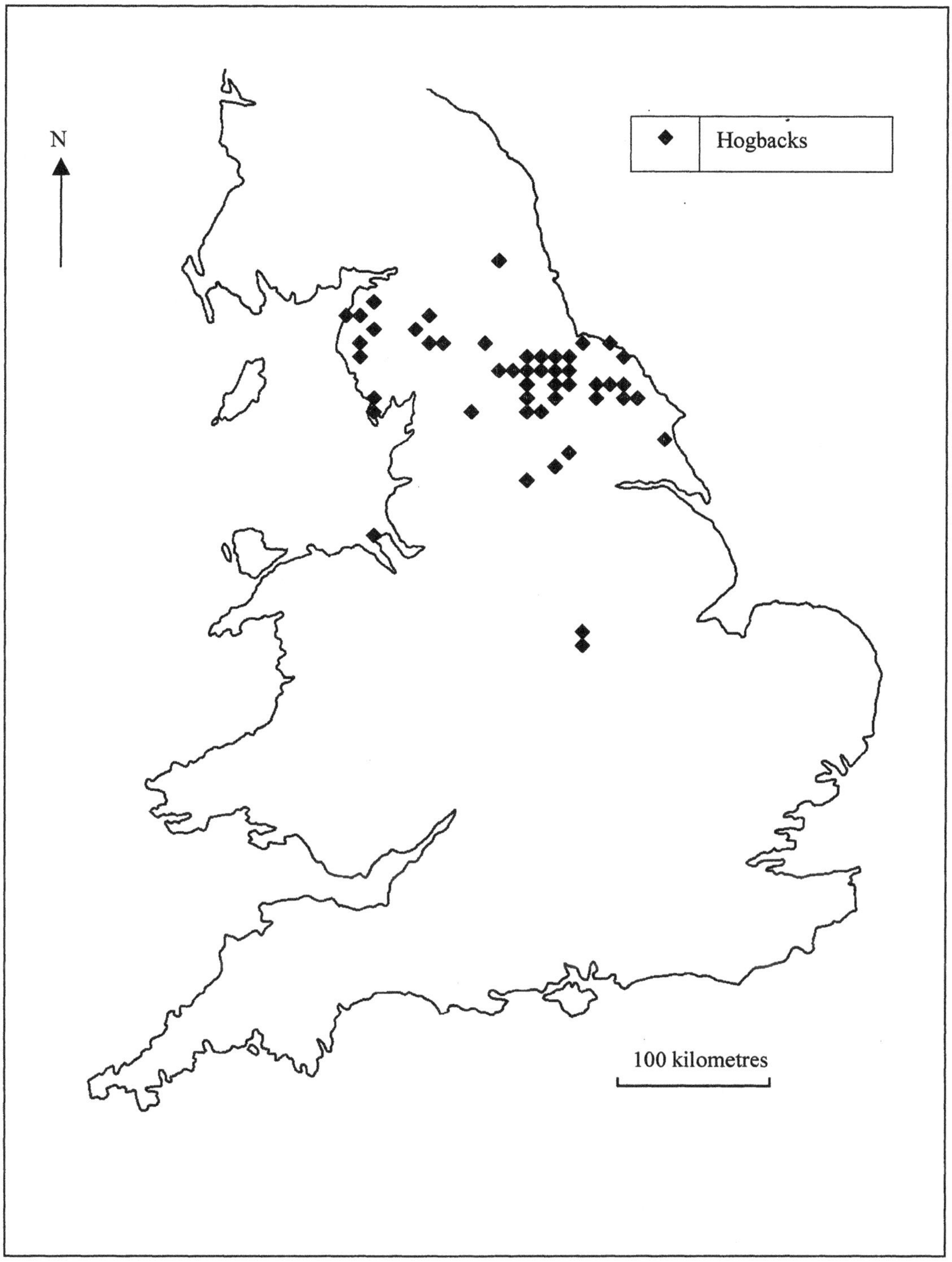

Fig. 8.4 *Hogbacks in Study Area (after Lang 1984: 86 with additions)*

Along with the runestone HARGM are in possession of a number of artefacts said to have come from the Pippin Castle site. These include the axe-head (figs. A8.7-8), a series of iron fragments (which may have been part of the saw) (figs. A8.9-11), pottery (figs. A8.12-15), pieces of timber (fig. A8.5), some flints, pieces of bone, a whetstone fragment (fig. A8.3), and three jars of soil and a concreted mass of what appears to be the same material (fig. A8.1). One of the jars carries the handwritten label '*From a Viking Cremation*' (fig. A8.1). The horseshoes are lost. The artefacts were taken for examination to the University of Bradford, and a description of the analysis is reproduced in appendix eight, with a selection of photographs and X-rays also contained. Briefly, examination of the soil provided no bone or any firm indication that it had been a part of a funeral hearth, despite some slight evidence of burning (fig. A8.1). The pieces of carved oak are likely to have been of medieval date, and appear to have been off-cuts used in the construction of a building (fig. A8.5). X-rays of the axe proved it to be an excellent weapon, made of steel rather than an iron object with a steel blade welded on (McDonnell 2003: pers. comm.) (figs. A8.7-8). No conclusions could be drawn from the other corroded iron fragments (figs. A8.9-11). X-ray fluorescence analysis of the whetstone fragment revealed no traces of metal (fig. A8.4). The three pieces of bone included whalebone (fig. A8.6), an ox humerus and a human tibia. The pottery shards were found to be representative of at least four of vessels from the Yorkshire Wares group, dating from the mid-twelfth to mid-fourteenth centuries (figs. A8.12-15).

The association of the runestone, axe, whetstone and piece of whalebone are highly suggestive of a Viking burial, settlement, or at the very least show very strong links with Scandinavian contacts. It is also tempting to associate the pieces of timber and early medieval pottery to the folk-memory of the chapel at the site, and again propose that the runestone had been a monument within the churchyard. The tibia may also owe its origin to this churchyard. However, no mention was ever made to the artefacts being found in association with human remains, inhumed or cremated. Quite what had been recognised by the person who collected the supposed cremation hearth sample will never be known.

Wensley, Yorkshire

In 1915 while grave digging in Wensley churchyard the sexton came across an inhumation, laid in an east-west direction at a depth of just over four feet (Bolton 1916: 228). With the inhumation was found a sword of Petersen Type L (*c* 900) (fig. A6.24), with a pommel decorated with silver and niello work, a spear complete with part of its wooden shaft and silver fixing pins, a knife and an iron sickle (Bolton 1916: 228-230). The sexton also noticed that the grave was very close to what looked like part of a series of mortared foundations, which were thought to be the foundations of the earlier Saxon church (Bolton 1916: 228).

Kildale, Yorkshire

During the late nineteenth century renovation work at Kildale Parish church there was uncovered eight or nine accompanied Viking period burials (Atkinson 1868: 52). Sadly much of the detail was over-looked, and the artefacts recovered subsequently stolen from a display within the church during the nineteenth century, and the information with regard to them is preserved in a series of sketches which were done at the time (fig, A6.15) (Elgee 1930: 220). On the first occasion during 1867, seven or eight inhumations were discovered laying in an east westerly direction, beneath the north wall of the nave (Atkinson 1874 (1988): 81, Atkinson 1868: 52-54). The first three of the group were partially listed with their associated grave-goods, which were as follows (Atkinson 1868: 52-4). The first inhumation was accompanied by a broken sword (most likely broken in the ground), a knife with a silver bound hilt, a pair of copper-alloy tweezers, a set of copper-alloy scales complete with pans, a lead weight, a small copper-alloy plate (possibly a scabbard mount), and a wooden box with a sliding lid containing what was probably a further lead weight (fig. A6.15) (Atkinson 1868: 53-54). The second and third inhumations were said to have both been accompanied by a sword and a dagger each, although it is more than likely that the daggers were in fact spearheads, a conclusion supported by a surviving illustration of some of the finds (fig. A6.15) (Atkinson 1874 (1988): 82, Atkinson 1868: 53-54). Other artefacts recovered from the site of the burials were an axe, a spear, a small domestic bone handled knife, spurs, a concave metal object with a rivet through it (shield boss?), a whetstone and some nails (Atkinson 1868: 53-54). Also said to have been found, although not directly reported to have been associated with the burials, was a stone slab with a cross carved in each corner (Atkinson 1868: 54). The cross-carved slab provokes comparison to those recovered from the boat burial at Kiloran Bay, Colonsay (figs 7.13-14).

It was recorded that all the swords were found lying across the legs, with the hilt resting on the right hip (Atkinson 1868: 54). The axe head was found resting by the right foot of its owner (Atkinson 1868: 54).

During work undertaken in 1868 a further inhumation was uncovered accompanied by a sword in its scabbard, a decorated copper-alloy buckle, and parts of the scabbard fittings and belt (Atkinson 1874 (1988): 84-5). The sword appears to be of Petersen Type X, dating to the tenth century (fig. A6.15; 3) (Atkinson 1874 (1988): 82). Swords of this type have also been recovered from Knock-y-Doonee and Larne.

From the artefacts recovered it seems safe to suggest that at least four were male. There is nothing to suggest from the remaining artefactual evidence that there were any female interments. It seems safe to suggest that they were buried either at the same time or within a short period of each other.

Camp Hill, near Carthorpe, Yorkshire

Unfortunately, as with so may of the possible Viking burials in England, the details of the discovery of a single inhumation grave near Camp Hill House just outside Carthorpe are very limited (Lukis 1870: 180). Sometime during the late nineteenth century a skeleton was found, accompanied by a sword and spearhead (fig. A6.5) (Lukis 1870: 180). The sword dates to *c*900 (Petersen Type L), a time span also attributable to the spear (fig. A6.5) (Bjørn & Shetelig 1940: 15). Interestingly Camp Hill House lies in the vicinity of Howe (from the Norse *haugr*) Hill, where a series of apparently Christian Anglo-Saxon graves were uncovered also during the late nineteenth century (see Eaglesfield, above) (Lukis 1870).

Repton, Derbyshire

As mentioned in earlier chapters the Great Army arrived in Repton in late 873 and fortified the ideally situated site of the monastery and church, which lay on a promontory above the River Trent (Biddle & Kjølbye-Biddle 1992: 36). Modern excavation (site report awaited) of the site recovered six inhumation burials of Viking type, along with a mid-Saxon sunken stone building containing the remains of at least two-hundred and sixty-four people (Biddle & Kjølbye-Biddle 2001:

68). Amongst some of the artefacts recovered from the heavily disturbed sunken building were an early medieval axe, part of a sword, a number of seaxes, knives, a chisel, a padlock key, seven fragments of jewellery, six pins and studs of gilded copper-alloy, part of a sword, and five silver pennies; four of which post date 872, the fifth dating to 873-4 (Biddle & Kjølbye-Biddle 2001: 68-9). The earliest recorded exploration of the mound began in the seventeenth century, and contains descriptions of human bones stored in charnel fashion around the centrally placed burial of a large person (Degge 1727-8 in Biddle & Kjølbye-Biddle 2001: 67). No mention was made of any grave-goods, even though the 'labourer' who opened it was observant enough to notice the remains of the joists within the structure (Degge 1727-8 in Biddle & Kjølbye-Biddle 2001: 67). Contrary to the beliefs of the excavators there is no evidence to suggest that this was the burial of a powerful Viking leader and even less likely contained the remains of Ivar the Boneless (Biddle & Kjølbye-Biddle 2001: 81-4). The normally reliable *Annals of Ulster* announces the death of Ivar in 873 and while does not state where he died, the lack of geographical stipulation leads to the logical assumption that it was Dublin, the seat of the kingdom he succeeded from Olaf (AU 873: pt. 3).

Studies of the remains of the two hundred and sixty-four people (male and female) in the mound have shown that they were disarticulated before inclusion in the building, and radiocarbon dates from then suggest that at least half of them were dead before the late seventh-early eighth century, that is, well before the Viking occupation of Repton (Biddle & Kjølbye-Biddle 2001: 79-80). It seems likely therefore, that rather than a huge Viking mausoleum, the building held the remains of an earlier Mercian king or church leader; or possibly a combination of the two in St Wigstan (died 840), surrounded by those important enough or wealthy enough to rest in perpetuity beside a saint. However, it does seem likely that the building would be used by the members of the camp to inter at least some of their dead, something perhaps supported by the artefacts recovered.

During the modern excavations another very important discovery was made, that of the intact inhumation of a Viking male (fig. A6.22) (Biddle & Kjølbye-Biddle 2001: 61-65). The grave had been marked by a large wooden post some thirty centimetres in diameter, and covered by a layer of stones, some of which came from broken Anglo-Saxon cross shafts (Biddle & Kjølbye-Biddle 2001: 60). The man had been the victim of a vicious death, and died of his perimortem injuries, a hard blow to the head and a cut to the top of the left leg, which would have severed the femoral artery (Biddle & Kjølbye-Biddle 2001: 61-62). He was buried in an east-west position, and was accompanied by a necklace with pendants of two glass beads, a silver-alloy Thor's hammer, a copper-alloy belt buckle, a sword (Petersen Type M, dated to the second half of the ninth century) still in its scabbard, a copper-alloy buckle from the scabbard harness, a folding knife, a knife of domestic type and an iron key which was resting on top of the scabbard (fig. A6.22) (Biddle & Kjølbye-Biddle 2001: 61-5). Possible ritually affiliated artefacts were also recovered; the tusk of a wild boar had been laid between his thighs, and there was evidence of the remains of an organic container further down, which had been the receptacle of the humerus of a jackdaw (Biddle & Kjølbye-Biddle 2001: 65).

Beside this grave was a further inhumation, which seemed to have been dug at or very close to the same time (Biddle & Kjølbye-Biddle 2001: 65). This grave held the remains of a younger man, who had suffered a blow to the skull (Biddle & Kjølbye-Biddle 2001: 65). His only accompaniment was an iron knife (Biddle & Kjølbye-Biddle 2001: 65). The likelihood that he had been buried at the same time as the older man and the nature of his injury being very similar to that of the (possible) sacrificial victim at Ballateare (Isle of Man) may offer some support to the hypothesis that this was the ritual killing of the older man's slave. Close to the burials was found a spear, evidently disturbed from its original position and possible evidence of a further accompanied burial (Biddle & Kjølbye-Biddle 2001: 65).

In 1923 an axe head was found buried in the graveyard between the crypt and the south aisle of the church (Biddle & Kjølbye-Biddle 2001: 55, Bjørn & Shetelig 1940: 14-15). The axe is of Petersen Type E (see Hesket-in-the-Forest and Pippin Castle, above), and dates to the late ninth century (Bjørn & Shetelig 1940: 14-15). The modern excavation discovered that it was very likely retrieved from a coffined inhumation that survived only as a shadow (Biddle & Kjølbye-Biddle 2001: 65).

Two swords have also been found within the vicinity of the camp, which may mark the sites of further accompanied burials (Biddle & Kjølbye-Biddle 2001: 55-56). The first, an Anglo-Saxon style, Petersen Type L (*c*900) was said to have been found amongst human bones close to the river (Biddle & Kjølbye-Biddle 2001: 55-57). A copy of a later, tenth century sword (Petersen Type X) was said to also have been found in the area, may have also come from a grave, (Biddle & Kjølbye-Biddle 2001: 57) albeit later than the winter camp at Repton.

Around the turn of the nineteenth century a hogback tombstone was recovered from the western part of the graveyard beyond the limit of the defensive earthwork (Biddle & Kjølbye-Biddle 2001: 55-56, Lang 1984: 160). Unfortunately it has subsequently been lost and survives only as a drawing (Biddle & Kjølbye-Biddle 2001: 55-56, Lang 1984: 160).

The excavations at Repton have shown quite conclusively the position of the camp of the Great Army as it wintered in England over 873-4. It has also shown how much human activity, its breadth and intensity, can actually take place in what we know historically to be a limited period of a few months before the army moved on. The later burial of a woman with a collection of small personal goods (see below), the tenth century sword and the hogback could also be taken as indicators that at least some of the Viking camp stayed behind and settled when the bulk of the army moved off, or perhaps the return of veterans of the army and camp followers. This is corroborated by the graves in 'Cemetery 3M', close to the sunken building, which was in use during the tenth century (see below) (Biddle & Kjølbye-Biddle 2001: 85).

8.2.1 Artefactual Analysis of Accompanied Burials in Christian Cemeteries

This section will consider the correlation and significance of the burials discussed above both as a discrete whole, and within the wider context of the rest of Britain and Ireland, and Scandinavia where appropriate. Owing to the nature of the analysis and in order to facilitate fluidity of structure where multiple sites will be compared within a sentence all general references to the sites are those listed in appendix five, and will be provided at the end of the sentence in numerical form (for example, Penrith would be (24)). Where specific points are drawn from particular sources full references will be made in the standard fashion. Analysis of the sites will be undertaken in traditional comparative manner via burial rites and artefactual analysis. This has been done not only to glean information from the archaeological remains, but show that the divisions used above are extremely valuable and more helpful in understanding interaction between immigrant and settled groups.

As with the Type I group above, by far the most commonly associated artefacts within these burials were items of weaponry, most particularly the sword, which is found at eight of the eleven sites, giving a total of fifteen. Of the eight, the swords from Penrith, Rampside (burial 2) and Kildale are all lost, although a drawing of the latter survives (fig. A6.15: 3) (24, 29, 33-7). The original sword believed to have come from a grave within Repton churchyard is now also lost, although a copy survives which can be allocated to the Petersen Type X group (tenth-eleventh century), that is, later than the date of 873-4 associated with the occupation of the great Army, and later than the sword in burial 511, which has been linked with the fortification of the winter camp (42). Ironically the sketch of the stolen sword from Kildale (fig. A6.15: 3) shows a weapon belonging to the same group. A Type X sword was recovered from one of two burials in Nottingham, and a Type X (or less likely Type W) sword was found in a gravel bank at West Seaton, near Workington, Cumbria (see appendix seven) (Bjørn & Shetelig 1940: 15). No swords of this type are known from the burial sites of Scotland, although swords of Type X were recovered from Knock-y-Doonee, Isle of Man; Larne, Co. Antrim; and three from the Dublin cemetery sites of Kilmainham and Islandbridge (92, 217, 231). This suggests that Scandinavian-influenced groups continued to be linked with the Repton site after the Great Army occupation; a hypothesis supported by the later graves discovered there, discussed below in Type III, and the one-time presence of a hogback tombstone (Lang 1984: 160).

The swords from Repton (grave 511) (fig. A6.22: 4), Ormside (fig. A6.18) and Rampside (fig. A6.19) are all Petersen Type M, dating from 850 to 900 (39, 27-8). The design is of simple type, and is the second most common form of Viking-period sword in Scandinavia (Peirce 2002: 84), which may account for the numbers occurring here. However, this being said, only a single example survives from Ireland, from Harley Park, Co. Kilkenny, which was not found in a grave-context (Walsh 1998: 232). The only other identified Type M sword recovered from a Viking-period burial in the British Isles was from Balladoyne Churchyard, Isle of Man (113). Of the one-hundred and ninety-eight Norwegian examples listed by Petersen in 1919, the majority were found in north-east Norway, which allied with the rarity of such examples in the British Isles and Ireland may indicate links with the deceased with this area.

The swords from Wensley (fig. A6.24), Camp Hill (fig. A6.5) and a further unprovenanced find from Repton belong to Petersen Type L (*c*900), whose typological date overlaps with that of Type M (32, 38, 42). This Type, also found in mound 1 at Heath Wood (fig. A6.9) and Crossmoor (fig. A6.6) (both Type I, above), is the predominant design recovered from the Scandinavian-influenced graves of the Viking-period on the Isle of Man, being found at Ballachrink, St Maughold, Ballabrooie and Ballaugh (7, 4, 101-3, 105). A Type L sword was similarly discovered from the graves at Torbeckhill, Kirkcudbright (fig. 7.3) (118), but there has yet to be found a sword of this type in a Viking-period burial in Ireland, although ten exist from other provenances (Walsh 1998: 233-4).

The final sword from Tendley Hill (fig. A6.23) belongs to the Petersen Type H group (850-950), which is the most common design of Scandinavian Viking-age sword (26). A sword of this type was recovered from mound 7 at Heath Wood; Scar, Sanday; and Ballinaby, Islay (fig. 7.10) (13, 148, 183). Sixteen swords of this type were found in the cemetery sites of Kilmainham and Islandbridge, Dublin (Walsh 1998: 231). As already discussed above, the Type H sword and its derivative Type I, are the most common form of sword in Viking period Norway (Walsh 1998: 229). It is most frequently found in Western Norway, but is very rare in Denmark (Walsh 1998: 229).

The next most commonly recovered artefact from the grave assemblages of the Type II group is the spear, occurring at six of the eleven sites; Tendley Hill (fig. A6.5), Heysham, Wensley, Camp Hill, Kildale (A6.15: 4) and Repton (26, 30, 32, 38, 33-7, 43). At Tendley Hill, Camp Hill, Wensley and Kildale the spears are accompanied by swords (26, 38, 32, 33-7). At Heysham the spear-head was apparently the only artefact accompanying an inhumation beneath a hogback (25). Across the corpus of Scandinavian influenced graves in the British Isles and Ireland spear-heads are a very common find, usually accompanied by other accoutrements of a martial nature (see chapter seven & appendix five). Spears were found at six of the seven sites in the Type I group discussed above.

The remains of shields were found at Ormside (fig. A6.17), and Kildale (27, 37). Sadly the shield from Kildale was stolen, and no illustration survives (37). The shield-boss from Ormside (fig. A6.17) is of the Irish Sea conical type, dating to 850-900, the period which corresponds exactly to the date of the accompanying Type M sword (fig. A6.18) (27). The shield-boss at Hesket is also of the same type (see above). The inhumations at Kiloran Bay, Colosay; Ballinaby, Islay (fig. 7.10); and Lamlash, Arran, also contained shields of this type, and at least twenty were recovered from the cemetery sites of Kilmainham and Islandbridge in Dublin (179, 183, 187, Bøe 1940: 35-8). Other shields of unidentified type from England were found at Aspatria (lost) and in mound 50 at Heath Wood, and are discussed above in Type I (2, 22).

Axes were found at three of the eleven sites; Pippin Castle (figs. A8.7 & A8.8), Kildale (fig. A6.15: 6) and Repton (31, 37, 41). All appear to be Petersen Type E (late ninth-early tenth century through to the eleventh), although evaluation of the Kildale example is reliant on a sketch, and Pippin Castle on an early twentieth century photograph and actual examination of a now extremely corroded artefact (figs. A6.15: 6 &A8.7-8) (31, 37). The axe from Repton was found in the churchyard, but not reported as being directly associated with a disturbed grave, although it is extremely likely (41). The axe-head recovered from the cremation at Hesket (Type I burial group, above) is also a Petersen Type E (1). The type is one commonly occurring as stray finds across England, and two axe-heads of this group were recovered from the Dublin sites of Kilmainham and Islandbridge (Bøe 1940:32-3). Axe-heads are a very common part of martial accoutrements in Scandinavian-influence graves of the Viking-period in Scotland and the Isle of Man (see chapter seven & appendix five).

Only two of the sites produced whetstones; Pippin Castle (fig. A8.3) and Kildale (fig. A6.15:2) (lost) (31, 37). A single whetstone was found amongst the Type I sites at Hesket (above) and Carlisle Cathedral (grave 251) amongst Type III sites (below) (1, 47). Small, pendant whetstones seem to be associated with the graves of children, being found with the Type III grave of the male adolescent at St Mary Bishophill Junior, York; a child at Cnip, Lewis; and also at Housegord, Shetland (see above and below) (72, 203, 173). Whetstones are an extremely common occurrence in Scandinavian-influenced graves in Scotland, Ireland and the Isle of Man (see chapter seven & appendix five).

Small knives were recovered from Kildale (fig. A6.15: 5) (lost), Ormside (lost) and Repton (37, 27, 39, 40, 43). The folding knife from grave 511 at Repton is similar to that found at Aspatria (fig. A6.3: 3) (above) and Carlisle Cathedral, grave 251 (Type III, see below) (39, 2, 47). Grave 295 at Repton, adjacent to 511, contained a male inhumation who wore a dagger at his waist (40). The description and surviving illustration of the flat-backed knife with its silver-wire bound handle (fig. A6.15: 5) draws immediate comparison to that recovered from grave 203, also at Repton (Type III, see below) (37, 81). Small domestic knives were also recovered from the Type III sites at Ripon Ailcy Hill (grave group 1064) and the grave of the adolescent male at St Mary Bishophill Junior, York (51, 72). Knives are extremely common in Scandinavian-influenced graves of the Viking-period across the corpus of burials discussed in chapter seven in Scotland, Ireland and the Isle of Man (see also appendix five).

The spur fragments (lost) reported from Kildale are the only pieces of riding equipment known from the Type II burials (37). Despite the recovery of two horse-shoes (lost) from the site at Pippin Castle, there is no further indication of any horse bone or riding gear being found alongside them (31). A piece of unworked whalebone from the Pippin Castle collection (fig. A8.6) is unparalleled in England, despite the forum being widely used for items across the Viking world. Animal bones and a horse-shoe were found at Kirk Lonan, Isle of Man, although to the south at Balladoole, no equine remains were reported alongside the discovery of riding equipment, including spurs of Carolingian type (111, 91). There is of course the chance that the animal bone was disregarded upon discovery. Heath Wood is the only site of the Type I group to have had animal bone finds recorded, probably owing to its more recent and modern excavations; a fact repeated at Repton the only other site to have recorded animal bone from a Viking-period grave (39). In grave 511 at Repton was discovered a jackdaw humerus (possibly contained in a charm bag) and a wild boar tusk (39).

Wensley was the only one of the Type II sites found to contain a sickle (32). It is paralleled in England only by that found at Hesket (see above) (1). They are, however, a common find in Scotland, occurring in the better appointed male and female graves (see chapter seven & appendix five). They have been recovered from at least nine sites; Reay, Caithness; Broch of Gurness, Orkney; Westness, Rousay; Scar, Sanday; Pierowall, Westray; Cnip, Lewis (fig. 7.8); Kiloran Bay, Colonsay; Cruach Mhor, Islay; and Kildonan, Eigg (115, 155, 146, 149, 144, 207, 179, 185, 188). Sickles were also recovered from the cemetery site at Islandbridge, Dublin; but as yet, no examples are known from the Isle of Man (231).

One of the burials at Kildale was the only Scandinavian-influenced Viking-period grave in England found to contain a set of weights and scales (fig. A6.15: 1) (33). Fragments of a copper-alloy scale pan and ingot were found in grave 251 in Carlisle Cathedral (see below, Type III) (47). Sadly the Kildale collection was stolen during the nineteenth century (33-7). Weights and scales were recovered from the Dublin cemeteries of Kilmainham and Islandbridge; Scar, Sanday; Broch of Gurness, Orkney; Kiloran Bay, Colonsay (fig. 7.15) and Tarbert, Gigha (231, 148, 156, 179, 191).

Items of personal equipment from the Type II group include a ring-headed pin from Brigham, paralleled in England by those found at Aspatria (fig. A6.3: 1), within mound 56 at Heath Wood and in grave 242 or 244 at Carlisle Cathedral(2, 23, 48) (see above, Type I and below, Type III). They are extremely common in the graves of Scotland, occurring at fourteen sites (see chapter seven & appendix 5). Ring-headed pins are also found at five of the nineteen burial sites on the Isle of Man, and at Larne, Co. Antrim; Cloghermore Cave, Tralee, Co. Kerry; and at the Dublin cemetery sites Kilmainham and Islandbridge (see chapter seven & appendix five) (217, 241, 231). Perhaps unsurprisingly they are believed to originate in the Irish Sea region, only Heath Wood of the English sites where they are found not on the Irish Seaboard.

The penannular brooch discovered in the grave at Tendley Hill is now lost, so further evaluation is denied, although the description of the terminals being formed of long-tongued beasts is intriguing (26).

The tweezers found at Kildale have no parallel in the English corpus, but were found in the female inhumations at Reay, Caithness and King's Cross Point, Lamlash Bay Arran (114, 186).

Similarly, the necklet comprising of a silver-alloy Thor's hammer amulet and two beads (fig. A6.22: 1-3) discovered in grave 511 at Repton has no equivalent in England, although such amulets are common in Scandinavia (39). A Thor's hammer amulet was discovered with the inhumation of a female at the Broch of Gurness, Orkney (155). The grave 511 from Repton also contained a key (fig. A6.22: 8), the only example from within the Type II group (39). A key was recovered from within the Type II group at York Minster (grave 68) (see below), and a latch-lifter form the Type I Red House burial, discussed above (64, 6). The only other key known to have been recovered from a Scandinavian-influenced burial of the Viking period in the British Isles and Ireland was found at Pierowall, Westray (144).

8.2.2 Accompanied Burials in Christian Cemeteries: results

Across the north of England study area there are eleven sites containing a minimum of twenty-two burials accompanied by Viking period artefacts other than small personal goods or dress-fittings. The nine Christian cemetery sites equate to the total number of churchyard burials in Scotland (three) and the Isle of Man (six) combined. Comparable use of Christian cemetery sites occurs in Dublin, but over a limited area, unlike the widely spread English examples.

As with the Type I group above and the corpus of burials from Scotland, Ireland and the Isle of Man, the most commonly associated artefacts within these burials were items of weaponry, most particularly the sword, examples of which occurred at eight of the eleven sites. The most common type of sword to be found belonged to the Petersen Type M group (850-900), being recovered from Repton (grave 511) (fig. A6.22: 4), and the North-West sites of Ormside (fig. A6.18) and Rampside (fig. A6.18). After Type H, it is the most common sword found in Viking-period Scandinavia; the majority of finds occurring in north-east Norway (Petersen 1919). The rarity of this type of sword in the rest of the British Isles and Ireland (the grave a Balladoyne Churchyard, Isle of Man; and an unprovenanced find in Kilkenny) gives reason to suggest that these men may have had origins in north-east Norway. Isotopic analysis on the remains of the man in grave 511 at Repton may prove instructive.

Three swords belong to the Anglo-Saxon type (Petersen Type L) were also recovered from, Wensley (fig. A6.24), Camp Hill (fig. A6.5) and again at Repton, although the exact provenance of the latter is now unknown (32, 38, 42). The introduction of this style of sword into Scandinavia is attributed to Viking groups who had been active in England during the late ninth century, and is the predominant design recovered from Scandinavian-influenced burials on the Isle of Man (101-3, 105). Type L swords were also the most common style recovered from the Type I sites above; occurring with the cremations at Heath Wood (mound 1) (fig. A6.9) and Crossmoor (fig. A6.6) (above) (7, 4).

Quite surprisingly only a single example of the most common type Scandinavian Viking-period sword Petersen Type H occurs in the Type II group at Tendley Hill (A6.23) (26). It is one of only two grave-provenanced examples in England (the other in mound 7 at Heath Wood), in comparison to the sixteen swords of this type recovered from the Dublin cemetery sites of Kilmainham and Islandbridge (Walsh 1998: 229) (13, 231). It is found most frequently in western Norway, its incidence in England and Ireland perhaps reflective of the Scandinavian origins of the deceased.

Two swords, now lost, one from Kildale (fig A6.15: 3), the other from Repton survive into modern times in the form of an illustration and a copy, respectively (36, 43). Both can be allocated to Petersen Type X (tenth to eleventh century); which is pertinent in the case of Repton as it is far later than the date of the Great Army's winter fortification of 873-4, and later indeed than the sword in the burial 511 (Petersen Type M, 850-900), directly associated with the martial occupation period (39). This suggests that Scandinavian-influenced groups continued to be linked with the Repton area beyond the evacuation of the Great Army, a hypothesis given more support by the discovery of further, later graves discussed below (Type III) and the one time presence of a hogback tombstone, now lost (39, 80-1) (Lang 1984: 160).

The records of accompanied Viking period interments recovered from beneath hogback tombstones (fig. 8.4) confirm that no list of Viking burials is complete without the inclusion of the one hundred and nine monuments in the study area (Edwards 1998, *Proceedings of the Cumberland & Westmorland Antiquarian & Archaeological Society* 1904, Lang 1984, Whitaker 1823, Kaye 1928). This addition alone drastically increases the number of burials under the Viking influence umbrella, and in doing so negates the question of why are there so few. However, only three of these hugely iconographic stones bear Christian motifs, an important and telling omission on the others on such a symbol of cultural assimilation, as parts of Christian cult practice are adopted and others manipulated to satisfy an assimilating community (Lang 1984).

Other than the modern excavations at Repton, the remaining burials were all sexed via the grave-goods. All were male. As shown above with Scotland and the Isle of Man there is no evidence whatsoever of any diagnostically Scandinavian female burials in the churchyards of northern England.

As with Heath Wood the burials at Repton can be directly associated with the presence of the winter camp of the Great Army (Richards 2003 *a* & *b*, Biddle & Kjølbye-Biddle 2001). It seems likely that the number of these type of burials far exceeded the known four, many no doubt having been disturbed and lost in earlier times and some perhaps still undiscovered. The discovery of artefacts dating to a period later than the Great Army occupation, such as the Petersen Type X sword (tenth to eleventh century), hogback and those graves containing small personal goods (Type III) are compelling evidence for the continued occupation of the area around Repton long after the Great Army had moved on.

All the burials can be dated with reasonable accuracy via the grave-goods, and all interments fit very credibly within the latter decades of the ninth century (fig. 8.2).

8.2.3 Accompanied Burials in Christian Cemeteries: conclusions

The use of Christian cemeteries as the receptacles of Scandinavian-influenced, apparently non-Christian funerary rites can only be seen as the reaction by two groups, immigrant and national, at a moment in time (probably a single generation) created to cater for the coalescing of different cultural practices within a community undergoing the processes of assimilation. In order for the ritual to take place there must have been close interaction between the groups involved with each part of the funerary rite; that is, between the Christian community and its leaders, and those immigrants with some knowledge of the funerary rites of the homeland with sufficient social influence within resident groups. In effect, it is a creation of a new facet of cultural practice – only able to take physical form by the agreement of both parts of the community. This mixing of cultural practice created a funerary tradition alien to both resident and immigrant communities. By this time Anglo-Saxon communities were interring their dead with no grave-goods beyond dress-fittings and the inclusion of occasional small personal items, such as cobs and finger-rings (Geake 1997). Larger, non-personal items, such as weaponry, however, accompanied the Vikings interred within Christian cemeteries. Similarly, the burial of these men in this fashion did not mirror the funerary rites and cultural practices of their homelands. There are no marker mounds, ditches or stone-settings, the grave goods are limited, there is a lack of large animal bone, a purely male artefactual demography, along with the use of Christian cemeteries, as the homelands during this period were still predominantly non-Christian. This apparent sloughing of large parts of basic funerary practices by the immigrants and adoption of the ways of the resident community is consistent with modern anthropological research and migratory principles, as discussed above, which demonstrates that only a specific group of people migrate, and are very unlikely to have a deep knowledge of cult practice or the need to perpetuate it (Laungani 1997, Rosenblatt 1997).

The use of hogback tombstones (fig. 8.4) is alien to both immigrant and national groups, and again appears to be an extremely visible, iconographic representation of the assimilation of two communities through cult practice at a particular period in time (see chapter five) (Richards 2002: 165). These monuments are perhaps more important than the accompanied burials themselves, some of which may or may not have been marked above ground as different to the other non-accompanied interments of the graveyard. The concealment of items during the burial process could mean that only those directly involved with the deposition of the goods, or witness to the burial would know that they were there. Hogbacks were above ground, and permanently on display. Recognition and an understanding of these hybrid Anglo-Scandinavian monuments within the community would have been vital, and their constructions involve many members from within the community. Firstly, there must have been a patron wealthy enough to pay for the carving of such a monument; secondly, he/she must have had the corresponding social influence to enable the hogback to be erected within a churchyard; thirdly, the patron or the stonemason must have had knowledge of the Scandinavian myths and legends in order for them to be recorded in this form. Finally, and most importantly, the priest and the majority Christian community would also have had to be willing to allow the erection and subsequent display of the hogbacks within their sacred space.

Arguably, the use of the Christian graveyard could have been achieved by force but it is more likely that social influence, bound up with the careful diplomacy of assimilation between resident and immigrant was key. The apparent lack of female Scandinavian type burials may be fundamental to the understanding of this. As discussed in chapter three the treatment of the dead in past societies and modern groups beyond the leading countries of what is seen to be the First World is dealt with principally by the immediate family, with support from the community as a whole (van Gennep 1977, Murray Parkes *et al* eds. 1997). The presence of only male Scandinavian-influenced Viking-period burials in Christian graveyards seems indicative of male settlers from Scandinavia intermarrying with local females (and hence their families), who along with any children they may have had, would be primarily responsible for the treatment of his body after death. There is no doubt the funerary rite would also be influenced by the presence of Scandinavian compatriots of the man also settled in the area, who would have had some knowledge of the funerary rites of the homelands and may have influenced or assisted the man's family in carrying out his wishes with regard to burial ritual.

The lack of evidence for diagnostically Scandinavian type female burials in Christian cemeteries may also be due to those performing the funerary rites having little knowledge of cult practice, or in the case of intermarriage within a Christian patriarchal society, swift conversion of religious belief and burial by a Christian family with scant regard for non-Christian beliefs, despite perhaps the wishes of the deceased.

The highly visible presence of male Viking burials and the invisibility of female migrants within Christian cemeteries is comparable to the Isle of Man, and could suggest, as on the Island, that intermarriage with women from resident groups was the norm.

The date range of the burials suggests that these types of interments took place within a single generation, probably during the latter decades of the tenth century, rather than over multiple generations as in Scotland. This must be due to the continuing absorption and assimilation of immigrant groups into Anglo-Saxon society, as ties and knowledge of Scandinavian cultural practice became further removed and diluted by intermarriage and the absence of colonial-type settlements, as in Ireland and Scotland, to perpetuate at least some facets of the funerary practices of the homelands.

The use of identifiable Scandinavian artefacts within a non-Scandinavian type burial site shows reasonably strong links with the homelands while at the same time an integration of cult practice between immigrant and resident groups. The prevailing types of Scandinavian sword to be recovered were Petersen type M (850-900) and the later Type X (tenth to eleventh century), two of a very common style in the homelands (Walsh 1998: 232-3). The plain Type M sword occurs predominantly in north-eastern Norway (Petersen 1919). Its scarcity in the British Isles and Ireland gives reason to suggest that these men may have had their origins in this area of Scandinavia.

These people could perhaps be reasonably linked to the primary settlers of the migration model, the pioneers and the very first migrants into the area. Chronologically it is likely (as with the pioneers) that these people may not be contemporary, and they need not necessarily be so, although the synchronous date ranges of the artefacts could conceivably support it. Migration and settlement is a sequence of perpetual cultural change, its players not governed by a timescale, but by levels of contact and interaction during assimilation processes.

8.3 Accompanied Burials of Viking Period Date in Christian Cemeteries (Type III) (fig. 8.5)

Cambois, Northumberland

During 1859 a mound by the side of the River Wansbeck at Cambois was opened by local antiquarians (Alexander 1987: 101). Inside the mound was found a cist, in which lay a skeleton accompanied by a copper-alloy disc-brooch (Alexander 1987: 101). Also recovered from the mound were a further two skeletons and a decorated bone comb (Alexander 1987: 101). The skulls of those disinterred still survive, and modern assessment identifies them as a woman aged between forty-five and sixty, and two men, one in his twenties, the other in his forties (Alexander 1987: 101-102).

Although the brooch has been dated to the ninth century, there is nothing to suggest it is of Scandinavian type or origin (Alexander 1987: 101-102). In the centre of the brooch is a bird carrying what looks to be a twig in its beak (Alexander 1987: 101). Champlevé enamel work surrounds the bird, bounded by a ring of punched circles (Alexander 1987: 101). This in turn is circled by a wider band of further, indistinguishable decoration (almost scallop shell like) edged by a series of scored lines (Alexander 1987: 101-102). The comb is plainly decorated on both sides with a series of incised lines and hatching (Alexander 1987: 102-3). Similar combs have been found in York and in the tenth century burial of a female at St Patrick's Chapel, Heysham (see below) (Alexander 1987: 103, Potter & Andrews 1994). Due to the manner of excavation it is unknown whether the three interments were contemporary, or whether they were secondary burials in an earlier mound. While the ninth and tenth century dates of the brooch and comb, respectively, insinuates a likely accompanied Viking period burial, it has no real compelling Scandinavian indicators. The use of cists and stone-lined graves, while commonly encountered in Viking burials, for example in Scotland, are by no means limited to this period or even non-Christian burials. If the burials were Viking and contemporary, then one would have expected far more in the way of grave goods, especially weaponry for the men. If the mound was primarily raised by Viking settlers for these people, the scarcity of the grave goods does not reflect the effort needed to raise such a monument. Surely if this person or people were deemed deserving of such a memorial then they would have been provided with more personal items of wealth to carry with them to the afterlife for use and indicators of their position in their society.

The iconography of the brooch is particularly Christian, the dove representative of the Holy Spirit. The design is one seen on enamelled brooches found in association with Christian contexts on the Continent, and is also strikingly similar to that found at Hyde Abbey, Winchester (Bersu & Wilson 1964: 85, Alexander 1987: 102). It is highly likely that these burials were part of a Christian cemetery, the church being in possession of the land where the burial was found since the tenth century (Alexander 1987: 103). Without knowledge of the dimensions, the tumulus from which the burials were recovered may have been simply a small rise in the ground.

Carlisle Cathedral, Cumbria

Recent excavations undertaken in the cathedral grounds at Carlisle uncovered a series of accompanied inhumations with the artefacts dating to the Viking period (Tweddle – unpublished, Anon, site report of Cathedral Green excavations, unpublished). The artefacts included a ring-headed pin, a dot and ring decorated buckle comparable to others found in Viking period contexts in the Scottish Islands and York, and a gold toggle decorated with a gold wire ball, similar to those recovered from Peel (Tweddle – unpublished, Anon, site report of Cathedral Green excavations, unpublished). Grave 251 was found to contain an inhumation accompanied by a buckle decorated in Scandinavian design, a knife in its sheath, a silver capped pendant whetstone, a copper-alloy scale pan fragment and a copper-alloy ingot (Tweddle – unpublished, Anon, site report of Cathedral Green excavations, unpublished).

Ripon, Yorkshire

Four combs and two cases of Scandinavian design, datable to between the ninth and mid-eleventh centuries, were recovered from a series of burials at the Ladykirk site on St Marygate (MacGregor 1987: 127, in Hall & Whyman 1987). The Sites and Monuments Record also lists the find of a hogback tombstone from the vicinity (NYM 19766).

Heysham, Lancashire

Next to St Peter's (see above) are the ruined remains of St Patrick's chapel, which formed part of an excavation undertaken during the nineteen-seventies and eighties. In grave sixty-three, situated just out side the chapel was found the remains of a female, accompanied by a poor quality cow bone comb, perhaps made specifically for use in a burial context, of a type commonly recovered from Viking graves in Scotland and from Anglo-Scandinavian contexts in York (Cook & Batey 1994: 122-124). Radiocarbon dates and artefactual analyses place the grave in the tenth century (Potter & Andrews 1994). Although accompanied by the comb, it is hard to imagine that this was the grave of a pagan Viking female, when one compares it to graves of a similar date in Scotland (see above). It seems more likely a personal rather than a ritual deposition connected with funerary rites, a wish of possibly the deceased or the people burying her. The likelihood that this was a Christian rather than a pagan burial is also compounded by the discovery of charcoal within the grave, a practice carried out in the past by church authorities to ensure that the land was perpetually marked for use by

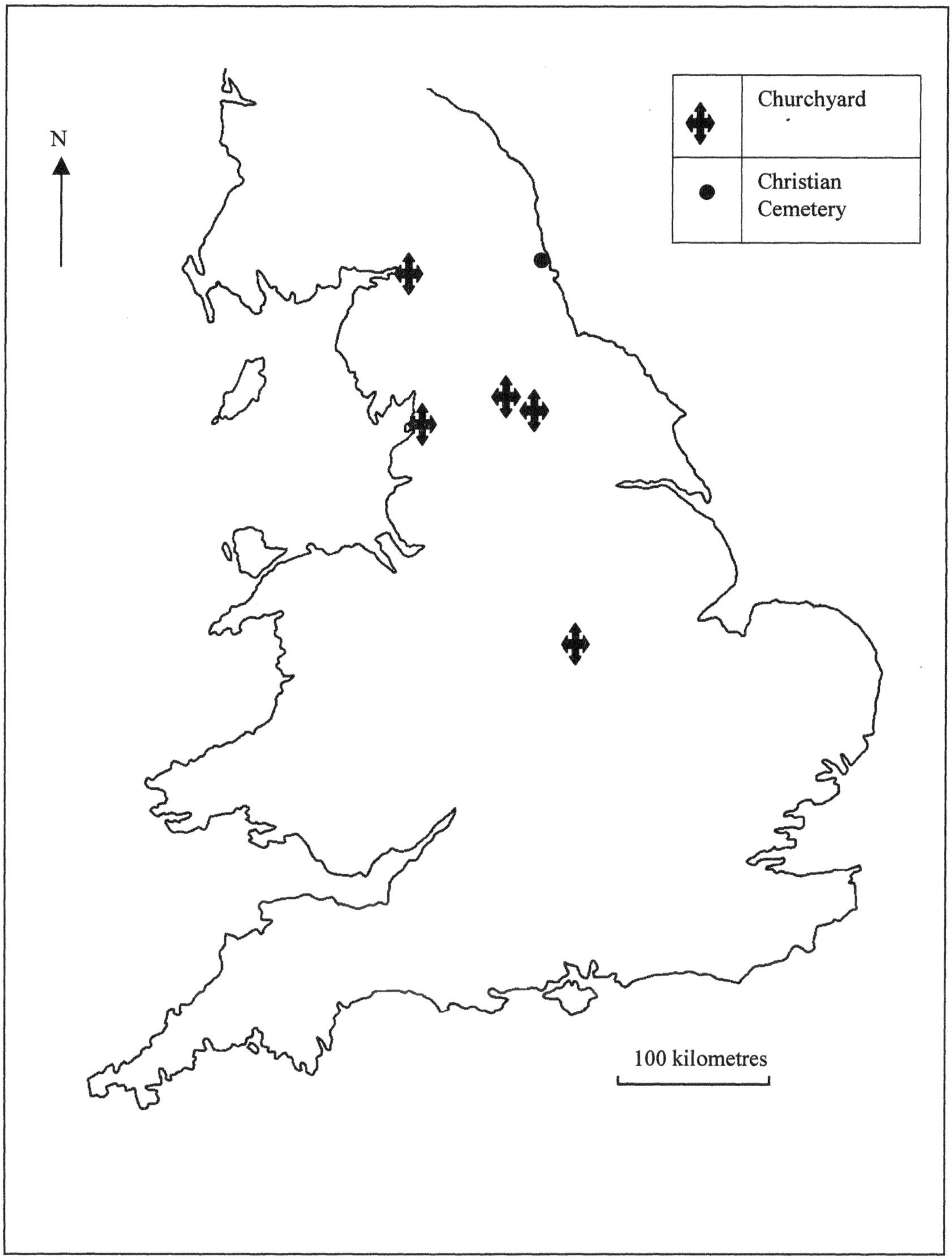

Fig. 8.5 *Accompanied Burials of Viking Period Date in Christian Cemeteries*

ecclesiastical authority (Anderson 1872: 529). The use of charcoal was also found during excavation of contemporary burials in York Minster (Phillips & Heywood 1995: 88-92). Interestingly the charcoal burials all seem to be associated with female graves.

York Minster, Yorkshire

Recent excavations within the Minster at York have recovered a series of inhumation burials datable to the Viking period, accompanied by a range of small personal items, ranging from finger-rings, comb fragments, grave-slabs of Scandinavian design, a key, chest fragments, ships' timbers reused as a coffin, pottery and glass (a full list of associated burials in appendix 3) (Phillips & Heywood 1995). Four of the inhumations were placed amongst a deposit of charcoal, a symbol of Christianity, found also in the female comb burial at Heysham (see above) (Phillips & Heywood 1995). Fragments of hogback tombstones also survive from the Minster site (Lang 1984: 170).

St Mary Bishophill Senior

Excavation prior to the demolition of the church during 1963 recovered a tenth century strap-end associated with the scattered remains of an inhumation (Ramm 1976: 45). A large piece of a hogback tombstone has also been provenanced to the churchyard (Lang 1984: 170).

St Mary Bishophill Junior

Excavations at the churchyard during the nineteen-eighties recovered a series of tenth century burials accompanied by small personal items. A St Peter's Penny, datable to between 905-915, a knife, whetstone and a buckle plate, were recovered from the grave of a young adult male (Wenham *et al* 1987: 80). A further burial was found to contain the remains of a young adult of unascertainable sex wearing a late ninth-early tenth century penannular silver arm-ring of Scandinavian design (Wenham *et al* 1987: 80). A further silver armlet was found interred with the remains of a young child (Wenham *et al* 1987: 81). The final accompanied burial was of a female, possibly associated with a bone pin (Wenham *et al* 1987: 81). The excavation also recovered four other associated unaccompanied burials of a male, two females and a child (Wenham *et al* 1987: 80-1).

A central fragment of a hogback tombstone also survives from the site (Lang 1984: 170).

Repton, Derbyshire

As discussed above there is evidence to suggest that the site of the Great Army's winter camp at Repton was only the beginning of Viking settlement in the area. A further Scandinavian type grave was also discovered during the excavations, although it had been dug some years after the Viking military occupation (Biddle & Kjølbye-Biddle 2001: 65). In it were the remains of a middle-aged woman who had been interred with a knife with its hilt decorated with silver wire, and a strike-a-light (Biddle & Kjølbye-Biddle 2001: 65).

Other than the female and the traditional type burials previously considered, a further accompanied burial of a male was found near the church building, wearing a gold finger-ring and accompanied by five silver pennies dating to the mid 870's (Biddle & Kjølbye-Biddle 2001: 65). From the grave goods, however, it seems more likely that he was a member of the local community rather than the Great Army.

The excavation of 'Cemetery 3M', close to the sunken building also produced a series of tenth century burials accompanied by small personal goods, including knives, richly ornamented garments, Scandinavian type jewellery and decorated silver wire balls of the sort found at Peel (Biddle & Kjølbye-Biddle 2001: 85-86).

The cemetery, later burial of the woman, the tenth century sword and the hogback could be evidence for some of the Viking camp staying behind and settling when the bulk of the army moved off, or perhaps the return of veterans of the army or camp.

8.3.1 Artefactual Analysis of Accompanied Burials of Viking Period Date in Christian Cemeteries

This section will consider the correlation and significance of the burials discussed above both as a discrete whole, and within the wider context of the rest of Britain and Ireland, and Scandinavia where appropriate. Owing to the nature of the analysis and in order to facilitate fluidity of structure where multiple sites will be compared within a sentence all general references to the sites are those listed in appendix five and will be provided at the end of the sentence in numerical form (for example, Carlisle grave 251 would be (47)). Where specific points are drawn from particular sources full references will be made in the standard fashion. Analysis of the sites will be undertaken in traditional comparative manner via burial rites and artefactual analysis. This has been done not only to glean information from the archaeological remains, but show that the divisions used above are extremely valuable and more helpful in understanding interaction between immigrant and settled groups.

By the very nature of the Type III burial (that is, with small personal goods) the collection of small objects within the group does not conform to any Viking-period Scandinavian-influenced stereotype or pattern seen in Types I and II, and the burials in the corpus from the rest of the British Isles and Ireland. The most common finds were bone combs, occurring at four of the nine sites; Cambois (fig. A6.4: 1); Ladykirk and St Marygate, Ripon; Heysham (fig. A6.14); and a very small fragment of a tooth was recovered from the fill of grave 50 at York Minster (44, 52, 53, 58). It was possible to identify the remains interred with the combs at Cambois, Heysham and York Minster as female (44, 53, 58). As discussed above, bone combs are an extremely common find in both domestic and grave contexts across the British Isles. The manner of deposition differs from those found in the traditional type Scandinavian-influenced burials of the Viking-period in Scotland, where the majority of females were accompanied by a pair of combs, and males, one (see above, also chapter seven & appendix five). This difference may be due to fashion or the incumbent possessing only one comb; although it seems far more likely that those people responsible for the burials were far more socially imbued by the mixing of Anglo-Saxon and Scandinavian immigrant cultural practices than the colonists of the Northern and Western Isles, who by the very nature of their settlement were able to maintain a greater part of the cultural practices of their homeland (see chapters six and seven). By comparison, of Types I and II above, only the cremation at Hesket was found to contain combs (1).

Pendant whetstones were recovered from the male inhumation at Carlisle Cathedral (grave 251) and the grave of the youth at St Mary Bishophill Junior, York (47, 72). With a length of 15.9cm, the whetstone from the grave of the adult is over twice the length of the example interred with the youth, which measured 6.5cm (47, 72, appendix 6). This is consistent with the miniature whetstones found in the burials of children at Cnip, Lewis, and Housegord, Shetland (203, 173). As discussed above, whetstones are a very common find in Scandinavian-influenced graves of the Viking-period across the British Isles and Ireland (chapter seven, appendix five). A whetstone was recovered from the cremation at Hesket (Type

I), amongst the artefacts from Kildale Church (Type II) (fig. A6.15: 2), and Pippin Castle (Type II) (fig. A8.3).

The whetstones in this Type III group were found in the graves containing the most artefacts, suggestive perhaps that those responsible for the interments were more influenced by immigrant traditions of settled Scandinavian groups. Although devoid of weaponry, the male interred at Carlisle had placed with him a folding knife, the remains of a set of scales and a copper-alloy ingot (47). The youth at York was also interred with a knife, along with a St Peter's Penny, dating to 905-15 (72). The folding knife in the Carlisle grave is similar to those recovered from Repton grave 511 (Type II) and Aspatria (Type I), and the scales find parallel with those recovered from Kildale (Type II) (47, 39, 2, 33). Weights and scales were also recovered from the Dublin cemeteries of Kilmainham and Islandbridge; Scar, Sanday; Broch of Gurness, Orkney; Kiloran Bay, Colonsay (fig. 7.15) and Tarbert, Gigha (231, 148, 156, 179, 191).

Along with Carlisle 251 and the burial of the youth at St Mary Bishophill Junior, small knives were also recovered from Repton (graves 295 and 203), and Ailcy Hill, Ripon (grave group 1064) (40, 81, 51). Grave 295 at Repton, adjacent to 511, contained a male inhumation who wore a dagger at his waist (40). The flat-backed knife with its handle decorated with silver wire recovered from the grave of a female (grave 203), also at Repton, draws immediate comparison to the description and surviving illustration of a knife from the Type II site of Kildale (fig. A6.15: 5) (lost) (37, 81). A knife was recovered from the Type I site Ormside, although this too has been subsequently lost (27). Beyond England, knives are extremely common in Scandinavian-influenced graves of the Viking-period across the corpus of burials discussed in chapter seven in Scotland, Ireland and the Isle of Man (see also appendix five).

In England only Type III sites produced coins. Along with the St Peter's Penny recovered from the burial of the youth at St Mary Bishophill, York, five silver Anglo-Saxon pennies dating to the 870's were recovered from grave 83 at Repton and a series of unprovenanced stycas found in the vicinity of Ailcy Hill, Ripon (72, appendix 6, 51). Three Northumbrian stycas, one dating to 808-40, another to 831-54, the third illegible, were recovered from the burial at Kiloran Bay, Colonsay; and a further example dating to 837-54 from King's Cross Point, Lamlash, Arran (179, 186). A coin of Edmund (940-6) was recovered from the burial at Buckquoy, Orkney; and of Eadred (946-55) with the inhumation of a child at Peel (161, 100). Nineteenth century accounts also report the discovery of Hiberno-Norse coins being discovered in the churchyard at St Magnen's, Kilmainham, Dublin, although it is not known whether they formed part of a hoard or a burial (251).
Items of personal adornment are limited to a single brooch at Cambois, whose Christian symbolism can be paralleled with similar finds in ecclesiastical contexts of Anglo-Saxon Southern England and the Carolingian Empire (Alexander 1987: 102). The ring-headed pin recovered from Carlisle Cathedral (grave 242/4), was very likely a shroud fastener, comparable to that recovered from Brigham above (Type II) (48, 25). As already discussed, such pins are ubiquitous across Viking-period contexts in the British Isles and Ireland, and their uses in dress manifold.

The gold wire toggle and sphere recovered from within Carlisle Cathedral are also thought to have been a decorative part of a robe, and are similar to those silver spheres recovered from the cemetery at Peel, Isle of Man (50, 95, 97). Gold finger-rings were found in grave 68 at York Minster and Repton, grave 529 (64, 80). A copper-alloy finger-ring was also recovered from grave 83 at Repton (appendix 6). No other finger-rings occur in the corpus of burials of the British Isles and Ireland, although they are a common unprovenanced find from the period.

The silver penannular arm-rings from the graves of the children at St Mary's Bishophill Junior, York, again has no parallel, although such objects are most commonly found in hoards (see chapter five) (75, 79).

The copper-alloy buckle, from Carlisle Cathedral grave 251, decorated with five bosses is similar to those recovered from Cnip, Lewis; Ardkinish, Colonsay; Eigg; and Coppergate, York (Tweddle, unpublished). Similarly, the dot and ring decorated copper-alloy buckle and strap-end from Carlisle Cathedral grave 269, finds parallel with the buckle-plate buried with the youth at St Mary Bishophill Junior, York, and from the burials at Peel, Isle of Man (Tweddle unpublished). The copper-alloy strap-end recovered from a grave at St Mary Bishophill Senior, York, is of common Anglo-Scandinavian type, bearing dot and ring marks on the underside and a Borre-style ring-chain on the upper (71).

The key accompanying the gold finger-ring in grave 68, York Minster, is paralleled only in England from the Type II context at Repton (grave 511) (fig. A6.22: 8) (64, 39). The only other key recovered from a Scandinavian-influenced burial of the Viking-period in the British Isles and Ireland occurred at Pierowall, Westray (144).

The pottery and glass fragments found in some of the graves within the Minster site at York have no parallels within the corpus of Scandinavian-influenced Viking-period graves, and must be seen as a product of an assimilating community, perpetuating and adapting traditions from within both Anglo-Saxon and Scandinavian cultural milieu. Out of the four cases where pottery was recovered on only one occasion did it accompany another item, which was the glass in grave 105 (57, 59, 61, 67). Grave 105, however, was the only inhumation not to be covered by a slab bearing Anglo-Scandinavian motifs (57, 59, 61, 67).

The final item to be considered is the strike-a-light recovered from the female inhumation at Repton (grave 203) (81). Which has parallels with the male inhumations at Balladoole, Isle of Man and Westness, Rousay (91) (Kaland 1993, Graham-Campbell & Batey 1998: 137).

8.3.2 Accompanied Burials of Viking Period Date in Christian Cemeteries: results

From the study there are nine sites containing upwards of thirty-five inhumations, accompanied by either small personal artefacts and/or marked by a grave-slab decorated by Scandinavian influenced designs.

The use of grave markers carved with Scandinavian motifs is visible alongside hogbacks within York Minster, non-Christian iconography being tolerated within the most important ecclesiastical building in the area, and housing the remains of the upper echelons of Northumbrian society (Phillips & Heywood 1995) (chapter five).

Where it could be ascertained, the sexing of the remains produced a balanced demography of nine females, eight males, and five children. The children all came from the burial sites within York, and while their survival may owe much to modern recovery techniques, no others have been found from the above-mentioned Viking type burial sites (Phillips & Heywood, Wenham *et al* 1987).

By the eclectic nature of small personal goods, the collection of objects within the group does not conform to any Viking-period Scandinavian-influenced stereotype or pattern seen in Types I or II, and the burials in the corpus from the rest of the British Isles and Ireland. Combs, pieces of glass and pottery, knives and other small domestic accoutrements, dress-fittings, trinkets and coins are all not unusual finds within Anglo-Saxon Christian graves of the period (Geake 1997), and their deposition here may owe as much to local origins than to Scandinavian influence.

Scandinavian-influence is perhaps visible in grave 251 at Carlisle cathedral and the graves of the children at St Mary Bishophill Junior, York (47, 72, 75, 79). The remains of a copper-alloy ingot and scale-pan found in Carlisle Cathedral 251 finds analogy with those recovered from Kildale (Type II) (fig. A6.15: 1), the Dublin cemetery sites of Kilmainham and Islandbridge; Scar, Sanday, Broch of Gurness, Orkney; Kiloran Bay, Colonsay (fig. A7.15); and Tarbert, Gigha (33, 231, 148, 156, 179, 191). The folding knife from the same burial is similar to those recovered from Repton 511 (Type II) and Aspatria (Type I), although it is worth pointing out here that such objects are a common find in Anglo-Saxon domestic contexts (for example, Thwing, E Yorks) (Ottaway 2000: 35).

The discovery of a miniature pendant whetstone in the grave of the youth at St Mary Bishophill Junior, York, provides more compelling evidence of Scandinavian influences at work in the circumstances of his burial (72), being consistent with the finds in the burials of children at Cnip, Lewis and Housegord, Shetland (203, 173). The silver-penannular arm-rings from the two other graves strongly hint at the scandinavianess of their influence, although such depositions find no analogy within the corpus (75, 79).

The decorated copper-alloy buckle from Carlisle Cathedral 251 is similar to those recovered from Cnip, Lewis; Ardkinish, Colonsay; Eigg; and Coppergate, York (Tweddle, unpublished), illustrative again of the links this man had with the Viking world of the Irish Sea region. The scenario is also seen in grave 269 at Carlisle Cathedral, which was found to contain a dot and ring decorated copper-alloy buckle and strap-end, a design found on the buckle-plate buried with the youth at St Mary Bishophill Junior, York, and from the Viking-period burials at Peel on the Isle of Man (Tweddle, unpublished). The dating of the burials has been done via artefactual analysis, and in the case of York Minster, radiocarbon dating. Unlike the rest of the burials discussed above, the date ranges are much broader, covering the eighth to the thirteenth centuries. Most, however, seem to fall around the mid-tenth century mark (fig. 8.2).

Amongst the grave goods there are no real diagnostically identifiable Scandinavian objects. Scandinavian influence is evident in Carlisle 251 and 242/4, and the graves of the two children at St Mary's Bishophill Junior, York, with their penannular arm-rings (Tweddle, unpublished) (47, 72-9). However, none could feasibly be used as strong evidence for the presence of a traditional Viking burial, given the other circumstances of the interment, and as argued above must be dealt with as a separate type, an accompanied burial of Viking-period date in a Christian cemetery.

8.3.3 Accompanied Burials of Viking Period Date in Christian Cemeteries: conclusions

There is little doubt that this list is already out of date and expanding with every excavation undertaken in or around the ecclesiastical centres of the towns in the north of England. What they do highlight, however, are the supposed *problems* of identifying *Viking* burials. All fall within the Viking period, some had token grave-deposits, and others had grave-markers decorated with Scandinavian influenced designs, and many were recovered from the so-called Viking capital of York, yet none are particularly identifiable as Viking graves. Small personal objects are regularly recovered from Anglo-Saxon burial contexts within Christian cemeteries across England throughout this later period, and the discovery of such artefacts in Viking-period contexts in the north should not automatically be seen as a direct result of Scandinavian influence. Links across the Viking world in the Irish Sea region are shown in the graves from Carlisle Cathedral and St Mary Bishophill Junior, York, where the same Anglo-Scandinavian designs are found in the Isle of Man and the Western Isles. This and the use of Scandinavian-influenced designs on grave-slabs in York Minster is physical evidence for further progress in the process of assimilation within the community, especially amongst the upper echelons of Northumbrian society. In most of the cases discussed it would be impossible to describe these people in ethnic terms, except possibly as Northumbrians, with reference to William of Malmesbury's tenth century account, who described the Norse, Danes, and Anglo-Saxons in Northumbria as being of one race (see chapter four), the blurring of cultural indicators becoming such in the process of assimilation, displayed again here in the case of burials (WM: 108).

Unlike the other types of burials discussed above, the date ranges are wide, evidence of different levels of interaction and assimilation between immigrants and nationals during different periods and circumstances.

8.4 Viking Immigrant Burials: discussion

"Placed in context of a particular ideological, social and economic systems, rituals of death begin to make sense in a way that they cannot if we pursue elusive cultural universals" (Metcalf & Huntington 1993: 75).

Although this study is primarily focussed on Viking burial in the north of England, it has proved vital to set it in context by comparing and contrasting the funerary rites of other immigrant groups in the British Isles and Ireland. While there are some similarities between regions, it is the differences that are far more conspicuous and offer the potential to further understanding of the archaeological record.

It can be seen that by dividing the corpus of burials into three distinct types it has been possible to better understand the socio-cultural processes surrounding those people involved in the disposal of the dead in the north of England during the Viking-period. There is little doubt that as time goes on more examples of each type will be discovered in the countryside and towns, but little is to be gained via the perpetuation of the Viking-burial numbers debate. In order to advance understanding of settlement processes, the archaeologist should be looking for evidence of possible Scandinavian-influence, and trying to appreciate why and how those subjects of deposition became interred. If the artefacts permit, or indeed isotopic analysis has been employed in order to ascertain the geographical region where the deceased spent their early years, the grave-group may be linked into the wider Scandinavian-influenced world. From examination of the corpus in chapters seven and eight, there is compelling evidence to suggest that those women interred with the same type of tortoise brooches (R647) and copper-alloy bowl at Red House; Ballyholme, Co. Down; and Westness, Rousay, perhaps shared a common origin.

By separating the burials into simple groups it has been possible to identify that those members of the Type I list are linked primarily by their positions in the landscape, via; the re-use of prehistoric burial mounds, the use of the extant funerary landscape, the association of all the sites with transport routes, and their situation beyond known limits of Anglo-Saxon village settlements. Although they share many artefactual similarities, and the tendency of using prehistoric burial sites with the rest of the British Isles and Ireland, there is no evidence to suggest that the Type I burials were anything other than a single event, carried out by transient groups at a specific moment in time. This is in contrast to the traditional type Scandinavian-influenced family burial sites of Scotland, and the Dublin cemetery sites during the Viking-period, which depict a period of use, and signs of a colony as the residents or at least those involved with the burial of the dead, were permitted by parochial circumstances to maintain some aspects of the cultural reaction to death carried out within the homelands at the time of their departure.

By comparison, those burials incorporated within Type II are representative of a period of early assimilation, a negotiation between resident groups and established settlers of Scandinavian origin over the disposal of those whose cultural background did not arise within Anglo-Saxon England. This adoption of national burial practices by Scandinavian settlers is entirely consistent with patterns observed within modern-day immigrant communities (Laungani 1997, Rosenblatt 1997). The use of the hogback tombstone is a concept alien to both immigrant and national groups, and should be seen in a similar light; as an object created by the interaction of two communities. These monuments are perhaps more important than the accompanied burials themselves in understanding integration and settlement between Anglo-Saxon and Scandinavian groups, as in direct contrast to the interred items, they were above ground and on permanent display.

The very nature of small personal goods defies compartmentalisation along religious lines (that is, Christian or non-Christian); without drawing analogy to the interment today (cremation or inhumation) of a person with his or her favourite items of attire or jewellery, it is not unknown for similar trinkets (combs, knives *etc*) and pieces of clothing to be recovered from what was acknowledged to be Christian Anglo-Saxon graves (Geake 1997).

As argued above, recognition of Scandinavian influence is a different matter. The copper-alloy scale-pan and ingot fragments found within grave 251 at Carlisle Cathedral draws immediate analogy to the burials at Kildale and Kiloran Bay, Colonsay, both sites where sets of weights and scales were recovered (47, 33, 179). However, there the similarity ends. The spectacular boat-burial of a socially-powerful male, attired with numerous martial accoutrements and a harnessed riding-horse, on a headland on Colonsay bears little resemblance to the confines of the ecclesiastical complex at Carlisle at the same date (179, 47). Even the church burial at Kildale is different, the set of weights and scales here associated with a burial containing a sword and spear; part of a series of eight inhumations all similarly martially attired (33-7). In contrast to both of these sites, Carlisle Cathedral 251 had with him a small folding pocket-knife and a sharpening stone (47).

Correspondingly, the burial of the youth at St Mary Bishophill Junior, York, with his small pendant whetstone is analogous with that of the child at Cnip, Lewis (208). While he lies alone in a town churchyard, the child at Cnip was buried in a small family graveyard alongside adults buried in traditional Scandinavian fashion (207-13).

While the dates of all these interments may be roughly contemporary, each burial took place under different sets of socio-cultural circumstances, and are reflective of that. The Scottish burials reveal the perpetuation of some Scandinavian burial practices, enabled by colonial style settlement; whereas the youth at York and the man at Carlisle were buried in a Christian town churchyard, no doubt under the direction of the priest who gave the attendant grave-side mass. The evidence for Scandinavian influence lies only in the link of a single object at each site, the miniature pendant whetstone at York, and the fragmentary remains of a copper-alloy scale-pan and ingot from Carlisle Cathedral 251 (47, 72). However, these links provide the opportunity to better understand the interaction and assimilation processes going on during the Viking-period in the north of England between resident and immigrant Scandinavian groups.

CHAPTER NINE - VIKING BURIAL IN THE NORTH OF ENGLAND: CONCLUSIONS

9.0 Introduction

The main aim of this research was to understand why there are apparently so few Scandinavian type burials in the north of England. The methods employed comprised of a multi-disciplinary approach, utilising not only the archaeological record, but primary historical sources, anthropology and theoretical modelling of culture contact during periods of assimilation between immigrant and resident groups. These methods were chosen to address the two key issues of the study; firstly, that the Viking groups were immigrants into a far from empty landscape; and secondly, that funerary rites are subject to a whole array of factors, dictated by the socio-cultural milieu in which the deceased had lived. These issues were fundamental to the study, and the theme of contact and interaction between immigrant and resident groups absolutely vital in the construction of hypotheses from the available evidence.

9.1 Conclusions

The research began by examining recent anthropological studies into funerary ritual and how they are inextricably linked to the society in which they are practiced (Radcliffe-Brown 1968: 163, Murray Parkes *et al* ed. 1997). During the period covered by the study the social fabric of the Viking homelands was undergoing a critical change, as the smaller, family owned estates were being incorporated into fledgling kingdoms. Correspondingly the state sponsored cult of Christianity was being introduced, and was to eventually replace the older, more personal community perpetuated farming based beliefs. Amongst these beliefs was a strong tendency towards ancestor worship, vividly recorded in the poetry and sagas of the Viking world. This facet of the religion was especially linked to the establishment of burial places, where the living validated claims to land by the very visible chronology of ancient ancestor mounds (see chapter three). The re-use of prehistoric burial sites is extremely evident in the archaeological records of the British Isles and Ireland (see chapters seven and eight), and it seems likely that immigrant groups were recognising and perpetuating funerary sites, as they had in their homelands.

However, as mentioned above, the Viking groups in the British Isles and Ireland were immigrants, and as such were subject to multiple and complex influences, some as a result of their own peculiar socio-cultural attributes and others from resident populations (see below and chapter six). By migrating, a person is removing himself/herself from the direct influence of their immediate community, which in the Viking period would be for the most part family members (Laungani 1997, Rosenblatt 1997: 38). Removed from these influences, anthropological research has shown that the discarding of cultural practice pertaining to funerary ritual is swift, and one of the primary cultural facets to be stripped during the settlement and assimilation processes in a new land (Laungani 1997). While it is shocking to think that such an intrinsic part of a belief system should be discarded so quickly, it is important to point out that this loss of ritual practice is not analogous with changes in religious belief (Laungani 1997, Rosenblatt 1997: 38). Such evidence of reactions by immigrant groups to personal and external socio-cultural influences upon a single, fundamental part of human behaviour, proved absolutely vital in the understanding of the Scandinavian type funerary evidence in the north of England.

The theme of contact and interaction and their subsequent effects on both immigrant and resident groups was continued in the study of the primary historical accounts relating to this period. For the most part they form a narrative of the conflicts between Viking raiders and resident Anglo-Saxon groups, although records survive pertaining to more peaceful interaction, including trade and during periods of subsequent settlement. Although from the contemporary sources it appears that all contact between war-bands and the resident Anglo-Saxon populace was solely aggressive, an army must be fed, equipped and entertained, crucial factors not perpetually sustainable from its own resources. With this in mind, it can be seen that non-martial contact did not begin pristinely during the historically attested settlements of the north in the late ninth century. Socio-cultural contact and with it, varying levels of assimilation had been proceeding for a great number of years prior to this, simply changing in manner and intensity as the needs and situations propelling it dictated the manner of interaction between Viking and resident groups at a particular time.

Vital to the process of assimilation, and overlooked by Viking period scholars, is the crucial effect the use of towns as winter camps would have had on both members of the Great Army and Anglo-Saxon residents. As discussed in chapter six, the speed of assimilation of immigrant and resident groups is vastly increased within towns (Beijer 1969: 54, Jansen 1969: 68). This use of towns continued throughout the settlement period, and the historical accounts of the early tenth century attest to the fact that they were still the focal points for the satellite communities in the surrounding countryside where immigrants and the descendents of immigrants lived alongside native Anglo-Saxons (see chapters four and five), some fifty years after the arrival and conquests of the Great Army.

From the study made of contemporary law codes and legal documents what is immediately clear is the speed at which Scandinavian settlers became involved in Anglo-Saxon law and practice. The Alfred-Guthrum Treaty is the first of the known extant legal documents to recognise and deal with Scandinavian and resident Anglo-Saxons as two separate ethnic groups, a tradition which was to continue in various forms until the ascension of Cnut in 1017. Similarly, the Alfred-Guthrum Treaty marked the first accommodation of Scandinavian terminology and aspects of law and practice into Anglo-Saxon statutes, again factors which were to occur and increase up until the Danish conquest. Overall, the legal documents of the period show an immediate and lasting influence by Scandinavian groups from all levels of society and in all manner of transactions, as successful integration of settled immigrant groups took place.

As with the historical documents of the period, analysis of Scandinavian-influenced stone-sculpture, language and settlement pattern showed the theme of contact and interaction between immigrant and resident populations to be very clearly in evidence throughout. In aspects of stone-sculpture, there is nothing to identify the patron of each example as being of Scandinavian descent, but there is no doubt that elite members of the immigrant community were the catalyst behind the boom in production and shift in market from majority ecclesiastical to secular consumption. Their continued display within churchyards also hints strongly of the manipulation of cultural fashion by the Anglo-Saxon clergy to facilitate the acceptance of Christianity, a method employed by missionaries since the earliest of times. The adoption of stone-sculpture as a commemorative technique, the introduction of new motifs by Scandinavian groups, combined with the continuation of Anglian traditions, fused to create an artistic schema entirely induced by the successful assimilation of immigrant and resident populations. The design and use of the hogback must also be recognized as a physical manifestation of the interaction between two groups during the assimilation process. The negotiations involved in the establishment of these monuments within churchyards, the majority of which bear no discernible Christian representations, cannot be underestimated or ignored.

This creation of a new cultural facet from two cultural origins is repeated in the study of place-names, and the recognition that a Scandinavian-influenced place-name arose within a district where both Old Scandinavian and Old English were spoken. The existence of a bi-lingual community is best illustrated by the fact that the majority of place-name forms are hybrid mixtures of the similar Old English and Old Scandinavian languages. This in itself reflects the level of assimilation taking place via the amalgamation of languages. The influence of Old Scandinavian on river names, whose forms are notoriously resistant to change, is a testament to the extent of its linguistic use in their vicinity; their adoption and perpetuation in Middle English a clear affirmation of successful and active assimilation. The use of Scandinavian and Scandinavian-influenced place-names within wapentakes is not surprising, but they are not exclusive and exist alongside districts bearing Old English names.

The most available archaeological evidence for Scandinavian-influence within settlement sites comes from the pre-construction archaeological evaluation work undertaken in towns such as York and Lincoln. Artefactual and structural remains demonstrate the use of Anglo-Scandinavian designs and economic vitality of the period; the growth and development of urban sites being dependent on the successful interaction between resident and incoming groups. In the countryside the high status site at Cottam provides evidence for the consumption of Anglo-Scandinavian goods amongst elite members of society, and encourages the exploration of further DMV sites to widen the field of knowledge of late Anglo-Saxon settlements. Such expansion of the dataset would also aid in placing Ribblehead, Simy Folds and Bryant's Gill in context, and perhaps establish once and for all whether they are examples of traditional upland construction techniques (which is likely) or an introduction into northern England by Scandinavian settlers.

Overall the picture provided by the Scandinavian-influenced archaeological resource of the late Anglo-Saxon period parallels that of the historical data, showing clear evidence of interaction and successful assimilation between resident and immigrant communities. The answers to why and how this took place was provided by analysis of migration and settlement of immigrant groups. As demonstrated in chapter six, migration is an extremely complex event, governed and driven by the human psyche. Despite this, it is also predictable, and there occurs a series of elements common between all migrating groups which make it possible to list a number of general rules (Anthony 1997: 22). Although the list of trends (see chapter six) cover different facets of observable behaviour by migrants, it is immediately clear that each element is based on some knowledge of the potential homeland. The importance of information flow in the decision to migrate cannot be over-emphasised. Such a venture, engendering as it does huge socio-economic risk on the chance of gain, are not made against the promise of an unknown land. Adventurers, traders or mercenaries, known as *pioneers*, all of whom are generally young adult males, relay reports and stories of new territories back to kin and friends at home (fig. 6.1). It is these reports that encourage the potential migrant. As discussed in chapter four, it would be inconceivable to think that the first contact the people of eighth century England had with Scandinavia was via piratical raids, and it is not beyond the realms of possibility to suggest that there had been, prior to this period, a certain amount of migratory movement and settlement. It would have been this knowledge of the landscape (people, geography, political and economic) that precipitated the first Viking raids on profitable Anglo-Saxon targets. The attack on Portland Harbour (789) is perfectly representative of this. At least one contemporary author was aware of the origins of the men (Æ, ASC), and in turn, they knew the Wessex coastline and where to execute a successful raid. A similar situation must be proposed for the raids carried out in Northumbria in 793 and 794. Stories and descriptions of the raids, alongside the tangible evidence of plunder, relayed by the men to kin and friends would have greatly increased knowledge of Anglo-Saxon England.

The establishment of semi-permanent camps from 850 onwards (see chapter four) would have provided opportunity for a great deal of non-martial contact with resident Anglo-Saxon groups, resulting in the accruing of further knowledge of the landscape and its people by the raiding parties. There is no doubt that this period of raiding provided the information to encourage the formation of the Great Army.

By combining the background research into the historical period of Scandinavia (chapter three) and Anglo-Saxon England (chapter four), along with the socio-economic traits identified from the migratory studies, it was possible to directly associate the members of the Great Army with the pioneers of the migration model. The use of these migratory principles proved to be the third dimension lacking in Viking period studies, and allied with the archaeological and historical resources opened the door to understanding the manner of socio-cultural interaction between immigrant and resident Anglo-Saxon communities, and then to understanding their burial practices. The very particular set of characteristics common to members of pioneer groups (and subsequent émigrés) produces four extremely important facts:

i. They are not a culturally homogeneous group,
ii. They are not representative of their particular cultural group,
iii. They are not a cross-section of their particular cultural group,
iv. They are not a representative cross-section of society.

Beyond the confrontational aspects, the contact and interaction between members of the Great Army and the resident Anglo-Saxon population would have been large, especially within the towns where over-wintering and before long, permanent capture, took place. The use of an urban environment cannot be overstated in the process of successful settlement; the proximity of the two groups a catalyst for assimilation (Beijer 1969: 54). As illustrated in chapter six, migration is not a one-way event, and there must have occurred the movement of men and camp followers to and from the Great Army and the homelands, each journey the bringer of further knowledge. Within a short period of time the Anglo-Saxon towns of the north would have became a focal point for the pioneers and a hive of social interaction, as the Great Army continued its movement and capture of kingdoms.

With the gradual break-up of the Great Army came the consolidation of the areas captured by it, and the first mention within the historical accounts of permanent, established settlements. The majority of its members, the young adult males, would have spent the greater part of their adult life within the social remit of Anglo-Saxon England. The influence and knowledge accrued of Anglo-Saxon culture that extended contact would bring cannot be underestimated. Similarly, the influence of some, albeit truncated, aspects of Scandinavian cultural practice would be familiar to resident Anglo-Saxon groups. This mutual familiarity, combined with the vital control of towns, paved the way for successful assimilation. Military domination was not a long-term option for the war-band leaders; skilful political manipulation was (see chapter four) and went hand-in-glove with assimilation into the Anglo-Saxon cultural milieu (see chapters four and five).

While this process of consolidation was being carried out, the movement of people around and between England and the Scandinavian homelands would have continued, carrying and spreading information regarding the fledgling Viking kingdoms. As the migration model shows (chapter six, figs. 6.1, 6.2 & 6.3) this transfer of knowledge would also include details of the pioneers' routes and settlement sites, which would subsequently determine the routes and settlement sites of primary and later migrants. The use of towns as focal points for initial settlements is corroborated by the archaeological record, which shows great expansion of York, Lincoln, Thetford and Norwich during the late ninth and early tenth centuries (chapter five) (Clarke & Ambrosiani 1995: 92-102). This can be seen as a result of the economic impetus an increasing population would bring. Again, choices of further occupation sites are predictable via patterns of migration (fig. 6.3) and show the propensity for development of satellite communities around sites of primary settlement. Once more this is evident within the archaeological and historical resource, supported this time by the cluster of Scandinavian-influenced place-names around many northern towns (see chapters four and five).

As with the pioneers, later migrants in no way represent the society or culture of their homeland. They are a very specific type of person with particular attributable social, economic, physiological and psychological traits necessary to undertake, endure, and most importantly, be successful (socially or economically) in their settlement of a foreign land (see chapter five). Assimilation is critical to this success. Contact, interaction and subsequent reaction between the two groups would all be quite different, albeit influenced to a certain extent by the knowledge and experiences shared between pioneer and new settler. Increased members drawn from a wider source of potentials than the pioneers would also extend further knowledge of some Scandinavian cultural practices amongst nationals. All these points are fundamentally important when trying to understand the archaeological record of this period and the burials. In short, migration and settlement is a sequence of perpetual cultural change, its players not governed by a timescale but by levels of contact and interaction during the assimilation process.

The funerary record, or more precisely, how particular groups deal with their dead, is seen within archaeology as culturally diagnostic, and to an extent, fixed (chapter six). However, research into migration and culture contact, religion and society has shown this to be untrue in the case of immigrant communities. For this reason it would have been misleading for the burial record of Viking period Scandinavia to be compared directly to those graves bearing Scandinavian influenced traits in the north of England. It was vital that the manner of funerary rites employed by other immigrant groups in the British Isles and Ireland be studied in order to set the research in context, and so derive a series of comparative analogies that could be used to understand socio-cultural interaction.

In Ireland only two of the twenty-seven known Viking burial sites are situated on the western seaboard. The remainder are to be found on the east coast, with thirteen in Dublin (fig. 7.1). This corresponds with the historical accounts provided by contemporary annalists who consistently record that Viking expansion beyond the Irish seaboard was prevented by the numerous Irish tribes (AU). This enforced limitation, in direct contrast to the situation in the north of England, resulted in the foundation of pristine settlements, or colonies, by immigrant groups, the largest of which being Dublin. This containment, while not prohibiting contact, severely curtailed assimilation between immigrant and resident groups, and allowed certain aspects of Scandinavian culture to be maintained, for example, accompanied burials with non-dress associated goods. However, even within the colonial burial record deviations from the norm exist, with amongst other things, the extensive use of Christian cemetery sites, no family groups, very few cremations, and the socio-political limitation to within the boundary of the colony by resident communities (chapter seven). The reuse of established burial mounds, both Christian and prehistoric is a trend repeated throughout the British Isles, and may be linked to ideas of ancestor mounds and land appropriation (see chapters three, seven and eight). Although the funerary record of Viking Ireland produces a predominantly male demography, the presence of diagnostically attributable Scandinavian female burials is evidence for the migration of women from the homelands, especially into the Dublin colony. In effect, the burial record in Ireland is mirroring the foundation of limited settlement, showing retention and perpetuation of some associated cultural traits because of the segregation of the immigrants by resident communities.

The Scandinavian type burial record on mainland Scotland was similarly limited to the coast (fig. 7.2), although no such limitation by the resident groups of the Islands is apparent (Graham-Campbell & Batey 1998: 54). The settlement of the Islands again resulted in the foundation of colonies, not restricted in the way Viking Dublin was from the rest of Ireland, but because of their geography. This geographical segregation and establishment of parochial communities allowed the continuation of cultural traits, for example, the accompanied burials encompass all Scandinavian demarcation techniques, boat burials and small family cemeteries. There are, however, still differences, and despite the majority of settlers having links to Norway, there are very few cremations, alongside the use of Christian graveyards and prehistoric settlement mounds (see chapter seven and eight). The increased evidence for female burials of Scandinavian type and children could demonstrate the settlement of families or at least the perpetuation of Scandinavian cultural traits within a family unit. No doubt the farming based settlements of the Northern and Western Isles were decided a safer option for migrating families to settle, rather than the trade based, martially dominated Dublin. However, in common with Dublin the Viking burials in the Scottish islands reflect the foundation of long-lived colonies, showing the retention and perpetuation of many cultural traits because of their parochial nature and continued links with the Scandinavian homelands.

Perhaps surprisingly the burial evidence from the Isle of Man differs quite substantially from both Ireland and Scotland (fig. 7.16). As yet there remains to be found a female burial of diagnostically Scandinavian type (for Peel, see chapter seven). The burial record seems to reflect and enforce the hypothesis that the ruling elite were replaced by Viking leaders, who found the land well populated, but small enough to control, and succeeded in introducing and maintaining a very strong Norse cultural milieu through social dominance.

As a result of the evidence drawn from the archaeological and historical sources, and the burial records of immigrant Scandinavian settlers in Ireland, Scotland and the Isle of Man, the corpus of burials from the north of England was divided into three distinct types. Separation into simple groups made it possible to identify that those members of the Traditional Burials (Type I) corpus are linked primarily by their positions in the landscape, via; the re-use of prehistoric burial mounds, the use of the extant funerary landscape, the association of all the sites with transport routes, and their situation beyond known limits of Anglo-Saxon village settlements. Although they share many artefactual similarities, and the tendency of using prehistoric burial sites with the rest of the British Isles and Ireland, there is no evidence to suggest that the Type I burials were anything other than a single event, carried out by transient groups at a specific moment in time. This is in direct contrast to the traditional type Scandinavian-influenced family burial sites of Scotland, and the Dublin cemetery sites, which depict a period of use, and signs of a colony as the residents or at least those involved with the burial of the dead, were permitted by parochial circumstances to maintain some aspects of the cultural reaction to death carried out within the homelands at the time of their departure.

By comparison, those burials incorporated within Type II (Accompanied Burials in Christian Cemeteries) are representative of a period of early assimilation, a negotiation between resident groups and established settlers of Scandinavian origin over the disposal of those whose cultural background did not arise within Anglo-Saxon England. This adoption of national burial practices by Scandinavian settlers is entirely consistent with patterns observed within modern-day immigrant communities (Laungani 1997, Rosenblatt 1997). The use of the hogback tombstone is a concept alien to both immigrant and national groups, and should be seen in a similar light; as an object created by the interaction of two communities (see chapter five). These monuments are perhaps more important than the accompanied burials themselves in understanding integration and settlement between Anglo-Saxon and Scandinavian groups, as in direct contrast to the interred items, they were above ground and on permanent display.

The very nature of small personal goods found within the Type III (Accompanied Burials of Viking-period Date in Christian Cemeteries) burial group, defies compartmentalisation along religious lines (that is, Christian or non-Christian); as it is not unknown for similar trinkets (combs, knives *etc*) and pieces of clothing to be recovered from what was acknowledged to be Christian Anglo-Saxon graves (Geake 1997). The recognition of Scandinavian influence is a different matter. The copper-alloy scale-pan and ingot fragments found within grave 251 at Carlisle Cathedral draws immediate analogy to the burials at Kildale and Kiloran Bay, Colonsay, both sites where sets of weights and scales were recovered (Tweddle, unpublished, Anon, unpublished Carlisle Cathedral excavation report, Atkinson 1867-70, 1874 (1988), Anderson 1906-7). However, there the similarity ends. The spectacular boat-burial of a socially-powerful male, attired with numerous martial accoutrements and a harnessed riding-horse, on a headland on Colonsay bears little resemblance to the confines of the ecclesiastical complex at Carlisle at the same date (Tweddle, unpublished, Anon, unpublished Carlisle Cathedral excavation report, Anderson 1906-7). Even the church burial at Kildale is different, the set of weights and scales here associated with a burial containing a sword and spear; part of a series of eight inhumations all similarly martially attired (Atkinson 1867-70, 1874 (1988)). In contrast to both of these sites, Carlisle Cathedral 251 had with him a small folding pocket-knife and a sharpening stone (Tweddle, unpublished, Anon, unpublished Carlisle Cathedral excavation report). Direct comparison of artefactual accompaniment without consideration of the socio-cultural conditions surrounding all three interments provides little help in furthering understanding of settlement processes at work during the Viking-period.

Similarly, the burial of the youth at St Mary Bishophill Junior, York, with his small pendant whetstone is analogous to that of the child at Cnip, Lewis (Wenham *et al* 1987, Welander *et al* 1987, Dunwell *et al* 1995). While he lies alone in a town churchyard, the child at Cnip was buried in a small family graveyard alongside adults buried in traditional Scandinavian fashion (Welander *et al* 1987, Dunwell *et al* 1995).

While the dates of all these interments may be roughly contemporary, each burial took place under different sets of socio-cultural circumstances, and are reflective of that. The Scottish burials reveal the perpetuation of some Scandinavian burial practices, enabled by colonial style settlement; whereas the youth at York and the man at Carlisle were buried in a Christian town churchyard, no doubt under the direction of the priest who gave the attendant grave-side mass. The evidence for Scandinavian influence lies only in the link of a single object at each site, the miniature pendant whetstone at York, and the fragmentary remains of a copper-alloy scale-pan and ingot from Carlisle Cathedral 251 (Tweddle, unpublished, Anon, unpublished Carlisle Cathedral excavation report, Wenham *et al* 1987). However, these links provide the opportunity to better understand the interaction and assimilation processes going on during the Viking-period in the north of England between resident and immigrant Scandinavian groups.

Chronological comparison of the artefacts recovered from all the discussed graves from the north of England (Types I-III) show quite conclusively what the migratory model predicts (fig. 8.2). While there is a possibility that at least some of the burials are concurrent (pioneer, primary and later settlers, and the later generations born to immigrant families) there is a strong probability that these people were not chronologically contemporary with others of the same migration group, for example the Hesket-in-the-Forest and Heath Wood cremations. And they need not necessarily be so. As argued throughout this thesis, the manner of deposition is entirely dependent on the socio-cultural circumstances surrounding those performing the funerary rites.

The research has also shown that the paucity of Viking burials in the north of England is a myth, created by an inability to recognise cultural reactions within the process of assimilation. A true figure is superfluous, but for arguments sake, if one were to include all those discussed in this study, the hogback tombstones, and the entire corpus of graveyard crosses bearing Scandinavian influenced designs; the number would be in the hundreds.

9.2 Future Research

This study has sought to apply a new analytical approach of analysis to Viking period research, and in doing so has highlighted a number of fundamental issues applicable beyond the confines of the research question. Within archaeology the funerary record is seen to be culturally diagnostic, and to an extent, fixed. However, this is untrue in the case of immigrant communities. Migrant groups are not a socio-cultural homogeneous community made up of a cross-section of their society, and as such cannot perpetuate all the socio-cultural traditions of their homeland. They are also extremely susceptible to change, and being removed from the social and cultural bonds of the homeland hastens this process. As shown, the primary adaptation in the behaviour of immigrant groups occurs in funerary rites, a direct result of the influence of the new environment in which they have placed themselves. All these factors must be taken into account wherever there is evidence to suggest the presence of migrating communities, from the prehistoric period, to the Romano-British, the Anglo-Saxons and beyond.

The study has also highlighted the dangers of applying chronologies using artefacts found within the graves of immigrants (for example, Scar, see chapter seven). Such typological dating may be valid in Scandinavia where burial is taking place within the socio-cultural boundaries of the homeland. However, these same boundaries do not exist within settled immigrant groups, and therefore cannot be used to the same extent. Again, such a fundamental point should be applied to other archaeological periods of study, which may result in the amendment of a number of chronologies.

Analysis of the evidence for Scandinavian farms and homesteads in the countryside shows the current level of knowledge and available evidence to be lacking. Although the study of migration demonstrates that it is extremely unlikely that a typical farmstead of western Norway will be found in the Yorkshire Dales – an immigrant population not comprising of a cross-section of society able to replicate such a structure exactly, and indeed perhaps unwilling to do so during the process of assimilation – research into upland settlement during and prior to the Anglo-Saxon period could establish whether Simy Folds, Ribblehead or Bryant's Gill are in fact examples of Scandinavian-influence or local traditions. On a similar vein, further exploration, and indeed where possible excavation of DMV sites would also increase knowledge of the period substantially.

Aspects of interaction between incoming settlers and resident Anglo-Saxon groups may also be investigated by analysis of a demarcated geographical area which contains a landscape high in numbers of Scandinavian-influenced place-names, sculpture, burials and miscellaneous artefactual finds. By combining non-intrusive landscape survey with the archaeology and any surviving historical evidence, along with a study of local traditions and dialect, a micro-landscape within the north of England may be constructed, from which evidence of settlement and interaction between incoming Scandinavian and resident groups may be seen. This could be expounded by repeating the process in a further area, so that comparisons might be made. Two such areas highly suited for this purpose would be those around the village of Wensley in the Yorkshire Dales, and Penrith in Cumbria.

Finally, this research has shown the benefit of combining archaeology with other fields of research in order to provide a deeper understanding of a particular facet of human behaviour. The use of isotopic analysis in the study of past human movement cannot be underestimated (for example, see Montgomery 2002), and must be fully utilised against the foundation and knowledge accrued from the archaeological, anthropological and historical resource. This combination would be more reliable than the use of DNA analysis in the identification of first generation migrants. Such work would not only be hugely important on those Viking period burials recovered from Ireland, Scotland and the Isle of Man, but the north of England churchyards and Christian cemeteries as well. Beyond the British Isles and Ireland this research would be invaluable in the tracing and understanding of Scandinavian migration across the North Atlantic and into south-east Europe and beyond, as adventurers and settlers made forays into what is now North America and the near east. However, the techniques are not limited to the Viking period alone. The combination of socio-cultural migration theory with isotopic techniques could be applied not only to prehistoric burials, but also Romano-British and Anglo-Saxon period cemeteries in order to better understand movement and social interaction during settlement and assimilation processes.

The new direction of this research and the results it has provided can be applied to many aspects of archaeology, and extend understanding of societies in the past. Migration is not a modern phenomenon, and its influence on the archaeological record has long been overlooked.

APPENDICES

Appendix 1 - Chronology

Where not otherwise indicated the events listed are taken from the Anglo-Saxon Chronicles (transl. & ed. by Swanton 2000). No recorded interaction where years not specified.

YEAR AD	RECORDED EVENTS OF VIKING INTERACTION
789	Killing of Beaduheard[1], reeve of King Beorhtric of Wessex, by Danes/Norse at Portland.
790-2	No accounts
793	Sack of Lindisfarne & raids on the north of England[2].
794	Northumbria ravaged, including the Tyne harbour of King Ecgfrith and his monastery at Jarrow looted. One of the Viking leaders is killed. Some of the Viking ships were damaged in a storm, resulting in some of the Vikings drowning in the sea. The Northumbrians killed the survivors[3]. Attacks recorded across Britain in Irish accounts[4].
795	Attacks made on Iona & Sky[5].
798	Increased attacks in Scotland & Ireland[6].
800	Churches of Hartness & Tynemouth plundered[7].
801-834	No accounts of attacks in England, although raids on Ireland continue unabated[8].
835	Sheppey ravaged.
836	Egbert, king of Wessex, at Carhampton, engages a Viking fleet of between 25-35 ships, & is defeated.
838	Egbert defeats a large raiding party who had joined with the Britons of Cornwall at Hingston Down.
840	A raiding party of 33 ships is defeated at Southampton. Another raiding group defeats an Anglo-Saxon force at Portland.
841	Defeat of an Anglo-Saxon force at Romney Marsh. Attacks made on Lindsey, East Anglia & Kent. The foundation of Dublin by raiding groups in Ireland[9]. Turgeis becomes first Viking king in Dublin[10]
842	Attacks made on London & Rochester.
843	Defeat of King Æthelwulf defeated by a force of 35 ships at Carhampton.
845	Turgeis, king of Dublin, is drowned in Lough Owel, Westmeath, by the king of the O'Neills[11].
848	A Viking force is defeated at the mouth of the River Parret.
850	Vikings defeated at Wicganbeorg. Winter at Thanet or Sheppey[12].
851	Vikings defeated at Sandwich, nine ships are captured. Three-hundred & fifty ships attack London & Canterbury, & over-run Mercia, but is subsequently defeated at Acleah. Arrival of raiding party (possibly from England) in Dublin & Anagasson[13].
852	Defeat of the fair foreigners by the dark foreigners at Carlingford Loch[14].
853	Skirmishes on Sheppey. Arrival of Olaf, the son of the king of Scandinavia, in Ireland, and submission of the Vikings there to him[15].
855	Vikings winter in Sheppey.
856	Horm, a Danish chief, was killed by Rhodri, son of King Mervyn of Wales[16].
857	First mention in the Annals of Ulster of Ivar the Boneless, acting in conjunction with Olaf to drive Caitil the Fair & his Norse-Irish fom Munster[17].
860	A raiding army storms Winchester, but is subsequently defeated.
865	The arrival of the Great Army. Winter quarters taken in East Anglia, with whom they had made peace. Fleet led by Ivar the Boneless[18].
866	The Great Army moves from East Anglia into Northumbria, where Ælla & Osberht were fighting over the kingdom. The Great Army takes York, and the claimant kings are subsequently killed[19]. Army subdues the populace & appoints an Anglo-Saxon Egbert who rules Northumbria north of the Tyne, for six years[20]. Ivar the Boneless plunders Scotland[21].
867	Great Army winters in Nottingham, Mercia.
868	The Great Army is besieged in Nottingham by King Æthelred & Alfred, but without any serious engagement. The Mercians make peace with the Great Army.
869/870	The Great Army return to York, then on to winter at Thetford, where they then defeated & killed King Edmund, & overran E Anglia. Viking personal names Ubba & Ingware (possibly Ivar the Boneless) are mentioned for the first time; said to be the killers of King Edmund[22].
870	The Great Army moved across into Reading, many battles take place in the vicinity. The arrival of the Summer Army. Olaf & Ivar the Boneless lay siege to Dumbarton; destroying & plundering when it fell[23].

[1] Chronicle of Æthelweard (Æ) p26
[2] Account from Simeon of Durham (SD)
[3] SD
[4] The Annals of Ulster (AU) part 7
[5] AU pt 3
[6] AU pt 2
[7] Roger of Wendover's, Flores Historiarum (RW)
[8] AU
[9] AU pt 4
[10] Cogadh Gaedhel re Gallaibh (The war of the Irish with the foreigners) from Logan 1991: 48
[11] Logan 1991: 48
[12] Swanton 2000: 64 fn 7
[13] AU pt 3
[14] AU pt 3
[15] AU pt 2
[16] AU pt 6
[17] AU pt 1
[18] Æ
[19] RW
[20] SD
[21] AU pt1
[22] Smyth 1978: 9
[23] AU pt 6

871	The Great Army moves from reading to London to winter, & makes peace with the Mercians. Olaf & Ivar return to Dublin with many slaves[24].
872	The Great Army moves into Northumbria & winters at Torksey in Lindsey. The Northumbrians revolt against Viking rule & expel the king Egbert & Archbishop Wulfhere, who fled to King Burgred of Mercia[25].
873[26]	Great Army moves from Lindsey to Repton, & over-winters there. King Burgred driven from Mercia, kingdom given to Ceolwulf. Death of Egbert, king of Northumbria[27]. Death of Ivar the Boneless, known as king of all the Norsemen of Ireland & Britain.[28].
874	Halfdan takes part of the Army into Northumbria; Ricsige is made king & Wulfhere reinstated as archbishop[29]. Halfdan winters on the River Tyne & raids across/conquers surrounding land. Guthrum, Oscytel & Anund, the 'three kings' of the Great Army move it to Cambridge.
875	Alfred defeats seven Viking ships at sea, & captures one. The Great Army reaches Wareham. Lindisfarne abandoned[30]. Halfdan slaughters many Picts in battle[31]. Halfdan kills Oistín, son of Olaf, one time king in Dublin[32].
876	A peace treaty with Alfred is made, but the Army takes Exeter regardless. Halfdan divides Northumbria amongst his followers & they begin to farm/settle[33]. One hundred & twenty raiding ships are lost off Swanage as the raiders venture west; some sailing, some by riding. Exeter is besieged by Alfred, & peace is struck. 876/7 death of Ricsige, king of Northumbria, ascension of Egbert II as king of the Northumbrians beyond the Tyne[34].
877	The remains of the Great Army depart into Mercia where the land is shared out. Some is given to Ceolwulf. Halfdan leaves Northumbria, apparently driven out by his own men[35]. Halfdan is killed in a skirmish with the Irish Vikings on Strangford Loch[36].
878	Year of many battles, beginning with Alfred being driven from Wessex, but ending with defeat for the Vikings at Edington. Guthrum & 30 of his leaders were baptised at Athelney. A brother of Ivar & Halfdan was defeated & killed along with his raiding party in Devon.
879	The Great Army moved from Cirencester into East Anglia, where the land is shared out. Other raiding parties are still active, including one in Fulham that subsequently left to fight the Franks in Ghent.
881	Alfred fights four Viking ships at sea.
883	Guthfrith, son of Hardacnut, becomes king in York following a ceremony combining both pagan & Christian rituals[37]. Lindisfarne monks re-established at Chester-le-Street[38].
884	A Viking raiding army from France laid siege to Rochester.
885	Alfred drives the army from Rochester out to sea.
886[39]	Alfred occupies London.
888	Sichfrith, king in Dublin, dies[40].
890	Guthrum dies, still held East Anglia, & was buried at Hadleigh (Suffolk)[41].
892	A large raiding army of some two hundred and fifty ships arrives from the continent at Appledore. Haesten, infamous Viking leader, arrives with eighty ships and builds a fort at Milton Royal.
893	The year is spent in continuous conflict between Alfred and his brother-in-law, Æthelred against the new raiding armies, bolstered by the Vikings settled in Northumbria and East Anglia. At on point the resident Vikings contribute some one hundred & forty ships. Included in this was one Sigfrith from Northumbria who brought his own pirate fleet to raid the south coast[42]. He subsequently sailed off from here to Ireland where he succeeded in splitting the Vikings in Dublin into two warring camps[43]. The raiding army then left their women, children & money in Northumbria & East Anglia & moved off to Chester.
894	The raiding army was driven out of Chester and across Wales, eventually seeking refuge in Northumbria & East Anglia. A winter camp was made on the River Lea, near Hertford[44]. Embassies are sent to York by King Alfred[45].
895	The army are driven from their River Lea camp & were forced to place their families again in East Anglia, before wintering at Bridgenorth. Guthfrith, king in York dies & is buried below what is now the Minster[46].
896	The raiding army went to settle in Northumbria and East Anglia, from which raids continued along the south coast. Those without property/money to enable them to settle joined other bands in France. Sihtric, king in Dublin, dies[47].
899	Unrest amongst the Vikings in Northumbria[48]. Alfred dies and is succeeded by his son Edward. Edward's cousin Æthelwold revolts against him, & joins the Vikings in Northumbria.
902	Æthelwold mentioned with a Viking fleet, & as king of the Danes & pagans[49]. The battle of the Holme is fought against the Vikings of East Anglia, who although victorious, had their king Eohric/Haruc killed there[50]. The Hiberno-Norse were driven from Dublin by Mael Finnia[51].

[24] AU pt 2
[25] RW
[26] Settlement of Iceland
[27] SD & RW
[28] AU pt 3
[29] RW & SD have 873 for return of Wulfhere, death of Egbert & ascension of Ricsige. No mention is made of Halfdan.
[30] SD
[31] AU pt 3
[32] AU pt 4
[33] RW
[34] SD
[35] HCD
[36] AU pt 5
[37] *History of St Cuthbert* (HSC)
[38] HSC fn 6
[39] Earliest year for Alfred-Guthrum Treaty, 886-890 (EHD 34)
[40] AU pt 9
[41] Annals of St Neots, Swanton 2000: 82 fn 7
[42] Æ
[43] AU
[44] Swanton 2000: 89 fn 7
[45] Æ
[46] Æ. SD dates his death as 894
[47] AU pt 3
[48] Æ
[49] ASC, Annals of St Neots, Swanton 2000: 92 fn 9
[50] Æ

903/4	Æthelwold raids with the Viking army, but is eventually defeated & killed by Edward along with the king of East Anglia, Eohric.
904	Ivar, grandson of Ivar the Boneless, king in Dublin, killed while raiding in Scotland[52].
905	Edward negotiates peace terms with Northumbria & East Anglia. Approximate start of issue of St Peter's pence in York[53]. Arrival of Hingamund & his followers from Ireland in the northwest of England: Æthelflæld gives them land to settle near Chester[54].
907	Chester refortified by the Anglo-Saxons.
910	The peace is broken & raids take place into Mercia & Wessex[55]. Edward retaliates, and they are defeated at a place names as Wednesfield, near Bridgenorth (ASC calls Tettenhall)[56]. The kings Halfdan, Eowils & Ivar were killed along with many other named jarls, holds & others in this heavy defeat[57]. The north is then harried by Edward for five weeks were many Viking settlers were killed.
911	Æthelred of Mercia dies, & Mercia falls under Edward's rule.
912	Æthelflæd fortifies Bridgnorth & Scergeat. Edward fortifies Hertford & Whitham, reclaiming his subjects here. Ragnald (a grandson of Ivar the Boneless) crosses from Ireland & sacks Dunblane with Jarls Ottar & Oswulf Crakabain.[58].
913	Æthelflæd fortifies Tamworth & Stafford. Viking raids across the surrounding country from Leicester & Northampton, resulting in local populace rising up & defeating them. 913/14 Ragnald defeats the English & Scots at Corbridge for the first time[59].
914	New raiders arrive from Brittany under jarls Ohtor & Hroald, who harried the Welsh coast. Bishop of Archenfield ransomed to Edward for forty pounds. Eventually driven out to Ireland. Fortification of Warwick & Buckingham. Jarl Thurcytel along with some of the other leaders from Bedford & Northampton submit to Edward. Victory in a sea battle off the Isle of Man by Ragnald over Barid son of Oitir[60].
915	Bedford fortified by Edward.
916	Jarl Thurcytel & others leave for France.
917	Towcester & Wigmore fortified. Raiding force leaves Leicester to unsuccessfully attack Towcester before moving across country. Another group from Huntington & East Anglia build a fort at Tempsford, drawing men to abandon the former. Attacks launched on Bedford from here, but were repulsed. A large Viking army drawn from East Anglia & Mercia lay siege unsuccessfully to Wigmore. Edward attacks & takes Tempsford fort, killing the king & other leaders. Another Viking army is raised, mostly from East Anglia, and Maldon is unsuccessfully attacked. Jarl Thurferth & the holds of Northampton along with their army, submit to Edward, giving him control of land up to the Welland. Huntingdon refortified by Edward, people submit. Colchester was similarly restored, & the people of East Anglia, the raiding army of East Anglia & Cambridge all submit. Æthelflæd takes Derby.
918	Stamford is fortified by Edward, & surrounding country submits. Æthelflæd dies at Tamworth, shortly after receiving the submission of York & Edward becomes ruler of Mercia. Nottingham is taken, refortified & manned by English & Danes. People of Mercia submit (English & Danes). Ragnald, so called king of the dark foreigners, leaves Ireland for Scotland with jarls Ottar & Oswulf (Oitir & Gragabai), & again defeats the Scots & English at Corbridge[61][62]. Ottar & Oswulf are killed during the battle[63]. Ragnald probably goes on to take York (refer to footnote at 923 for discrepancies in dates of the AU & ASC).
919	Thelwall & Manchester fortified.
920	Second fort built at Nottingham. Bakewell fortified. Constantine king of Scotland, Ragnald & the earls of Bamburgh, along with the people of Northumbria (English, Danes, Norwegians) & the king of the Strathclyde Britons submit to Edward. Sihtric, another grandson of Ivar, leaves Dublin[64] & destroys Davenport[65].
921	Fortress built at the mouth of the Clwyd. Guthfrith, another grandson of Ivar, becomes king in Dublin[66].
923	?Ragnald takes York[67].
924	Edward dies & is succeeded by Æthelstan.
925	Sihtric king in York meets with Æthelstan at Tamworth & makes peace[68]. Sihtric marries Ædgyth, Æthelstan's sister after baptism – a faith he soon deserts along with his English bride[69].
927	Sihtric dies[70] & Æthelstan assumes Northumbria after putting down a rebellion, probably sourced from Bamburgh[71] and an attack by Guthfrith (Sihtric's brother)[72] from Ireland attempting to claim the crown of his kinsman[73]. Olaf Sihtricson flees to Ireland, & Guthfrith Sihtricson to Scotland[74]. Guthfrith Sihtricson escapes being handed to Æthelstan at Dacre & unsuccessfully lays siege to York with one Thurferth[75]. Eventually turns to Æthelstan & was baptised at his court, before leaving, probably for Ireland[76].
934	Æthelstan invades Scotland. Guthfrith (grandson of Ivar the Boneless) dies in Dublin, his son Olaf Guthfrithson becomes king [77].
937	Æthelstan defeats a combined force of Olaf Guthfrithson & Constantine of Scotland at Brunanburh.
938	Olaf Guthfrithson back in Dublin[78]

[51] AU pt 2
[52] AU pt 4
[53] Dolley 1978: 26
[54] The Three Fragments (Smyth 1975:62)
[55] Æ
[56] Æ
[57] Æ & ASC Swanton 2000: 97 fn 14 for full list
[58] SD
[59] HSC
[60] AU pt 4
[61] AU pt 4
[62] HSC
[63] AU pt 4
[64] AU pt 5
[65] SD
[66] AU pt 5
[67] Discrepancy in dates between AU & ASC. AU reports Ragnald's death in 921, so it is likely he held York prior to Sihtric leaving Dublin; most likely on his way to take over. Smyth (1975: 103) argues Ragnald held York as early as 910 following the crushing of the Northumbrian Viking army at Tettenhall.
[68] William of Malmesbury (WM)
[69] RW
[70] AU pt 2
[71] WM
[72] SD
[73] AU pt 3
[74] WM
[75] WM
[76] WM
[77] AU pt 1 & Smyth 1978: 10
[78] AU pt 5

939	Death of Æthelstan, Edmund accedes.
940	Arrival of Olaf Guthfrithson in York[79]. Lead his army to unsuccessful siege of Northampton before raiding across country towards Tamworth. Armies of Olaf & Edmund met at Leicester, but no battle took place, peace being negotiated by Archbisops Wulfstan of York & Oda of Canterbury[80]. Olaf marries Aldyth, daughter of an Anglo-Scandinavian jarl, Orm, who had helped him secure his new kingdom[81].
941/2	Olaf Guthfrithson dies after raids in Lothian, & Lindisfarne is attacked by the men of York[82]. He is succeeded by his cousin Olaf Sihtricson (Cuarán)[83]. Ragnald Guthfrithson arrives in York. Edmund reclaims the Five Boroughs.
943	Olaf & Ragnald are baptised with Edmund as sponsor.
944	Olaf & Ragnald are driven out as Edmund retakes Northumbria. Death of Ragnald[84].
945	Olaf Sihtricson expels his cousin Blacaire Guthfrithson & becomes king on Dublin[85]. Edmund raids Cumbria & cedes it to Malcolm, king of Scotland after deposing King Dunmail & maiming his two sons[86].
946	Edmund is killed, & is succeeded by his brother Eadred who brings Northumbria under control. Eric Bloodaxe (son of King Harald Finehair of Norway) is taken as king in York by the Northumbrians[87].
948	Eric Bloodaxe is driven out by Northumbrian nobles, owing to threat of force from Eadred[88].
949	Olaf Sihtricson returns to Northumbria.
952	Olaf Sihtricson is driven out of York & replaced by Eric Bloodaxe as king.
954	Eric was driven out of York by the Northumbrians & subsequently murdered along with his son Haeric & his brother Ragnald by Earl Maccus at Stainmore, after being betrayed by Earl Oswulf[89]. Eadred becomes king of Northumbria, appointing Oswulf earl[90].
955	Eadred dies & is succeeded by Eadwig.
956	Archbishop Wulfstan of York dies.
959	Eadwig dies, succeeded by Edgar.
966	Thored, son of Gunner, raids Westmorland.
975	Edgar dies, succeeded by Edward the Martyr
978	Edward murdered, Æthelred the Unready accedes.
980	Olaf Sihtricsson relinquishes Dublin crown & retires to Iona[91].
981	Renewed Viking attacks, seven ships at Southampton, raids on Thanet, Padstow, Devon, Cornwall & Cheshire.
987	Watchet & a mint on the Somerset coast attacked.
991	Olaf Tryggvason (later king of Norway) arrives in Folkestone with ninety-three ships & over-runs Sandwich, Ipswich & surrounding countryside. Æthelred is defeated at Maldon, & a tribute of ten thousand pounds is paid. Olaf is baptised. Æthelred's treaty (c991-4) with the Vikings[92].
992	Ælfric btrays Æthelred, allowing Viking raiders to escape a sea battle.
993	Bamburgh is destroyed, with raids continuing up the Humber, attacking Linsey & Northumbria. Local forces raised, but leaders fled.
994	Olaf Tryggvason & King Sven of Denmark arrive in London with a fleet of ninety-four ships, which were driven off at great cost. Raid through surrounding countryside, & are bought off by sixteen thousand pounds. Olaf Tryggvason vows not to attack England again.
997	Devon, Cornwall and Wales are harried via the Severn & Tama estuaries.
998	Raids into Dorset via the River Frome. Bases set up on the Isle of Wight, with supplies running from Hampshire & Sussex.
999	Sail up the River Medway to Rochester & defeat English forces there. Æthelred unable to muster a fleet.
1000	Æthelred raids across Cumbria & attacks the Isle of Man on his way back south. The raiding army of Vikings of the south had left for France.
1001	A raiding army at Æthelingadene defeats Æthelred, & attacks continue unchecked. The raiding army is joined by Pallig, a one time ally of the king.
1002	Twenty-four thousand pounds is paid in tribute. Year Æthelred orders that all Danes in Briton be killed on St Brice's Day[93].
1003	Exeter is attacked & Sven is allowed to progress once more across country to Salisbury.
1004	Sven burns Norwich, but the people of East Anglia give him battle.
1005	Famine in England. Raiding army returns to Denmark.
1006	Raiding army returns again & attacks a defenceless Sandwich. Over-winter on the Isle of Wight, & harry inland. Æthelred again defeated at East Kennet.
1007	Tribute of thirty to thirty-six thousand pounds paid.
1008	Æthelred orders ships to be built.
1009	Wulfnoth, father of earl Godwine, seizes twenty of these ships & undertakes his own raids along the south coast. The fleet is subsequently abandoned by the king. Thorkell arrives at Sandwich, & is paid three thousand pounds to keep out of Canterbury. The raiding army winters in England & continues to harry.
1010	Levies are defeated near Thetford. English forces give up.
1011	Raids continue across southeast, & Archbishop Ælfheah of Canterbury is captured.
1012	Archbishop killed since he refused any suggestion that a ransom be paid. Eight thousand pounds was paid to the raiders. Thorkell & forty-five ships from the raiding army join Æthelred.
1013	Sven arrives & England north of Watling Street submits, followed by the rest. Æthelred leaves for the Isle of Wight & then Normandy.
1014	Death of Sven & his son Cnut chosen as king. Æthelred returns to England & drives Cnut out at Lindsey.
1015	Cnut returns to harry the south.

[79] SD fn 2
[80] SD
[81] RW
[82] SD
[83] SD
[84] Angus 1965: 165
[85] AU pt 6
[86] RW
[87] SD & fn 5
[88] SD & fn 6
[89] RW
[90] SD & fn 2
[91] Smyth 1979:264
[92] EHD 42, II Æthelred
[93] EHD 127

1016	Cnut returns with a large force & attracts English followers. Edmund, son of Æthelred, raids the north of England in preference to attacking the Danish army, but ultimately marches south[94]. Æthelred dies, & Edmund succeeds. Many battles fought through the year between Edmund & Cnut, ending with the final defeat of the English at Ashingdon. A treaty between them at Alney left Edmund with Wessex, East Anglia, Essex & London, & Cnut the north. Death of Edmund.
1017	Cnut elected as king of England. England divided into four districts – Wessex for himself, East Anglia for Thorkell, Mercia for Ealdorman Eadric & Northumbria for Earl Eric.

[94] Swanton 2000: 147 fn. 15.

Appendix 2 - The Movements of the Great Army around England

866 – Move from East Anglia (possibly Thetford) over the mouth of Humber and into Northumbria. Ships sail from the Wash up to Humber estuary, then into the Ouse and up to York. Possible some rode across country.
867 – York-Nottingham. Ouse-Humber estuary-River Trent-Nottingham.
869 – Nottingham-York- reverse above.
York-Thetford. Ouse-Humber estuary-sea-Great Ouse estuary-Great Ouse-Little Ouse (Great Ouse splits into R. Ouse & Little Ouse)-Thetford. NB-Santon Downham in Thetford Forest.
870 – Thetford-Reading. Little Ouse-Great Ouse-Estuary-Sea-Thames-Reading.
871 – Reading-London. Straight back down Thames.
872 – London-Torksey. Thames-Sea-R.Witham to Lincoln-Fossdyke (Roman canal)-Torksey.
873 – Torksey-Repton. Fossdyke joins River Trent at Torksey – River Trent leads straight to Repton.
874 – Halfdan – Repton-Tyne mouth. River Trent-(Torksey)-Fossdyke-(Lincoln)-River Witham-Sea (Likely army split here)-Tyne estuary.
874 – Guthrum, Oscytel & Anund – Repton-Cambridge. River Trent-(Torksey)-Fossdyke-(Lincoln)-River Witham-Sea (Likely army split here)-Great Ouse-River Ouse (which becomes)-River Cam-Cambridge.
875 – Cambridge-Wareham (Poole Harbour, Swanton ASC p74). River Cam-River Ouse-Great Ouse-Sea-Poole Harbour.
876 – Wareham-Exeter. Some rode it. Sea-River Exe-Exeter. 120 ships lost of Swanage on way (ASC).
Exeter-Mercia (Probably Gloucester, according to Æthelwaerd's Chronicle, where they set up a camp-Swanton ASC p75). River Exe-Sea-River Severn-Gloucester.
877 – Halfdan's expulsion with only 3 ships (HCD). Tyne mouth-Sea-Strangford Loch.
878 – Gloucester-Chippenham (fall of Wessex). Probably a land march from base at Gloucester, where ships would have been left.
Chippenham-Cirencester. Land march after Guthrum's baptism at Athelney and defeat at Edington.
879 – Cirencester-East Anglia. Possibly sailed from Gloucester, round into the Channel/North Sea.

Appendix 3 – Maps showing Viking-period sculpture in the north of England

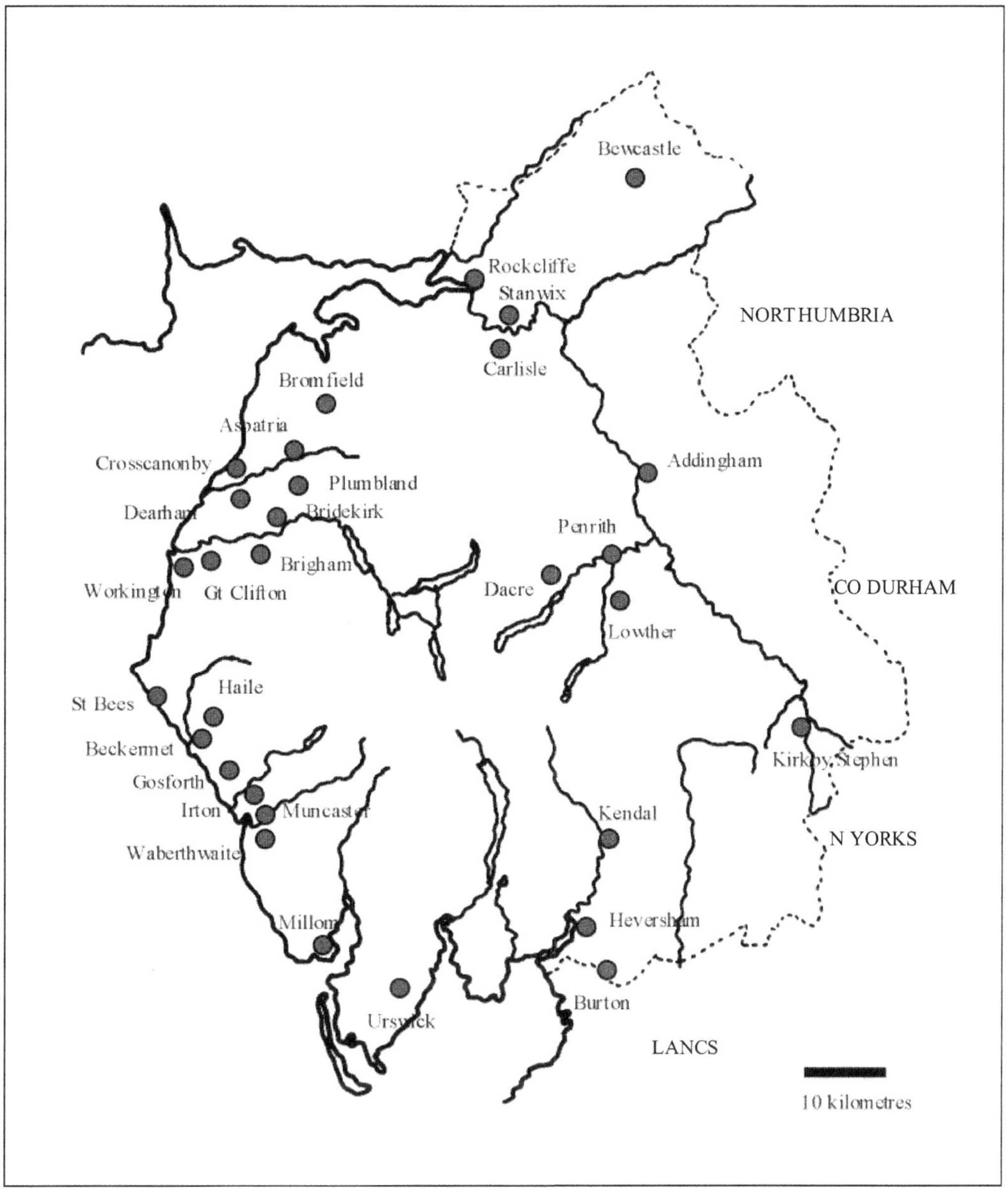

Fig. A3.1 *Map showing sites of Viking-period sculpture in Cumbria and Westmorland (after Bailey 1980: 261)*

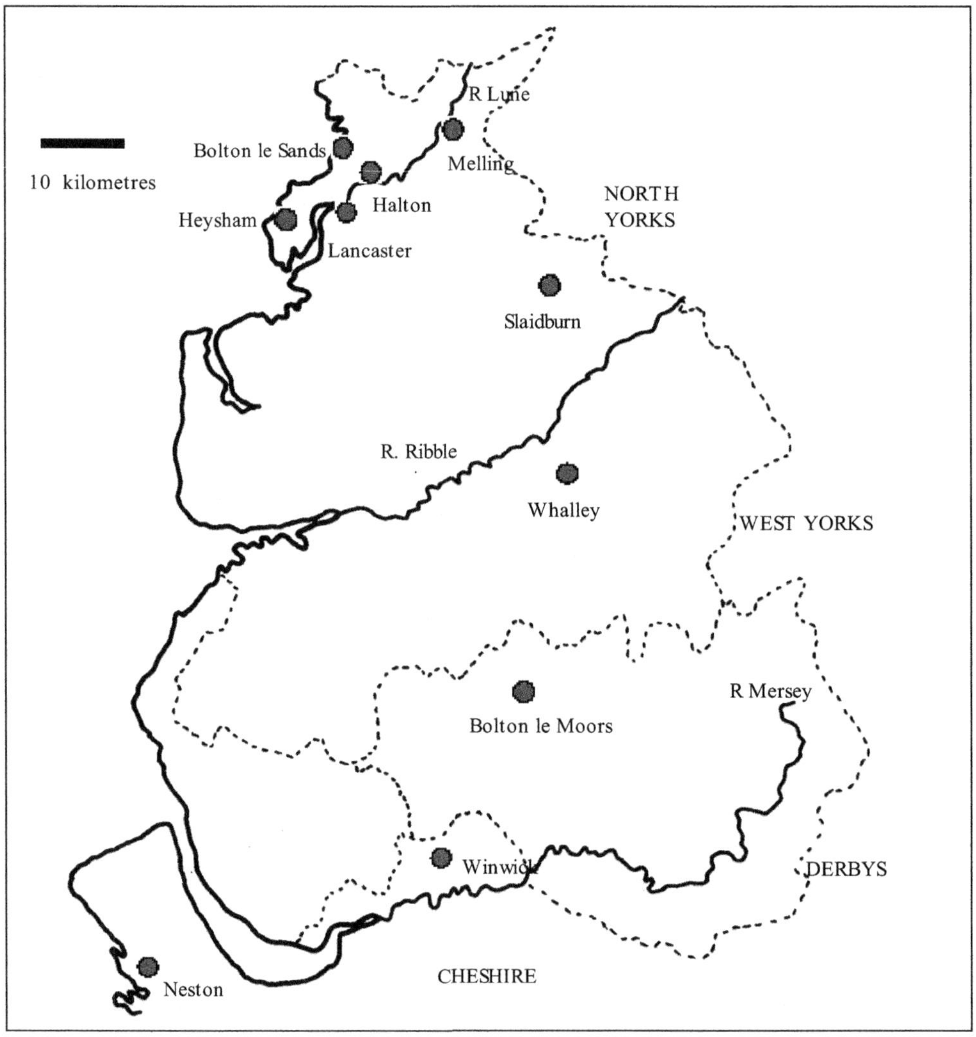

Fig. A3.2 *Map showing sites of Viking-period sculpture in Lancashire (after Bailey 1980: 262)*

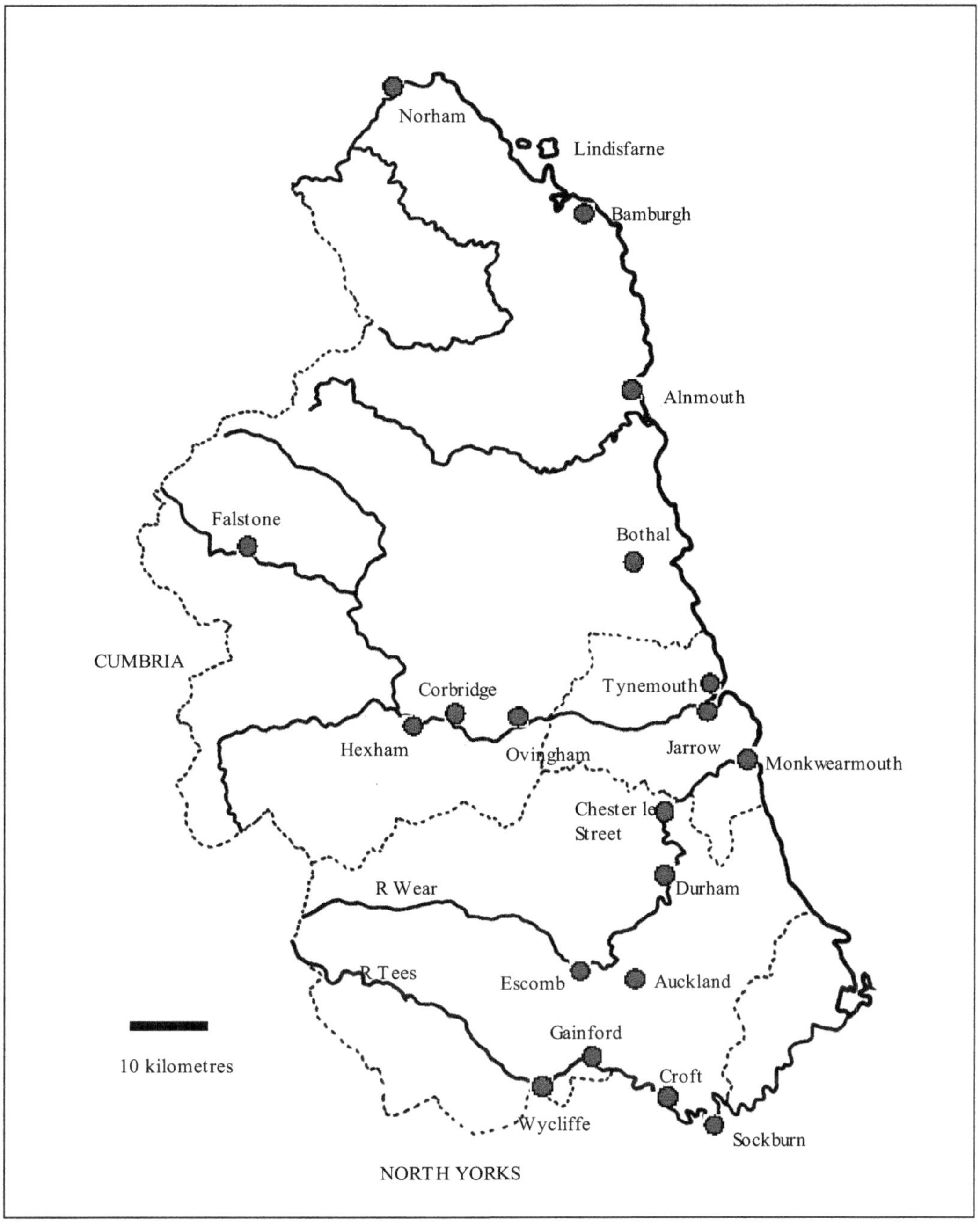

Fig. A3.3 *Map showing sites of Viking-period sculpture in Northumberland, Durham, Tyne & Wear (after Bailey 1980: 257)*

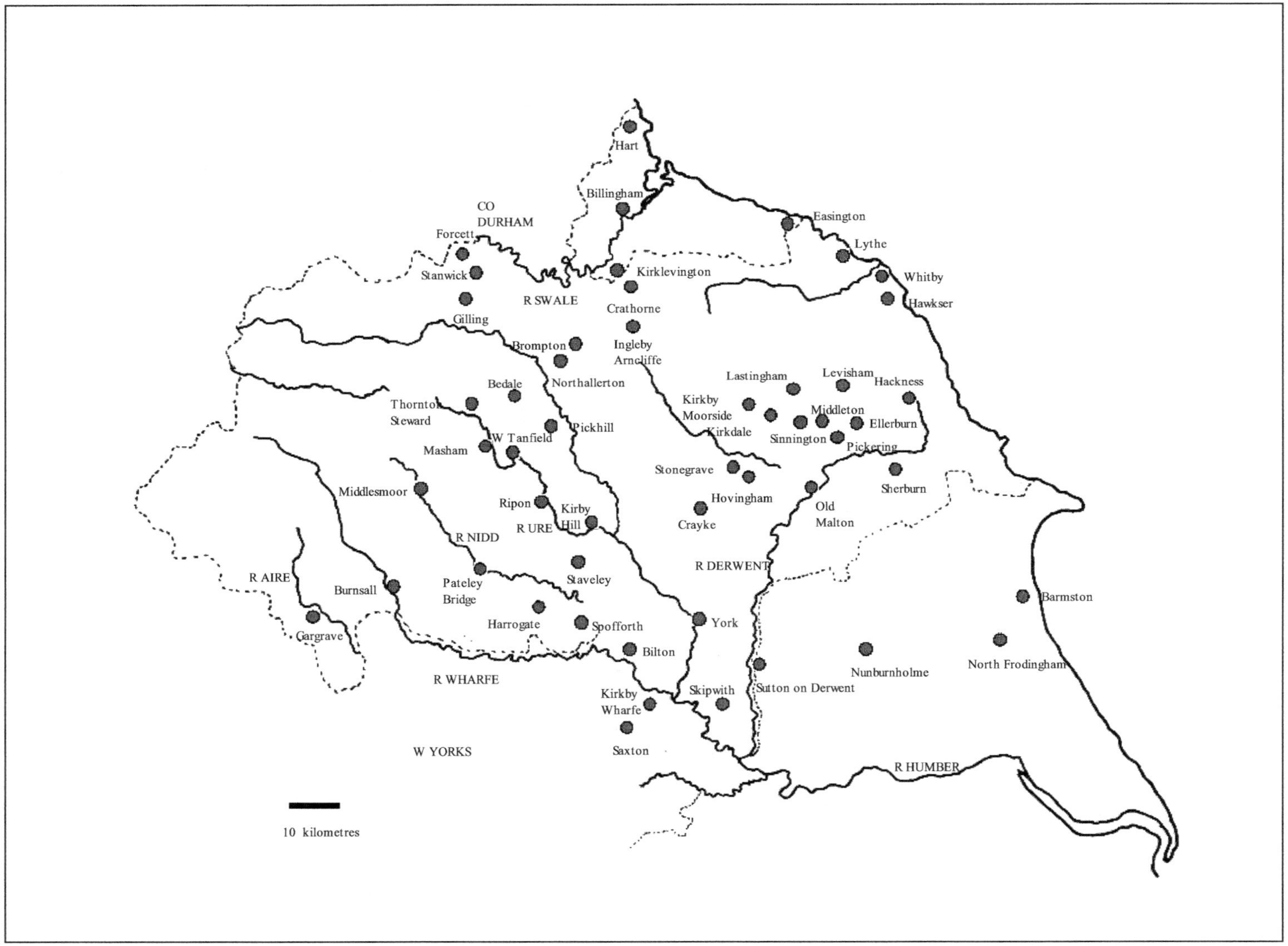

Fig. A3.4 *Map showing sites of Viking-period sculpture in North Yorkshire, Humberside & Cleveland (after Bailey 1980: 258-9)*

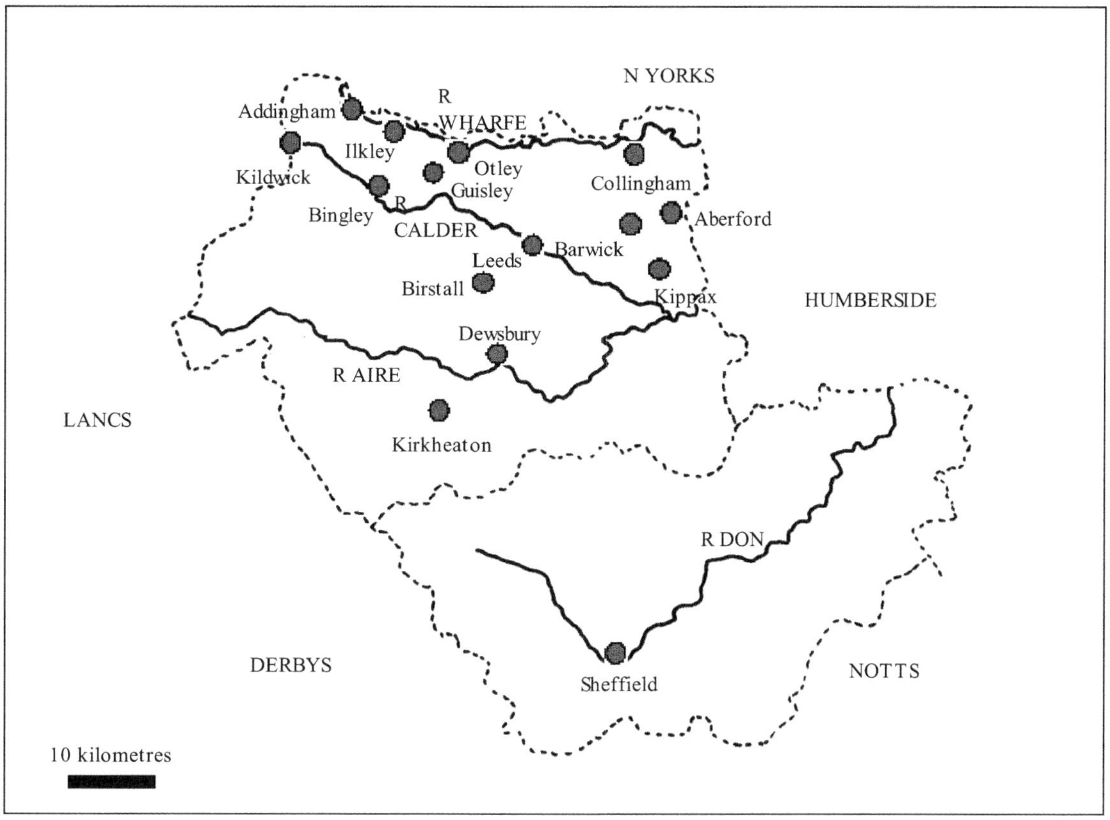

Fig. A3.5 *Map showing sites of Viking-period sculpture in South & West Yorkshire (after Bailey 1980: 260)*

Appendix 4 – Major finds of Scandinavian-influence of the Viking-period in the north of England

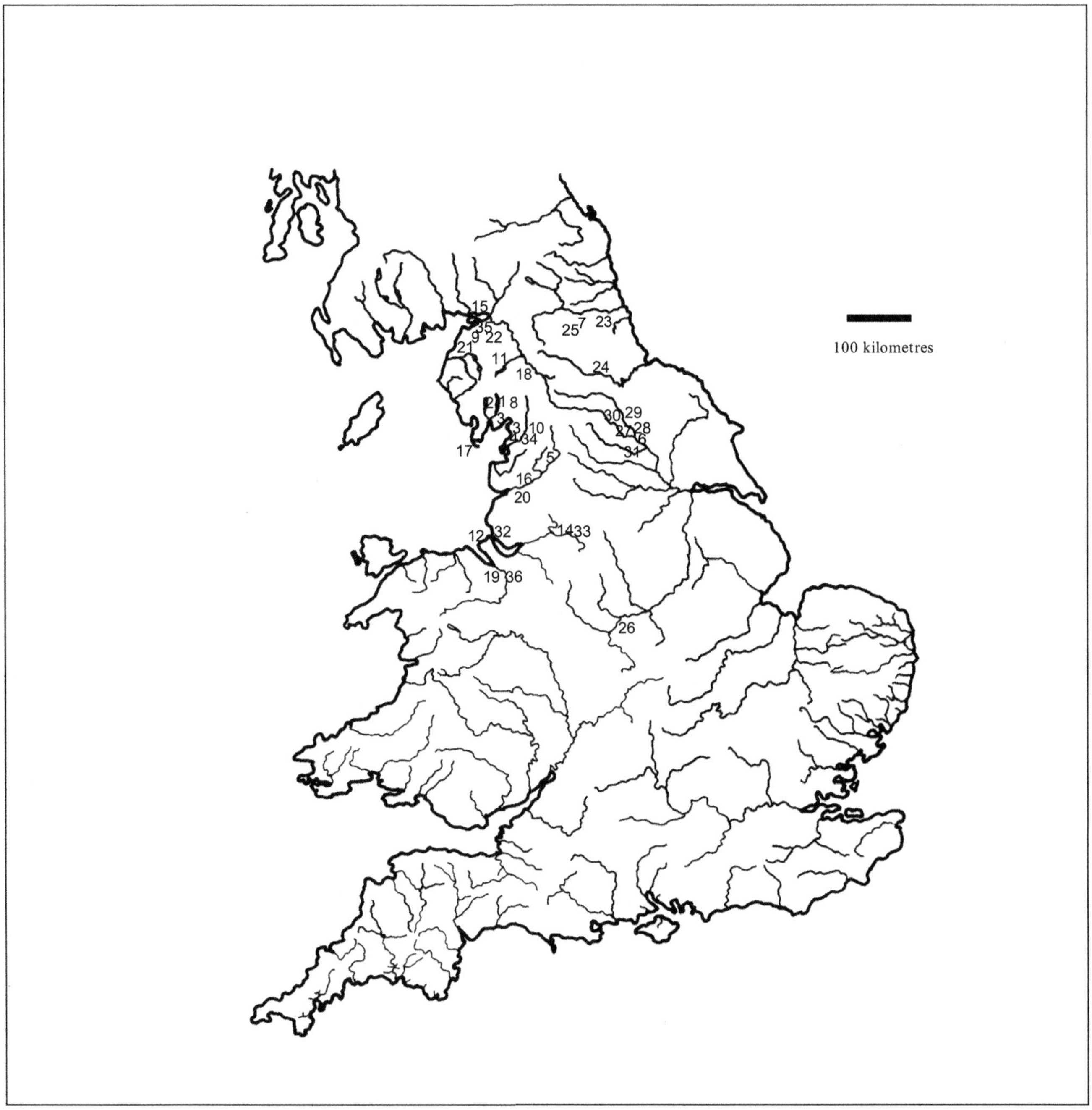

Fig. A4.1 *Map showing sites of major Scandinavian-influenced finds of the Viking-period in the north of England. Key below.*

Weapons

1	2 spear-heads, Kentmere
2	Spear-head, Esthwaite Water
3	Spear-head, Nan Bield Pass, Lake District
4	Spear-head, Lancaster
5	Chape, Chatburn, Ribble Valley
6	York, multiple finds
7	Axe-head, Harbuck, Lanchester, Durham

Jewellery

8	Silver bossed penannular brooch & torque, Orton Scar, Cumbria
9	Silver penannular brooch, Brayton Park, Aspatria, Au armlet with runic inscription, Aspatria Parish, Cumbria
10	Silver ball-type (thistle) brooch, Casterton Hall, Lancs
11	6 silver penannular brooches, Flusco, nr Penrith, Cumbria
12	Ring-headed pin, Meols, Wirral
13	Ring-heade pin, Arnside Towere, Lancs
14	Brooch, Castlefield, Manchester
15	Silver arm-ring, Gretna, Solway
16	Decorated Cu-alloy boss, Ribchester, Lancs
17	Cu-alloy head, nr Furness Abbey, Furness
18	Ormside Bowl, Ormside, Westmorland
19	Gold-plated finger-ring, Chester
6	York, multiple finds

Hoards

20	Cuerdale, Lancs
21	Dean, Cumbria
22	Kirkoswald, Cumbria
23	Heworth, Gateshead
24	Gainford, Durham
25	Satley, Durham
26	Repton, Derbys
27	Goldsborough, Yorks
28	Bossall, Yorks
29	Easingwold, Yorks
30	Ripon, Yorks
31	Bolton Percy
32	Harkirke, Lancs
33	Castle Hill, Manchester
34	Halton Moor, Lancs
35	Scotby, Cumbria
36	Chester

(Edwards 1998, Richards 2000, Björn & Shetelig 1940, Ferguson & Cowper 1892-3 Victoria County History (Yorkshire), Graham-Campbell 1992)

Appendix 5 - Quick reference tables of Scandinavian-influenced burials in the north of England, Isle of Man, Scotland and Ireland
Traditional Viking Burials in the north of England (Type I)

Site	Inhumation/ Cremation	Artefacts	Date	Sex	Nr Scandinavian Settlements	Nr Transport Routes	Other burials	High Ground	Identifying Feature	Reference
Hesket-in-the-Forest, Cumbria	C	sword, 2 spears, shield, axe, bridle-bit & fittings, 3 bone combs, whetstone, sickle, spurs, 3 pieces of stone	MC10th	M	?	Y	N	N	mound	1
Aspatria, Cumbria	I	sword, spear, axe, spur, shield, bridle-bit, Au strap-end, Au buckle, ring-headed pin, Fe buckle, folding knife, nails, Fe frags & cauldron	LC9thE10th	M	?	Y	Y	Y	mound	2
Claughton Hall, Garstang, Lancs.	C	sword, spear, pair tortoise brooches, Ag-gilt Carolingian brooch, 2 beads, molar tooth, axe head, hammer, urn, BA stone axe-hammer	EC10th	M/F	?	Y	Y	N	mound	3
Crossmoor, Inskip, Lancs.	C	sword, spear, urn	*c*900	M	?	N	N	N	?	4
Leeming Lane, Bedale, Yorks.	I	spear, pair tortoise brooches	900-950	F	?	Y	N	N	?	5
Red House Park, Adwick-le-Street, Doncaster, Yorks.	I	2 tortoise brooches, Cu-alloy bowl, knife, latch-lifter	LC9th	F	?	Y	Y	N	N	6
Heath Wood, nr Ingleby, Derbyshire (1)	C	sword, suspensory loop, buckle, strap-slider, animal bone, Cu-alloy fragments	LC9th	M	Y	Y	Y	Y	mound	7
Heath Wood (2)	?		LC9th	?	Y	Y	Y	Y	mound	8
Heath Wood (3)	C	buckle, nails, Cu-alloy fragments	LC9th	?	Y	Y	Y	Y	mound	9
Heath Wood (4)	?		LC9th	?	Y	Y	Y	Y	mound	10
Heath Wood (5)	C	nails, animal bone	LC9th	F	Y	Y	Y	Y	mound	11
Heath Wood (6)	C	2 buckles, nails, strap-end, fibula, Cu-alloy fragments, animal bone	LC9th	F(?)	Y	Y	Y	Y	mound	12
Heath Wood (7)	C	sword, nails, Fe fragments	LC9th	M	Y	Y	Y	Y	mound	13
Heath Wood (8)	unrec'd excav.		?	?	Y	Y	Y	Y	mound	14
Heath Wood (9)	?		LC9th	?	Y	Y	Y	Y	mound	15
Heath Wood (10)	?		LC9th	?	Y	Y	Y	Y	mound	16
Heath Wood (11)	C	spade, Ag embroidery, nails, animal bone	LC9th	?	Y	Y	Y	Y	mound	17
Heath Wood (12)	?		LC9th	?	Y	Y	Y	Y	mound	18
Heath Wood (13)	?		LC9th	?	Y	Y	Y	Y	mound	19
Heath Wood (14)	natural		?	?	?	?	?		mound	20
Heath Wood (15)	?		LC9th	?	Y	Y	Y	Y	mound	21
Heath Wood (50)	C	sword hilt, shield, knife, 2 cu-alloy tacks, nails, chest hinge-pivot	LC9th	F & juvenile	Y	Y	Y	Y	mound	22
Heath Wood (56)	C	ring-headed pin	LC9th	?	Y	Y	Y	Y	mound	23

Accompanied Burials in Christian Cemeteries (Type II)

Site	Inhumation/ Cremation	Artefacts	Date	Sex	Nr Scandinavian Settlements	Nr Transport Routes	Other burials	High Ground	Identifying Feature	Reference
Penrith, Cumbria	I	sword	?	M	?	Y	Y	N	hogback	24
Brigham, Cumbria	I	ring-headed pin, hogback	?	?	?	Y	Y	N	hogback	25
Tendley Hill, Eaglesfield, Cumbria	I	sword, spear, penannular brooch	850-950	M	?	N	Y	Y	?	26
Ormside, Westmorland	I	sword, shield, knife	LC9th	M	?	Y	Y	N	?	27
Rampside, Lancs.	I	sword	LC9th	M	?	Y	Y	N	?	28
Rampside.	I	sword	?	M	?	Y	Y	N	?	29
Heysham, Lancs.	I	sword, spear	?	M	?	Y	Y	N	hogback	30
Pippin Castle, Harrogate, Yorks.	C?	axe, Fe fragments, 2 horseshoes, pottery, timber, flint cores, animal bone, whetstone	LC9th EC10th	?	?	N	Y	Y	hogback	31
Wensley, Yorks.	I	sword, spear, knife, sickle	*c*900	M	?	Y	Y	N	?	32
Kildale, Yorks.	I	sword, dagger, tweezers, weights & scales, box for weights, scabbard fitting	?	M	?	N	Y	N	N	33
Kildale, Yorks.	I	sword, dagger	?	M	?	N	Y	N	N	34
Kildale	I	sword, dagger	?	M	?	N	Y	N	N	35
Kildale	I	sword, belt & fittings	C10th	M	?	N	Y	N	N	36
Kildale (misc. finds)	*c*5I	dagger, axe, spear, small knife, spur frags., shield boss, whetstone, buckle, nails	?	?	?	N	Y	N	N	37
Camp Hill, Carthorpe, Yorks.	I	sword, spear	*c*900	M	?	Y	Y	Y	?	38
Repton, Derbyshire	I	sword, scabbard, belt, Thor's hammer pendant & necklace fittings, glass beads, key, knives, animal bone	LC9th	M	Y	Y	Y	N	stone setting & wood post	39
Repton	I	knife	?	M	Y	Y	Y	N	stone setting & wood post	40
Repton	I	axe	LC9th	M	Y	Y	Y	N	?	41
Repton	I	sword	*c*900	M	Y	Y	Y	N	?	42
Repton (misc. finds)	?	axe, sword, spear, seaxes, knives, chisel, padlock key, Fe fragments, Ag band with garnets, gilded Cu-alloy tacks, pennies *c*872-4, hogback (lost)	?	?	Y	Y	Y	N	?	43

Accompanied Burials of Viking Period Date in Christian Cemeteries (Type III)

Site	Inhumation/ Cremation	Artefacts	Date	Sex	Nr Scandinavian Settlements	Nr Transport Routes	Other burials	High Ground	Identifying Feature	Reference
Cambois, Northumberland	I	disc brooch, comb	LC9thEC10th	F	?	Y	Y	N	mound	44
Cambois	I		LC9thEC10th	M	?	Y	Y	N	mound	45
Cambois	I		LC9thEC10th	M	?	Y	Y	N	mound	46
Carlisle Cathedral Cumbria (ref. 251)	I	decorated buckle, knife in sheath Ag-capped pendant whetstone cu-alloy scale pan fragment Cu-alloy ingot	LC9thEC10th	M	?	Y	Y	N	?	47
Carlisle Cathedral (ref. 242 or 244)	I	ring-headed pin	C10th	?	?	Y	Y	N	?	48
Carlisle Cathedral (ref. 269)	I	ring & dot Cu-alloy buckle & strap-end	EC10th	?	?	Y	Y	N	?	49
Carlisle Cathedral (misc.)	?	Au toggle with Au wire ball attachment	EC10th	?	?	Y	Y	N	?	50
Ailcy Hill, Ripon, Yorks (misc.)	?	hogback, stycas	?	?	?	?	?	Y	?	51
Ladykirk & St Marygate, Ripon (ref.7009)	?	four combs & two cases	LC9th-MC11th	?	?	?	?	?	?	52
Heysham, Lancs.	I	comb, charcoal deposit	C10th	F	?	Y	Y	N	?	53
York Minster (ref. 37)	I	charcoal deposit	C8-10th	?	Y	Y	Y	N	?	54
York Minster (ref. 38)	I	charcoal deposit	C8-12th	F	Y	Y	Y	N	?	55
York Minster (ref. 40)	I	charcoal deposit	C8-11th	?	Y	Y	Y	N	?	56
York Minster (ref. 48)	I	pottery	C8-11th	child	Y	Y	Y	N	slab	57
York Minster (ref. 50)	I	comb fragment	C10-11th	F	Y	Y	Y	N	slab	58
York Minster (ref. 51)	I	pottery	C10th	child	Y	Y	Y	N	slab	59
York Minster (ref. 54)	I		C10th	?	Y	Y	Y	N	slab	60
York Minster (ref. 56)	I	pottery	C9-10th	?	Y	Y	Y	N	slab	61
York Minster (ref. 57)	I		C11th	M	Y	Y	Y	N	slab	62
York Minster (ref 58)	I		C10th	?	Y	Y	Y	N	slab	63
York Minster (ref 68)	I	key, Au finger-ring	?	?	Y	Y	Y	N	?	64
York Minster (ref. 79)	I	chest fragments	LC9thEC10th	child	Y	Y	Y	N	?	65
York Minster (ref. 93)	I	boat timbers	C10-11th	M	Y	Y	Y	N	?	66

Site	Inhumation/ Cremation	Artefacts	Date	Sex	Nr Scandinavian Settlements	Nr Transport Routes	Other burials	High Ground	Identifying Feature	Reference
York Minster (ref. 105)	I	pottery, glass	900-1050	?	Y	Y	Y	N	?	67
York Minster (ref. 107)	I	charcoal deposit	C9-13th	F	Y	Y	Y	N	?	68
York Minster (ref. 52)	I		C11th	?	Y	Y	Y	N	slab	69
York Minster (ref. 53)	I		?	?	Y	Y	Y	N	slab	70
St Mary Bishophill Senior, York	I	strap-end	C10th	?	Y	Y	Y	N	?	71
St Mary Bishophill Junior, York	I	coin d905-15, knife, whetstone, buckle-plate	C10th	M	Y	Y	Y	N	?	72
St Mary Bishophill Junior, York	I		C10th	F	Y	Y	Y	N	?	73
St Mary Bishophill Junior, York	I		C10th	F	Y	Y	Y	N	?	74
St Mary Bishophill Junior, York	I	Ag penannular arm-ring	LC9thEC10th	?	Y	Y	Y	N	?	75
St Mary Bishophill Junior, York	I	pin, coffin fittings	C10th	F	Y	Y	Y	N	?	76
St Mary Bishophill Junior, York	I		C10th	child	Y	Y	Y	N	?	77
St Mary Bishophill Junior, York	I		C10th	M	Y	Y	Y	N	?	78
St Mary Bishophill Junior, York	I	Ag penannular arm-ring	C10th	child	Y	Y	Y	N	?	79
Repton, Derbyshire	I	Au finger-ring, 5 Ag pennies	LC9th	M	Y	Y	Y	N	?	80
Repton	I	knife, strike-a-light	*c*900	F	Y	Y	Y	N	?	81

Possible Viking Burials in the north of England

Site	Inhumation/ Cremation	Artefacts	Date	Sex	Nr Scandinavian Settlements	Nr Transport Routes	Other burials	High Ground	Identifying Feature	Reference
West Seaton, Workington, Cumbria	?	sword	C10th	?	?	N	N	N	?	82
Whitbarrow Scar, Witherslack, Cumbria	?	sword	?	?	?	N	N	N	N	83
Sayle Bottom, Great Asby, Cumberland	I	sword	?	M	?	?	Y	?	mound	84
Sandford Moor, Westmorland	?	sword, 2 spears, shield	?	M	?	Y	Y	Y	mound	85
Brockhall, Billington, Lancs	I	spearhead(s)	?	M	?	Y	?	N	mound	86
Hasty Knoll, Blackrod, Wigan, Lancs.	C?	Fe weapons	?	M	?	Y	?	?	mound	87
Meols, Lancs.	?	sword, axe, spear	?	M	?	Y	?	N	?	88

Viking Burials in the Isle of Man

Site	Inhumation/ Cremation	Artefacts	Date	Sex	Nr Scandinavian Settlements	Nr Transport Routes	Other burials	High Ground	Identifying Feature	Reference
Ballateare, Jurby	I	sword, scabbard, baldric, 3 spears animal bone, ring-headed pin, knife & sheath, fragments of wood & leather	LC9thEC10th	M & F	?	Y	Y	Y	mound	89
Cronk Mooar, Jurby	I	sword, scabbard & fittings, strap-end, spear, shield, knife & sheath	LC9thEC10th	M	?	Y	Y	?	mound	90
Balladoole, Arbory	I	boat, horse tack, spurs, ring-headed pin, Ag-gilt belt buckle, cauldron, strike-a-light, whetstone, shield, 2 knives, animal bone	LC9thEC10th	M & F	?	Y	Y	Y	mound	91
Knock y Doonee, Andreas	I	boat, rivets & anchor stone, sword, scabbard, animal bone, axe, spear, 2 knives, shield, smith's tools (tongs & hammer), cauldron, Ag decorated pin, bridle parts, belt & fittings,	C10th	M	?	Y	Y	?	mound	92
Claghbane, Ramsey	?	sword, spear, shield, bead	LC9thEC10th	M	?	Y	N	?	?	93
Peel Castle, St Patrick's Isle	I	goose wing, cooking spit, knife, shears, belt, workbag & 2 needles, 71 amber & glass necklace beads, cloth, decorated knife, comb, pestle & mortar amulet, pendant of 2 amber beads, fossil, herbs	LC9thEC10th	F	?	Y	Y	N	?	94
Peel Castle, St Patrick's Isle	I	ring-headed pin, buckle, 18 Ag wire balls	LC9thEC10th	?	?	Y	Y	N	?	95
Peel Castle, St Patrick's Isle	I	ring-headed pin, strap-end, buckle, comb, Fe awl	LC9thEC10th	?	?	Y	Y	N	?	96
Peel Castle, St Patrick's Isle	I	4 Ag wire balls	LC9thEC10th	?	?	Y	Y	N	?	97

Site	Inhumation/ Cremation	Artefacts	Date	Sex	Nr Scandinavian Settlements	Nr Transport Routes	Other burials	High Ground	Identifying Feature	Reference
Peel Castle, St Patrick's Isle	I	knife in dec. scabbard, buckle, gilt strap-end, box, rivets, Cu-alloy frags.	LC9thEC10th	?	?	Y	Y	N	?	98
Peel Castle, St Patrick's Isle	I	bell, necklace of 6 glass & 2 amber beads	LC9thEC10th	child	?	Y	Y	N	?	99
Peel Castle, St Patrick's Isle	I	coin of Eadred d946-955	MC10th	child	?	Y	Y	N	?	100
Ballachrink, Jurby	?	sword, spear, perforated stone disc	*c*900	M	?	Y	N	?	mound	101
Ballaugh, Ballaugh	I	sword, spear	*c*900	M	?	Y	N	?	mound	102
St Maughold's, Maughold	?	sword	*c*900	M	?	Y	Y	?	?	103
Kirk Michael	?	spear	?	?	?	Y	Y	?	?	104
Ballabrooie, Patrick	?	sword, scabbard	*c*900	M	?	Y	N	Y	mound	105
St John's Kirk German, Tynwald Hills	?	sword, stirrup, axe, beads	?	M	?	Y	Y	N	mound	106
Ballelby, Patrick	I	axe, sword	?	M	?	Y	N	?	mound	107
Old Kirk Braddan, Braddan	I	sword	?	M	?	Y	Y	?	?	108
Malew Parish Church, Malew	I	2 swords	?	M	?	Y	Y	?	?	109
Ronaldsway, Kirk Malew	I	spear	?	M	Y	Y	Y	N	?	110
Orry's Grave, Gretch Veg, Kirk Lonan	?	animal bone, sword, horse-shoe,	?	M	?	Y	N	?	mound	111
Jurby Parish Church, Jurby	?	sword,	MC9th	M	?	Y	Y	?	?	112
Balladoyne Churchyard, St John's	?	sword, shield, spear wrapped in fabric	850-950	M	?	Y	Y	?	?	113

Viking Burials in Scotland

Site	Inhumation/ Cremation	Artefacts	Date	Sex	Nr Scandinavian Settlements	Nr Transport Routes	Other burials	High Ground	Identifying Feature	Reference
Reay, Caithness	I	horse bone, 2 tortoise brooches, ring-headed pin, 2 buckles, steatite spindle whorl, tweezers, bridle-bit	?	F	Y	Y	Y	N	?	114
Reay, Caithness	I	sickle, axe, belt buckle, whetstone, ring-headed pin, knife, 2 flints, shield, rivet, mounting	950-1000	M	Y	Y	Y	N	?	115
Balnakeill, Durness, Sutherland	I	sword, scabbard, spear, shield, strap-end, beads, ring-headed pin, 14 gaming pieces & board, comb, needles & case, fish-hook, textiles	?	youth	?	Y	N	N	N	116
St Cuthbert's, Kirkcudbright	I	sword, scabbard, ring-headed pin, bead	?	M	?	Y	Y	N	?	117

Site	Inhumation/ Cremation	Artefacts	Date	Sex	Nr Scandinavian Settlements	Nr Transport Routes	Other burials	High Ground	Identifying Feature	Reference
Torbeckhill, Ecclefechan, Kirkcudbrightshire	I?	sword	*c*900	M	?	Y	Y	?	mound	118
Boiden Mound, Lower Bridge of Froon, Argyll & Bute	C	sword, shield, spear	?	M	?	Y	N	?	mound	119
Gordon Bay, Argyll	?	boat rivets	?	?	?	Y	?	?	?	120
Dunrobin Castle, Golspie, Sutherland	?	pair tortoise brooches	?	F	?	Y	?	?	?	121
Dunrobin Castle, Golspie, Sutherland	?	axe, ring	?	M	?	Y	?	?	?	122
Ospisdale House, Dornoch, Sutherland	?	tortoise brooch, urn	?	F	?	Y	?	?	standing stone	123
Castletown, Caithness	I	pair tortoise brooches, arm-ring, bodkin	C10th	F	Y	Y	N	?	mound	124
Haimer, nr Thurso, Caithness	?	weaponry	?	?	Y	Y	?	?	?	125
Huna, Caithness	I	boat rivets, timber, chain fragments, 2 rope restrainers	?	?	?	Y	N	?	?	126
St Peter's, Thurso, Caithness	I	runic cross slab	?	?	Y	Y	Y	?	slab	127
Longhills in Westerseat, nr Wick, Caithness	?	2 tortoise brooches,	?	F	?	Y	?	?	mound	128
Ballindalloch, Morayshire	I	horse bone, shield, rings, bridle-bit, Fe fragments	?	M	?	?	?	?	?	129
Pierowall, Westray, Orkney	I	sword, spear, shield, comb	?	M	?	Y	Y	N	standing stone	130
Pierowall,	I	pair tortoise brooches, knife/weaving sword, ring-headed pin	?	F	?	Y	Y	N	?	131
Pierowall,	I	pair tortoise brooches, ring-headed pin, needle case & needles, spindle whorl, sickle, comb	?	F	?	Y	Y	N	?	132
Pierowall,	I	pair tortoise brooches, beads, 2 ring-headed pins, pin, 2 combs	?	F	?	Y	Y	N	cist	133
Pierowall,	I	axe, shield, Fe fragments	?	M	?	Y	Y	N	?	134
Pierowall	I	animal bone, bridle-bit, buckle, spear, Fe fragments, bone with Fe fragments	?	M	?	Y	Y	N	?	135
Pierowall	I	animal bone, knife, bridle-bit	?	?	?	Y	Y	N	?	136
Pierowall	I		?	?	?	Y	Y	N	?	137
Pierowall,	I	sword, shield, whetstone, comb, bead, Fe fragments with wood attached	?	M	?	Y	Y	N	stone-setting	138
Pierowall,	I	pair tortoise brooches, trefoil brooch, pin	?	F	?	Y	Y	N	?	139

Site	Inhumation/ Cremation	Artefacts	Date	Sex	Nr Scandinavian Settlements	Nr Transport Routes	Other burials	High Ground	Identifying Feature	Reference
Pierowall,	I	pair tortoise brooches, ring-headed pin, 2 decorated combs & cases	?	F	?	Y	Y	N	?	140
Pierowall,	I		?	?	?	Y	Y	N	?	141
Pierowall,	I	pair tortoise brooches, ring-headed pin, 2 combs	?	F	?	Y	Y	N	?	142
Pierowall,	I	shield, spear, tool-axe, Fe fragments	?	M	?	Y	Y	N	?	143
Pierowall	I	2 knives, sickle, key, drinking horn terminal, bead, Fe with wood attached, nails	?	?	?	Y	Y	N	?	144
Pierowall,	I	21 boat rivets, animal bones, 2 buckles, button fragment, Fe fragment	?	?	?	Y	Y	N	?	145
Westness, Rousay, Orkney	I	pair tortoise brooches, 40 beads, Irish brooch pin, gilt mount, 2 A-Saxon strap-ends, comb, sickle, cu-alloy bowl, weaving-sword, shears, pair heckles	C9th	F & infant	Y	Y	Y	N	cist	146
Westness, Rousay, Orkney	I		?	F	Y	Y	Y	N	?	147
Scar, Sanday, Orkney	I	sword, 8 arrows & quiver, 22 gaming pieces, comb, scale weights, mount	950-1050	M	?	Y	Y	N	N	148
Scar, Sanday, Orkney	I	whalebone plaque, gilt equal-armed brooch, sickle, comb, 2 spindle whorls, weaving-sword, shears, needle case, maple wood box	950-1050	F	?	Y	Y	N	N	149
Scar Sanday, Orkney	I		950-1050	child	?	Y	Y	N	N	150
Lamba Ness, Sanday, Orkney	?	sword, spear	?	M	?	Y	?	?	?	151
Lamba Ness, Sanday, Orkneys	?	pair tortoise brooches, jet armlet, bead, ring-headed pin	?	F	?	Y	?	?	?	152
Braeswick, nr Lamba Ness, Sanday, Orkneys	?	tortoise brooch, beads	?	F	?	Y	?	?	?	153
Lyking, Mainland Orkney	C	spear, buckle, comb (unburnt)	?	M	?	Y	N	?	mound	154
Broch of Gurness, Mainland Orkney	I	pair tortoise brooches, necklet with amulets one a Thor's hammer, sickle, knife, pin	LC9thEC10th	F	Y	Y	Y	?	stone-setting, mound	155
Broch of Gurness	?	glass linen smoother, scales, bead, whetstone, Fe fragments	?	F	Y	Y	Y	?	?	156
Broch of Gurness	?	shield	?	M	Y	Y	Y	?	?	157
Broch of Gurness	?	shield	?	M	Y	Y	Y	?	?	158
Broch of Gurness	?	ring-headed pin, amber bead, human cranium	?	?	Y	Y	Y	?	?	159
Broch of Gurness	?	5 rings	?	?	Y	Y	Y	?	cist	160

Site	Inhumation/ Cremation	Artefacts	Date	Sex	Nr Scandinavian Settlements	Nr Transport Routes	Other burials	High Ground	Identifying Feature	Reference
Buckquoy, Mainland Orkney	?	coin of Edmund d940-6, knife, whetstone, bone mount, buckle, ring-headed pin, spear	C10th	M	Y	Y	N	?	mound	161
Stenness, Mainland Orkney	I	ring-headed pin	?	?	?	Y	?	?	mound	162
Howe, Cairnton, Stromness, Mainland Orkney	?	glass linen smoother	?	?	?	Y	?	?	mound	163
Gyron Hill, Sandwich-under-Skaill, Mainland Orkney	?	oblong steatite vessel	?	?	?	Y	?	?	cist	164
Skaill Bay, Mainland Orkney	I	animal bone, comb & case, needle, whetstone, knife, spear, rivet, Fe fragments, stone disc	?	M	?	Y	?	?	cairn	165
Mainland Orkney	C	pair tortoise brooches, spindle whorl, jet bangle, pin	?	F	?	Y	?	?	mound	166
Styes, Sanday, Orkney	?	sword	?	M	Y	Y	Y	?	mound	167
Sweindrow, Westness, Rousay, Orkney	?	sword, shield, Fe fragments	?	M	?	Y	?	?	?	168
St Olaf's White Ness, Mainland Shetland	I	axe	?	?	?	Y	Y	?	slab-lined grave	169
Unst, Shetland	?	tortoise brooch, circular Cu-alloy box	?	?	?	Y	?	?	?	170
Clibberswick, Unst, Shetland	I	pair tortoise brooches, trefoil brooch, Ag armlet, beads	?	F	?	Y	?	?	?	171
Clivocast, Unst, Shetland	I	armour	?	M	?	Y	N	?	mound	172
Housegord, Weisdale, Mainland Shetland	?	whetstone pendant, beads	?	?	?	Y	Y	?	mound	173
Sumburgh, Mainland Shetland	I	tortoise brooch, sword, shield	?	M & F	?	Y	Y	?	?	174
Wick of Aith, Fetlar, Shetland	?	tortoise brooch, rivets,	?	F	Y	Y	?	N	mound	175
Carn nan Bharraich, Oronsay, Western Isles	I	pair gilt rectangular brooches, beads, bone object, penannular brooch	C9th	F	?	Y	Y	N	mound & standing stones	176
Carn nan Bharraich	I	knife, ring	C9th	M	?	Y	Y	N	mound & standing stones	177

Site	Inhumation/ Cremation	Artefacts	Date	Sex	Nr Scandinavian Settlements	Nr Transport Routes	Other burials	High Ground	Identifying Feature	Reference
Carn nan Bharraich	I	pair tortoise brooches, ring-headed pin, needle case & needle, shears, socket, Fe bar, Fe fragments, rivets, nails	C9th	F	?	Y	Y	N	mound	178
Kiloran Bay, Colonsay, Western Isles	I	boat, sword, animal bones, stycas, sickle, buckle, axe, spear, shield, cauldron, arrows, mounts, nails & rivets, whetstone, scales & weights	*c*900	M	?	Y	N	N	oblong stone-setting	179
Ballinaby, Islay, Western Isles	I	miscellaneous finds of 3 swords, spear, shield	?	?	?	Y	Y	N	3 standing stones & stone settings	180
Ballinaby, Islay, Western Isles	I	tortoise brooches, heckle, glass linen smoother, needle case & needles, beads, Ag ring-headed pin, ladle, decorated discs, Ag chain, mount,	?	F	?	Y	Y	N	stone-setting	181
Ballinaby, Islay, Western Isles	I	sword & scabbard, shield, spear, 2 axes, fishing spear, adze, tongs, hammer, drinking horn, cauldron	?	M	?	Y	Y	N	stone-setting	182
Ballinaby, Islay, Western Isles	I	sword, shield, knife, axe, decorated buckle, ring-headed pin	C9th	M	?	Y	Y	Y	cist	183
Ballinaby, Islay, Western Isles	?	pair tortoise brooches	?	F	?	Y	Y	Y	standing stone	184
Cruach Mhor, Islay, Western Isles	I	pair tortoise brooches, beads, spindle whorl, knives, sickle, socket of weaving sword	LC9thEC10th	F	Y	Y	?	?	?	185
King's Cross Point, Lamlash Bay, Arran, Western Isles	C	whalebone plaque, Fe mounting, casket hasp, rivets, nails, Cu-alloy fragment, tweezers, styca d837-54, piece of black rock	C9th	F	?	Y	?	?	mound	186
Millhill, Lamlash Bay, Western Isles	?	scramasax, shield	MC8th	M	?	Y	?	Y	mound	187
Kildonan, Eigg, Western Isles	I	single-edged sword, whetstone, penannular brooch, cloth bag & fragmentary contents, buckles, axe, sickle, beads, bead, spear	C10th	M	Y	Y	Y	?	mound	188
Kildonan, Eigg, Western Isles	I	sword, penannular brooch, buckle, beads, whetstone, flints	C10th	M	Y	Y	Y	?	mound	189
Kildonan, Eigg, Western Isles	I	sword, cu-alloy fragment, decorated mounts, whetstone	C9th	M	Y	Y	Y	?	mound	190
Tarbert, Gigha, Western Isles	?	scales & weights	?	?	?	Y	N	?	cist & stone marker	191
Newton Distillery, Islay, Western Isles	I	pair tortoise brooches, bead	?	F	?	Y	N	Y	?	192
Lochan Kill Mhor, Oronsay, Western Isles	?	Fe fragments, teeth, charcoal	?	?	?	Y	?	?	?	193
Colonsay, Western Isles	I	2 swords, shield, Fe fragments, & bar, knife, rivets, nail & rivets, melted cu-alloy fragments, Fe plates with textile, anchor shaped boat rivet,	?	M	?	Y	?	?	?	194
Ardskinish, Colonsay, Western Isles	?	ring-headed pin, buckle, rivet hood	?	?	?	Y	?	?	?	195

Site	Inhumation/ Cremation	Artefacts	Date	Sex	Nr Scandinavian Settlements	Nr Transport Routes	Other burials	High Ground	Identifying Feature	Reference
Cnoc-Nan-Gill, Colonsay, Western Isles	?	boat rivets, ox tooth, human tooth	?	?	?	Y	?	N	mound	196
Mull, Western Isles	?	pair tortoise brooches	?	F	?	Y	?	?	?	197
Tiree, Western Isles	?	pair tortoise brooches, large pin	?	F	?	Y	Y	?	?	198
Cornaigbeg, Tiree, Western Isles	(multiple) I	animal bones swords, spears, shields	?	?	?	Y	Y	?	?	199
Tote, Sheabost, Skye	C	axe, pin, bead, whetstone, wood with Fe inset, Fe fragments	?	M	?	Y	N	?	mound	200
Ardvonrig, Barra, Western Isles	?	pair tortoise brooches, comb, penannular brooch, heckle, drinking horn mount & terminal, knife, buckle, Cu-alloy rod, slate whetstone (also likely weaving-sword & heckles)	LC9th/C10th	F	?	Y	?	?	mound	201
Eriskay, Western Isles	?	sword, spear	?	M	?	Y	?	?	?	202
South Uist, Western Isles	?	comb	?	?	?	Y	?	?	mound	203
Bhaltos, Uig, Lewis, Western Isles	I	pair tortoise brooches, circular brooch, buckle, penannular brooch all Celtic style, Cu-alloy chain bead	LC9th	F	N	Y	Y	Y	mound	204
Ensay, Western Isles	I	Cu-alloy scales, small hammer	?	?	?	Y	?	?	?	205
Sangay, Western Isles	I	pair tortoise brooches, pin, needle	?	F	?	Y	Y	?	?	206
Cnip, Uig, Western Isles	I	pair tortoise brooches, whetstone, needle case, knife & sheath, sickle, beads, comb, strap-end with studs & buckle, rivet, ring-headed pin with incised cross	C10th	F	N	Y	Y	Y	mound	207
Cnip, Uig, Western Isles	I	bead, stone pendant, nails	LC9thC10th	child	N	Y	Y	Y	N	208
Cnip, Uig, Western Isles	I		LC9thC10th	M	N	Y	Y	Y	stone-setting	209
Cnip, Uig, Western Isles	I	cow molar	LC8thLC9th	M	N	Y	Y	Y	stone-setting	210
Cnip, Uig, Western Isles	I	bone pin, perforated Fe plate	LC8thLC9th	F	N	Y	Y	Y	stone-setting	211
Cnip, Uig, Western Isles	I	beads, decorated pin	?	child	N	Y	Y	Y	N	212
Cnip, Uig, Western Isles	I	rivet	?	child	N	Y	Y	Y	N	213
Barra, Western Isles	?	comb	?	?	?	Y	?	?	cist	214
Machrins Machair, Colonsay, Western Isles	I	animal bone, metal plaque of Celtic design, ring-headed pin, knife, nail, textile	LC9th	F	Y	Y	Y	?	cist	215

Site	Inhumation/ Cremation	Artefacts	Date	Sex	Nr Scandinavian Settlements	Nr Transport Routes	Other burials	High Ground	Identifying Feature	Reference
Machrins Machair, Colonsay, Western Isles	I	sword, shield, axe, spearhead, Fe pot, boat rivets, bridle-bit, bead, penannular brooch, pin,	?	M	Y	Y	Y	?	mound	216

Viking Burials in Ireland

Site	Inhumation/ Cremation	Artefacts	Date	Sex	Nr Scandinavian Settlements	Nr Transport Routes	Other burials	High Ground	Identifying Feature	Reference
Larne, Co. Antrim	I	sword, spear, ring-headed pin, comb, penannular brooch	LC9thEC10th	M	?	Y	N	?	N	217
Church Bay, Rathlin Island, Co. Antrim	I	Ag penannular brooch, beads	?	F	?	Y	Y	Y	standing stone	218
Church Bay, Rathlin Island, Co. Antrim	I	Sword	?	M	?	Y	Y	Y	mound	219
Church Bay, Rathlin Island, Co. Antrim	I	Cu-alloy ladle, cauldron, rings	?	F	?	Y	Y	Y	?	220
Church Bay, Rathlin Island, Co. Antrim	I		?	?	?	Y	Y	Y	nr standing stone, above	221
Ballyholme, Co. Down	I	pair tortoise brooches, cu-alloy bowl & pieces of wool, linen	LC9th	F	?	Y	N	Y	mound	222
Phoenix Park, Dublin	I	pair tortoise brooches, gilt mounting	?	F	Y	Y	Y	?	?	223
Phoenix Park, Dublin	I	brooch	?	F	Y	Y	Y	Y	?	224
Aylesbury Road, Donnybrook, Dublin	I	sword, spear, arrows, (possibly assoc. dagger, pin, penannular brooch, 3 rings)	LC9thEC10th	M	Y	Y	Y	?	mound	225
Bully's Acre, Kilmainham, Dublin	I	sword, spear, pin, axe, Fe fragments	?	M	Y	Y	Y	?	?	226
Islandbridge, Dublin	I	sword, dagger, spear	?	M	Y	Y	Y	?	?	227
Islandbridge, Dublin	I	animal bone	?	M	Y	Y	Y	?	?	228
Islandbridge, Dublin	I	2 swords, axe, spear, shield	?	M	Y	Y	Y	?	?	229
Kilmainham, Dublin	I	sword, spear, beads	?	M	Y	Y	Y	?	?	230
Kilmainham & Islandbridge Cemeteries, Dublin	*c*36 I	many unprovenanced artefacts – see chapter 6	LC9thEC10th	?	Y	Y	Y	?	?	231
Bride Street, Dublin	C	sword, spear, shield	?	M	Y	Y	N	?	?	232

Site	Inhumation/ Cremation	Artefacts	Date	Sex	Nr Scandinavian Settlements	Nr Transport Routes	Other burials	High Ground	Identifying Feature	Reference
Royal Arcade, College Green, Dublin	?	sword, single edged sword, axes, 4 spears, shields, arrows, buckle	?	?	Y	Y	Y	?	mound	233
Suffolk Street, Dublin	I	weaponry	?	M	Y	Y	Y	?	?	234
Palace Row (now Parnell Square North), Dublin	I	sword, shield	?	M	Y	Y	Y	?	?	235
Granby Row, Dublin	I	sword, spear, rivets	?	M	Y	Y	Y	?	?	236
Dollymount, Dublin	?	sword	?	M	Y	Y	N	?	?	237
Cork Street, Dublin	?	sword	?	M	Y	Y	?	?	?	238
Kildare Street, Dublin	?	sword	?	M	Y	Y	?	?	?	239
Eyrephort, Co. Galway	I	sword, shield, spear, dagger	MC9th	M	?	Y	?	?	?	240
Cloghermore Cave, Tralee, Co. Kerry	I	Ag ring-headed pin, whetstone, knife, animal bone, Ag button, Fe fragments	?	M	?	Y	Y	?	cave	241
Barnhall, Co. Kildare	I	axe, weaponry	?	M	?	N	?	?	?	242
Milltown, Co. Kildare	I	animal bone	?	?	?	?	?	?	?	243
Navan, Co. Meath	I	animal bone, mountings, bridle fittings & decoration – Celtic design	LC9thEC10th	?	?	N	?	?	?	244
Three-Mile Water, Arklow, Co. Wicklow	?	pair tortoise brooches & chain	900-950	F	?	Y	N	?	?	245
The Morragh, nr. Wicklow, Co. Wicklow	?	sword	?	M	?	?	N	?	?	246
Tybroughney, Co. Kilkenny	I	swords	?	?	?	Y	N	?	?	247
St John's Point, Co. Down	I	swords	?	?	?	Y	?	?	?	248
Croghan Erin, Co. Meath	?	spear	?	?	?	?	Y	?	cairn	249
Templemoyle, Lamavady, Co. Londonderry	C	sword, urn, whetstone, hammer, speckled pebble	?	?	?	?	Y	?	cairn & cist	250
St Magnen's Churchyard, Kilmainham, Dublin	?	Irish-Norse coins, 2 swords	?	?	Y	Y	Y	?	carved stone	251

References

1	**Hodgson C (1832)**, An Account of some Antiquities found in a cairn, near Hesket-in-the-Forest, in a letter from Mr Christopher Hodgson to the Rev. John Hodgson, Secretary, *Archaeologia Aeliana* first series, 2, 1832, pp106-109 **Cowen JD (1934)**, A Catalogue of objects of the Viking period in the Tullie House Museum, Carlisle, *Transactions of the Cumberland & Westmorland Antiquarian Archaeological Society (C & W)* new series, vol. 34 (174-180) pp166-187 ***Addenda Antiquaria,* (1905)**, The Viking-age Hoard from Hesket, now in Tullie House Museum, *C & W*, n/s vol. V pp305-308
2	**Rooke H (1792)**, Druidical and other British Remains in Cumberland… *Archaeologia* 10, pp105-13 **Abramson P (2000)**, A re-examination of a Viking Age burial at Beacon Hill, Aspatria, *C & W*, vol. C, pp79-88
3	**Edwards BJN (1969)**, The Claughton Viking Burial, *Historical Society of Lancashire & Cheshire*, vol. 121, pp109-116 **Jones M (1846)**, Remains of a Viking Burial, *Archaeological Journal (AJ)* 6, pp74-75 **Kendrick T (1928-1945)**, The Claughton Hall Brooches, *Saga-Book of the Viking Club* vol. XI, pp117-24, pl I & II, 1930-36
4	**Fishwick H (1891)**, *The History of the Parish of St Michael's-on-Wye, in the County of Lancashire*, printed for the Chetham Society new series 25, pp2-3
5	**Archaeological Intelligence (1848)**, *AJ*, vol. V, pp220-221
6	**Speed G & Cardwell P (2003), (Northern Archaeological Associates), pers. comm..**
7-12	**Clarke C & Fraser W (1946)**, Excavation of Pagan Burial Mounds: Ingleby, Derbyshire, *Derbyshire Archaeological Journal (DAJ)*, pp1-23
13	**Clarke C, Fraser W & Munslow FW (1949)**, Excavation of Pagan Burial Mounds at Ingleby, Second Report, *DAJ*, vol. 69, pp78-81
14	Accredited by Posnansky M, to Clarke et al 1949, but they only record opening Mound 7. RCHME records mound disturbed by excavation, possibly Clarke or even Bateman
15-21	**Posnansky M (1956)**, The Pagan-Danish Barrow Cemetery at Heath Wood, Ingleby. 1955 Excavations, *DAJ* vol. 76, pp40-56
22-23	**Richards J (2003)**, pers. comm., lecture given on the burial ground at Heathwood, nr. Ingleby, at the Yorkshire Archaeological Society 8th February **JD Richards JD (2003)**, Heathwood, Ingleby, *Current Archaeology*, no. 184, vol. XVI, no. 4, pp170-3
24	**Edwards BJN (1998)**, *Vikings in North West England. The Artifacts*, Centre for North-West Regional Studies, University of Lancashire, p96
25	**Proceedings (1904)**, *C & W* n/s vol. 4 p340 **Lang (1984)**, as above in note 33-9, p116
26	**Cowen JD (1967)**, Viking Burials in Cumbria: a Supplement, C & W n/s vol. 67, pp31-4 ***The Cumberland Pacquet***, 18th October 1814
27	**Ferguson RS (1899)**, Various finds in Ormside Churchyard, *C & W* series 1, vol. XV 1899, pp377-380 **JD Cowen (1934)**, A Catalogue of objects of the Viking period in the Tullie House Museum, Carlisle, *C & W*, vol. 34, new series, pp166-187
28-9	**Gaythorpe H (1910)**, The Rampside Sword; with Notes on the Church & Churchyard of Rampside in Furness, *C & W* vol. 10 n/s, pp298-306 **Cowen JD (1948)**, Viking Burials in Cumbria, *C & W*, vol.47 n/s, pp73-76
30	**Whitaker TD (1823)**, *A History of Richmondshire* (2 vols.) London, vol. II p319 **Edwards (1998)**, as above in note 40, p24
31	**Kaye WJ (1928)**, A Viking Grave Near Harrogate, *Durham University Journal*, vol. XXV, pp381-384 ***Harrogate Herald,*** 28th March 1928
32	**Lord Bolton (1916)**, Proceedings, *Proceedings of the Society of Antiquaries (PSA)*, vol. XXVIII, 2nd series, pp228-230
33-7	**Atkinson JC, (1867-70)**, Proceedings Thursday, January 9th 1868, *PSA*, Series 2, IV, pp52-54 **Atkinson JC (1874)**, *History of Cleveland Ancient and Modern*, vol. I, MTD Publications, Leeds (facsimile reprint from 1874 edition) pp81-85
38	**Lukis WC (1870)**, On some Anglo-Saxon Graves on Howe Hill, near Carthorpe, in the Parish of Burneston, North Riding of Yorkshire, *Yorkshire Archaeological Journal (YAJ)* vol. I, pp175-181
39-43	**Biddle M & Kjolbye-Biddle B (1992)**, Repton and the Vikings, *Antiquity* vol. 66, pp36-51 **Biddle M & Kjolbye-Biddle B (2001)**, Repton and the 'great heathen army', 873-4, in Vikings and the Danelaw, in *Select Papers from the Proceedings of the Thirteenth Viking Congress*, ed. J Graham-Campbell, R Hall, J Jesch & D Parsons, Oxbow, Oxford, pp45-96 **Bjørn A & Shetelig H (1940)** *Viking Antiquities in England – with a supplement of Viking antiquities on the continent of western Europe*, part IV of Viking Antiquities in Great Britain and Ireland, ed. Shetelig H, The Scientific Research Fund of 1919, H Aschehoug & Co. (W. Nygaard), Oslo **Lang JT (1984)**, The Hogback: a Viking colonial monument, in *Anglo-Saxon Studies in Archaeology and History III*, ed. by S Chadwick Hawkes, J Campbell and D Brown, Oxford University Committee for Archaeology, Oxford, pp85-176, @ p160
44-6	**Alexander ML (1987)**, A Viking-Age Grave from Cambois, Bedlington, Northumberland, *Medieval Archaeology (MA)*, vol. 31, pp101-105 **The Greenwell Papers**, 16 MSS 12 No 13 p3, British Museum, London
47-50	**Tweddle D**, *Carlisle, Cathedral Green Decorated Metalwork*, Unpublished **Anon**, *Site Report of Excavated Graves at Cathedral Green, Carlisle*, Unpublished
51	**Sites & Monuments Record**, no. NYM19766
52	**Hall RA & Whyman M (1987)**, Settlement & Monasticism at Ripon, North Yorkshire, From the 7th to 11th Centuries AD, *MA*, vol. 31, pp62-161
53	**Potter TW & Andrews RD (1993-4)**, Excavation & Survey at St Patrick's Chapel & St Peter's Church, Heysham, Lancashire, 1977-8, *AJ*, vol. 74, pp55-134
54-70	**Phillips D & Heywood B (1995)**, *Excavations at York Minster, vol. I, From Roman Fortress to Norman Cathedral*, ed. Carver MOH, RCHME, HMSO London. Burial details from MOH Carver's table 2, pp88-92
71	**Ramm HG (1976)**, The Church of St Mary, Bishophill Senior: Excavations 1964, *YAJ*, vol. 48 pp35-68
72-79	**Wenham LP, Hall RA, Briden CM & Stocker DA (1987)**, *St Mary Bishophill Junior & St Mary Castlegate*, The Archaeology of York, Anglo-Scandinavian York 8/2, published for York Archaeological Trust by CBA London
80-1	As above in note 39-43
82	**Collingwood WG (1904)**, Proceedings, *C & W*, vol. 4, n/s, p335 **Collingwood WG (1904)**, The Workington Sword, *Saga-Book of the Viking Club*, vol. III, pt. III, pp302-4
83	**Hutton FRC (1901)**, Witherslack Church & Manor, *C & W*, vol. 1, n/s, pp186-193 & Plate
84	**Greenwell W (1878)**, *British Barrows. A record of sepulchral mounds in various parts of England. Together with a description of figures of skulls, general remarks on prehistoric crania and an appendix by G Rolleston*, Clarendon Press, Oxford, p386 **O'Sullivan D (1996)**, A group of pagan burials from Cumbria?, in *Anglo-Saxon studies in Archaeology & History 9*, ed. D Griffiths, Oxford University Committee for Archaeology, Oxford, pp15-23 @ pp17-18
85	**Preston W (1766)**, An Account of opening one of the largest barrows on Sandford Moor, Westmorland, letter dated Warcop Hall Sept 5th to Bishop Lyttleton, read at the Society of Antiquaries Nov 6th 1766: *Archaeologia*: or miscellaneous tracts relating to Antiquity vol. III, MDCCLXXXVI (1766), p273
86	**Gastrell F (1850)**, *Notitia Cestriensis or Historic Notices of the Diocese of Chester*, from the original manuscript of FR Raines, vol. II part II printed for the Chetham Society, vol. 21, p286
87	**Whitaker J (1775)**, *History of Manchester*, vol. 2, Saxon Period, pp36-37
88	**Griffiths D (2001)**, *pers.comm.*, & also *Settlement & Acculturation in the Irish Sea Region*, paper given at the Viking-period Settlement in Britain & Ireland Conference, Cardiff University
89	**Bersu G & Wilson DM (1966)**, *Three Viking Graves in the Isle of Man*, The Society of Medieval Archaeology, Monograph Series, No 1, London, pp45-62
90	**Bersu & Wilson (1966)**, as above in note 89, pp63-83
91	**Bersu & Wilson (1966)**, as above in note 89, pp1-44

92	**Kermode PMC (1930)**, Ship-Burial in the Isle of Man, *AJ* vol. X, pp126-133
93	**Cubbon M (1983)**, The archaeology of the Vikings in the Isle of Man, in *The Viking Age in the Isle of Man, Select Papers from the Ninth Viking Congress*, Isle of Man 4-14 July 1981, ed by C Fell, P Foote, J Graham-Campbell & R Thomson, Viking Society for Northern Research UCL, p18 **Cubbon AM (1982)**, Find of a Viking Sword, Spear & Shield… *Proceedings of the Isle of Man Natural History & Antiquarian Society (PIMNHAS)* VIII: 4, pp439-57
94-100	**Freke D (2002)**, Excavations on St Patrick's Isle, Peel, Isle of Man 1982-88, Prehistoric, Viking, Medieval and Later, Centre for Manx Studies Monographs 2, Liverpool University Press, pp66-71
101	**Megaw BRS (1937)**, Weapons of the Viking Age found in Man, *Journal of the Manx Museum (JMM)*, vol. III, p234
102	**Megaw (1937)**, as above in note 101, pp235-6
103	**Megaw (1937)**, as above in note 101, p235
104	**Megaw (1937)**, as above on note 101, p235
105	**Cubbon AM (1965)**, A Viking Sword from Ballabrooie, Patrick: with evidence of pattern-welding, *JMM* vol. VI, pp249-253
106	**Megaw (1937)**, as above in note 101, p235
107	**Megaw (1937)**, as above in note 101, p235
108	**Megaw (1937)**, as above in note 101, p235
109	**Megaw BRS (1938)**, An Ancient Cemetery at Balladoyne, St Johns, *JMM*, vol. IV, p13
110	**Neely G (1940)**, Excavations at Ronaldsway, Isle of Man, *AJ*, vol. XXX, pp72-86 **Higgins DA (1999)**, Survey & Trial Excavations at the Ronaldsway Village site, Ronaldsway Airport, Isle of Man, in *Recent Arc Research in the Isle of Man*, ed. PJ Davey, BAR British Series 278, pp139-152
111	**Megaw (1937)**, as above in note 101, p236
112	**Megaw (1937)**, as above on note 101, p235
113	**Megaw (1938)**, as above on note 109, pp12-13
114-15	**Curle J (1913-14)**, On recent Scandinavian grave finds from the island of Oronsay & from Reay, Caithness…, *Proceedings of the Society of Antiquaries of Scotland (PSAS)*, vol. 48, pp292-315, @pp292-9 **Edwards AHJ (1926-7)**, Excavations of graves at Ackergill and of an earth house at Freswick Links, Caithness & a description of the discovery of a Viking grave at Reays, *PSAS*, vol. LXIII, pp196-209 @ pp202-207 **Edwards AHJ (1928-9)**, Excavations at Reay Links & at a Horned Cairn at Lower Dounreay, Caithness. *PSAS*, vol. LXIII, pp138-50
116	**Batey CE (1993)**, The Viking & Late Norse Graves of Caithness & Sutherland, *The Viking Age in Caithness, Orkney & the North Atlantic* (Papers from 11th Viking Congress), ed. CE Batey, J Jesch & CD Morris, Edinburgh University Press, pp148-64 @ pp157-8
117	**Batey (1993)**, as above in note 116, p144 **Greig S (1940)**, *Viking Antiquities in Scotland*, part II of Viking Antiquities in Great Britain & Ireland, ed. Shetelig H, The Scientific Research Fund of 1919, Oslo: H Aschehougt & Co (W. Nygaard), p13
118	**Curle AO (1913-14)**, Notices of the discovery of a hoard of rapier-shaped blades of bronze at Drumcoltran and the Stewartry of Kirkudbright & of a Viking sword at Torbeckhill nr Ecclefechan, *PSAS*, vol. XLVIII, pp333-5
119	**Anderson J (1874-5)**, Notes on the Relics of the Viking Period of the Northmen in Scotland, Illustrated by Specimens in the Museum, *PSAS*, 1874-5 vol. X, pp536-594 @ p569 **Stewart HJ (1853)**, Notice of the discovery of some ancient arms & armour near Glenfruin on the estate of Sir James Colquhoun of Luss, *PSAS*, vol. I, p143
120	**Greig (1940)**, as above in note 117, p15
121-2	**Anderson (1874-5)**, as above in note 119, p554 **Greig (1940)**, as above in note 117, pp15-17
123	**Greig (1940)**, as above in note 117, p17 **Anderson (1874-5)**, as above in note 119, p554
124	**Anderson (1874-5)**, as above in note 119, p549-50 **Greig (1940)**, as above in note 117, p24
125	**Greig (1940)**, as above in note 117, p25
126	**Batey C (1987)**, *Freswick Links, Caithness. A re-appraisal of the Late Norse site in its context*, BAR British Series 179 (vols. I & II), Oxford, p38
127	**Batey (1987)**, as above in note 126, pp39-40
128	**Anderson (1874-5)**, as above in note 119, p551
129	**Anderson (1874-5)**, as above in note 119, p569-70
130-	**Thorsteinsson A (1968)**, The Viking Burial Place at Pierowall,
145	Westray, Orkney, *The 5th Viking Congress*, Torshavn 1965, ed. Niclasen B, Foroya Landsstyri, pp156-73
146-147	**Kaland SHH (1993)**, The settlement of Westness, Rousey, *The Viking Age in Caithness, Orkney & the North Atlantic* (papers from 11th Viking Congress), ed Batey CE, Jesch J, Morris CD, Edinburgh University Press pp308-17 @ pp312-17 **Letter from C Paterson to Sellevold (1999)**, appendix B part 10, p56 in BJ Sellevold, *Picts & Vikings at Westness. Anthro inverstigations of the skeletal material from the cemetery at Westness, Rousay, Orkney Islands.* Norsk institutt for kulturminneforskning, Oslo **Graham-Campbell J & Batey CE (1998)**, *Vikings in Scotland. An Archaeological Survey*, Edinburgh University Press, pp135-8
148-150	**Owen OA & Dalland M (1999)**, *Scar: a Viking boat burial on Sanday, Orkney*, Tuckwell Press in Association with Historic Scotland, East Lothian
151-2	**Greig (1940)**, as above in note 117, p86-8 **Graham-Campbell & Batey (1998)**, as above in note 146-7, p57, 144 Donations to the museum *PSAS*, vol. XII 1877-78, p599 Donations to the museum *PSAS*, vol. XLIX 1914-15, p15
153	**Curle (1913-14)**, as above in note 118, pp333-5 **Greig (1940)**, as above in note 117, p88 **Graham-Campbell & Batey (1998)**, as above in note 146-7, p57
154	Donations to the Museum from TS Traill, *PSAS* IX 1872-73 p5 **Greig (1940)**, as above in note 117, p80 **Graham-Campbell & Batey (1998)**, as above in note 146-7, p144
155-160	**Hedges JW (1987)**, *Bu, Gurness & the Brochs of Orkney*, Part II: Gurness (vols. I-III), BAR British Series 164, pp73-4, 86-7 **Robertson WN (1968-9)**, A Viking grave found at the Broch of Gurness, Aikerness, Orkney, *PSAS*, vol. 101, pp289-90
161	**Ritchie A (1976-7)**, Excavation of Pictish and Viking-age farmsteads at Buckquoy, Orkney *PSAS*, vol. 108, pp174-227
162	**Charleson MM (1903-4)**, Notice of Some Ancient Burials in Orkney. *PSAS*, vol. XXXVIII, pp559-566, @ p566 **Greig (1940)**, as above in note 117, p80
163	**Marwick JG (1927)**, Notes on some relics from Orkney, exhibited before the society, *PSAS*, vol. LXIII, p121-2 **Greig (1940)**, as above in note 117, p80-81 **Graham-Campbell & Batey (1998)**, as above in note 146-7, p60
164	**Greig (1940)**, as above in note 117, p81
165	**Greig (1940)**, as above in note 117, p81-84 **Graham-Campbell & Batey (1998)**, as above in note 146-7, p59 **Watt WGT (1887-88)**, Notice of the discovery of a stone cist with an iron age interment at Skaill Bay, *PSAS*, vol. XI, pp283-5
166	**Charleson MM (1903-4)**, Notice of some ancient burials in Orkney, *PSAS* vol. XXXVIII, pp559-566 **Greig (1940)**, as above in note 117, p86 **Graham-Campbell & Batey (1998)**, as above in note 146-7, p59
167	**Anderson (1874-5)**, as above in note 119, p566 **Bond J (2003)**, pers. comm.
168	**Greig (1940)**, as above in note 117, p88-90 **Anderson (1874-5)**, as above in note 119, pp563-66
169	**Graham-Campbell & Batey (1998)**, as above in note 146-7, p64 & 144
170	**Greig (1940)**, as above in note 117, p103
171	**Anderson (1874-5)**, as above in note 119, p556 **Greig (1940)**, as above in note 117, p103-5 Purchases for the Museum, *PSAS* (1882-3), vol. XVII, pp17-8
172	**Graham-Campbell & Batey (1998)**, as above in note 146-7, p64
173	**Graham-Campbell & Batey (1998)**, as above in note 146-7, p64
174	**Graham-Campbell & Batey (1998)**, as above in note 146-7, p64
175	**Graham-Campbell & Batey (1998)**, as above in note 146-7, p64
176-178	**Greig (1940)**, as above in note 117, pp44-46 **Graham-Campbell & Batey (1998)**, as above in note 146-7, pp113-118 **McNeill M (1890-1)**, Notice of excavations in a burial mound of the Viking time in Oronsay, *PSAS* vol. XXV, pp432-5 **Anderson J (1906-7)**, Notice of Bronze Brooches and personal ornaments from a ship-burial of the Viking time in Oronsay, *PSAS*, vol. XLI, pp437-50 **Grieve S (1913-14)**, More Upon Carn nan Bharraich, or Cairn of the men of Barra, a burial mound of the Viking time on the island of Oronsay Argyllshire. *PSAS*, vol. 48, pp272-91 **Curle J (1913-14)**, On recent Scandinavian grave finds from the island of Oronsay, *PSAS*, vol. 48 1913-14 pp292-315

179	**Greig (1940)**, as above in note 117, pp48-61 **Graham-Campbell & Batey (1998)**, as above in note 146-7, pp118-122 **Anderson J (1906-7)**, Notice of bronze brooches..with a description of..a ship-burial of the Viking time at Kiloran Bay, Colonsay *PSAS*, vol. 41, pp443-9
180-4	**Graham-Campbell & Batey (1998)**, as above in note 146-7, pp122-125 **Anderson J (1879-80)**, Notes on the contents of two Viking graves in Islay, Discovered by William Campbell Esq. of Ballinaby, *PSAS*, vol. XIV, pp51-2 **Edwards AJH (1933-4)**, A Viking cist-grave at Ballinaby, Islay, *PSAS*, vol. 68, pp74-78 **Anderson (1874-5)**, as above in note 119, p554
185	**Gordon K (1990)**, A Norse Viking-age grave from Cruach Mhor, Islay, *PSAS*, vol. 120, pp151-60
186	**Graham-Campbell & Batey (1998)**, as above in note 146-7, p144 **Greig (1940)**, as above in note 117, pp26-27 **Balfour JA (1908-9)**, Notice of a Viking Grave mound, King's Cross, Arran, *PSAS* vol. XLIII, pp371-5
187	**Greig (1940)**, as above in note 117, pp27-28 **Graham-Campbell & Batey (1998)**, as above in note 146-7, pp95-96
188-90	**Greig (1940)**, as above in note 117, pp63-70 **Graham-Campbell & Batey (1998)**, as above in note 146-7, p84 **Macpherson N (1872-79)**, Notes on Antiquities from the Island of Eigg, *PSAS* vol. XII, pp586-92
191	**Greig (1940)**, as above in note 117, pp29-30 **Graham-Campbell & Batey (1998)**, as above in note 146-7, p92 **Bryze T (1912-13)**, Note on the balance & weights of the Viking period found in the island of Gigha *PSAS*, vol. XLVII, p436
192	**Greig (1940)**, as above in note 117, pp42
193	**Greig (1940)**, as above in note 117, pp46
194	**Greig (1940)**, as above in note 117, pp46-48
195	**Greig (1940)**, as above in note 117, pp61 **Graham-Campbell & Batey (1998)**, as above in note 146-7, p91 **Anderson J (1907)**, Notice of brooches & personal ornaments from a ship-burial of the Viking time in Oronsay, & other bronze ornaments from Colonsay, *PSAS*, vol. XLI, p441
196	**Greig (1940)**, as above in note 117, pp61-62 **Graham-Campbell & Batey (1998)**, as above in note 146-7, p91
197	**Anderson (1879-80)**, as above in note 180-4, p72
198	**Anderson (1874-5)**, as above in note 119, p554 **Greig (1940)**, as above in note 117, pp63
199	**Greig (1940)**, as above in note 117, pp63 **Graham-Campbell & Batey (1998)**, as above in note 146-7, p87 **Anderson (1874-5)**, as above in note 119, p554
200	**Lethbridge TC (1920)**, A Burial of the Viking Age in Skye, *AJ*, vol. LXXVII, pp135-6 **Greig (1940)**, as above in note 117, pp 70-71 **Graham-Campbell & Batey (1998)**, as above in note 146-7, pp78
201	**Greig (1940)**, as above in note 117, pp72-73 **Graham-Campbell & Batey (1998)**, as above in note 146-7, pp83 **Curle J (1913-14)**, On Recent Scandinavian Grave-finds from the Island of Oronsay & from Reay, Caithness, with notes on the development & chronology of the oval brooch of Viking time, *PSAS*, vol. XLVIII, pp292-315, @pp308-309
202	**Greig (1940)**, as above in note 117, pp73
203	**Greig (1940)**, as above in note 117, pp73-74 Donations to the Museum, *PSAS*, vol. IX, 1870-72, p446,
204	**Macleod DJ (1915-16)**, An Account of a find of ornaments of the Viking time, from Valtos, Uigg, in the Isle of Lewis, *PSAS*, vol. L, pp181-9 **Greig (1940)**, as above in note 117, pp75-78 **Graham-Campbell & Batey (1998)**, as above in note 146-7, p74
205	**Greig (1940)**, as above in note 117, p79 **Anderson J (1874-5)**, as above in note 119, p556
206	**Anderson J (1874-5)**, as above in note 119, p555 **Greig (1940)**, as above in note 117, p79
207-213	**Welander RDE, Batey C & Cowie TG, with contributions by Bender Jørgensen L, Harman M, Scott MacKenzie C (1987)**, A Viking Burial from Kneep, Uig, Isle of Lewis, *PSAS*, vol. CXVII, pp149-74 **Dunwell AJ, Cowie TG, Bruce MF, Neighbour T, Rees AR with contributions by B Finlayson, N Kerr, N Murray, RJ Strachan (1995)**, A Viking Age Cemetery at Cnip, Uig, Isle of Lewis, *PSAS*, vol. CXXV, pp719-752
214	**Graham-Campbell & Batey (1998)**, as above in note 146-7, p83
215-16	**Graham-Campbell & Batey (1998)**, as above in note 146-7, pp90-91 **M'Neill M (1891-2)**, Notice of the Discovery of a Viking Interment, in the Island of Colonsay, *PSAS*, vol. XXVI, pp61-2 **Ritchie JN (1981)**, Excavations at Machrins, Colonsay, *PSAS*, vol. 111 pp263-81
217	**Smith JH (1841-44)**, An Account of the Discovery, in the month of November last, of a Human Skeleton, accompanied by Weapons, Ornaments, etc., *Proceedings of the Royal Irish Academy (PRIA)*, vol. II, pp40-46 **Fanning T (1970)**, The Viking Grave Goods Discovered near Larne, Co. Antrim in 1840, *(JRSAI)*, vol. C, pp71-78 **Bøe J (1940)**, *Norse Antiquities in Ireland*; part III of Viking Antiquities in Great Britain & Ireland, ed. Shetelig H, H Aschehoug & Co (W Nygaard) Oslo, The Scientific Research Fund of 1919, p76
218-21	**Warner R (1973-4)**, The re-provenancing of two important Viking period penannular brooches, *Ulster Journal of Archaeology (UJA)*, 3rd series vols. 36-7, pp58-70 @ pp61-3 **Northern Island Sites and Monuments Record** **Ó Floinn R (1998)**, The Archaeology of the Early Viking Age in Ireland, in *Ireland & Scandinavia in the Early Viking Age*, eds. Clarke HB, Ni Mhaonaigh M & Ó Floinn R, Four Courts Press, Dublin, pp131-165 @ pp144-145
222	**Dr. Cochrane (1906)**, Proceedings, *JRSAI*, vol. XXXVI, pp450-454 **Smith R (1905-6)**, Proceedings, *PSA* vol. XXI, pp72-79 **Bøe (1940)**, as above in note 217, p75
223	**Hall RA (1974b)**, A Viking Grave in the Phoenix Park Co. Dublin, *JRSAI*, vol. CIV, pp39-43 **'H' (1861-2)**, On the use of certain antique bronze articles, supposed by some to be musical instruments, *UJA*, 1st series, pp271-277 @ p274 **Worsaae J (1846-7)**, *Viking Ireland*, Jens Worsaae's accounts of his visit to Ireland: 1846-47, transl. Ase Goldsmith, ed by D Henry. The Pinkfoot Press: Balgavies Angus 1995 p64 **Ó Floinn (1998)**, as above in note 218-21, @pp132-3
224	**Ó Floinn (1998)**, as above in note 218-21, pp131-165 @ pp132, 134
225	**Frazer W (1879-88)**, On a Great Sepulchral Mound, *PRIA*, 2nd series, vol. II, pp29-55 **O'Brien E (1992)**, A Reassessment of the 'Great Sepulchral Mound' containing a Viking burial at Donnybrook, *MA*, vol. 36, pp170-3 **Bøe (1940)**, as above in note 217, p66-7 **Hall RA (1978)**, A Viking-age Grave at Donnybrook, Co. Dublin, *MA*, vol. 22, pp64-83
226	**Bøe (1940)**, as above in note 217, p58 **O'Brien E (1998)**, The location and context of Viking burials at Kilmainham and Islandbridge, Dublin, in *Ireland and Scandinavia in the Early Viking Age*, ed. by Clarke HB, Ni Mhanaigh M & Ó Floinn R, Blackrock: Fourcourts, Dublin, pp202-221
227	**O'Brien (1998)**, as above in note 226, pp202-221
228	**Bøe (1940)**, as above in note 217, p59 **O'Brien (1998)**, as above in note 226, pp202-221
229	**O'Brien (1998)**, as above in note 226, pp202-221
230	**Briggs CS (1985)**, with contributions by Guido M & Walsh A, A Neglected Viking Burial with Beads from Kilmainham, Dublin, discovered in 1847, *MA*, vol. XXIX, pp94-108
231	**Bøe (1940)**, as above in note 217, p65 **O'Brien (1998)**, as above in note 226, pp202-221
232	**Bøe (1940)**, as above in note 217, p65
233	**Bøe (1940)**, as above in note 217, p65 **Worsaae (1846-7)**, as above in note 223, p64 **Ó Floinn (1998)**, as above in note 218-21, pp135-6
234	**Ó Floinn (1998)**, as above in note 216, pp135-136
235	**Bøe (1940)**, as above in note 217, p67 **Ó Floinn (1998)**, as above in note 218-21, p134
236	**Ó Floinn (1998)**, as above in note 218-21, p134
237	**Bøe (1940)**, as above in note 217, p85 **Ó Floinn (1998)**, as above in note 218-21, pp134
238	**Ó Floinn (1998)**, as above in note 218-21, p132 **Bøe (1940)**, as above in note 217, pp65-68
239	**Ó Floinn (1998)**, as above in note 218-21, p132 **Bøe (1940)**, as above in note 217, pp65-68
240	**Raftery J (1960-1)**, A Viking Burial in Co. Galway, *Journal of Galway Archaeology & Historical Society (JGAHS)*, vol. 29, pp3-6 **Sheehan J (1987-8)**, A reassessment of the Viking burial from Eyrephort, Co. Galway, *JGAHS*, vol. 41, pp60-72

241	**Connolly M & Coyne F (2000)**, Cloghermore Cave. The Lee Valhalla, *Archaeology Ireland*, vol. 14, no. 4, winter 2000, pp16-19
242	**Ó Floinn (1998)**, as above in note 218-21, pp144-145
243	**Harrison SH (2001)**, Viking Graves and Grave-goods in Ireland, in *The Vikings in Ireland*, ed. Larsen A-C, Viking ship Museum, Roskilde, pp66 **Anon (1859)**, Presentations, *PRIA*, vol. III, p121
244	**Armstrong ECR (1922)**, Some Irish Antiquities of Unknown Use, *AJ*, vol. II pp6-12 **Bøe (1940)**, as above in note 217, p76

245	**Coffey G (1902)**, A Pair of brooches and chains of the Viking Period, recently found in Ireland, *JRSAI*, vol. XXXII, pp71-73 **Bøe (1940)**, as above in note 217, p73
246	**Ó Floinn R (1998)**, Two Viking Burials from Co. Wicklow, *Journal of the Co. Wicklow Archaeological Society (JCWAS)*, vol. 1, pp29-35
247	**Harrison (2001)**, as above in note 243, p68-9
248	**Harrison (2001)**, as above in note 243, p68-9
249	**Harrison (2001)**, as above in note 243, pp61-75
250	**Northern Island Sites and Monuments Record**
251	**Worsaae J (1846-7)**, as above in note 223, p64

Appendix 6 – Gazetteer of Scandinavian-influenced burials in the north of England

Listed below is a concise catalogue *raisonné* of the Viking burials in the north of England. The reference numbers provided correlate to those listed at the end of appendix 5. Where not stipulated the dimensions of the artefacts are given in centimetres.

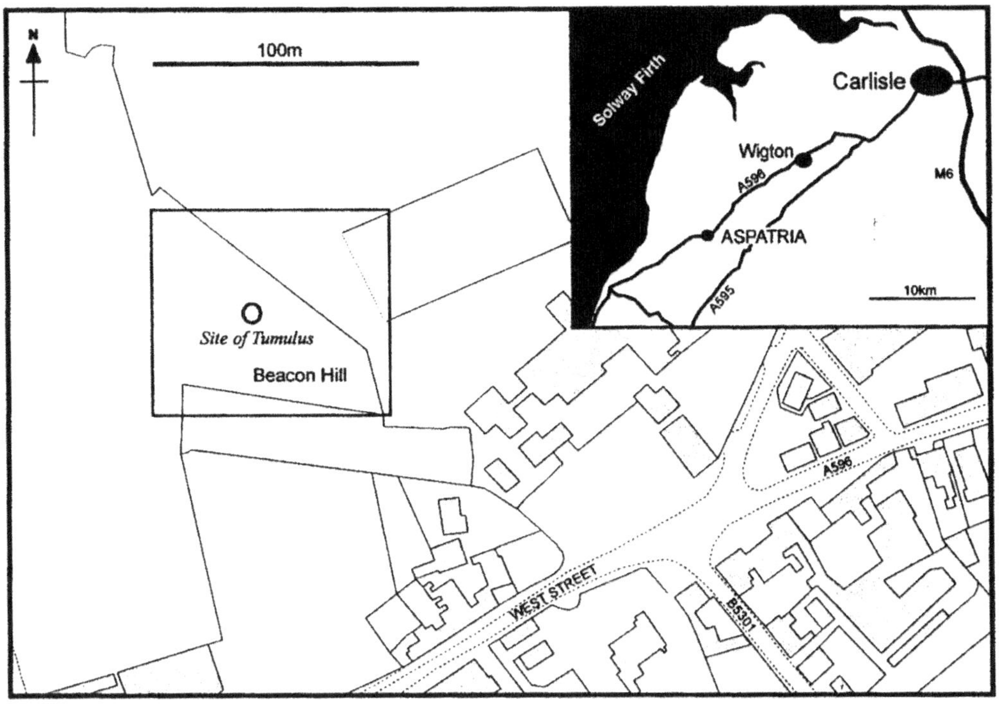

Fig A6.1 *Map to show position of Viking burial at Aspatria, Cumbria (from Abramson 2000: 80)*

Aspatria, Cumbria (NY469455) (figs A6.1-3) (ref. 2)

Secondary inhumation of a male accompanied by Viking-period goods (late 9th early 10th century) in a Bronze Age mound on a hillside promontory above the village. Along with the artefacts two cup and ring marked stones were also recovered (fig. A6.2: 8). The mound was originally opened during the late 18th century, and the area re-excavated in 1997 in advance of the erection of a telecom mast. The line of the Roman road from Maryport to Old Carlisle lies less than a kilometre to the south.

Artefacts, late C18th excavation (lost) - Iron sword (fig. A6.2: 1): lower guard ornamented with silver (Ag) flowers. The length of the sword was said to have been 5 feet, which is unlikely.
Fe Dagger or more probably a spear-head (fig. A6.2:2): its socket studded with silver, L=46.4
Gold (Au) strap-end (fig. A6.2: 3): Carolingian in style, L=5.5, W=2
Au buckle (fig. A6.2: 4): L=2.9, W=3.5, D=3.9
Fe shield fragments
Fe axe head (fig. A6.2: 5): possibly Petersen Type D (LC9^{th} EC10^{th})
Fe spur (fig. A6.2: 6)
Fe bridle-bit (fig. A6.2: 7)
Two cup and ring-marked stones (fig.A6.2: 8)

Artefacts from 1997 (extant) - Copper (Cu)-alloy ring-headed pin (fig A6.3: 1): L=9.9, T= 0.4, Ring D=2.2, T=0.3
Fe buckle, plate & Cu-alloy strap-guide (fig. A6.3: 2): L=2.1, W=4.2/L=2.4, W=3.1/W=3.8
Fe folding-knife (fig. A6.3: 3): L=7.6, W=2.3, T=1.1
Fe spur fragment, tin-plated (fig. A6.3: 4): L=6.9, W=1.1 T=0.7
Fe axe-head fragment, some wood remaining in socket (fig. A6.3: 5): L=5
Fe nails & Fe fragments
Fe cauldron fragments (?): L=6.8, W=6.4
Fragments of left and right human tibiae, possibly female

Extant finds are on display in Beacon Hill School, Aspatria.

Brigham, Cumbria (NY086309) (ref. 25)

10th century ring-headed pin found in vicinity of broken hog-back tombstone during renovations of the church building in the 19th century. L=14.6, D=2.

Artefact in the Tullie House Museum, Carlisle (TH).

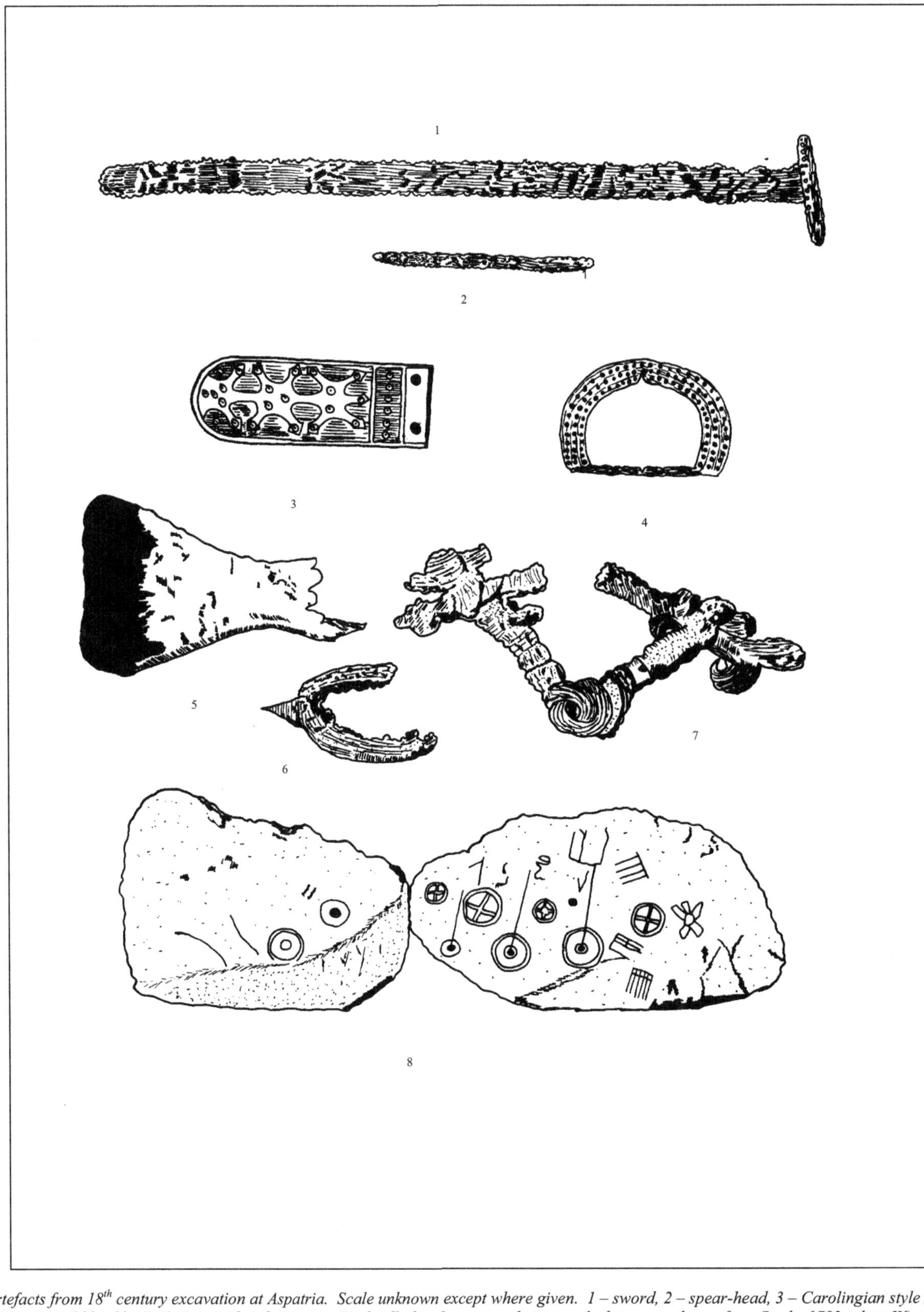

Fig. A6.2 *Artefacts from 18th century excavation at Aspatria. Scale unknown except where given. 1 – sword, 2 – spear-head, 3 – Carolingian style strap-end (1:1), 4 - gold buckle (1:1), 5 – axe-head, 6 – spur, 7 – bridle-bit, 8 – cup-and-ring marked stones redrawn from Rooke 1792: plate IV)*

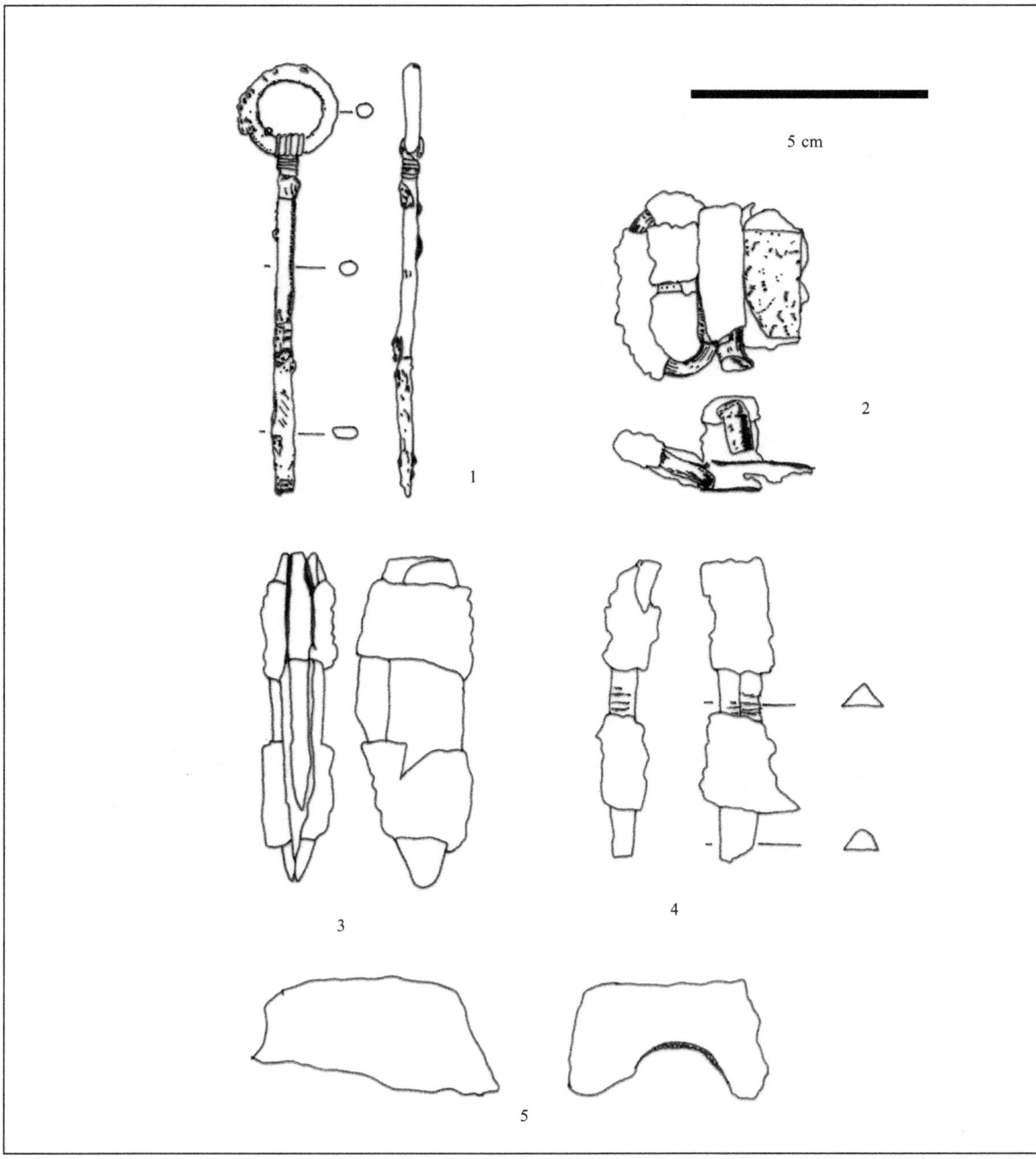

Fig. A6.3 *Extant finds, Aspatria. (1- ring-headed pin, 2 – buckle, 3 – folding-knife, 4 – spur fragment, 5 – axe-head) (redrawn from Abramson 2000: 86)*

Cambois, Northumberland (NZ303843) (fig. A6.4) (ref.45-6)

Three inhumations were removed from a mound beside the River Wansbeck during the mid 19th century. Two were the unaccompanied burials of males. The third, a female, was found in a cist accompanied by a brooch. Also recovered from the mound was a bone comb, comparable to those recovered from Coppergate, York.
Artefacts - Cu-alloy disc brooch (fig. A6.4: 1): the brooch has been cast, & is of a type dating to the 9th century found in Southern England & the Carolingian Empire. The edges are decorated in a scallop fashion; *Champlevé* enamel work surrounds the depiction of a bird carrying a twig in its beak. D=4.4
Bone comb (fig A6.4: 2): badly damaged, decorated with cross-hatching along its length. L=10.5
One female & two male skulls.

Artefacts in the British Museum (BM); the skulls stored at the Natural History Museum (NHM).

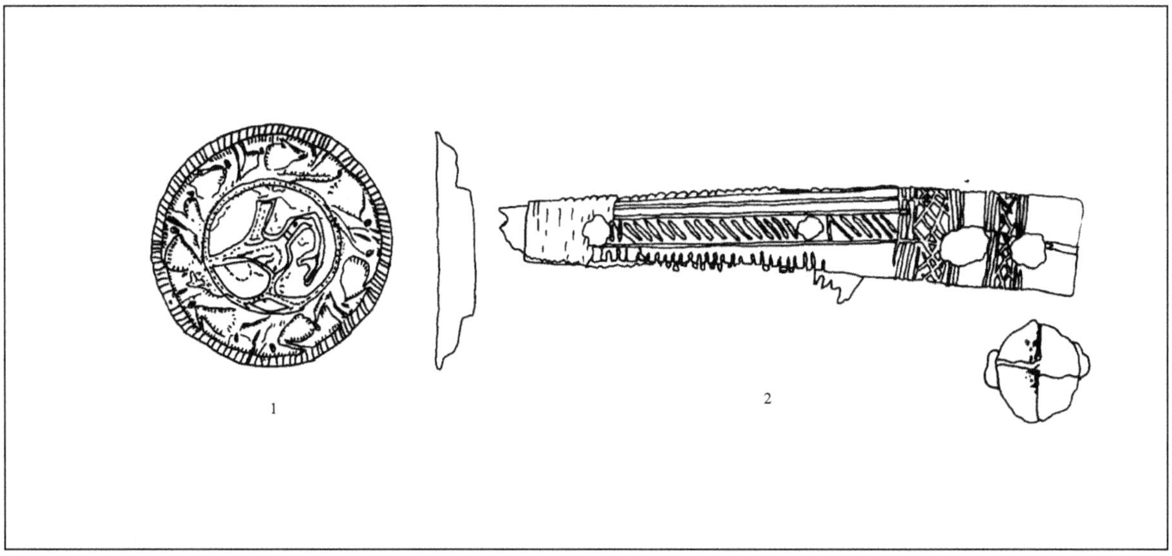

Fig. A6.4 *Disc brooch & comb from Cambois, Northumbria (scale 1:1) (redrawn from Alexander 1987: 102-3)*

Camp Hill, nr Carthorpe, Yorkshire (SE312824) (fig. A6.5) (ref. 38)

Inhumation accompanied by a sword and spear-head, recovered during the early 19th century. An early Christian Anglo-Saxon cemetery was also found within the vicinity at the time.
Artefacts - Fe sword (fig. A6.5: 1): Petersen Type L (*c*900), missing its tip & pommel. L=54.8
Fe spear-head (fig. 6.5: 2): L=30.0

Artefacts are in the BM.

Carlisle Cathedral (NY403555) (ref. 47-50)

Recent excavations within the Cathedral precincts revealed a series of burials dating to the Viking-period accompanied by dress-fittings and small personal goods.
Artefacts (Grave 251) - Cu-alloy strap-end buckle, D-shaped loop, decorate with 5 bosses. Late 9th early 10th century. L=9.08, W=2.27
Cu-alloy fragments of small scale-pan. L=3.46, W=1.72
Cu-alloy ingot, sub-circular section. L=2.28, D=0.39
Slate whetstone with Ag looped suspension mount. Square cross-section. L=15.9, W=1.05, T=0.94
Fe folding knife
Artefacts (Grave 242 or 244) - Cu-alloy pin shank, probably part of a 10th century ring-headed pin. L=6.46, W=0.32
Artefacts (Grave 269) - Cu-alloy buckle & strap-end, decorated with dot & ring marks. L=5.4, W=3.62/L=5.0, W=2.14
Artefacts (misc.) - Au pendant toggle made up of 4 wire-work spheres. L=3.37, D=1.31

Artefacts in Carlisle Cathedral treasury.

Claughton Hall, nr. Garstang, Lancashire (SD513425) (fig. A6.6) (ref. 3)

Secondary use of a Bronze Age burial mound. Viking-period (early 10th century) cremation of possibly male & female, along with artefacts discovered early 19th century.
Artefacts - Pair Cu-alloy gilt tortoise brooches (fig. A6.6), type Rygh 652 (10th century). L=9.7
Carolingian Ag-gilt & nielloed ornamental mount, converted into a brooch with the addition of a hinged pin: L=4.8, W= 2.4
2 beads, one blue glass, one red paste
Artefacts lost - Bronze Age stone axe-hammer, cinerary urn & bones, Fe axe, sword (possibly Petersen Type L), Fe spear-head, human molar tooth, wooden structure

Extant finds in private hands, owned by the Fitzherbert Brockholes family of Claughton Hall.

Crossmoor, nr Inskip, Lancashire (SD440380) (fig. A6.7) (ref. 4).

Viking-period cremation (*c*900) discovered during quarry work in the late 19th century. Five miles from Claughton, above.
Artefacts - Fe sword (fig. A6.7): blade broken approximately half-way down and remainder missing. Petersen Type L (*c*900)
Artefacts lost - Fe dagger or more likely a spear-head
Pottery urn bearing scorch marks

Sword in Blackburn Museum.

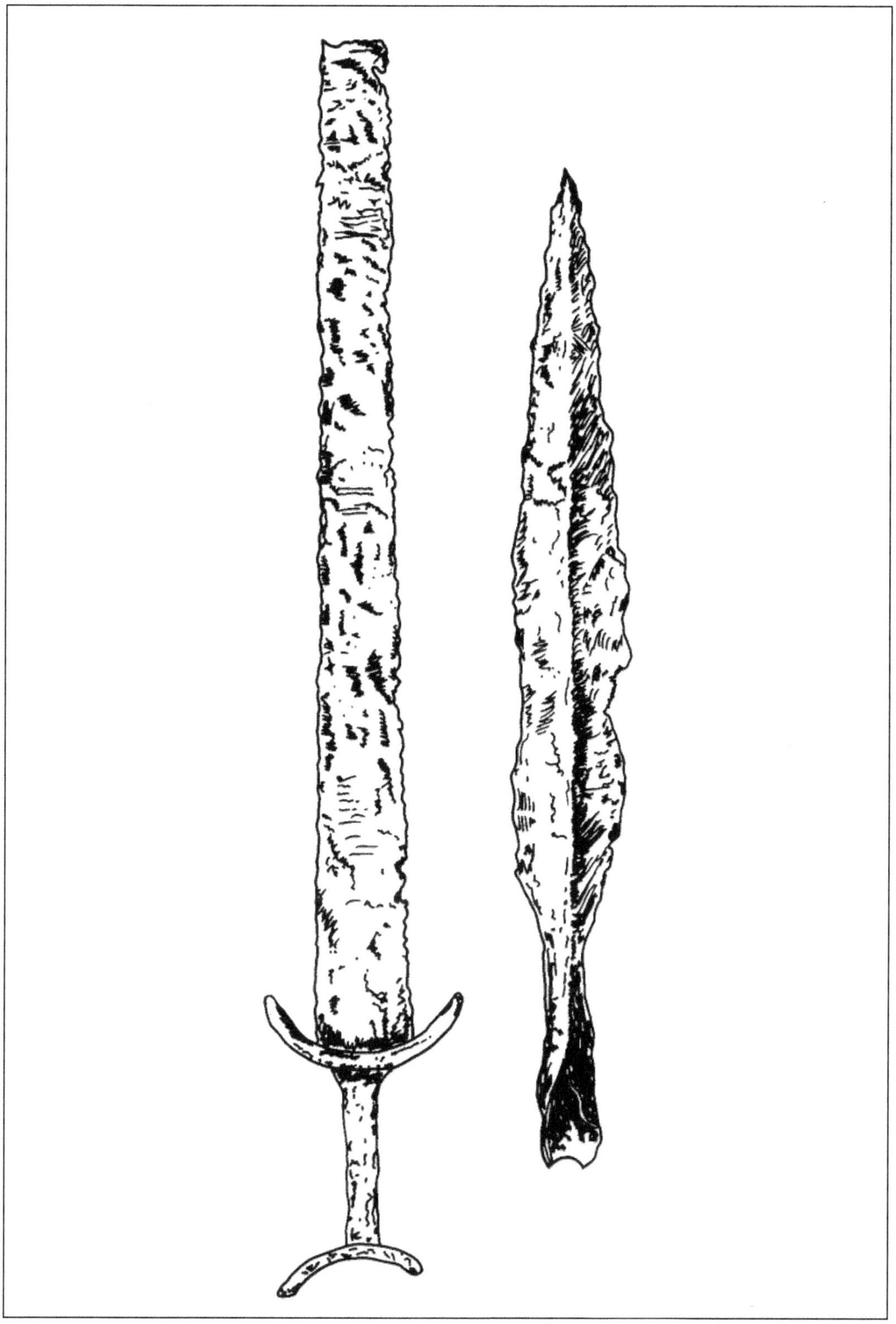

Fig. A6.5 *Sword (third actual size) & spear-head (half-size) from Camp Hill, Yorks (redrawn from Lukis 1870: plate opposite p176)*

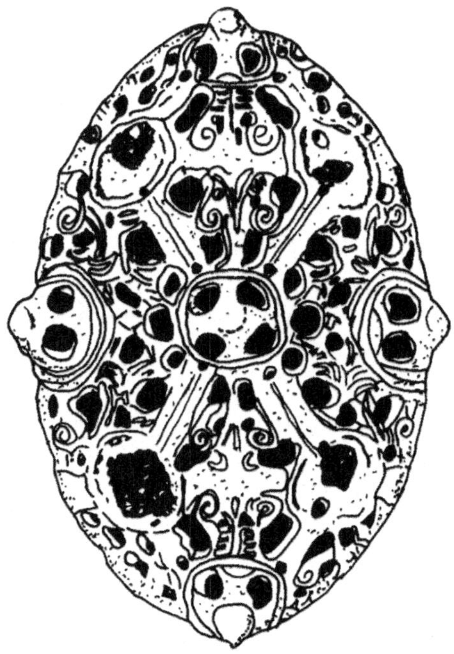

Fig. A6.6 *Tortoise brooch from Claughton, Lancs (seventh-eighths size) (redrawn form Edwards 1998: 16)*

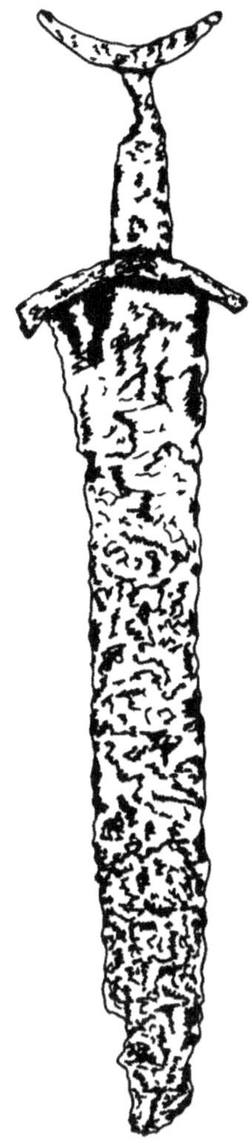

Fig. A6.7 *Sword from Crossmoor, Inskip, Lancs (half-size) (redrawn from Edwards 1998: 20)*

Heathwood, Ingleby, Derbyshire (SK342259) (fig. A6.8-9) (ref. 7-23)

Cremation cemetery utilised during Viking-period, probably linked to winter camp of the Great Army at nearby Repton (873-4). The cemetery is made up of 59 mounds and lies on rising ground above the River Trent. At least five mounds are known to have been excavated during the 19th century, but were unrecorded.

Artefacts – mound 1 - Fe sword (fig. A6.9): only parts of lower & upper guards pommel knob and hilt fragment remain. All show evidence of fire damage. Petersen Type L (*c*900). L=40.6
Cu-alloy suspensory loop: L=4.1, W=4.6
Fe buckle, tongue missing, circular in section: L=6.35, W=3.8
Fe strap-slider: W=1.9
Cremated bone of sheep & dog: unburnt ox skull fragment & 7 teeth.
Cu-alloy fragments.
Artefacts – mound 2 - Natural feature.
Artefacts – mound 3 - Fe buckle, plate & tongue. L=4.8, W=2.2
2 Fe collared nails with spherical heads. L=3.81, collar W=1.3-1.9
Cu-alloy fragments, tubular in shape, possibly a vessel rim. L=1.27, W=1, rod, L=3.2
Artefacts – mound 4 - Sandstone structure within mound, but devoid of hearth & artefacts.
Artefacts – mound 5 - 2 Fe nails: L=3.8/L=7.6, W=1.27, disc-head D=4.5 cremated animal bone of ox or horse.
Artefacts – mound 6 - Uncremated animal bone, ox, pig & a sheep's tooth.
2 Fe buckles, complete with tongues, one with strap-slider. Both L=5.7, W=3.8
6 Fe nails with disc heads: L=2.54
Cu-alloy strap-end: L=3.8, W=1.3
Cu-alloy fibula-type brooch, very damaged: L=2.5
3 Cu-alloy fragments, one a thin rod
Artefacts – mound 7 - Fe sword: only lower part of the blade & lower guard extant: L=26, W=5.1/L=12.7, W=1.8. Petersen Type H (800-950).
*c*24 Fe rivets, some clenched
Fe fragments, all very damaged; one possibly a buckle tongue
Artefacts – mound 8 - Mound disturbed, but unrecorded. Possibly opened by Bateman in the 19th century.

Artefacts – mound 9 - Sandstone structure within mound, but devoid of hearth & artefacts.
Artefacts – mound 10 - Sandstone structure within mound, but devoid of hearth & artefacts.
Artefacts – mound 11 - Cremated animal bone: dog, sheep/goat & horse.
Unburnt Fe spade.
Ag-wired headband: L=3, W=*c*0.8
Artefacts – mound 12 - Sandstone structure within mound, but devoid of hearth & artefacts.
Artefacts – mound 13 - Sandstone structure within mound, but devoid of hearth & artefacts.
Artefacts – mound 14 - Natural feature
Artefacts – mound 15 - Sandstone structure within mound, but devoid of hearth & artefacts.

Artefacts – mound 50 (female & juvenile) - Unburnt jaw of a cow
Ag sword mount decorated in Trewhiddle style: L=2.6, W=0.8
Fe shield fragments
Fe knife
2 Cu-alloy tacks
Fe hinge pivot from a chest
Selection of Fe nails in 3 different sizes
Cremated bone of horse, dog, sheep/goat, cattle & side of pork
Artefacts – mound 56 - Cu-alloy ring-headed pin: L=10, D=2
Fragments of pig bone

Artefacts in Derby Museum.

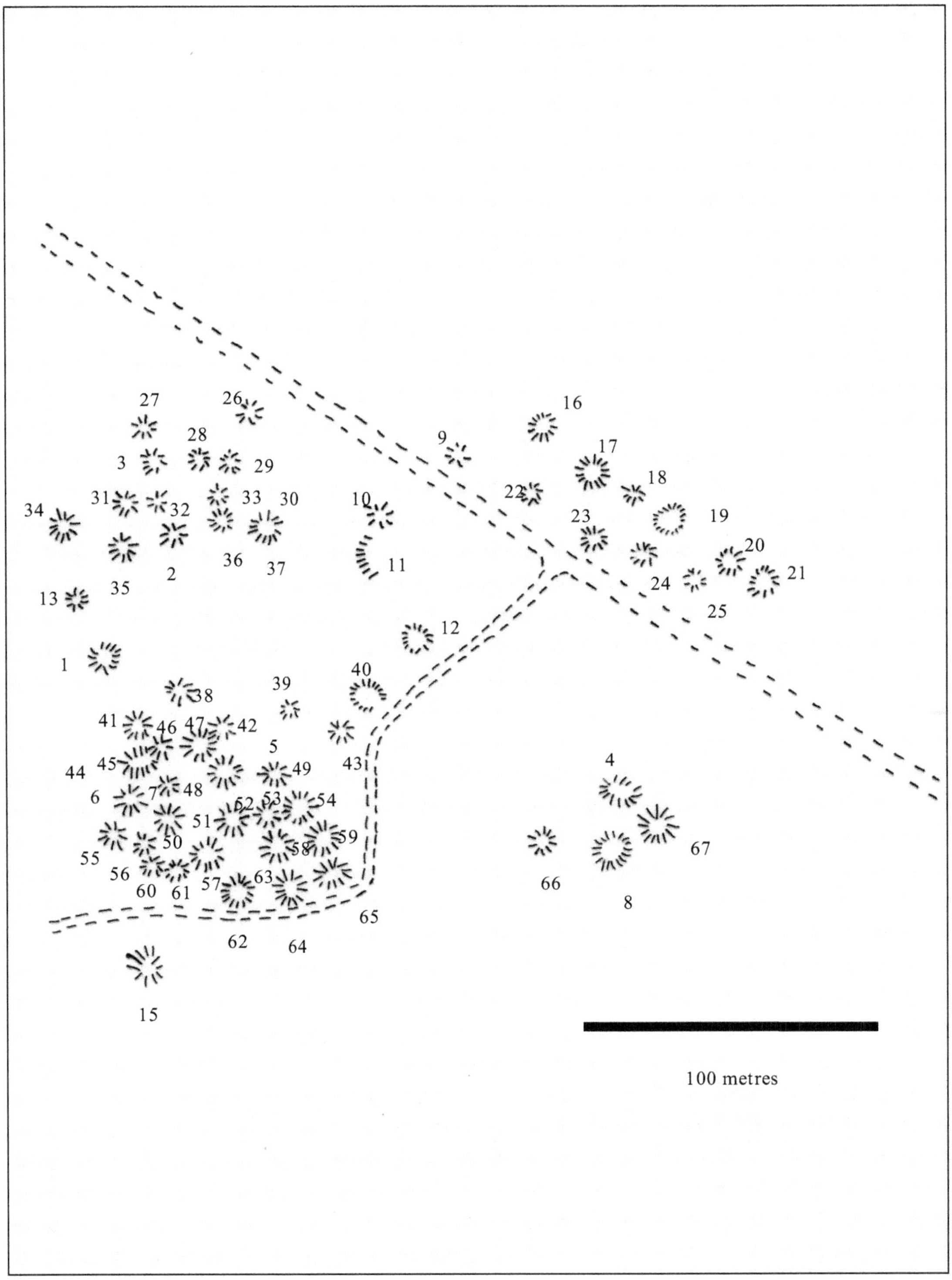

Fig. A6.8 *Sketch map of burial mounds at Heathwood, Ingleby, Derbys (mound 14 proved to be natural, & is therefore unmarked) (after Richards et al 1995: 57)*

Fig. A6.9 *Sword (fifth size) from mound 1, Heathwood, Ingleby, Derbys (redrawn from Clarke & Fraser 1946: 15)*

Hesket-in-the-Forest, Cumbria (NY469455) (figs. A6.10-A6.13) (ref. 1)

A large mound was removed during the early 19th century during road improvements along the line of the Roman road between Penrith & Carlisle (fig. A5.10). In it was found a cremation hearth and a collection of Viking-period artefacts, datable to the mid 10th century. Early nineteenth century accounts also record the presence of further, possibly Bronze Age, tumuli in the vicinity.
Artefacts - Fe sword (fig. A6.12), blade broken & point missing, but otherwise in remarkably good condition. Clear evidence of ritual damaged, the blade bent back round against itself. Lower guard decorated with Ag plate engraved with ring-chain pattern. Possibly repeated on the upper-guard, but hard to tell as fire-damaged; pommel knob missing. Petersen Type O (900-50): L=92.1
Fe spear-head: tip missing, 7 rivet holes in socket with remains of several Cu-alloy rivets. Petersen Type I: L= 44.8
Fe spear-head: bent in the middle, socket decorated with 6 closely spaced rings, each pierced by a pair of rivet holes. A single Cu-alloy rivet remains. Petersen Type F: L=27.9
Fe axe-head (fig. A6.11): Petersen Type E: L=18.4
Fe bridle-bit, pieces of melted Cu-alloy still adhering in places: L=24.1
Fe rectangular buckle: lacking tongue, W=5.1
Fe circular buckle, lacking tongue, plate intact, L=5.7
Fe sickle, L=21
Whetstone, square section, L=11.4
3 decorated bone combs and cases (fig. A6.13): fragmentary, largest piece L=18.1, the back & case decorated with bands of angular interlacing; the spandrels and ends are filled with cross-hatching.
Fe shield boss of Irish Sea conical type (850-900): broken in two pieces; D=14
Artefacts lost - Pair Fe spurs

Artefacts in TH.

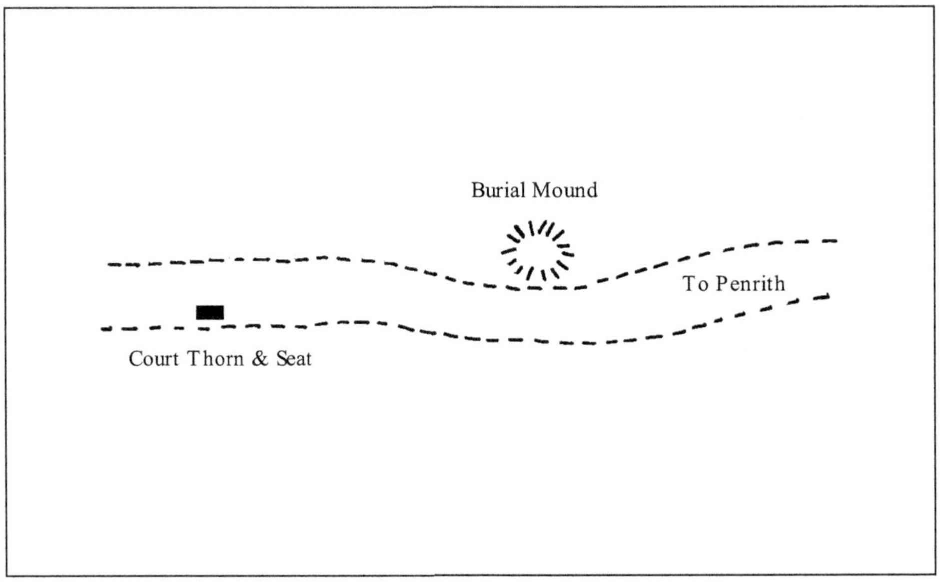

Fig. A6.10 *Sketch map showing position of the cremation at Hesket-in-the-Forest, Cumbria (redrawn from Hodgson 1832: plate opposite p107, no. 5)*

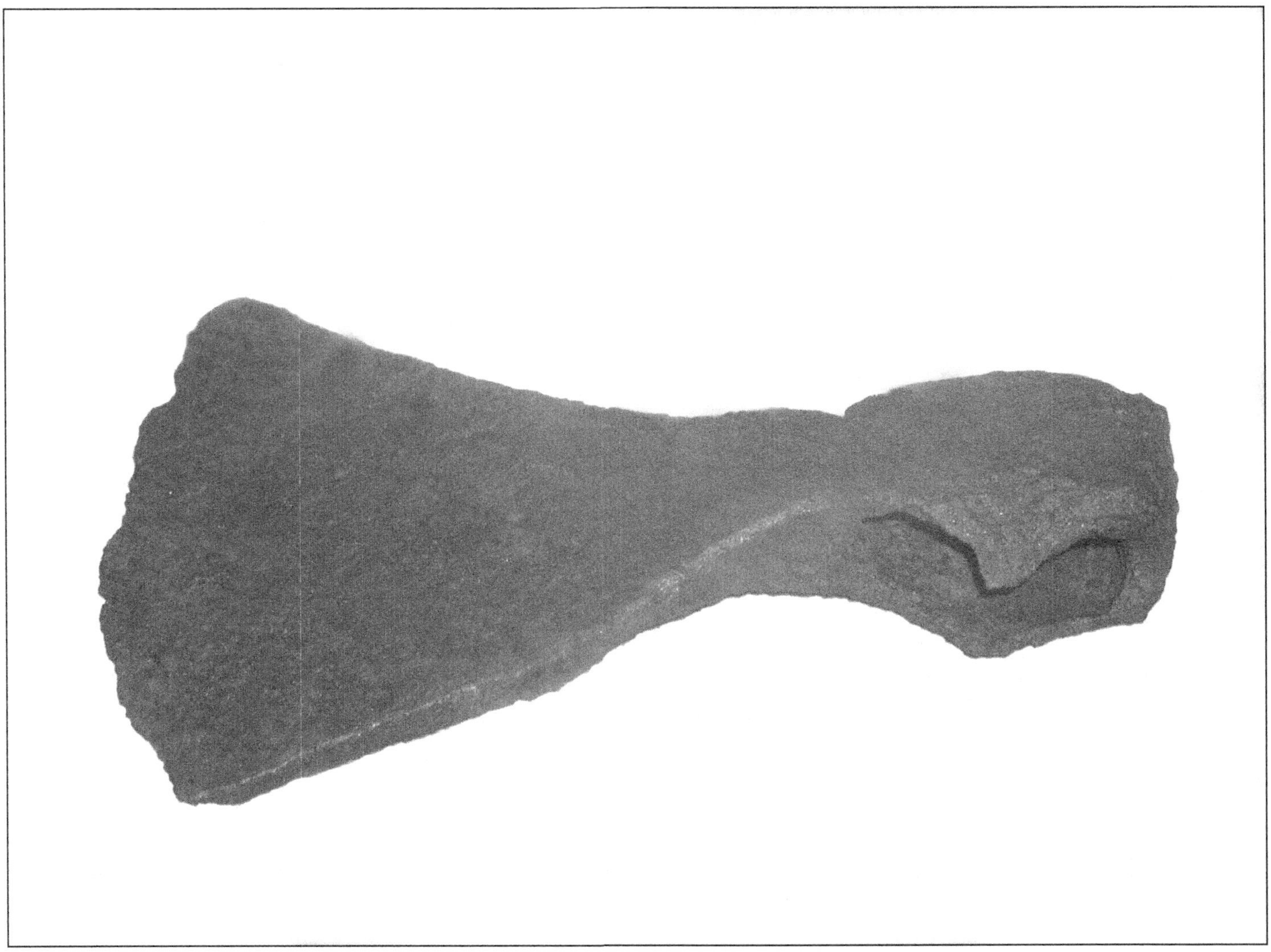

Fig. A6.11 *Axe-head, from Hesket-in-the-Forest, Cumbria (Tullie House Museum & Art Gallery, Carlisle)*

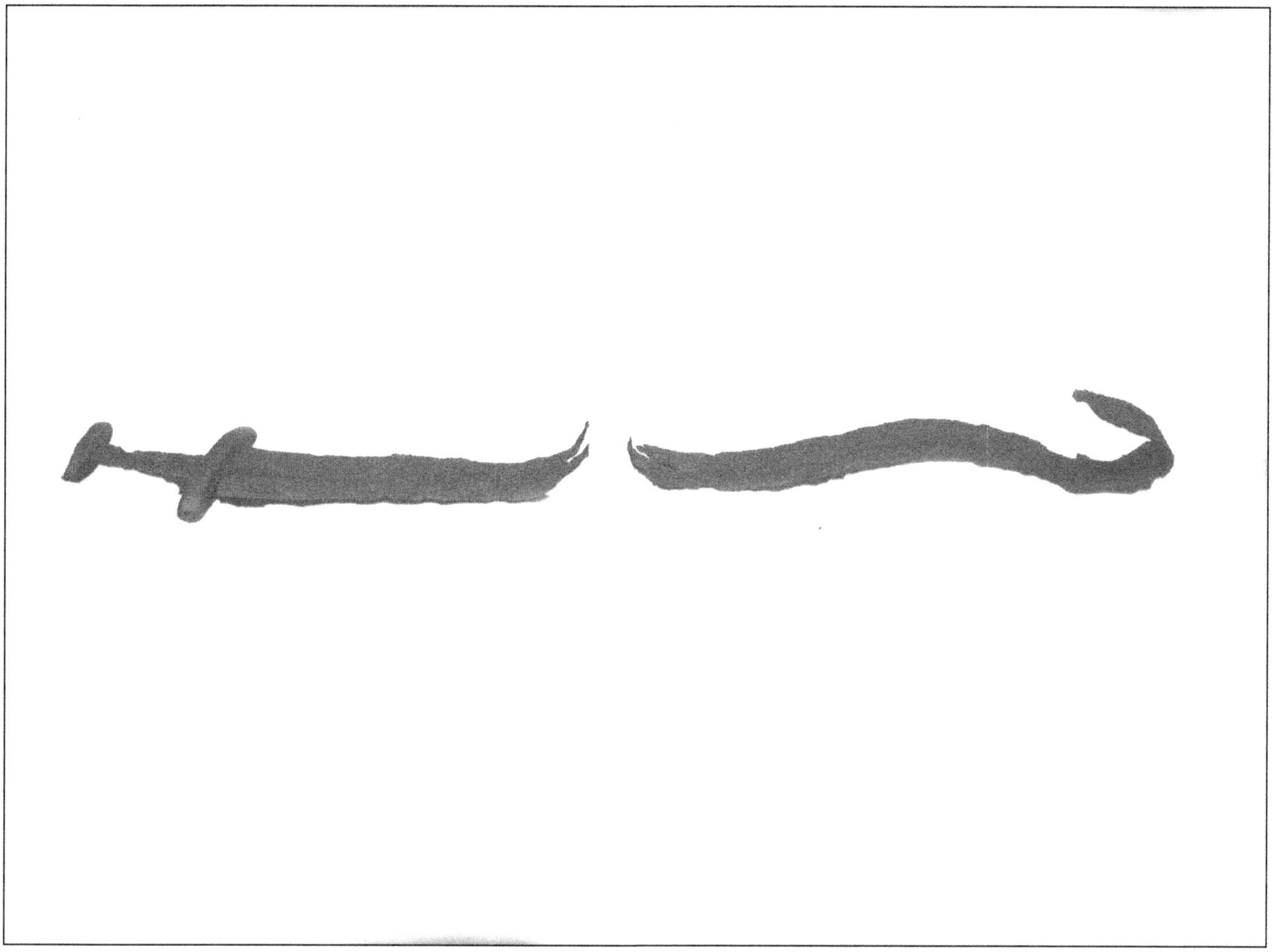

Fig. A6.12 *Sword from Hesket-in-the-Forest, Cumbria (Tullie House Museum & Art Gallery, Carlisle)*

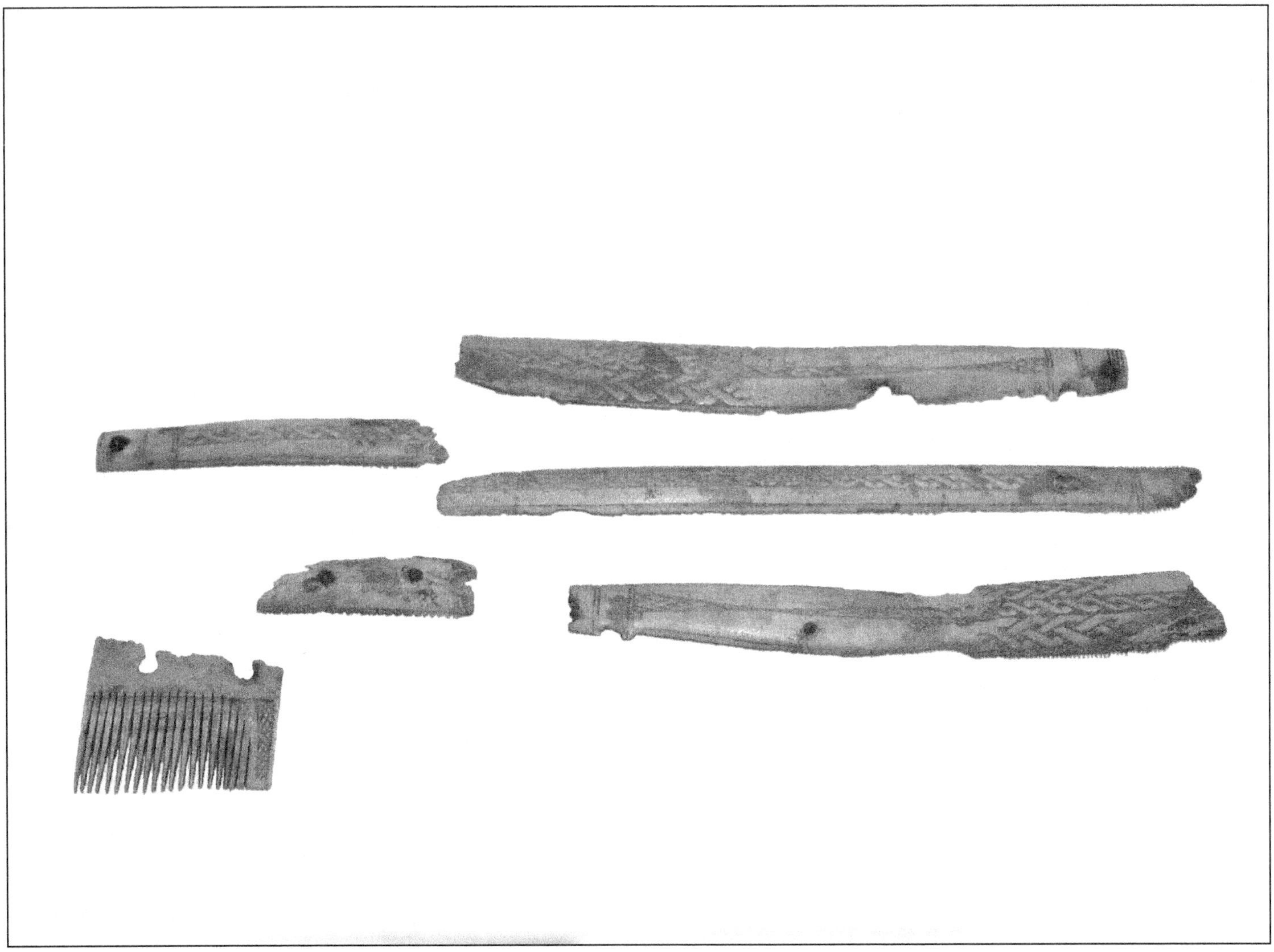

Fig. A6.13 *Combs and cases, from Hesket-in-the-Forest, Cumbria (Tullie House Museum & Art Gallery, Carlisle)*

Heysham, Lancashire (SD412604) (fig. A6.14) (ref. 30 & 53)

In St Peter's Churchyard and inhumation accompanied by a spear-head was found beneath a hogback during the early 19th century. The spear-head was subsequently lost, but the hogback is preserved inside the church. During excavations during the 1970's in the ruins of the adjacent St Patrick's chapel, a 10th century female inhumation (grave 63) was found to contain a poor quality cow-bone comb, of a type common across the north of England and the Scottish Isle of the period. The grave was charcoal lined in accordance with ecclesiastical land demarcation practices of the time (see also York Minster, below).
Comb (fig. A6.14): L=16.5, W=3.1

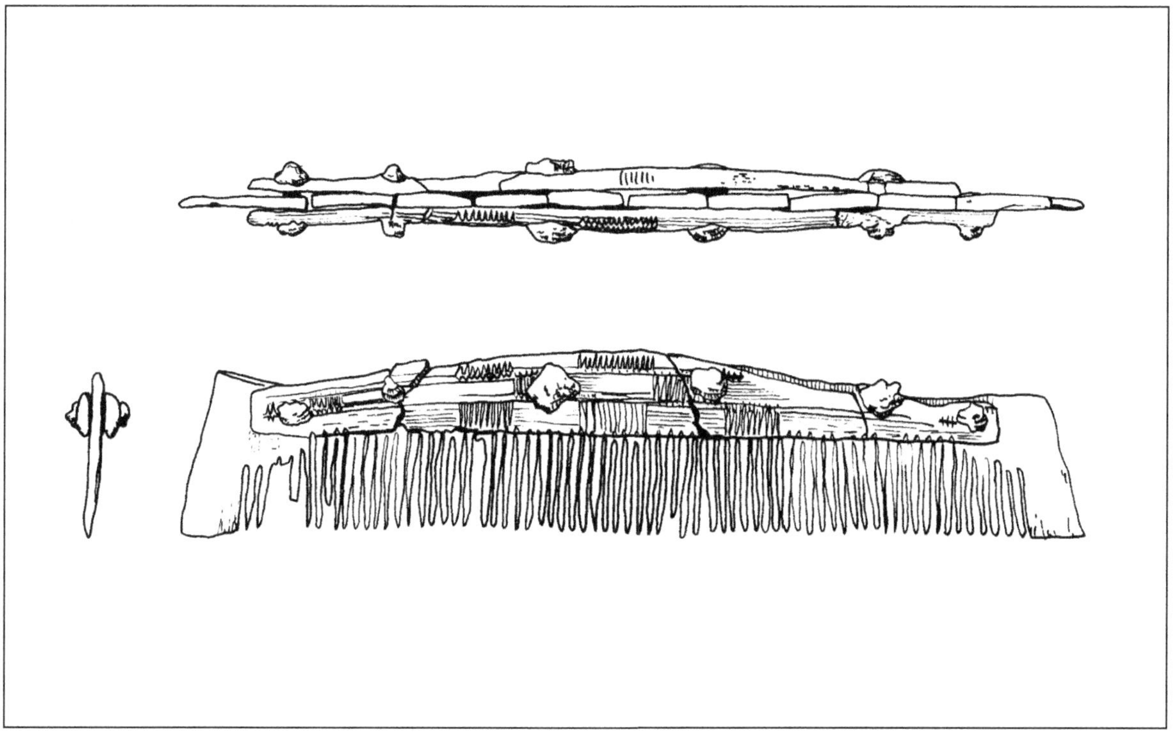

Fig. A6.14 *Comb (1:1) from Heysham, Lancs (redrawn from Potter & Andrews 1994: 123)*

Kildale, Yorkshire (NZ600100) (fig. A6.15) (ref. 33-7)

During the mid 19th century a series of 10th century accompanied inhumation burials were recovered from within Kildale parish church. They numbered between 8 & 9, much of the detail being overlooked, a difficulty compounded by the subsequent theft of the artefacts from the church a short while after. Some details of the artefacts were obtainable from contemporary drawings & accounts.

Artefacts – 1st inhumation - Fe sword
Fe flat-backed knife with Ag-wire bound hilt (fig. A5.15:5): L=14
Cu-alloy tweezers
Cu-alloy scales (fig. A6.15: 1), beam L=6.4, & pans
Pb weight
Cu-alloy plate, possibly a scabbard mount
Wooden box with sliding lid, containing another Pb weight

Artefacts – 2nd inhumation - Fe sword
Fe spear-heads

Artefacts – 3rd inhumation - Fe sword, possibly Petersen Type X (10th century) (figA6.15: 3): L=83.8
Cu-alloy buckle (fig. A6.15: 7): oval in shape: L=2.6, W=1.7
Cu-alloy buckle & plate (fig. A6.15: 8): scalloped decoration, L=2.9, W=2.5/L=2.7, W=2
Further unspecified belt fittings

Artefacts, miscellaneous - Fe axe-head (fig. A6.15: 6): L=19, possibly Petersen Type E
Whetstone (fig. A6.15: 2): L=10.2
Fe spear-head
Fe knife, small domestic type
Fragments of shield boss & rivets

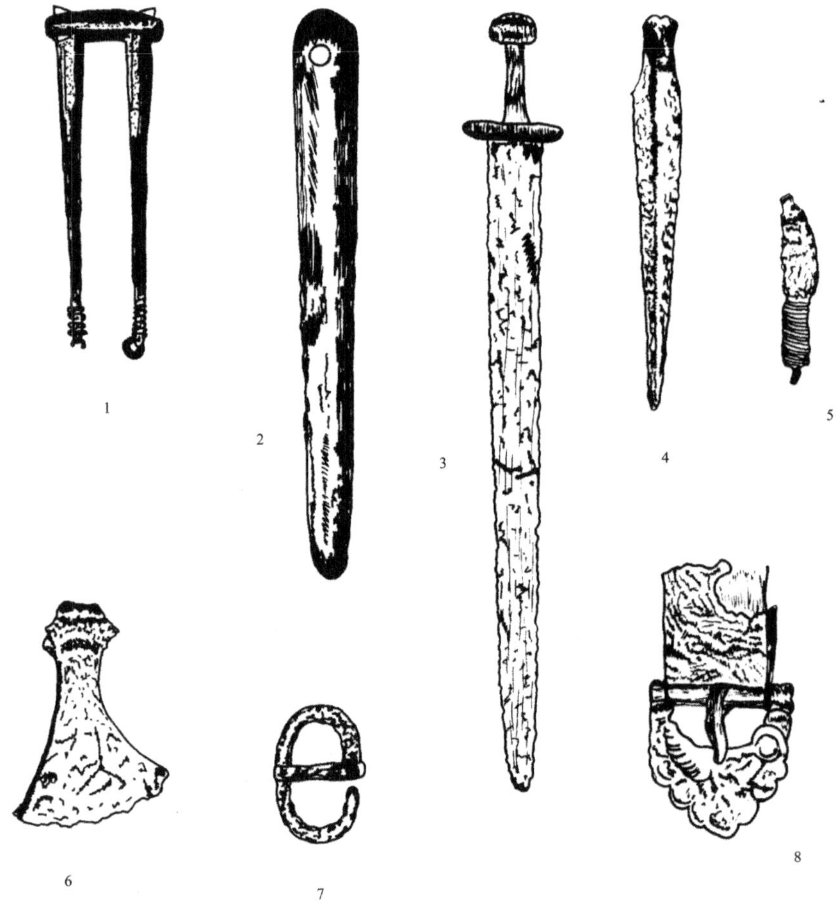

Fig. A6.15 *Sketch of Artefacts from Kildale. 1 - scales (1:1), 2 – whetstone (1:1), 3 - sword, 4 - spear-head, 5 – knife, 6 – axe-head, 7 – oval buckle (1:1), 8 – scalloped buckle (1:1) (redrawn from Elgee 1930: 221 & Atkinson 1874 (1988): 84-5)*

Leeming Lane, nr Bedale, Yorkshire (*c*SE280893) (fig. A6.16) (ref. 5)

A female inhumation was uncovered while workmen undertook repair of the road which follows the line of the Roman road between Catterick & Piercebridge in the early 19th century. The remains were found to be accompanied by a pair of tortoise brooches and a spear-head.

Artefacts - Cu-alloy tortoise brooches type Rygh 652 (900-50) (fig. A6.16): L=8, W=5
Artefacts lost - Spear-head & a brooch

A single brooch is held by the Nat. Mus. of Scot. Edinburgh, & is currently on display in the Yorkshire Museum, York (YM). The second brooch is lost.

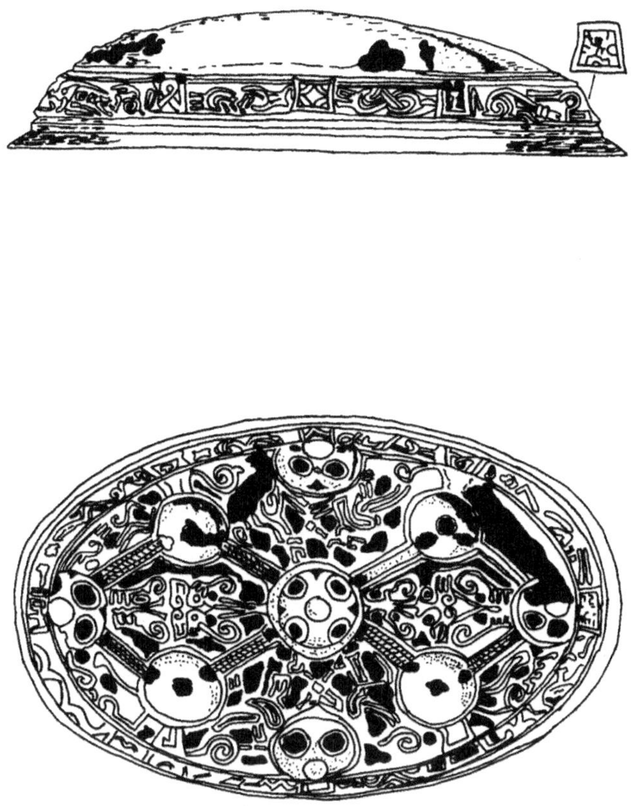

Fig. A6.16 *Tortoise brooch from Leeming Lane, nr Bedale (scale 1:1) (redrawn from Anon 1848: fig. opposite p220)*

Ormside, Westmorland (NY702177) (figs. A6.17-18) (ref. 27)

Accompanied inhumation found in 19th century while grave-digging in the churchyard. The Ormside bowl was also discovered here. The church appears to have been built upon a prehistoric mound.
Artefacts - Fe sword (fig. A6.18): despite being in 2 pieces it is virtually compete. Petersen Type M (850-900). L=91.4
Fe shield boss (fig. A6.17), Irish Sea conical type (850-900). D= 11.4, H= 9.5, flange W=3.2, rim L=30.5, D=1.6: 4 nails also remain, spaced at 6.4cm intervals.
Artefacts lost - Fe flat-backed knife: L=11.8, blade L=5.7

Artefacts in TH. Ormside Bowl in YM.

Fig. A6.17 *Shield boss, from Ormside, Westmorland (Tullie House Museum & Art Gallery, Carlisle)*

Plate A6.18 *Sword from Ormside, Westmorland (Tullie House Museum & Art Gallery, Carlisle)*

Penrith, Cumbria (NY513305) (ref. 24)

17th century account of the discovery of an inhumation accompanied by a sword beneath a hogback in the parish churchyard. The sword has been lost, but the hogback forms part of the Giant's Grave in the churchyard.

Pippin Castle, Scargill, nr Harrogate, Yorkshire (SE221544) (ref. 31 & appendix 8)

A series of mounds & earthworks were destroyed at the turn of the 20th century by reservoir building. The finds recovered date from the prehistoric to early medieval period (see appendix 6 for complete inventory and analysis of artefacts).
Artefacts - Crude hogback (fig. A8.4), with runic inscription *SUNA*: L=56, H=33, W=17.6
3 jars of soil (fig. A8.1) marked, 'from Viking Cremation': analysis found no burnt bone
Whetstone fragment (fig. A8.2): L=6.1, W=4.0
Human tibia, possibly female: L=35 W(proximal)=6.6, W(distal)=40, mid W=6.6
Whalebone (fig. A8.6), possibly rib, no evidence of working: L=17.5
Steel axe-head (figs. A8.7-8) possibly Petersen Type E (late 9th-early 10th century): L=19.1, D along haft=19.5
9 corroding Fe fragments (figs. A8.9-11), possibly from a saw

Artefacts held by Harrogate Museums & Art Galleries.

Rampside, Lancashire (SD239674) (fig. A6.19) (ref. 28-9)

Churchyard site of 2 separately recovered accompanied inhumations during the 19th century. The first burial was accompanied by a single-edged sword of Petersen Type M (850-900). The second inhumation, also accompanied by a sword (now lost) was covered by a grave-slab. As with Ormside (We) above, the church seems to have been situated on a prehistoric mound; 19th century records attesting to numerous suggestive finds.
Artefacts – 1st burial - Fe sword (fig. A6.19): single edged, Petersen Type M (850-900). The upper quarter of the blade is missing, and grip bent with pommel towards lower guard. L=56.8
Artefacts lost – 2nd burial - Grave-slab
Fe sword, very damaged, the hilt & some of the blade surviving to a L=30.5

Extant sword in Barrow Museum.

Fig. A6.19 *Sword from Rampside, Lancs (quarter size) (redrawn from photograph, Gaythorpe 1910: plate opposite p301)*

Red House Park, Adwick-le-Street, nr Doncaster, Yorkshire (SE529093) (figs. A6.20-21) (ref. 6)

The inhumation of a female accompanied by late 9th century Viking-period artefacts was undertaken in 2001 by NAA, prior to the laying of utility services. The burial was found in a ditch beside a Romano-British track-way.

Artefacts - 2 tortoise brooches, an unmatched pair, but of same type Rygh 647 (Petersen P37:12 & P37:3) (fig. A6.20). L=9, W=6
Cu-alloy bowl (fig. A6.21): D=*c*20, depth=0.5
Fe flat-backed knife: L=6.5, W=1.5
Fe latch-lifter: L=8.2

Artefacts in Doncaster Museum.

Fig. A6.20 *Tortoise brooches from Red House Park, Adwick-le-Street, Yorks (Photograph by Bill Marsden Photography, reproduced with kind permission of Northern Archaeological Associates)*

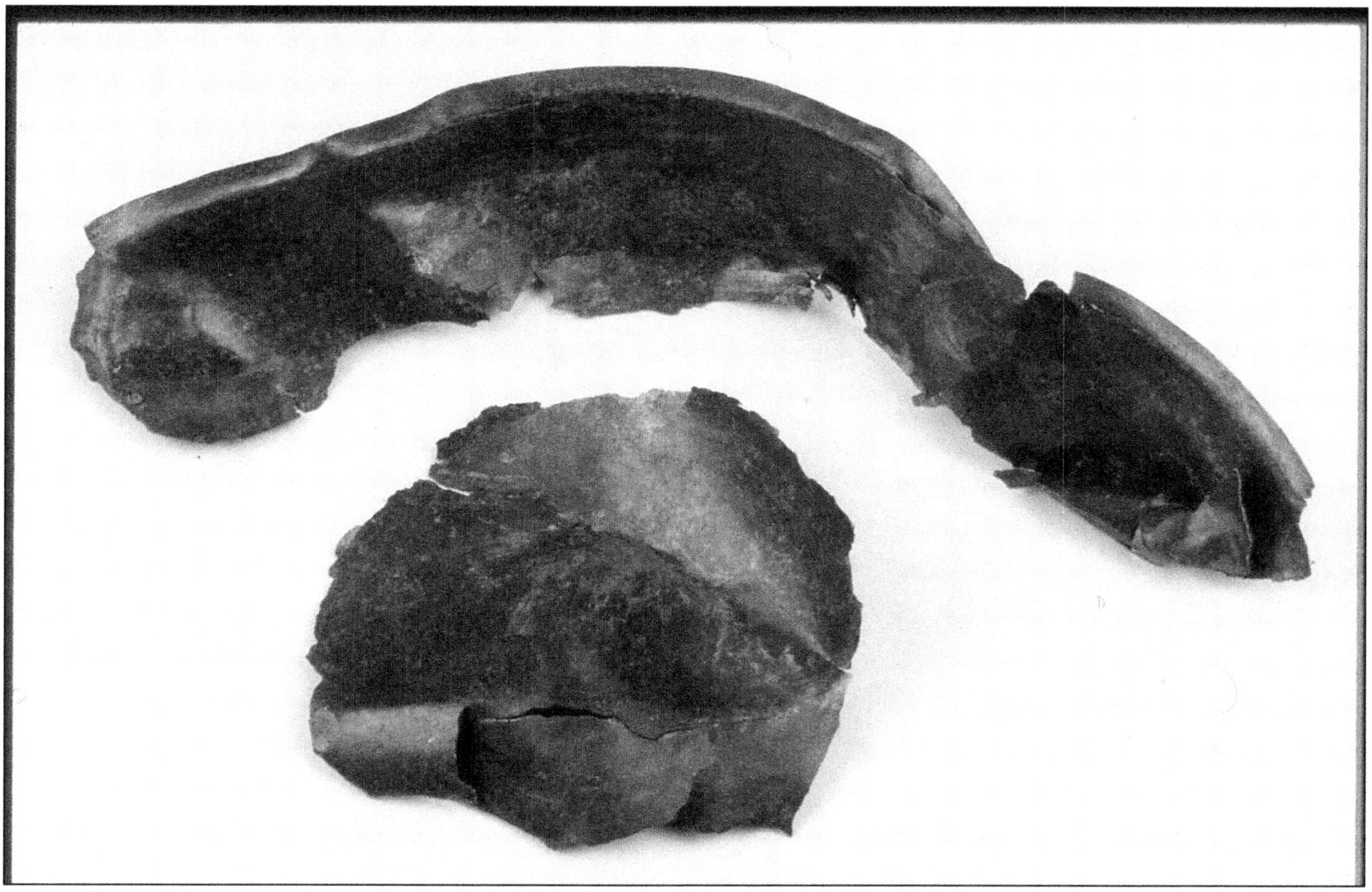

Fig. A6.21 *Copper-alloy bowl from Red House Park, Adwick-le-Street, Yorks*
(Photograph by Bill Marsden Photography, reproduced with kind permission of Northern Archaeological Associates)

Repton, Derbyshire (SK303272) (fig. A6.22) (ref. 39-43, 80-1)

The ecclesiastical site beside the River Trent, fortified by the Great Army in the winter of 873-4, has produced many Viking-period artefacts, not least those recovered from modern excavations. These have yet to be fully published.
Artefacts, miscellaneous - Fe axe-head, Petersen Type E (850-900): L=22.8, W=16.8, external haft width=4
Fe sword, badly corroded, upper part only extant. Petersen Type L (*c*900): L=40.8
Copy of a sword found (& now lost) in Repton vicinity. Petersen Type X (10th century). Copy replicates virtually complete sword, with tip folded over. L=88.2
Artefacts (Grave 511) male inhumation - Necklace group – Ag-alloy Thor's hammer (fig. A6 22:2). Suspension loop broken. L=16.5, W=1.5. White glass bead (fig. A6.22: 1), square cross-section, D=2, D of hole=0.7. blue glass bead (fig. 22: 3), 3 circular insets, circular cross-section: D=2.5, D of hole=0.8
Cu-alloy & Ag fastener (fig. A6 22: 5), pierced at wide end. L=2.5, W=0.5, T=0.1
Cu-alloy belt buckle with Fe rivets, plate & loop decorated with dot & ring marks (fig. A6.22: 6). L=4.1, W=3.2/plate W=1.9
Cu-alloy buckle & plate from scabbard suspensory strap (fig. A6.22: 7). L=4.5, loop W=2.6, plate W=1.8
Fe sword (fig. A6.22: 4): Petersen Type M (850-900). L=89.7. Oak scabbard bound with leather and lined in sheepskin
Fe key (fig A6.22: 8), badly corroded, simply design with single ward cut. L=7.8, bit W=1.8, stem W=1.5
Fe folding knife, badly corroded. L=10.8, W=2.8, T=2
Fe flat-backed knife, badly corroded. L=16.5,blade W=2
Jackdaw humerus: L=4.6
Wild boar tusk. L=8.5
Artefacts (Grave 295) male inhumation - Fe knife
Artefacts (Grave 529) male inhumation - Au finger-ring, loop fastening, trapezoid centre, decorated with dot marks. D=2
5 Anglo-Saxon pennies of 870's
Artefacts (Grave 83) male inhumation - Cu-alloy finger-ring
Artefacts (Grave 203) female inhumation - Fe knife with handle bound with Ag wire (see Kildale, above)
Fe strike-a-light
Artefacts, uncatalogued - Viking-period spear-head, seaxes, knives, chisel, padlock-key, Fe fragments, Ag band with garnets, gilded Cu-alloy tacks, Anglo-Saxon pennies *c*872-4, hogback (lost)

Artefacts in Derby Museum. Human remains in NHM.

Ripon, Yorkshire (SE310710) (ref. 51-2)

Recent excavations in the vicinity of Ripon Cathedral have resulted in the recovery of several artefacts of Viking-period date.
Artefacts from Ladykirke & St Marygate - Antler comb, decorated with horizontal striation: L=15.5
Antler comb, decorated with lozenges: L=9.3
Antler comb: L=9
Antler comb fragment, decorated by long striations: L=4.2
Antler comb-case, decorated with intersecting cuts; L=11.2
Antler comb-case, decorated with incised lines; L=124.4
Artefacts from Ailcy Hill (Grave group 1064) - Fe flat-backed knife: L=15, W=1.6
Cu-alloy D-ringed double tongued buckle: L=4.2, W=1.6

Artefacts held by Harrogate Museums & Art Galleries: selected items on display within Ripon Cathedral.

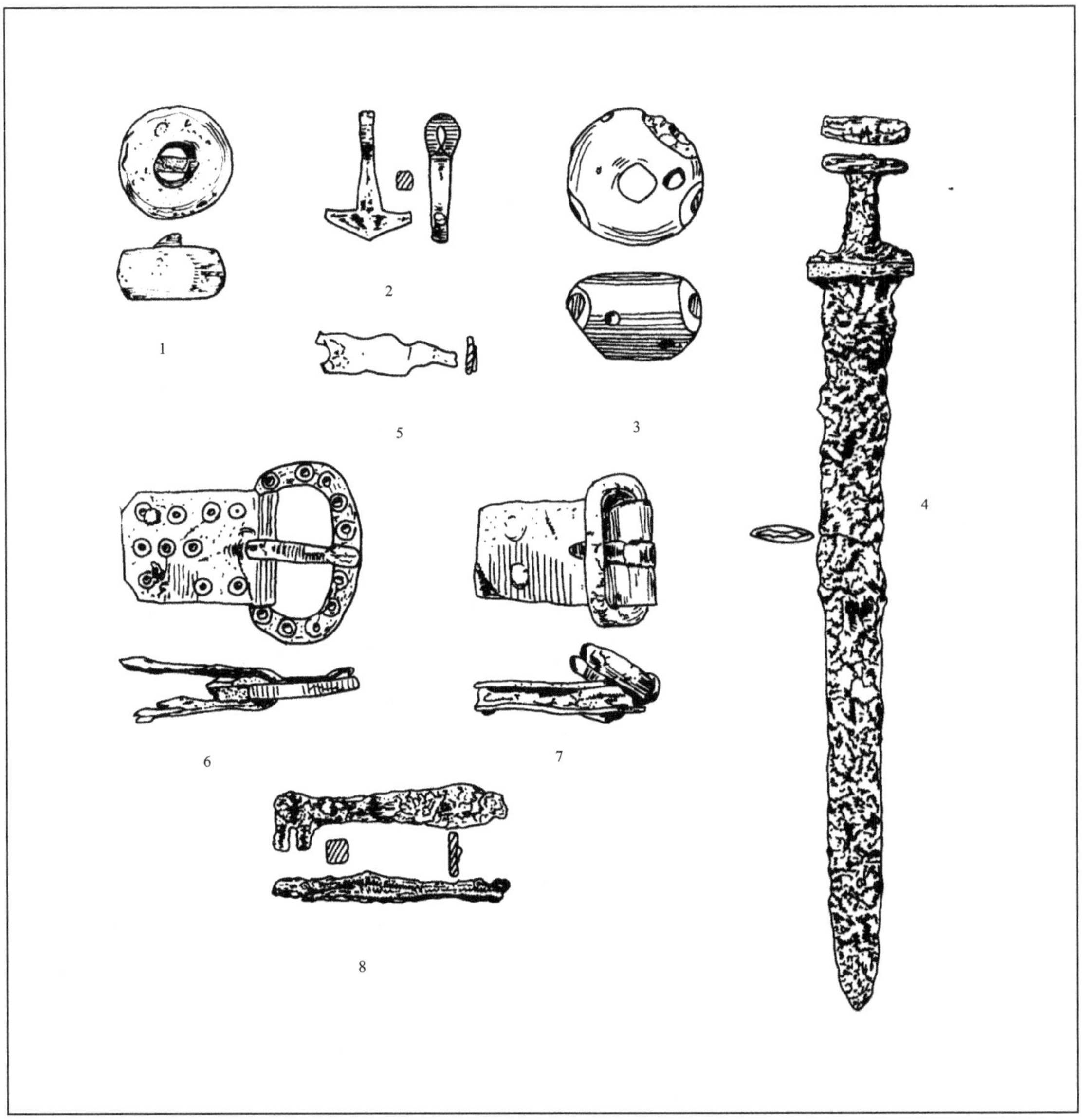

Fig. A6.22 *Artefacts from Grave 511, Repton, Derbys. 1 – white glass bead (1:1), 2 – Thor's hammer pendant (1:1), 3 - blue glass bead (1:1), 4 – sword (1;6), 5 – fastener fragment (1:1), 6 – decorated buckle (1:1), 7 – undecorated buckle (1:1), 8 – key (1:2) (redrawn from Biddle & Kjølbye-Biddle 1992: 43)*

Tendley Hill, Eaglesfield, Cumbria (NY091287) (fig. A6.23) (ref. 26)

Accompanied inhumation found in the hilltop promontory during the 19th century in the vicinity of a likely Christian Anglo-Saxon cemetery.
Artefacts - Fe sword (fig. A6.23), missing tip, half of grip, upper guard & pommel. The hilt bears traces of Ag inlay. Petersen Type H (800-950) or I (850-900), most common types of Viking-period sword. L=50.8
Artefacts lost - Fe halberd, or more probably a spear-head: L=27.9
Cu-alloy penannular brooch, with a pair of beasts forming the ring, their heads separated by the pin

Sword in Black Gate Museum, Newcastle-Upon-Tyne.

Wensley, Yorkshire (SE093895) (fig. A6.24) (ref. 32)

Inhumation accompanied by Viking-period artefacts comprising a sword, spear-head, knife & sickle found while grave-digging in the parish church during the early 20th century.
Artefacts - Fe sword (fig. A6.24), virtually complete, small fragments missing from upper & lower guards only. The pommel is highly ornate & decorated with Ag & niello work. Petersen Type L (*c*900). L=91.6
Fe spear-head: has remains of wooden shaft in the socket, along with 4 of the Ag fixing pins. L=55.9
Fe sickle: L=15.2
Fe knife: flat-backed type. L=15.2

Artefacts in Wensley Church.

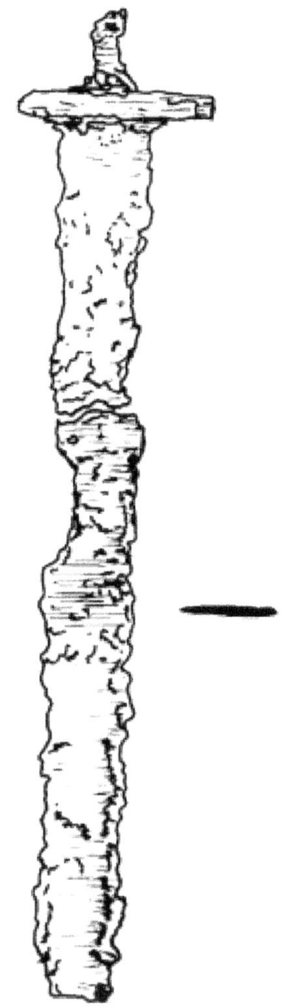

Fig. A6.23 *Sword (quarter size) from Tendley Hill, Eaglesfield, Cumbria (redrawn from Cowen 1967:200)*

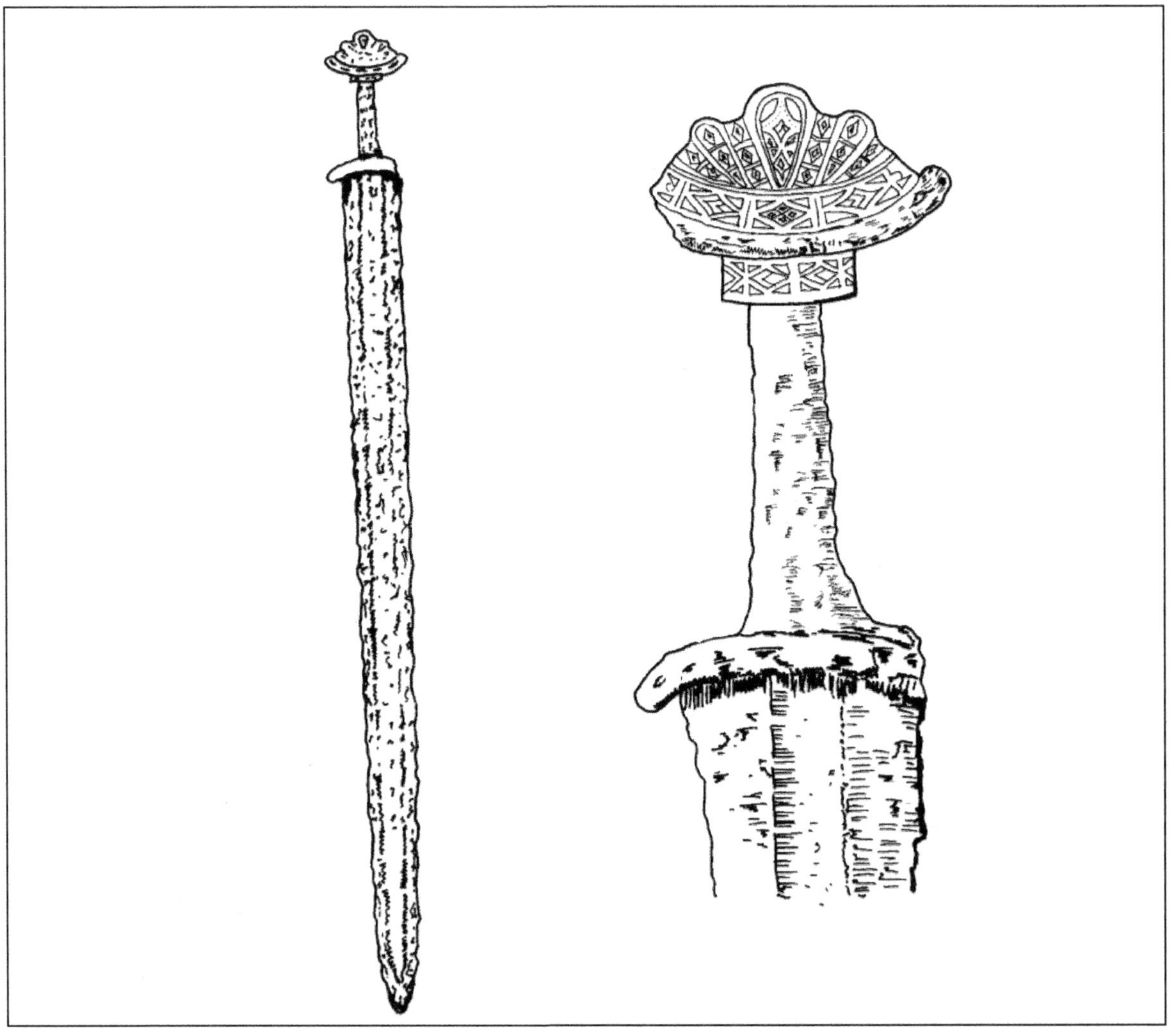

Fig. A6.24 *Sword (one-sixth size) & hilt detail (two-thirds size) from Wensley (redrawn from Bolton 1916: 229)*

York Minster, Yorkshire (SE601522) (ref. 54-70)

Recent excavations within the Minster revealed a series of inhumation burials accompanied by small personal items dating to the Viking-period. Some of the burials were marked with Viking-period stone-sculpture. Three hogback fragments (one lost) were also recovered during excavations.
Inhumation: grave 37 - Legs only, charcoal burial
Male inhumation: grave 38 - Wooden coffin, charcoal
Grave 40 - Disturbed, possibly charcoal
Child inhumation: grave 48 - Buried in stone-lined cut, grave-slab (YM 41) decorated by incised cross with interlacing between the arms (11th century). L=67.3, W=38.8, T=22.8
Pieces of 8-9th pottery
Male inhumation: grave 50 - Covered by 10th century grave-slab (YM 39), decorated with cable-moulding around edges, stylised cross in the centre, with curving arms formed of two beast heads. Panels decorated with 3 interlocking beasts: L=67.5-67.8, W=40-42.5, T=15.5. Comb tooth fragments.
Child inhumation: grave 51 - Covered by 3 end-stone markers. First (YM 38), edges decorated with cable-moulding, super-imposed cross with animal heads on terminals, panels decorated with York winged-beasts: L=71.5, W=30, T=16, 10th century. Second (YM 32), 2 interlocking beasts with human figure below jowls (repeated on each face), L=37.5, W=33, T=14.7, mid 10th-11th century. Third (YM 33), 2 addorsed demi-beasts on each side, sides incised to represent bodies of animals, L=54.6, W=43.8, T=16.5.
10th century pottery fragments
Grave 54 - Cut covered by decorated slab (YM 34), the Sigurd Stone (see chapter five). Top face perimeter cable-moulding; panel shows knotted dragon & human figure, hands to mouth. Beyond him is a headless torso, above the figure of a horse. Worn figure amongst borders. Long side B, patterned with interlace & ring-knots. Short side C, 2 profiled animals in combat, between them is a squatting bear. Long side D, in the centre is a human figure wielding a sword, with legs spread. Behind and in front of him are coiled dragons; at his feet a dragon's head. Short side E is lost. 10th century. H=130, W=47.3, T=28.3
Grave 56 - Cut covered by decorated slabs. First (YM 36), perimeter decorated with cable-moulding, broken at the centre of each end by facing animal head. Panels on each side depict York winged-beast. Sides decorated with cable-moulding. Late 9th-mid 10th century. L=32.6, W=38.2, W=22. Second (YM 37), broken in 2. Made from Roman half-column, perimeter cable-moulding, centre carved with incised cross with inward facing animal masks at the terminal of each arm. Panels above arms show animals of York winged-beast style. Late 9th-mid 10th century. L=63 & 69.5, W=36.5-41, T=20.1
Male inhumation: grave 57 - Covered by slab (YM 42), re-used Roman inscribed stone. One end inscription survives, '+OR ATEPR/OANIMA/CO(S)T(A/V)N/C (….). 11th century. L=175.4, W=48.3, T=11.4
Grave 58 - Cut covered by grave-slab (YM 35), broken in 2, bottom lost. Bears incised cross with animal heads on terminal. Facing York-winged beasts fill each panel. Cross continues on further fragment, also depicts a further winged beast in the panels formed by the cross. Sides are dressed & tooled. L=51.5, W=54.7, T=14.7
Grave 68 - No information on burial. Wooden coffin with fittings of which a broken hinge fragment remains: 10.5x3.4x0.1-0.5 Fe pre-Conquest key, L=11.6, circular cross-section, broken loop. Bit pierced by a single hole. Cu-alloy finger-ring, undecorated, D=2.2
Child Inhumation: grave 79 - 2 Fe hinges *in-situ*, possible remains of a chest burial: 19x5.5, 19.5x3.5
Male inhumation: grave 93 - Lines of surviving clench nails & wooden clinker built structure of coffin indicates that the remains were interred in a boat. Original L=175, W=0.61. Head surrounded by 3 unadorned pillow stones.
Grave 105 - Uncertain grave. Ring-headed pin with swollen head marked with dot: L=12.8, D of ring=1.4. Fe coffin fittings heavily corroded, included lock, hasps and hinges. Piece of yellow-brown glass: 0.36x8.5, T=0.25

Female inhumation: grave 107 - Charcoal deposit.
Grave 52 - Coped grave-cover (YM 45), Undecorated save for moulded perimeter line. 11th century. L=208, W=57, T=23.5
Grave 53 - Coped grave cover (YM 44), undecorated: L=148, W=46.5, T=26

Artefacts in YM.

St Mary Bishophill Senior, York, Yorkshire (SE601522) (ref. 71)

Excavations were undertaken when the church was demolished in 1963. A 10th century Cu-alloy strap-end was found 'associated with human bone'. No further detail given. Strap-end is of common Anglo-Scandinavian type, decorated with Borre-style ring-chain, reverse decorated with dot and ring marks: L=4.9, W=1.7.

Artefacts in YM.

St Mary Bishophill Junior, York, Yorkshire (SE601522) (ref. 72-9)

Recent excavations recovered a series of burials associated with Viking-period artefacts.
Adolescent male inhumation - St Peter's Penny 905-15
Fe knife: L=10.2, W=2.1
Schist whetstone pendant: L=6.5, W=1.2
Cu-alloy buckle & plate, decorated with *repoussé* bosses: L=3.7, W=2.2
Inhumation, possibly female adolescent - Ag arm-ring, trapezoid section, tapering towards hooked end fastenings, decorated with rows of punched dots: D=6.8
Threaded through the arm-ring was a damaged Ag ring, D=2
Inhumation of a child (*c*4yrs), remains scattered - Fragments of a Ag arm-ring of type similar to above.

Artefacts in YM.

Appendix 7 - Possible Scandinavian-influenced burial sites in the north of England

West Seaton, Workington, Cumbria

In 1903 a sword was discovered by workmen in a gravel ridge called Oysterbanks, near West Seaton (Collingwood 1904: 302-303). Although the sword (now lost) was reportedly broken and bent at the end like the example from the Hesket burial, pieces of the scabbard were found still adhering to the rust concretion of the blade (Collingwood 1904: 302). Since it would be impossible to replace a sword so damaged in its scabbard, it follows that the damage must have been done while it was still sheathed. This leads to a more unlikely scenario, as it would then suggest that the scabbard was metallic, something unknown from archaeological or contemporary sources, which have shown the scabbards of this period to be made of wood, bound with leather, which would have burned away during any introduction of furnace heat needed to bend the sword in such a manner. This being so, it is perhaps safe to assume that the sword was damaged in its burial environment. It is quite possible, however, that it came from a burial, ridges or natural promontories being a frequent choice for interment (see Aspatria, Tendley Hill, Camp Hill, etc). The site was only eighty yards away from the river Derwent, and not far from Derwentmouth where the river empties into the Irish Sea (Collingwood 1904: 302), so perhaps it was a site chosen because it was both visible to land travellers and ships moving along the river. When examined by Bjørn and Shetelig (1940: 21-22) before the Second World War the sword was identified as a Petersen Type W or X, dating to the tenth century.

Whitbarrow Scar, Witherslack, Cumbria

Another sword, found presumably in the nineteenth century, was recovered eight feet below the surface of a gravel bed, beneath Whitbarrow Scar, near Witherslack (Hutton 1901: 193). The place where it was recovered was said to be in the path of moorland winter run-off, so there may be a chance of re-deposition from a site further up the hill (Hutton 1901: 193). However, nothing is known of the circumstances surrounding the find, which may have been part of a burial or simply casual loss. The sword is missing its tip and pommel, and so cannot be given a type or date with any certainty (Hutton 1901: Plate, facing 193).

Sayle Bottom, Great Asby, Cumbria

Unfortunately all that remain of a burial ground comprising of several mounds in the vicinity of Sayle Bottom are a series of slightly differing antiquarian accounts from the nineteenth century (O'Sullivan 1998:17-18). The earliest account describes the mounds as differing in shape and size, some being rectangular, others circular (Hodgson 1820, in O'Sullivan 1998:17). One of the mounds was opened during the late eighteenth century and a series of human remains and a sword recovered (Hodgson 1820: 724, in O'Sullivan 1998:17). In the late nineteenth century Canon Greenwell visited the site, and recounts the discovery of an inhumation with a knife at its waist from a further mound sometime before his arrival (Greenwell 1878:386).

From the surviving accounts it seems that there were at least two burials likely to date from the Anglo-Saxon period. Whether they were indeed Viking or Anglo-Saxon is open to speculation.

Sandford Moor, Westmorland

During the late eighteenth century one of the barrows lying beside the Brough to Carlisle Roman road was opened by William Preston on behalf of Bishop Lyttleton (Preston 1766: 273). From his description it appears that the large mound contained at least two burials (Preston 1766: 273). The primary burial appears to have been an unaccompanied cremation, covered by a layer of sand and a cairn of stones (Preston 1766: 273). Approximately a metre above this was found an urn containing ashes, which had been place inside a further pottery vessel (Preston 1766: 273). To one side and slightly lower, directly above the primary cremation, was recovered sword with a decorated hilt, a spear and another iron fragment that Preston was unable to identify (Preston 1766: 273). From the account it is difficult to state with any certainty that the mound contained a secondary Viking cremation burial, although close parallels can be made with Claughton, which was recovered from a Bronze Age mound.

Brockhall, Billington, Lancashire

In 1836 the removal of a substantial mound at Brockhall Eases, around five hundred yards away from the River Ribble next to the road leading to the farm at Brockhall, uncovered the remains of a large cist (Raines 1850: 286). Inside the cist was an inhumation accompanied by the '*rusty remains of some spearheads of iron*' (Raines 1850: 286). The account then goes on to say that the bones and weaponry disintegrated when disturbed (Raines 1850: 286). Sadly, this is the extent of the description of the burial, which may have been Viking, suggested by the mound, cist and weaponry.

Hasty Knoll, Wigan, Lancashire

In 1770 a large cairn known locally as Hasty Knoll was dismantled (Beamont 1872:87 Whitaker 1775: 36-7). It was said to be constructed of stones taken from the bed of the nearby River Douglas, and legend had it that it was the burial site of the Arthurian era (Beamont 1872:87, Whitaker 1775: 36-7). Inside the mound were found numerous fragments of iron and weaponry, and below ground level a hole of some seven feet in length which was described as being filled with black earth and decomposed remains (Beamont 1872:87, Whitaker The History 1775: 36-7). This could be, as Edwards (1998:19) suggests, the remains of a cremation, of the type found at Hesket. However, with no further knowledge of the items recovered it is really quite impossible to label the burial any more firmly than Anglo-Saxon or Viking.

Meols, Wirral Coast, Lancashire

Nineteenth century antiquarian accounts of the recovery of an axe, spearhead and part of a sword on the seashore of the Wirral, may point to a one time Viking burial that has been washed into the sea (Griffiths pers. comm. 2001).

Appendix 8 - Results of artefact analysis from Pippin Castle, Scargill, Yorkshire (photographs in assoc. with Harrogate Museums & Arts, Harrogate Borough Council)

Cremation Samples (HARGM: 1158.2) (fig. A8.1)

The possible cremation samples comprise of three soil filled glass jars and a concreted mass of what appears to be a similar material. The two larger jars were sealed with brown paper and string, one bearing a handwritten label, '*From Viking Cremation*'. The third, smaller jar, was sealed with red wax.

Examination of the concreted mass proved it to be a lump of puddle clay mixed with gravel. There was no evidence of burning or cremated bone.

The paper seal on one of the large jars had been torn, and it was decided to empty its contents to examine the soil for any remains of cremated bone (fig. A8.1). A single, unidentifiable fragment was recovered, approximately 6x4mm. Minimal evidence of burning was confined to a few reddened clay fragments, but not enough to suggest they had ever been part of a cremation hearth.

Examination of the soil through the glass in the remaining two jars, backed by the lack of evidence from the former samples, prompted the decision to leave them both sealed. Advancement in scientific understanding in future years may prove beneficial to further analysis.

Fig. A8.1 *Possible cremation deposit (HARGM 1158.2), from Pippin Castle, Scargill, Yorks*

Stone (HARGM: 11518.1 & 10155)

There were five pieces of stone, incorporating two pieces of sandstone (marked 11518.5) and three flint cores (HARGM 11518.9). The first piece of sandstone was rounded but did not appear to have been worked or otherwise used as an artefact. The second, more rectangular example appears to have been worked into a single flat edge, but shows no marks of use.

The largest piece of stone in the collection is the crude hog-back tombstone (fig. A8.2) inscribed with the eleventh or twelfth century runes reading, SUNA (son) (Kermode in Kaye 1901: 55, Baldwin-Brown 1928: 384). Its dimensions are, length 560mm, height 330mm, and is approximately 176mm wide at the base.

A single fragment of sandstone whetstone (10155) was recorded, of length 61mm, and width 40mm (fig. A8.3). The whetstone was subject to x-ray fluorescence (XRF settings at 250 live secs., 35 kilo-vaults and 200 micro-amps), but no traces of metal fragments from use were found (fig. A8.4). The traces of green substance on the upper surface appear to be organic, possibly wax or some fixative used for display purposes at an earlier date.

Fig. A8.2 *Hogback with runic inscription from Pippin Castle, Scargill, Yorks (HARGM)*

Fig. A8.3 *Whetstone fragment (HARGM 10155) from Pippin Castle, Scargill, Yorks*

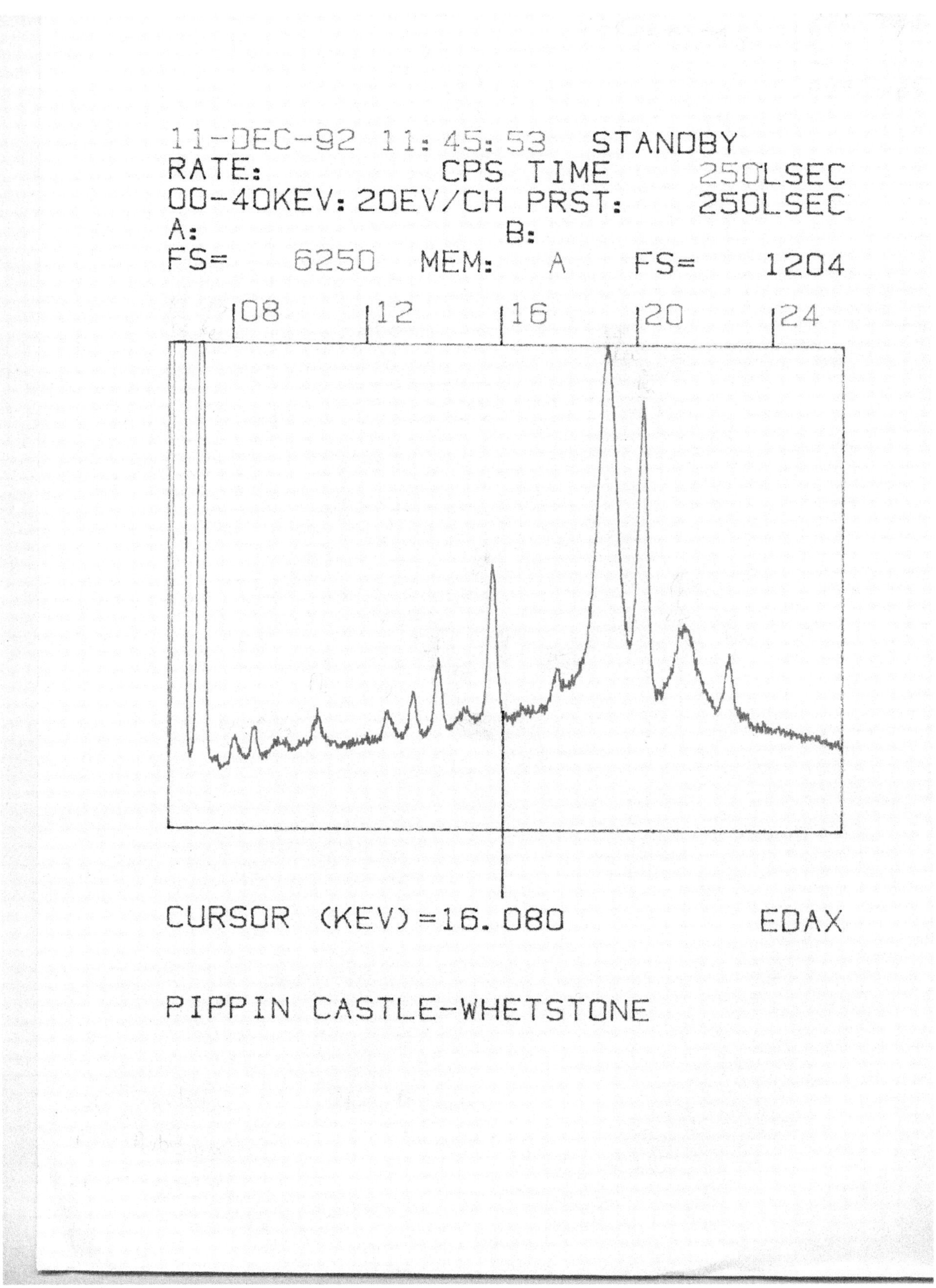

Fig. A8.4 *XRF results from whetstone fragment from Pippin Castle, Scargill, Yorks*

Wood (HARGM 11518.1)

The four pieces of carved wood in the collection were all made from oak. The two objects both numbered 11518.7 have been carved and polished into a Maltese cross and a flat square at some time post recovery. Their original archaeological state is unknown.

The other two pieces (11518.6) were an irregular flat trapezoid (fig. A8.5) and an octagonal peg with tapered ends. The nature of both pieces was such that they could both have been off cuts from the construction of a building.

Fig. A8.5 *Worked oak (HARGM: 11518.1) from Pippin Castle, Scargill, Yorks*

The marks of manufacture are still visible on the trapezoid piece (fig. A8.5), and appear to have been shaped by a very sharp axe, the blade placed on the surface and knocked through, the jambs (or tool marks) clearly visible on the smooth wedged end of the wood. The other end has been roughly hacked off from its parent piece, which suggests salvage rather than trimming. The length of the object is 155mm, and depth 15mm.

The peg is octagonal in shape, with each end cut to a tapered, wedge point. Its overall length is 185mm.The marks of manufacture are also visible on the peg, and again indicate that it was made by a very sharp axe, with the blade placed against the surface and knocked through. The sloping cut of the longer end indicates that it had been trimmed from a parent piece, so as not to split the piece remaining in use. There were insufficient rings to allow dendrochronological dating. The apparent provenance from the museum along with the appearance of the wood and tool marks indicates a broadly medieval date.

Bone (HARGM 11518.1)

There are three pieces of bone in the collection. The first is a right bovine humerus (11518.8), with evidence of dog chew marks; length 230mm, width across proximal end, 66mm. The second is a piece of whalebone 175mm long (11518.8), possibly rib, which shows no evidence of working (fig. A8.6). The third piece of bone is a human left tibia (11518.8), showing evidence for a squatting facet. Its overall length is, 350mm, diameter around centre, 66mm, proximal width, 66mm, and distal width, 40mm. Owing to its size it may have belonged to a female, but without the rest of the skeleton it is impossible to be certain.

Fig. A8.6 *Whalebone fragment (HARGM 11518.8) from Pippin Castle, Scargill, Yorks*

Iron (HARGM: 11518.1 & HARGM: 10156)

The iron in the collection comprised of an axe-head (HARGM: 10156), possibly identifiable with Petersen Type E, of the ninth/early tenth century (figs. A8.7-8), and nine pieces of corroding fragments (11518.3) (figs. A8.9-12). Comparison of these fragments to a photograph taken in 1928 in the *Harrogate Herald* may prove them to be a part of a flat-backed iron implement, possibly a large knife, or part of a decayed saw recorded by the excavators in 1901. The comparison also shows a large part of the underside of the axe that is now missing, presumed corroded away or fragmented and now lost.

All the iron was x-rayed (figs. A8.8, A8.11-12). The axe head and a larger piece of the corroding iron (K304B) were exposed for 3 minutes at 120 kilo-vaults. The smaller fragments were exposed for 1 minute 30 seconds, at 120 kilo-vaults. The larger fragment (K304B) was also exposed again on this setting.

Little could be ascertained from the fragments due to corrosion. The axe however, appears to be an excellent weapon, made from steel and not just an iron shape with a steel cutting edge welded on. No samples were taken for further analysis, although pieces could be used to confirm that it is indeed good quality steel and to see if it has passed through a cremation fire. This analysis would assist in the understanding of Viking period axes and their metallurgy, about which very little is known. The length of the axe along the top is 191mm, and depth along the haft edge, 195mm.

Fig. A8.7 *Axe-head (HARGM 10156) from Pippin Castle, Scargill, Yorks*

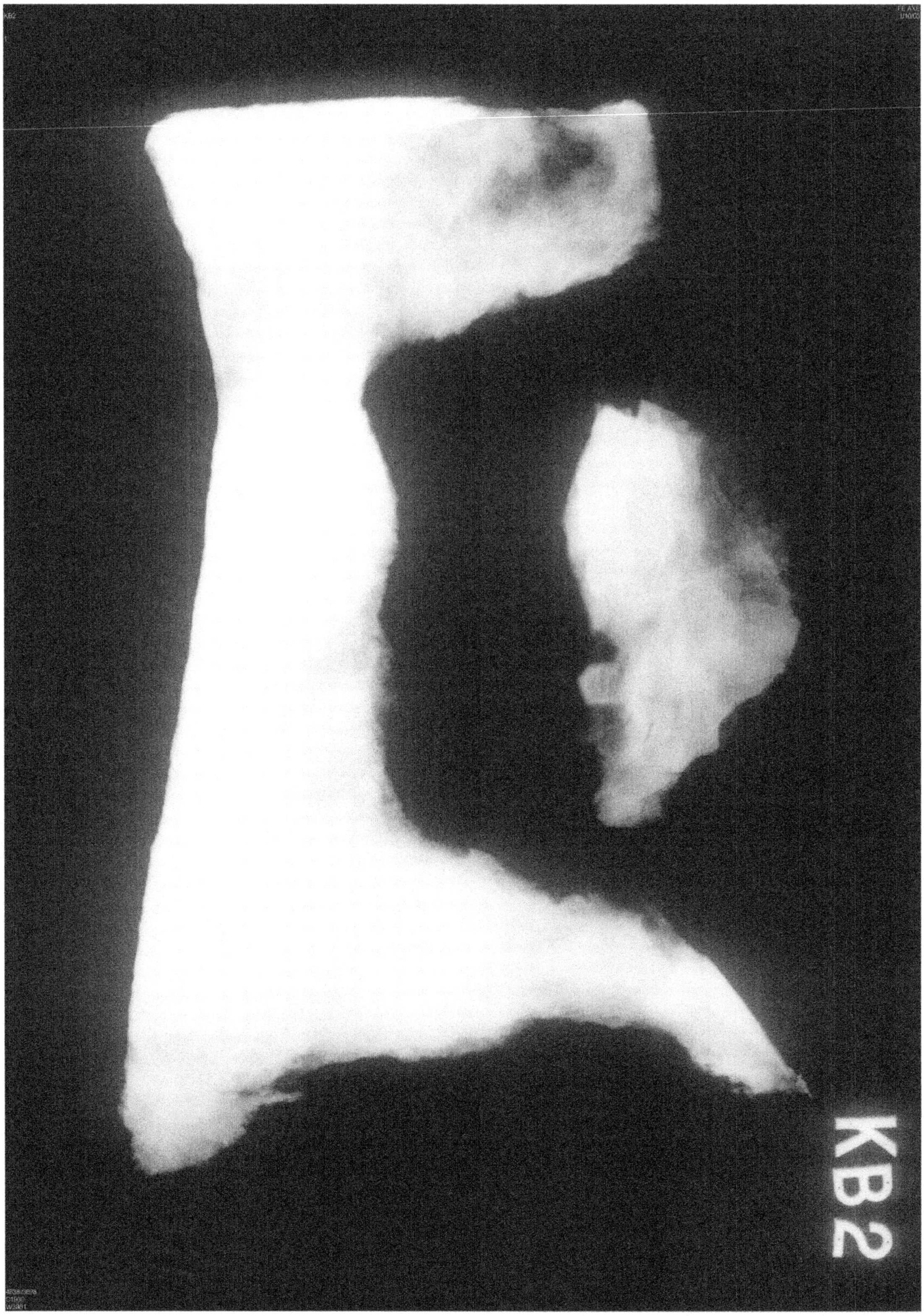

Fig. A8.8 *X-ray of axe-head (HARGM 10156) from Pippin Castle, Scargill, Yorks*

Fig A8.9 *Iron fragments 1 (HARGM : 11518.3) from Pippin Castle, Scargill, Yorkshire*

Fig. A8.10 *Iron fragments 2 (HARGM: 11518.3) from Pippin Castle, Scargill Yorks*

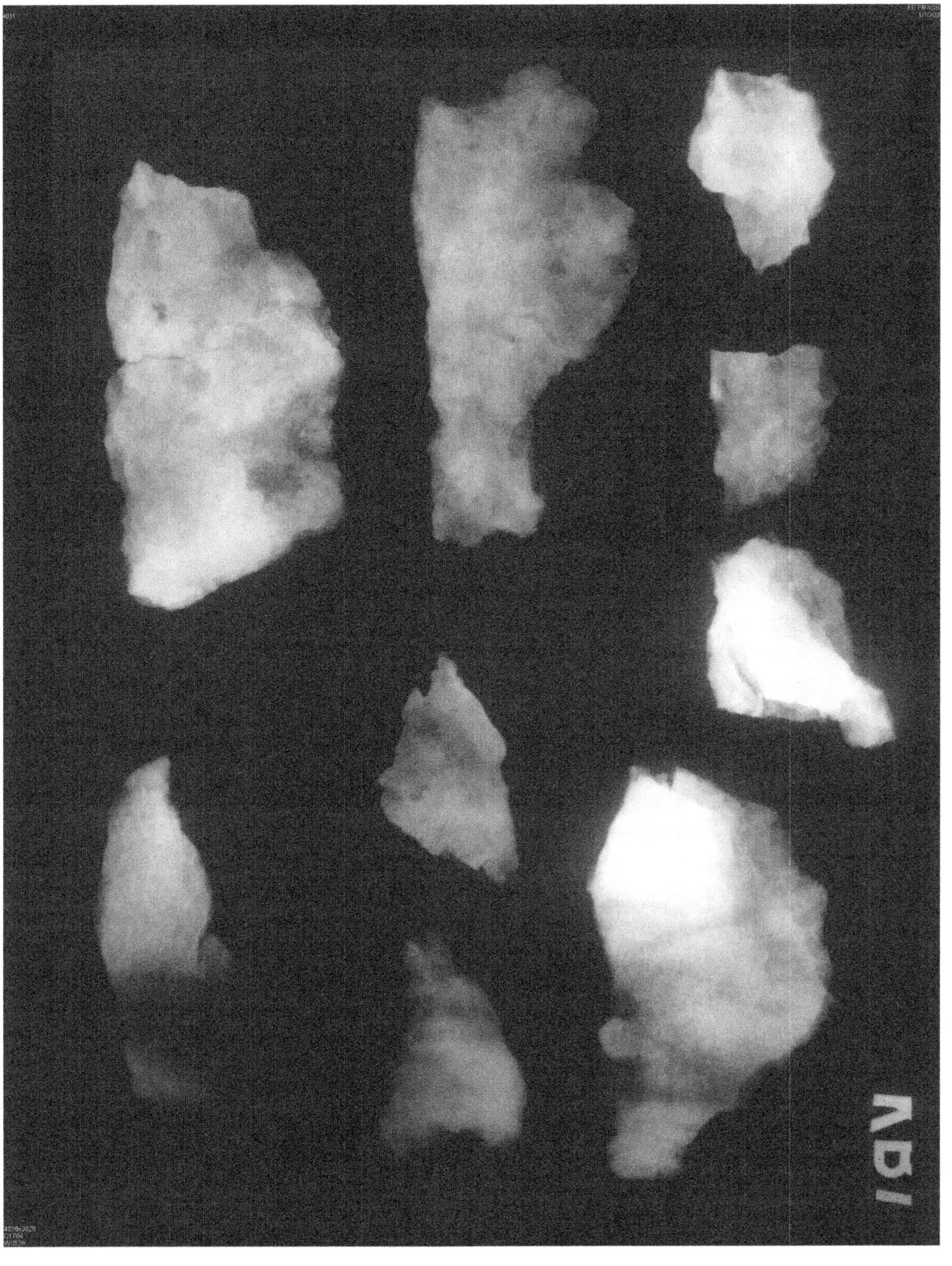

Fig. A8.11 *X-ray of iron fragments (HARGM: 11518.1 & HARGM: 11518.3) from Pippin Castle, Scargill, Yorks*

Pottery (HARGM 11518.1, 10163 & 10818) (figs. A8.12-15)

From the collection of pottery fragments it has been possible to identify with any certainty a minimum of 4 vessels, dating to between the mid 12th and mid 14th centuries. They appear to be local coarse earthenwares and form part of the Yorkshire Ware group.

Vessel 1 (fig. A8.12) – 7 sherds including handle fragment, light buff sandy fabric, with a light into dark green glaze with speckles. Two thumb marks at the base of the handle. Appears to be part of a jug with a simple rod handle.

Vessel 2 (fig. A8.13) – 1 sherd, part of the base, fine grained burnt sandy fabric. Outer surface pale pink in colour, with traces of glaze on base.

Vessel 3 (fig. A8.14) – 10 sherds, buff fabric with coarse inclusions. Externally the upper body is glazed a dark khaki colour. The lower part is grey in colour, with a slightly pitted surface. The vessel appears to have been a jug, with clearly defined thumbing around the base.

Vessel 4 (fig. A8.15) – 1 sherd, sandy buff fabric. Unglazed. Internally slightly pitted surface, outer surface smoother. Appears to have been another jug, with thumbed decoration around base.

Fig. A8.12 *Pottery, vessel 1, from Pippin Castle, Scargill, Yorks*

Fig. A8.13 *Pottery, vessel 2, from Pippin Castle, Scargill, Yorks*

Fig. A8.14 *Pottery, vessel 3, Pippin Castle, Scargill, Yorks*

Fig. A8.15 *Pottery, vessel 4, Pippin Castle, Scargill, Yorks*

REFERENCES

Primary Sources

Primary Texts (beginning with abbreviated terms used in main text)

Æ – The Chronicle of Æthelweard, ed. by A Campbell, Thomas Nelson & Sons Ltd, London, 1962
ASC – The Anglo-Saxon Chronicles, ed. & transl. by M Swanton, Phoenix Press, London, 2000
Asser – Asser's Life of King Alfred, in Alfred the Great. Asser's Life of King Alfred & other contemporary sources, transl. by S Keynes & M Lapidge, Penguin, Harmondsworth, 1983
AU – Annals of Ulster (to AD 1131) – ed. by S MacAirt & G MacNiocall, part I text and translation, Dublin Institute for Advance Studies, 1983
EHD – English Historical Documents, c500-1042, vol. 1, ed. by D Whitelock, 2nd edition, Eyre Methuen, London, 1979
FW – Florence of Worcester
HCD – History of the Church of Durham, Simeon of Durham, transl. by J Stevenson, reprint in 1993 from 1855 edition of the Church Historians of England, Llanerch Press, Lampeter
HK – A History of the Kings of England, Simeon of Durham, transl. by J Stevensen, reprint in 1987 from 1858 edition of the Church Historians of England, Llanerch Press, Lampeter
HSC - History of St Cuthbert, anonymous, in English Historical Documents, c500-1042, vol. 1, ed. by D Whitelock, 2nd edition, Eyre Methuen, London, 1979, document 6, pp286-288
RW – Roger of Wendover's *Flowers of History*, formerly ascribed to Matthew Paris, vol. I, part I 447-1066 AD, transl. by JA Giles reprint in 1993 from 1849 edition, Llanerch Press, Lampeter
Saxo – The History of the Danes Books I-IX by Saxo Grammaticus, transl. by P Fisher, ed. by H Ellis Davidson, DS Brewer (Boydell & Brewer), Woodbridge, 2002
WM – William of Malmesbury, *The History of the Kings of England, and of his own times*, transl. by J Stevenson, reprint in 1989 from 1854 edition of the Church Historians of England, Llanerch Press, Lampeter
Accounts of Othere & Wulfstan, ed. & transl. by N Lund & CE Fell, Two Voyagers at the Court of King Alfred. The Ventures of Othere and Wulfstan together with the Description of Northern Europe from the Old English Orosius, William Sessions Ltd, New York, 1984
Annals of Ireland: Three Fragments copied…, by Dubhaltach Mac Firbisigh, ed. by J O'Donovan, Dublin, 1860
Annals of St-Bertin, ed. & transl. by JL Nelson, 1991, Manchester University Press
Annals of St Neots, ed. by D Dumville & M Lapidge, The Anglo-Saxon Chronicle: A Collaborative Edition, 17, Cambridge 1984
Chronicle of John of Peterborough, ed. by JA Giles, D Nutt, London, 1845
Cogadh Gaedhl re Gallaibh: The War of the Gaedhil with the Gaill or the invasions of Ireland by the Danes and other Norsemen, ed. JH Todd, Rolls series 1867
Egil's Saga, transl. by B Scudder, in *The Sagas of the Icelanders. A Selection*, Allen Lane, The Penguin Press, London, 1997, pp3-184
Eirik the Red's Saga, transl. by K Kunz, in *Sagas of the Icelanders*, Allen Lane The Penguin Press, London 1997, pp653-674
Heimskringla, Snorri Sturluson, transl. by S Lang, revised with notes by P Foote, Dent, London 1964, vols. I & II
History of the Archbishops of Hamburg-Bremen, Adam of Bremen, transl. by FJ Tschan, Columbia University Press, New York, 2002
The Earliest Norwegian Laws. Being the Gulathing Law and the Frostathing Law, transl. by LM Larson, Columbia University Press, New York, Morningside Heights, 1935
The Saga of the People of Laxardal, transl. by K Kunz, in *The Sagas of the Icelanders. A Selection*, Allen Lane, The Penguin Press, London, 1997, pp270-421

Grants and Charters

Grant by Cenwulf, king of Mercia, and Cuthred, king of Kent, to the abbess of Lyminge, of land in Canterbury as a refuge (804), in English Historical Documents, c500-1042, vol. 1, ed. by D Whitelock, 2nd edition, Eyre Methuen, London, 1979, document 82, pp514
Grant by Ceolwulf I, king of Mercia, to Archbishop Wulfred, of land at Mylentum near Kemsing, Kent (17th September 822), in English Historical Documents, c500-1042, vol. 1, ed. by D Whitelock, 2nd edition, Eyre Methuen, London, 1979, document 83, pp514-6
Grant by Burgred, king of Mercia, to Ealhhun, bishop of Worcester, of a privelege for lands mainly in Gloucester (855), in English Historical Documents, c500-1042, vol. 1, ed. by D Whitelock, 2nd edition, Eyre Methuen, London, 1979, document 90, pp526-7
Privilege of Ceolwulf II of Mercia, freeing the diocese of Worcester from the charge of feeding the kings horses, in return for spiritual benefits and the lease for four live of land at Daylesford, Worcester (dated 875), in English Historical Documents, c500-1042, vol. 1, ed. by D Whitelock, 2nd edition, Eyre Methuen, London, 1979, document 95, pp533
Grant by King Edward the Elder of land in Wylye to Æthelwulf (901), in English Historical Documents, c500-1042, vol. 1, ed. by D Whitelock, 2nd edition, Eyre Methuen, London, 1979, document 100, pp541-3
Grant by King Æthelstan to his thegn Ealdred of the land at Chalgrave and Tebwirth, Bedfordshire (dated 926), in English Historical Documents, c500-1042, vol. 1, ed. by D Whitelock, 2nd edition, Eyre Methuen, London, 1979, document 103, pp546-7
Grant by King Æthelstan, of Amounderness to the Church of York (7th June 934), in English Historical Documents, c500-1042, vol. 1, ed. by D Whitelock, 2nd edition, Eyre Methuen, London, 1979, document 104, pp548-551
Grant by King Eadred to Wulfric, of land in Warkton, Northamptonshire (946), in English Historical Documents, c500-1042, vol. 1, ed. by D Whitelock, 2nd edition, Eyre Methuen, London, 1979, document 105, pp551-2
Grant by King Eadwig of Southwell to Oscetel, Archbishop of York (956), in English Historical Documents, c500-1042, vol. 1, ed. by D Whitelock, 2nd edition, Eyre Methuen, London, 1979, document 108, pp556-7
Old English Charter of King Æthelred confirming the will of Æthelric of Bocking (995-999), in English Historical Documents, c500-1042, vol. 1, ed. by D Whitelock, 2nd edition, Eyre Methuen, London, 1979, document 121, pp579-80

Laws

The treaty between Alfred and Guthrum (dated 886-890), in English Historical Documents, c500-1042, vol. 1, ed. by D Whitelock, 2nd edition, Eyre Methuen, London, 1979, document 34, pp416-7
II Æthelstan (c926-30) (Æthelstan's laws issued at Grately, Hampshire), in English Historical Documents, c500-1042, vol. 1, ed. by D Whitelock, 2nd edition, Eyre Methuen, London, 1979, document 35, pp417-22
II Edmund (939-46), in English Historical Documents, c500-1042, vol. 1, ed. by D Whitelock, 2nd edition, Eyre Methuen, London, 1979, document 38, pp427-9
The Hundred Ordinance (c939-961), in English Historical Documents, c500-1042, vol. 1, ed. by D Whitelock, 2nd edition, Eyre Methuen, London, 1979, document 39, pp429-30
IV Edgar (962-3), in English Historical Documents, c500-1042, vol. 1, ed. by D Whitelock, 2nd edition, Eyre Methuen, London, 1979, document 41, pp434-7
II Æthelred (King Æthelred's treaty with the Viking army) c991-994, in English Historical Documents, c500-1042, vol. 1, ed. by D Whitelock, 2nd edition, Eyre Methuen, London, 1979, document 42, pp437-439
III Æthelred (c978-1008), in English Historical Documents, c500-1042, vol. 1, ed. by D Whitelock, 2nd edition, Eyre Methuen, London, 1979, document 43, pp439-42
V Æthelred (1008), in English Historical Documents, c500-1042, vol. 1, ed. by D Whitelock, 2nd edition, Eyre Methuen, London, 1979, document 44, pp442-6
Extracts from the laws of Cnut (1020-3), in English Historical Documents, c500-1042, vol. 1, ed. by D Whitelock, 2nd edition, Eyre Methuen, London, 1979, document 49, pp454-467

Miscellaneous Historical Sources

Archbishop Oswald's Old English memoranda on the estates of the see of York (975-992), in English Historical Documents, c500-1042, vol. 1, ed. by D Whitelock, 2nd edition, Eyre Methuen, London, 1979, document 114, pp565
Ratification by King Æthelred for Æscwig, bishop of Dorchester, of an estate at Risborough, Buckinghamshire, granted to him by Archbishop Sigeric in exchange for money to buy off the Danes (994), in English Historical Documents, c500-1042, vol. 1, ed. by D Whitelock, 2nd edition, Eyre Methuen, London, 1979, document 117, pp569-70
Renewal by King Æthelred for the monastery of St Fridewide, Oxford, of a privilege for their lands at Wichendon, Buckinghamshire, and Whitehall, Cowley, and Cutslow, Oxfordshire, after their church and deeds had been burnt down during the massacre of the Danes (7th December 1004), in English Historical Documents, c500-1042, vol. 1, ed. by D Whitelock, 2nd edition, Eyre Methuen, London, 1979, document 127, pp590-592
Old English will of King Eadred (951-955), in English Historical Documents, c500-1042, vol. 1, ed. by D Whitelock, 2nd edition, Eyre Methuen, London, 1979, document 107, pp554-556

Old English Will of Wulfric Spott (1002-1004), in English Historical Documents, c500-1042, vol. 1, ed. by D Whitelock, 2nd edition, Eyre Methuen, London, 1979, document 125, pp586-89
Old English letter, in English Historical Documents, c500-1042, vol. 1, ed. by D Whitelock, 2nd edition, Eyre Methuen, London, 1979, document 232, pp895-6
Ynglinga Saga, in *Heimskringla*, by Snorre Sturlason, ed. By E Monsen, transl. by AH Smith, W Heffer & Sons Ltd, Cambridge 1932, pp1-35

Secondary Sources

Abramson P (2000), A re-examination of a Viking Age burial at Beacon Hill, Aspatria, *Transactions of the Cumberland and Westmorland Antiquarian and Archaeological Society* vol. C, pp79-88
Alexander ML (1987), A Viking-Age Grave from Cambois, Bedlington, Northumberland, *Medieval Archaeology*, vol. 31, pp101-105
Ammerman A & Cavalli-Sforza LL (1984), *The Neolithic transition and the genetics of populations on Europe*, Princetown University Press
Anderson J (1872), Description by Ahmed Ibn-Fozlan (an eye-witness) of the ceremonies attending the incremation of the dead body of a Norse chief, written in the early part of the tenth century. Translated from Holmboe's Danish version of the Arabic original, with notes on the origin of cremation, and its continuance, *Proceedings of the Society of Antiquaries of Scotland,* 1872-3 vol. IX, pp518-531
Anderson J (1874), Notes on the Relics of the Viking Period of the Northmen in Scotland, Illustrated by Specimens in the Museum, *Proceedings of the Society of Antiquaries of Scotland*, 1874-5 vol. X, pp536-594
Anderson J (1879), Notes on the Contents of two Viking Graves in Islay, Discovered by William Campbell, Esq., of Ballinaby; with notices of the burial customs of the Norse sea-kings, as recorded in the sagas and illustrated by their grave-mounds in Norway and in Scotland, *Proceedings of the Society of Antiquaries of Scotland* vol. XIV, pp51-89
Anderson J (1907), Notice of bronze brooches and personal ornaments from a ship-burial of the Viking time in Oronsay, and other bronze ornaments form Colonsay, *Proceedings of the Society of Antiquaries of Scotland*, 1906-7 vol. XLI, 4th series vol. V, pp437-50
Andersson J (1998), Pagan Viking Burials in the Isle of Man - implications for the afterlife, in *Cult & Belief in the Viking Age: a period of change*, Socrates Interdisciplinary Intensive Course, pre-circulated discussion papers part II, University of Uppsala, pp1-10
Angus WS (1965), Christianity as a political force in Northumbria in the Danish and Norse Periods, in *The Fourth Viking Congress (York 1961)*, ed. A Small, Oliver & Boyd, Edinburgh & London, pp142-165
Anon (1848), Archaeological Intelligence – Anglo-Saxon Period, *Archaeological Journal*, vol. V, pp220-1
Anon (1859), Presentations, *Proceedings of the Royal Irish Academy*, vol. III, p121
Anon (unpublished), *Site Report of Unexcavated Graves at Cathedral Green, Carlisle*
AnthonyDW (1990), Migration in Archaeology: The Baby and the Bathwater, *American Anthropologist*, vol. 92 no. 4, pp895-914
Anthony D (1997), Prehistoric Migration as a Social Process, in *Migrations and Invasions in Archaeological Explanation*, ed. J Chapman & H Hamerow, BAR International Series 664, pp21-32
Armstrong ECR (1922), Some Irish Antiquities of Unknown Use, *Antiquaries Journal*, vol. II, pp6-12
Atkinson JC (1868), Proceedings Thursday, January 9th 1868, *Proceedings of the Society of Antiquaries of London*, series 2, vol. IV, (1867-70), pp52-54
Atkinson JC (1874), *History of Cleveland Ancient and Modern*, vol. I, MTD Publications, Leeds (facsimilie reprint from 1874 edition), pp81-85
Attenborough FL (ed. & transl.) (1922), *The Laws of the Earliest English Kings*, reprinted in 2000 by Llanerch Press
Bailey RN (1978), The Chronology of Viking-Age Sculpture in Northumbria, in *Anglo-Saxon and Viking Age Sculpture*, ed. by J Lang, BAR British Series 49, pp173-203
Bailey RN (1980), *Viking Age Sculpture in the North of England*, Collins, London
Bailey RN (1981), The Hammer and the Cross, in *The Vikings in England and in their Danish homeland*, ed. by E Roesdahl, J Graham-Campbell, P Connor & K Pearson, The Anglo-Danish Viking Project, London pp83-87
Bailey RN (1985), Aspects of Viking-Age Sculpture in Cumbria, in *The Scandinavians in Cumbria*, ed. by JR Baldwin & ID Whyte, Scottish Studies for Northern Studies, Edinburgh, pp53-64
Bailey RN & Lang JT (1975), The date of the Gosforth sculptures, *Antiquity*, vol. 49 pp290-3
Baldwin-Brown G (1928), In WJ Kaye (1928), A Viking Grave near Harrogate, *Durham University Journal*, vol. XXV, pp381-384
Balfour JA (1909), Notice of a Viking grave-mound, Kingscross, Arran, *Proceedings of the Society of Antiquaries of Scotland,* 1908-9 vol. XLIII 4th series vol. VII, pp371-5
Balfour JA (1910), Notes on a Viking grave-mound at Millhill, Lamlash, Arran, *Proceedings of the Antiquaries of Scotland,* 1909-1910 vol. XLIV, 4th series vol. VIII, pp221-4
Bateman T (1978 from 1861), *Ten Years Diggings in Celtic and Saxon Grave-hills, in the Counties of Derby, Stafford & York from 1848 to 1858*, Moorland Reprints, Buxton
Batey CE (1987), *Freswick Links, Caithness. A re-appraisal of the Late Norse site in its context*, BAR British Series 179 (vols. I & II), Oxford
Batey CE (1988), A Viking-Age bell from Freswick Links, Caithness, *Medieval Archaeology*, vol. 31, pp213-6
Batey CE (1993), The Viking & Late Norse Graves of Caithness & Sutherland, *The Viking Age in Caithness, Orkney & the North Atlantic* (Papers from 11th Viking Congress), ed. CE Batey, J Jesch & CD Morris, Edinburgh University Press, pp148-64 @ pp157-8
Batey CE (1995), Aspects of rural settlement in Northern Britain, in D Hooke & S Burnell ed., *Landscape and Settlement in Britain AD400-1066*, Exeter University Press, pp69-94
Batey CE (2002), Viking and late Norse re-use of broch mounds in Caithness, in *In the Shadow of the Brochs. The Iron Age in Scotland*, eds. B Ballin-Smith & I Banks, Tempus, Stroud, pp185-190
Beamont W (1872), The Fee of Makerfield; with an account of some of its lords, the Barons of Newton, *Lancashire and Cheshire Historical Society Transactions* vol. XXIV, p87
Beijer G (1969), Modern International Migratory Movements, in *Migration*, ed. Jackson JA, Cambridge University Press, pp11-59
Bersu G & Wilson DM (1966), *Three Viking Graves in the Isle of M*an, The Society of Medieval Archaeology, Monograph Series, no. 1, London
Biddle M & Kjølbye-Biddle B (2001), Repton and the 'great heathen army', 873-4, in Vikings and the Danelaw, in *Vikings and the Danelaw, Select Papers from the Proceedings of the Thirteenth Viking Congress*, ed. J Graham-Campbell, R Hall, J Jesch & D Parsons, Oxbow, Oxford, pp45-96
Birkedahl P & Johansen E (1994), The Sebbersund Boat-graves, in O Crumlin-Pedersen & B Munch Thye, *The Ship as a Symbol. Prehistoric and Medieval Scandinavia*, Papers from an International Research Seminar at the Danish National Museum, Copenhagen, pp160-4
Bjørn A & Shetelig H (1940), *Viking Antiquities in England – with a supplement of Viking antiquities on the continent of western Europe*, part IV of Viking Antiquities in Great Britain and Ireland, ed. H Shetelig, The Scientific Research Fund of 1919, H Aschehoug & Co. (W. Nygaard), Oslo
Blackburn M (2001), Expansion and control: aspects of Anglo-Scandinavian minting south of the Humber, in *Vikings and the Danelaw. Select Papers from the Proceedings of the Thirteenth Viking Congress*, ed. J Graham-Campbell, R Hall, J Jesch & DN Parsons, Oxbow Books, Oxford, pp125-142
Bøe J (1940), *Norse Antiquities in Ireland*, part III of Viking Antiquities in Great Britain and Ireland, ed. H Shetelig, The Scientific Research Fund of 1919, H Aschehoug & Co. (W. Nygaard), Oslo
Bolton, Lord (1916), Proceedings, *Proceedings of the Society of Antiquaries of London*, vol. XXVIII, 2nd series, pp228-230
Bond JM & Worley FL (forthcoming), *Cremated animal bone from the mounds at Heath Wood, Ingleby*
Braudel F (1972), *The Mediterranean and the Mediterranean Worlds in the Age of Phillip II*, vols. I & II, transl. by S Reynolds, 2nd revised edition, Collins, London
Brøndsted J (1936), Danish Inhumations of the Viking Age, *Acta Archaeologica* vol. 17, pp6-22
Bruce JR & Cubbon W (1930), Cronk ny Howe, *Archaeologia Cambrensis* vol. LXXXV, pp267-308
Bursche A (1996), Archaeological Sources as Ethnical Evidence. The case of the Eastern Vistula mouth, in *Cultural Identity and Archaeology. The construction of European communities*, ed. P Graves-Brown, S Jones, & C Gamble, Routledge, pp228-237
Byock J (2001), *Viking Age Iceland*, Penguin, London
Calverley WS (1899), *Early Sculptured Crosses, Shrines and Monuments in the Present Diocese of Carlisle*, ed. by WG Collingwood, T Wilson, Kendal
Camden W (1722), *Britannia, or a Chorographical Description of Great Britain and Ireland, together with the adjacent Islands*, 2nd ed. amended and transl. by E Gibson, printed by M Matthews for Awnsham Churchill, vol. II
Cameron K (1975), Scandinavian Settlement in the Territory of the Five Boroughs: the Place-Name Evidence, parts I-III, in *Place-Name Evidence for the Anglo-Saxon Invasions and Scandinavian Settlement*, ed. by K Cameron, English Place-Name Society, pp115-71
Carver MOH (1999), The Anglo-Saxon Cemetery at Sutton-Hoo: an interim report, in *The Age of Sutton Hoo*, ed. M Carver, Boydell Press, Woodbridge, (reprint from 1992) pp343-371

Cave AJE (1946), Report Nos. IV-V, in C Clarke & W Fraser, Excavation of Pagan Burial Mounds: Ingleby, Derbyshire, *Derbyshire Archaeological Journal*, pp1-23 @ pp20-2
Chapman J & Hamerow H (1997), On the Move Again: Migrations in Invasions in Archaeological Explanation, in *Migrations and Invasions in Archaeological Explanation*, ed. J Chapman & H Hamerow, BAR International Series 664, pp1-10
Charleson MM (1904), Notice of some Ancient Burials in Orkney, *Proceedings of the Society of Antiquaries of Scotland,* 1903-4, vol. XXXVIII, 4th series vol. II, pp559-566
Childe VG (1929), *The Dawn of European Civilization,* Routledge & Kegan Paul
Clarke C & Fraser W (1946), Excavation of Pagan Burial Mounds: Ingleby, Derbyshire, *Derbyshire Archaeological Journal*, pp1-23
Clarke C, Fraser W & Munslow FW (1949), Excavation of Pagan Burial Mounds at Ingleby, Second Report, *Derbyshire Archaeological Journal*, vol. 69, pp78-81
Clarke DL (1978), *Analytical Archaeology,* second edition (revised by B Chapman), Methuen & Co. Ltd
Clarke H & Ambrosiani B (1995), *Towns in the Viking Age*, Leicester University Press
Coffey G (1902), A pair of brooches and chains of the Viking period recently found in Ireland, *Journal of the Royal Society of Antiquaries of Ireland*, vol. XXXII, pp71-73
Coggins D, Fairless KJ & Batey CE (1983), Simy Folds: An Early Medieval Settlement Site in Upper Teasdale, Co. Durham, *Medieval Archaeology* vol. 27, pp1-26
Collingwood WG (1899), The Ormside Cup, *Transactions of the Cumberland & Westmorland Antiquarian and Archaeological Society*, series 1, vol. XV, pp381-7
Collingwood WG (1904), The Workington Sword, *Transactions of the Cumberland & Westmorland Antiquarian and Archaeological Society,* new series vol. IV, pp302-3
Collingwood WG (1907), Anglian and Anglo-Danish Sculpture in the North Riding, *Yorkshire Archaeological Journal* vol. XIX pp267-413
Collingwood WG (1911), Anglian and Anglo-Danish Sculpture in the East Riding with addenda to the North Riding, *Yorkshire Archaeological Journal* vol. XXI pp254-302
Collingwood WG (1927), *Northumbrian Crosses of the Pre-Norman Age*, London
Cook A & Batey C (1994), The Bone Comb, in TW Potter & RD Andrews, Excavation and Survey at St Patrick's Chapel and St Peter's Church, Heysham, Lancs., 1977-8, *Antiquities Journal* vol. 74, pp55-134
Connolly M & Coyne F (2000), Cloghermore Cave: The Lee Valhalla, *Archaeology Ireland*, vol. 14, no. 4, pp16-19
Cowen JD (1934), A Catalogue of objects of the Viking period in the Tullie House Museum, Carlisle, *Transactions of the Cumberland & Westmorland Antiquarian and Archaeological Society*, 2nd series, vol. 34 (174-180) pp166-187
Cowen JD (1948), Viking Burials in Cumbria, *Transactions of the Cumberland & Westmorland Antiquarian Society*, vol. 47, pp73-6
Cramp R (1978), The Anglian Tradition in the Ninth Century, in *Anglo-Saxon and Viking Age Sculpture*, ed. by J Lang, BAR British Series 49, pp1-32
Cramp R (1984), *Corpus of Anglo-Saxon Stone Sculpture, vol. I County Durham and Northumberland (parts 1 & 2)*, Oxford University Press on behalf of the British Academy
Cramp RJ & Bailey RN (1988), *Corpus of Anglo-Saxon Sculpture vol. II, Cumbria West and Lancashire North of the Sands*, Oxford University Press on behalf of the British Academy
Crawford BE (1987), *Scandinavian Scotland*, Leicester University Press
Crawford IA & Switsur VR (1977), Sandscaping and C14: the Udal, North Uist, *Antiquity*, 51, pp124-36
Crawford IA (1986), *The West Islands and Highlands: A View of 50 Centuries. The Udal (N. Uist) Evidence*, Great Auk Press, Cambridge
Crawford IA (1988), Structural discontinuity and associable evidence for settlement disruption: five crucial episodes in a continuous occupation 250-1689 (the Udal evidence), in *Settlement and Society in Scotland: Migration, Colonisation and Integration*, ed. R Mason, Association of Scottish Historical Studies, pp1-34
Craigie WA (1914), *The religion of Ancient Scandinavia*, Constable & Company Ltd, London
Crossley-Holland K (transl.) (1980), *The Norse Myths*, Andre Deutsch, London
Crowfoot EG (1956), Appendix I, in M Posnansky, The Pagan-Danish Barrow Cemetery at Heath Wood, Ingleby. 1955 Excavations, *Derbyshire Archaeological Journal*, vol. 76, pp40-56 @pp52-3
Cubbon AM (1965), A Viking Sword from Ballabrooie, Patrick, with evidence of pattern welding, *Journal of the Manx Museum*, vol. VI, pp249-53
Cubbon M (1983), The archaeology of the Vikings in the Isle of Man, in *The Viking Age in the Isle of Man, Select Papers from the Ninth Viking Congress, Isle of Man 4-14 July 1981*, ed by C Fell, P Foote, J Graham-Campbell, R Thomson, Viking Society for Northern Research University College London 1983 pp13-26
Curle AO (1914) a, Notices of the discovery of a hoard of rapier-shaped blades of bronze at Drumcoltran and the Stewartry of Kirkudbright and of a Viking sword at Torbeckhill near Ecclefechan, *Proceedings of the Society of Antiquaries of Scotland,* 1913-14, vol. XLVIII, 4th series vol. XII, pp333-335
Curle J (1914) b, On Recent Scandinavian Grave-finds from the Island of Oronsay, and from Reay, Caithness, with Notes on the Development and Chronology of the Oval Brooch of the Viking Time, *Proceedings of the Society of Antiquaries Scotland*, 1913-14 vol. 48, pp292-315
Dalton JP (1814), *The Cumberland Pacquet* of 18th October 1814, in JD Cowen, More about the Viking Grave at Eaglesfield, *Archaeologia Aeliana,* 4, vol. XLV, pp197-203 @ p198
Dalton JP (1841), Personal correspondence reproduced in JD Cowen, More about the Viking Grave at Eaglesfield, *Archaeologia Aeliana,* 4, vol. XLV, pp197-203 @ pp197-8
DeCorse CR (1994), Material aspects of Limba, Yalunka and Kuranka ethnicity: archaeological research in northeastern Sierra Leone, in *Archaeological Approaches to Cultural Identity*, ed. SJ Shennan, Routledge, pp125-140
Degge S (1727-8), An account of a humane skeleton of an extraordinary size, found in a repository at Repton in Derby-shire…, *Philosophical Transactions*, 35, pp363-5
Dīaz-Andreu M (1996), Constructing Identities Through Culture. The past in the forging of Europe, in *Cultural Identity and Archaeology. The construction of European communities*, ed. P Graves-Brown, S Jones, & C Gamble, Routledge, pp48-61
Dickinson S (1985), Bryant's Gill, Kentmere: Another 'Viking-Period' Ribblehead?, in *The Scandinavians on Cumbria*, ed. by JR Baldwin & ID Whyte, Scottish Society for Northern Studies, Edinburgh, pp83-88
Dolley M (1978), The Anglo-Danish and Anglo-Norse coinages of York, in *Viking Age York and the North*, ed. RA Hall, CBA Research Report no. 27, The Council for British Archaeology, pp26-31
Dolukhanov PM (1994), Cultural and ethnic processes in prehistory as seen through the evidence of archaeology and related disciplines, in *Archaeological Approaches to Cultural Identity*, ed. SJ Shennan, Routledge, pp267-277
Dommasnes LH (1982), Late Iron Age in Western Norway, Female Roles and Ranks as Deduced from Analysis of Burial Customs, *Norwegian Archaeological Review* vol. 15 nos. 1-2, pp70-84
Dommasnes LH (1991), Women, Kinship, and the Basis of Power in the Norwegian Viking Age, in *Social Approaches to Viking Studies*, ed. by R Samson, Cruithne Press, Glasgow, pp65-73
Donations to the Museum (1872), Donation from Prof. TS Traill, *Proceedings of the Society of Antiquaries of Scotland*, 1872-3, vol. IX, p5
Donations to the Museum (1878), *Proceedings of the Society of Antiquaries of Scotland*, 1877-78, vol. XII p599
Donations to the Museum (1893), *Proceedings of the Antiquaries of Scotland,* 1893-4, vol. XXVIII
DuBois TA (1999), *Nordic Religions in the Viking Age*, University of Pennsylvania Press, Philadelphia
Dunwell AJ, Cowie TG, Bruce MF, Neighbour T, Rees AR with contribs. by B Finlayson, N Kerr, N Murray, RJ Strachan (1995), A Viking Age Cemetery at Cnip, Uig, Isle of Lewis, *Proceedings of the Society of Antiquaries of Scotland*, vol. CXXV, pp719-752
Edwards AHJ (1927), Excavation of graves at Ackergill and of an earth house at Freswick Links, Caithness & a description of the discovery of a Viking grave at Reay, Caithness, *Proceedings of the Society of Antiquaries of Scotland,* 1926-7, vol. LXI pp196-209 at pp202-207
Edwards AHJ (1928), Excavations at Reay Links and a Horned Cairn at Lower Dounreay, Caithness, *Proceedings of the Antiquaries of Scotland*, 1928-9, vol. LXIII, 6th series, vol. III, pp138-150
Edwards AJH (1934), A Viking Cist grave at Ballinaby, Islay (with a note on the skeletal remains by Prof. TH Bryce), *Proceedings of the Society of Antiquaries of Scotland*, 1933-4 vol. LXVIII, 6th series vol. III, pp74-8
Edwards BJN (1969), The Claughton Viking Burial, *Historical Society of Lancashire & Cheshire*, 1969, vol. 121, pp109-116
Edwards BJN (1998), *Vikings in North West England: The Artifacts*, Centre for North-West Regional Studies, University of Lancaster, Lancaster
Edgren T (2000), The Eastern Route; Finland in the Viking Age, in *Vikings: the North Atlantic Saga*, ed. by WW Fitzhugh & EI Ward, Smithsonian Institution Press, Washington & London, pp103-115
Ekwall E (1968), English River Names, Oxford University Press

Ekwall E (1981(1960)), *The Concise Dictionary of English Place-names*, fourth ed., Oxford University Press

Eldjárn K (1984), Graves and Grave-goods: Survey and Evaluation, in *The Northern and Western Isles in the Viking World: Survival, Continuity and Change*, ed. by A Fenton & H Pálsson, John Donald Ltd, Edinburgh, pp2-11

Elgee F (1930), Early Man in North-East Yorkshire, John Bellows, Gloucester, pp220-1

Ellmers D (1995), Valhalla & the Gotland Stones, in *The Ship as s symbol in Prehistoric & Medieval Scandinavia*, Papers from an International Research Seminar at The Danish National Museum, Copenhagen 1994, ed. by O Crumlin-Pedersen & B Munch Thye, Publications from the National Museum, Studies in Archaeology & History, vol. I Copenhagen, pp165-171

Encyclopaedia Britannica, 15th edition

Fanning T (1970), The Viking Grave Goods Discovered near Larne, Co. Antrim in 1840, *Journal of the Royal Society of Antiquaries of Ireland*, vol. 100, pp71-78

Fell C (1986), Old English *wicing*: a question of semantics, *Proceedings of the British Academy*, vol. 72, pp295-316

Fell C (1987), Modern English Viking, in *Studies in Honour of Kenneth Cameron, Leeds Studies in English*, New Series 18, eds. T Turville-Petre & M Gelling, pp111-122

Fellows-Jensen G (1972), *Scandinavian Settlement Names in Yorkshire*, Navnestudier-Institut for Navneforkning vol. 25, CA Reitzels Forlag, Copenhagen

Fellows-Jensen G (1978), Place-names and Settlements in the North Riding of Yorkshire, *Northern History*, vol. 14, pp19-46

Fellows-Jensen G (1981), Scandinavian Settlement in the Danelaw in the light of the place-names of Denmark, in *Proceedings of the Eighth Viking Congress*, ed. by H Bekker-Nielsen, P Foote & O Olsen, Odense University Press, Odense, pp133-145

Fellows-Jensen G (1983), Scandinavian Settlement of Man, in *The Viking Age in the Isle of Man, Papers from The Ninth Viking Congress*, ed. by C Fell, P Foote, J Graham-Campbell & R Thomson, Viking Society for Northern Research, University College London, pp37-52

Fellows-Jensen G (1985a), *Scandinavian Settlement Names in the North-West*, Navnestudier-Institut for Navneforkning vol. 25, CA Reitzels Forlag, Copenhagen

Fellows-Jensen G (1985b), Scandinavian Settlement in Cumbria and Dumfriesshire: The Place-Name Evidence, in *The Scandinavians on Cumbria*, ed. by JR Baldwin & ID Whyte, Scottish Society for Northern Studies, Edinburgh, pp65-82

Fellows-Jensen G (1992), Scandinavian Place-Names of the Irish Sea Province, in J Graham-Campbell ed. *Viking Treasure from the North West. The Cuerdale Hoard in its Context*, National Museums & Galleries on Merseyside, Liverpool Museum, pp31-42

Fellows-Jensen G (1994), From Scandinavia to the British Isles and back again. Linguistic Give-and take in the Viking Period, in *Birka Studies 3, The Twelfth Viking Congress, Developments Around the Baltic and the North Sea in the Viking Age*, ed. by B Ambrosiani & H Clarke, Stockholm, pp253-268

Fellows-Jensen G (1995), Scandinavian Settlement in Yorkshire – through the rear-view mirror, in Scandinavian Settlement in Northern Britain. Thirteen Studies of Place-Names in their Historical Context, ed. by BE Crawford, Leicester University Press, pp170-186

Fellows-Jensen G (2001), In the Steps of the Vikings, in *Vikings and the Danelaw. Select Papers from the Proceedings of the Thirteenth Viking Congress*, ed. by J Graham-Campbell, R Hall, J Jesch & DN Parsons, Oxbow Books, Oxford, pp279-288

Gelling M (1973), Review of G Fellows-Jensen, *Settlement Studies in North Yorks.*, in Notes & Queries, April, pp144-6

Gelling M (1981), The word 'church', in English place-names, *Bulletin of the CBA Churches Committee 15*, pp4-9

Gelling M (1988), *Signposts to the Past, Place-Names and the History of England*, 2nd ed., Phillimore

Ferguson RS (1899), Various finds in Ormside Churchyard, *Transactions of the Cumberland & Westmorland Antiquarian and Archaeological Society*, series 1, vol. XV, pp377-380

Ferguson RS & Cowper HS (1892-3), An Archaeological Survey of Cumberland and Westmorland; and of Lancashire North-of-the-Sands, *Archaeologia* vol. LIII, pp485-537

Fishwick H (1891), *The History of the Parish of St Michael's-on-Wye, in the County of Lancashire*, printed for the Chetham Society new series 25, pp2-3

Fletcher R (1997), *The Conversion of Europe. From Paganism to Christianity 371-1386 AD*, Harper Collins, London

Foote P & Wilson DM (1979), *The Viking Achievement. The Society and Culture of Early Medieval Scandinavia*, Book Club Associates, London

Frazer W (1879-88), On a Great Sepulchral Mound, *Proceedings of the Royal Irish Academy* 2nd series II, pp29-55

Freke D (1995), *The Peel Castle* Dig, The Friends of Peel Castle

Freke D (2002), *Excavations on St Patrick's Isle, Peel, Isle of Man 1982-88, Prehistoric, Viking, Medieval and Later*, Centre for Manx Studies Monographs 2, Liverpool University Press

Gage (Mrs) (1851), *History of the Island of Rathlin* (M/S in private possession), pp12-14

Gaythorpe H (1910), The Rampside Sword; with Notes on the Church & Churchyard of Rampside in Furness, *Transactions of the Cumberland & Westmorland Antiquarian and Archaeological Society* new series vol. X, pp298-306

Geake H (1997), *The Use of Grave-Goods in Conversion-Period England c600-850*, BAR British Series 261, Oxford

Gelling PS (1984), The Norse buildings at Skaill, Deerness, Orkney, and their immediate predecessor, in *The Northern and Western Isles in the Viking World*, eds. A Fenton & H Pálsson, John Donald, Edinburgh, pp12-39

Gelling PS (1990), Excavations at Skaill, Deerness, Orkney, in *The Prehistory of Orkney BC4000-1000 AD*, ed. C Renfrew, Edinburgh University Press, pp176-82

Gordon K (1990), A Norse Viking-age grave from Cruach Mhor, Islay, *Proceedings of the Antiquaries of Scotland,* vol. 120, pp151-60

Graham-Campbell J (1980), *The Scandinavian Viking-Age Burials of England – some problems of interpretation,* in, Anglo-Saxon Cemeteries 1979 – The Fourth Anglo-Saxon Symposium at Oxford, ed. P Rahtz, T Dickinson and L Watts, BAR British Series 82, Oxford, pp379-382

Graham-Campbell J (1989), The Archaeology of the Danelaw: an introduction, *Les Mondes Normands (VIIIE-XIIES)* La Simarre/Societe d'archeologie me dievale universite de Caen, Caen France, ed. H Galinie, pp69-76

Graham-Campbell J (1992), The Cuerdale Hoard: Comparisons and Context, in *Viking Treasure from the North West. The Cuerdale Hoard in its Context, Selected papers from The Vikings of the Irish Sea Conference*, ed. by J Graham-Campbell, National Museums & Galleries on Merseyside Occasional Papers, no. 6, pp107-115

Graham-Campbell J (1998), The Early Viking Age in the Irish Sea Area, in *Ireland and Scandinavia in the Early Viking Age*, eds. HB Clarke, M Ní Mhaonaigh & R Ó Floinn, Four Courts Press, Dublin, pp104-130

Graham-Campbell J (2001), Pagan Scandinavian burial in the central and southern Danelaw, in *Vikings and the Danelaw. Select Papers from the Proceedings of the Thirteenth Viking Congress*, 1997, ed. J Graham-Campbell, R Hall, J Jesch and DN Parsons, Oxbow Books, Oxford, pp105-123

Graham-Campbell J & Batey CE (1998), *Vikings in Scotland. An Archaeological Survey*, Edinburgh University Press

Grainge W (1871), *The History and Topography of Harrogate and the Forest of Knaresborough*, John Russell Smith, London

Gräslund A-S (1980), *Birka IV. The Burial Customs. A study of the Graves on Björkö*, Kungl Vitterhets Historie Och Antikvitets Akademien, Ailmqvist & Wiksell International, Stockholm

Gräslund A-S (2000), Religion, Art and Runes, in *Vikings – The North Atlantic Saga*, ed. by WW Fitzhugh & EI Ward, Smithsonian Institute in assoc. with the National Museum of Natural History, Washington & London, pp55-69

Graves-Brown P (1996), All Things Bright and Beautiful? Species, ethnicity and cultural dynamics, in *Cultural Identity and Archaeology. The construction of European communities*, ed. P Graves-Brown, S Jones, & C Gamble, Routledge, pp31-95

Greenwell W (1878), *British Barrows. A record of sepulchral mounds in various parts of England. Together with a description of figures of skulls, general remarks on prehistoric crania and an appendix by G Rolleston*, Clarendon Press, Oxford

Greig S (1940), *Viking Antiquities in Scotland*, part II of Viking Antiquities in Great Britain and Ireland, ed. by H Shetelig, H Aschehoug & Co. (W. Nygaard) The Scientific Research Fund of 1919, Oslo

Grieve S (1914), Note upon Carn nan Bharraich, or Cairn of the Men of Barra, a burial mound of the Viking time on the Isle of Oronsay, Argyllshire, with an outline of the political history of the Western Isles during the latter half of the ninth century, *Proceedings of the Society of Antiquaries of Scotland*, 1913-14 vol. XLVIII, 4th series vol. XII, pp272-291

Hadley DM (1997), 'And they proceeded to plough the land and support themselves': the Scandinavian settlement of England, *Anglo-Norman Studies*, 19, pp69-96

Hadley DM (2000*a*), *The Northern Danelaw. Its Social Structure, c800-1100*, Leicester University Press

Hadley DM (2000b), 'Hamlet and the Prince of Denmark': Lordship in the Danelaw, c. 860-954, in *Cultures in Contact: Scandinavian settlement in England in the ninth and tenth centuries*, Studies in the early Middle Ages: vol. 2) ed. by DM Hadley & JD Richards, Brepols, Turnhout, Belgium, pp107-132

Hadley DM (2002), Burial Practices in Northern England in the Later Anglo-Saxon Period, in *Burial in Early Medieval England and Wales*, ed. S Lucy & A Reynolds, Society for Medieval Archaeology Monograph 17, Society for Medieval Archaeology, Maney Publishing, Leeds, pp209-227

Haley S (1999), Death after Death, in *The Loved Body's Corruption. Archaeological Contributions to the Study of Human Mortality*, Cruithne Press, Glasgow, pp1-8

Hall RA (1974*a*), The Pre-Conquest Burgh of Derby, *Derbyshire Archaeological Journal*, vol. 94. pp16-23

Hall R (1974*b*), A Viking Grave in the Phoenix Park Co. Dublin, *Journal of the Royal Society of Antiquaries of Ireland*, vol. CIV, 39-43

Hall RA (1978), A Viking-age Grave at Donnybrook, Co. Dublin, *Medieval Archaeology*, vol. 22, pp64-83

Hall RA (1989), The Five Boroughs of the Danelaw: a review of present knowledge, *Anglo-Saxon England*, vol. 18, pp149-206

Hall RA (2000), Anglo-Scandinavian Attitudes: Archaeological Ambiguities in Late-Ninth-to-Mid-Eleventh Century York, in *Cultures in Contact: Scandinavian Settlement in England in the Ninth and Tenth Centuries*, ed. by DM Hadley and JD Richards, Brepols, Turnhout, Belgium, pp311-324

Hall RA (2001), Anglo-Scandinavian urban development in the East Midlands, in *Vikings and the Danelaw. Select Papers from the Proceedings of the Thirteenth Viking Congress*, ed. by J Graham-Campbell, R Hall, J Jesch & DN Parsons, Oxbow Books, Oxford, pp143-155

Hall RA & Whyman M (1987), Settlement and Monasticism at Ripon, North Yorkshire From the 7th to 11th Centuries, *Medieval Archaeology*, vol. 31, pp62-161

Halsall G (2000), *The Viking Presence in England? The Burial Evidence Reconsidered*, in, Cultures in Contact: Scandinavian Settlement in England in the Ninth and Tenth Centuries, ed. By DM Hadley and JD Richards, Brepols, Turnhout, Belgium, pp259-276

Hamilton JRC (1956), *Excavations at Jarlshof, Shetland*, Ministry of Works Archaeological Report no. 1, Edinburgh

Hamilton W (1822), *Letters concerning the North Coast of the County of Antrim*, letter 2 written 1784, pp20-21

Harrison SH (2001), Viking Graves and Grave-goods in Ireland, in *The Vikings in Ireland*, ed. by A-C Larsen, The Viking Ship Museum, Denmark, pp61-75

Hart C (1992), *The Danelaw*, The Hambledon Press, London

Haslam J (1987), Market and Fortress in England in the reign of Offa, World Archaeology, vol. 19, no. 1, pp45-52

Hedges JW (1987), *Bu, Gurness and the Brochs of Orkney (Part II: Gurness)* (vols. I-III), BAR British Series 164 pp73-4, 86-7

Hertz R (1907), Contribution á une étude sur la representation collective de la mort (A Contribution to the Study of the Collective Representation of Death), *Année Sociologique* 10, pp48-137, (English transl. in Needham & Needham (1960)

Higgins DA (1999), Survey and Trial Excavations at the 'Ronaldsway Village' site, Ronaldsway Airport, Isle of Man, in PJ Davey ed. *Recent Archaeological Research on the Isle of Man*, BAR British Series 278, Oxford, pp139-152

Higham N (1985), The Scandinavians on North Cumbria: Raids and Settlement in the later Ninth to mid tenth Centuries, in *The Scandinavians on Cumbria*, ed. by JR Baldwin & ID Whyte, Scottish Society for Northern Studies, Edinburgh, pp37-52

Higham NJ (1992), Northumbria, Mercia and the Irish Sea Norse, 893-926, in J Graham-Campbell ed. *Viking Treasure from the North West. The Cuerdale Hoard in its Context*, National Museums & Galleries on Merseyside, Liverpool Museum, pp21-30

Higham MC (1995), Scandinavian settlement in north-west England, with a special study of *Ireby* names, in *Scandinavian Settlement in Northern Britain. Thirteen Studies of Place-Names in their Historical Context*, ed. by BE Crawford, Leicester University Press, pp195-205

Hodder I (1982), *Symbols in Action*, Cambridge University Press

Hodgson C (1832), An Account of some Antiquities found in a cairn, near Hesket-in-the-Forest, in a letter from Mr Christopher Hodgson to the Rev. John Hodgson, Secretary, *Archaeologia Aeliana*, 1st series, 2, pp106-109

Hodgson J (1820), *Topographical and Historical Description of the County of Westmorland* (London)

Holman K (2001), Defining the Danelaw, in *Vikings and the Danelaw. Select Papers from the Proceedings of the Thirteenth Viking Congress*, ed. by J Graham-Campbell, R Hall, J Jesch & DN Parsons, Oxbow Books, Oxford, pp1-11

Holmqvist W (ed.) (1970), *Excavations at Helgö. Report for 1960-64*, Kungl Vitterhets Historie Och Antikvitets Akademien, Stockholm

Hutchinson W (1794-1797) (1974), *The History of the County of Cumberland*, vols. I & II, F Jollie, Carlisle, republished by EP Publishing Ltd in collaboration with Cumberland County Library

Hutton FRC (1901), Witherslack Church & Manor, *Transactions of the Cumberland & Westmorland Antiquarian and Archaeological Society*, new series, vol. I pp186-193

Innes M (2000), Danelaw Identities: Ethnicity, Regionalism, and Political Allegiance, in *Cultures in Contact: Scandinavian settlement in England in the ninth and tenth centuries*, Studies in the early Middle Ages: vol. 2) ed. by DM Hadley & JD Richards, Brepols, Turnhout, Belgium, pp65-88

Insley J (1986), Toponymy and settlement in the north-west, *Nomina*, vol. 10, pp169-72

Isaac J (2000), *Economics of Migration*, reprint of 1947 edition, Routledge

Jackson JW (1946), Report No. VI, in C Clarke & W Fraser, Excavation of Pagan Burial Mounds: Ingleby, Derbyshire, *Derbyshire Archaeological Journal*, pp1-23 @ pp22-3

Jackson WJ (1956), Appendix IV, in M Posnansky, The Pagan-Danish Barrow Cemetery at Heath Wood, Ingleby. 1955 Excavations, *Derbyshire Archaeological Journal*, vol. 76, pp40-56, @p55

Jansen C (1969), Some Sociological Aspects of Migration, in *Migration*, ed. JA Jackson, Cambridge University Press, pp60-73

Jesch J (2001*a*), Skaldic verse in Scandinavian England, in *Vikings and the Danelaw, Select Papers from the Proceedings of the Thirteenth Viking Congress*, ed. by J Graham-Campbell, R Hall, J Jesch & DN Parsons, Oxbow Books, Oxford, pp313-325

Jesch J (2001*b*), *Ships and Men in the Late Biking Age. The Vocabulary of Runic Inscriptions and Skaldic Verse*, Boydell Press, Woodbridge

Jespersen O (1967), *Growth and Structure of the English Language*, ninth edition, Blackwell

Jones G (1973), *A History of the Vikings*, Oxford University Press, Oxford

Jones M (1849), Remains of a Viking Burial, *Archaeological Journal*, vol. VI, pp74-5

Jones S (1997), *The Archaeology of Ethnicity. Constructing Identities in the Past and Present*, Routledge

Jørgensen L (1987), Family Burial Practices and Inheritance Systems. The Development of an Iron Age Society from 500BC to AD 1000 on Bornholm, Denmark, *Acta Archaeologica*, vol. 58, pp17-53

Jørgensen L (2000), Political Organisation and Social Life, in *Vikings – The North Atlantic Saga*, ed. by WW Fitzhugh & EI Ward, Smithsonian Institute in assoc. with the National Museum of Natural History, Washington & London, pp72-83

Kaland SHH (1993), The settlement of Westness, Rousey, *The Viking Age in Caithness, Orkney & the North Atlantic* (papers from 11th Viking Congress), ed Batey CE, Jesch J, Morris CD, Edinburgh University Press pp308-17 @ pp312-17

Kaye WJ (1902), Reading presented in the *Proceedings of the Society of Antiquaries of London*, vol. XIX, pp55-6

Kaye WJ (1928), A Viking Grave Near Harrogate, *Durham University Journal*, vol. XXV, pp381-384

Kemp RL (1996), *Anglian Settlement at 46-54 Fishergate*, The Archaeology of York, 7/1, CBA

Kermode PMC (1902), In WJ Kaye (1902), *Proceedings of the Society of Antiquaries of London*, vol. XIX, pp55-6

Kermode PMC (1930), A Ship Burial on the Isle of Man, *The Antiquaries Journal*, vol. X, pp126-133

Kershaw P (2000), The Alfred-Guthrum Treaty: Scripting Accommodation and Interaction in Viking Age England, in *Cultures in Contact: Scandinavian Settlement in England in the Ninth and Tenth Centuries*, ed. by DM Hadley & JD Richards, Brepols, Turnhout, Belgium, pp43-64

Keynes S (1980), *The Diplomas of King Æthelred 'the Unready' 978-1016. A Study in their use as Historical Evidence*, Cambridge University Press, Cambridge

King A (1978), Gauber high pasture, Ribblehead – an interim report, in *Viking Age York and the North*, ed. by RA Hall CBA Research report 27, pp21-5

Kossinna G (1911), *Die Herkunft der Germanen*, Kabitzsch, Leipzig

Kossinna G (1921(1914)), *Die Deutsche Vorgeschichte: eine Hervorragend Nationale Wissenschaft*, Mannus-Bibliothek 9

Krogh KJ (1983), The Royal Viking Age monuments at Jelling in the light of recent archaeological excavations. A preliminary report, *Acta Archaeologica* vol. 53 (1982), pp183-216

Lamb R (1993), Carolingian Orkney and its Transformation, in *The Viking Age in Caithness, Orkney and the North Atlantic*, ed. by CE Batey, J Jesch & CD Morris, Edinburgh University Press, pp260-271

Lambarde W (1568), *APXAIONOMIA, sive de priscis Anglorum legibus libri & c*

Lang JT (1971), The Castledermot Hogback, *Journal of the Royal Society of Antiquaries of Ireland*, vol. 101, pp154-8

Lang JT (1973), Some Late Pre-Conquest Crosses in Ryedale, Yorkshire: a Reappraisal, *Journal of the British Archaeological Association*, 3rd series vol. 86 pp17-20

Lang JT (1976*a*), Sigurd and Weland in Pre-Conquest carving from Northern England, *Yorkshire Archaeological Journal*, vol. 48 pp83-94
Lang JT (1976*b*), The Sculptors of the Nunburnholme Cross, *Archaeological Journal* vol. 133 pp75-94
Lang JT (1978), Continuity and Innovation in Anglo-Scandinavian Sculpture, in *Anglo-Saxon and Viking Age Sculpture*, ed. by J Lang, BAR British Series 49, pp145-172
Lang JT (1984), The Hogback: a Viking colonial monument, in *Anglo-Saxon Studies in Archaeology and History III*, ed. by S Chadwick Hawkes, J Campbell and D Brown, Oxford University Committee for Archaeology, Oxford, pp85-176
Lang JT (1988), *Anglo-Saxon Sculpture*, Shire, Princes Risborough
Lang JT (1991), *Corpus of Anglo-Saxon Stone Sculpture, vol. III York and Eastern Yorkshire*, Oxford University Press on behalf of the British Academy
Lang JT (1995), Pre-Conquest Sculpture, in Phillips D & Heywood B (1995), *Excavations at York Minster*, vol. I part 2, From Roman Fortress to Norman Cathedral, ed. MOH Carver, RCHME, HMSO London, pp433-467
Lang JT (2001), *Corpus of Anglo-Saxon Stone Sculpture, vol. VI Northern Yorkshire*, Oxford University Press on behalf of the British Academy
Langston J (2000), Human bone, in P Abramson, A re-examination of a Viking Age burial at Beacon Hill, Aspatria, *Transactions of the Cumberland and Westmorland Antiquarian and Archaeological Society,* vol. C, pp79-8 @ pp80-1
Langston J (2001), Assessment of Human Skeletal Material: Skeleton 4, in *Red House Park Adwick-le-Street, Doncaster, South Yorkshire*, Archaeological Post-Excavation Assessment by Northern Archaeological Associates for Earth Tech Morrison on behalf of Yorkshire Water Services Ltd, NAA 01/64, July, pp51-3
Larcom T (1849), Donations, *Proceedings of the Royal Irish Academy*, vol. IV, pp388-9
Laungani P (1997), Death in a Hindu family, in *Death and Bereavement Across Cultures*, ed. by C Murray Parkes, P Laungani & B Young, Routledge, London & New York, pp52-72
Leahy K & Paterson C (2001), New light on the Viking presence in Lincolnshire: the artefactual evidence, in *Vikings and the Danelaw, Select Papers from the Proceedings of the Thirteenth Viking Congress*, ed. J Graham-Campbell, R Hall, J Jesch & D Parsons, Oxbow, Oxford, pp181-202
Lee ES (1966), A Theory of Migration, *Demography,* vol. 3, pp47-57
Leeds ET (1946), Report No. II, in C Clarke & W Fraser, Excavation of Pagan Burial Mounds: Ingleby, Derbyshire, *Derbyshire Archaeological Journal*, pp1-23 @ pp14-19
Leeds ET (1949), Second Report in C Clarke, W Fraser & FW Munslow, Excavation of Pagan Burial Mounds at Ingleby, *Derbyshire Archaeological Journal*, vol. 69, pp78-81 @ pp80-1
Lehtosalo-Hilander P-L (1987), Christians and Pagans in 9th Century Scandinavia, *The Christianization of Scandinavia*, ed. by B Sawyer, P Sawyer & I Wood, Report of the Symposium held at Kungälv, Sweden, 4-9th August 1985, Viktoria Bokförlag, Alingsås, pp31-61
Lethbridge TC (1920), A Burial of the 'Viking Age' in Skye, *Archaeological Journal*, vol. LXXVII, pp135-6
Levy JF (1956), Appendix V, in M Posnansky, The Pagan-Danish Barrow Cemetery at Heath Wood, Ingleby. 1955 Excavations, *Derbyshire Archaeological Journal*, vol. 76, 1956, pp40-56 @ p56
Liebermann F (1903-16), *Die Gesetze der Angelsachsen*, Halle
Logan FD (1991), *The Vikings in History*, 2nd ed., Routledge, London & New York
Lucy S (2000), *The Anglo-Saxon Way of Death*, Sutton, Stoud
Lukis WC (1870), On some Anglo-Saxon graves on Howe Hill, Nr Carthorpe, in the Parish of Burneston, North Riding of Yorkshire, *Yorkshire Archaeological Journal*, vol. I, pp175-181
Lund N (1976), 'Thorp-names', in *Medieval settlement: Continuity and Change*, ed. by PH Sawyer, pp223-5
Lund N (ed.) & Fell CE (transl.) (1984), *Two Voyagers at the Court of King Alfred. The Ventures of Othere and Wulfstan together with the Discription of Northern Europe from the Old English Orosius*, William Sessions Ltd, New York
M'Neill M (1891), Notice of excavations in a burial mound of the Viking time in Oronsay, *Proceedings of the Antiquaries of Scotland*, 1890-91 vol. XV pp432-5
M'Neill M (1892), Notice of the Discovery of a Viking Interment, in the Island of Colonsay, *Proceedings of the Society of Antiquaries of Scotland*, 1891-2 vol. XXVI pp61-2
MacGregor A (1987), Combs and Comb Cases, in Settlement and Monasticism at Ripon, North Yorkshire From the 7th to 11th Centuries AD, RA Hall & M Whyman, *Medieval Archaeology*, vol. 31, pp62-161 @ p127
Macleod DJ (1916), An account of a find of ornaments of the Viking time from Valtos, Uig, in the Isles of Lewis, *Proceedings of the Antiquaries of Scotland*, 1915-16 vol. L, 5th series vol. II, pp181-189
MacPherson N (1878), Notes in Antiquities from the Island of Eigg, *Proceedings of the Society of Antiquaries of Scotland,* 1877-78 vol. XII, pp577-597
Margary ID (1967), *Roman Roads in Britain*, John Baker, London
Margeson S (1997), *The Vikings in Norfolk*, Norfolk Museums Service
Marwick JG (1928), Notes in some relics from Orkney exhibited before the Society, *Proceedings of the Society of Antiquaries of London,* 1927-8, vol. LXII, 6th series vol. II, pp121-122
Megaw BRS (1937), Weapons of the Viking Age Found in Man, *The Journal of the Manx Museum*, vol. III, pp234-237
Megaw BRS (1938), An Ancient cemetery at Balladoyne, St. John's: New Discoveries near Tynwald Hill, *The Journal of the Manx Museum*, vol. IV, pp11-14
Metcalf P & Huntington R (1993), *Celebrations of Death. The Anthropology of Mortuary Ritual*, 2nd ed., Cambridge University Press
Montgomery J (2002), *Lead and strontium isotope compositions of human dental tissues as an indicator of ancient exposure and population dynamics*, unpublished PhD thesis, University of Bradford
Morris CD (1977), Northumbria and the Viking Settlement: the Evidence for Land-Holding, *Archaeologia Aeliana*, 5th series, vol. V
Morris CD (1981), Viking and native in northern England. A case study, in *Proceedings of the Eighth Viking Congress* 1977, ed. by H Bekker-Nielsen, P Foote & O Olsen, Odense University Press, Odense, pp223-244
Morris CD (1989), *The Birsay Bay Project. Coastal Sites beside the Brough Road, Birsay, Orkney Excavations 1976-1982*, University of Durham, Dept. of Archaeology Monograph series no. 1, vol. I
Morris CD (1996), *The Birsay Bay Project. Sites in Birsay Village and on the Brough of Birsay, Orkney*, University of Durham, Dept. of Archaeology Monograph series no. 1, vol. II
Morris CD (1998), Raiders, Traders and Settlers: the Early Viking Age in Scotland, in *Ireland & Scandinavia in the Early Viking Age*, eds. HB Clarke, M Ní Mhaonaigh & R Ó Floinn, Four Courts Press, Dublin, pp73-103
Morrison PA & Wheeler JP (1978), The Image of "Elsewhere", in *Human Migration Patterns and Policies* ed. WH McNeill & RS Adams, Indiana University Press, pp75-84
Murray Parkes C, Laungani P & Young B (1997), Introduction, in *Death and Bereavement Across Cultures*, ed. by C Murray Parkes, P Laungani & B Young, Routledge, London & New York, pp3-9
Murray Parkes C, Laungani P & Young B (eds.) (1997), *Death and Bereavement Across Cultures*, Routledge, London & New York
NAA Archaeological Post-Excavation Assessment (2001), *Red House Park, Adwick-le-Street, Doncaster, South Yorkshire*, by Northern Archaeological Associates for Earth Tech Morrison on behalf of Yorkshire Water Services Ltd, NAA 01/64, July
Needham R & Needham C (1960), A Contribution to the Study of the Collective Representation of Death, in *Death and the Right Hand*, Free Press, New York
Neely G (1940), Excavations at Ronaldsway, Isle of Man, *The Antiquaries Journal*, vol. XXX, pp72-86
Nicolaisen WFH (1969), Scottish place-names, 29: Scandinavian personal names in the place-names of south-east Scotland, *Scottish Studies*, vol. 11, pp223-36
Ó Floinn R (1998*a*), The Archaeology of the Early Viking Age in Ireland, in *Ireland & Scandinavia in the Early Viking Age*, eds. HB Clarke, M Ní Mhaonaigh & R Ó Floinn, Four Courts Press, Dublin, pp131-165
Ó Floinn R (1998*b*), Two Viking Burials from Co. Wicklow, *Journal of the County Wicklow Archaeological Society*, vol. 1, pp29-35
O'Brien E (1992), A Reassessment of the 'Great Sepulchral Mound' containing a Viking burial at Donnybrook, *Medieval Archaeology* (notes & news), vol. 36, pp170-3
O' Brien E (1998), The location and context of Viking burials at Kilmainham and Islandbridge, Dublin, in *Ireland & Scandinavia in the Early Viking Age*, eds. HB Clarke, M Ní Mhaonaigh & R Ó Floinn, Blackrock: Four Courts Press, Dublin, pp203-221
O'Sullivan D (1998), A Group Of Pagan Burials from Cumbria?, in *Anglo-Saxon Studies in Archaeology and History 9*, 1996, ed. D Griffiths, Oxford University Committee for Archaeology, pp15-23
Osborn A (1994), Multiculturalism in the eastern Andes, in *Archaeological Approaches to Cultural Identity*, ed. SJ Shennan, Routledge, Multiculturalism in the eastern Andes, in *Archaeological Approaches to Cultural Identity*, pp141-156
Ottaway P (1992), *Archaeology in British Towns. From the Emperor Claudius to the Black Death*, Routledge, London

Ottaway P (2000), Metal objects, in P Abramson, A re-examination of a Viking Age burial at Beacon Hill, Aspatria, *Transactions of the Cumberland and Westmorland Antiquarian and Archaeological Society,* vol. C, pp79-8 @ pp81-7

Owen OA & Dalland M (1999), *Scar: a Viking boat burial on Sanday, Orkney*, Tuckwell Press in Association with Historic Scotland, East Linton

Page RI (1971), Scandinavian Runes in the British Isles, *Reading the past: Runes*, British Museum Publications, London, pp53-9

Page R (1983), The Manx Rune-Stones, in *The Viking Age in the Isle of Man, Select Papers from the Ninth Viking Congress, Isle of Man 4-14 July 1981*, ed by C Fell, P Foote, J Graham-Campbell, R Thomson, Viking Society for Northern Research University College London 1983, pp133-146

Page RI (1995), How long did the Scandinavian language survive in England? The epigraphical evidence, in *Runes and Runic Inscriptions: Collected Essays on Anglo-Saxon and Viking Runes*, pp181-95

Parsons D & Abrams L pers. comm. (2001), *Place-name studies and settlement history: ploughing the same furrow or stuck in a rut?,* Viking Period Settlement in Great Britain and Ireland, Conference Cardiff University

Parsons DN (2001), How long did the Scandinavian language survive in England? Again, in *Vikings and the Danelaw. Select Papers from the Proceedings of the Thirteenth Viking Congress*, eds. J Graham-Campbell, R Hall, J Jesch & D Parsons, Oxbow, Oxford, pp299-312

Paterson C (1999), Letter from, to Sellevold at appendix B part 10, p56 in BJ Sellevold, *Picts & Vikings at Westness. Anthropological investigations of the skeletal material from the cemetery at Westness, Rousay, Orkney Islands.* Norsk institutt for kulturminneforskning, Oslo

Pedersen A (1997*a*), Weapons and Riding Gear in Burials – evidence of military and social rank in 10th century Denmark?, in, *Military Aspects of Scandinavian Society in a European Perspective, AD1-1300*, publications of the National Museum studies in Archaeology & History vol. 2 Copenhagen, Papers from an International Research Seminar at Danish National Museum Copenhagen 2-4th May 1996, ed. A Nøvgård Jørgensen & BL Clausen, pp123-135

Pedersen A (1997*b*), Similar Finds – Different meanings? Some preliminary thoughts on the Viking-age burials with riding equipment in Scandinavia, in *Burial and Society. The Chronological and Social Analysis of Archaeological Burial Data*, ed. by CK Jensen & KH Nielsen, Aarhus University Press, Aarhus, pp171-183

Peirce I (2002), *Swords of the Viking Age*, Boydell Press, Woodbridge

Petersen J (1919), *De Norske Vikingesvaerd. En Typologisk – Kronologisk Studie over Vikingetidens Vaaban,* Kristiana. Videnskapsselskapets skrifter, II, histfilos, no. 1, Oslo

Phillips P (1989), *Archaeological Landscape Studies in Northern Lincolnshire*, BAR British Series 208, part 1, Oxford

Phillips D & Heywood B (1995), *Excavations at York Minster*, vol. I, From Roman Fortress to Norman Cathedral, ed. MOH Carver, RCHME, HMSO London. Burial details especially from MOH Carver's table 2, pp88-92

Posnansky M (1956), The Pagan-Danish Barrow Cemetery at Heath Wood, Ingleby. 1955 Excavations, *Derbyshire Archaeological Journal*, vol. 76, 1956, pp40-56

Potter TW & Andrews RD (1994), Excavation and Survey at St Patrick's Chapel and St Peter's Church, Heysham, Lancs., 1977-8, *Antiquities Journal* vol. 74, pp55-134

Preston W (1766), An Account of opening one of the largest barrows on Sandford Moor, Westmorland, letter dated Warcop Hall Sept 5th to Bishop Lyttleton, read at the Society of Antiquaries Nov 6th 1766: *Archaeologia*: or miscellaneous tracts relating to Antiquity vol. III, MDCCLXXXVI (1766), p273

Price C (1969), The Study of Assimilation in Migration, in *Migration*, ed. JA Jackson, Cambridge University Press, pp181-237

Price N (1998), *Different Vikings? Towards a cognitive archaeology of religion and war in late Iron Age Scandinavia*, in pre-circulated discussion papers part I of the Socrates Interdisciplinary Intensive Course. Cult & Belief in the Viking Age: a Period of Change, University of Uppsala, pp1-13

Price N (2000), The Scandinavian Landscape. The People and the Environment, in *Vikings – The North Atlantic Saga*, ed. by WW Fitzhugh & EI Ward, Smithsonian Institute in assoc. with the National Museum of Natural History, Washington & London, pp31-41

Price NS (2002), *The Viking Way. Religion and War in Late Iron Age Scandinavia*, Dept. of Archaeology & Ancient History, University of Uppsala, Sweden

Purchases for the Museum (1882), *Proceedings of the Antiquaries of Scotland,* 1882-3, vol. XVII, new series vol. V

Radcliffe-Brown AR (1968), *Structure and Function in Primitive Society. Essays and Addresses*, Cohen & West Ltd, London

Raftery J (1960-1), A Viking Burial in Co. Galway, *Journal of Galway Archaeology and History Society*, vol. 29, pp3-6

Raines FR (1850), Gastrell F, *Notitia Cestriensis or Historic Notices of the Diocese of Chester,* from the orig. manuscript. of FR Raines, vol. II part II printed for the Chetham Society, vol. 21, p286

Ramm HG (1976), The Church of St Mary, Bishophill Senior: Excavations 1964, *Yorkshire Archaeological Journal*, vol. 48 pp35-68

Ramskou T (1950), Viking Age Cremation Graves in Denmark, a Survey, *Acta Archaeologia*, vol. 21, pp137-182

Randsborg K (1980), *The Viking Age in Denmark. The Formation of a State*, Duckworth, London

Richards JD (1991), *Viking Age England*, Batsford

Richards JD (1999), Cottam: Anglian and Anglo-Scandinavian settlement on the Yorkshire Wolds, *Archaeological Journal*, vol. 156, pp1-110

Richards JD (2000*a*), *Viking Age England*, Tempus, Stroud

Richards JD (2000*b*), Identifying Anglo-Scandinavian Settlements, in *Cultures in Contact: Scandinavian Settlement in England in the ninth and tenth centuries*, ed. DM Hadley & JD Richards, Brepols, pp295-309

Richards JD (2001), Finding the Vikings, in *Vikings and the Danelaw, Select Papers from the Proceedings of the Thirteenth Viking Congress*, ed. J Graham-Campbell, R Hall, J Jesch & D Parsons, Oxbow, Oxford pp269-277

Richards JD (2002), The Case of the Missing Vikings: Scandinavian Burial in the Danelaw, in *Burial in Early Medieval England and Wales*, ed. S Lucy & A Reynolds, Society for Medieval Archaeology Monograph 17, Society for Medieval Archaeology, Maney Publishing, Leeds, pp157-170

Richards JD (2003*a*), Heath Wood, Ingleby, *Current Archaeology*, no. 184, vol. XVI, No. 4, February, pp170-3

Richards JD (2003*b*), *Pers. comm.*, Lecture given on the Viking Cemetery at Heath Wood, Ingleby, at The Yorkshire Archaeological Society, Leeds, 8th February

Richards JD, Jecock M, Richmond L, & Tuck C (1995), The Viking Barrow Cemetery at Heath Wood, Ingleby, Derbyshire, *Medieval Archaeology*, vol. 39, pp51-70

Ritchie A (1976-7), Excavation of Pictish and Viking-age farmsteads at Buckquoy, Orkney, *Proceedings of the Society of Antiquaries of Scotland,* 1976-7 vol. 108, pp174-227

Ritchie JN (1981), Excavations at Machrins, Colonsay, *Proceedings of the Society of Antiquaries of Scotland,* vol. 111, pp263-81

Roberts BK (1989), Late *-bý* names in the Eden Valley, Cumberland, *Nomina*, vol. 13, pp25-40

Robertson WN (1968-9), A Viking Grave found at The Broch of Gurness, Aikerness, Orkney, *Proceedings of the Society of Antiquaries of Scotland*, vol. 101, pp289-90

Roesdahl E (1991), *The Vikings* (transl. by SM Margeson & K Williams), The Penguin Group, London

Rooke H (1792), Druidical and other British Remains in Cumberland *Archaeologia*, vol. X, pp105-13

Rosenblatt PC (1997), Grief in Small-Scale Societies, in *Death and Bereavement Across Cultures*, ed. by C Murray Parkes, P Laungani & B Young, Routledge, London & New York, pp27-51

Ross EJ (1941), *Fundamental Sociology* (no publisher given)

Sass T (transl.) (1995), The Funeral of the Rus Chief, in ML Warmind, Ibn Fadlan in the Context of his Age, in *The Ship as a Symbol in Prehistoric and Medieval Scandinavia*, Papers from an International Research Seminar at the Danish National Museum, Copenhagen, 1994, ed. by O Crumlin-Pedersen & B Munch Thye, Publications from the National Museum Studies in Archaeology & History, vol. I, Copenhagen, pp 136-7

Sawyer P (2000), Scandinavia in the Viking Age, in *Vikings – The North Atlantic Saga*, ed. by WW Fitzhugh & EI Ward, Smithsonian Institute in assoc. with the National Museum of Natural History, Washington & London, pp27-30

Schäferdiek K (1987), Missionary Methods, *The Christianization of Scandinavia*, ed. by B Sawyer, P Sawyer & I Wood, Report of the Symposium held at Kungälv, Sweden, 4-9th August 1985, Viktoria Bokförlag, Alingsås, pp24-26

Scudder B (transl.) (1997), Egil's Saga, in *The Sagas of the Icelanders. A Selection*, Allen Lane, The Penguin Press, London, pp3-184

Sellevold BJ (1999), *Picts & Vikings at Westness. Anthropological investigations of the skeletal material from the cemetery at Westness, Rousay, Orkney Islands.* Norsk institutt for kulturminneforskning, Oslo

Sheehan JA (1987-8), A Reassessment of the Viking Burial from Eyrephort, Co. Galway, *Journal of Galway Archaeology and History Society*, vol. 41, pp60-72

Shennan SJ (1994), Introduction: archaeological approaches to cultural identity, in *Archaeological Approaches to Cultural Identity*, ed. SJ Shennan, Routledge, pp1-32

Shetelig H (1910), Traces of the custom pf suttee in Norway during the Viking Age, *Saga-Book of the Viking Club* vol. VI, pp180-208

Sidebottom P (2000), Viking Age Stone Monuments and Social Identity in Derbyshire, in *Cultures in Contact: Scandinavian Settlement in England in the Ninth and Tenth Centuries*, ed. by DM Hadley and JD Richards, Brepols, Turnhout, Belgium, pp213-235
Simek R (2000), *Dictionary of Northern Mythology*, (transl. by A Hall), D S Brewer, Woodbridge
Smith R (1905-6), Notes on two Viking Brooches and a bowl found at Ballyholme between Bangor and Groomsport Co. Down, *Proceedings of the Society of Antiquaries London*, vol. XXI, pp72-79
Smith, JH (1841-44), An Account of the Discovery, in the month of November last, of a Human Skeleton, accompanied by Weapons, Ornaments, etc., *Proceedings of the Royal Society of Antiquaries of Ireland*, vol. II, pp40-46
Smyth AP (1975), *Scandinavian York and Dublin I. The History and Archaeology of Two Related Viking Kingdoms*, Templekieran Press, Dublin
Smyth AP (1977), *Scandinavian Kings in the British Isles 850-880*, Oxford University Press
Smyth AP (1978), The Chronology of Northumbrian History in the ninth and tenth centuries, in *Viking Age York and the North*, ed. RA Hall, CBA Research Report no. 27, The Council for British Archaeology, pp8-10
Smyth AP (1979), *Scandinavian York and Dublin: The history and archaeology of two related Viking kingdoms*, II, Dublin New Jersey Humanities Press, Dublin Templekieran Press
Speed G (2003), *Pers. comm.*, (Northern Archaeological Associates)
Stamper P & Croft R (2000), *Wharram: A Study of Settlement in the Yorkshire Wolds VIII: The South Manor*, York University Archaeological Publications 10
Stenton F (1998), *Anglo-Saxon England*, 3rd edition, Oxford University Press, Oxford
Stephens G (1884), *Old Northern Runic Monuments of Scandinavia and England, now first collected and deciphered*, vol. I (vols. I-III, 1866-1884), London & Kjobenhavn
Stewart HJ (1853), Notice of the discovery of some ancient arms & armour near Glenfruin on the estate of Sir James Colquhoun of Luss, *PSAS*, vol. I, p143
Stocker D (2000), *Monuments and Merchants: Irregularities in the Distribution of Stone Sculpture in Lincolnshire and Yorkshire in the Tenth Century*, in, Cultures in Contact: Scandinavian Settlement in England in the Ninth and Tenth Centuries, ed. By DM Hadley and JD Richards, Brepols, Turnhout, Belgium, pp179-212
Stocker D & Everson P (2001), Decoding Diversity in Danelaw Stone Sculpture, in, *Vikings and the Danelaw, Select Papers from the Proceedings of the Thirteenth Viking Congress*, ed. J Graham-Campbell, R Hall, J Jesch & D Parsons, Oxbow, Oxford pp223-243
Styles T (2001), Scandinavian elements in English place-names: some semantic problems, in *Cultures in Contact: Scandinavian Settlement in England in the Ninth and Tenth Centuries*, ed. by DM Hadley and JD Richards, Brepols, Turnhout, Belgium, pp289-298
Swanton M (1969), A Rune-stone from Victoria Cave, Settle, Yorkshire, *Medieval Archaeology* vol. 13 (1971), pp211-14
Swanton M (ed. & transl.) (2000), *The Anglo-Saxon Chronicles*, Phoenix Press, London
Taylor RC (1969), Migration and Motivation, in *Migration*, ed. JA Jackson, Cambridge University Press, pp99-133
Thomas G (2000), Anglo-Scandinavian Metalwork from the Danelaw: Exploring Social and Cultural Interaction, in *Cultures in Contact: Scandinavian Settlement in England in the ninth and tenth centuries*, ed. DM Hadley & JD Richards, Brepols, pp237-255
Thorpe B (1840), *Ancient Laws and Institutes of England*, vol. I, London Record Commission
Thorsteinsson A (1968), The Viking Burial Place at Pierowall, Westray, Orkney, *The 5th Viking Congress, Torshavn 1965*, ed. by B Niclasen, Føroya Landsstýri. Tórshavnar Býráđ. Føroya Fróđskaparfelag. Føroya Fornminnissaun, Torshavn, pp156-73
Thorvildsen K (1975), *The Viking Ship of Ladby*, 2nd edition, National Museum, Copenhagen
Townend M (2000), Viking Age England as a Bilingual society, in *Cultures in Contact: Scandinavian Settlement in England in the Ninth and Tenth Centuries*, ed. by DM Hadley and JD Richards, Brepols, Turnhout, Belgium, pp89-105
Trafford S (1997), *Theoretical Approaches to early Medieval Migration*, DPhil Thesis, University of York
Trafford S (2000), Ethnicity, Migration Theory and the Historiography of the Scandinavian Settlement of England, in *Cultures in Contact: Scandinavian Settlement in England in the ninth and tenth centuries*, ed. DM Hadley & JD Richards, Brepols, pp17-39
Trotzig G (1985), An Axe as a Sign of Rank in a Viking Community, in *Archaeology and Environment in Honorem Evert Baudau 4*, ed. M Backe, I Bergman-Hennix, L Forsberg, L Holm, L Liedgren, A-K Lindqvist, I-M Mulk, M Nejati, P Perstrand, PH Ramqvist, Society fot Norrlandic Archaeology and Prehistory, Dept. of Archaeology University of Umeå, Umeå pp83-87
Turville-Petrie EOG (1964), *Myth and religion of the North. The Religion of Ancient Scandinavia*, Weidenfeld & Nicolson, London
Tweddle D (unpublished), *Carlisle, Cathedral Green Decorated metalwork*
Van Gennep A (1977), *The Rites of Passage*, transl. by MB Vizedom & GL Caffee, Routledge & Kegan Paul, London & Henley
Wainwright FT (1942) (2000), North West Mercia AD 871-924, in *Wirral and its Viking Heritage*, ed. P Cavill, SE Harding & J Jesch, English Place-name Society, Nottingham, 2000, pp19-42, reprinted from Transactions of the Historic Society of Lancashire and Cheshire vol. 94, 1942, pp3-55
Walker JC (1788), *An Historical Essay on the Dress of the Ancient and Modern Irish addressed to the Right Honourable of the Earl of Charlemont. To which is subjoined, a memoir on the arms and weapons of the Irish*, Dublin
Wallace-Hadrill JM (1975), *The Vikings in Francia*, The Stenton Lecture 1974, University of Reading
Walsh A (1998), A Summary Classification of the Viking Age Swords in Ireland, in *Ireland & Scandinavia in the Early Viking Age*, eds. HB Clarke, M Ní Mhaonaigh & R Ó Floinn, Four Courts Press, Dublin 1998, pp222-235
Walton Rogers P (2001), Scandinavian Oval Brooches in *Red House Park Adwick-le-Street, Doncaster, South Yorkshire*, Archaeological Post-Excavation Assessment by Northern Archaeological Associates for Earth Tech Morrison on behalf of Yorkshire Water Services Ltd, NAA 01/64, July, pp45-47
Warmind ML (1995), Ibn Fadlan in the Context of his Age, in *The Ship as a Symbol in Prehistoric and Medieval Scandinavia*, Papers from an International Research Seminar at the Danish National Museum, Copenhagen, 1994, ed. by O Crumlin-Pedersen & B Munch Thye, Publications from the National Museum Studies in Archaeology & History, vol. I, Copenhagen, pp 130-7
Warner R (1973-4), The re-provenancing of two important penannular brooches of the Viking period, *Ulster Journal of Archaeology*, 3rd series 36-7, pp58-70 at pp61-2
Watt WGT (1888), Notice of the Discovery of a Stone Cist, with an Iron Age Interment, at Skaill Bay, *Proceedings of the Society of Antiquaries of Scotland*, 1887-1888, vol. X, pp283-285
Watts V (1995), Northumberland and Durham: the place-name evidence, in *Scandinavian Settlement in Northern Britain. Thirteen Studies of Place-Names in their Historical Context*, ed. by BE Crawford, Leicester University Press, pp206-213
Waugh DJ (1996), *Shetland's Northern Links: Language and History*, Scottish Society for Northern Studies, Edinburgh
Wenham LP, Hall RA, Briden CM & Stocker DA (1987), *St Mary Bishophill Junior & St Mary Castlegate*, The Archaeology of York, Anglo-Scandinavian York 8/2, published for York Archaeological Trust by CBA London
Welander RDE, Batey C & Cowie TG, with contribs by L Bender Jorgensen, M Harman, C Scott MacKenzie (1987), A Viking Burial from Kneep, Uig, Isle of Lewis, *Proceedings of the Antiquaries of Scotland,* vol. CXVII: pp149-74
Whitaker J (1775), *The History of Manchester*, vol. II, Saxon Period, pp36-7
Whitaker TD (1823), *A History of Richmondshire* (2 vols.) vol. II, London, p319
Whitelock D (1941), The Conversion of the Eastern Danelaw, *Saga Book of the Viking Society*, vol. 12, part 3, pp159-176
Whitelock D (1959), The Dealings of the Kings of England with Northumbria in the Tenth and Eleventh Centuries, in *The Anglo-Saxons; studies on some aspects of their history and culture*, presented to Bruce Dickins on his seventieth birthday, ed. P Clemoes, Bowes & Bowes, London, pp70-88
Whitelock D (ed. & transl.) (1930), *Anglo-Saxon Wills*, Cambridge University Press, Cambridge
Whitelock D (ed.) (1979), *English Historical Documents*, c500-1042, vol. 1, 2nd edition, Eyre Methuen, London
Williams A (1986), 'Cockles Amongst the Wheat': Danes and the English in the Western Midlands in the First Half of the Eleventh Century, *Midland History*, vol. 11, pp1-22
Wilson DM (1967), The Vikings' Relationship with Christianity in Northern England, *Journal of the British Archaeological Association*, vol. 30, series 3, pp37-46
Wilson DM (1968), Archaeological Evidence for the Viking settlement and raids in England, *Fruhmittelalt Studien 2*, pp291-304
Wilson DM (1976), The Scandinavians in England, in The Archaeology of Anglo-Saxon England, ed. DM Wilson, Cambridge University Press, pp393-403

Wilson PA (1978), Eaglesfield, the place-name, the burials, *Transactions of the Cumberland and Westmorland Antiquarian and Archaeological Society*, vol. 78, pp47-54
Wilson DM & Klindt-Jensen O (1980), *Viking Art*, 2nd ed., Allen & Unwin, London
Winchester AJL (1987), *Landscape and Society in Medieval Cumbria*, Donald, Edinburgh
Worsaae J (1846-7), *Viking Ireland, Jens Worsaae's accounts of his visit to Ireland: 1846-47*, transl. Ase Goldsmith, ed. by D Henry. The Pinkfoot Press: Balgavies Angus, 1995
Wright D (1983), Slag and Thermoluminescence Dating in, Coggins D, Fairless KJ & Batey CE (1983), Simy Folds: An Early Medieval Settlement Site in Upper Teesdale, Co. Durham, *Medieval Archaeology* vol. 27, pp1-26

Lightning Source UK Ltd.
Milton Keynes UK
UKOW07f0710240817
307819UK00004B/31/P

9 781407 300504